RECORDS OF EARLY ENGLISH DRAMA

Records of Early English Drama

CUMBERLAND
WESTMORLAND
GLOUCESTERSHIRE

EDITED BY AUDREY DOUGLAS AND
PETER GREENFIELD

UNIVERSITY OF TORONTO PRESS

TORONTO BUFFALO LONDON

© University of Toronto Press 1986
Toronto Buffalo London
Printed in Canada
ISBN 0–8020–5669–5

1000685792 T

Canadian Cataloguing in Publication Data

Main entry under title:
Cumberland, Westmorland, Gloucestershire

(Records of early English drama)
Bibliography
Includes index.
ISBN 0–8020–5669–5

1. Performing arts – England – Cumberland – History –
Sources. 2. Performing arts – England – Westmorland –
History – Sources. 3. Performing arts – England –
Gloucestershire – History – Sources. 4. Theater –
England – Cumberland – History – Sources. 5. Theater –
England – Westmorland – History – Sources.
6. Theater – England – Gloucestershire – History –
Sources.   I. Douglas, Audrey, W., 1935–
II. Greenfield, Peter   III. Series.

PN2581.C85 1986   790.2'09427'8 C86–093275–3

The research and typesetting costs of
Records of Early English Drama
have been underwritten by the
Social Sciences and Humanities Research Council of Canada.

Contents

GLOUCESTERSHIRE

Records of Early English Drama

The aim of Records of Early English Drama (REED) is to find, transcribe, and publish external evidence of dramatic, ceremonial, and minstrel activity in Great Britain before 1642. The general editor would be grateful for comments on and corrections to the present volume and for having any relevant additional material drawn to her attention.

ALEXANDRA F. JOHNSTON   University of Toronto   GENERAL EDITOR
SALLY-BETH MACLEAN   University of Toronto   ASSOCIATE EDITOR

EXECUTIVE BOARD

PETER CLARK   University of Leicester
JOANNA DUTKA   University of Toronto
DAVID GALLOWAY   University of New Brunswick
R.W. INGRAM   University of British Columbia
STANLEY J. KAHRL   The Ohio State University
IAN LANCASHIRE   University of Toronto
PETER MEREDITH   The University of Leeds
J.A.B. SOMERSET   University of Western Ontario
PRUDENCE TRACY   University of Toronto Press

EDITORIAL ADVISORY BOARD

HERBERT BERRY   University of Saskatchewan
DAVID BEVINGTON   University of Chicago
A.C. CAWLEY   The University of Leeds
L.M. CLOPPER   Indiana University
DAVID MILLS   The University of Liverpool
A.G.R. PETTI   University of Calgary
RICHARD PROUDFOOT   King's College, London
JOHN WASSON   Washington State University (Pullman)

Symbols

BL	British Library	GCL	Gloucestershire County Library
BRO	Bristol Record Office	GRO	Gloucestershire Record Office
CCRO	Carlisle, Cumbria Record Office	KAO	Kent Archives Office
CH	Chatsworth House	KCRO	Kendal, Cumbria Record Office
CPL	Carlisle, Public Library	KTC	Kendal, Town Council
CRO	Cheshire Record Office	PRO	Public Record Office
DDPD	University of Durham, Department of Paleography and Diplomatic	SA	Stadtarchiv, Augsburg
		SRO	Staffordshire Record Office

A	Antiquarian Compilation
BR	*Boke off Recorde*
CWAAS	Cumberland and Westmorland Antiquarian and Archaeological Society
DNB	*Dictionary of National Biography*
EES	*Early English Stages*
MS	*Mediaeval Stage*
STC	*Short-Title Catalogue*
TBGAS	*Transactions of the Bristol and Gloucestershire Archaeological Society*
VCH	*Victoria County History*
*	(after folio, page, or membrane number) see endnote
〈...〉	lost or illegible letters in the original
[ ]	cancellation in the original
(*blank*)	a blank in the original where writing would be expected
° °	matter in the original added in another hand
⌐ ⌐	interlineation above the line
∟ ⌐	interlineation below the line
^	caret mark in the original
...	ellipsis of original matter
		change of folio or membrane in passages of continuous prose
®	right-hand marginalia
†	marginalia too long for the left-hand margin

Preface

Cumberland/Westmorland/Gloucestershire marks a new direction for the REED series. The pattern established for civic volumes by *York* will continue with publication of records from other important urban centres such as Beverley and Bristol. Some research areas have been defined by county rather than by borough, however, and their records will be issued in the form of county collections.

There are some items of general editorial policy relating to county volumes which may be usefully set forth at this time. Although the progress of several centuries has obscured or drastically redesigned some county boundaries, REED will observe county limits as recognized by their contemporary, pre-1642 records. Thus, modern Cumbria reverts to its earlier division into Cumberland and Westmorland. While it is clearly desirable to issue county records as discrete units, some collections will not be large enough to warrant separate publication. Smaller collections such as Cumberland and Westmorland therefore will be bound together in one volume. As far as possible, these multiple collections will share a boundary, diocese, or general region; thus, we anticipate single volumes for Herefordshire/Worcestershire or Shropshire/Staffordshire. Occasionally, smaller collections from very different areas of Britain will be ready for simultaneous publication; our determination to make our records available to others at the earliest possible date will then lead to such pragmatic but unexpected combinations as Cumberland and Westmorland with Gloucestershire.

Within these volumes of multiple collections, the autonomy of individual counties will be observed. Where one editor has responsibility for two counties, there will be a common introduction, as illustrated by Dr Douglas' discussion of Cumberland and Westmorland (pp 5–52). In addition, patrons' list, glossaries, and index will be shared.

The diversity of locations and sources for county records presents more complex problems in organization. County records volumes will have two or more of the following major divisions: Boroughs and Parishes; Monasteries; Households; Diocese; County.

Within the Boroughs and Parishes or Monasteries division, records will be presented according to the location they refer to, in alphabetical order. Under each location, entries will then be arranged chronologically along the same pattern established in REED's civic volumes. Thus, in the Gloucestershire collection, records relating to the parish of Bisley are printed as a chronological unit before the numerous entries from varied civic and ecclesiastical sources for the important borough of Gloucester.

The Household section differs only in its style of heading. Important families sometimes had more than one residence in a county and occasionally it has proved difficult to identify the exact location for family entertainments. Households, therefore, are sorted alphabetically by family name, with chronological arrangement of records within each household.

Many ecclesiastical records refer to specific parishes in a county and may be placed under the correct location within the Boroughs and Parishes section. Other documents, such as statutes or visitation articles, relate to a diocese as a whole; these are organized chronologically in a separate section and identified by diocese (as, for example, Diocese of Gloucester, pp 345–6).

Similarly, there are county or quarter session records which cannot be pinpointed to a particular location. Such general regulations, usually from county justices of the peace, will be grouped in chronological order within a County section.

General Editorial Procedures

Editorial policy common to all three collections included in this volume is discussed below. More specialized concerns such as the selection and dating of entries are to be found in the introductions of the two editors.

LAYOUT

Entries are preceded by date (wherever required to mark a change of year), MS or book identification, and folio, page, or membrane number. Where folio or page numbers have been supplied editorially, they are enclosed within square brackets. Italics are used to indicate dating and account subtitles supplied by the editors (eg, *Extraordinary fees*). An antiquarian source is indicated in the left-hand margin by the letter A (Antiquarian Compilation).

Every effort has been made to preserve manuscript layout (though not precise lineation). Right-hand marginalia have been set in the left margin of the text but this transposition is indicated by the symbol ®. Routine marginal account or date headings have been modernized as part of the editorial subtitles in the interests of consistency and ease of reference.

Emendations, scribal errors, and duplicate entries in related MSS are noted at the foot of the page. Textual notes are also used to identify dates, place-names, or persons mentioned in the text. Notes to the Kendal records in the Westmorland collection supply full personal names as a reference guide to the Appendix of Kendal Tradesmen (pp 220–5), which contains short biographies of the borough's officials and tradesmen, arranged alphabetically by surname. Endnotes are used for more extensive discussion of textual and dating difficulties and to provide biographical or historical material necessary for intelligible context.

PUNCTUATION

The punctuation of the MSS has been retained. Virgules have been indicated as / and //. MS braces, line-fillers, otiose flourishes, and diacritics used to distinguish 'y' from 'þ' and 'u' from 'n' have been omitted.

SPELLING, CAPITALIZATION, AND EXPANSION

The spelling and capitalization of the original MSS have been preserved. 'ff' has been retained for 'F' while the standard and elongated forms of 'I' have been uniformly transcribed as 'I'. Ornamental and oversized capitals have been rendered as regular capitals. Where it has been difficult to tell whether a letter is upper or lower case, the lower case has been preferred.

Abbreviated words have been expanded according to scribal practice, with supplied letters italicized and superior letters lowered to the line. Where scribal spelling practice cannot be determined, abbreviations in Latin have been expanded to standard classical forms and in English to modern British forms. Abbreviations still in common use (eg, 's,' 'd,' 'lb,' '&c,' 'viz,' and 'Mr' with a title or surname) and those cumbersome to expand, such as those typical of weights and measures ('ob'), have been retained. Generally, a 'punctus' is supplied where there is some sign of abbreviation in the MS. 'xp' and 'Xp' have been expanded as 'chr*ist*' and 'Chr*ist*.' The sign ℮ has been expanded as '*es*' in the English records except when it follows an 'e'.

Treatment of the superscript 'r' in the Westmorland records is an exceptional case. In WMB/K Chamberlains' Accounts and PRO: STAC/8/4/4, there is a clear distinction between a simple superscript 'r' (usually written 'ɛ' as in 'receiuᵉ') and a mark of abbreviation sometimes combined with superscript 'ɛ' (receiꝸ' or 'westmꝰland'). These two forms have been distinguished by transcribing the first group as 'receiur' without expansion, and the second group as 'receiu*er*' or 'westm*er*land' with expansion.

Place-names, personal names, and surnames have only been expanded to modern spelling where that is ascertainable. Marks of abbreviation were sometimes omitted in antiquarian copies of original documents; the resulting eccentricities, such as 'Ite' (for 'Item'), have been preserved without emendation in the text.

Sally-Beth MacLean
Associate Editor

CUMBERLAND/WESTMORLAND

Acknowledgments

Various people have eased the passage of Cumberland and Westmorland dramatic records from archival identification to print. To all, my thanks. In particular I am grateful to Mr Bruce Jones and Miss Sheila Macpherson of the Cumbria Record Office (Carlisle and Kendal), together with their staff, for warm interest and help; to Dr Henry Summerson for advising me of the reference to the Carlisle miracle play; and to Dr Diana Wyatt, Professor John Elliott, and Professor David George for locating respectively material in the Public Record Office, the Library of Queen's College, Oxford, and the Cheshire Record Office. With respect to the German Miners' Accounts I am indebted for help to Dr Wolfram Baer, Archivdirektor, Stadtarchiv, Augsburg and to Herr Paul Warmbrun for identification of extracts from the accounts. Professor Eckehard Catholy of St Michael's College, Toronto, and Professor Michael Sheehan of the Pontifical Institute of Mediaeval Studies, Toronto, gave welcome assistance with problems of translation.

All the REED staff, past and present, have been consistently cheerful and supportive. I am especially grateful to Anne Quick and Abigail Young for prepararation of the glossaries, and to Ian Lancashire and Theodore R. De Welles for invaluable bibliographic work. I also thank Donna Best, William Cooke, Cameron Louis, Darlene Money, Heather Phillips, William Rowcliffe, and Elza Tiner for their meticulous help; and of course Sally-Beth MacLean whose unfailing good sense and humour have gracefully sustained – and where necessary curbed – editorial zeal.

AWD

Historical Background

Cumberland and Westmorland

The popular conception of Cumberland and Westmorland, lit by images of England's Lake District, is often tinged with nineteenth-century romanticism, for which Wordsworth's poetry perhaps provides the literary starting-point. While the rugged grandeur of the Cumbrian Mountains does indeed dominate the area, the topography is more varied than this picture normally admits.

The two counties are roughly confined to the most northwesterly bulge of England from which the Furness area (historically part of Lancashire but now in the new county of Cumbria) formerly took a large bite. The mountains at their oldest and highest form craggy peaks of slate and volcanic rock. On the west they are bounded by a narrow coastal plain of red sandstone and carboniferous limestone that runs north from the tip of Furness, eventually swinging eastwards and broadening into the low lying basin of Solway Firth, the border with Scotland. Geologically one with this plain are two principal river valleys, one formed by the Eden, flowing north into Solway Firth from its source in northern Westmorland, and the other by the Kent, flowing south through Westmorland into Morecambe Bay. The Eden and the Kent form an angled axis between the Cumbrian mountain range to the west and the Pennines to the east; along this axis are strung some of the more important towns of the two counties: Carlisle, Penrith, Appleby, and Kendal. Kendal itself is surrounded by a great northerly arc of Silurian rock, rolling moorland that stretches from Lake Windermere and Coniston Water in the west to well beyond the river Lune at the county border in the east.

Archaeology and place-name evidence attest a history that stretches back at least to Celtic and Roman times. An important legacy of Roman occupation was a network of roads converging on this strategic area – Roman Carlisle stood at the western end of Hadrian's Wall – that continued to serve generations of travellers well into the Middle Ages.[1] From the seventh to the twelfth centuries, first Anglian, then Norse settlers moved in, the latter from Irish bases as well as from Scandinavia. It was not until the time of Henry II, however, that the institution of the counties of Cumberland and Westmorland brought the inhabitants into the overall pattern of English local government. Carlisle was grouped with the honours of Coupland and Allerdale to become the county of Cumberland, the baronies of Appleby and Kendal forming Westmorland. Some years earlier, in 1133, a new bishopric had been established at Carlisle. With the exception of certain Durham peculiars, Carlisle had jurisdiction over the major part of Cumberland and northern Westmorland, while the diocese of York, through the western deaneries of the archdeaconry of Richmond (Copeland, Kendal, and Lonsdale) had jurisdiction over the remainder of the two counties.

Even with the county structure, royal government continued to be remote, necessarily dependent in earlier centuries on the loyalty and co-operation of strong local lords (the Percys, Cliffords, and Dacres). The fifteenth century saw the introduction of new administrative measures. The Council of the North was created towards the end of the century and wardens were appointed for the West, Middle, and East Marches of the border. In this way the government sought not only to expedite matters of local administration, including criminal jurisdiction, but to stem the constant forays of borderers intent upon horse- and cattle-thieving, sometimes with wholesale destruction of local communities. About this time local obligations of border service were systematized and peel towers erected throughout the area as places of defence and refuge from raiders who penetrated through narrow valleys well into Westmorland. In 1537, after the Pilgrimage of Grace, the king's Council of the North took its final form as a solely administrative and judicial body. Wardens continued to exercise military powers, reporting directly to the central government. Both the council and the wardenries provided a solid training ground for the talents of the northern nobility and gentry. In 1603, with the union of the Scottish and English crowns in the person of James VI and I, a theoretical peace came to the border and the old military organization was superseded by extensive commissions addressed to prominent local men.

In the sixteenth century most of the population of Cumberland and Westmorland was still scattered over the region in small settlements, distinct from the larger compact villages of southern counties. The prevalent form of land tenure was a customary tenant right that gave relative security of tenure while requiring certain services and fines. Pastoral farming was dominant, though communities might co-operate in a strip system for hay and arable, together with common grazing on moor or fell for sheep and cattle. The production of wool, stimulated by thirteenth-century monastic initiative, provided a coarse-textured export and raw material for local cloth.

Among the larger communities the most important was Carlisle, not only in virtue of its age and royal charter, but as the seat of the bishopric and of the wardenry of the West March, with quarters for a permanent garrison. Kendal and Appleby, both in Westmorland, were the only other royal boroughs in the two counties. Kendal, incorporated in 1575 by royal charter, continued to function with close links to its manorial and agrarian origins. Elsewhere small market towns such as Egremont and Cockermouth in Cumberland, though styled boroughs, were dominated by a manorial structure of government that operated through a leet court. Other local communities were each governed by a select vestry or elected body of twelve or more members, who dealt without discrimination in church or secular matters arising within the parish.[2]

The later sixteenth and the seventeenth centuries brought social and economic change to the region. The Reformation and its aftermath stirred movements ranging from the Pilgrimage of Grace, a rebellious outpouring of religious, political, and economic grievances, to the growth of Puritanism (especially in the Quaker communities of the seventeenth century) and the persecution of Catholic recusants. Organizational change established the new diocese of Chester in 1541, to which were transferred the western deaneries of the archdeaconry of Richmond. Properties confiscated at the suppression of historic abbeys (St Bee's, Lanercost, Holme Cultram, Shap) and of hospitals, chantries, and religious guilds passed into the hands of a new breed of gentry, intent upon the accumulation of lands and rents, and venturing into industry and trade. These men now gratified a taste for public service primarily in borough and county rather than as formerly in border administration. Their 'halls,' already distinguished by stone structure and fortified towers, were enlarged and ornamented as country seats. At the same time customary tenants were fighting to establish a basic right to security of tenure and precision of service in the apparent face of increased, or simply more efficient, landlord exploitation.

Famine and plague also brought disturbance to the economy of Cumberland and Westmorland in the late sixteenth and early seventeenth centuries. Compared with southern England, the north at this period was more easily pushed 'past the edge of subsistence' by fluctuations in trade and failures of harvest.[3] The seventeenth century also saw significant new factors in the economy of the region: the establishment after 1603 of relative stability on the border, with consequent improvement in the security of traffic and market conditions; the emergence of the statesman, or yeoman farmer of the northwest counties, whose interests were closely allied to those of the textile trades; and an overall rise in urban population partly created by a changing rural land-market that forced men to leave the countryside for the towns.

In the sections that follow some brief details will be given to pinpoint the various locations and households that supply evidence of dramatic and musical activity within the two counties. As preamble the reader must bear in mind certain points that condition the outcome of such inquiry and that warn us not to expect a rich dramatic vein comparable to that mined elsewhere in England. First, until 1603 the region, especially its eastern half, was under perpetual threat from border warfare and raids destructive of life, of material goods (including documentary records), and of a sense of security and continuity. Second, the rural pattern of settlement was at all times sparse, with many small communities spread over the two counties; those people isolated in narrow mountain valleys or remote moorland dales probably maintained at most an intermittent contact with the outside world. Third, we must note the absence of any towns or cities possessed of both a long history and substantial economic importance, conditions necessary for an elaborate civic ceremonial, or at least for a propensity to lavish expenditure.

Boroughs

CARLISLE, CUMBERLAND

The medieval history of Carlisle as an English town begins with William Rufus. In 1092 the king made it his northern outpost against the Scots, driving out their allies, the Northumbrians, from the region and effectually establishing a frontier that ran from Solway Firth along the line of the Cheviot Hills to the river Tweed. Commanding the western plain encircling the firth, Carlisle and its castle, built by William Rufus, straddled various strategic routes, often utilizing portions of existing Roman roads. These ran south by way of Penrith and Shap to meet sundry ways through the Pennine dales; north into the Scottish lowlands; west into coastal Cumberland; and east into Northumbria along the old Roman Stanegate south of Hadrian's Wall. Well sited as a garrison town and market centre, Carlisle was also an obvious target for repeated Scottish onslaught.

Internally, the city's life is amply illustrated in the incident that marred the performance of a miracle play in 1342.[4] As a garrison town Carlisle had to cope with the demands and excesses of a resident body of troops and their commander, housed in the castle and its precincts. With the creation of the see of Carlisle in 1133, the Augustinian priory church had become the cathedral, the canons forming its chapter. When, as in 1342, episcopal and military powers were concentrated in the hands of one quick-tempered man, the bishop, John de Kirkeby, violence must have seethed close to the surface of civic life. In the early seventeenth century relations with the bishop were more cordial; he regularly entertained the mayor and brethren during Christmas, sometimes at Rose Castle, his country seat south of Carlisle, and Henry Robinson (1598–1616) in particular favoured at least one of the city's guilds with his patronage.[5]

In the late fifteenth century the garrison status of Carlisle was reinforced when, with the creation of the Council of the North, the northern border area was divided into East and West Marches. Carlisle, the seat of the warden of the West March, was linked by a chain of beacons with the countryside of Cumberland and Westmorland, and with part of Lancashire. Fire kindled on the high tower of the castle summoned forth border service owed by customary tenants in the region.

Carlisle had escaped absorption into the various baronies created by Henry I in the northwest of the kingdom, being kept in crown hands. A rudimentary burgage grant may have preceded a charter of Henry II that conferred on the burgesses of Carlisle quittance of tolls and a free merchant guild; by 1221 the citizens were farming the revenues of the city, thus obtaining some degree of self-government.[6]

Details of city government incidentally given by jurors testifying about the miracle-play fracas in 1342 are confirmed in a charter of 1353. The city had evidently attained a high degree of autonomy, with its own mayor, bailiffs, and coroners, and judicial privileges that encompassed 'pleas of the crown and all things belonging to the office of ... sheriff.' A market was held on Wednesday and Saturday, with a two-week fair each year starting on 15 August.[7] Early in the reign of Elizabeth I, at the time the Dormont Book, the city's first extant register, was begun, the government is described as vested in a mayor and eleven other citizens, with a further group of twenty-four chosen by the eleven.[8] Some seventy years later, in 1636, a charter of Charles I confirms the existing municipal government of mayor, eleven citizens now termed aldermen, and twenty-four capital citizens, empowered to make and enforce by-laws; the mayor, the recorder, and two senior aldermen act as justices of the peace; there is a sword-bearer with three sergeants-at-mace; and the city has a leet court and view of frankpledge.[9]

In the seventeenth century Carlisle had eight occupations or guilds. The Dormont Book emphasizes their active and important role in municipal government: four members from each occupation were required to assist the mayor and brethren in the annual audit, the removal as necessary of civic officials, and the creation of new freemen; in addition they had custody of two of the four keys to the city's common chest.[10] The fullness of power delineated here is in sharp contrast to the subordinate role in civic government accorded the Kendal trades in the same period.

APPLEBY AND KENDAL, WESTMORLAND

In the early seventeenth century Appleby was governed by a mayor, twelve aldermen, and a common council of sixteen burgesses. The office of mayor is mentioned in the reign of Edward I, but Appleby's history as a royal borough goes back to the twelfth century, when Henry II granted a charter c. 1179. While no written record exists of any earlier creation of a borough, it is probable that burgage tenements were in fact laid out at the foot of Appleby Castle when it was built in about 1110. The church of St Lawrence, dating from the early twelfth century, together with the castle and the 'new town,' lay on the west bank of the river Eden, distinct from an older village and church on the opposite bank (the present Bongate).[11] The castle, as the seat of the barony of Westmorland, was held from the thirteenth century by the Cliffords, who also served as hereditary sheriffs of the county.

In 1200 King John granted the borough the right to farm its own revenues, a significant sign of municipal independence.[12] From 1295 Appleby sent two members to Parliament and from the mid-thirteenth century assizes were held in the town.

In the twelfth century the borough had also acquired generous trading privileges, modelled on those held by York. Appleby's geographic position, however, in the path of periodic Scottish incursion, hampered its economic development. The town was twice occupied by the Scots in the twelfth century and twice ravaged and burnt by the Scottish raiders in the fourteenth. Economically, its medieval history was that of a small, struggling market-town. Only after 1603, as hostilities in the border area gave way to a period of security, did Appleby show signs of a new, stable prosperity.[13]

Appleby's neighbour, Kendal, about twenty miles to the southwest in the valley of the Kent, was the seat of Westmorland's other barony. Kendal's recorded history as a market town goes back to 1189, when Gilbert, son of Roger fitz Reinfred and husband of an heiress to the barony of Kendal, procured for the community a Saturday market. Subsequent royal grants in 1268 and 1333 provided annual three-day fairs in early summer and mid-October.[14] From the fourteenth century, Kendal's fortunes were linked to the manufacture of coarse woollen cloth, the famous 'Kendal green'; by the end of the fifteenth century booths, shops, shambles, and court-houses emerge as descriptive features of the town in rentals and surveys.[15] By this time also the barony as a whole – and thus also the manor of Kendal of which the town formed a part – had been partitioned among three fees. As a result the rents, tolls, and profits of justice arising from Kendal were now divided among the holders of properties subsequently known as the Richmond fee (representing half the barony), and the Marquis and Lumley fees (each representing one quarter of the barony).

Early in its history some form of burgage grant had been made to the inhabitants of Kendal by a holder of the barony. The earliest extant grant of liberties, made by William de Lancastre III, dates from the thirteenth century; subsequently Peter de Brus III, who married William's sister, Helewise, confirmed to the burgesses customs granted by his 'uncle' ('advinculus'), William de Lancastre.[16] The term, 'advinculus,' is ambiguous and perhaps misleading. The original borough may well have been founded by William de Lancastre II, grandfather to Helewise and steward to Henry II; thus the grant of a market in 1189 would have been for the support of an existing community.

It is evident from the various records documenting the history of Kendal that here as elsewhere in England burgage tenure, held for a free rent, conferred the basic right to alienate property and to answer to a borough court separate from that held for the manor.[17] In this way Kendal's burgesses were marked off from a number of customary tenants in the town whose burdens (heriot, gressum, and border service), shared with the mass of Westmorland tenantry, were the subject of widespread protest in 1621.

By 1575, when Kendal obtained a royal charter of incorporation, the Marquis and Richmond fees were both in the hands of Queen Elizabeth I, a circumstance that probably facilitated the grant. The Lumley fee had come to the Bellingham family; living at Levens, near Kendal, members of the family appear in the seventeenth-century chamberlains' accounts as patrons of the corporation and as supporters of the Kendal Stage Play of 1621.

The effect of the royal charter of 1575 was to strengthen and define the authority and jurisdiction of the existing borough, while retaining elements of the old manorial organization within which it had originated. The government of the newly incorporated borough was put in the hands of an alderman, twelve burgesses, and twenty-four assistants, with common seal. Two sergeants-at-mace executed processes and mandates. The alderman and senior burgess also served as justices of the peace together with the recorder, 'skilled in law,' who effectually replaced the old manorial steward.

The court of record, which met every three weeks, and the leet courts at Michaelmas and Easter were taken over from the older jurisdictional framework, though with the significant difference that profits now went to the corporation rather than to the holders of fees. Similarly the Richmond and Marquis tolls, still so designated in the new chamberlains' accounts, were now leased by the corporation for its own profit. The charter also confirmed the two annual fairs (now centred on holidays that fell on 25 April and 28 October) together with accompanying courts of piepowder.[18] In 1636 the original structure of the corporation was replaced by a mayor, twelve aldermen, and twenty burgesses; the enhanced status of the corporation was symbolized by the appointment of a sword-bearer.[19]

The real influence of the new borough government, however, was based in the power it received to make by-laws, allowing it to regulate trade and industry in the town and to make provision for all matters of municipal welfare and concern. From 1575 such acts, set down in the Boke off Recorde, the first register of the corporation, show that overall supervision of the various Kendal trades was an integral part of the corporation's business. Each of the twelve trades or guilds listed in the register elected either two or four wardens as officers responsible to the alderman and brethren. The wardens' oath of office, outlining their duties, shows that the corporation approved or amended draft orders brought forward by each trade after discussion in its own assembly, punished wrongdoers and profited from consequent fines, kept apprenticeship records, and supervised the activities of 'strangers' engaged in business in the town.[21]

Unfortunately, the role of the trades in Kendal before 1575 – a crucial consideration, as will be shown later in discussion of the Kendal Corpus Christi Play – cannot be traced, as there appears to be no extant documentation of their activities within the old manorial borough. The long history of Kendal as a borough, however, some hundreds of years before incorporation by royal charter, and the growth of its trade and manufactures from the fourteenth century, provide grounds for the assumption that industrial and trade associations were organized long before 1575 and that some form of regulatory supervision, perhaps shared between borough and lord, was in place before that date.

Towards the end of the sixteenth century there appears to have been a decline in the population of Kendal from a figure in 1576 that was possibly as high as 3300. Throughout the seventeenth century the number of inhabitants remained relatively stable, close to 2500. Not a large town by contemporary standards, Kendal nevertheless survived regional bouts of famine, disease, and high prices in the first four decades of the century to maintain itself as a relatively prosperous community. It continued to depend upon textile and, to a lesser extent, leather industries (though by the later seventeenth century the composition of these industries and their attendant work-force was changing) and to function in both local and long-distance trade. By the eighteenth century it was supplying its 'new' draperies or cottons to the competitive London market.[22]

Households

AUGSBURG MINERS: KESWICK, CUMBERLAND

German miners were brought to Keswick as part of a project aimed at developing an English metalworking industry. In 1564 the Company of Mines Royal was formed under royal licence. Daniel Hechstetter, an original party to the agreement then drawn up, acted as agent for David Haug and Hans Langnauer, an Augsburg business company with wide European connections in textiles, spices, and banking, that had recently acquired mining interests from the Austrian house of Fugger. Twenty-four shares in the new English company were sold, some on a fractional basis; while English shareholders of varying social degree outnumbered the German, the majority of shares were in the hands of Haug and Langnauer. The initial terms of the agreement gave the Company of Mines Royal rights in various northern and western counties and in Wales, but mining operations were from the start confined to the Keswick region – for example, in Borrowdale, Grasmere, Newlands, and Buttermere. Not only expertise and equipment were imported from the continent but workers as well, whose needs, from lodging to clothing, food, and utensils, were supplied by their employers on credit allowed against their earnings.

Management was provided by the Augsburg company's agent, who took up residence in Keswick. As records show, he was responsible for accounting to his superiors in Augsburg for all expenditures, not only those strictly related to the mining operation but also sundry items of a household or domestic nature. The various company men, whether Hechstetter himself, his occasional replacement, or his subordinates, seem with few exceptions to have been on good terms with local gentry, engaging them in company business and exchanging seasonal gifts. After a period of apparent hostility, the miners too were evidently accepted in the area; some of them married English women, lending an exotic flavour to the nomenclature found in local parish registers.

The expenses involved in funding the Keswick venture, however, were considerable and for a large part were consumed in buildings erected for the various mining and smelting operations. In 1577 Haug and Langnauer withdrew from the Company of Mines Royal. Daniel Hechstetter opted to remain in England to oversee the work he had initiated, but in 1580 the company was reorganized under new management and the German business interest was to all intents and purposes at an end.

LOWTHERS OF WHITEHAVEN, CUMBERLAND AND LOWTHER, WESTMORLAND
CURWEN OF WORKINGTON, CUMBERLAND

Among the local names that occur in the sixteenth-century Keswick accounts are those of the Lowther and Curwen families. For these members of the gentry the first four decades of Stuart rule in the following century were generally prosperous and peaceful years in which personal fortunes were repaired or enhanced and the responsibilities of public life undertaken with conscientious energy. Connections with other families of similar social and economic standing were maintained through property transactions and intermarriage, often perversely reinforced through constant estate litigation. For the most part the Cumberland and Westmorland gentry were solidly royalist in sentiment and conservative in religion; a minority, among them the Curwens, were numbered actual recusants in the seventeenth century.[23]

At the heart of an influential county standing was the careful management of landed properties and interests, a policy that held it 'noe lesse good husbandry to improve the wast and baren ground, as to purchas new.'[24] From 1617 until his death twenty years later, Sir John Lowther, a lawyer, frugally husbanded his revenues in order to amass a considerable number of properties, especially in the immediate area of Lowther itself; by the time his son and eventual heir, the second Sir John, died in 1675, the family's interests reached from Westmorland into the neighbouring counties of Cumberland, Durham, and Yorkshire. Another son, Sir Christopher Lowther, was as a young man assigned an estate at Whitehaven in Cumberland that eventually became his inheritance; here he developed thriving commercial interests.

Sir Patricius Curwen succeeded his father Sir Henry, at Workington Hall, Cumberland, in 1623 when he was twenty-two years old, holding in addition other properties and manors in the immediate vicinity. Apart from landed revenues Sir Patricius shared the commercial interests of his Lowther neighbour at Whitehaven. The Curwen income was enhanced by the exploitation of resources such as fisheries and coal and iron mines, and by ventures into sea trade. Like the Lowthers, Sir Patricius took a keen personal interest in the management of his estates and income, keeping a careful eye on the accounts kept by his steward.

Both the Lowther and Curwen families had a longstanding role in public life. Sir John Lowther the elder was a justice of the peace and member of the Council of the North; his grandfather, Sir Richard Lowther, had briefly served as warden of the West March. Elected to Parliament, Sir John was also steward of the Richmond fee, negotiating the agreement made in 1619 between Prince Charles, the holder of the fee, and protesting tenants. The second Sir John succeeded his father in 1637. Also a member of Parliament and steward of the Richmond fee, he went on to become sheriff of the county of Cumberland in 1661.

Sir Patricius Curwen was created a baronet in 1627 and had a varied experience in public life. As a young man he helped levy and lead Cumberland forces for the expedition to relieve La Rochelle and its Huguenot garrison. In 1630 he became sheriff of Cumberland, as his father had been, and was later involved in the king's defensive preparations in face of Scottish invasion. As a royalist, he took an active part in the Civil War, sending on one occasion provisions at his own expense to the beleaguered garrison of Carlisle. Like the Lowthers, he was named among the delinquents who lost property by parliamentary sequestration for their part in the war.

While each of these families maintained a principal residence in the country, the nature of their public and economic interests brought them into constant contact with the wider world of borough and county. The shrievalty gave the Curwens stature in Carlisle where the county assizes were held. Workington Hall itself, with its peel tower and medieval hall, went back to the fourteenth century, though two wings were added late in Elizabeth's reign. The Curwens' home overlooked the small town, the village of the manor of Workington, with its Wednesday market and two annual fairs. But the family's own commercial and mercantile interests were based on the little port of Workington, whose real growth took place in the next century. Even in the earlier period, however, it provided the Curwens with a seagoing link for trade in iron and coal to Scottish and Irish ports. In 1641 'Barronett Curwen' joined forces with the Lowther interests to lobby for a fixed customs duty for the export of coal throughout the king's dominions.[25]

In the middle years of the seventeenth century Lowther Hall was substantially re-built, though most of the work was done after 1642. Lowther Hall and its park, a few miles south of Penrith, stood close to the route south to Shap, which then branched to Kendal and Kirkby Stephen. In 1640 Sir John the younger, recently created a baronet, noted that the bulk of the extant structure consisted of two towers between which lay his father's new building (1630) on the site of an older traditional hall. The lead and wood of the new roof, stripped from Kirkoswald Castle in Cumberland, had been bought from the castle's owner, Lord William Howard.[26]

Within the northwest the Lowthers' interests gave them a varied connection with town life. In his early years the elder Sir John had divided his time largely between his estate at Maulds Meaburn, where a house was built in 1610, and Kendal where he stayed in winter, 'attendeing,' as he wrote in his memoir, 'the markett daye in my house for the resorte that come to me for my profession.'[27] This policy paid off not only in profits used to purchase land but in his appointment just before his death as recorder of Kendal under the new charter of 1636. The Lowthers also had firm con-nections with Appleby, where Sir John had attended the grammar school. In later years Lowther livestock was brought into Appleby to be sold, as well as to Penrith and Carlisle. In fact, trading interests prompted the second Sir John to buy a burgage tenement in Appleby about 1639, a trifle that recompensed him with freedom from toll.[28] His standing in the borough was eventually rewarded there (as in Kendal) with the post of recorder.

HOWARD OF NAWORTH, CUMBERLAND

Influential and prosperous as they were, the Lowther and Curwen families ranked far below Lord William Howard of Naworth Castle, a younger son of the fourth duke of Norfolk and without doubt the most powerful English border magnate of his time. At the beginning of the period for which his household books are extant (1612), he had settled with his large family to a prosperous and stable life at Naworth, enjoying a propertied existence that included the barony of Morpeth in Northumberland and the Dacre and Greystoke baronies in Cumberland which were the inheritance of his wife Elizabeth. The Cumberland baronies had been finally secured in 1601, though only after a dozen years of litigation in which much money and labour had been spent fighting first a rival Dacre claimant, Elizabeth's uncle, and then the crown. (The fact that two members of the Lowther family acted for the queen in this matter sowed the seeds of enmity between the two houses.)

Built on an escarpment jutting towards the river Irthing, Naworth Castle lies a few miles northeast of Carlisle, close to the ancient Stanegate road that runs into Northumberland. For the Howard family the castle was well placed for the management of their affairs in the border counties. An old Dacre fortress, it no longer maintained a garrison, though on occasion it housed prisoners before they came to trial or sped Howard sons in pursuit of border trouble-makers.

Until 1618 the Howards seem to have been busy with the repair, maintenance, and consolidation of their various properties, making up for past losses and outlays by careful management. But in that year Lord William Howard was named as a commissioner for the government of the Middle Shires, which had replaced the old administrative units of the East and West Marches; thereafter he was active in the prosecution of the theft and violence that continued to plague the border area. As a young man, Lord William Howard had become a Roman Catholic. In later life, at a time when recusancy was seen as a threat to national security, his religion confined him to a local role in justice and administration. His Catholicism earned him the enmity and suspicion of government and neighbours alike. Sir John Lowther's hostility towards Lord William Howard was compounded of distrust of his religion and inevitable dislike of his frequent appearance in court as litigant, using methods that Sir John professed to find questionable.[29]

Educated at Cambridge, Lord William Howard retained all his life a scholarly interest in theology and history, in manuscripts (of which he had a fine collection), and in Roman antiquities. He had his own library in the castle, and corresponded with several literati of his time. In September 1640, an ailing old man, he left Naworth for Greystoke in face of threatened Scottish invasion and died there two weeks later.

CLIFFORD OF APPLEBY AND BROUGHAM, WESTMORLAND

In 1617 when James I came south from Carlisle on his return from Scotland, he was entertained at Brougham Castle, about twelve miles northwest of Appleby, by Francis Clifford, fourth earl of Cumberland, who had succeeded his brother George in 1605. George's daughter and only surviving offspring, the Lady Anne Clifford, had visited the Clifford estates in Westmorland as a child in 1607. In 1616 she was at Brougham to attend the funeral of her mother, Margaret, who had died after a brief residence in the castle. Apart from these interludes, Francis Clifford's reception of the king at Brougham in 1617 seems to have been the only occasion in the early seventeenth century when the Clifford family made any display of residence in Westmorland. No doubt this was partly because prolonged lawsuits were waged against Francis Clifford, first by the countess Margaret on her daughter's behalf, and then by Anne herself, pressing a strong claim to the Clifford barony in Westmorland and the properties, such as Brougham and Appleby, that went with it. Francis Clifford's reception for James I in 1617 was certainly linked to a recent royal award in the current round of litigation, favourable to the earl. Nevertheless, the earl, who died in 1641, and his son and successor, who died two years later, seem to have prudently shunned Clifford properties west of the Pennines in favour of residence at Londesborough and Skipton in the North Riding of Yorkshire.[30]

In 1643 Anne was the twice widowed countess of Dorset and of Pembroke. By the fifth earl's death in this year she came into her long disputed inheritance, acquiring Clifford properties not only in Westmorland but in Yorkshire as well. From that time on she lived exclusively in the north, devoting a good deal of her fortune to the restoration of Clifford castles, including Appleby, Brough-under-Stainmore, Brougham, and Pendragon in Westmorland.

Drama, Music, Ceremony, and Custom

In summarizing the evidence presented largely by borough and household records, I shall examine first activity that is local in origin – plays, civic waits, drummers, and other performers – including comment on the particular round of events that distinguished the civic life of Carlisle. Second, I shall look at the incidence of visiting performers, such as players, waits, and musicians – 'visiting' in the sense that such groups came from outside the locality of the borough or household whose records note their appearance; in all but a few cases these visitors are also from outside the two counties. In particular I hope to show that Kendal and Carlisle as boroughs each display distinct characteristics: Kendal, a small market town, newly incorporated, its rudimentary ceremonial and entertainment largely linked to municipal events rooted in its economic and administrative structure; Carlisle, with a long history as a troubled border and garrison town, nevertheless marking its seventeenth-century calendar with customary celebrations stemming from an even older folk tradition.

Local Activity

PLAYS

The performance of a miracle play ('quoddam miraculum') in Carlisle in 1345 is only incidentally remarked by a jury concerned with the violence that brought the performance to a sudden end. Thus, while the date (31 July), the location ('in foro ... ciuitatis'), and the performers ('clerici') are named, nothing of substance is gleaned about the play itself. It may be noted, though, that 31 July was not marked by any customary observance in the chamberlains' accounts of the early seventeenth century. The role of 'clerks' in the performance suggests a play still close to its liturgical origins in which guild organization had no part. Unfortunately we can only speculate whether the clerks were cathedral personnel (though presumably the canons themselves would have been termed 'canonici' in the record) or whether they were perhaps drawn from St Cuthbert's, a neighbouring parish church equally accessible to the market-place.

   The Kendal Corpus Christi play, still in existence at the beginning of the seventeenth century, was possibly unique in English town life at this late period. Various sources, both manuscript and antiquarian, document the history of the Kendal play between 1575 when the borough was incorporated and 1605 when the play was apparently suppressed. The *terminus a quo*, however, is misleading. Any assumption that the play sprang forth simultaneously with the birth of the corporation, based on a clause within a borough ordinance of 2 February 1575/6, breaks down when that evidence is examined in detail. Rather than an enactment providing for the establishment of the play, the ordinance is an attempt to limit attendance at dinners within the borough; it makes passing reference to the play in excluding from its terms such dinners 'as have bene comonlye vsed/at or vpon/Shotinges in long bowes, or metynges of men off Occupacions/aboute orders for their severall pagiandes of Corpus Christi playe.' The overall wording of this clause implies that the play's performance was already an established fact at the very beginning of Kendal's history as an incorporated borough.

The clause quoted is also important in two other respects. First, it reveals that the organization of the play lay in the hands of the occupations or guilds; a few years later we find additional evidence of this in a Shearmen's ordinance entered in the Boke off Recorde (1580–1), demanding a payment from all freemen admitted to the occupation 'besides Custome for the Playe.' Second, the clause is important in that it incidentally gives some solid detail about the play by referring to the 'severall pagiandes' that made up its content. Even so, it is clear that the Kendal play was stationary and not processional. An ordinance of 22 September 1586, aimed at better control of the licensing of plays, refers to the 'Playe of Corpus christi,' adding 'or any other stage playes,' while an entry in the chamberlains' accounts for 1600–1 indicates that the play was enacted in one particular street location. In 1612 Thomas Heywood referred to Kendal's 'stage-playes' in a curious statement about their origin and longevity.[31] A lingering memory of this nomenclature probably lies behind the wording of the Star Chamber interrogatories of 1622–3, which sought to elucidate details of the Kendal 'staige plaie' mounted in July 1621 by customary tenants of the barony.

Evidence confirming the religious content of the play comes from antiquarian writers later in the seventeenth century. In his diary John Shaw noted an interview in 1637 with an old man who had seen the Kendal play in his youth and was able to recall details of what must have been the crucifixion scene. Another diarist, Thomas Crosfield, alludes in 1638 to debate with his Oxford colleagues on whether the Kendal play ran contrary to canon law, constituting 'a kind of preaching or setting out of ye scripture to edification.' John Weever, in his *Ancient Funerall Monuments* (1631), claimed to have seen the Kendal play early in the reign of James I, before its suppression 'vpon good reasons' in circumstances he does not describe.[32] Entries in the chamberlains' accounts for 1605 show that an inquiry was carried out by commissioners (unidentified) at the time of the Easter leet court; journeys to York later that year, made by the vicar and the schoolmaster of Kendal, raise the possibility that the ecclesiastical high commission, which sat at York, was investigating charges against the corporation. Some years later Anthony Ducket, in his deposition concerning the Kendal Stage Play of 1621, revealed that Rowland Dawson, alderman at that time, had retained so strong a memory of the circumstances of the suppression in 1605 that he was reluctant to license yet another stage play in the town.

The Boke off Recorde yields some further evidence about the play in the late sixteenth century. For play days as on other festival days, members of the corporation were required in 1575/6 to wear black caps and gowns, then in 1586 their 'best vyolat gownes'; these clauses were subsequently cancelled or repealed from their respective ordinances, possibly in or after 1605. The ordinance of September 1586 reveals that the borough was already divided over the play's performance. Ostensibly the enactment is concerned with the proper licensing of this and other plays, but the preamble suggests that public demand for the play was an embarrassment to the corporation, possibly on economic grounds – 'waste' was a constant cry in Kendal – or through fear of intervention by the authorities.

Entries in the chamberlains' accounts alluding to 'the play' (rather than to 'players') fall into two groups. One group associates performance with named individual citizens: we hear of the play 'at mr wilsons' and of 'mr Ingall play' (1587–8), and of a payment to John Collen 'for his lofte for ye playe' (1589–90); in the summer of 1594 a total of twenty-eight shillings is paid out for 'Sir potters' stage play. Without other detail it is impossible to elaborate on these entries, which provide food less for thought than for speculation. The second group, three entries for the early years of the seventeenth century, are more significant. 'Wine off the play daie' and 'paven of stret whear play was' (1600–1) point to a performance of Kendal's own play, especially in the usage, 'play daie,' consistently found in Boke off Recorde entries. In 1601–2 the chamberlain, John Robinson, was reimbursed for thirty shillings 'which he layd ovt abovt the play by appoyntment.' As far as the chamberlains' accounts are concerned, these entries mark what were apparently the last performances of the Kendal play, and perhaps therefore the events that occasioned the commissioners' inquiry of 1605.

CIVIC WAITS AND DRUMMERS

Both Carlisle and Kendal employed waits and drummers on certain civic occasions. The records show, however, that there were distinctions in status and function. Minimal evidence also exists for waits at Appleby.

There are only eight entries in the Carlisle chamberlains' accounts concerning waits' liveries; a coat is mentioned in 1602/3 and cloaks in 1624 for which broad red was purchased (as again in 1627). The waits' cash remuneration seems to have consisted of rewards at time of performance. Apart from his livery, the wait mentioned in 1602/3 has no recorded remuneration. All succeeding references are to 'waits', in 1624 specifically to two, who together received two shillings on each of two occasions. Thereafter the more usual payment appears to be two shillings and sixpence. A payment for cloth for 'pipers' (1638–9) is the sole indication over the whole period that the waits of Carlisle may have employed the smallpipes characteristic of the

northern region, bellows-blown, with chanter and drones. The only personal identification is provided in 1616 when Mr Thompson is named as the city's wait.
Thompson is also rewarded, though not specifically as wait, twice in October
1614 (once at the election), with further payments to 'his boyes' both in that month
and again in 1618.

The piecemeal evidence of Carlisle sources suggests that the waits performed a
variety of functions. The leet court of October 1629 requested that with the sabbath
excepted, the waits 'goe' from that time until Candlemas, morning and evening, and
all Christmas. Four years later the leet made a similar request alluding to 'former
Custome,' which may only date back to 1629, and 'such allowance as formerly they
[the waits] haue had.' If this allowance was a particular fee allotted to midwinter duties,
then it is not recorded in the chamberlains' accounts. Apart from liveries, the accounts
enter payments for the waits' attendance at festivities on St John's and St Peter's Eves
(1614), for 5 November, when the mayor usually held a dinner (1616), on Shrove
Tuesday (1635–7), on All Hallow Thursday, and at the horse-race (1635). The Tanners
reward the city's waits on All Hallow Thursday 1614 and 'waits' in their chamber on
that day in 1613. One of the problems encountered here, as at Kendal, is the terminology employed. The Tanners consistently paid for 'waits' (1627–31) at their annual
dinner on 28 October; earlier they paid 'musicions or waits' (1626) and 'musicians'
(1618–25). The conclusion that these terms are synonymous with 'city waits' is supported by entries in the chamberlains' accounts for the period 1617–25. Here there
are consistent references to musicians where, on other evidence, we should expect the
city's waits to be named: for 5 November (1617, 1620), at the election (1620, 1624),
on Shrove Tuesday (1620, 1622), All Hallow Thursday (1621, 1625), and at the horse-
race (1621). Gaps in livery allowances that exist for the years 1618–19 and 1628 do
not necessarily mean that waits were not appointed; in the Kendal accounts such gaps
exist even while duties are maintained – we may suspect that liveries were simply
handed on until they wore out.

During the period 1583–1640 twenty-four payments at irregular intervals were
made for the Kendal waits' liveries, described as coats until 1613, and thereafter, with
exceptions in 1615 and 1627–8, as cloaks. The fabric varied: 'blv' was bought in 1595,
and grey and black frieze respectively in 1600 and 1603; after this date the choice was
consistently broadcloth, described in 1603–4 and 1619 as red. The Kendal waits were
not paid a fixed stipend on any periodic basis. On 7 November 1601 they received
a reward of one shilling 'at theyr first Coming'; the occasion is not otherwise detailed,
but the wording suggests a term of office coincident with the civic year that began
at Michaelmas. As with the Carlisle waits, cash remuneration was routinely made at
time of performance rising from one shilling, normally, in earlier years, to two shillings in 1618–19, and two shillings and sixpence in 1621–2, a sum which was more
or less constant over the remainder of the period.

The actual number of waits employed by the corporation, or the number attending
any one function, cannot always be determined with certainty. Several entries,

however, are indicative of numbers. In the autumn of 1603 sixpence was paid to Robert Hodgson who 'shold have beine the wait' – a circumstance unexplained – and the following spring a small allocation of cloth was made to 'the wayte.' Payment was made to Jasper Hey and his man for music at the Easter leet court of 1618, the only occasion when a wait (presumably) is identified by name and in a context that suggests a professional or experienced musician working with a subordinate. Three cloaks were purchased for the waits in 1636, the year in which Kendal elected its first mayor. Oddly enough, the enhanced status of the corporation does not seem to have generated more employment for the waits; thereafter they are noted as attending only one function, a leet dinner in 1637, although purchases continued to be made for their livery (1637–8, 1639–40).

The chief function of the Kendal waits was to attend the round of corporation dinners. During most of our period three dinners were routinely held during each alderman's term of office – those marking his election at Michaelmas, the immediately following leet court, and the Easter court of the next year. Occasionally the waits attended the alderman's dinner,[33] and for a period of time (1617–31) the corporation venison feasts held in late summer.

It is evident from the bare bones of entries in the accounts that these dinners were relatively informal affairs, at which leading citizens (alderman, burgesses, assistants, and their wives) sat down with whatever guests the occasion allowed or demanded. Sometimes we glimpse that the event was housed in a local inn or tavern – the 1590 election dinner at Christopher Fox's, for instance, and the venison feast of 1626 at Peter Huggon's. More often wives of local men in good standing with the corporation are named as catering the victuals for the company. It is probable (and sometimes documented) that they ran taverns or eating-houses to supplement their husbands' living. The wives of James Ayrey, William Warriner, and William Chamber (at various times sergeants-at-mace) performed this service, Mrs Chamber holding almost uninterrupted sway for twenty years (1616–36). Whether these women always provided the accommodation for the dinners is not clear from the accounts, though it is very likely. The Moot Hall, built in 1592, would have been the only other contender for this honour, but no confirmatory glimpse of it as a location for corporation dinners is afforded in the accounts. Wherever the dinner was held, however, some distinction of status seems to have been preserved in the seating and serving of guests.[34] From about 1620 until the middle 1630s the corporation dinners moved through their heyday. Numbers were large (eighty-two persons at the 1629 election dinner), with the consumption of wine with the meal and 'drinke' after (probably beer), accompanied from 1628 by a choice of tobaccos. This was also the period of the venison feast, with meat supplied by courtesy of local nobility and gentry. In this sort of atmosphere, we can visualize Kendal's waits as providing not ceremony but entertainment for the added pleasure of the company bidden to dine at corporation expense.

Kendal's waits were rarely employed outside these routine functions. In 1587 they helped celebrate Queen's Day (17 November) for which the bells of Kendal parish church were always rung; they greeted Dr Henry Robinson, the provost of Queen's College, Oxford, as he passed through Kendal (1591–2), and in 1596 they sped a contingent of Kendal men on the way to answer a summons to border service 'at bvrning of bekens.'

Terminology other than 'waits' occurs in the Kendal accounts. The 'minstrels' mentioned at dinners in 1588 and in each year 1596–8 were probably the waits; coats had already been provided for them before that time so they must have been an established feature of town life. Similarly we should probably read 'waits' for 'minstrel' references that occur for 5 August 1604 and for 1617 at the venison feast. The mention of 'pipers' at the 1595 election dinner and two dinners in 1600–1 (a year when they are also provided with liveries) suggests that, as in Carlisle, the waits employed the local smallpipes.

For Appleby there is only scant information about the wait (or waits), and it is impossible to form any picture of a civic function. The extant chamberlains' accounts (1585, 1609–30 with gaps) refer only three times to the possible existence of a wait, in the form of payments for the 'piper': ten shillings for his coat in 1609–10, and for his wages ten shillings in 1610–11 and sixpence in 1614–15. The waits of Appleby (in plural form) are noted in the Carlisle accounts as visiting the city twice in early spring (1610/11, 1614) and again in 1618/19. The apparently contradictory evidence of numbers and the suddenly deflated wage pose problems that cannot be answered within the context of the documents transcribed. Both are symptomatic, however, of a more universal difficulty rooted in problems of terminology: the term 'waits,' for instance, whenever it occurs in a municipal context should be allowed a good deal of flexibility. It may denote a well-developed professional organization such as the York waits. At the other extreme we may be dealing with no more than a fluctuating group – one or more local musicians – who receive little but sporadic patronage, if that, from their home town. Among the latter, in all likelihood, were the waits of the various small communities – Keswick, Millom, Kirkby Thore, Askrigg, even Appleby – named in the Carlisle accounts.

Both Carlisle and Kendal employed a drummer, though each on entirely different terms. While references to the drummer or the drum in Kendal are sporadic, we have some indication of who played it and when. The drum was beaten at the dispatch of border service in 1596 and 1601, and on 5 August (Gowrie Day) in 1604. Garnett, the man who twice played for Queen's Day (1587, 1593) is probably the cobbler, Edward Garnett, who mended the drum in 1594 (WMB/K, Chamberlains' Accounts, Book 8 f[17]). Similarly Edward Archer, sworn to the occupation of Wrights, was twice paid for beating on Queen's Day (1601–2), again in 1608, and also for repairs in 1602 (Book 16 f [21]). Rewarded on an ad hoc basis, the Kendal drummer was drawn from the artisan ranks of society, perhaps as much for his ability to keep the instrument in good repair as for his ability to play it.

Carlisle's drummer, on the other hand, enjoyed a certain status and security of tenure, signs of a more professional standing. He was retained on an annual or quarterly basis for a fixed fee that stood at twenty shillings per annum until halved in the account for 1616–17 to ten shillings, a sum constant to the end of the period. In addition there are eight disbursements for the drummer's livery or coat (broadcloth in 1604, red kersey in 1627–8). Until he died, apparently in the winter of 1621–2, Nicholas Hudson was named as the city's drummer and another Hudson, probably a relative, was listed as drummer for the first quarter of 1642. Apart from regularly recurring entries for fees, however, there is scant information on the role of the drummer in Carlisle's civic life. Nicholas Hudson is among the 275 people who received in 1614 a gift of money customarily distributed at Midsummer, with a further charitable gift at the time of a sickness that probably led to his death. In 1635 the city's drummer attended the horse-races on Kingmoor for two days, while Richard Hudson, (probably the same 'Hudson' who is named in 1642) performed on Shrove Tuesday 1638/9.

From 1638, with the approach of civil war, the town drummers of Kendal and Carlisle were drawn into an increasingly military role. As the need for defensive preparations became apparent, payments for drum and drummer become more frequent. In Kendal these are linked to the activities of the locally raised 'trained soldiers.'[35] In the Carlisle chamberlains' accounts, payments also begin to appear for trumpeter and drummers belonging to the military, perhaps to the garrison itself.[36]

OTHER LOCAL PERFORMERS

Discussion of waits and drummer form the only grounds for direct comparison between Kendal and Carlisle, for the latter's accounts feature individuals not paralleled in the former. For instance, in Carlisle sums varying from one shilling to two and sixpence were paid to John Burton or John Trumpeter over the years 1602–20. Specific information for some years, coupled with the placing of entries for others, indicates that his most regular appearance was on election day, sometimes with waits or musicians. John Burton also took part in festivities on All Hallow Thursday in 1603, 1617, and 1618; on this occasion in 1615 he was described as an 'intruder' (interluder). He was also paid for his services on 1 January 1602/3 and with a New Year's gift in January 1608/9. Of added interest is the fact that a 'John Trumpeter' visited Naworth five times in the years 1612–20; the virtual coincidence of his subsequent absence from the Naworth accounts and from the Carlisle accounts after 1620 confirms his identity as John Burton of Carlisle and suggests, moreover, that he died shortly afterwards.

While we may speculate about the death of John Trumpeter in the winter of 1620–1, it is certain that a more colourful character, 'Willyam miller the Citye foule,' died about then, since his funeral expenses are entered early in the account for that year. Entries for Willy the Fool occur regularly from December 1610 and give us some glimpses of his role in the life of the city. In the 1614–15 account he is described as 'ye naturall ffoole'; shirts, shoes, hose, and coat were routinely purchased for him, with expenses entered for fabric, tailoring, and repair. Red and white kersey for his coat, with a small quantity of canvas, were bought three times 1614–17; other distinctive items include two bells and a feather (1614), a 'sack,' and a pair of 'dulle sole' shoes (1617–18).

There is some tenuous evidence that the fool, or if not always he then some other person, had a special part to play in entertainment at Christmas. Fabric for the fool's coat in 1617 is grouped with other such purchases for the city's 'Christames sportes.' Similarly in 1614 and 1619 shoes and stockings were bought for Willy just before Christmas. Further details from the beginning and end of Willy's tenure suggest that a 'lord' or 'abbot' presided over the Christmas festivities. In December 1610 an entry for Willy's shoes is followed on 26 December by the purchase of other items of clothing – a hat, coat, and red broadcloth – delivered not to the fool this time but to 'my lord Abbot.' In 1620 there is a payment for 'the lords coat against Christinmes.' Willy died, however, probably in the winter of 1620–1, so that the role of Christmas lord may on that occasion have been played by someone else.

Other glimpses of the fool's activities are seen in the summer of 1614. The kersey, bell, and feather bought then were probably intended for him to wear at the celebrations on St John's and St Peter's Eves in the last week of June. In the same period he is named as present at the mayor's house, carrying (perhaps dispensing) wine and sugar. Later he was outfitted with clothes for the assizes, possibly for an appearance at an entertainment or dinner following the court session.

On All Hallow Thursday 1605 payment was made for 'one that was foole'; unfortunately, gaps in the accounts make it impossible to determine whether this character was Willy himself, since we cannot pinpoint the beginning date of his career with certainty. But the noncommittal phrasing of the entry suggests that even if the reference was to Willy Miller, he had not yet become an acknowledged protégé of the city of Carlisle.

When we turn to household accounts we catch a glimpse of local musicians who had a role not only in the domestic life of gentry and noble families but in the work place on their estates. At Naworth the Howards employed John Mulcaster to entertain during the Christmas season (1629/30, 1633/4). At Workington the Curwens had Bodell, a local fiddler, and a piper often named as Anthony Troughton; here too there was piping at Christmas on a good many occasions between 1625 and 1640, as also at Hackthorpe Hall, Westmorland when Sir John Lowther the younger was in residence in 1635/6. The Workington piper was also employed at harvest time in almost every year between 1628 and 1640, a season when he earned twopence a day for periods ranging from nine to seventeen days. It is not clear whether he entertained at a meal concluding each day's work (which the small sum would suggest) or whether his airs, like functional reapers' songs, kept the harvest workers advancing in a steady and even line through the fields.

CARLISLE'S CUSTOMARY CALENDAR

A varied schedule of events was encompassed in Carlisle's mayoral year, distinguishing the borough from Kendal, whose municipal entertainment was chiefly linked to routine events in the corporation's administrative round. In Carlisle the first significant occasion in the mayor's term of office was Gunpowder or Conspiracy Day on 5 November, normally marked by a dinner with accompanying entertainment sometimes detailed in the accounts. Scholars from Carlisle Grammar School appear four times in the period 1619–36, performing a 'speach play' or oration before the mayor's guests assembled at dinner, and in 1639 they were responsible for the bell-ringing (CA/4/2 f [190]), a consistent feature of the city's celebration of 5 November. In other years various musicians entertained at the dinner (1617, 1620; in 1616 together with a juggler) and in 1616 and 1620 payment was also made for a wake.

The next event on the mayoral calendar was the Shrove Tuesday games. These are occasionally called 'silverplay,' 'play,' or 'silver' games, but in such cases evidence of date and content confirms a Shrove Tuesday context. Except for the accounting years 1621–2 and 1624–5, there are entries for this event in every year for which chamberlains' accounts are extant. Apart from small itemized payments a lump sum was normally laid out, rising from a low of 15s 6d (10 March 1602/3) to erratic peaks in later years, of which the highest was £1 8s (21 February 1636/7.) The city merchant, Edward Dalton, acted as something of a Shrove Tuesday impresario, receiving a number of these large payments from 17 February 1617/18 to 21 February 1636/7.

The games traditionally took place at the Swifts, a low lying area of land just east of the modern Eden Bridge, on the south bank of the river.[37] On 5 February 1610/11 the accounts give their first indication that the Shrove Tuesday event centred on a game of football, with payment for the ball; on 8 March 1613/14 there was a reward for the boy 'that wonn the foote Ball.' While entries for this sport continue throughout the period, repair to the hammer shaft is mentioned for the first time on 9 February 1618/19 and again on 26 February 1627/8, when 'acocke … & … makeinge his pitts' forms yet another item. These two events each appear twice more in the next decade. On 21 February 1636/7 one shilling was paid for a piece of cloth on which to put the games: was this simply a custodial measure, or does it indicate a new event, such as bowls, for instance? More problematic are allusions to gunners, who made use of a door (sometimes with a sheet of 'pastboard') at the games in 1627/8 and on four occasions in the next decade. What sort of activity the gunners engaged in and who they were, cannot be elucidated from the accounts. It is conceivable that in the interest of good public relations the city invited a contingent from the garrison to display its prowess in a performance that may have involved a mock battle or some other form of scenic representation. On several occasions the accounts show that music was part of the Shrove Tuesday celebrations, with payments made to waits or musicians, or to named individual performers; the drummer, Richard Hudson, and musicians, performed in 1638/9 at the last Shrove Tuesday celebration recorded in the accounts.

All Hallow Thursday (Ascension Day) was another major occasion for the city of Carlisle, not relinquished even in the troubled year of 1643, when performances on two drums were paid for (CA/4/2 f [205]). Chamberlains' and guild accounts show that the celebration focused on a circuit of local boundaries, an activity long associated in Christian tradition with the Rogation days immediately preceding Ascension Day. At Carlisle, all the occupations joined the mayor and brethren of the corporation in a riding of the boundaries of Kingmoor to the north of the city. From 1593 to 1635 payments are frequently entered for entertainment on this day, variously the trumpeter, waits, musicians, a fool, a fiddler, a juggler, and in 1611 simply 'the plaie.' These presentations were probably given publicly, the trumpeter and waits perhaps accompanying the riding with other forms of entertainment reserved for the procession's return to the city. Later on in the day the occupations assembled in their individual chambers for fare such as bread, cheese, cakes, and ale, sometimes enjoying their own music, as did the Tanners in 1613, 1614, and 1636, and the Merchants in 1629 and 1633. The twenty shillings uniformly paid out to the occupations on this day evidently broke down into a traditional gratuity of 2s 6d given to each of them by the mayor. After retiring with the brethren to the high chamber for refreshments, the mayor went on to visit the other chambers, sharing wine with the assembled members of each occupation. On most occasions disbursements for the day included money spent on gunpowder and we may speculate that the holiday ended with a gunnery, or more probably a fireworks display, an event to which the occasional but distinct label of 'summer games' in the chamberlains' accounts may apply.[38]

Kingmoor was the scene of another Carlisle event, though one only intermittently staged during the period 1621–37. This was the horse-race, run in May according to the chamberlains' accounts, some days after the boundary-riding had taken place. Horse racing in Carlisle had late sixteenth-century antecedents.[39] In the first twenty years of the seventeenth century it seems to have been discontinued, for it receives no explicit mention in extant civic records until April 1619, when the leet court requested that racing be resumed, urging the mayor and brethren to 'call for' (seek out from a previous holder, perhaps) 'the silver broad Arrowes and the Stock and the horse … Bels'; these, with an additional silver-gilt cup to the value of £5 were to maintain a yearly race under an articled agreement that the cup be awarded not outright but on a year-to-year basis. Items concerning a case for this 'boule' and for the writing of the articles were entered in the 1620–1 account. The chamberlains' accounts, however, afford evidence of the race itself only for 1621, 1631, 1635, and 1637, other sources pointing to a possible fifth event in 1636. Entries provide glimpses of weights and a scale carried to Kingmoor, of halberdiers needed to control the crowd, and of the mayor entertaining favoured visitors such as the sons of Lord William Howard of Naworth. On two occasions (1621, 1635) musicians or waits form part of the day's entertainment. In March 1635/6 an ordinance forbade the city's waits to receive what must have been a customary gratuity when they attended the horse-race.

Details, not always cogent, of prizes awarded may also be gleaned from the Chamberlains' Audit Book and guild accounts. Possibly the silver-gilt cup was never brought in after its first presentation or else other races were added, for we find the city paying for a gilt bowl in 1631 and plate in 1635 and 1636. In 1632–3 the occupations began to subscribe to further awards, perhaps sensing benefits accruing to the city's commercial life from the popularity of the event. The Tanners contributed to the purchase of one dozen silver spoons (as apparently did the other occupations) intended for a 'third Course of Horse rase.' The Merchants in the same year gave money towards the renewing of 'a Runninge Bowle,' with further sums collected for plate over the years 1633–6.

St John's Eve and St Peter's Eve, towards the end of June, together provide the last traditional event in the mayoral year. In 1614 we have a glimpse of what was already a vestigial remainder of a Midsummer celebration, with payments for butchers' and sergeants' wakes, watchers either night, the waits, and a corporation banquet perhaps held as part of the festivities. In subsequent years the twofold occasion is seen as a time for the distribution of money to the corporation's pensioners, the chamberlains' accounts providing no further evidence of Midsummer revelry.

Visiting Performers

PLAYERS

According to the Kendal chamberlains' accounts, forty visits from groups of players occurred between 1585 and 1637. The Carlisle accounts show thirty-four visits from players between 1602–3 and 1639. Bearing in mind the gaps in the latter source, we may estimate that Carlisle was in fact the more popular venue, one factor perhaps being that the cash reward earned there was on the average higher than in Kendal. Matching years in borough and/or household accounts occasionally allow us to see players' companies visiting two locations within a period of weeks or even days: for instance, players of the earl of Sussex visited both Carlisle and Kendal in the autumn of 1617, as did the queen's players in the following spring, and the king's players in the latter days of February 1622/3 and early August 1627. Similarly the prince's players were at Carlisle and Naworth in the winter of 1621/2 and Lord Strange's players at Workington and Kendal in October 1636. There is only rare indication of whether players' visits were timed to exploit local events or circumstances. In November 1585 Lord Morley's players enlivened the banquet given for the auditors at Kendal, players performed there in the newly built Moot Hall in 1592–3, and the visit of the prince's players in 1623 (and also possibly the king's in 1625/6) coincided with the period of the Easter leet court. Local patrons are in evidence. The players of Edward, Lord Morley, and of his son, William, Lord Mounteagle, whose family seat was at Hornby Castle in Lancashire, appear five times between 1585 and 1614. The players of Philip, Lord Wharton, who died in 1625, and of his grandson and heir, also Philip, appear sixteen times between 1600 and 1638.

Several groups of players are denoted by provenance rather than by patron. The sums paid to them are large enough to discount the theory that 'players' is a term here synonymous with 'waits' or 'musicians.' With one exception – the Penrith players at

Naworth in November 1622 – payments fall within the January–February period. Payments to players visiting Carlisle from Penrith (1602/3) and to the local Warwick players at Naworth (1624/5) are dated from early January, indicating that performances were linked with Christmas or Epiphany celebrations. Visits of the Cockermouth players to Workington, however, in February 1628/9 and 1633/4 may hint at a Shrovetide connection.

WAITS AND MUSICIANS

A noticeable feature of the Kendal accounts is that no entries are recorded for waits from outside the town. In Carlisle, however, 'stranger' waits are frequently rewarded. The poverty of Kendal citizens as compared to those of Carlisle may explain this difference, or perhaps the fact that there were better opportunities for performance in the various traditional outdoor events of Carlisle's calendar. As a garrison town and the major crossing point between Scotland and England, Carlisle may well have exercised a unique attraction. It is difficult to see, though, why this attraction would not also have influenced the itinerary of players by drawing the various companies northward to the exclusion of Kendal. Furthermore, it is unlikely, though not impossible, that the waits of Kendal were able to maintain the same kind of closed shop as did their more prestigious counterparts at York, though they would certainly have won the backing of the corporation had they tried.

Judging from the number of entries in the Carlisle, Naworth, and Lowther accounts, the most frequently heard visiting waits travelled from their home towns of Penrith, Cumberland (26 entries); Kendal, Westmorland (18); and Lancaster, in the next county (11) – statistics that reflect the comparative distance of each borough from Carlisle. Other waits, local in that they originated in the western Pennines area, came from the Westmorland communities of Appleby (3 entries), Kirkby Thore, Kirkby Stephen, Orton, and Kirkby Lonsdale, and from Cockermouth, Keswick, and Millom in Cumberland. A diverse group of visitors hailed from north and west Yorkshire, journeying westward through the Pennines to arrive in Carlisle as early as March. These included waits from Barnard Castle in Teesdale; Richmond at the bottom of Swaledale (4 entries); Middleham (6 entries), Askrigg, Bedale, and Thirsk in or near Wensleydale; Ripon (11 entries) and Knaresborough in the Vale of York, with the city of York itself; and finally a concentration of communities in the Aire-Calder region: Wakefield (7 entries), Halifax (5), Leeds, Bradford, and Doncaster. From farther away came the waits of Durham, Newcastle upon Tyne, Lincoln (8 entries), and – farthest of all – the waits of Edinburgh, Bristol, and Canterbury. While in sum these entries reflect a wide provenance of waits visiting the northwest of England, several groups are named only once in the overall period of the accounts; in fact only visits from the waits of Penrith, Kendal, and Middleham (from 1608–9) span the entirety of the period covered in the accounts.[40]

The Documents

The transcriptions have been primarily organized by county; within each county they are subdivided into two sections, Boroughs and Households. It must be stressed that these are titles descriptive of institutions rather than of classes of record. Under the former, for each borough, are grouped various classes of records: 'public' or government, borough (court records, chamberlains' accounts), and guild, all bearing upon dramatic activities within the context of civic life. The latter title, on the other hand, comprises accounts drawn from private sources – household or estate – that illustrate such activities in the context of domestic of household life. Each borough and household is thus dealt with as an entity, its materials organized chronologically under yearly headings.

For the descriptions that follow, two points should be noted. First, in the case of a series or collection of manuscripts, a detailed description is given only of those volumes or individual documents from which material is transcribed. Second, errors in foliation in original manuscripts (folios omitted, gaps or repetition in numbering) and details of torn or missing folios are noted only where relevant to a particular problem in transcription.

Cumberland

BOROUGHS

Carlisle

Parliamentary and Council Proceedings
London; Public Record Office, C49/46/16; 26 September 1345; Latin; parchment; 10 membranes of varied size; modern numbering 1–10; bound in file, stiff back, limp front, white buckram, with title on front cover.
Mb 8: 240mm × 288mm (227mm × 275mm); fair condition, 2 small holes in text. Mb 10: 394mm × 315mm (300mm x 300mm); poor condition, but repaired, with some discolouration obliterating text, small cuts at sides, tear at right side, and two small holes at left side.

Letter of Henry Scrope
London, British Library, Egerton MS 2598; 1589–93; English; paper; ii (modern) + 279 (original) + ii (modern); folio size varies (f 82, 305mm × 196mm); manuscript made up of single leaves; late 19th century foliation; good condition, with repairs throughout; British Library binding, 19th century, red leather over board covers stamped with Egerton arms in gold, spine has shelf mark and title: 'Correspondence and Papers of William Asheby, of Loseby, co. Leicester, during his embassy to Scotland ... July 1588 [–] January 1589/90 [and continuing to] 1593.' The document was transcribed by Anna Jean Mill, *Mediaeval Plays in Scotland* (Edinburgh, 1927), p 299.

Chamberlains' Accounts 1
Carlisle, Cumbria Record Office, CA/4/1; 1602–19; English; paper; iii (modern) + 76 (interspersed original and modern) + vi (modern); average original folio size 301mm × 190mm (275mm × 156mm), 37 lines per page; six paper booklets gathered between and individually separated by blank modern folios of uniform size; unfoliated; poor to fair condition, discolouration or fading at upper and lower edges, marginal decay, minor repairs; bound in leather (325mm × 201mm), covered with heavy mottled grey paper originally sealed to cover inside with wax, spine labelled, 'Chamberlains' Accounts|Vol I|1602–3|1605–6|1608–9| 1610–11|1618–19.'

Chamberlains' Accounts 2
Carlisle, Cumbria Record Office, CA/4/2; 1613–44; English; paper; iii (modern) + 215 (interspersed original and modern) + iii (modern); average original folio size 393mm × 148mm (360mm × 130mm), 55 lines per page (except 1617–18: 308mm × 104mm (294mm × 77mm), 30 lines); 20 paper booklets, gathered between and separated by blank modern folios of uniform size; unfoliated; poor to good condition, discolouration and fading, some ff torn or perforated, decay at margins (occasionally severe); bound in brown calf (410mm × 155mm), scroll decoration at edges, civic crest stamped in gold, bottom front and spine, title in gold, centred front: 'Corporation of Carlisle, Chamberlains' Accounts, Vol II. Various Years, 1613–1644.'

For each volume I have ascribed sequential foliation from the first to the last original folios, including all blank folios, both original and modern, that lie between; thus for volume 1, ff [1–76v], and for volume 2, ff [1–215v].

Two chamberlains (occasionally one towards the end of the period) were chosen annually at or after Michaelmas to handle the revenues and expenditures of the corporation. REED items are found only in the record of disbursements. These are not uniformly recorded 1602–42. Certain groups may be categorized under separate heads (eg, Benevolences, Rewards) or by marginal notation (eg, 'Re*ward*,' 'ffoole') throughout an untitled disbursements section. Fees are always listed under separate title. Up to 1628, with some exceptions, the accounts are drawn up annually; from 1634 they are given on a quarterly basis for each year, the periods ending at St Thomas's Day (21 December) or Christmas, Our Lady Day (25 March), St John's Day (24 June) and

Michaelmas (29 September). Chamberlains might assume joint responsibility for the whole year, or divide the quarters between them (as described in the endnotes).

In the chronological table that follows, each account is briefly described with reference to titles (abbreviated and modernized) from which material is excerpted in the text.

There is no actual account for 1605–6, though f [30v] is endorsed as the chamberlains' account for that year. This folio may be the last of the 1604–5 account, the endorsement based on a misunderstanding of a heading, f [28v], for demissions made by Henry Baines, mayor in 1604, to be accounted for by John Raven and William Raven at Our Lady Day (25 March), 1606. Baines's demissions (authorization of leasing of city revenues – see p 159, endnote to CA/4/9 f [25]) would have been made for the year 1604–5 at his retirement (September 1604); the Ravens, as chamberlains for that year, would have accounted for these demissions six months after their own retirement (Michaelmas 1605), that is, in the following March (see below, Chamberlains' Audit Book). The date, Our Lady Day 1606, given in the heading, may thus have been misinterpreted as the end date of the accounting period, rather than being more correctly understood as the date of the subsequent audit. A summary of the account categories for 1602–43 follows:

1602–3	CA/4/1	ff [1–20v]	Disbursements, Fees, Benevolences, Wine (annual)
1604–5	CA/4/1	ff [22–8v]	Disbursements, Fees, Benevolences, Wine (annual)
1608–9	CA/4/1	ff [32–47v]	Disbursements, Fees (annual)
1610–11	CA/4/1	ff [49–61v]	Disbursements, Fees (annual)
1613–14	CA/4/1	ff [1–15v]	Disbursements, Fees (annual); Disbursements on St John's Eve and St Peter's Eve
1614 15	CA/4/2	ff [17–22v]	Disbursements, Fees (annual)
1616–17	CA/4/2	ff [24–33v]	Disbursements, Fees (annual)
1617–18	CA/4/2	ff [35–41]	Receipts
		ff [42–57]	Disbursements with marginal categorization, Fees (quarterly)
1618–19	CA/4/1	ff [63–76v]	Ordinary, Rewards, Fees, Liveries (annual)
1619–20	CA/4/2	ff [78–86v]	Disbursements in two separate but concurrent accounts, Fees (annual)
1620–1	CA/4/2	ff [88–94v]	Disbursements, Fees (annual)
1621–2	CA/4/2	ff [96–101v]	Disbursements with marginal categorization, Fees (annual)

1621–2	CA/4/2	ff [103–7v]	Draft of above – Disbursements (annual)
1622–3	CA/4/2	ff [109–14v]	Disbursements (annual)
1624–5	CA/4/2	ff [116–25v]	Disbursements (annual); Fees (quarterly)
1626–7	CA/4/2	ff [127–33v]	Disbursements (annual); Fees (quarterly)
1627–8	CA/4/2	ff [135–42v]	Disbursements (annual); Fees (quarterly)
1634–5	CA/4/2	ff [144–51v]	Disbursements, Fees (quarterly)
1635–6	CA/4/2	ff [153–63v]	Disbursements, Fees (quarterly)
1636–7	CA/4/2	ff [165–78v]	Disbursements, Fees (quarterly)
1638–9	CA/4/2	ff [180–7v]	Disbursements, Fees (quarterly)
1639–40	CA/4/2	ff [189–97v]	Disbursements, Fees (quarterly)
1642–3	CA/4/2	ff [199–207v]	Disbursements, Fees (quarterly)

Chamberlains' Day Book
Carlisle, Cumbria Record Office, CA/4/9; 1569– ; English; paper; 24 + ii; average folio size 300mm × 205mm (270mm × 130mm), 30 lines per page; unfoliated; poor condition; fragmentary portion of original binding (taken from a Latin parchment manuscript), measuring approximately 230mm × 190mm with many holes, is attached to f [1] and f [24v], the whole, plus 2 additional ff, is stitched into stiff grey paper covers (310mm × 202mm).

The Day Book, very faded in parts, contains some orders and various rough jottings; there are many blank folios.

Court Leet Rolls
Carlisle, Cumbria Record Office, CA/3/21, 28–9; 1619, 1629, 1633; English; paper; written top to bottom; unnumbered. CA/3/21: 4 mbs, attached at top; 380mm × 290mm restored to 424mm × 302mm (360mm × 260mm), 36 lines per mb 1–3; faded script, mbs restored, newly sewn at top. CA/3/28: 5 mbs, attached at top; 402mm × 315mm restored to 445mm × 325mm (340mm × 270mm), 25 lines per mb; faded script; now stitched at top between modern paper folios. CA/3/29: 8 mbs, loose, formerly attached at top; 395mm × 295mm, mb 3 restored to 420mm × 302mm (310mm × 250mm), 25 lines per mb; clear script; all mbs wrinkled, marginal decay; mbs 5–8 with increasingly larger hole, bottom left, from 15mm diameter to loss of whole corner (90mm diameter) mb 8.

The leet court, or mayor's tourn, usually sat twice a year, in the spring and autumn. Ten rolls are extant for the period 1597–1633. These record, first, presentments from the leet jury for various offences that range from treason to infringement of local ordinances; second, ordinances agreed upon in court as necessary for the city's continuing welfare. REED items are transcribed from the second group.

Chamberlains' Audit Book
Carlisle, Cumbria Record Office, CA/4/139; 1597–1684; English; paper; ii (modern)
+ i + 158 + i (original) + ii (modern); average folio size 295mm × 190mm (265mm × 140mm),
32–52 lines per page; 4 gatherings; foliated 1–158 in red ink, probably at later date (placing
allows for wear at folio corners); good condition; bound in brown calf (310mm × 200mm),
civic crest, lower front and spine, title, centred front, stamped in gold: 'Corporation of Carlisle
Audit Book 1597–1684.'

The chamberlains' accounts were audited roughly six months after their retirement
from office; eg, the accounts for the fiscal year Michaelmas 1613–Michaelmas 1614
were audited on or about the following 24 March (information from sources varies
slightly). The city held throughout the period to a chronological year starting on 25
March; thus the audit took place roughly at the turn of the chronological year (24
March 1614/15). The current mayor and 'ye fower of ye Election of every Occupation'
(f [47]) were in attendance. The accounts were prepared for audit under approximately four summary heads: arrears owing and paid; incoming revenues from sources
such as tolls, rents, farmed revenues; the chamberlains' expenditures or 'allowances
craved'; an estimate of the existing deficit. The 'allowances craved' (often of a grouped
nature) occasionally contain items of interest to REED, either supplementing information from CA/4/1–2, or filling in gaps in that source.

Merchants' Book
Carlisle, Cumbria Record Office, D/GC/4; 1580–1733 (approximately); English; paper; 227
leaves; average folio size 330mm × 210mm (320mm × 160mm), 36 lines per page; original and
restored folios (including fragments); some earlier ink foliation preserved, modern pencil
foliation 1–227; blank folios throughout; modern brown leather binding (340mm × 215mm).

The merchants formed one of Carlisle's eight occupations or trades. The carefully
restored Merchants' Book contains various orders from c.1580, including those
appointing days for the annual dinner and quarterly meetings, ff 2–3; also a roll of
members, admission oath, and various memoranda. Minutes of the quarterly meetings
include undermasters' annual accounts; these detail routine items for the annual dinner
and Ascension Day festivities excerpted below. The undermasters presented their
accounts on the Friday after the feast of St Peter (29 June); the actual date is noted in the
manuscript and is given editorially in the transcription.

Tailors' Guild
Carlisle, Public Library, A453, 1652–1867; English; paper; 5 (modern) + 130 (original) +
approximately 135 (modern) leaves; intermittent pagination, different inks, variously
positioned, ff [4–6], 7–11, [70v–97v], 142–96; f [126]: 290mm × 174mm (255mm × 160mm),
32 lines; bound in mottled board (304mm × 185mm), miscellaneously printed, coloured end-
papers, calf spine, inside front cover: 'George Thorpe, 9 Howard Terrace, Carlisle'; front end-

paper, recto, book-plate inscribed 'Tullie House' and verso, 'This Book came into the possession of Dixon Losh Thorp 1898...'; loose sheet of paper (75mm × 190mm), inscribed 'Volume of Receits of the Tailors' Guild Carlisle (see Ferguson and Nanson's Municipal Records pp. 143 etc/.)'

Foliation has been ascribed to exclude modern folios (and to ignore the intermittent pagination), numbering the first to the last of the original, ff [1–130].

The material comprises various orders, admissions and fines, not always in chronological order (ff [1–114], 1652–1867; f [115], 1705–34; ff [125–130], 1659–96); f [125] heads a section described as orders copied (1659) out of an earlier book (see endnote, p 163, to A453 f [126]).

Tailors' Guild
Carlisle, Cumbria Record Office, D/Lons/L13/11, 'Taylors' Guild, No 1'; 18th century transcription of original material 1659–1703; English; paper; 96 leaves; average folio size 320mm × 195mm (275mm × 150mm), 30 lines per page; unfoliated; good condition; bound in grey board (320mm × 207mm), title written upper third front cover: 'Taylors' Guild No 1' with added comment, 'Finished Examined by R: Yarker January 1706' and modern label 'City of Carlisle 1659–1703 Tailors' Guild Minute Book (copy).'

This 1703 copy was evidently made from A453 (described above) when that volume was still in use by the guild. Material continued to be entered in A453, however, well beyond 1703; hence this D/Lons/L version is only a partial transcript of A453.

Tanners' Guild
Carlisle, Cumbria Record Office, D/Lons/L, 'No 1 Tanners' Guild'; 18th century transcription of original material c.1566–; English; paper; 108 leaves; average folio size 320mm × 200mm (300mm × 150mm), 27 lines per page; 9 gatherings; unfoliated; good condition; bound in grey board (320mm × 200mm), title written twice, upper third front cover: 'No 1 Tanners Guild' and 'Tanners Guild No 1–'.

An order made 8 Elizabeth I, f [6v], establishes a possible starting date c.1566 for the material transcribed in this antiquarian volume. The earlier folios are taken up with various orders, including those relating to quarterly meetings, f [5–5v], and the annual dinner, ff [6], [9]. Minutes of quarterly meetings, with masters' accounts detailing receipts and expenses, run from 1610 through 1642, ff [13v–55v], and include items for the occupation's dinner and All Hallow Thursday, some of which have been transcribed here. The masters presented their accounts on Friday after All Hallows Day (1 November); the accounts are dated by the All Hallows Quarter in the manuscript, but the probable date has been editorially supplied in the transcription.

HOUSEHOLDS

Augsburg Miners

Agent's Accounts
Augsburg, Stadtarchiv, Handelsbücher Nr. 20, Fasz. 1, 6–8; 1569–74; German; paper; annual
volumes of accounts for the Augsburg mining company of David Haug and Hans Langnauer;
original foliation for individual accounts (therefore not sequential through each volume); all
in good condition with exceptions noted; each volume in parchment, with title (upper portion,
front cover), eg, '1569 Journal der Bergwerksandlungen in Engellant, dass 69. Jar Betreffennt'
(others similarly descriptive). Fasz. 1, 1569: 269 + iii; folio size 296mm × 202mm. Fasz. 6,
1571: 186 leaves; folio size 323mm × 221mm; binding damaged. Fasz. 8, 1573: 122 leaves; folio
size 322mm × 223mm. Fasz. 7, 1574: 118 leaves; folio size 320mm × 222mm.

Handelsbücher Nr. 20 consists of 12 volumes, 1569–77, of which seven relate to
the Keswick and five to the London ends of company business. In the Keswick volumes, disbursements are grouped under various heads for the company's operations
in the area. Details concerning the domestic life of the company officials and their
household needs are also included in the accounts, occasionally yielding information
of interest to REED. Collingwood (*Elizabethan Keswick*) deals in some detail with these
volumes, excerpting and summarizing material of local interest rather than providing
actual detailed transcriptions. He points out (p 6) that the accounts, made up seven
times a year, covered periods roughly ending at Shrovetide, Easter, Whitsun, St James
Day (25 July), Holy Cross Day (14 September), All Saints' Day (1 November) and
Christmas (end of December). Foliation is editorially ascribed sequentially throughout each volume.

Curwen of Workington

Curwen Account Book
Carlisle, Cumbria Record Office, Account Book of Sir Patricius Curwen, Bart. (Workington
Estate); 1625–46; English; paper; 254 leaves; average folio size 315mm × 195mm
(290mm × 155mm), 54 lines per page; unfoliated; good condition overall, first folio fragmentary; bound in folded flexible board (340mm × 525mm), sheets bound in with pink tape, remains of pink tie on front binding, title on labels (modern), front cover and spine: '1625–46
Account Book of Sir Patricius Curwen, Bart. (Workington Estate).'

Curwen himself began this book (f [3], 'a booke of my receates and disbursements')
ending towards the bottom of f [5v] where his steward, William Thwaite, continues.
Receipts and disbursements are not recorded on any consistent periodic basis, but

cover several weeks to several months, each group audited by Curwen himself (with signature). Disbursements are not categorized, household and estate items being intermingled.

Howard of Naworth

Household Books
University of Durham, Department of Paleography and Diplomatic, Howard of Naworth C706; 1612–34; English; paper; 11 household books; Books 2–10 with initials WM near title, Book 1 title, front cover, '1612 Naward Ephemeris seu Liber Expensis domes*ticis* ib*idem* a Primo Ianu*arij* ... Thomas Widmerpoole' (most others similar).

Book 1: January 1612/13–30 December 1613; ii + 58 + i; average 312mm × 195mm (275mm × 165mm), 44 lines per page; contemporary foliation; good condition, worn margin; bound in parchment (recording loan to which Richard, bishop of Coventry, is a party), 305mm × 210mm.

Book 2: 1 August 1618–31 July 1619; i + 67; average 310mm × 195mm (280mm × 175mm), 38 lines per page; contemporary foliation 1–65; good condition; bound in parchment, back 302mm × 210mm, front 295mm × 168mm.

Book 3: 1 August 1620–end July 1621; i + 56; average 304mm × 192mm (275mm × 185mm), 39 lines per page; contemporary pagination 1–79; fair condition, 17 ff missing (probably unwritten); bound in parchment, front 303mm × 205mm, back 303mm × 185mm.

Book 4: 1 August 1621–July 1622; i + 62; average 305mm + 195mm (275mm × 165mm), 40 lines per page; contemporary foliation 1–61; fair condition; bound in parchment, front only remains, 304mm × 185mm.

Book 5: 1 August 1622–31 July 1623; i + 56; average 304mm × 198mm (275mm × 175mm), 42 lines per page; contemporary foliation; fair condition; bottom outer corners ff 1–17 crumpled, bottom two thirds f 52 missing; bound in parchment, front only remains, 290mm × 195mm.

Book 6: 1 August 1624–end July 1625; i + 54; average 305mm × 195mm (255mm × 160mm), 43 lines per page; contemporary foliation 1–57; good condition, f 10 missing; bound in parchment, front 287mm × 204mm, back 295mm × 187mm, title severely faded.

Book 8: 1 August 1626–beginning of June 1627; ii + 46; average 305mm × 195mm (265mm × 155mm), 42 lines per page; contemporary foliation 1–41; fair condition, some ff mutilated or missing (index, f [ii], gives last section at f 50); bound in parchment, front 285mm × 215mm, back 286mm × 183mm (holed).

Book 9: 19 May–5 November 1628; i + 39; average 320mm × 195mm (300mm × 170mm), 45 lines per page; contemporary pagination 1–77; good condition; blank spaces filled in with material *temp.* 1671–75; bound in parchment, front only remains, 328mm × 212mm, title, p 1.

Book 10: 5 November 1629–October 1630: iii + 59; average 320mm × 185mm (295mm × 155mm), 48 lines per page; contemporary foliation 1–64; fair condition; marginal decay (especially ff 1–10, 58–64), 5 ff missing, probably unwritten; bound in parchment, front 330mm × 210mm, back 315mm × 195mm (several holes 2–15mm diameter), title severely faded.

Book 11: 1633; i + 89; average 290mm × 190mm (265mm × 155mm), 44 lines per page; contemporary foliation 1–80; bound in parchment (or fine leather), backed with original first and last ff of book, front 284mm × 198mm, back 285mm × 182mm (six holes 4–10mm diameter); spine holed, remains of two pairs of leather ties attached to front and back covers, labels pasted front, top right and bottom, probably contemporary, inscribed '5' and 'Digging coal …' respectively, title severely faded.

The Naworth Household Books, kept by Thomas Widmerpoole, Lord William Howard's steward, record incoming revenues from various manors and expenses under a variety of heads (My Lord's Parcels, My Lady's, Rewards, Extraordinary).

A twelfth book, for 1640, contains nothing of interest to REED. Book 7, August 1625–July 1626, lacks f 51, on which, according to the book's index, was 'Extraordinary Payments,' the section normally relevant.

Ornsby (*Household Books*) excerpted these accounts, for 1612–13 and 1640 in full, and elsewhere *in extenso*. He errs, however, in summarizing the years covered (p vi), nor does he indicate clearly his editorial method. Ornsby also examined a book of accounts kept by John Pildrem which gives the expenses of Lord William Howard on a journey to and from 'Spa' in 1623, with partial records for the years 1619, 1622, and 1627. From this Ornsby transcribed extensively the full record for 1619, with extracts from other years. He states that (*c.*1838) the book had been in the possession of 'Mr Lawson of Longhirst in Northumberland,' but at the time of writing (1878) it was in Naworth Castle (p vii). It does not appear to have been included among the records deposited in Durham and I have not been able to trace its history or location.

Lowther of Whitehaven

Sir Christopher Lowther's Notebook
Carlisle, Cumbria Record Office, D/Lons/W1/4; 1635–7; English; paper; vi + 67 + ii; 145mm × 85mm (145mm × 75mm); contemporary foliation; good condition; fly leaves i–vi with notes of purchases, living costs, etc at Hamburg *c.*1637, recipes, part of a letter, and index I–W; end leaves i–ii with index A–H.

This paper booklet, in the hand of Sir Christopher Lowther of Whitehaven, Cumberland, is the last of three notebooks or diaries (1632–7) recording his domestic and business activities. The notebooks, with other documents, have been transcribed and edited by D.R. Hainsworth, *Commercial Papers of Sir Christopher Lowther*.

Westmorland

BOROUGHS

Appleby

Chamberlains' Accounts
Kendal, Cumbria Record Office, 1585, 1609–30; 16 separate accounts, variously receipts and disbursements, 1–16 leaves; English; paper; all leaves pierced 2 holes, top; all accounts endorsed 'RB 102.' Account 2: 1609–10; 1 leaf; 305mm × 193mm (270mm × 160mm), 31 lines recto, 6 verso; receipts and disbursements, title (f [1] at foot): 'anno domini 1610 / the accompt of Iames Marton and Charles Emerson Chamberlains for the aforesaid yeare.' Account 4: 1610–11; 1 leaf; 398mm × 153mm (260mm × 140mm), 34 lines recto; untitled disbursements. Account 8: 1614–15; 8 leaves; ff [1], [3–6] 395mm × 150mm (225mm × 140mm), average 27 lines per page; ff [2], [7–8] from 125mm × 100mm to 190mm × 105mm; the whole sewn together at top of folios, folded once; receipts and disbursements, endorsed f [6v]: 'The Chamberlaynes accompt in Anno 1615' (contemporary or approximate) and 'Accounts of Receipts & Disbursements & other papers etc / No: 102 / being 40 in Number' (possibly later hand).

Two chamberlains were chosen annually to handle receipts and disbursements for the borough. The volume of business transacted was not large; the pierced holes in the leaves of the accounts indicate that they were originally kept fairly casually, probably tied in bundles. Disbursements were not categorized under separate titles, except as in Account 8, 1614–15, which includes special building or repair projects. Accounts, where titled, are given one chronological year; but Account 11 f [1], headed 1618, notes that the chamberlains were sworn 9 October 1617, and Account 15 f [1], headed 1629, dates the first receipt 20 October 1628. This evidence suggests that the chamberlains entered office in the Michaelmas season preceding the year given as the date for each account. Thus for Account 11, the fiscal year effactually runs 1617–18, for Account 15, 1628–9, with presumably a similar span for the rest of the accounts. But as at Kendal the fiscal year sometimes seems to have extended beyond Michaelmas itself: Account 13, 1620–1, is endorsed with the note that the account was made by the chamberlains, 2 December 1621, f [2v]; both Account 15 f [1] and Account 16 f [1] 1629–30 refer to their respective accounts as ending 30 November.

The material has been numbered editorially in chronological sequence; each number refers to a separate item, whether this is a single leaf containing, for example, one receipts account or several leaves stitched together as in Account 8. Thus Account 4, disbursements for 1610–11, is separate from Account 3, receipts for the same period; the date of Account 4 has been ascertained from internal evidence (the balancing of the sum of receipts in Account 3 with the sum of disbursements and remainder in Account 4).

Kendal

Chamberlains' Accounts
Kendal, Cumbria Record Office, WMB/K; 53 books, 1582–1641; English; paper; average leaves 27 (highest 48, Book 52; lowest 12, Book 23); unfoliated except modern Book 1, 1–34, and contemporary (sometimes not in correct sequence or with gaps) Book 10, 1–8; Books 12, 22, 2–10; Books 16, 18, 19, 2–11; Book 41, 2–21; Book 43, 1–26; paginated, contemporary, Book 14, 4–10; Book 47, 2–26; Book 15, 1–26; average folio size 401mm × 151mm (380mm × 128mm), 56 lines per page (except Book 11, 300mm × 100mm (285mm × 90mm), 48 lines); leaves variously arranged and stitched, 1–12 gatherings; overall condition fair, marginal decay, some discolouration, loose or missing stitching, torn or excised folios throughout; bound with heavy greyish paper, Books 30, 31, 43; same binding, but with fragments of blue-grey end-papers in red scroll pattern, Books 45, 50, 51; bound with light board, Book 4 (lower third front and back missing), Book 34; bound with parchment, Book 37 (dilapidated), Book 38 (with leather thonging), Book 39 (light tooling at edges); remaining books unbound, first and last folios forming covers, all books, title centred, front cover, top portion. Unbound and unfoliated books have been numbered editorially from front title/cover page to back cover.

Two chamberlains, elected annually at Michaelmas, were responsible for receipts and disbursements for the corporation; the accounts were audited at Martinmas (or roughly mid–November) for the preceding fiscal year. Many books keep separate titles for routine categories of payments, such as those made in respect of the town's mills or profits from town by-laws. Disbursements of a general kind, among which REED items are found, are most frequently listed in the 'Extraordinary' section. Book 1 contains accounts for 1582–7; in succeeding years the record was entered in one paper booklet per year. No REED items are found in Book 2, 1582–3, a book of receipts, or in Book 20, 1605–6, which lacks an Extraordinary Payments account (perhaps originally written on ff [15–16], now missing). A second book of receipts, Book 11, 1596–7, includes disbursements that duplicate those in Book 10, the chamberlains' book for that year. Numbers 29A, a special assessment account, and 29B, an audit voucher (both 1617 and boxed with the chamberlains' books) are described in the endnotes.

Kendal, Cumbria Record Office, WD/AG/Box 5; 1593–4; English; paper; 32 unnumbered leaves; 205mm × 142mm (195mm × 125mm), average 35 lines per page; 4 gatherings; good condition; bound in portion of parchment music manuscript, with red four-line stave and ornamentation, black notes and words ('videt Iacob vestimenta …'), 215mm × 155mm, edges folded to inside and sewn.

This account is an alternative version of Chamberlains' Accounts, Book 7, with which it is collated in the transcription.

Boke off Recorde
Kendal, Cumbria Record Office/Kendal Town Council; 1575–early 18th century; English; paper; iii + 351; 298mm × 200mm; contemporary foliation; bound in worn brown leather, 3 decorative thonged panels back and front, evidence of linear decoration at edges, title page: 'A boke off Recorde or Register, Contayninge all the acts and doings in or concerning The Corporation within the Towen off Kirkbie Kendall. Begynnynge … the Eighte day off Ianuarij … 1575' (abstract of title also on label inside front cover).

The Boke off Recorde is the first register of the borough, dating from its incorporation in 1575. The book includes lists of free inhabitants, aldermen, mayors, civic officers, and occupation members, as well as ordinances for the borough and occupations and various memoranda. Many pages are blank. It is written in several hands, the first (1575–1580s) recurring throughout the book, but separated by later hands as blank pages were subsequently filled. R.S. Ferguson edited a transcript of the register, based on two earlier transcripts, in *A Boke off Recorde*.

Diocese of Chester: Consistory Court Paper
Chester, Cheshire Record Office, EDC5/1625/13; Latin heading, English text; paper; single sheet; 305mm × 195mm (140mm × 150mm); fair condition (one small hole and creases in paper); endorsed in different hand 'Responsa personalia Willelmi Miller parochie de Kendale Capta 22ᵈᵒ Octobris Anno domini 1625.'

HOUSEHOLDS

Clifford

Household Accounts
Chatsworth House, Bolton Abbey MS 97; English; paper; i + 209 + i; 244mm × 190mm (265mm × 115mm); foliated 1–204; good overall condition except ff 201–4 detached from binding; bound in parchment, 168mm × 195mm, front and back, with remnants of green tape ties, front cover, stained, with title, '1616,' top third, centred, '97' in blue pencil at top left, '24' in pencil at bottom left.

This account book records disbursements, dated 3 November 1616–23 March 1616/ 17, for the fourth earl of Cumberland, under such headings as Rewards, Riding Charges, Extraordinary. It includes reference to preparations for the visit of James I to Brougham, one of the earl's castles in Westmorland. The book is one of an extensive series of accounts (estate and household) kept for the Clifford earls from the late sixteenth century to 1643 when the fifth earl died. This material is numbered, not always in chronological order, in the Chatsworth finding-aid, 'Manuscripts of his Grace the Duke of Devonshire: List of Household Accounts etc. at Bolton Abbey'; numbers 94–100 (1610–25) are household accounts prepared by Thomas Litton, primarily for charges at Londesborough. As indicated on p 16 and in note 30, though they continued to draw revenues from their Westmorland estates, the Clifford earls of this period confined their residence to Yorkshire.

Diary of the Lady Anne Clifford
Maidstone, Kent Archives Office, U269 F48/2; 1616–20; paper; 38 leaves; unnumbered; 230mm × 90mm; each leaf folded to form two folios; each folio written recto only in two vertical columns, the smaller about 51mm wide; no binding, except the whole wrapped in one leaf.

The document has been transcribed, with an introductory note, by V. Sackville-West, *The Diary of the Lady Anne Clifford.*

Lowther of Lowther

Estate Accounts
Carlisle, Cumbria Record Office, Lowther Estate Accounts (John Lowther of Lowther), D/Lons/L3/1/5; 1638–71; English; paper; 293 leaves; average 390mm × 148mm (370mm × 120mm), 55 lines per page; unfoliated; early folios marginally worn, top outer corners missing, folios bound with tape into folded flexible board, overall 410mm × 380mm.

Disbursements account for undifferentiated household and estate items; these are grouped in periods of seven days and upwards, each group summarized as a total disbursed up to a particular date.

MISCELLANEOUS

State Papers Domestic
London, Public Record Office; English; paper. Within each group (designated by letter and number), documents are bound into a series of volumes and numbered within each volume. SP1/134, No 1346: articles of accusation; 9 July 1538; 1 leaf, partly restored; 302mm × 210mm. SP1/134, No 1370: letter dated 13 July 1538, originally accompanying No 1346; 1 leaf, partly restored; 301mm × 182mm; endorsed in same hand as text 'To the right honorable and my Singulere goode lorde my lord preuy seall be this yeuyne' (and see p 214, ll 14–16). SP 14/40, No 11: rough memorandum; undated; 2 ff, partly restored, each with 2 holes 10mm apart, centred in top margin; originally one folded sheet, 338mm × 245mm; endorsed f [2v] 'Concerninge the Lord William Howard.' SP14/86, No 34: memorandum; 2 ff; originally one folded sheet, 596mm × 390mm; endorsed in hand distinct from text '1616//Mr Saundersones Note.'

Star Chamber Records
London, Public Record Office, STAC/8/34/4; 1621–2; English; parchment and paper; 59 leaves; modern numeration at foot of folios, 1–59 in smaller hand, 1–56 in larger hand (used here for reference purposes) added at time of microfilming, omitting blank folios; large bundle of individual documents of varying sizes, tied together with string at top left corners; fair condition; unbound. Ff 14–15, examination of defendants, 16 February 1621/2; paper; 330mm × 210mm. Ff 18–19, sworn deposition, 19 November 1622; paper; 325mm × 210mm. F 26, interrogatories, undated; parchment; 1325mm × 215mm. Ff 31–8, sworn depositions, 10 September 1622; parchment; 8 leaves numbered 1–8 (contemporary) in top and bottom margins; 500mm × 225mm (f 35). F 40, interrogatories, undated; parchment; 774mm × 320mm. F 49, joint answers of defendants, undated; parchment; 3 membranes stitched bottom to top forming one leaf; 1006mm × 520mm. F 51, portion of interrogatories, undated; parchment; 716mm × 320mm. F 54, portion of answers of individual defendants, 29 April 1622; parchment; 737mm × 280mm. F 55, bill of plaintiff; parchment; 510mm × 785mm; endorsed 5 December 1621.

Problems presented by ff 49–54 are further discussed below, pp 236–7, endnote to STAC/8/34/4 f 49.

Thomas Crosfield's Diary
Queen's College, Oxford, MS 390; English and Latin, some French and Greek; paper; 228 leaves; 182mm × 130mm; contemporary foliation; original binding, leather and board.

Entries in the diary (ff 16–81v, 84v, 87–92v, 173v–177) are interspersed with notes on books read, almanacs, and sermons. Entries are dated 6 January 1626–9 November 1638, 15 November–25 December 1638, January 1640, 2 February 1653–1 February 1654, and 1 November 1632–10 September 1638 (ie, a second set of entries for this period).
Thomas Crosfield was a student and fellow at Queen's College from 1618 until 1640. His diary, recording his thoughts and activities, together with events of local interest, has been edited by Frederick S. Boas, *The Diary of Thomas Crosfield* M.A., B.D. *Fellow of Queen's College, Oxford.*

Life of John Shaw
London, British Library, Add. MS 4460; c. 1707; English; paper; iii (modern) + 84 (original) + iii (modern); contemporary pagination, with subsequent foliation 1–84; 250mm × 140mm; narrow paper booklets bound together; small hole (from burn) at top inner corner on f 43; 19th c. British Library binding, marbled paper over board covers with leather corners, stamped front and back with scroll device and 'E Bibliotheca "Birchiana",' leather spine has shelf mark and title, 'Bibliographical Notes: Mus. Brit.; Bibl. Birch 4460,' f 1 inscribed 'Tho. Birch – bought at the sale of the Museum of Ralph Thoresby Esq. 7th March 1764.'

The manuscript (ff 3–16v) contains 'a transcript of the life of Mr. *John Shawe* formerly vicar of *Rotherham* and Preacher afterwards at Kingston upon *Hull* wr⟨....⟩n by himself' (f 2); it was copied from the original by Ralph Thoresby. Additional material follows, relevant to the lives of Dr Tobias Matthews (bishop of Durham and archbishop of York), Dr Samuel Winters, and others.

Shaw's 'Life' has been published as *Memoirs of the Life of Master John Shawe* and as 'The Life of Master John Shaw' in Surtees Society, vol 65.

Editorial Procedures

Principles of Selection

Included for each location or group of household records are all references to local
and visiting waits, players or plays, minstrels and musicians, and entertainers such
as jugglers, bearwards, puppet-players, and fools.[41] Entries for the Carlisle and
Kendal drummers are routinely transcribed with the exception of duties carried out
at the time of local musters, levy of trained bands, or similar militia acitivities. Items
for the purchase and repair of drums are omitted from all accounts. Payments to the
Kendal waits and/or drummer, related to the summons of border service, have been
retained. This service, regional in scope, was performed as a traditional obligation by
customary tenants within the barony of Kendal; as such it also provides illustrative
detail of the tenant protest that sparked the Kendal Stage Play of 1621.

Where waits, musicians, or other forms of entertainment are noted for civic or guild
dinners, catering details and numbers in attendance are also transcribed for context
purposes.[42] The Tailors' Guild ordinance for the observance of Corpus Christi Day
is included in Appendix I (p 146), largely because it is the sole basis for the conjecure
that Carlisle mounted a procession on that day in which all the guilds took part.

All references to the visit of James I to Carlisle, Brougham Castle, and Kendal in
August 1617 have been included. Omitted, however, are items for the ringing of bells
on those royal or national occasions that were routinely observed throughout the kingdom.[43]

The civic life of Carlisle, as instanced in the chamberlains' and guild accounts, neces-
sitates some selective culling of material. The primary concern of the selection process
has been to preserve the sense of a traditional calendar of events, as the city moves
each year from the Michaelmas election through to the Midsummer celebration of St
John's Eve and St Peter's Eve. In the early seventeenth century a round of time-
honoured activities still gave Carlisle a strong corporate identity that distinguished
it from a relatively new royal borough such as Kendal.

The records, however, pose particular problems for the transcriber. These include
the fact that certain events do not *consistently* reveal evidence of a dramatic or ceremonial nature, that entries from more than one source have sometimes to be pieced

together to document the whole of a particular event, and that while a number of items appear to be germane to REED, both their origin and their contemporary significance remain obscure. The short discussion that follows will illustrate ways in which these problems have been variously approached.

Full details for the Shrove Tuesday games, a traditional event, have been transcribed for every recorded occasion, including not only entries for entertainment, but details of the games themselves and the equipment required. The celebration of All Hallow Thursday, however, has been treated differently. A perambulation of Kingmoor was the core of the occasion, and the day's events, taking a set form, would normally fall outside REED's scope.[44] A variable factor, however, occurs in occasional payments for entertainment made on that day. These entries appear either in the chamberlains' accounts or in guild records. Where such payment is noted, all entries for that particular All Hallow Thursday are transcribed.[45] Thus the day's events (for which the two sets of records provide complementary information) are documented as fully as possible in order to furnish an intelligible context for the entertainment item. Entries for gunpowder, included in this scheme, present a subsidiary problem; they are transcribed in the hope that future research may shed light on a possible connection with an older 'summer games' tradition.[46]

The third and final event singled out for comment here is the Carlisle horse-race on Kingmoor, run in May in occasional years. Horse-racing in Carlisle went back at least to the sixteenth century, and may have had a Shrove Tuesday connection. Resumed after 1619 by public demand, the event appears to have had a strong claim to inclusion in the traditional schedule of civic events. All recorded entries for the race have been transcribed, including those descriptive of the guilds' role in the presentation of plate.

For household records a few additional points should be noted. Payments made for waits, players, or other forms of entertainment have been omitted where the location patently falls outside the counties of Cumberland and Westmorland.[47] In the Howard household books sums sometimes noted as spent 'at play' or 'at a play' have been omitted since they appear to be gambling expenses (however phrased).[48] Payments for an 'instrument' and for 'organs' that occur in the Curwen accounts have not been transcribed.[49]

Dating and Chronology

The bulk of the Cumberland and Westmorland transcriptions are taken from the chamberlains' accounts for Carlisle and Kendal. The chamberlains' term of office, in both cases coincidental with the mayoral or aldermanic term, ran from Michaelmas to Michaelmas. For this reason I have chosen a chronology for the transcriptions as a whole based on the chamberlains' accounting year: eg, the heading '1618–19' indicates a year that runs from 29 September 1618 to 28 September 1619. Furthermore, the preservation of documentary integrity is more crucial for these boroughs than for other areas dealt with in this volume. In the case of Carlisle especially, each annual chamberlains' account records a traditional succession of events, a local calendar, which if at all possible ought not to be fragmented by the imposition of an alien chronology.

Of course no system is ideal. This one, presenting the line of least resistance and obviating the problems of old and new style chronology, must still bend to accommodate certain inconsistencies. In particular, the chamberlains' year, while linked to the mayoral and aldermanic term, sometimes extended beyond Michaelmas – well into October in Kendal. This overrun probably stems from the fact that while the alderman was elected on or close to 29 September, the chamberlains themselves were not chosen until the burgesses and assistants met for the first time in the new aldermanic year, obviously at a later and more flexible date; there would then be delays in settling up the old account and handing over office. In Kendal also the annual audit, which took place at Martinmas (mid-November), probably came to represent a more realistic climax to the chamberlains' term of office than Michaelmas itself. In the transcription, items specifically dated after 28 September are given an extended editorial date that includes the year, to avoid any inference that they belong to the preceding September or October: eg, WMB/K 1, f 20v, is dated 30 September 1587[+], indicating that the payment date falls within the succeeding year (1587–8), but for the sake of documentary integrity the entry has been kept within the original account. Similar inconsistencies presented by guild and household accounts are dealt with below.

The editorial dating of entries is also affected by other aspects of the chamberlains' accounting procedures, in particular the methods employed for cash rewards made, for instance, to visiting players and waits, or for the more routine payments made to those responsible for the Carlisle Shrove Tuesday games or the provisioning of the Kendal corporation dinners. The accounts of both boroughs indicate that a large number of payments were handled on the authority of the mayor or alderman, being made by his 'appointment' or 'command.' For want of actual evidence we may infer that a written instruction authorized the chamberlains to make specific payments on many such occasions and to claim these expenses at the end of the accounting year. At other times it is clear, especially in Kendal, that on-the-spot payments were made by the alderman or individual citizens as the occasion demanded; subsequent reimbursement was claimed from the chamberlains, though sometimes at a date much later than that of the event itself.[50] The final account, made up with the help of hired penmanship, was presumably based on a day-to-day record of vouchers and receipts detailing claims and payments made throughout the year – evidently a ticklish process that was understandably eased by recourse to the amenities of a local tavern.[51]

What the system, if it may so be described, presents to the modern editor is a series of possible dates, all relative to the accounting process, any one or none of which may be given in the final form of the account. A dramatic entry, for example, may conceivably be dated in the account by the event itself, the act of payment, or the reimbursement of the payer; where none of these details is supplied, it is in a sense dated according to the time at which the final account containing this information was made up. Which of these dates are we to select for editorial purposes as (1) sound, (2) consistent, (3) useful to the researcher? Unfortunately the answer to (1) and (2) is not always the answer to (3), though (3) of course should have priority.

The editorial solution here is based on the self-evident premiss that the account itself is primarily concerned with documenting the record of payments; to those who kept such accounts the events themselves are only of interest insofar as they pin down the occasion or purpose of expenditures. In keeping with this premiss, and with the aim of preserving documentary integrity, editorial dates assigned in parentheses, eg, (9 May), refer to the date of payment as indicated in the account itself. As demonstrated above, the payment date may in fact be quite distinct from the date of the event or activity for which it was made. In such a case the date of the event, if known, is supplied in a textual note. In some instances, of course, the date of payment and of event coincide, but this is normally clear from the context of the entry.

The difficulties of dating are compounded by the actual format of the chamberlains' accounts, where dates if included at all are not always given on a consistent basis. Two basic approaches are found: one dates items 'externally,' usually in the left margin or centred; the other dates them 'internally,' that is, as part of the entry itself. Normally I have not transcribed marginal or centred dates; instead these have been given editorially in parentheses. Internally dated entries have been left to speak for themselves. More problematic is the fact that very few accounts take either approach consistently, so that we are often faced with an entry for which there is no explicit date in the account. Where an account is intermittently dated I have assigned payment periods in parentheses for undated items, using the immediately previous and immediately following explicit dates for this purpose, eg, *(4 June–5 July)*, or where there is no *terminus ad quem*, using the format *(21 September⁺)*. I have done this, however, only where two criteria are met: first, the account must demonstrate a reliable chronology of successive items, tested by the proper sequence both of dates, where they occur, and of references to known routine events (eg, the Michaelmas and Easter leet courts in Kendal); second, the intermittent dates must be spaced in such a way as to make the payment periods significant: *(4 June–15 July)* not *(3 January–6 June)*. The most that can be said for this method is that it narrows down the date of payment and hence possibly the date of the event if otherwise unknown. The reader may not agree that because a particular entry occurs between two sequential dates it records a payment made within the period, but he or she has at least a glimpse of where it occurs on the face of the document, with the option of repudiating the editorial conclusion. It should also be added that a parenthetical payment date refers to all items that follow without other editorial interruption.

The adoption of a Michaelmas year poses some minor problems also in the incorporation of other types of accounts into the edited text. Almost all the material excerpted from the Carlisle Merchants' and Tanners' accounts concerns either the occupations' dinners – for the former the first Sunday after 8 September (Our Lady's

Nativity), for the latter St Simon's and St Jude's Day (28 October) – or their role in the All Hallow Thursday celebrations (May–early June). The Merchants' under-masters accounted to the occupation on the Friday after the feast of St Peter (29 June); the Tanners' masters made their account on the Friday after All Hallows Day (1 November). Thus we know only the date when the final account was rendered, and cannot pin down the actual date or period when money changed hands, though in most cases it was probably close to the events for which payments in the account are recorded. Again this circumstance means some accommodation both of the basic premiss that the edited accounts date the record of payments, not events, and also of the Michaelmas accounting year format. With the occupations' records it seems unwise to separate either single events such as dinners or intrinsic parts of an event such as All Hallow Thursday from the year of their occurrence. For this reason entries of this type are incorporated into the Michaelmas year according to the date of the events themselves (given in the textual notes). The editorial ascription, however, is extended to indicate that the entries are from an account of a particular date, one that may fall outside the year of occurrence. Hence in the transcription under the year 1618–19, the Tanners' All Hallow Thursday entries are headed 'f [26v] (Masters' Accounts dated 5 November 1619),' that is, information relative to the event (6 May 1619) is taken from an account whose date falls after 28 September 1619, the terminal date of the Michaelmas accounting year, and within what is properly 1619–20. On the other hand, information relative to the annual dinner (28 October 1618), taken from the annual account rendered a few days later, is headed 'f [24v] (Masters' Accounts dated 6 November)', the account and the event both falling within the Michaelmas year 1618–19.

Household accounts, while not conforming in the original to the Michaelmas year, present less of an editorial problem than the occupations' accounts. Entries in the Curwen account book are dated internally with some frequency; the Lowther account book contains dated summaries of expenses at roughly ten-day intervals. Thus entries from both sources may be assigned narrow payment periods, if not specific dates. This has facilitated fitting dramatic entries into the Michaelmas year. Naworth account entries are also closely dated, normally within two to three days of one another. These accounts, however, were kept annually in separate books, usually beginning in August. To preserve a consistent Michaelmas year it has occasionally been necessary to split entries from one household book between two years: thus Howard Household Book 4 runs from August 1621 to July 1622; transcribed entries dated in August (ff 30–30v) are given under 1620–1, while those dated from 12 November (f 30v) are given under 1621–2.

Finally, it should be stated that in the introduction and notes frequent reference is made under date to material in the text. Events that fall on dates in the period 1 January–24 March are given as, for example, 2 February 1575/6; where an exact date is lacking, material is referred to under the accounting year, as, for example, Shearmen's ordinance, 1580–1. In all other cases the references are straightforward, eg, 7 November 1601.

Notes

1 For an historical approach to the development of roads, see Brian Paul Hindle, *Lakeland Roads: From Early Tracks to Modern Highways* (Clapham, N. Yorks, 1977), and 'Roads and Tracks,' *The English Medieval Landscape*, Leonard Canter (ed) (London, 1982), pp 193–217. The main Roman road from the south followed the Lune valley to Low Borough Bridge, Ewe Close, Brougham, Old Penrith, and Carlisle; the Gough map (1360) shows it running from Carlisle to Penrith and Shap, thence branching to Kendal and Kirkby Lonsdale. Roman routes west through the mountains ran from Watercrook (south of Kendal) via Ambleside and Hardknott Pass to Ravenglass, and from Old Penrith through Keswick to Cockermouth, Papcastle, and Maryport. In the Middle Ages a dangerous southerly route crossed Morecambe Sands from Furness to Lancashire. Monasteries founded on the edges of the Lake District had a stake in the upkeep and development of roads for estate and marketing purposes. Stimulus also came from the creation of peel towers and from the need for 'corpse' roads that communicated with distant parish churches. The foundation of Keswick in 1276 and the establishment of small market-towns in the south and west of the Lake District also spurred road development, as did the growth of mining in the sixteenth century.

2 C.M.L. Bouch and G.P. Jones, *A Short Economic and Social History of the Lake District Counties 1500–1830* (Manchester, 1961), pp 150–5, summarize the evidence for select-vestry government in Cumberland and Westmorland.

3 See Andrew B. Appleby, 'Disease or Famine? Mortality in Cumberland and Westmorland 1580–1640,' p 430. Appleby discusses four major crises: an outbreak of typhus, probably accompanied by famine (1587); plague (1598); and famine (1597 and 1623).

4 See pp 63–4, PRO: C49/46/16

5 See p 152, endnote to D/Lons/L, f [16v], f [17].

6 Adolphus Ballard, *British Borough Charters 1042–1216* (Cambridge, 1913), pp 185, 205; and Adolphus Ballard and James Tait, *British Borough Charters 1216–1307* (Cambridge, 1923), p 303.

7 Richard S. Ferguson and William Nanson (eds), *Some Municipal Records of the City of Carlisle*, pp 10–11.

8   Ferguson and Nanson, *Municipal Records*, p 12; the only duty laid on the twenty-four is to help elect the mayor.

9   Oaths of office and ordinances in the Dormont Book, begun in 1561 (Ferguson and Nanson, *Municipal Records*, pp 47–87) suggest that the new charter added little to the city's existing administrative and judicial framework; the sword-bearer is a new feature. Names of the mayor and bailiffs, given in the charter, checked against the chamberlains' accounts (CA/4/2 f [166], account title) show that its terms took effect at Michaelmas 1636.

10 Ferguson and Nanson, *Municipal Records*, pp 29–30; the occupations comprised Merchants, Weavers, Smiths, Tailors, Tanners, Cordwainers, Glovers, and Butchers.

11 Maurice Beresford, *New Towns of the Middle Ages* (London, 1967), p 502.

12 Ballard, *British Borough Charters 1042–1216*, p 27.

13 Taxation assessments for 1334 show that Appleby ranked below the average village assessment of some southwestern counties (Beresford, pp 262–3). Henry VIII cited Scottish incursion when he reduced its fee-farm rent from twenty to two marks (*Appleby and its People*, Curwen Archives Trust (1979), p 3), while the cursory nature of extant seventeenth-century chamberlains' accounts suggests a continuing paucity of economic life. By the middle decades of the century Appleby played an important role in the economic life of the Lowther family (see above, p 14 and note 28). By 1700 it had added a small suburb (Roy Millward, 'The Cumbrian Town between 1600 and 1800,' *Rural Change and Urban Growth*, C.W. Chalklin and M.A. Havinden (eds) (London, 1974), p 222).

14 J.F. Curwen (ed), *Records relating to the Barony of Kendale*, vol 1, pp 2, 9, 18.

15 Curwen, *Records*, vol 1, pp 50, 53, 55.

16 Curwen, *Records*, vol 1, pp 6 (1222–46), 8 (1247–60). Julian Mumby analyses a newly found *full* text of William's grant in CWAAS, Transactions (forthcoming).

17 Curwen, *Records*, vol 1, p 37 (burgage tenement held for money rent and suit of court), p 54 (alienation of tenement with delivery of seisin). A Kendal court roll of 1441–2 shows that the three-weekly court sat for the borough on Mondays and for the manor on Tuesdays (PRO: SC2/207/110).

18 BR pp 275–8.

19 BR, pp 310–11, 332–3. Frequent references to provision for 'judges' (WMB/K, Chamberlains' Accounts, Books 1, f [5]–52, f [25], 1583–1639), normally in or about the month of August, indicate that assizes were held in the borough.

20 The trades listed c. 1578 are those of Chapmen, Mercers, Shearmen, Tailors, Cordwainers, Tanners, Innholders, Butchers, Cardmakers, Surgeons, Smiths, and Carpenters, each with subsidiary or allied trades (BR, pp 110–11).

21 BR, pp 47–8.

22 C.B. Phillips, 'Town and Country: Economic Change in Kendal c. 1550–1700,' *The Transformation of English Provincial Towns: 1600–1800*, Peter Clark (ed) (London, 1984), pp 99–131; I am indebted to the author and the editor for

allowing me to read the proofs of this chapter. Signs of municipal self-confidence after 1575 include improvements to Kendal parish church designed to accommodate corporation dignitaries (WMB/K, Chamberlains' Accounts, Books 42, f [22]; 43, f [20]; and 46, f [31]; numerous benefactions to Kendal Grammar School and local charities (BR, pp 222–54); and evidence of well-attended municipal feasts in the peak years 1620–36 (see p 21).

23 J.A. Hilton, 'The Cumbrian Catholics,' *Northern History* 16 (1980), p 49. The percentage of Cumberland and Westmorland gentry families who were Roman Catholic rose from 13% in 1600 to 19% in 1642.

24 'Memorable Observations' of Sir John Lowther (died 1675), *Lowther Family Estate Books 1617–1675*, C.B. Phillips (ed), Surtees Society, vol 191 (Gateshead, 1979) p 237.

25 *Commercial Papers of Sir Christopher Lowther 1611–1644*, D.B. Hainsworth (ed), pp 224, 226.

26 'Memorable Observations,' p 233.

27 'Autobiography' of Sir John Lowther (died 1637), Phillips, *Lowther Family*, p 213.

28 Phillips, *Lowther Family*, p 60.

29 'Autobiography,' pp 214–19; see also Appendix 1, p 218.

30 Walter L. Woodfill's indication that the Bolton Abbey MSS have dramatic materials for the Westmorland castles of Appleby and Brougham (*Musicians in English Society from Elizabeth to Charles* I (Princeton, New Jersey, 1953), p 256) is not borne out by research at Chatsworth. Extant Clifford household books and accounts for 1610–25 (Bolton Abbey MSS 79, 94–100) and for 1632–42 (ibid, MSS 169–70, 173–80) show that Clifford household life in the north was conducted at Londesborough and Skipton and in the surrounding areas.

31 *An Apology for Actors* (London, 1612), sig. G3: '... to this day, in diuers places of *England*, there be townes that hold the priuiledge of their Faires, and other Charters by yearely stage-plays, as at *Manningtree* in *Suffolke*, *Kendall*, in the *North*, & others.' The Kendal play's alleged origin cannot be documented from any known charter; no record documents a stage play at this date for Manningtree.

32 A manuscript chronicle of 1736, written by Bartholomew Noble (buried in Kendal parish church in 1773), noted a performance of the Corpus Christi play in 1604 (*Local Chronology*, p vii). I have been unable to trace the original manuscript. It is unlikely that a subsequent reference to 'the play' in the chamberlains' accounts for 1607–8 is evidence of a Corpus Christi performance.

33 See endnote on p 229 to WMB/K [Book 3] f [16v].

34 The alderman's table was served with apples and nuts at the 1615 election dinner and sometimes, as at the 1630 Michaelmas leet dinner, a higher price per head was charged for the fare served to its occupants. The leet jurors had to be content with bread, cheese, and beer, and were presumably served in a separate location.

35 WMB/K, Chamberlains' Accounts, Book 51, f [22v], repairs to town drum; ff [24], [25], and Book 52 f [27], to Webster for drumming and for his suit.

36 CA/4/2 f [183], beating the drum (twice); f [184v], Colonel Trayford's trumpeter, Irish drummers; CA/4/139 f 90, Lord General's trumpeter, Captain Warriner's drummer; CA/4/2 f [191v], four trumpeters; f [195], Corporal Brown's boy 'for beating with our company.'

37 J.A. Wilson, 'Some Early Sporting Notes relating to Cumberland,' CWAAS, Transactions, O.S., 12 (1891), p 193, cites an opinion that horse-racing on Kingmoor took place on Shrove Tuesday. Contemporary sources transcribed here, however, clearly distinguish between Shrove Tuesday games at the Swifts held in February or March, and the Carlisle horse-race held on Kingmoor in May (discussed below). It is conceivable that the Shrove Tuesday term, 'playsilver games,' alluded to competitive cock-fighting or horse-racing of an informal or local kind. See p 158, endnote to CA/4/2 f [128v], for the Shrove Tuesday 'running of naggs' at the Swifts at an earlier time. For either activity the silver bell was a possible prize (Wilson, p 193).

38 See p 153, endnote to CA/4/2 f [6].

39 J.A. Wilson, 'Some Early Sporting Notes,' pp 191–3, includes a description of the racing bells belonging to this period, which were awarded as prizes; these are now in the museum in Tullie House, Carlisle.

40 Household accounts frequently record payments to itinerant pipers; with players, waits, and other musicians, they made up the main body of visitors rewarded at Workington and Naworth. Such callers are often anonymous. Administrative and legal records, however, occasionally identify persons who probably earned a living as casual or itinerant performers. The following constitute examples noted during research. Pipers: John Batie al. Sudby, John Bell, William Robinson, 1611; William Smith al. Piper, 1615; Robert Corbett, 1616; Thomas Bell, 1617 (CCRO: Esther C. Beattie, 'The City of Carlisle, Quarterly Records of the Mayor's Court, Index and Guide,' vol 1, pt 2); William Caldbeck, Hugh Machell, 1630; William Heslop, 1632 (ibid, vol 2); William Rigg of Kirkland, 3 July 1614 (KCRO: WMB/K, Kendal Court Records, Quarter Sessions, Recognizances, 1612–16, f [9]). Waits: John Docker of Carlisle, 17 May 1584 (KCRO: WMB/K, Kendal Court Rolls, Easter–Michaelmas 1584, mb 3); John Pattinson 1625 (CCRO: Beattie, 'Quarterly Records,' vol 1, pt 2). Minstrels: John Warryner of Kirkland, 3 February 1584/5 (Kendal Court Rolls, Michaelmas 1584–Easter 1585, mb 15d); John Armstrong, (1641 Protestation return for [Nichol] Forest in Kirkandrews in Esk parish – CCRO copy of original in the Record Office, House of Lords). Also Beatrice 'la harpereste' [of Brandhouse in Natland], 6 Edward II (Sizergh Castle, Westmld: Thomas West, 'An Abstract of the Ancient Writings belonging to Thomas Strickland of Sizergh, Esq.,' vol 1, modern transcript, p 38); John Decker, fiddler, 5 October 1612 (Kendal Court Records, Quarter Sessions, Recognizances 1612–16, f [1]); John Bird, fencer, 1614 (CCRO: Beattie, 'Quarterly Records,' vol 1, pt 2).

41 An exception is Howard Household Book 3, f 39, 3 January 1620/1, 'to the foole of Brampton ij s vij d,' probably a charitable donation.

42 Small amounts of wine and sugar for toasts are omitted unless providing useful detail; see p 93, CA/4/2 f [80v], ll 35–6, for Shrove Tuesday 1619/20.

43 Kendal ringers observed Queen Elizabeth's accession day, 17 November 1583–1602, WMB/K, Chamberlains' Accounts, Book 1, f 3v–17, f [16], and 5 November 1608–40, Book 22, f [13]–53, f [20], continuing at least through the Interregnum to Book 70, 1660. Carlisle marked 5 November 1613–42, CA/4/2 ff [1v–201v].

44 In the sixteenth century Kendal citizens spent the three Rogation days perambulating town boundaries, followed by a 'comon walk' on Easter Day; on 1 May and the Sunday next there were 'certayn pastymes and recreacons' on the town's outskirts (in the Barnhills), the young people gathering birch boughs, and the populace then returning up Stramongate and 'so to the churche' (BR, p 130).

45 Extant chamberlains' and/or guild records include no entertainment payments for All Hallow Thursday as celebrated in the years 1609–10, 1612, 1616, 1622–8, 1630–2, 1634, 1637–42.

46 See p 153, endnote to CA/4/2 f [6].

47 See, for example, Howard Household Book 11, f 36v, 4 March 1633/4, a payment to Lady Arundel's dwarf for bringing a gift to Lord William Howard. Surrounding payments indicate that this occurred during a visit to London.

48 Frequent sums in the Howard household books were allocated for gambling. Doubtful readings include Howard Household Book 4, f 53, 17 December, 'Giuen at a play in Brampton for mrs mary etc vij s vj d'; and Book 11, f 15, 29 June 1622, 'to my lady a play sent by mr w. Charlton xx s' following a payment dated 27 June, 'to mr William as lent by him to my lady at play.'

49 Curwen Account Book, 1631, f [63v], 16–21 May, nails and glue for the instrument; f [65v], 27–9 June, cords; 1635, f [127v], 25–6 March, dressing and tuning the organs, leather, glue, cords, a key and a band for it, f [129], 8–14 May, the organist for a second tuning.

50 'pd mr Alderman the 7th of Ianuarij as appeareth by his note money disbursed per him to souldiers etc from the 13th Novembr, till this daye' (WMB/K, Chamberlains' Accounts, Book 43, f [19v]).

51 'Paid at the Taverne when we received the accomptes of ould Chamberlaines by mr Mayors appointment' (WMB/K, Chamberlains' Accounts, Book 50, f [23v]).

Select Bibliography

This list comprises books, articles, or published facsimiles of printed works that contain primary transcriptions or the originals of records edited in the text, as well as books and articles that have proved useful in the preparation of this volume.

Appleby, Andrew B. 'Disease or Famine? Mortality in Cumberland and Westmorland 1580–1640,' *Economic History Review*, 2nd Series, 26 (1973), 403–32.

Boas, Frederick S. (ed). *The Diary of Thomas Crosfield* M.A., B.D. *Fellow of Queen's College, Oxford: Selected and Edited from the* MS. *in Queen's College Library for the Royal Society of Literature* (London, 1935).

Bouch, C.M.L. and G.P. Jones, with contributions by R.W. Brunskill. *A Short Economic and Social History of the Lake Counties 1500–1830* (Manchester, 1961).

Boumphrey, R.S., C. Roy Hudleston, and J. Hughes, with a foreword by Roger Fulford. *An Armorial for Westmorland and Lonsdale*. Cumberland and Westmorland Antiquarian and Archaeological Society, Extra Series, vol 21 (Northumberland Press, 1975).

Campbell, Mildred. *The English Yeoman Under Elizabeth and the Early Stuarts* (New Haven, 1942).

Collingwood, W.G. (transcr and trans). *Elizabethan Keswick: Extracts from the Original Account Books, 1564–1577, of the German Miners, in the Archives of Augsburg*. Cumberland and Westmorland Antiquarian and Archaeological Society, Tract Series, no 8 (Kendal, 1912).

Curwen, John F. *The Castles and Fortified Towers of Cumberland, Westmorland, and Lancashire North-of-the-Sands, together with a brief Historical Account of Border Warfare*. Cumberland and Westmorland Antiquarian and Archaeological Society, Extra Series, vol 13 (Kendal, 1913).

– (ed). *Records relating to the Barony of Kendale by William Farrer, Litt.D.* Cumberland and Westmorland Antiquarian and Archaeological Society, Record Series, vol 4 (Kendal, 1923).

– (ed). *Records relating to the Barony of Kendale by the Late William Farrer, Litt.D.* Cumberland and Westmorland Antiquarian and Archaeological Society, Record Series, vol 5 (Kendal, 1924).

– (ed). *Records relating to the Barony of Kendale*. Cumberland and Westmorland Antiquarian and Archaeological Society, vol 6 (Kendal, 1926).

Ferguson, Richard S. (ed). *A Boke off Recorde or Register Containing All the Acts and Doings on or Concerning the Corporation within the Town of Kirkbiekendall beginning at the First Entrance or Practicing of the Same which Was the Eighth Day of January in the Year of the Reign of Lady Elizabeth by the Grace of God of England France and Ireland Queen Defender of the Faith etc. etc. the Eighteenth 1575. Kirkbie Kendall A.D. 1575. To Which Are Added the Several Charters Granted by Q. Elizabeth, K. Charles., and K. Charles II*. Cumberland and Westmorland Antiquarian and Archaeological Society, Extra Series, vol 7 (Kendal, 1892).

– and W. Nanson (eds). *Some Municipal Records of the City of Carlisle, viz., the Elizabethan Constitutions, Orders, Provisions, Articles, and Rules from the Dormont Book, and the Rules and Orders of the Eight Trading Guilds, Prefaced by Chapters on the Corporation Charters and Guilds, Illustrated by Extracts from the Court Leet Rolls and from the Minutes of the Corporation and Guilds*. Cumberland and Westmorland Antiquarian and Archaeological Society, Extra Series, vol 4 (Carlisle and London, 1887).

G[eorge] E[dward] C[okayne]. *The Complete Peerage of England, Scotland, Ireland, Great Britain and the United Kingdom, Extant, Extinct or Dormant*. Rev ed (London, 1910–59).

Great Britain. Royal Commission on Historical Monuments: England. *An Inventory of the Historical Monuments in Westmorland* (London, 1936).

Hainsworth, D.R. (ed). *Commercial Papers of Sir Christopher Lowther 1611–1644*. Surtees Society, vol 189 (Gateshead, 1977).

Local Chronology; Being Notes of the Principal Events Published in the Kendal News papers since their Establishment. Compiled by the Editors. Reprinted from the 'Kendal Mercury' and 'Westmorland Gazette' (London and Kendal, 1865).

Mill, Anna Jean. *Mediaeval Plays in Scotland: Thesis Submitted for the Degree of Ph.D. of the University of St Andrews, July 1924*. St Andrews University Publications, no 24 (Edinburgh and London, 1927).

Murray, John Tucker. *English Dramatic Companies 1558–1642*. 2 vols (London, 1910).

Nicolson, Joseph and Richard Burn. *The History and Antiquities of the Counties of Westmorland and Cumberland*. 2 vols (London, 1777).

Ornsby, George (ed). *Selections from the Household Books of the Lord William Howard of Naworth Castle: With an Appendix, Containing Some of his Papers and Letters, and Other Documents Illustrative of his Life and Times*. Surtees Society, vol 68 (Durham, 1878).

Pearsall, W.H. and Winifred Pennington. *The Lake District: A Landscape History* (London, 1973).

Reid, Rachel Robertson. *The King's Council in the North* (London, 1921).

Sackville-West, V. (intro). *The Diary of Lady Anne Clifford* (London, 1923).

[Shaw, John]. 'The Life of Master John Shaw,' *Yorkshire Diaries and Autobiographies in the Seventeenth and Eighteenth Centuries*. Charles Jackson (ed). Surtees Society, vol 65 (Durham, 1877), pp 119–62.

– *Memoirs of the life of Master John Shawe ... Written by Himself. With Notes Explanatory and Biographical by John Broadley ...* (Hull, 1824).

Spink, Ian. 'Campion's Entertainment at Brougham Castle, 1617,' *Music in English Renaissance Drama*. John H. Long (ed) (Lexington, 1968), pp 57–74.

The Victoria History of the Counties of England. *The Victoria History of the County of Cumberland*. Vol 1 (London, 1901). *The Victoria History of the County of Cumberland*. Vol 2. James Wilson (ed) (London, 1905).

Weever, John. *Ancient Fvneral Monvments Within the Vnited Monarchie of Great Britaine, Ireland, and the Islands adiacent, with the dissolued Monasteries therein contained* (London, 1631). STC: 25223. [Facs ed, *The English Experience: Its Record in Early Printed Books Published in Facsimile*, no 961 (Amsterdam and Norwood, N.J., 1979).]

The Westmorland Note-Book. Vol 1, 1888–9 (Kendal and London, 1888–9).

Whellan, William. *The History and Topography of the Counties of Cumberland and Westmorland* (Pontefract, 1860).

Whitaker, Thomas Dunham. *The History and Antiquities of the Deanery of Craven, in the County of York*. 3rd ed. 2 vols. A. W. Morant (ed) (Leeds and London, 1878; rpt Manchester and Skipton, 1973).

Whitwell, John. *The Old Houses of Kendal; or the Local Perambulator* (Kendal, 1866).

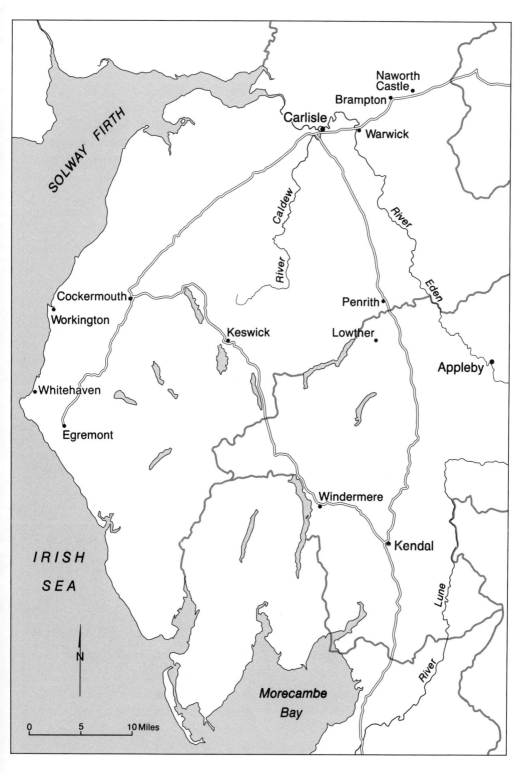

Cumberland and Westmorland with principal renaissance routes

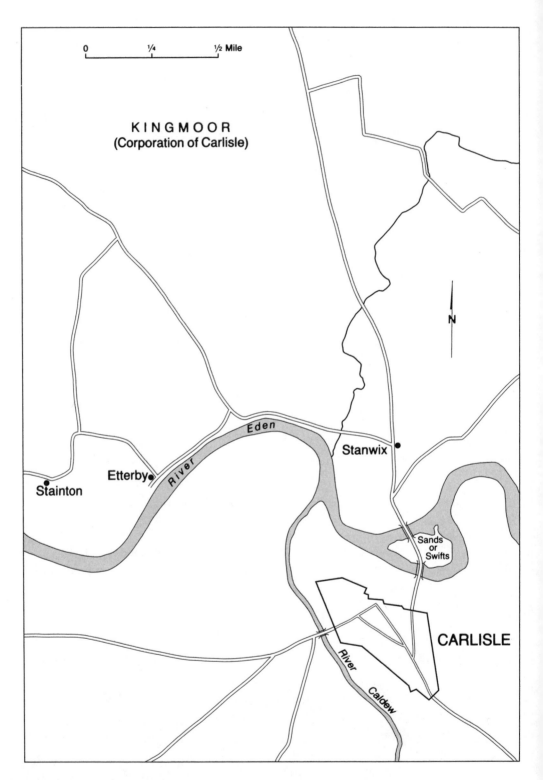

Carlisle and environs 1597: a conjectural map adapted from J. Hughes, 'The Plague in Carlisle 1597/98,' CWAAS, NS 71 (1971), by kind permission of the author

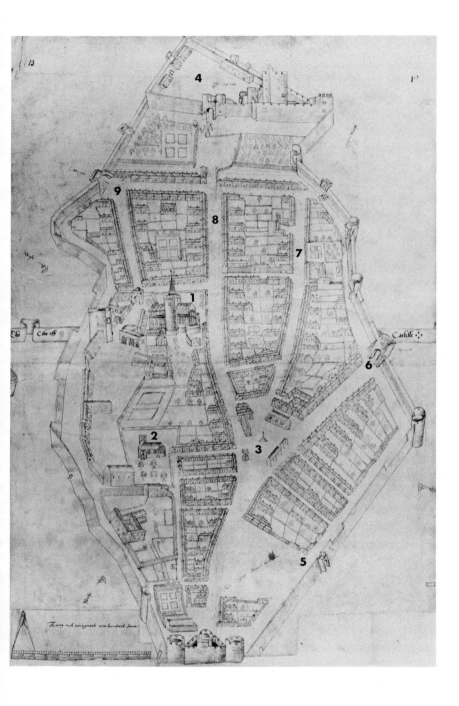

16th c Carlisle, from BL: Cotton Augustus i.i.13 by permission of the British Library

1 Cathedral	4 Castle	7 Fiskergate
2 St Cuthbert's	5 Botchergate	8 Castlegate
3 Market-Place and Cross	6 Rickergate	9 Caldewgate

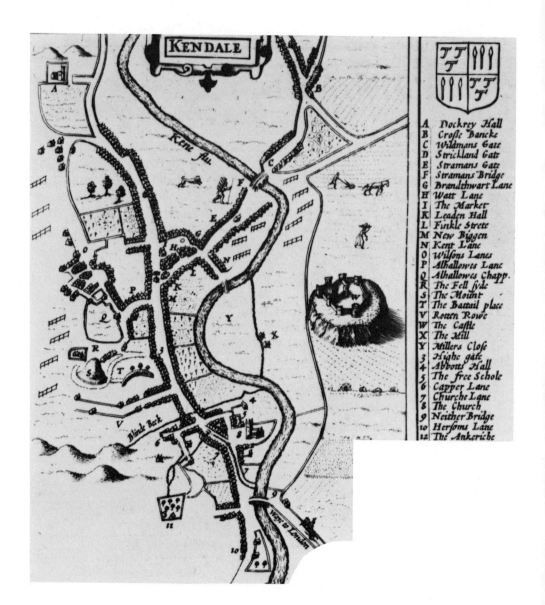

Map of Kendal from John Speed, *The Theatre of the Empire of Great Britaine*, by courtesy of the Huntington Library

CUMBERLAND RECORDS

Boroughs

CARLISLE

1345–6
Parliamentary and Council Proceedings   PRO: C49/46/16
mb 8* *(26 September)*

Inquis*icio* capt*a* ap*u*d karl*iol*u*m* die Lune *proxima* ante *f*est*u*m *s*ancti   5
mich*ae*l*i*s anno *r*eg*n*i *r*egis Edwardi t*er*cij a conq*uestu* decimo nono
coram d*omi*no Thoma de Lucy Ric*ar*do ⟨...............⟩ ⟨...⟩g'ton p*er*
Commissione*m* d*omi*ni Regis assign*at*is sup*er* quibusdam
dissenc*i*onib*us* et discordijs int*er* homin*es* in munic*i*one Castri d*omi*ni
Regi*s* karl*iol*i existent*es* & C*om*munitat*em* Ciuitat*i*s karl*iol*i   10
⟨....................⟩ p*er* Adamu*m* de Kyrkeby Petrum ffrankys Thom*am*
de Neuby Ioh*ann*em de mulcastre Ric*ar*du*m* de Scraityngham
Ric*ar*du*m* del sandes ⟨..........⟩ Thom*am* de Canonuby Ioh*ann*em de
Ireby Ioh*ann*em de Agillonuby Ioh*ann*em de Cokedene & Ioh*ann*em
filiu*m* simonis de kyrkandres Iur*at*ores Qui dic*un*t sup*er* sacra ⟨......⟩   15
q*u*od die dom*in*ica in vig*i*lia *s*ancti Petri aduinc*u*la anno supradicto
Cum Clerici fecer*un*t quendam ludu*m* in foro d*i*cte ciuitatis karl*iol*i
quedam contumelia mota fuit inter Ed*mundu*m Walays s*er*uient*em*
d*omi*ni Ep*iscop*i karl*iol*i & Walterum Cole homin*em* d*omi*ni Petri de
Tillioll' eo q*u*od idem Ed*mundu*s percussit d*i*ctu*m* Walterum cum   20
quadam virga grossa ter in capite ⟨..⟩ d*i*ct*us* Walterus cepit ips*um*
Ed*mundu*m per capuc*i*um & delacerauit capuc*i*um & tunicam et
Ric*ar*dus del Botelry s*er*uiens d*i*cti d*omi*ni Ep*iscop*i karl*iol*i videns hoc
p*er*cussit d*i*ctu*m* Walterum cu*m* quodam cultello in dorso fere ad
mortem & sup*er* hoc ludus recessit Et tunc d*i*ct*us* Petrus de Tillioll'   25

9/ dissenc*i*onibus *for* dissensionibus
16/ in vig*i*lia *s*ancti Petri aduinc*u*la: *31 July 1345*

videns hominem suum sic esse in periculo mortis misit Willelmum ⟨...⟩
Wyclyf Coronatorem domini Regis & cum eo Iohannem de stapelton'
& Thomam de Neuby ad dictum dominum Episcopum karlioli
supplicando eidem domino Episcopo quoniam cum haberet dictum
Ricardum del Botelria in comitiua sua in Castro karlioli qui hominem   5
predictum percussit quod faceret ipsum responsurum de predicta
transgressione secundum legem ⟨.... ⟩ predictus Episcopus karlioli
concessit pro se & hominibus suis quod nulla mala fieri deberent
quousque veritas fuerit inde inquisita ...

mb 10* *(26 September)*   10

Acta apud karliolum die Luna proxima ante festum sancti michaelis
archangeli anno regni regis Edwardi tercij a conquestu decimo Nono
coram domino Thoma de Lucy ⟨..........⟩ assignatis per Commissio⟨...⟩
domini Regis ad inquirendum de diuersis articulis in Commissione   15
contentis per Adamum de Crofton' Robertum de Tybay Nicholas le
spenser Willelmum de morley Thomam kaskell' stephanum de Acton'
gilbertum de kirkandres Robertum growce henricum de musgraue
Iohannem de Tybay stephanum aurisfabrum & Adamum de Appylby'
Iuratores qui ⟨...⟩ super sacramentum suum quod die dominica in   20
vigilia sancti petri ad uincula sicut clerici inceperunt ludere quoddam
miraculum in foro karlioli in medio Ciuitatis quid⟨.....⟩iger Episcopi
Edmundus Walays percussit in capite Walterum Cole de Skaleby cum
grossa virga ter & Walterus volens impedire dictum Edmundum ne
ampl ⟨..........⟩ cepit eum per capucium & interim Ricardus frater   25
Walteri de Botellar' percussit dictum Walterum Cole retro in dorso
cum quodam cultello fere ad mortem propter quod populus erat
perter⟨..........⟩ vnde maior & balliui multum moti Connotauerunt
Communitatem ad aulam Communem ad inquirendum veritatem de
dicta contumelia et interim vicecomes maior Ciui ⟨..........⟩Crofton'   30
juerunt ad Episcopum & rogauerunt eum vt pacificaret homines suos
ne amplius delinquerint quousque veritas de transgressione predicta
fuerit inquisita ...

1,14/ 2 holes, *vertically spaced in the* MS, *each about 8mm wide*
12/ Luna *for* Lune
14/ Commissio⟨...⟩: *probably* Commissionem
20/ ⟨...⟩: *probably* dicunt
22/ ⟨.....⟩iger, *ie*, armiger

1588–9
Letter of Henry Scrope   BL: Egerton MS 2598
f 82*

After my verie hartie Comendacions: vpon a letre receyved from Mr   5
Roger Asheton, Signifying vnto me that yt was the kinges earnest
desire for to have hir Majestes players for to repayer into Scotlande
to his grace I dyd furthwith dispatche a servant of my owen vnto them
where they were in the furthest parte of Langkeshier, whervpon they
made their returne heather to Carliell, wher they are, and have stayed   10
for the space of ten dayes, wherof, I thought good to gyue yow notice
in respect of the great desyre that the king had to have the same, to
Come vnto his grace: And withall to praye yow to gyve knowledg
therof to his Majestie / So for the present, I bydd yow right hartelie
farewell / Carlislie the xxth of Septembre / 1589   15
...

1602–3
Chamberlains' Accounts   CCRO: CA/4/1
f [1v]*   *(7–22 December) (Disbursements)*   20

Item for Clothe vnto the drummer belman and beadell
with Clarke to be theyre leveryes   xlvj s
...
(10 March)   25
Item for silver playgames vpon Shrovetewesdaie   xv s vj d
...

f [3v]   *(Fees and Annuities)*
...   30
Item vnto nycholas hudson   xx s
...

ff [4–4v]   *(13 October–19 November) (Benevolences)*
...   35
Item vnto Iohn troumpeter   ij s
...

22/ the drummer: *Nicholas Hudson*   36/ Iohn troumpeter: *John Burton*
26/ Shrovetewesdaie: *8 March*

(19 November–14 December)
Item vnto a blinde harper   xij d

...

(1 January)
Item vnto Iohn troumpeter capteine boyer Droommer   5
and other ij musitians   iiij s

...

(1 January–8 February)
Item vnto the players of penrethe   x s

...   10
Item vnto Iames baines and his felowe players   x s
Item for a Coatt vnto the waitte   xx s
Item for Candles to the players   iij d
(8 February)
Item vnto my lorde morleyes players   xxx s   15

...

(8 February–2 June)
Item vnto the waittes of penreth   xij d

...

(2 June, All Hallow Thursday)   20
Item vnto Iohn troumpeter   xij d
(2 June+)
Item vnto Iohn grayson waitt of Cokermouthe   xij d

...

Item vnto ij Scotes minstrels   xij d   25

...

Item vnto Iohn nixon piper   vj d

...

Item vnto j scotes gentlewomanminstrell   ij s
Item vnto my lorde evers players   xiij s iiij d   30

...

Item vnto the waittes of lankaster   iij s iiij d
Item vnto Certeine players in december   x s

...

                                                                                         35

f [5]   *(Wine, Ale, and Cakes)*

...

Item in chardgies in the highe chamber vpon mr Maior

29/ gentlewomanminstrell: *ie*, gentlewoman's minstrel
38/ mr Maior: *Richard Warwick, f [1], account title*

and his bretheren vpon hallowe thursdaie   xvj s ij d

…

1604–5
Chamberlains' Accounts   CCRO: CA/4/1   5
f [22v]*   *(November–3 December) (Disbursements)*

…

Item for vj q*uar*tes stamell brodclothe vno the droum*m*er   xx s

…

                                                                                10

f [22]   *(10 February–7 April)*

…

Item for playgames vpon shrovetewesdaie   xviij s ⟨....⟩ d

…

                                                                                15

f [23]   *(9 May)*

…

Item vnto the eighte occupations vpon halow thursdaie   xx s

…

                                                                                20

f [23v]*   *(Fees and Annuities)*

…

Item vnto nycholas hudson droum*m*er   xx s

…

                                                                                25

f [24]   *(2 October) (Benevolences)*
first vnto Iohn troumpeter   ij s

…

(6 April–9 May)
Item vnto the waittes of Penrethe   ij s   30

…

Item vnto the waittes of leaddes   ij s
Item vnto the waittes of kendall   xij d
Item vnto the waittes of Rychmonde   ij s

…   35

(9 May)
Item vnto one that was foole vpon hallow thursdaie   xij d

…

13/ shrovetewesdaie: *12 February*
13/ ⟨....⟩d: *marginal repair*

f [24v]   *(13 May⁺)*
Item vnto Craggell the singer   xij d
…
Item vnto the waittes of waikfeald   ij s
…   5

f [25]   *(9 May) (Wine, Cakes, and Spices)*
…
Item for one gallon of Secke one potle Clared wine one
quarte whitt wine j li of Suger 3 pottes beare one box of   10
comfittes and wheatt Caikes vpon halowethursdaie at
afternoone in the heighe Chamber   [⟨…⟩ s ⟨…⟩ d] ⌐xiij s⌐
…

1608–9   15
Chamberlains' Accounts   CCRO: CA/4/1
f [34]   *(October) (Disbursements)*
…
Item to Iohn Burton trumpiter vpon the election day at
mr maior comand   ij s vj d   20
…

f [37v]   *(January)*
…
Item vnto Iohn Burton trumpiter for his Newyeares gifte   xij d   25
…
(28 January–1 February)
Item vnto the waits of Newcastle at mr maior command   ij s vj d
…
                                                                                       30
f [38]   *(February)*
…
Item the 3 day vpon the waits of kendall at mr maior
commande   ij s vj d
…   35
Item the 7 daie vpon the waits of peareth at mr maior
command   ij s
…

20/ mr maior: *John Pattison, elected 3 October, f [34], account title*

ff [38v–39v]

...

Item the last day In the citties games		
beinge Shrovetewesday	xviij s	
Item vpon Iohn blacke fydler pip*er*		5
the same day	xij d/	

(March)

...

Item the 3 day to the waits of hallifax at mr maior		
commande	ij s vj d	10
Item vnto a musition of mr dudleys at mr maior		
com*m*ande	xij d	
Item the 5 day vnto one maior vavicers musitions at		
mr maior com*m*ande	ij s vj d	
Item the 6 day vnto the waits of durham at mr maior		15
com*m*ande	ij s vj d	

...

Item the 10 day vnto the waits of Lemin at mr maior		
com*m*ande	ij s vj d/	

...   20

Item the 24 day vpon the waits of midlam at mr maior		
com*m*ande	xij d	

...

f [39v]   *(30 March)*   25
Item ... vpon the waits of wakeffeilde at mr maior
com*m*ande   ij s vj d

...

f [40v]   *(April)*   30

...

Item the 18 day vpon a Tru*m*piter at mr maior		
com*m*ande	vj d	

...

Item the xxiiij day [for] vpon my lord stafforde players at   35
mr maior commande   x s

4/ Shrovetewesday: *28 February*
18/ Lemin/ *Leeming in North Riding or Leeming in West Riding, Yorkshire*

f [41]   *(13–25 May)*

...

Item vnto the waits of Richmonde at mr maior com*m*ande   xv iiij d

...

f [42]   *(July)*

...

Item the xxiiijth day vpon my lord of lincolne players at
mr maior com*m*ande   xx s

...

f [43]   *(28 August)*

Item ⟨...⟩to the waits of york at mr maior com*m*ande   ij s vj d

...

f [43v]   *(29 September)*

...

Item to nicholas hudson for his hex   xx s

...

f [47] *(Fees and Annuities)*

...

To Nicholas hudson the drumer   ⟨...⟩

...

1610–11
Chamberlains' Accounts   CCRO: CA/4/1
f [52]   *(October) (Disbursements)*

...

Item to Iohn Burton trumpiter vpon the election day at
mr Maior com*m*ande   ij s vj d
Item vnto the waits of peareth the same daie at mr maior
com*m*ande   ij s vj d

...

18/ hex *for* hexpenses *(?), possibly for livery; preceding and following items respectively for
     sergeants' cloaks and beadles' liveries*
23/ ⟨...⟩ *triangular tear 60mm wide at outer edge of folio, penetrating 45mm*
31/ mr Maior: *Edward Aglionby, elected 1 October, f [52], account title*

f [53]   (28 November)

...

Item to my lord wharton players at mr Maior
commande...   xx s

...   5

(19–24 December)
Item for a paire of shoes to willy the fowle at mr maior
commande   xviij d

...
                                                                                    10

f [53v]   (December)

...

Item the xxvjth day for a coat to my lord Abbott at mr
Maior commande   xvij s
Item for a hat vnto [my] ⌜the⌝ said lord read in the   15
makinge of his coat & hat & for candles   viij s vj d

...

f [54]*

...   20

Item for the games vpon Shrove tewesday   xxix s
Item to the waits of peareth at mr maior command the
same day   iij s iiij d
Item for a foat ball the same day at mr maior commande   viij d

...   25

f [54v]
Item the xxth of februarij to the waits the waits of
lancaster at mr Maior commande   iiij s vj d
Item the xxiijth daie to the waits of Midlam at mr maior   30
command   ij s

...
Item the iiijth of March to the waits of Appleby at
mr Maior commande   ij s

...   35

Item the xxvjth day to the waits of wackefeilde at
mr Maior commande   iij s iiij d

...

21/ Shrove tewesday: 5 February
28/ the waits the waits: dittography

f [55]*   *(April)*

…

Item to the drummer for his coat	xx s

…

f [55v]

…

Item the seconde of Maie being alhallowe thursday to the chambers at mr Maior commande	xx s
Item to Philip Burtholme the same day at mr Maior commande	xij d
Item to musitions the same day	iiij s
Item to the plaie hase at mr maior commande	xij d
Item to henry mounk for xviij li of powder at mr Maior commande	xxiiij s
Item to Michaell warde for x li of powder at mr Maior commande	xiij s iiij d
Item to Iohn Iackson for xvij li of powder	xxij s viij d

…

f [56] *(1–15 July)*

…

Item vnto the waits of lincolne at mr Maior commande	iiij s
Item to the waits of peareth at mr Maior commande	xviij d

…

f [56v]* *(July)*

…

Item to the waits of leads at mr Maior commande	iiij s

…

Item to george wilson & his thre sones being waits who offerd them selves to be hird at mr Maior command	ij s vj d

…

f [57] *(15–27 August)*

…

Item to my lord Awbeny plaiers at mr Maior commande	xx s

…

(18 September⁺)

Item payed for Makinge of the fowles coat and his stockins at mr Maior commande	iiij s

Item for his coat & his stockins to Michaell warde   xiiij s ij d
...

f [6ov]   *(Fees and Annuities)*
...   5
Item to nicholas hudson dru*mm*er   xx s
...

A   ***Tanners' Guild Minute Book***   CCRO: D/Lons/L
     f [14]*   *(Masters' Accounts dated 2 November)*   10
     (Disbursements)
     ...
     Ite for ye settinge of ye occupacion dinn*er*   vj s:–
     Ite for wylde foole Capons & cunyes   xij s. v d.
     Ite to [Minstrels] ˄ ⌜minstrells⌝ at ye Dinner   xiiij d.   15
     Ite for Strangers at ye same Dinnere   viij s. vj d.
     Ite ffor wyne & suger then   xvij s. –
     ...

     f [14v]   *(Masters' Accounts dated 8 November 1611)*   20
     (Receipts)
     ...
     Ite rec of the Cittyes benevolence ffor accopaininge
     Mr Maior to the kinge moore   ij s– vj d
     ...   25

     f [15]   *(Disbursements)*

     Inprimis disbursed in Charges at our Chamber uppon yė
     Rydinge with Mr Maior of the bounder of the kings   30
     moore   xxij s iiij d./
     ...

     1611–12
A   ***Tanners' Guild Minute Book***   CCRO: D/Lons/L   35
     f [15] *(Masters' Accounts dated 8 November)*
     (Disbursements)
     ...
     Ite for ye settinge of [the] ˄ ⌜ye⌝ Occupacion Dinn*er*   v s.

13/ ye occupacion dinn*er*: *28 October*   23–31/ *for All Hallow Thursday, 2 May*
23/ accopaininge *for* accompaininge   39/ ⌜ye⌝ Occupacion Dinner: *28 October*

Ite for Capons, wyled foole & Connyes   xj s.–
Ite for sertayne Strangers   vj s. vj d.–
Ite for wyne & Sewger in all   xxj s:–
...
Ite to minstralls at ye Dinner   xij d   5
...

1612–13

A   *Tanners' Guild Minute Book*   CCRO: D/Lons/L
f [16v]*   *(Masters' Accounts dated 6 November)*   10
(Disbursements)
...
Ite ffor settinge of ye Dinner   ij s
Ite for [⟨.⟩]wyldefoole and Capons   vj s.
Ite for Strangers   vj s– vj d–   15
Ite for wyne over my lords allowance of x s and x s to
ye howse   xvij s vj d.–
...
Ite to the Minstrells   xij d
...   20

f [17]*
...
Ite geven to ye Chamberlens to paye the howse where ye
Dinner was madd   x s–   25
...

f [17v]   *(dated 5 November 1613)(Receipts)*
...
Ite off Mr Maiors gifft & ye Cittyes for ryding ye kings   30
moore   ij s vj d.
...

f [18]   *(Expenses)*
...   35
Ite bestowed upon Mr Maior & his brethren in ye
Chamber upon hallowe Thursdaye   v s. vj d.
Ite to ye wates & Drummer   xij d.–
...

13/ ye Dinner: *28 October*   30–8/ *for All Hallow Thursday, 13 May*

1613–14
Chamberlains' Accounts   CCRO: CA/4/2
f [1]*   *(4–11 October) (Disbursements)*

Imprimis given to Iohn Bvrton trumpeter	ij s vj d	5
to Iohn Gyles and other his Men dwelling in		
Cockermouth being sir henry Curwens Muzistians	iij s iiij d	

...
(13–16 October)

given to A blind harper called hingerham Stewart A scotes		10
Man	xij d	

...

the 19th given to george Little pip*er*	xviij d	

...

15

f [1v]   *(4–5 November)*
...

payed to Mr maior wic'h he gave to A blind harp*er* with		
other of his Companye	ij s	

...
20
(6–13 November)

Given to Muuiissians that came from yorkshire	iij s 4 d	

...

f [2]   *(28 November–10 December)*   25
...

to my lor*d* Quarton plaires	xiij s 4 d	

...
(14–22 December)

to willye Milner A paire shoes and paire hoisen	⟨....⟩	30

...

f [2v]   *(4–7 January)*
...

to sir Mvngo and the boyes for singing at Mr Maiors	v s	35

...

18/ Mr maior: *Thomas Blenerhassett, CA/4/139 f 47, account title*
30/ willye Milner: *the city's fool*
30/ ⟨....⟩ *bottom right corner of folio missing*

(8–9 January)
to the waytes of lancaster   iij s 4 d

...

to kendall players not permiting yem to play   iij s 4 d

...   5

given to sir henrye Curwens Musissians at last court   iij s 4 d

...

ff [3–3v]   *(9–15 January)*

...   10

given to the players came from barnycastle   v s

...

to the waiytes of pearith   ij s vj d

...

(15–16 January)   15
to my lord Staffordes players   xiij s 4 d

...

the ffirst day March to the waites of Canterburye   iij s 4 d

...

(1–8 March)   20
when my lord Cumberland dynned with yow pottle sack
pottle Clared dli suger   iiij s 8 d
to his man & his three boyes that was our waites   iij s 4 d

...

(8 March, Shrove Tuesday)   25
A foote Ba⌐w⌐lle vpon the sandes   [⟨....⟩] vj d–

...

to a Boy that wonn the foote Boll   xij d

...

given to Mr maior & John Hoddye to bestowe of waites   30
Riton and other passengers   iiij s 4 d

...

(26 March–1 April)
to the whaites of Appelby   ij s

...   35

6/ *ie, at quarter sessions, mentioned 4–7 January, f [2v]*
21/ *yow: ie, Thomas Blenerhassett, mayor*
22/ *dli: di. li.*
26/ *entry interposed at top of folio*

(1–3 April)
given to waites of Midlam   iij s 4 d
...

f [4]   *(3–30 April)*   5
...

given to the waites of Lancaster   iij s 4 d
...

given to the waites of Hellifax   iij s 4 d
...   10
(3–11 May)
°giuen to the waytes of Altherton   iij s 4 d°
...

f [4v]*   *(16–27 May)*   15
...

[th] To threre munisseners that Came frome Barwick   iij s 4 d
...

f [6]*   *(2–23 June)*   20
...

To the occupations   xx s
ffor Games   xviij s
ffor powder fortie shillinges
for Carridg and browne paper   xij d   25
Mr Maior in the merchantes chamber two quarts of white
wyne and Suger 8 d   ij s
Shoemaker Chamber a quart of white and Suger   xij d
...

To Iohn Earle when you brought in the Games   xij d   30
...

f [6v]   *(23 June–8 July)*
...

At yor awne house Carried by lytell Wille a quart of   35
Clarrit & suger   xij d
...

12/ Altherton: *probably Atherton, Lancs*
35/ yor awne house: *ie, referring to Thomas Blenerhassett, mayor*
35/ lytell Wille: *William Milner, the city's fool*

Paied to henrie Monk for three yeardes of white Carsay
for the fooles Cotte v s 8 d and white threed and read
threed 8d for a yeard and a halfe of harne 8 d
Paied to Thomas hodg for three yardes of Read Carsaie
for the foole ix s   5
paied to Mathewe Cape for two bells for
the foole and a fether   vj d
...

f [7]
...   10
ffor makeing of the fooles Cotte   [v s] v s
...
°To the waytes of Bristo not sufferinge them to play°   v s
...   15
f [7v]   *(8 July–10 August)*
...
given to the waites of knarshbrough   v s
...   20
f [8]   *(18–25 August)*
...
for a paire of Shooes and hose to the foole at the Sizes   ij s
...
(25 August+)   25
to three mussishiners one of them said he was borne in
Carelell   *(blank)*
...

f [8v]   30
...
given to the waites that was last here at Mr Maiors
appointment   iij s 4 d
...
to william ffoole half yeard half quarter saye   xviij d   35
f [9v]   *(Fees)*
...
to the Cittyes dromer   xx s
...   40

39/ ff [9v–10], *untitled list of fees and annuities*

f [13]*   *(Disbursements on St John's Eve and St Peter's Eve)*

...

Nicho*las* hudson   xij d

...

® x8:   the two waites   ij s   5

...

f [14v]*

...   10

ffor the bouchers waike and the seargantes waike   ij s
to the watchers either night one pott of Ale   xij d

...

°Giuen to the Cities waites St Iohn Euen and St Peters
even°   ij s   15

Chamberlains' Audit Book   CCRO: CA/4/139
f 48   *(Allowances Craved)*

...

Ite*m* to ye wates ffor their wages   iiij li.   20

...

A   ***Tanners' Guild Minute Book***   CCRO: D/Lons/L
f [19]   *(Masters' Accounts dated 4 November) (Receipts)*

...   25

Ite rece*aved* of Mr Maior as his gifte for Rydinge
kingmoore   ij s vj d

...

(Expenses)
Ite bestowed in ye Cha*m*ber upon ye Daye of Rydinge   30
the kinge moore   xvj–viij
Ite to ye wates of ye Cittye   xvj d

...

1614–15   35
Chamberlains' Accounts   CCRO: CA/4/2
f [18]   *(3–10 October) (Disbursements)*

...

Ite*m* to Iohn Trumpiter by mr maiors Coma*n*d   ij s. vj d.

26–32/ *for All Hallow Thursday, 2 June*
39/ mr maior: *Richard Bell elected mayor 3 October, f [18], account title*

Item to Mr Thompson ye musicion at mr maiors com*and*   vj s viij d
Item to his boyes then by mr maiors Comand   xviij d.

...

Item to ye fforesayde Thompson musicion ye xth of
october mr Aglionby mr hasset & others   v s.   5

...

(5 November–2 December)

Item to ye wates of kirkbesteven   xviij d

...   10

f [18v]*

Item the 2 of december to my lord whartons players, at
Comand of mr maior   vj s viij d.   15

...

(2–8 December)

Item to the wates their leveres cost   iiij li. iiij s

...   20

(Disbursements of Henry Baynes, mayor)

Item ye last daye of december to one Iohn dockara ye
wate of lancaster   ij s vj d.

...

25

f [19]   *(15 January*+*)*
...

Item to ye wates of pearethe   xviij d.
Item to ye lord Staffoordes playeres   v s:

...   30

Item to ye waites of kerkbethure   xviij d.
Item the newers gift by mr maior to ye Cittyes wates   ij s vj d.

...

®Caldew Bridge   Item ffor ye Summergames   xx s.

...   35

34/ Caldew Bridge: *written on scrap of paper 10mm x 22mm pasted in margin*

Item ffor A ffooteball to yonge men vpon Shraffe
tewsdaye   vj d

...

Item to ye Chambers and occupacions of ye Cittye vpon
all hallow daye   xx s.   5
Item in ye merchantes Chamber then a quart of Sacke sett
vpon mr maores head   xij d

...

Item to Iohn Trumpeter as an intruder vpon alhallowes
thursdaye   ij s   10
Item in powder wasted ye same daye   xliii s iiij d

...

Item to ye wates of kendall   ij s

...

Item to ye wates of lincoln   ij s   15
Item ffor A Coote to ye naturall ffoole miller tow payer of
showes & tow payer of hosse   xxviij s:/

...

f [20]*   20

...

Item to ye wates of knasburghe   ij s

...

Item to Sir Thomas metcalfes musicions   ij s
                                                                        25
Item to ye wates of Bristowe   ij s vj d

...

Item to ye wates of lancaster   ij s vj d

...

(Fees)   30

The wates ffee   (blank)

...

Item to ye Cittyes drummer   xx s:

...

1–2/ Shraffe tewsdaye: 21 February
5/ all hallow daye: 18 May
22–8/ each entry is preceded by a dot in left margin

A   *Tanners' Guild Minute Book*   CCRO: D/Lons/L
f [20]   *(Masters' Accounts dated 3 November) (Receipts)*
...
Imprimis receaved of Mr Maior as a Gratuity for
accompaining him & his brethren to ye kinge moore upon   5
Allhallowe Thursday   ij s. vj d.
...
(Expenses)
Inprimis at ye Rydinge of the bounder bestowed in o*u*r
Chamber   xiij s. iij d.   10

1616–17
Chamberlains' Accounts   CCRO: CA/4/2
f [24]   *(1 October) (Disbursements)*
...   15
Item to Iohn burton trum*p*iter vpon the election day at
mr Maior com*m*ande   ij s
...

f [24v]   *(26 October)*   20
...
Item to ⟨..⟩ Thompson the cities wate   xxij d
Item to the waits of thriske at mr Maior com*m*ande   xij d
...
Item the vth of Nove*m*ber to mr Maior for his diner the   25
same day   xx s
Item to the Iudgler the same day at mr Maior com*m*ande   vj s
Item to mr thompsone the wait   xxij d
...
Item for a shert to wille the ffowle   xx d   30

f [25]   *(18–22 December)*
...
Item to wille the ffoall for a paire of shoes & hoas   iij s [⟨....⟩]
...   35

4–10/ *for* All Hallow Thursday, *18 May*
17/ mr Maior: *Adam Robinson, elected mayor 30 September, f [24], account title*
22/ ⟨..⟩ / *stained; probably* Mr

f [25v]   *(22 January–22 February)*

...

Item to one william hutton a musitian & 3 of his company
at mr Ma commande   xviij d

...

Item for the games vpon Shrovetewesday   xx s
Item for a foat ball   iiij d

...

f [26v]*   *(Mayor's Disbursements)*

...

°Item payde ffor leadinge 8: Carfull of wood ffrom
Corbye, beinge for Rayles againste his majesties Cominge
to Carlell, ye 27 of Iune   vij s iiij d:

...

Item in rewarde to ye waytes of Barwicke   ij s vj d.

...

Item to ye paynter ffor ye kinges Armes vpon Richard
gayte, & payntinge ye Crosse with ye ffayne over &
besydes. 40 s . payde to him by Iohn Iackson   iiij li. iiij s.

...

Item geuen to A tumbler & his musicions   iiij s.

...

Item to Anthony Sanderson, Thomas Blackelocke
Mychaell pattinson, William hynde, Robart watson &
Richard Stodart for wating of mr Maior when ye kinges
Majestie was heare°   xxx s.

...

f [27]   *(John Jackson's Disbursements)*

first to the occupations vpon alhallowe thursday in theire
chambers   xx s
to Iohn Burton trumpiter   xij d
to the waits of lincolne   xviij d
In wine & sugar the brethren beinge present the same day   ij s vj d

...

In powder the same day   xvj s viij d

...

6/ Shrovetewesday: *4 March*   32/ alhallowe thursday: *29 May*

Item to the waits of lancaster   xij d

...

f [27v]

...   5

Item for whit & Read carsey to the foalls coat   xiiij s 4 d
Item for harne to his clothes   ix d

...

Item for Makinge the foall coat   v s

...   10

f [30v]*   *(Fees and Annuities)*

...

to nicholas hudson dru*mm*er   x s

...   15

Chamberlains' Audit Book   CCRO: CA/4/139
f 53*

The Accounte...bigininge At Mychaelmes 1616 And endinge At   20
Mychaelmes 1617: In w*hi*ch yeare his Ma*j*estie kinge Iames the ffirst
was at Carelell & did Solemnise his ffeast their vpon Gowryes daye.
ye vth of August:/...

...

                                                                           25

f 54
The Alowances now Craved with ye nessesarye expences disbursede
Againste his Ma*j*estie Comminge, As also in fees to his offisers, At his
heighnes beinge their...

...   30

Ite*m* ffor a present to his Ma*j*estie w*hi*ch was a Cupp of
goulde duble giltt with a Cover of three full quarters
heigh   xxvij li:
Item to Thomas Blackelocke ffor goinge to London
aboute ye same to Robe*r*t pattinson their   xx s: 35
Item ffor ffortye duble peaces of goulde with a purse of
blewe Silke & Silver, presented w*i*th ye Cupp: to his
Ma*j*estie & for ye Charge & procuringe ye said gould   xlv li:
Item in ffees to all offisers of his Ma*j*esties howsholde as
by A p*ar*ticuler vnder mr hebburns hande, beinge   40
gentilma*n* vsher to his Ma*j*estie appearede   xxix li xij s:
Item in more ffees to ye offisers of his Ma*j*esties querye as

by a particuler appeared vnder Sir Robert Osburnes
hande   vj li vj s viij d:

...

Item alowede in mr Robinsons hande ffor his
extraordinarij Chargis in entertayninge ye kinges   5
servantes & for his howse kepinge to ye more worshipp
of ye Citty   xv li:

A   *Tanners' Guild Minute Book*   CCRO: D/Lons/L
        f [23]   *(Masters' Accounts dated 7 November 1617)*   10
        (Receipts)
        ...

Ite of Mr Maior for accompainge him at ye kinge moore   ij s. vj d
...

(Expenses)   15
Item at ye Rydinge of our bounder bestowed in ye
Chaber   xvij s—
...

f [22v]*   20

Memorandum that the kings most excellent Majestie Iames ye firste
was heare at Carelell ye ffourth Daye of Auguste where ye maior of
the Cittye Mr Adam Robinson with Mr Thomas Carelton Recorder
and ye Brethren of [ye]ᴧ⌐the¬ Cittye presented him first with a Speatche   25
then a cupp of gold vallewed at 30 li: and a purse of Sylk with 4ᵗⁱᵉ
Iacobusies or peaces in ye same his Majestie vouchsafed very
pleasinglye the Speatch & Gifte & thanked Mr Maior & all [the]ᴧ⌐ye¬
cittizens theirfore and then presentlye went to [the]ᴧ⌐ye¬ Churche
accompanied with his nobles bothe of Englande & Scotlande The next   30
Daye he did keepe a feast Royall went agayne to ye Churche in State
with his nobles / beinge gowryeidaye / where preached before him
Robert Snadon Bishopp of Carelell And ye maior that Daye goinge
before him to & from [the]ᴧ⌐ye¬ Church at ye Courte gate kissed his
Hand & so⟨....⟩At his Departure ye third Daye ye Maior & his   35
Brethren tooke their leves of his Majestie who used all of them very
graciouslye talkinge a good Space with them./

4–7/ *for All Hallow Thursday, 29 May*
13/ accompainge *for* accompaninge
17/ Chaber *for* Chamber
33/ Snadon: *Robert Snowden, bishop of Carlisle, 1616–21*

1617–18
Chamberlains' Accounts   CCRO: CA/4/2
f [42]*   *(Disbursements)*

Rewarde *Imprimis*	disbursed to Iohn Trumpetter …	xviij d	5

f [43]

	…		
rew	disbursed to the musetions at mr mayre the v^t of november beinge gowres day …	xviij d	10

f [43v]

	…		15
ffoole	disbursed for willy*a*m miller the Citye foule for a sacke	ij s iiij d	
foole	disbursed for a pare of hose	xviij d	
foole	disbursed for a pare of dulle sole shewes …	xx d	
Rewarde	geauen to me Lo*r*d Quarton players …	v s	20

f [44v]

	…		
	disbursed to mr mayre for gonpowdr diner the v^t of november …	xx s	25
Rewarde	geauen to the Earle of Sussex players …	xiij s iiij d	

	30

f [46v]   *(St Thomas Day) (Benevolences)*

	…		
ffee dr*um*mer	to nicho*la*s hudson …	ij s vj d	

	35

f [47]

	…		
Rewarde	geauen to the wates of kendall …	xviij d	

10/ mr mayre: *Thomas Pattinson, signature at end of account,* f *[56]*
11/ beinge gowres day *added after payment entered*

ffoole   disbursed to willye foule for a pare of shewes   iij s vj d

                ...

                f [47v]
                ...   5
rewarde   geauen to hobbye Corbutt   xviij d
                ...
not.   disbursed to Edward dalton for the games   xxvj s viij d
                ...
ffoole   disbursed for leadder to men willye foule shewes   ij d   10

                f [49]*
                ...
Rewarde   geauen to a tumler   xij d
                ...   15
Rewarde   geauen to the Irishe wates   xij d
                ...
Rew   geauen to the wates of Durham   xviij d
Rewarde   geauen to sir Iohn dalton musetions   xij d
                ...   20

                f [49v]   (Lady Day)(Benevolences)
                ...
ffee   to nychols hudson   ij s vj d
drummer
                ...   25

                f [50]
                ...
Rewarde   geauen to the quenes players   xxij s
                ...   30

                ff [50v–1]
                ...
Rew   geauen to the wates of Penreathe   iij s iiij d
ffoole   disbursed to Thomas Raylton for makeing willye foule   35
                cotte   v s

                ...
                disbursed for Clothe delivered to the Chamberlayns for
                the Citye vse at Christames sportes

                6/ hobbye Corbutt: *a musician, see p 95, l.6*
                8/ the games: *Shrove Tuesday, 17 February*

Impr*imis*	vj yeardes of read kersaye at iijs iiijd a yeard	xx s
	disbursed for vj yeardes of kersaye whit and read	
	Peniston	xiij s
	iij qurtrs of Peniston and Coulert thred	j s x d
	iij yeardes and a halfe of grey kersaye	viij s ix d/
	for the saregantes Clokes Lace and neckes	iiij li.
ffoole	for Willym myller cott vj yeardes of whit and read	
	kersaye	xv s
foole	for Canvice	xij d
	...	
	disbursed for puder	xxvij s
	disbursed to ye eight Occupations	xx s
Rew	geauen to Iohn Tru*m*petter	xij d
Rew	geauen to the Wates of hellefax	xij d
	...	
Rew*arde*	geauen to the wates of wakfeld	xviij d
Rew*arde*	geauen to mr Thompson boyes	xviij d
Rew	geauen to a Iugler	xij d
	...	

f [51v]

...

Rew*arde*	disbursed to the fidler on Allathursdaye	xij d

...

f [52]   *(St John's Day)*   *(Benevolences)*

...

ffee	to nichols hudson	ij s vj d

...

f [53]

...

ffoole	disbursed for read and white for mending	
	willye foule cott	iij s

...

11–12/ *for All Hallow Thursday, 14 May*
23/ Allathursdaye: *All Hallow Thursday, 14 May*

f [53v]*

...

Rewarde   geauen to me Ladye Elibethe players   xxvj s viij d

...

Rewarde   geauen to musetions of hellefax at the dynner at   5
           Besse Parker   ij s

...

f [54]

...   10

Rew   geauen to the players the xij° of September by
           mr mayre derection   x s

...

f [54v]*   (12-29 September)   15

Rew   geauen to Sir Iohn sawell musetiones   xij d
Rew   geauen to the wats of Bedell   xij d
Rew   geauen to the wates of Linkon   xviij d
           ...   20

f [55]   (Benevolences)(Michaelmas Day)

ffee   to nycholas hudson   ij s vj d

           ...   25

A   *Tanners' Guild Minute Book*   CCRO: D/Lons/L
     f [24v]   (*Masters Accounts dated 6 November*)(*Receipts*)
     ...
     Ite of Mr Maior a gratuetie for accompainge him to ye   30
     kinge moore   ij s. vj d.

     ...
     (*Expenses*)
     Ite at ye Rydinge of ye bounder bestowed in [the]ᴧ ⌈ye⌉
     Chaber   xiiij s. viij d. 35

     ...

3/ Elibethe *for* Elizabethe   30–35/ *for All Hallow Thursday, 14 May*
30/ accompainge *for* accompaninge   35/ Chaber *for* Chamber

1618–19
Chamberlains' Accounts   CCRO: CA/4/1
f [63]   *(Ordinary Disbursements)*

In primis geuen to Iohn Trumpeter ye ffirste daye of		5
October, beinge ye election day	ij s	
...		
Item to Edwarde dalton ffor ye Sommergames	xxvij s: vj d:	
Item ffor a ffote ball, & ye breatch of a hammer shafte	viij d.	
Item to ye occupacions vpon alhallowe daye	xx s:	10
Item ye same daye to Iohn trumpeter	xij d.	
...		

f [64v]   *(Rewards)*

...		15
Item to ye wates of Millam	iij s.	
...		
Item to Sir wilfryde lawsons Musecions	iij s.	
...		
Item to ye wates of pearethe	ij s. vj d.	20
...		
Item to ye wates of Barnardcastle	xij d.	
...		
Item to ye wates of Rippon	ij s. vj d.	
...		25
Item to ye wates of wakeffeelde	ij s.	
...		
Item to A knightes musicions yat Came oute of		
yorkshyer	iij s iiij d.	
		30

f [65]*

...		
Item ye 20^tie of November geven to my lord whartons		
playeres	xiij s. iiij d.	
		35
...		
Item to ye wates of kendall	ij s	
Item to ye wates of Applebye	xij d:	

8/ ye Sommergames: *Shrove Tuesday, 9 February*
10/ alhallowe daye: *6 May*

Item to hobbye Corbett & lebodye vpon hall thursdaye   xij d.

...

(5 June)
Item to the Bearwarde...   vj s.

...   5

(5 June⁺)
Item to George Bell & other tow wates   ij s

...

Item to ye kinges playeres   xxx s:

...   10

f [66]   (Fees)

...

The drummers ffee   x s.

...   15
(Liveries)
The Seriantes leueries
The Beedles leueries
The hirdes leuerye
The wates leverey   xi li xij s viij d.   20
The drummers leverey
The Bellmans leverey
The ffooles Cote & other Chargis ffor him   xxvij s xj d./

...

                                                                             25

f [76v]*

Trumpeter.   (blank)

...

Leveres 11 li. 5s. 2d: 7s 6d:/–11 li: 12s. 8d:/   30
ffoole 18d. 23d. 5s: 16s: 12d 2s 6d–1 li: 7s: 11d.

...

Court Leet Rolls   CCRO: CA/3/21
mb [2]   (21 April)   35

...

Item we Request that Mr Maior and his breathren shall call for the
silver broad Arrowes and the Stock and the horse ˄ ⌈nages⌉ Bels with
all expedytion[s] and the same so called [into] in to bestowe the same
and ffive poundes more in A silver Cup gilded to be Imployed for   40

1/ hall thursdaye: 6 May   1/ lebodye: Robert Lebody, a musician, see p 95, l.21

manteyning of A horse Rase for the Cytties vse (vpon the kinges more)
at such tyme yearely as theye shall thinke convanient, And to Article that
the same cup shall be brought in yearely as they shall thinke ffittinge
...

5

A   ***Tanners' Guild Minute Book***   CCRO: D/Lons/L
f [24v]   *(Masters' Accounts dated 6 November) (Expenses)*
...

Ite for [ye] Strangers at o*ur* Dinner	vj s–
Ite for wyne & Sewger then	viij s vj d.
Ite for wylde foole Cunnyes & Capons	vij s. iij d.
Ite at ye settinge of ye Dinner	ij s.–

10

...

f [25]

15

...
Ite to ye Musicians at o*ur* Dinner   viij d.
...

f [26v]   *(Masters' Accounts dated 5 November 1619)*
(Receipts)

20

...
Ite from Mr Maior of hallow Thursdaye   ij s. vj d.
...
(Expenses)   25
Ite bestowed in ye Chamber upon hallowe Thursday   xvj s. viij d.
...

1619–20
Chamberlains' Accounts   CCRO: CA/4/2   30
f [79]*   *(William Simson's Disbursements)*
...
Item to Iohn Burton trumpiter vpon the election day at
mr maior comm*a*nde   ij s vj d
Item to 2 musitions beinge mr navell his men at mr Ma*i*or   35
comm*a*nde   xviij d
...

9/ o*ur* Dinner: *28 October*
23/ hallow Thursdaye: *6 May*
34/ mr maior: *Thomas Blenerhassett, elected 4 October, f [79], account title*

Item for Amending wille the ffoale his clothes   xvj d
…
Item for 2 shertts to wille the foale & for makeinge of
them   iiij s x d
Item bestowed vpon my lord dudley players at mr Maior   5
commande   x s
…
Item to the waits of kendall at mr Maior commande   ij s vj d
…
                                                                                    10

f [79v]
…
Item to a piper & a drummer at mr Maior commande   vj d
…
Item bestowed vpon Sir wilfrid lawson foale at mr Maior   15
commande   xij d
…
Item for a paire of shoes to wille the foale vpon christmas
even   ij s vj d
Item for a paire of stockins & making them to him   ij s vj d   20
…

f [80]*
…
Item to the schollers for a speach play   ij s vj d   25
…
Item to a scotts foale   vj d
…

f [80v]   30
…
Item to 2 musitions at thomas Atkinson mariage   xij d
…
Item for the cites gams vpon Shrove tewesday   xxv s
Item in wine & sugar after the brethren came from the   35
meadowe   vs viij d
Item for a foatball   4 d
Item for a bar   ij d
…
Item to 2 pipers vpon Shrovetewesday at night at   40

34,40/ Shrove tewesday: *29 February; see also p 95, ll.6–7*

mr Maior commande	vj d

...

Item to puppie players	xij d
Item to 3 musitions at mr Maior commande	xij d

...   5

f [81]

Item to a Iudgler that would have gone in the town at divers tyms	xviij d 10

...

Item vpon alhallow thursday in the occupations chambers	xx s
In powder the same day	xxiiij s

...   15

Item vpon the late quenes Maiesties players	xxj s

...

f [81v]

...   20

Item for a coat to wille the foal	xj s
Item for sherts to him & making them	vs vj d
Item for a paire of stockins	xx d
Item for a paire of shoes	ij s vj d
Item for making his coat	iij s 4 d 25

...

Item to the waits of kendall	xviij d
Item to one of mllam that playd vpon a drume & a pipe	vj d

...

Item to a piper when the veneson was eaten at mr Maior	vj d 30

...

Item for a band to wille the foale	iiij d

...

f [82]   (*Dalston Dalton's Disbursements*)   35

...

Item to one Iohnston a ffoole at mr Maior commande	vj d

...

16/ xxj s: *folio torn through descenders of* xx; j *written over* x
28/ Item: *word almost obliterated by a marginal tear*

Item to my lord hume his ffoole   vj d

...

f [82v]*

...   5

Item vpon hobby corbat vpon shrove tewesday for
musicke   ij s vj d

...

Item to the waits of Aske at mr Maior com*m*ande   ij s
Item to the waits of midlam   xviij d   10

...

Item to the waits of peareth   xviij d

...

f [83]   15

...

Item to the waits of Rippon   ij s vj d

...

Item to a Iudgler vpon alhallowe thursday   ij s vj d

...   20

Item to Robert lebody for musicke vpon alhallowe
thursday   ij s

f [83v]

...   25

Item to the waits of lincolne at mr Maior com*m*ande   ij s

...

Item bestowed vpone my lady elizabeth players   xv s

...

                                                                               30

f [85]   *(Fees)*

...

The dru*m*mers ffee   x s

...

                                                                               35

A   *Tanners' Guild Minute Book*   CCRO: D/Lons/L
    f [26v]   *(Masters' Accounts dated 5 November) (Expenses)*

...

Ite for xiij Strangers at o*u*r Dinner   vj s. vj d.

6/ shrove tewesday: *29 February; and above,* pp 93 *l.34 -* 94 *l.1*
19/ alhallowe thursday: *25 May*

Ite for wyne & (Sewger besydes Mr [gents] ‸ ⌈Gents⌉) o*ur*
Dinner   vj s. vj d (vj d.
Ite for wylde fowle Cunnyes & Capons   viij s. viij d.–
Ite at ye settinge of o*ur* Dinner   ij s.–

                                                                                5

f [27]
...
Ite to ye Musecions for playing at o*ur* Dinner   vj d.
...

                                                                               10

f [28]   *(Masters' Accounts dated 3 November 1620) (Receipts)*
...
Ite frome Mr Maior of hallowthursdaye   ij s. vj d–
...

                                                                               15

f [28v]   *(Expenses)*

Ite bestowed in [the] ‸ [ye] Chaber upon hallow Thursdaye   iiij s–
...

                                                                               20

1620–1
Chamberlains' Accounts   CCRO: CA/4/2
f [89]*   *(Disbursements)*
...
Ite*m* to Iohn Trumpiter   xij d   25
Ite*m* to the Musitians att Mr Maior comand   ij s
...

f [89v]
...
                                                                               30
Ite*m* giuen for makinge awake the fifte day of nouember
att Mr Maior comand   xviij d
Ite*m* giuen to Mrs Maioras ‸ ⌈for⌉ the dyner the vth of
nouember   xxiij s iiij d
...   35

1–2/ o*ur* Dinner: *28 October*   18/ Chaber *for* Chamber
13/ hallowthursdaye: *25 May*   26/ Mr Maior: *Thomas James, f [89], account title*

Item giuen to the Musitians the same day att Mr Maior
comand   ij s

…

Item giuen to the kings players att Mr Maior comand   xxiij s

…   5

f [90]

…

Item disbursed for william Mylners buriall and his
funerall expenses att mr maior com*and*   x ⟨…⟩   10

…

f [90v]

…

Item giuen to towe Musitians of Ednebrough att Mr   15
Maior comand   xij d

…

Item giuen to Edward Dalton vpon shroufe theusday for
the gams Mr Maior comand   xxxij s
Item giuen for a foot ball the same day att Mr Maior   20
comand   viij d

f [91]

⟨……………⟩ the Musitians the same   25
⟨………⟩ Maior comand   ⟨……⟩
Item giuen to the princis players the xxth of december att
mr Maior comand   xxij⟨..⟩

…

Item giuen to thre Musitioners goeinge to workington att   30
Mr Maior comand   xviij d

…

Item giuen to the waits of penrith att Mr Maior comand   xij d

…

1/ Mr Maior: *Thomas James, f [89], account title*
10/ x ⟨…⟩: *remainder of payment obliterated by heavy discolouration*
18/ shroufe theusday: *13 February*
25/ *first three words obliterated by a hole 80mm in diameter, placed 32mm from the left edge*
   of folio and 10mm from top, with fading in surrounding area; probably Item giuen to
26/ *first three words faded–probably* day at Mr; *payment obliterated by discolouration*
28/ *payment partly illegible because of discolouration*

Item giuen to the waites of midlim In yorke shire att Mr
Maior comand   xviij d

…

Item giuen to Edmond Chraister ˏ ⌜for⌝ the lords coat
against Christinmes Mr Maior comand   x s   5

…

f [91v]

…

Item giuen for powder vpon allhallow thursday   xxxviij s   10

…

Item giuen vpon allhallowthursday to the chambers of the
ocupations   xx s
Item giuen to the Musitians the same day att Mr Maior
comand   ij s vj d   15

…

f [92]

Item giuen for makinge a case for the giltinge bo⟨.⟩le att   20
Mr Maior comand   vj d

…

Item bestowed vpon my lord william sonnes the horsrace
day In beare att Mr Maiors   ij s
Item giuen the Musitioner for plainge the same daye att   25
Mr Maior comand   xij d

…

Item giuen for parchment for writtinge the Artickels for
the giltinge boule   vj d

…   30

f [92v]

…

Item giuen to the waites of durham   ij s

                                                                                                        35

f [93]

…

Item giuen to the waites of Rippin att Mr Maior comand   xviij d

…

10/ allhallow thursday: *10 May*   23/ my lord william: *Lord William Howard of Naworth*

Item giuen to the waites of kendall   iij s

...

f [93v]

...   5

Item giuen att the assize to Sir Henry Curwen Musitians   xviij d
Item giuen to the waites of kendall   xij d
Item giuen to the waites of Millam   xij d
Item giuen to the kings players   xxij s

...   10

f [94v]   *(Fees and Annuities)*

...

To the drummer   x s

...   15

A   ***Tanners' Guild Minute Book***   CCRO: D/Lons/L
     f [28v]   *(Masters' Accounts dated 3 November) (Expenses)*

...

Ite ffor v: Strangers at our Dinner   ij s. vj d.   20
Ite ffor wyne then   xx s
Ite in towpences ffor everye brothers Dinner & Strangers
amountinge to 82. psons   xv s. vj d.

...

Ite to Musetions of ye Dinner   vj d.   25

...

f [29v] *(Masters' Accounts dated 2 November 1621) (Receipts)*

...

Ite of Mr Maior [⟨.⟩]ₐ ⌈a⌉ benevolence to [the]ₐ ⌈ye⌉   30
Company   [⟨....⟩d] ii s. vi d.

...

(Expenses)
Ite bestowed in [the]ₐ ⌈ye⌉ Chamber upon hallow
Thursday   xv s. ij d   35

...

20/ our Dinner: *28 October*   30–5/ *for All Hallow Thursday, 10 May*
23/ psons *for persons*

1621–2
Chamberlains' Accounts   CCRO: CA/4/2
f [97]*(Disbursements)

...

Reward   Item to a poore singingman one Busse Cominge out of
Irelande   ij s   5

...

ordnere   Item ffor a dinner to the bretheren vpon ye gunpowder
daye Sir Iohn dalston & other Strangers ther   xx s

Reward   Item to ye Scollers ffor an exercyse or an oracion
deliuered by them to Mr Maior & his Company then   ij s   10

...

f [97v]*

...   15

Reward   Item to ye wates of Boston in linconshyer   ij s

...

Reward   Item to my Lorde Wharton playeres   x s

...

Reward   Item to Nycholas hudson in ye tyme of him self & his
howsouldes vicitacion   ij s vj d   20

...

Reward   Item geuen to offiseres in Christinmes at nawart ye Maior
& bretheren beinge ther   x s

Reward   Item to a musicion their at ye same tyme   ij s   25

...

Reward   Item to Richeson ye Ieaster or Counterfeete   xij d

...

(February)

Reward   Item to ye kinges Iugler   xx s   30
Reward   Item to ye wates of kirkbylonesdell   xviij d

...

f [98]   (March)

...   35

ordnere   Item payde vnto Edmonde Craster ffor ye seriantes
ffreese Cotes & viij^th yeardes and a halfe of brode Reed
ffor ye beadles drumme & hirdes leveres   v li ij s iij d

...

8–9/ ye gunpowder daye: 5 November   11/ Mr Maior: Henry Baines, f [97], account title
27/ Item to a poore man one Richeson a Iester f [104v]

Reward	Item to ye wates of lincon	xviij d	

(April)

Reward	Item to ye wates of lancaster	xviij d	
	...		
Reward	Item to ye wates of pearethe	xij d	5
Reward	Item to ye wates of kirkbyelonesdell	xviij d	
Reward	Item to ye wates of Rippon	xviij d	
	...		

(May)

ord'	Item to Edward dalton ffor ye Summergames	xxviij s	10
Reward	Item to ye wates of Barwicke	ij s	
	...		

f [98v]*   *(May–June)*

	...		15
Reward	Item to ye wates of kendall	ij s	
	...		
Reward	Item to ye kinges playeres ye 13 of September	xx s	

f [99]   *(Fees)*

	...		20
	Item to ye drummer of ye Cittye	x s	

A	***Tanners' Guild Minute Book*** CCRO: D/Lons/L	
	f [29v–30] *(Masters' Accounts dated 2 November) (Expenses)*	25

...		
Ite for two Strangers at ˏ ⌈our⌉ Dinner	xij d	
Ite bestowed in Wine then	v s viij d	
Ite in towpences for every Brothers dinner beinge		
Parsons	xvj s	30
Ite for setting of [the] ˏ ⌈ye⌉ Dinner	ij s	
Ite to Musitions	vj d	
...		

3/ xviij d: xij d f *[104v]*
10/ ye Summergames: *see p 153, endnote to CA/4/2 f [6]*
11/ ij s: xviij d f *[104v]*
27/ ⌈our⌉ Dinner: *28 October*

1622–3
Chamberlains' Accounts   CCRO: CA/4/2
f [110v]   *(Disbursements)*

...

More giuen to my lord wharton players att Mr Maior   5
Comand   xij s

...

f [111]

...   10

More given to the princes players att Mr Maior comand   xx s

...

More given to the Musitians vpon ffastineven day att Mr
Maior comand   ij s vj d

...   15

f [112]

...

More given to the kinges players att Mr Maior comand   xx s

More given for the games vpon fastineven day   xx s   20

...

A   *Tanners' Guild Minute Book*   CCRO: D/Lons/L
f [31]   *(Masters' Accounts dated 8 November) (Expenses)*

...

Ite for [the]ᴧ ⌜sex⌝ Strangers   iij s   25
Ite ffor wylde foole Cunyes & Capons   vj s. xj d:& vj d.
                                                         for a malert
Ite in Wyne   [⟨.⟩s iiij d] v s:iiij d.
Ite at ye setting of ye dinner   ij s
...   30
Ite to ye Musicions   vj d

...

1623–4
A   *Tanners' Guild Minute Book*   CCRO: D/Lons/L
f [32]   *(Masters' Accounts dated 7 November) (Expenses)*   35

...

Ite ffor Settting of our dinner   iiij s
Ite ffor viij Strangers invyted to ye same at 8 d   [v s iiij d]ᴧ ⌜v s. iiij d⌝
Ite ffor wyne beinge both Sacke & Claried   v s. iiij d

5/ Mr Maior: *Thomas Gent, f [110], account title*   29/ ye dinner: *28 October*
13,20/ ffastineven day: *Shrove Tuesday, 25 February*   37/ our dinner: *28 October*

Ite ffor wylde ffooll Capons & Cunyes   vj s.

...

Ite to [the]ᵥ ⌈ye⌉ Musicions   vj d

...

Merchants' Book   CCRO: D/GC/4
f 87   *(Undermasters' Accounts dated 2 July 1625)*
(Disbursements)

...

Item at our dinner for 16 Straingers   00–08–00   10
Item for the Occupation and weadoes being in Nomber
36. at 6 d   00–18–00
Item 13 quartes of Clared wine   00–08–08
Item for 5 quartes of secke   00–05–00
Item to the Cookes, and vnder Cookes   00–03–04   15
Item to the Musitians   00–01–06

...

1624–5
Chamberlains' Accounts   CCRO: CA/4/2   20
f [117]   *(Disbursements)*

Imprimis given to the musitians at michaelmas at mr
maior Command   00 02 06

...   25

f [117v]   *(30 November–14 December)*

...

Item given to the waitts of lincoln at mr maior Command 00 01 00

...   30

Item the 14th of december given to balife ward *pro*
15 yard [of] & aquarter of brod read *pro* the waitts Clocks
the 3 beadles Cotts the belman Cotte the drum*mer*Cotte
& the hird Cotte at 7s *per* yard at mr Maior Com*m*and   05 6 9

...   35

f [118]   *(11 January–22 March)*

...

Item given to George tayler *pro* makeinge of aplay at mr

10/ our dinner: *12 September*
23–4/ mr maior: *Thomas Blenerhassett, f [117], account title*

maior Command   00 02 6

...

f [118v]

...

Item to the waitts of Rippon at mr maior Command   00 01 04

...

(21 April–30 May)
Item given to the waits of peareth   00 01 00

...

f [119] (11 June–5 July)

...

Item given to the waitts of lincoln at mr maior Command 00 01 00

...

Item given to the ˏ ⌈kings⌉ players vpon the 5th of Iulij at
mr maior Command   01 00 00

...

(5 July–17 August)
Item given to the waitts of peareth   00 01 00

...

f [119v]   (24 August[+])

...

Item to the waytes of wakefeild   00 01 00

...

Item to the waytes of kendall   00 01 00

...

Item to the waitts of darinton   00 01 00

...

f [121]*   (Fees) (Christmas)

...

Item to the drummer pro his ffee   00 02 6

...

(Our Lady Day)
Item to the drumer pro his ffee   00 02 6

...

(St John's Day)
Item to the drummer pro his ffee   00 02 06

...

f [121v] *(Michaelmas)*

...

Item to the dru*mm*er *pro* his ffee   00 02 6

...
                                                                                                                                 5

A   ***Tanners' Guild Minute Book***   CCRO: D/Lons/L
f [33] *(Masters' Accounts dated 5 November) (Expenses)*

...

Ite ffor Setting ye Occupacions Dinner   ij s vj d in ye hands
Ite ffor viij Stranges invyted to ye same at 8 d apeace   v s. iiij d   10
Ite ffor Wyne bothe Sacke and Clarrede   vij s ij d
Ite bestowed in wyld ffoole Capons and Cunyes   vj s vj d

...

Ite to the Musitions   vj d

...
                                                                                                                                15

f [34] *(Masters' Accounts dated 4 November 1625) (Receipts)*

...

Ite ffrome Mr Maior as A gratuetie to ye Companie ffor
Rydinge with him of he Cittyes bounder   ij s vj d.   20

...

(Expenses)
Inprimis bestowed upon ye Companye at ye Rydinge
of ye kings moore upon ye assention daye in breede
cheese drinke & Cake   x s—   25
Ite ffor our quarter of Sacke & one quart whyte wine   xx d.
Ite ffor [⟨...⟩]ₐ ⌈dressinge & trinning of ye⌉ Chamber   vj d
Ite to ye Musisions that daye   iiij d

...
                                                                                                                                30

Merchants' Book   CCRO: D/GC/4
f 88   *(Undermasters' Accounts dated 29 June 1626)*
(Disbursements)

...

Imprimis 45 *per*sones that were at our dinner   01–02–6   35
ffor wine at our dinner   0–13–0
to the Cookes and vndercokes   0–03–0
ffor Musik   0–01–0

9/ ye Occupacions Dinner: *28 October*   27/ [⟨...⟩]: *6 words of about 25 letters*
19–28/ *for All Hallow Thursday, 26 May*   35/ our dinner: *11 September*

ffor beare   0–06–06

...

1625–6

A   *Tanners' Guild Minute Book*   CCRO: D/Lons/L   5
    f [34]   *(Masters' Accounts dated 4 November) (Expenses)*

...

Ite ffor setting of [the] ⸢ye⸣ occupacons dinner   ij s
Ite ffor vij Strangers at ye dinner   iiij s. viij d
Ite ffor wyne both Sacke & Clarred to ye sayd dinner   vij s viij d.   10

...

Ite to ye musisions at ye dinner   vj d

...

Merchants' Book   CCRO: D/GC/4   15
f 89   *(Undermasters' Accounts dated 6 July 1627)*
(Disbursements)

...

ffor 57 persones at our dinner   01–08–06
ffor wine the same tyme   00–15–08   20
ffor Musike   00–01–06
to the Cookes   00–03–00
Bestowed in beare   00–01–00

...

                                                                             25

1626–7
Chamberlains' Accounts   CCRO: CA/4/2
f [128v]*   *(Disbursements)*

...

Item given to tho*mas* porter *pro* makeinge of the games at   30
⟨................⟩ the 6th of feabruarij   1. 7. 0

...

Item given *pro* afoott balle on shrough tuesday   0. 0. 6

...

Item given to the waitts of kendall the 8th of feabruarij at   35
mr maior Com*mand*   0. 1. 0

...

8/ ⸢ye⸣ occupacons dinner: *28 October*   31/ 6th of feabruarij: *Shrove Tuesday*
19/ our dinner: *10 September*

f [129]   *(8 February–3 May)*

...

Item given to the waitts of Ripon at mr maior Com*m*and   o. 1. o

...

Item to the waitts of peareth at mr maior Com*m*and   o. o. 8   5

...

f [129v]*   *(3 May–11 June)*

...

Item bestowed vpon the waitts of lancaster   o. 1. 4   10

...

Item given to the lord dudles players ye 18 Iune   o. 3. 4.

...

Item payde the 5th of auguste to Edward dalto*n* *pro*
adrume to the Cittye at mr maior Command   1. 6. 8.   15

...

f [130]*   *(5 August* + *)*
Item given to the kings players at mr maior Com*m*and   1 l. 10. o

...   20

Item bestowed vpon the waitts of lancaster ⌐Darinto*n*⌐ and
S*i*r thomas Medcalfe [Mu] players   o. 3. 4

...

(Christmas) (Fees)
Item to the drumer   o. 2. 6.   25

...

f ⌐130v⌐   *(Our Lady Day)*

...

Item to the drumer   o. 2. 6.   30

...

(St John's Day)
Item to the drumer   o. 2. 6.

...

                                                                              35

f [131]   *(Michaelmas)*

...

Item to the drumer   o. 2. 6.

...

A   *Tanners' Guild Minute Book*   CCRO: D/Lons/L
f [35]   *(Masters' Accounts dated 3 November) (Expenses)*
...

Ite to ye setting of ye Occupacons dinner	ij s	
Ite for x Strangers at ye same dinner	vj s viij d	5
Ite ffor wyne bothe Sacke & Claret to ye sayd dinner	v s: ij d	
Ite ffor wylde ffowle Capons & Cunnyes	v s 2 d.	
...		
Ite to ye Musicions or wates	vj d	
...		10

1627–8
Chamberlains' Accounts   CCRO: CA/4/2
f [136]   *(Disbursements)*
...   15

Item given to mr maior for the dinner that was bestowed
vpon the brethren and other gentlemen and Cittizens
vpon the gunpowther day   1. 0. 0.
...
                                                                                         20

f [136v]
...
Item given to the schollers that maid the oration ye 5th of
november at mr maior Command   0. 02. 9.
...   25
Item given to Edward dalton of Shrougtuesday for
makeinge of the gaimes at mr maior Command   01. 07. 4
Item for 2 foott balles j s pro ahammer shaftinge ij d   00. 01. 2.
Item for acocke that day & for makeinge his pitts   00 00 10
Item for adoore for the gunners that day   00. 00. 10   30

f [137]*
...
Item given to ye waitts of kendell at mr maior Command   0. 02. 0.
Item given to ye waitts of peareth at mr maior Command   0. 01. 0.   35
...

4/ ye Occupacons dinner: *28 October*
16/ mr maior: *Matthew Cape, f [136], account title*
18/ gunpowther day: *5 November*
26/ Shrougtuesday: *26 February*

Item given the 10th of martch to ye waitts of Rippon   o. oi. 6.

...

Item given to william heslehead for playinge at Caldowe   o. oo. 6.

...
                                                                                        5

f [138]

...

Item given to hobbye Corbitt for playinge at Michaelmas
when mr maior was Elected and other times   o. 5. o.

...   10

Item given to the waits of hallifacke at mr maior
Command   o. i. o

...

f [139v]*   *(Christmas) (Fees)*   15

...

Item to the drumer   o. 2. 6.

...

f [140]*   *(Mayor's Disbursements)*   20

...

Item payed to the kings Ravelles ye 29 of Iulij   oi. oo. o

...

Item for the waitts vj yeard of fine Read at 8 s   2. o8. o.

...   25

Item for 3 yeard of Read kersay for the drumer   o. io. o.

...

A   **Tanners' Guild Minute Book**   CCRO: D/Lons/L
    ‡ [36]   *(Masters' Accounts dated 2 November) (Expenses)*   30

...

Ite at ye settinge of ye occupacions dinner   ij s.
Ite payed ffor 8 Strangers invited by thoccupacion   v s : iiij d :
Ite ffor wyne & Sacke to ye sayd dinner   v s vj d
Ite ffor wyld ffowle Capon & Cunyes   vj s iiij d   35

...

Ite to ye Wates in benevolence   vj d

...

22/ ye 29 of Iulij *added after payment entered*   32/ ye occupacions dinner: *28 October*

Merchants' Book   CCRO: D/GC/4
f 91* *(Undermasters' Accounts dated 5 July 1629)*
(Disbursements)

Imprimis to Thomas Blaymer who had the Occupation		5
dinner	1–9–0	
ffor wine the same tyme	0–16–0	
More given to the Cookes	0–3–0	
To the Musike	0–1–0	
More for setting the dinner in beare	0–2–0	10

...

1628–9
Chamberlains' Day Book   CCRO: CA/4/9
f [25] col a* *(Fees quarterly)* 15

...

To ye drummer	ij s vj d	

...

A   *Tanners' Guild Minute Book*   CCRO: D/Lons/L 20
f [37] *(Masters' Accounts dated 7 November)*
(Expenses)

...

Ite at ye setting of ye occupacions dinner	ij s	
Ite ffor aleavene Strangers at ye sayde dinner	vij s. iiij d	25
Ite ffor wyldeffowle, Capons & Cunyes	vij s. iiij d	
To wyne & Sacke	ix s iiij d	

...

Ite to ye Wates for ther musycke at dinner	vj d	

... 30

f [38] *(Masters' Accounts dated 6 November 1629)*
(Receipts)

...

Ite Mr Maiors gift at ye Rydinge of his bounder	ij s vj d	35

...
(Expenses)
Inprimis bestowed in this Chamber upon thassencion
Daye, havinge accompaned Mr Maior upon ye rydinge of
ye Cittyes Bounder upon ye kings moore, in wyne Ayle, 40

5–6/ the Occupation dinner: *14 September*   35–40/ *for Ascension Day, 14 May*
24/ ye occupacions dinner: *28 October*

breed, Cakes & Cheese   xviij s. ij d./

...

Merchants' Book   CCRO: D/GC/4
f 90v   *(Undermasters' Accounts dated 5 July) (Receipts)*   5

...

More of the Chamberlines vpon Assention daye   0–2–6

f 91   *(Disbursements)*

...   10

More vpon assention day disbursed   0–10–0
the Musike same daye   0–0–6

f 92v   *(Undermasters' Accounts dated 2 July 1630)*
(Disbursements)   15

...

Payed at our dinner for comp & Strangers   01–08–00
More ffor wine at our dinner   0–13–04
payed to the Cookes and Musicke   0–04–06
payed at setting our dinner   0–01–00   20

...

1629–30
Court Leet Rolls   CCRO: CA/3/28
mb 5   *(23 October)*   25

...

[Item we order that the waytes of this cyttie Shall goe eu*er*ye day
Morning and evening vntill candlemas, (saving onely the saboath daye)
And likewise that goe all Christenmasse tyme except sabaoth daye]
...   30

A   **Tanners' Guild Minute Book**   CCRO: D/Lons/L
    f [38]   *(Masters' Accounts dated 6 November)*
    (Expenses)

...   35

Ite At ye settinge of ye occupacions dinnere   ij s
Ite ffor Strangers at ye dinner x: vj s. viij d
Ite ffor wilde ffoole Capons & Cunnyes   vj s

7/ Assention daye: *14 May*   20/ our dinner: *13 September*
36/ At *written over* to   36/ ye occupacions dinnere: *28 October*

Ite ffor wyne & Sacke   vij s iiij d
...
Ite to ye Wates for musicke at dinner   vj d
...

5

Merchants' Book   CCRO: D/GC/4
f 93v   *(Undermasters' Accounts dated 1 July 1631)*
(Disbursements)

Imprimis at our dinner for 54 persones at 6 d   01–07–00   10
ffor wine at our dinner   0–13–04
Payed to the Musicke   0–02–00
To the Cookes and vndercookes   0–03–00
ffor setting the dinner   0–01–00
...   15

1630–1
Chamberlains' Audit Book   CCRO: CA/4/139
f 78v   *(Allowances craved)*
...   20
Item ffor a ffree gilt Bowlle provyded by ye Cittye to be
Rune ffor vpon ye kinges moore   vj li
Item ffor Chargis to Mr Maior that he was att to Strangers
at those Rases   ij li
Item bestowed vpon sertayne Scittizens beinge halbert   25
men to se good order kept vpon ye moore   vj s viij d:
...

A   **Tanners Guild Minute Book**   CCRO: D/Lons/L
f [39]   *(Masters' Accounts dated 5 November) (Expenses)*   30
...
Ite at ye setting of the occupacion Dinner   ij s
Ite ffor Strangers at our dinners   ij s
Ite ffor Wylde ffoole Capons & Cunyes   vj s:
Ite ffor Wyne & Sacke   v s. iiij d   35
...
Ite to ye Wates in benevolence   vj d.
...

10/ our dinner: *12 September*
32/ the occupacion Dinner: *28 October*

1631–2

A   *Tanners' Guild Minute Book*   CCRO: D/Lons/L
f [40]   *(Masters' Accounts dated 4 November) (Expenses)*
...

Ite at the settinge of the Occupacions Dinner	ij s	5
Ite ffor Strangers bidd to o*u*r Dinner	vij s iiij d	
Ite ffor Wylde ffowle & Capons	v s. x d.	
Ite ffor wyne & Sacke	viij s	

...

Ite to ye Wates in benevolence	vj d	10

...

Merchants' Book   CCRO: D/GC/4
f 95v   *(Undermasters' Accounts dated 5 July 1633)*
(Disbursements)   15

...

Item given to the Musicke	0–2–00	
for setting the dynner	0–01–00	

...

for 47 at our dinner	1–3–6	20
ffor wine at the same tyme	0–13–4	

...

1632–3

A   *Tanners' Guild Minute Book*   CCRO: D/Lons/L   25
f [42]   *(Masters' Accounts dated 8 November 1633)*
(Receipts)
...

Ite of ye Chaberlens as frome Mr Maior	ij s vj d	
...		30

(Expenses)

Ite upon all hallowe Thursdaye (with ye Collection of the		
Brotherhoode) in accompaninnge Mr Maior in rydinge of		
ye bounder upon ye Kings more spent in this our		
Chamber as by pticuler note appeared	xix s iiij d./	35
Ite gene towards ye price of one dosan of Silver spoones		
by consent upon ye motion of Mr Iohn Baynes then		
maior as every of other 7 Companyes did ffor a third		

5/ the Occupacions Dinner: *28 October*	29/ Chaberlens *for* Chamberlens
18/ the dynner: *9 September*	29–35/ *for All Hallow Thursday, 30 May*
35/ pticuler *for* perticuler	

Course of Horse rase   x s./

...

Merchants' Book   CCRO: D/GC/4
f 95   *(1 February)*   5

Receaved of Mr William Barwicke ╲[ffor] ⌈in⌉ money
towardes the renewing of a Runninge Bowle   iij li
          [and deliuered to Edward dalton]
...   10

f 95v   *(Undermasters' Accounts 5 July) (Receipts)*
...
of the Chamberlines   0–02–6
...   15
(Disbursements)
on assention day for a cheise   0–3–4
ffor bread and Cakes   0–3–04
ffor beare same tyme   0–3–06
ffor wine the same tyme   0–1–6   20
to the Musike   0–0–6
...
The whole stocke of Money now remayinge due to the
occupation the 5 of Iuly 1633   13–07–00
of wch the money for the plate is a parte thereof   01 li–0–206   25

1633–4
Court Leet Rolls   CCRO: CA/3/29
mb 3   *(23 October)*
...   30
Item we request mr maior that the three wates wche now are
allowed may continue and commanded to play begininge presently
and soe to continue vntill Candlemas and to play both att Christmas
and at all other times according to former Custome excepted onely
the Sabbaoth dayes and to haue such allowance as formerly they   35
haue had, this is resone to the whole Company
...

14–21/ *for All Hallow Thursday, 30 May*   23/ remayinge *for* remayninge
25/ 0–206 *recte* 02–06

Merchants' Book   CCRO: D/GC/4
f 96*   *(Undermasters' Accounts dated 3 July)*
...

...resting in Ed*ward* dalton handes for the plate   02–0–0
...   5
more to him for the plate   iij li 4 s ij d

f 99   *(Undermasters' Accounts dated 3 July 1635) (Disbursements)*
...

More for 35 at our dinner	0–17–6 10
Payed ffor 5 widdoes	0–02–6
ffor 6 Straingers	0–03–00
More given to the Cookes	0–03–00
More to the Musicke	0–02–00
ffor wine at our dinner	0–13–00 15
More for settinge the dinner	–01–00

1634–5
Chamberlains' Accounts   CCRO: CA/4/2
f [146]*   *(Henry Sewell's Disbursements, first quarter) (Fees)*   20
...
Item to the drum*m*er   0. 2. 6
...

f [146v]   *(Thomas Wawby's Disbursements, second*   25
quarter) (12 February)
...

ffor the siluer games against Shroftuesday	1. 8. 0
for expenses about them	0. 2. 8
one sheet pastboard for the Gun*n*ers	0. 0. 6 30
two footballs	0. 1. 0
for carrying and bringing home the doore	
for the Gun*n*ers and bar fro*m* the sandes	0. 1. 0

...
(Fees)   35
To the drum*m*er   0. 2. 6
...

8/ MS *incorrectly numbers f 97 as f 99*   28/ Shroftuesday: *10 February*
10/ our dinner: *14 September*   31/ 1. 0 *written over* 0. 6

f [147v]   *(Thomas Wawby's Disbursements, third quarter)*
(19 April–7 May)

...

paid to the waites of Askrig	0.	0.	6
paid to the Waites of Orton	0.	0.	6
paid to the Waites of Bradforth	0.	0.	6
to the waites of Cockermoth	0.	0.	6
to the waites of Orton	0.	1.	0

...

(7 May, Ascension Day)
Paid to william Atkinson & Allexander dalton for 36. li.

3 ounces of powder	2.	10.	10
paid to the seuerall companies vpon ascension day	1.	0.	0

...

(13 May)
ffor carrying the weightes and scales to ye kinges moore

two daies at our courses	0.	2.	0
To the halbyteers for attending there	0.	2.	0
To the drummer	0.	2.	0
To the Waites	0.	2.	0
bestowed on the Waites of Penreth	0.	0.	6

...

Bestowed on the Waites for their attendance on

shroftuesday and ascension day	0.	5.	0

...

(Fees)

To the drummer	0.	2.	6

...

f [148v]   *(Thomas Wawby's Disbursements, fourth quarter) (4–16 August)*

...

Item bestowed vpon ye waites of Barwicke	0.	1.	0

...

f [149]   *(Fees)*

...

Item To the drummer	0.	2.	6

...

24/ shroftuesday: *10 February*   24/ ascension day: *7 May*

Chamberlains' Audit Book   CCRO: CA/4/139
f 85*   *(General Disbursements)*

...

Item to ye Scolleres ffor their Oracion   vij s. vj d.

...

Item ffor ye plate ffor ye horsrace   vj li. xiij s. iiij d.
Item to Mr Maior ffor his expenc then   xx s

...

Item in Rewarde to dyveres strangeres wates   xx s

A   ### Tanners' Guild Minute Book   CCRO: D/Lons/L
f [44]   *(Masters' Accounts, dated 6 November 1635) (Receipts)*

...

Ite Receaved of Mr Maior ffor accompaning him in
Rydinge of ye kings moore   ij s vj d

...

(Expenses)
Inprimis upon hallow Thursdaye spent in ye Cha⸢m⸣ber
(over yat was Collected of everye brother towards ye
defrayinge of yat expence beinge: ix s x d: x s j d the some
oute of the Stocke   xx s. xj d
Ite ffrom Dressinge of the Chamber then   vj d

...

Merchants' Book   CCRO: D/GC/4
f 96v*   *(3 April)*

...

Thes following are to pay arrerages behind for plat the last
yeare 1634
Edward Barwis
Thomas Atkinson
Iohn: Iacksoun
Thomas Robinson
Iohn hewart
Edward durrance
Thomas Blaymer
Mdum yt is agreed by consent of the whole trade this quarter day 1635

7/ Mr Maior: *Ambrose Nicholson, f 84, account title*
14–22/ for All Hallow Thursday, 7 May
22/ ffrom *instead of* ffor; *written over prior word*
37/ Mdum *for* Memorandum

that thes whose Names are vnder written shall pay every of them
towardes the Maintenance of the Plate this next yeare ffor that they have
payed nothing heretofore
Mathew wilkinson
[Ioseph Ieffersoun   5
Thomas Warde
William Slee
Thomas Monke]

Merchants' Book   CCRO: D/GC/4   10
f 97   *(Undermasters' Accounts dated 3 July) (Receipts)*
...
of the Chamberlines vpon assen day   02–6
...
                                                                         15
f 98   *(Undermasters' Accounts dated 1 July 1636) (Disbursements)*
...
ffor settinge the dinner   0–01–00
ffor wine at the dinner   0–09–00
...   20
ffor Strangers at our dinner   0–05: 6
...
ffor Musicke at the dinner   0–02–00
...
                                                                         25
f 97v   *(25 September 1635)*
...
owing by Edward dalton towardes a New pece of plate to
be Run the next yeare 1636   03–0–0
...   30

1635–6
Chamberlains' Accounts   CCRO: CA/4/2
f [149]*   *(24 March)*
...   35
°An Act   made & Consented vnto at ye Last Auditt by Mr Maior & his bretheren
with the ffowers of ye occupacions that no Barr monnye was heareafter
to be alowte to ye seriantes nor no monnyes to ye wates at ye goinge

4–6/ *irregular double line in left margin*   13/ assen *for* assention
13/ assen day: *7 May*   18/ the dinner: *13 September*

to ye kinges more or ye horsrace°

...

f [154v]*   *(John James's Disbursements, first quarter) (Fees)*

...

Item to the drumer   00: 02: 6

...

f [156]   *(Christopher Knagge's Disbursements, second quarter)*

...

Item given for 2 ffoott balles & acocke of
shroughtuesday   00: 01: 06:
Item for a doore and paisboard *pro* the gunners y*at* day   00: 01: 00:
Item given to Ed*ward* dalto*n* for the games   01: 14: 00

...

Item given to the Citties whaitts   00: 02: 6

...

f [156v]   *(Fees)*

...

Item to ye drumer   0: 02: 6:

...

f [157]   *(John James's Disbursements, third quarter)*

...

Item given to ye waitts of kendell   00: 01: 00

...

f [157v]

...

Item given vpon Assentio*n* day amongst the
occupations   01: 00: 00
Item given for 36 lb of powther   03: 10: 00

...

f [158]   *(Fees)*

...

Item to the drumer   0: 02: 6

...

12/ shroughtuesday: *1 March*   31/ Assentio*n* day: *26 May*

f [159]   *(Christopher Knagge's Disbursements, fourth quarter)*
(Fees)

...

Item to the drumer   0: 02: 6

...   5

Chamberlains' Audit Book   CCRO: CA/4/139
f 87*   *(General Disbursements)*

...

Item ffor a peace of plate ffor ye horse Course   5 18 11   10

...

A   *Tanners' Guild Minute Book*   CCRO: D/Lons/L
f [45]   *(Masters' Accounts dated 4 November 1636) (Receipts)*

...   15

Ite Rec ffrome Mr Maior   ij s vj d

...

(Expenses)
Inprimis for 1 quart of Sacke & Musyk   xviij d
Ite upon hallowe Thursdaye in cheese 4 s. 4 d.   20
in breede & Cakes - 5 s. 8 d. Ayle 6 s. 9 d.
wyne 20 d. Rishes 2 d. in all   xviij s. vij d:

...

Merchants' Book   CCRO: D/GC/4   25
f 98   *(Undermasters' Accounts dated 1 July) (Receipts)*

...

ffrom the Chamberlines   0–02–6

...

(Disbursements)   30
vpon assention day 1 quarte of wine i p sacke   0–01–02

...

f 97v   *(1 July)*

...   35

Remaining in Mr William Iames Maior for the plate   1–10

16/ Rec *for* Received
16–31/ *for All Hallow Thursday, 26 May*

1636–7
Chamberlains' Accounts   CCRO: CA/4/2
f [166v]*   *(Charles Crookbane's Disbursements, first quarter) (Fees)*
...

to the drum*m*er   0–2 6   5
...

f [170]*   *(John Nicholson's Disbursements, second quarter)*
(6 February–23 March)
...   10
Item given to Edward dalto*n* for makeinge the games
against Shroughtuesday & for apeace Cloth to put
them on   01: 18: 10
Item given that day for 2 foott balles   00: 01: 02
Item given for a Cocke that day   00: 00: 08   15
Item given for adoore and paysbourd for the guners   00   01: 00
Item given for makeinge 2 new hammer shaftes that
was broken that day   00: 00: 04
Item given to the Citties whaitts of Shroughtuesday   00: 02: 06
...   20
Item given to the skhollers for makeinge an Oratioun
the 5th of november before mr maior & his brethren   00: 10: 00:
...
Item given to the waitts of Rippon at mr maior
Com*m*and   00: 02: 06   25
...

f [170v]   *(Fees)*
...
Item to the drumer   00: 02: 06   30
...

f [168] *(Charles Crookbane's Disbursements, third*
quarter) (18–25 May)
                                                                            35
Item more the 25th May for careing of the weights to
the moore 2 times   0–2–0
more for packthred   0–1–0

12, 19/ Shroughtuesday: *21 February*

Item more that was bestowed in wine at the Crosse   0–3–4
Item given to them that caried halbertes to the Moore   0–5–4
…
(Fees)
to the drumer   0–2–6   5
…

f [171]   *(John Nicholson's Disbursements, fourth quarter)*
(2 September⁺)
…   10
Item given to the waitts of darinton   00: 02: 06:
…

f [171v]
…   15
Item given to the waytts of Barwicke   00: 02: 00
…
Item given to the waitts of kendell   00: 01: 06
…
                                                                              20
f [172]   *(Fees)*
…
Item to the drumer   00: 02: 0
…
                                                                              25
1638–9
Chamberlains' Accounts   CCRO: CA/4/2
f [181v]*   *(Disbursements, first quarter)*
…
To my lord Whartons players by the command of Mr   30
Maior November the 15th   0–10–0
…

f [182]   *(Fees)*
…   35
To ye drummer   0–2–6
…

1/ Crosse *perhaps for* Corsse   30–1/ Mr Maior: *John Aglionby, f [182], signature*

(Poor)

In cloth for the Sergiants, pipers, Beadles and drum*m*er   13–14–⟨.⟩

f [182v]   *(Disbursements, second quarter) (7–26 February)*

...   5

To the Waites of Keizwicke   0–1–0
To the Waites of kendaill   0–1–6

...

To the musitions vpon fasten Euenday by the comand of
Mr Maior   0–2–0   10

...

ffor the playes for fasteneuenday   1–12–6
To one for carrienge the doore   0–0–4
ffor two footebals   0–0–8

                                                                                        15

f [183]

...

To Richard Hudson for fastenuen day & the same day   0–0–6
...

(Fees)   20

To the drum*m*er   0–2–⟨6⟩
...

f [184v]   *(Disbursements, third quarter)*

...   25

To the waites of Rippon Aprill 10th   0–1–0

f [185]   *(Fees)*

...

To the drum*m*er   0 2 6   30

...

2/ *placed at foot of 'Poor' account, the payment included in combined totals for 'Fees' and 'Poor'*
2/ ⟨.⟩: *bottom outer corner of folio decayed*
9/ fasten Euenday: *26 February*
12/ playes: *ie, games*
18/ the same day: *8 March*
21/ ⟨6⟩: *marginal decay of folio*

f [186v]   *(Fees)*

...

To ye drum*m*er   0 2 6

...

1639–40
Chamberlains' Accounts   CCRO: CA/4/2
f [191]   *(Fees)*

...

It*em* to the drummer   00: 0[3]⌈2⌉: 0[4]⌈6⌉

...

f [191v]   *(Disbursements, second quarter)*

...

It*em* giuen to the players att Chrisinmas by the
Commaund of mr mayor   00. 10. 00

...

f [192]

...

It*em* 7 feb*ru*ary giuen to the waites of kendall by the
Commaunde of mr mayor   00: 01: 00

...

f [192v]

...

It*em* 17 feb*ru*ary giuen to the waites of askrigg by the
Commaund of mr mayor   00. 01. 00

...

f [192v]   *(Fees)*

...

It*em* to the drummer   00: 02: 06

...

f [193]   *(Disbursements, third quarter)*

...

It*em* 20 Aprill giuen to the waites of Rippon by the
Commaund of mr mayor   00: 01: 00

...

f [194]   *(Fees)*
...
Item to the drummer   00: 02 06
...

f [194v]   *(Disbursements, fourth quarter) (9–26 August)*
...
Item bestowed by mr mayor on the waites of *(blank)*   00. 01. 00
...

f [195v]   *(Fees)*
...
Item to the drummer   00: 02: 06
...

Chamberlains' Audit Book   CCRO: CA/4/139
f [91]   *(Disbursements)*
...
to William Iames the drummer   01 00 00
to a drummer for teachinge of Heslop   00 10 00
...

1642–3
Chamberlains' Accounts   CCRO: CA/4/2
f [201v]*   *(Disbursements, first quarter) (19 November)*
...
To Robert Browne a puppie player   00: 10: 00
...

f [202]   *(Fees)*
...
to the drummer hudson   00: 02: 06

f [202v]*
...
to William Iames drummer   00: 05: 00
...
paid for cloath for the Sergiants Cooke and waits   13 18 00
...

32/ hudson *added after payment entered*

Households

AUGSBURG MINERS

1568–9
Agent's Accounts   SA: Handelsbücher Nr. 20, Fasz. 1
f [19v]*   *(Account dated 22 January) (George Needham's expenses)*

...

Verehrt Spilleütten In Weihennächt Feirtagen   £–.1.–   5

f [114]*   *(Account dated 30 May) (Daniel Ulstät's expenses)*

...

Des Lord Moundtÿadt Spileüten verehrt.   £–.2.–

...   10

Ettlichen Spilleüten In Weÿhenächten   £–.3.–

f [114v]

...

Den Knappen verehrt, so Ine am 3 Konigstag   15
angesungen.   £–.5–.

...

1570–1
Agent's Accounts   SA: Handelsbücher Nr. 20, Fasz. 6   20
f [8v]   *(Account dated 26 February)*

...

In 2 malen Comedias oder Spil Zustehen verert Jedes mals
3 s   –.6.–/

...   25

f [69]   *(Account dated 4 June)*

...

Mer Spilleütten In 2 mal als frembde leutt sein hier
gewesen verert.   –.2.–/

...   30

15/ so: *adverb replacing pronoun, here with sense 'who'*

1571–2
Agent's Accounts   SA: Handelsbücher Nr. 20, Fasz. 6
f [134v]   *(Account dated 3 November)*
...

Einem frembden Spilman verert.   –.–.8/   5
...

1572–3
Agent's Accounts   SA: Handelsbücher Nr. 20, Fasz. 8
f [4]   *(Account dated 1 January)*   10
...

Den Hofierern alhie, Geiger und Pfeiff*er*.   –.4.–
...

1573–4   15
Agent's Accounts   SA: Handelsbücher Nr. 20, Fasz. 8
f [89v]   *(Account dated 26 December)*
...

Milorts Scrups Dinern so ein Comedi gehalten verert.   –.2.–
...   20

Fasz. 7, f [4]   *(Account dated 1 January)*
...

Den Spilleüten alhie.   –.2.–
...   25

f [6]*   *(Account dated 27 March)*
...

Dem Schuelmaister von Bireth verert, so ein Comedi
gehalten.   –.1.4.   30
...

12/ Hofierern: *musicians*; alhie: *here*
19/ Milorts: *my lord's*
19,29/ so: *adverb replacing pronoun, here with sense* 'who'
24/ alhie: *here*

CURWEN OF WORKINGTON

1625-6
Curwen Account Book   CCRO
f [5]   *(25 October–14 February) (Disbursements)*   5
...
Item to the players this last Chistinmas   v s
...

f [5v]   10

Item to the piper for his wages this last Christenmas   x s
...

f [7]   *(3–14 May)*   15
...
To the pypers at newbiggin & penrith   xij d
...

1626-7   20
Curwen Account Book   CCRO
f [23v]   *(28 July–4 August) (Disbursements)*
...
To the Musicions...   xij d
...   25

f [25v]   *(7 September–15 October)*

To Troughton the pyper   xiij s iiij d
...   30

1627-8
Curwen Account Book   CCRO
f [29]   *(3–19 January) (Disbursements)*
...   35
To Troughton the pyper in Christmas   x s
...

7/ Chistinmas *for* Christinmas
17/ newbiggin: *Newbiggin, Cumberland, about 3 miles southwest of Penrith*

f [33v]   *(15–24 September)*

…

To my Lady, for Anthony the [p] pyp*er*   ij s

…

    5

1628–9
Curwen Account Book   CCRO
f [35]   *(14–18 October) (Disbursements)*

…

To the pyp*er* in harvest   ij s   10

…

f [35v]   *(9–15 November)*

…

To my Lo*rd* Whartons players   ij s vj d   15

…

f [36]   *(12–13 December)*

…

To the Earle of derbyes players   xx s   20

…

f [37v]   *(11–14 February)*

…

To Cockermoth players   x s   25

…

f [43v]   *(24–8 August)*

…

To Bodell the fidler   v s   30

…

f [44v]   *(27–9 September)*

…

To the pyper, for 16. dayes in harvest   ij s viij d   35

…

1629–30
Curwen Account Book   CCRO
f [45]   *(4–6 November) (Disbursements)*
    40
…

To my Lo*rd* Whartons players   ij s vj d

…

f [47]

…

To my Master for the players. 6. Ianuarij   xiij s iiij d
To Anthonie the pyper   x s

…   5

f [48]

…

To Bodle the fiddler. 26: februarij   iij s

…   10

f [53v]   (31 July–7 August)

…

To a pyper   xij d

…   15

f [55]

To a Companie of players 2: september   v s

…   20

f [55v]   (26 September–4 October)

…

To the Musicions for my Lady   ij s vj d

…   25

1630–1
Curwen Account Book   CCRO
f [56]   (16–17 October) (Disbursements)

…   30

To henrye the pyper for harvest   ij s

…

f [56v]   (29–30 October)

…   35

To Will Bodle the fiddler   ij s

…

f [57]   (8–10 November)

…   40

To a Company of players   iij s

…

f [58]   (*16–20 November*)

...

To the players   v s

...

5

f [63]   (*18–23 April*)

...

To players, by my Lady   v s

...

10

1631–2
Curwen Account Book   CCRO
f [69v]   (*23 October*)(*Disbursements*)

...

To the pyper in harvest   ij s iiij d   15

...

f [72v]   (*6–7 January*)

...

To the pyper in Christmas   x s   20

...

f [74v]

To two Trumpetters, 8. Mart*ch*   xviij d   25

...

1632–3
Curwen Account Book   CCRO
f [79]   (*28 October–3 November*)(*Disbursements*)   30

...

To the pyper in harvest. for 9. dayes   xviij d

...

f [83]   (*4–7 January*)   35

...

To the pyper for Christmas   x s

...

f [83v]   40

...

To my Lord Whartons players. 21: feb*ruarij*   x s

...

f [84]   *(1–3 March)*

...

To a poor fidler   iiij d

...

(16 March)
To yorkshyre Musicions...   xij d

...

f [89v]   *(28 September–6 October)*

...

To the pyper for 15. dayes   ij s vj d

...

1633–4
Curwen Account Book   CCRO
f [92]   *(Disbursements)*

...

To my Lor*d* Whartons men. 7. dece*mber*   x s

...

f [93v]   *(5–12 January)*

...

To Troughton the pyper   x s

...

f [94v]   *(15–20 February)*

...

To my Maister, for Cockermoth players   x s

...

f [103]   *(4–5 September)*

...

To Bodle the fidler   ij s vj d

...

(5–6 September)
To the Pyper for watching horses   viij d

...

1634–5
Curwen Account Book   CCRO
f [109v]*   *(Disbursements)*

...

To Troughton the pyper, 9 Ian*uarij*   xx s   5

...

1635–6
Curwen Account Book   CCRO
f [122]   *(4–10 October)(Disbursements)*   10

...

To the pyper for harvest   ij s vj d

...

f [132v]   *(1–5 August)*   15

...

To a Company, of Musicians   0. 2. 0

...

f [134]   *(22–6 September)*   20

...

To the pyper, for 15. dayes in harvest   0 2: 6.

...

1636–7   25
Curwen Account Book   CCRO
f [134v]   *(3 October)(Disbursements)*

...

To my Lor*d* Strange men   0 2. 0.

...   30

f [148]   *(9–12 September)*

...

To the pyper for . 16. dayes in harvest   0 2. 8

...   35

f [149]*   *(28 September–1 October)*

...

For making the Ialor and Trumpiters Cloakes   0 5 0

...   40

1637–8
Curwen Account Book CCRO
f [159]   *(4–8 September) (Disbursements)*
...
To the pyper for 16: dayes   0 2 8   5
...

1640–1
Curwen Account Book CCRO
f [175]   *(12–14 October) (Disbursements)*   10
...
To the pyper, in harvest, for 17.dayes at 2 d   0 2: 10
...

f [178]   *(11–16 January)*   15
...
To Anthony troughton the pyper in Christmas   0 10 0
...

1641–2   20
Curwen Account Book CCRO
f [187]   *(10–16 October) (Disbursements)*
...
To the pyper, for 15: dayes in harvest, at 2 d   0 2 6.
...   25

f [190v]   *(31 December–8 January)*
...
To Anthony troughton, the pyper   0 10 0
...   30

1642–3
Curwen Account Book CCRO
f [200]   *(4–5 November) (Disbursements)*
...   35
To the pyper, for his harvest wages   0 2: 8.
...

12/ at 2 d *added after payment entered*

HOWARD OF NAWORTH

1612-13
Household Books 1   DDPD: Howard C706
f 10*   *(1 August) (My Lady and the Little Gentlemen)*   5

...

[.] ⌐3.⌐ pair of ⌐red⌐ dauncing pumpes for the child*en*   iiij s

...

f 21   *(3 January) (Rewards)*   10

...

To Iohn Trumpetor   v s.

...

(14 January)
To iij pipers at the gates   iij s.   15

...

(15 January)
To the wates at Carlyle   ij s vj d.

...

(23 January)   20
to *Sir Henry* Curwens iij waites   xij d.

...

(21 March)
To ye waites of Pearoth   ij s.

                                                                          25

f 21v *(25 March)*

...
To the waites of Rippo*n*   ij s vj d

...

(31 March)   30
To ye waites of Carlyle   ij s

...

(26 April)
to a pyp*er* at ye gate   vj d

...   35

(9 May)
To ye wates of doncaster   iij s

...

f 22   *(28 June)*
...
To I*ohn* Trumpeter   v s.
...

                                                                        5

f 22v   *(13 July)*
...
To a musicia*n* sent from Mrs Tayler   xx s.
...

                                                                        10

f 23   *(12 August)*
...
To Rbert for teaching the gent*lemen* to daunce   xl s.
...
(2 September)   15
The waites of wakefield   ij s vj d.
...
I*ohn* Trumpeter   v s.
...

                                                                        20

1617–18
Household Books 2   DDPD: Howard C706
f 33   *(1 August)* *(Rewards)*
...
To iij pipers at the gates   ij s vj d.   25
...
(5 August)
To iiij musicians at the gates   ij s vj d.
...
(12 August)   30
To the Princes players   x s.
...
(13 August)
Carlile   ...iij consorts of musicians vij s vj d....
...   35

13/ Rbert *for* Robert
13/ the gent*lemen*: *the sons and/or grandsons of Lord William Howard*

1618–19
Household Books 2   DDPD: Howard C706
f 34   *(12 November) (Rewards)*
...
To a pip*er* y*at* came out of Lankyshire   ij s.   5
...

f 34v   *(9 January)*
...
Io*hn* Trumpetor. ij s vj d ...   10
...
(19–21 January)
Carlile   ... musicians iiij s vj d ....
...
(22 January)   15
To a iugler   xij d.
...

f 35   *(14 February)*
...   20
To a cornetter   ij s.

...
(27 February)
to iij minstrells giue*n* by m*rs* mary   xviij d.
to ij other   xij d.   25
...
(13 March)
to 2. pipers   xij d.
...

                                                                                        30

f 35v*   *(28 April)*
...
to a pip*er* ij d ...
...
Giue*n* at Askerton by my lady . 12 of Iune .   35
... a pip*er* vj d
...

(20 June)
To iij musicians at the gate   xij d.
…

f 36*   *(27 July)*   5
…
To the waites of Carlyle   ij s vj d.
…
(31 July)
To the musicians of Penreth   ij s vj d.   10
…

f 62   *(23 July) (Extraordinary Payments)*
…
to mr Heymore for teaching to daunce in part   xx s.   15
…

1620–1
Household Books 3   DDPD: Howard C706
f 20v*   *(My Lady's Expenses)*   20
…
mr Gray for   a pair of daunsing pumpes   ij s vj d.
mrs mary.
per bill.   …
december. 1620.
               f 38v*   *(31 October–10 November) (Rewards)*   25
…
To the poor at my lady going to Thornthwate v s …
mr Radclif   …
to the dawncer   xx s.
To the players   x s.   30
…

f 39   *(31 December)*
…
To Iohn trumpeter   v s.   35
…

f 39v   *(16 February) (Rewards)*
…
To the princes players   x s.   40
…

(28 February)
To the waites of Penreth   ij s.
to a minstrell at the gates vij marcij   xij d.
...

(16 March)   5
To the waites of midlam   xij d.
...

(18 March)
To the waytes of Richmond   xij d.
...   10

(24 April–1 May)
To the waites of Carlyle   xij d.
...

Household Books 4   DDPD: Howard C706   15
f 30   *(14 August)(Rewards)*
...

To ij. fidlers at the gate   xij d.
...

(30 August)   20
To the waites of kendall   xviij d.
...

f 30v*   *(15 August)*
...   25
mr Radclif   To a company of players   v s.
...

1621–2
Household Books 4   DDPD: Howard C706   30
f 30v   *(12 November)(Rewards)*
...

To mrs mary to giue vnto 2. fidlers   ij s vj d.
...

(30 November)   35
To Players   v s.
...

f 31v   *(6 April)*
...   40
to iij waytes of Rippon   ij s
...

(*22 April*)
To a harper　　　　　　　　　　　　　　　　　　　vj d.
...

　　　　　　　　　　(*23–6 April*)　　　　　　　　　　　　　　　　　5
mr Radcliff　　To pypers at ye gate　　　　　　　　　　　ij s.
　　　　　　　　　...

(*5 May*)
To the waites of lancaster　　　　　　　　　　　xij d.　10
...

f 32　(*26 June–2 July*)
　　　...
mr *william*　to ye waites of berwick　　　　　　　　　ij s.　15
Radclif
　　　...

Household Books 5　DDPD: Howard C706
f 28　(*18 September*)(*Rewards*)
　　　...　　　　　　　　　　　　　　　　　　　　　　20
To a harper at the gates　　　　　　　　　　　　vj d.

1622–3
Household Books 5　DDPD: Howard C706
f 28　(*10 October*)(*Rewards*)　　　　　　　　　　　25
　　　...
To a piper　　　　　　　　　　　　　　　　　　iiij d.
(*14 October*)
To a cornetor　　　　　　　　　　　　　　　　　ij s.
　　　...　　　　　　　　　　　　　　　　　　　　　30

f 28v*　(*17 November*)
　　　...
To ye players of Penreth　　　　　　　　　　　iij s.
(*18 November*)　　　　　　　　　　　　　　　　　35
[Sent to them afterward for mrs Howard　　　　vj s]
　　　...

6/ *first of 3 items enclosed in marginal brace under Radclif's name*
15/ *fourth of 30 items enclosed in marginal brace under Radclif's name*

f 29v*   (8 May)

...

To a company of players at [Brampton] Coomcach.   v s.

...

(11 May)   5

To the waites of lancaster   xviij d.

...

1624–5

Household Books 6   DDPD: Howard C706   10

f 31v*   (5 January) (Rewards)

...

To the Players of warwick   xxij s.

...

                                                                                  15

f 32   (11 April)

...

to the waytes of Penreth   ij s.

...

                                                                                  20

f 32v   (22 May)

...

to the waites of Carlyle   ij s.

...

                                                                                  25

1625–6

Household Books 7   DDPD: Howard C706

f 27v   (5 June) (Rewards)

...

to the waites of Penreth   ij s.   30

...

(24 June)

to iij trumpeters   iij s.

...

                                                                                  35

1626–7

Household Books 8   DDPD: Howard C706

f 26v   (30 December) (Rewards)

...

To ye scottish piper   ij s vj d.   40

...

f 27   *(30 December–5 January)*
...
To the piper of Brampton   ij s vj d.
...
(8 January)   5
To ye piper by my ladyes commaund   ij s vj d.
...
(14 March)
To the waites of Penreth   xij d.
...   10

1627–8
Household Books 9   DDPD: Howard C706
p 42   *(26 May) (Rewards)*
...   15
To the waites of Carlile   xij d
...

p 43   *(26 September)*
...   20
To 2 Pypers   ij s
...

1629–30
Household Books 10   DDPD: Howard C706   25
f 31   *(1 January) (Rewards)*
...
To a Piper by my ladie   ij s vj d
...
f 31v   *(8 January)*   30

To Iohn Mulcaster the Piper for playinge at Naward this
Cristenmas time   xv s.
...
(5 March)   35
To thre Pypers the waytes of Richmonde   ij s vj d
...

f 32v   *(13 July)*
...   40
To a Companie of Players   v s.

f 33 *(12 August)*

...

To a Companie of Players by my ladies Commaund   v s

(13 August)

To a Companie of ffidlers   ij s vj d   5

...

1630–1

Household Books 10   DDPD: Howard C706

f 33v* *(19 October) (Rewards)*   10

...

To a Pyper at [Carlile] ⌜Corbie⌝   xij d

...

1633–4   15

Household Books 11   DDPD: Howard C706

f 36 *(30 December) (Rewards)*

...

To a fellow with a Hobbie Horsse by my ladies
Commaund   ij s vj d.   20

...

(1 January)

To the Piper by my lady vpon New yeares daye v s ...

...

(6 January)   25

To Iohn Mulcaster the Piper for playinge here all
Christenmas   xx s.

...

f 36v *(4 March)*

...   30

To 3 Pypers at Corbye   xviij d.

...

(7 March)

To the waytes of darneton   ij s.

                                                       35

f 37 *(14 March)*

...

To 3 ffidlers   ij s

(17 March)

To a Companie of Pipers   ij s vj d   40

...

(28 March)

To 2 Pipers the waites of Durham ij s.
...

(1 April)

To 3 Severall Companies of Musitions at the Gate, by
Io*hn* Porter v s vj d
...

f 37v *(21 May)*
...
To the waites of Penreth ij s.
...

(17 June)

To the waites of Durham v s.
To a fiddler xij d.

(21 June)

To a blinde Herper by my ladies Com*m*aund v s.
...

f 38 *(24 July)*
...
To a Herper by my ladies Com*m*aund xij d.
...

f 38v *(12 September)*
...
To a Companie of Players x s.
...

f 74v *(22 August)* *(Extraordinary Payments)*
...
To Mr Robert Hymes for one Moneth Teachinge Mr
William Howard and Mrs Elizabeth ˌ ⌈his Sister⌉ to daunce xl s
...

LOWTHER OF WHITEHAVEN

1634–5
Sir Christopher Lowther's Notebook   CCRO: D/Lons/W1/4
f 30v   *(4 December)*   5

...

Gyuen Fiddlers 4 d: *y*at came to *y*e doors   –0–4

...

f 32*   *(30 December)*   10

...

I gaue piper 6 d: & Coocke 6 d. and came to Whithauen   –0–1–0

...

f 34v   *(14 January)*   15

...

Gaue pipers at house   0–0–4

...

APPENDIX 1
Undated Document

Tailors' Guild CPL: A453
f [126]* *(transcribed 5 January 1659)*
...
Also it is ordained & appointed by ye *said* Occupac*i*on that vpon
Corpus Christy day, as old vse & Custome was befor time, the whole   5
Light, with ye whole Occupac*i*on & Banner to be in St Maries
Churchyard at ye Ash tree at [x] ⌜10⌝ of ye clock in ye forenoon, &
he yt comes not befor ye banner be rased to come away ⟨..⟩ pay vj d.
each offender toties quoties.

7/ ⌜10⌝ *above* [x]
8/ ⟨..⟩: *ink blot or erasure; probably* to

Translations

CARLISLE

1345–6
Parliamentary and Council Proceedings   PRO: C49/46/16
mb 8   *(26 September)*

Inquisition taken at Carlisle, Monday next before the feast of St Michael
in the nineteenth year of the reign of King Edward, the third from the
Conquest, before Sir Thomas de Lucy, Richard ⟨..........⟩g'ton, assigned
by a commission of the lord king concerning some dissensions and
discords between the men (who) are in munition of the lord king's castle
at Carlisle and the community of the city of Carlisle ⟨....................⟩;
by the jurors, Adam de Kyrkeby, Peter Frankys, Thomas de Neuby,
John de Mulcastre, Richard de Scraityngham, Richard del Sandes
⟨..........⟩ Thomas de Canonuby, John de Ireby, John de Agillonuby,
John de Cokedene, and John, son of Simon de Kyrkandres, who say on
their ⟨oath⟩ that on Sunday, the vigil of St Peter ad vincula, in the year
mentioned above, when the clerks performed a certain play in the
market-place of the said city of Carlisle, a dispute broke out between
Edmund Walays, servant of the lord bishop of Carlisle, and Walter Cole,
man of Sir Peter de Tilliol, because the same Edmund struck the said
Walter three times on the head with a certain large stick ⟨and⟩ the said
Walter took him, Edmund, by the hood and tore both hood and tunic,
and seeing this, Richard del Botelry, servant of the said lord bishop of
Carlisle, struck the said Walter with a knife in the back, almost killing
him and thereupon the play stopped. And then the said Peter de Tilliol,
seeing his man was for this reason in danger of death, sent William ⟨...⟩
Wyclyf, the lord king's coroner, and with him John de Stapleton and
Thomas de Neuby, to the said lord bishop of Carlisle, beseeching the
same lord bishop, since he had in his retinue in Carlisle Castle the said
Richard del Botelria, who struck the aforesaid man, that he would make
him answer for the said offence according to the law ⟨...⟩; the said

bishop of Carlisle agreed on behalf of himself and his men that no wrongful acts ought to be committed until the truth of the incident should be ascertained ...

mb 10   *(26 September)*

Transacted at Carlisle, Monday next before the feast of St Michael the Archangel in the nineteenth year of the reign of King Edward, the third from the Conquest, before Sir Thomas de Lucy ⟨..........⟩ (they) having been assigned by a ⟨commission⟩ of the lord king to inquire into various articles contained in the commission; by the jurors, Adam de Crofton, Robert de Tybay, Nicholas le Spenser, William de Morley, Thomas Kaskell, Stephen de Acton, Gilbert de Kirkandres, Robert Growce, and Adam de Appylby, who ⟨say⟩ on their oath that on Sunday, the vigil of St Peter ad vincula, just as the clerks began to perform a certain miracle play in the market-place of Carlisle in the middle of the city, Edmund Walays ⟨a certain squire⟩ of the bishop, struck Walter Cole of Scaleby on the head three times with a large stick, and Walter, wishing to prevent the said Edmund from ⟨further ....⟩, grasped him by the hood and meanwhile Richard, brother of Walter de Botellar, struck the said Walter Cole from behind in the back with a knife, almost killing him, and on this account the people were ⟨angry⟩; whereupon the mayor and bailiffs, much disturbed, summoned the commons to the common hall to find out the truth about the said outbreak of violence and meanwhile the sheriff, the mayor ⟨of the city .....⟩ Crofton, (these men) went to the bishop and asked him to restrain his men lest they commit further offences, until an inquiry should be made concerning the truth of the said offence ...

AUGSBURG MINERS

1568–9
Agent's Accounts   SA: Handelsbücher Nr. 20, Fasz. 1
f [19v]*   *(Account dated 22 January) (George Needham's expenses)*
...
Given to players at Christmas-time   £–.1.–

f [114]*   *(Account dated 30 May) (Daniel Ulstät's expenses)*
...
Given to Lord Mountjoy's players   £–.2.–
...

To some players at Christmas   £–.3.–

f [114v]

…

Given to the miners who sang for him (Daniel
Ulstät) at the feast of Epiphany   £–.5–.

…

1570–1
Agent's Accounts   SA: Handelsbücher Nr. 20, Fasz. 6
f [8v]   *(Account dated 26 February)*

…

For 2 comedies or plays, given each time 3 s   –6–

f [69]   *(Account dated 4 June)*

…

More given to players on 2 occasions when
visitors were here.   –2–

…

1571–2
Agent's Accounts   SA: Handelsbücher Nr. 20, Fasz. 6
f [134v]   *(Account dated 3 November)*

…

Given to a visiting player   –8/

…

1572–3
Agent's Accounts   SA: Handelsbücher Nr. 20, Fasz. 8
f [4]   *(Account dated 1 January)*

…

To musicians here, fiddlers and pipers   –4–

…

1573–4
Agent's Accounts   SA: Handelsbücher Nr. 20, Fasz. 8
f [89v]   *(Account dated 26 December)*

…

Given to my lord Scrope's men who presented a
comedy   –2–

…

Fasz. 7, f [4]   *(Account dated 1 January)*
...
To players here   −2−
...

f [6]*   *(Account dated 27 March)*
...
Given to the schoolmaster from Penrith who presented a
comedy   −.1.4.
...

Endnotes

63–4 C49/46/16 mb 8, 10

Portions of these two leaves, especially at the margins, are severely faded. Dots within diamond brackets represent approximate numbers of illegible letters.

The episode described in this documentation, of which the play's interruption was only a part, has all the elements of a widespread feud between the citizenry of Carlisle and the garrison. Both John de Kirkeby, bishop of Carlisle 1332–52, and Peter de Tilliol of Scaleby Castle, about six miles northeast of the city, were men of standing with an active role in public and military life. The bishop, before he ever came to the see, had incurred the hatred and contempt of the citizens while prior of St Mary's, Carlisle; at the time of this incident he was serving as governor of Carlisle and hence commanded the garrison. Peter de Tilliol had been sheriff of the county 1327–30 and was at various times elected knight of the shire for Edward III's parliaments. The initial clash between the two parties, described here, escalated in a series of progressively more violent incidents in which the garrison fired indiscriminately on the citizenry, killing a woman. In ensuing resistence to attempts by the city authorities to arrest individual members of the garrison, a city bailiff was also killed.

65 Egerton MS 2598 f 82

Henry Scrope, ninth Lord Scrope, was at this time warden of the West March and captain of Carlisle. Scrope's letter, though unaddressed, was presumably sent to William Asheby, England's ambassador to Scotland (1588–90), in whose collection of papers it is found.

65 CA/4/1 f [1v]

The 'belman,' entered annually in the Fees account, was the town crier. In the 1622–3 Disbursements account he is paid 2d 'for going through the towne twise for the heighe Chamber dore key'; payment for a new key entered in the same account suggests that the 'belman' was used in this instance to publish a case of loss or theft (CA/4/2 ff [111–11v]).

67 CA/4/1 f [22v]

This account begins f [22v] (account title and payments for October) and continues f [22] before moving to f [23]. Repair to the outer edge of the lower two-thirds of the folio masks wholly or partially marginal dates for f [22v] and portions of payments for f [22].

67   CA/4/1   f [23v]
The Fees account is repeated [f 27] with some additional items; the entry concerning Nicholas
Hudson is identical (except 'drom*m*er' f [27] for 'droum*m*er' f [23v]).

71   CA/4/1   f [54]
The three items for Shrove Tuesday (5 February) are included in the account under the marginal
heading for January. While two out of the three may conceivably have been prepaid, the waits
of Penrith were surely paid on the day of performance. Hence the marginal heading for February, lined up with the item succeeding those for Shrove Tuesday, is misplaced.

72   CA/4/1   f [55]
This item may be approximately dated mid-April: the fifth preceding payment is for 13 April,
the next succeeding for 12 April.

72   CA/4/1   f [56v]
It is impossible to narrow down the date of these payments. The first of the thirteen entries
on f [56v] is given for 'the last of July'; the next folio ([57]) has a marginal heading for August.
It would, however, be misleading to ascribe any of the intervening twelve items, all undated,
to 31 July.

73   D/Lons/L   f [14]
In 1594 the membership ordered that no strangers be bidden to the Common Dinner except
the mayor and bailiffs and the 'preacher'; their table was to be allowed two bottles of wine
'& no more,' 2s 6d worth of wild fowl, 2s worth of capons, 16d in conies, and 16d at the setting
of the table, that is, a further allowance for drink, such as beer (f [9v], 34th order).

74   D/Lons/L   ff [16v], [17]
From 1609 until his death in 1616, Henry Robinson, bishop of Carlisle, annually provided
the membership with 10s for wine at the dinner (Receipts, ff [12v], [13v], [14v], [17v], [19],
[20]). On this particular occasion, however, the bishop gave 20s. The account indicates that
the extra 10s (l. 16), was used 'to paye the howse where ye Dinner was madd' (ll. 24–5), that
is, the eating-house or tavern that catered to the event and possibly accommodated it. These
lines are the only suggestion in the Tanners' accounts that the dinner may have taken place
at such a location, rather than in the occupation's chamber itself.

75   CA/4/2   f [1]
Two hands are evident in the Disbursements account: the first writes ff [1–4], roughly
October–April, f [7v], 8 July–10 August, and f [8v], the last nineteen items of the account;
the second writes ff [4–7], 1 May–end of June, and f [8], 10–25 August. The two hands may
indicate a division of work between alternating chamberlains, though they do not coincide
with the traditional quarters of the fiscal year established at Carlisle.

77   CA/4/2   f [4v]
'Munisseners' (l. 17) is probably an errant form of 'musicioners.' Scribes seem to have had particular trouble with this word, in whatever form they penned it. Waits from 'Barwick' visited

Carlisle five times in the period 1614–37; waits from 'Berwick' were at Naworth in 1622. Both orthographical forms may refer to Berwick-upon-Tweed; alternatively either or both may refer to Barwick-in-Elmet (Yorkshire, West Riding). The latter suggestion is supported by the fact that waits from other West Riding communities (Bradford, Darrington, Doncaster, Halifax, Leeds, and Wakefield) visited Carlisle at roughly the same period (1605–37).

77 CA/4/2 f [6]
The payment of 20s to the occupations and expenditures in the Merchants' and Shoemakers' chambers are relative to All Hallow Thursday (2 June), as are, probably, items for powder, carriage, and brown paper. More problematic are references to 'the Games'; possibly these sums are late entries for Shrove Tuesday (9 March), 'you' (l.30) being the mayor, Thomas Blenerhassett, who may have closed the games with some ceremony. Elsewhere in the chamberlains' accounts, however, are entries for 'summer games,' one of which, entered for the month of May 1622, may refer to All Hallow Thursday (30 May 1622). In the two remaining instances – p 80, l.34 and p 90, l.8 – the allusion is less clear. In both cases the positioning of the item in the account, the absence of any other lump sum payment for Shrove Tuesday, and the naming of Edward Dalton (responsible in five other instances for the Shrove Tuesday games) as the payee suggest that 'summer games' is a misnomer for the Shrove Tuesday event. (It may of course be an alternative usage for that occasion, though hard to believe for Carlisle in February.) The 1614–15 entry, however, is apparently lined up with the marginal notation, 'Caldew Bridge,' as the location of the games; this information is not consonant with other evidence showing that the Shrove Tuesday games were staged at the Swifts (see Introduction, p 25). Overall, there is some indication that an event known as 'summer games' was staged in Carlisle on or close to All Hallow Thursday; what its component parts were remains a mystery, though in the context of payments for 'powder' (l.24), it may have been at this period a gunnery or fireworks display terminating the All Hallow Thursday holiday.

79 CA/4/2 ff [13–14v]
A separate account detailing expenditures on St John's Eve and St Peter's Eve was retained for this year; in other years the total amount spent on that occasion was normally entered without details in the Disbursements account. The sums for Nicholas Hudson, the city's drummer, and 'the two waites,' (ll.3, 5) are included in a list of almost uniform payments of one shilling made to approximately 275 individuals; the second entry for 'the Cities waites' (ll.14–15) probably represents a reward for performing on the two occasions. The general Disbursements account for this year contains items for wine at a banquet (f [6v] 23 June–8 July) that was perhaps part of the celebration.

The feast of the nativity of St John the Baptist falls on 24 June, the feast of St Peter and St Paul on 29 June. In Carlisle 24 June was a quarter-day when, for instance, fees were due. Quarterly chamberlains' accounts from 1634–5 split payments for the two saints' days between the end of the third and the beginning of the fourth quarters, thus confirming that 29 June is the feast of St Peter intended in the record (rather than, for example, the feast of St Peter ad vincula, 1 August).

The connotation of 'Eve' needs some discussion. In the early seventeenth century we are witnessing the vestiges of an event at least partly rooted in a folk celebration of Midsummer; in this context the 'Eve' (ie, the preceding night or vigil of the feast) had particular significance for the feast of St John the Baptist, marking a time when Midsummer revelry traditionally took place. Occasional terminology in the accounts (CA/4/2 f [26], 1617, 'midsomer eave' and f [98v], 1622, 'at midsomer & st peters eaven') points to the popular maintenance of this tradition and hence to the nights of 23 June and 28 June as the occasions for the twofold celebration. By the seventeenth century, however, the old Midsummer element is already in decline as St John's quarter-day exerts its fiscal influence. In 1603 we catch a vestigial glimpse of banquets together with the princely sum of £12 8d spent on pots of ale (CA/4/1 ff [2], [5v]) – enough to slake the thirst of some hundreds of citizens. The 1614 celebration was probably one of the last of such occasions marked by any kind of traditional revelry. Certainly the sum then dispensed, £14 6d, though matched in the following year (CA/4/2 f [19v]), was never approached again. In the years that followed, the chamberlains' accounts show that the eves of St John and St Peter were used for the distribution of fluctuating sums of money among a limited group of citizens often described as those who had borne office -- in other words, corporation pensioners (eg, CA/4/1 f [63], 1619; CA/4/2 f [92], 1621; f [129v] 1627); in 1639 a calendar of such persons is mentioned (CA/4/2 f [185v]). The distribution was carried out in some traditional form, however, for in 1635 a gratuity was paid to one 'going about with ye Chamberlaine both nightes' (CA/4/2 f [148]). Nevertheless in later years sums denoted as paid out on St John's Eve and St Peter's Eve were virtually assimilated to the third-quarter distribution of fees.

80   CA/4/2   f [18v]
Starting 11 December, items in the Disbursements account are headed 'Heare Beginnithe the disbursements Comanded by Mr henrye Baynes Maior of the Cittye Elected ye 9th daye off december [vpon ye deathe of mr Bell] 1614....'

81   CA/4/2   f [20]
Sir Thomas Metcalfe (l.24) of Nappa Hall, Yorkshire, married Elizabeth, daughter of Sir Henry Slingsby of Scriven, Yorkshire, and his wife, Francis, who was half-sister to Maior Vavasour (see p 456). Colourful details of his life are given in Joseph Foster, *Pedigrees of the County of Families of Yorkshire*, vol 4. Metcalfe was known as 'The Black Knight of Nappa' for his armed assault on the Robinson family of Raydale House in furtherance of an hereditary claim to the property; summoned to Star Chamber for this breach of the peace, he was fined £1500. James I is said to have stayed at Nappa Hall while on progress, hunting with his host in Raydale. Metcalfe's 'roystering hospitality' and personal extravagance, together with losses suffered for the Royalist cause in the Civil War, eventually left his successors impoverished.

83   CA/4/2   f [26v]
The chamberlains' disbursements conclude at f [26]. There follow (i) in a second hand, 'Mr Maiors disbursmentes in behalf of his Chamberlens,' (f [26v]), a self-contained account dated internally June–August in which, apart from the king's visit, most expenditures are for repairs and maintenance, wine, and benevolences; (ii) in the first hand, 'Iohn Iacksons disbursements in behalf of ye Chamberlens,' f [27–7v], starting with All Hallow Thursday (29 May), similar in content to (i) but with no items dated. John Jackson was a city bailiff 1614–15 (CA/4/2 f [18], account title). It is possible that the chamberlains, Thomas Gent and Rowland Edgden

(account title, f [24] – 'hegdell' for 'Edgden,' CA/4/139 f 53), were unable to carry out their duties in the latter part of their term.

The principal route from the north into Carlisle crossed the river Eden and entered the city by way of 'Richard gayte' (ll. 18–19, modern Rickergate). Evidently James entered Carlisle by this gate on his return from Scotland on 4 August. Other items for this year refer to 'Riddinge & dressinge Richard gate' f [26v], 'pavinge of Richardgate' f [27], and 'cariage of the painter oiles from yorke' f [27v].

84   CA/4/2   f [30v]
Yearly fees and annuities are given three times for this year. The first list (f [30v]) is transcribed here, perhaps being a fair copy of those that follow (ff [31v] and [32v]), which are marred by frequent cancellations; items on f [32v] are each preceded by a cross in the left margin. Information about Nicholas Hudson is identical on all lists.

84   CA/4/139   f 53
On 5 August 1600, three years before he came to the English throne, King James VI of Scotland survived what he claimed was an attempt on his life at Gowrie House, Perth; his hosts (the alleged would-be assassin, the master of Ruthven, and his brother, the earl of Ruthven) were killed in the ensuing fracas. In spite of contemporary scepticism about James' version of the event, the Scottish Kirk was coerced into proclaiming a day of thanksgiving for the king's deliverance, held annually thereafter on 5 August (David Harris Willson, *King James VI and I* (London, 1959), pp 126–30). After James's accession to the English throne this episode was eclipsed by an authentic conspiracy much closer to home as far as the English were concerned – the Gunpowder Plot of 1605. The annual celebration of 'conspiracy' or 'gunpowder' day on 5 November was fairly quickly taken up by the English population; the 5 August thanksgiving, as exemplified in Carlisle at least, seems to have had much less continuing impact. Early in James' reign, in 1604, 'a waike' is recorded for that date, with payments for wood, peats, and ale (CA/4/1 f [26]), but thereafter the observance drops from sight until 1617 when the king himself visited the city and formally celebrated Gowrie(s) Day on 5 August (see also Tanners' Guild Minute Book, p 95). Bruce Jones, archivist at the Carlisle Record Office, points out that in the northern counties 'gowrie,' a variant of 'gowdy' or 'gaudy,' may mean 'festive' or 'frolicsome' in local usage (*The English Dialect Dictionary*, Joseph Wright (ed), vol 2 (London, 1900), pp 695, 698). Certainly this or some other circumstance soon blurred the strict origin of the term as applied to one particular event and date (5 August); three months after the king's visit, the words 'beinge gowres day' are added as an afterthought to an entry for 5 November 1617 (p 86, l. 11) and towards the end of his reign, in 1624, payments occur for 'the gowries day' again on this date (CA/4/2 f [117]).

85   D/Lons/L   f [22v]
The illegible word (l. 35) appears to be made up of four letters with brevigraph, perhaps 'parted' in the original from which the antiquarian scribe made his copy. M. Creighton, *Carlisle*, 2nd ed (London, 1889), p 151, quotes this passage, modernizing the spelling and giving no citation; 'gowryeidaye,' however, appears as 'a Saint's Day' and the mayor kisses the king's hand 'at their departure.'

86   CA/4/2   f [42]
Though lacking specific quarterly titles, the chamberlains' general disbursements this year are
recorded – undated with few exceptions – on a quarterly basis. Items normally headed Fees
and Poor are not given under separate annual titles; instead these payments are lumped together
as being disbursed '... on St Thomas daye in benevolence for the Citye' (f [45v]) and so on
for each of the quarter-days. As such these lists are interpolated chronologically into the general disbursements, ff [45v–6v], [49v–50], [54v–6], marking the end of each quarter.

87   CA/4/2   f [49]
Hasler, *History of Parliament*, vol 2, p 8, gives the last known date for Sir John Dalston (l. 19)
as 1609; according to the Chamberlains' Accounts, however, Sir John attended the mayor's
dinner on 5 November 1621 (CA/4/2 f [97]).

89   CA/4/2   f [53v]
The location of this event (ll. 5–6) together with an item for wine and sugar at Bess Parker's,
dated 12–29 September (f [54]), suggests that the dinner comprised a corporation venison feast.
This is also arguable from evidence in 1614 in the form of a bill pasted on the lower portion
of f [14v]; dated 17 September, it includes 2s 6d owing to Margaret Barwick for wine supplied
to the venison feast at Bess Parker's (evidently an inn or eating-house). The venison on that
occasion was a present from Lord William Howard.

89   CA/4/2   f [54v]
The letter 'w' as in 'sawell' appears to be occasionally substituted in the manuscript for 'v' – eg,
in 'sewerall' (several) at f [51v]; hence Savell, an alternate form of Savile, is intended here.

90   CA/4/1   f [65]
George Bell and the two waits (p 91, l. 7) were probably itinerant musicians. Carlisle's waits
are usually named as 'the waits' or 'the city's waits' in the accounts. The date of the item does
not suggest that George Bell and his fellows performed in connection with any civic event.

91   CA/4/2   f [76v]
Rough summaries of expenditures are given under categorized heads on this the last page of
the 1617–18 account. These calculations, however, are relevant to the 1618–19 account
(CA/4/1 ff [63–76v]) and appear to be written in the same hand. The categorized titles that
appear in the 1618–19 account are repeated for the most part on CA/4/2 f [76v]; in addition
other categories are excerpted from the account, as 'Trumpeter,' 'wyne in presentes,' 'ffoole,'
and 'Paper.' In the 1618–19 account sums for liveries (£11 12s 8d) and the fool (£1 7s 11d)
are given (CA/4/1 f [66]); these are identical with those in CA/4/2 f [76v], where the component
parts of each sum are also recorded.

92   CA/4/2   f [79]
William Simson and Dalston Dalton, (p 94, l. 35) each account for disbursements as chamberlains for the year 1619–20, (f [79], account title). Internal evidence shows that Simson and
Dalton kept their accounts separately but concurrently, rather than dividing the quarters or
the halves of the year between them. For example, Simson accounts for items for election day,

4 October, f [79]; Christmas Eve, f [79v]; 5 November, f [80]; Shrove Tuesday, 29 February, f [80v]; and the venison dinner (normally an early autumn event). Dalton accounts for 5 November activities, f [82]; Shrove Tuesday, f [82v]; and All Hallow Thursday, 25 May, f [83]. Payments are not specifically dated in these accounts.

93   CA/4/2   f [80]
Grammar school pupils performed their speech play at the mayor's dinner on 5 November (see Introduction, p 25). An entry in Dalton's disbursements noting a payment of 10s for 5 November (f [82]) represents payment for the dinner this year.

95   CA/4/2   f [82v]
Aske Hall, near Richmond in North Riding, Yorkshire, may be intended here (l. 9). Until his death in 1622 Sir Thomas Wharton, son of Philip, third Baron Wharton, lived at Aske Hall, the home of his sister Lady Eleanor, who had married the owner, Robert Bowes.

96   CA/4/2   f [89]
The full form 'comand' (l. 26) is found frequently in this account. Brevigraphs appearing over the word in this orthographical form are therefore treated as superfluous.

100   CA/4/2   f [97]
There are two versions of this account. The first, ff [97–9], from which the transcription is excerpted, is fuller and appears to be the final version: the general disbursements are each marginally designated by category ('Reward,' 'reparacion'); separate titles appear for 'power' (poor), 'ffees,' and 'Rentes,' f [99]; the signature 'Henry: Baines. Mayor' appears at the end, f [99]. The second account, ff [104–5], bears a pencilled note (?modern) stating 'This next is a draft of the last'; here the payments are grouped under marginal heads for October, f [104]; February–May, f [104v]; and July–August, f [105]. Both top and bottom outside corners of f [104] are missing to a depth of 25–30mm square, a fact that may explain the absence of marginal heads for November–January and for June. Items in the transcription, ll. 5–11, 20–1, 23–7, and p 101, l. 22 are omitted in the draft version. Editorial months and collation notes where significant are supplied from the draft.

100   CA/4/2   f [97v]
The word 'vicitacion' (l. 21) suggests that some calamity befell Nicholas Hudson and his household. It is a word sometimes synonymous with an outbreak of plague; but the steep rise in the burial rate for Cumberland and Westmorland parishes occurs later, in 1623–4, and even then is arguably attributable to famine rather than disease (Andrew B. Appleby, 'Disease or Famine?' pp 424–30). This occasion, however, is the last on which the name of Nicholas Hudson appears in the Chamberlains' Accounts.

101   CA/4/2   f [98v]
'Reward' (l. 18) is written beneath a small oblong of original paper, 15mm × 24mm, apparently attached to the folio with a dab of sealing wax.

104   CA/4/2   f [121]
Fees are accounted for here, and in all accounts that follow, under the four quarter-days; the third is mistakenly given as 'Our Lady Day' in the manuscript, f [121] and has here been corrected with reference to the 1617–18 account, f [52], where it is named as St John's Day, 24 June.

106   CA/4/2   f [128v]
There is a horizontal tear 55mm long, narrowing from 30mm wide at the outer edge of the folio to 4mm, through the first approximately sixteen letters of the line, which are all but illegible. From what is visible, Bruce Jones of the Carlisle Record Office suggests the reading 'kings meede bridge,' a location equivalent to the Sands, or the Swifts, the land lying between Eden Bridge and the former Priestbeck Bridge on the south bank of the river Eden. This reading is supported by information relative to the Swifts given by Anthony Curwen, a native of Carlisle, in the early seventeenth century:

> Many old men and women about Karliell do well knowe and rememr. that
> all the grounds was one contynuse ground, and when I was a scholler at
> Karliell no hinderance to the footeball play nor to the essayes of running
> of naggs, men and women leaping dauncing &c. upon every Shrove
> Tuesday.

Curwen was agent for crown lands in Carlisle and his reminiscence, noted in a survey of 1612, is cited by J.A. Wilson, 'Some Early Sporting Notes relating to Cumberland,' CWAAS, Trans. O.S., vol 12 (1893), 195, as from a document 'amongst the archives of Bolton Abbey.' I did not locate this manuscript at Chatsworth, and a check of LR2/212, Misc. Books, Carlisle, 8 James I, in the Public Record Office in London, an evidently similar survey of the same date, did not yield the passage quoted.

107   CA/4/2   f 130v
In the manuscript 'darinton' is centred in very small script above 'lancaster' (l.21), suggesting that the scribe may have intended to delete the latter.

107   CA/4/2   f [130]
One obvious dating difficulty should be noted: the penultimate date given in the account is 5 August, but the seventh item thereafter is dated 29 July, f [129v]. Nevertheless, in order to preserve textual chronology, I have ascribed entries from f [130] to the date 5 August[+].

108   CA/4/2   f 137
Entries immediately preceding the payment to 'william heslehead' (p 109, l. 3) refer to the repair of Caldew Bridge (provision of lime, gravel, and clay, and workmanship); William's 'paving' rather than 'playinge' may have been intended. Or was William perhaps a piper, employed to encourage the workers?

109   CA/4/2   f 139v
Fees for 1627–8 are itemized for the first quarter (Christmas), and total £3 3s 9d; only this

total is repeated for each of the remaining quarter-days. The drummer's total annual fee would have been the 10s usually noted in the later period of the accounts.

109 CA/4/2 f [140]
Items transcribed from this folio are part of a list for which it is noted: 'these disbursments *per* mr maior are nott to be Craved allowance by this Chamberlaines booke'; ie, they cannot be claimed at time of audit as the chamberlains' expenses.

110 D/GC/4 f 91
This entry suggests that Thomas Blaymer, an occupation member (p 117, l. 36), also ran an eating-house or tavern that may have accommodated the 1628 dinner as well as catering to it. As in the case of the Tanners' Guild (see p 74, ll. 24–5), this is the sole indication that the annual dinner did not take place in the occupation's own chamber.

110 CA/4/9 f [25] col a
This Fees account seems to be part of an *aide-mémoire* to the chamberlains for the year 1628–9 (Thomas Syde and Robert Nicholson, account title, f [25]). It instructs them as to what revenues to collect, from whom, and when, and then itemizes necessary expenditures from these revenues under Rents and Fees and Poor (both quarterly). All but two of the incoming and outgoing items are preceded by a cross (or four). Fees and Poor accounts are in parallel columns. This record may be connected with the demissions of the outgoing mayor; the Audit Book (CA/4/9, f 47) makes it clear that customarily one of the retiring mayor's last acts (on St Matthew's Day, 21 September) was to authorize the farming or leasing of certain city revenues to particular individuals.

115 D/GC/4 f 96
Details in the account show that the entry of £3 4s 2d for the plate was made up of the initial sum of £2, plus an allocation from stock funds of £1 4s 2d.

115 CA/4/2 f [146]
For the first quarter Henry Sewell accounts for all disbursements including Fees; Thomas Wawby similarly for the three remaining quarters. Wawby's neatly kept accounts have marginal monthly heads and occasional dates, allowing payment-periods to be ascribed to excerpted entries.

117 CA/4/139 f 85
In the chamberlains' account for this year (CA/4/2, f [145]) payment of £1 15s is entered for the mayor's dinner of 5 November, the occasion when the scholars performed their oration or speech play.

117 D/GC/4 f 96v
The heading and seven names listed (ll. 30–6) form the second of two parallel columns of names under the general heading of Amercements. The whole entry for 3 April 1635 indicates a lack of interest in a prize for the horse-race, for which money was collected from as early as the previous accounting year, 1633–4 (p 115, ll. 4–6). Presumably the plate referred to was offered

in one of the races run a few weeks later on 13 May 1635 (p 116, ll. 16–21). A subsequent entry for 25 September 1635 in the Merchants' Book (p 118, ll. 28–9) also indicates that a new piece of plate was assigned to the coming year (1636).

118   CA/4/2   f [149]
This act was probably passed on or about 24 March 1635/6 when the account for the fiscal year Michaelmas 1634 to Michaelmas 1635 was presented for audit. The act is recorded in a hand distinct from that used in either chamberlain's account; the signature of Ambrose Nicholson (mayor 1634–5) appears between this passage and the preceding final entry of Wawby's account, suggesting that the record was entered on the folio after the audit had taken place. In fact the sergeants continued thereafter to receive bar money: for 1636–7, ff [166–6v], [170], [171v]; for 1638–9, ff [181v], [183]; and for 1639–40, f [189v].

119   CA/4/2   f [154v]
John James and Christopher Knagge account respectively for the first and third, and second and fourth quarters of 1635–6, including quarterly portions of Fees.

120   CA/4/139   f 87
This entry and a further isolated reference to plate in the Merchants' Book (l. 36) provide the only indication that the horse-race may have been run in 1636; the Chamberlains' Accounts, however, lack the detail that they normally record for this event. Possibly the plate was held over for the race run the following year (p 121, l. 36–p 122, l. 2).

121   CA/4/2   f [166v]
Although the two chamberlains for this year accounted for alternate quarters, each kept his own book; that is, each book has a distinctly characteristic hand, paper, and watermark, with separate audit signatures of Richard Barwis, mayor (ff [168v], [171v]). These books were subsequently bound into CA/4/2 consecutively so that Charles Crookbane's quarters (the first and third) precede John Nicholson's quarters (the second and fourth).

121   CA/4/2   f [170]
A payment of twenty shillings to the mayor for 5 November is entered in disbursements for the first quarter (CA/4/2 f [166]) – that is, for the dinner at which the scholars performed (ll. 21–2).

122   CA/4/2   f [181v]
Receipts and disbursements are accounted for each quarter by only one chamberlain, Mathew Wilkinson.
   Two unabbreviated forms ('comand' and 'command') both appear in this account; the brevigraph in a third form, 'cõmand,' has been taken as a sign of abbreviation and the word transcribed 'command' (l. 30).

125   CA/4/2   ff [201v], 202v
Again only one chamberlain, 'Chamberlane Crookbane,' kept the account for this year, though on a quarterly basis. The payment for cloth (l. 38) is one of two disbursements

interposed between the Poor Account and second-quarter payments. Hudson's 2s 6d (l. 32) continues as a quarterly payment throughout the fiscal year 1642–3.

126   Handelsbücher Nr. 20, Fasz. 1 f [19v]
George Needham was holding a quarter-share in the Company of Mines Royal in February 1565/6, and was still listed in 1580 when the company was reorganized. Throughout much of 1567 Needham was in the Keswick area transacting company business. In the late autumn he returned again for this purpose, remaining in the area for well over a year (W.G. Collingwood, *Elizabethan Keswick* (Kendal, 1912), pp 3–4, 22–3, 26–9).

126   Handelsbücher Nr. 20, Fasz. 1 f [114]
Daniel Ulstät, who was in Keswick as resident agent for company affairs in 1568, returned to Germany the following year. Lord James Mountjoy was a shareholder in the Company of Mines Royal from February 1565/6 (Collingwood, *Elizabethan Keswick*, pp 3–4, 62).

127   Handelsbücher Nr. 20, Fasz. 8 f [6]
The Penrith schoolmaster was John Davis, first master of the Free Grammar School of Penrith (1569–76) (Percy H. Reaney, *Records of Queen Elizabeth Grammar School, Penrith*, CWAAS, Tract Series, vol 10 (Kendal, 1915), p 16). An historical account compiled in the early eighteenth century by Dr Hugh Todd, the vicar of Penrith, draws on earlier sources and includes a confirmation, dated 1708, of ten general rules for the school. Two of these (Reaney, pp 57–8), both based on ecclesiastical ordinances of 1571, are possibly significant in the case of the performance at Keswick. The eighth rule urges that the master and usher 'so form the Speech and Language of all their Scholars, by constant and frequent Exercise, that they may speak with a Clear, Audible and Distinct Voice.' The tenth rule lists authors whose works will prove beneficial to the scholars' language and manners; among these is the Roman playwright, Terence (Publius Terentius Afer, 195?–159 BC), one of whose comedies may have provided the text for the performance brought to Keswick from Penrith.

133   Curwen Account Book   f [109v]
This payment was first entered on f [108v] ('to Anthony Troughton') with fifteen other items, headed 'disbursed since 31 december 1634.' These were subsequently cancelled when the steward presumably realized that he had forgotten to enter the receipts for the period, which were normally given before the disbursements. All the cancelled items were included in the disbursements that begin on f [109v].

133   Curwen Account Book   f [149]
These payments probably stem from Sir Patricius Curwen's responsibilities as sheriff of Cumberland, an appointment he received in 1637; the allusion to 'the Ialor' is perhaps connected with the county jail in Carlisle.

135   Howard C706 [Book 1]   f 10
Payments made for children in the family, either as individuals or as a group, are frequently entered in Lady Elizabeth's account. For this year there are entries for her fifth son Thomas; youngest daughter Mary; and grandsons William, son of Sir Philip Howard, and Thomas, son

of Sir Henry Bedingfield (who married the eldest daughter, Elizabeth). All seven sons (Philip, Francis, William, Charles, Thomas, Robert, and John) were at Naworth in 1612 – those who married remained until the last decade of Lord William Howard's life. Sir Philip's widow continued to live there with her six children after her husband's death in 1616 (George Ornsby, *Household Books*, pp viii–x, xxxviii–xli; pp 9–10, notes).

137   Howard C706 [Book 2]   f 35v
Through his wife, Lord William Howard became lord of the barony of Gilsland, part of the Dacre inheritance. Askerton Castle, Cumberland, was a small border fortress within the barony, manned by the Land Serjeant of Gilsland, and a small garrison (Ornsby, *Household Books*, pp xxiv, xxxv).

138   Howard C706 [Book 2]   f 36
The Penrith musicians (?waits) were probably heard in Carlisle. The payment recorded is the second of a bracketed group of four, one of which was for 'loan of sheets at Carlyle'; another was made 'at the assyeses.'

138   Howard C706 [Book 3]   f 20v
Cuthbert Gray, described in a letter of 1608 as a Newcastle merchant, also farmed the revenues of Newbiggin, Northumberland (Heddon with Newbiggin, a Howard estate). He frequently supplied the household with goods and, more in the role of agent, performed a variety of services for the family (Ornsby, *Household Books*, pp 69, 412). The dancing pumps are fifth in a list of seven items attributed to him, enclosed in a marginal brace.

138   Howard C706 [Book 3]   f 38v
Lord William Howard purchased Thornthwaite, near Hawes Water, Westmorland, from Sir Henry Curwen of Workington; the estate lay in the parishes of Shap and Bampton (Ornsby, *Household Books*, pp 5, 222, notes). It was in the latter parish that the misrule episode, involving Lord William Howard's tenants, allegedly took place (see p 218). Mr Radclif (William Radclif, p 140, ll. 15–16) was auditor and receiver-general to Lord William Howard (Ornsby, *Household Books*, p 90, note). Payments for the poor, the dancer, and the players are included in a bracketed list of five payments attributed to Mr Radclif and apparently all connected with the Thornthwaite visit.

139   Howard C706 [Book 4]   f 30v
The item for 15 August is one of fourteen grouped with marginal brace under the name of 'mr Radclif.' The chronological sequence of the Rewards account is interrupted here since these entries are variously dated October, August, and September.

140   Howard C706 [Book 5]   f 28v
Mary Howard, daughter of Lord William Howard, is probably intended here (l. 36). A marginal cross precedes this item.

141   Howard C706 [Book 5]   f 29v
The name of the month, usually found as a marginal heading in the Household Books, has

been omitted from the group of ten items among which these payments are included. Listed between groups for April and June, they are almost certainly for the month of May, which is nowhere else recorded in this Rewards account. Cumcatch and the manor of Brampton (both in Cumberland) were Howard lands; the latter, about three miles southwest of Naworth, was the market town nearest the castle.

141   Howard C706 [Book 6]   f 31v
There are numerous entries in the Household Books for Warwick (Warwick and Wetherall, Cumberland, a Howard estate about four miles east of Carlisle). The date suggests that the players came to Naworth in connection with festivities for the Christmas season.

143   Howard C706 [Book 10]   f 33v
Corby, Cumberland, lies about six miles east of Carlisle. The moieties of the manor were successively purchased by Lord William Howard in 1606 and 1624 (Ornsby, *Household Books*, p 111, note).

145   D/Lons/W1/4   f 32
During Christmas 1634 Sir Christopher Lowther was in Westmorland en route home from a business trip to York. According to the notebook (f 32) he dined with his brother John on 29 September at Hackthorpe Hall (not far from Lowther), where presumably he slept before setting out for Whitehaven the next day.

146   A453   f [126]
This ordinance is one of several headed by the statement that in 1659 they were copied out of an earlier book (see Document Descriptions, p 34), without any indication of the date(s) of their original enactment. The remainder of A453 contains other entries for the guild 1652–1734 in various contemporary hands, indicating that the 1659 transcription of older ordinances was an administrative measure designed to restore and maintain continuity of guild records, probably undertaken because of loss, damage, or interruption suffered during the preceding period of the interregnum.
      This volume in turn evidently provided the exemplar for the version of the Corpus Christi Day ordinance given in R.S. Ferguson and W. Nanson, *Municipal Records*, p 147, and in D/Lons/L13/11, Tailors' Guild Minute Book, an eighteenth-century copy. Collation of all three reveals no substantial differences between them and in the two latter versions only minor variants in spelling or expansion: eg, at line 6, Ferguson gives 'gt Maries church yard' where in A453 the elongated 's' in 'st' has been read as 'g'; and the D/Lons/L13/11 version consistently substitutes 'the' for 'ye.'
      In a footnote to the transcription of the ordinance, Ferguson remarks: 'This is a most interesting entry, and carries us back to the pre-Reformation Corpus Christi procession in Carlisle. Great Mary's church would be the parish church in the cathedral nave, and its churchyard is now known as S. Mary's burial ground.' The cathedral in Carlisle was served by canons of the Augustinian priory, and as was usual in such cases parishioners were confined to the nave for the purposes of worship. Ferguson's reference to 'the pre-Reformation Corpus Christi procession' is given uncorroborated by any other evidence and must remain speculative. It is admittedly unlikely that Corpus Christi Day was simply one of the guild's

quarter-days – the movability of the feast, ranging from 21 May to 24 June, would have made the choice impractical. Nevertheless, as it stands, the ordinance merely provides for an assembly of the guild brethren (and probably sisters, as implied by the phrase 'the whole light'); whether this was for an event confined to the guild itself or a preliminary to a full-scale turnout of the eight occupations cannot be determined from the ordinance alone.

The reference to the banner is not in itself significant of any extraordinary ceremonial nor of activities dating from the pre-Reformation period. Well after the Reformation the Carlisle Merchants, for example, had their yard wand (or standard) and banner; at St Peter's quarter these were ritually delivered by outgoing to incoming undermasters (Merchants' Book, ff 86-6v, 87v, 88v, 1624–7); in 1629 a long table covering was purchased (f 91) and in 1631 a new banner, described as 'cullers,' was made for the guild (f 93v). The two purchases were added to those items delivered to incoming undermasters (f 94v, 1632, and f 99, 1635). These few objects seem to have furnished a minimal ceremonial for guild events – probably quarter-day assemblies, the annual dinner, and the All Hallow Thursday perambulation of Kingmoor in which all the guilds took part before returning to their chambers for refreshments. Cautiously, therefore, we should refrain from jumping with Ferguson to any conclusion, based on the transcribed ordinance, about the existence of a pre-Reformation Corpus Christi procession, unless evidence can be adduced from other sources.

WESTMORLAND RECORDS

Boroughs

APPLEBY

1609–10
Chamberlains' Accounts 2   KCRO
f [1]   *(Disbursements)*
...
Item to Iohn Simpson for the pipers cote   x s   5
...

1610–11
Chamberlains' Accounts 4   KCRO
f [1]   10

To Mr. smith for the piper wages x s
...

1614–15   15
Chamberlains' Accounts 8   KCRO
f [3]   *(Disbursements)*
...
to Iohn simpson for ye piper wayge   vi d
...   20

KENDAL

1575–6
Boke off Recorde   KTC
f 219*   *(2 February)*   5

Item it is Orderide & Constitutid: lykewise by the Alderman / and
Burgesses, withe the hole assennte and advise aforesaid / That no
person or personns. off what callinge or estate so ever. he. she. or they
bee off / Whiche either. be nowe dwellinge / or whiche hearafter. shall   10
fforton to be dwellinge & residente. within this Boroughe / or liberties
hearoff / ffrome & after / the sayd sevynth daye off ffebruarij nexte
comynge / shall. / either provide. prepare. desyer. byd. warne. have or
make / or cause or suffer to be had provided prepared. desyerid bydden
warnyd. or made / at or with in / any his. hers. or their seuerall howse /   15
or in or at any other howsse or place / within this / Boroughe. / or
liberties hearoff / any dynner. super or ffeaste / ffor moneye offor. for
personns ˯ ⌜towne ffolkes, to any Nomber moore or lesse⌝ above the
Nomber off / twelve which makes vpp. three measses off ffolkes (Suche
lyke dynners supers. ffeastes or drynkyns / as have bene comonlye   20
vsed / at or vpon / Shotinges in long bowes, or metynges of men off
Occupacions / aboute orders for their severall pagiandes of Corpus
Christi playe / ˯ ⌜Or at the Aldermans electyon / Or at any court day⌝
at accustomyed tymes in the yeare / onely exceptyd and resserved) Or
shall provide / prepair / desyer. byd. warne make. or have/or cause or   25
suffer to be provided. prepaired desyerid. bydden warnyd or made any
open or generall drynkynges Nutcastes. merye nyghtes. aplecastes. or
others suche lyke at all / ffor moneye offor ffor any nomber ˯ ⌜of
townsfolkes⌝ greate or. small vpon payn to fforfeite & losse to thusse
off the Chamber /. off this Boroughe ffor everye ffault so comytted   30
& donne x s....

f 224v*

An Other Order for metinges off Burgesses & xxiiij^ti etc on: Certayn   35
stacion & apoyntyd dayes
14°:day Iune [⟨....⟩] ˯ ⌜1576⌝†

7/ Item *in heavily stroked larger script*   7/ the Alderman: *Henry Wilson*
18–19/ above ... ffolkes: *12 words underlined* MS   31/ x s *preceded by small sign*
35/ An Other Order for *in larger heavily stroked script;* ✔*in left margin*

Item it is Ordeyned & Constitutyd by the Alderman Burgesses and
xxiiii^{ti} Assistauntes off this Boroughe / that aswell everye one off the
xxiiij^{ti} Assistauntes, as the xij° Pryncipall Burgesses off this Boroughe
/ nowe & frome hencefurthe, ffrome tyme to tyme beinge in some
convenyente tyme after he be called into either off the same ij°   5
companys and have receyved his Othe, shall provide & have A playne
Clothe gowen off black or off some other sad color, or mor at his
°caps repealed° pleasure, and the same gowen shall putt & wear vpon hym with A
rownd black capp on his head moost commonlye on all Sondayes in
the year, and on all holye dayes lykewise when the wether is ffayr &   10
vphold, But especiallye on theis dayes ffollowinge, (as many as be at
home & in healthe / or have not some busynes or presente occacion
to go furthe off this Boroughe, abowte some busynes tollerable, that
°Stacion Dayes: is to say, on the dayes off the Election / etc & othe takynge of every
repealed   Alderman, The day off every Alderman his pryncypall ffeaste or   15
22 Maij 1578;   dynner, [On Alhallowe day], On Christenmes day [On Newe years
viz: daye / The Twelfth day], On Easter day [Thassencion day], & On
Alhallowe daye: Whitsondaye ([Excepte some of the same holye dayes happen on any
Newe yeare &
xijth: Dayes: Setterdaye]) And shall on everye of the same dayes before or at tyme
Thassencion   off Rynnginge off the Third peall, be redye accordinglye to   20
Daye: etc°   accompanye the Alderman or his deputie ffor the tyme alwayes beinge
everye one at and ffrome the Alderman or his deputye his owen
dwellinge howsse, to the Churche, bothe to mornynge & evnynge
prayer, every one in his order rowem & place / as he nowe is or
hearafter may be lawfullye called & placyd and not otherwise, And   25
agayne ffrome the Churche in lyke order to accompany the sayd
Alderman or his deputye to anempste everye one his owen dwellinge
howse, [And also] °Sub pena forisfacturae tocies quocies / xij d to be
levyed etc°
...   30

f 225*

in like maner & order to and ffrome the proclamacion on the ffayer
vacat   dayes and play dayes and ffrome thence to and ffrome the hall, as   35
occation shall requyer, Sub pena fforisfacturae tocies quocies xij d
...

1/ Item *in larger heavily stroked script*
11/ vphold: *the phrase or clause which should follow this verb has been left out*

1580–1
Boke off Recorde   KTC
f 237v

Stet:
18. Maij 1581
ad Cur*iam*
ib*idem*

Shearmen   5
Item it is likewise Ordeyned / that all & every *person* & *per*sons beinge
A Shearman (when he hath Served owte [of] his Apryntishippe / and
before he be admyttid ffreeman of the same Company), shall pay to
thuse of the hole Companye of Shearmen aforesaid / besides Custome
for the Playe) xij d (suche *per*sons as have alredie pa*id* to the   10
corporac*ion* / only exceptid)
...

1582–3
Chamberlains' Accounts I   KCRO: WMB/K   15
f 5v   *(23 September)*
...

payd to edward garnett for waites cootes   xxiij s 4 d
...
                                                                             20

1584–5
Chamberlains' Accounts I   KCRO: WMB/K
f 13   *(Payments)*
...

pd ... by mr edward potter   ij s 25
...

pd to him for ye waites cotes   xxv s vj d

1585–6
Boke off Recorde   KTC   30
f 225*   *(25 April)*
...

St: Mark 1586   And it is further declaryde to be the trewe meaninge & entente of
the same Alderman & Burgesses that everye one of them on everye
of the foresayd: three Cheiff ffestivall dayes of chr*i*stenmas . easter &   35
penticost [and also on every of the sayd dayes of the ffayres &
playdayes], shall have vpon them & weare their best vyolat gownes
[⟨............⟩] S*u*b pen*a* xij d

18/ edward garnett: *Edward Garnett (1)*   34/ the ... Alderman: *John Armer*
34/ ✔ *in left margin*   38/ *2–3 words of about 12 letters illegible*

f 244

ffor the Playe

Forasmuche as verry many & dyvers of the common Inhabitantes of   5
this Incorporacion (suche of them onlye as rather preferr ther owne
pryvate commodities / and the common customes & vsages hear / and
more respecte the Satisfyinge of their / owne delightes & fantasyes,
by A greate deale than the Benyfite & common welthe of all others
in generall (beinge the greater parte) doo covytt & earnestlye Crye for   10
the havinge of Corpus christi play, yearlye vsuallye to be had played
and vsed heare as in former tymes without admyttinge or allowinge
almost any occacion or necessitie for the stayinge therof in any yeare
Holdinge pryvate opynyons sometymes and affirmynge that the
havinge or denyinge therof onlye restethe in the Alderman / for the   15
tyme beinge) Althoughe (that in trewth) in all matters & causes
belonginge this Bourghe he is (at it were) tyed to the Societie Counsell
and Brotherhead of others with hym Not havinge power in hymselff,
to appoynte & sett downe Orders & constitucions of hymselff [to
appoynte & sett downe] in all thinges specially in suche as generallye   20
Concerne the Common state & affayrs of the same Bourghe without
the ayde & counsell & grave advise & assistaunce of his Bretherne the
head Burgesses adioyned vnto hym / ffor the redresse & certayntye
of reformacion wherof / It is Ordeyned & constitutid by the Alderman
and head Burgesses of this Bourghe of Kyrkbykendall / That it shall   25
not be lawfull at no tyme hearafter / ffor the Alderman of the same
Bourghe for the tyme beinge or any his deputie or deputies, to
appoynte & geve lycence ffor the same Playe of Corpus christi / or
any other stage playes to be had or vsed heare, onlye of hymselff in
any yearc at or aboute the accustomyde tyme therof, or at any other   30
tyme Excepte it shalbe lyked of and consentid vnto by his sayd
Brethern the head Burgesses or the more parte of them frome tyme
to tyme beinge vpon payne to forfeyte & losse to the vse of the
Chamber of this Bourghe tocies quocies C s

5/ Forasmuche *in larger heavily stroked script*
17/ at *for* as
34/ C s *preceded by small sign*

Chamberlains' Accounts 1   KCRO: WMB/K
f 16*   *(Wine and Sugar)*

...

pd to william fox wif for Ale bread & Apples at A banket
when ye Auditor & receiueres was ther at martinmas   iij s   5
pd to mr dickson for comffites ye same tyme   xxj d
pd to ye players of my lord [of] morlaies at ye same tyme   v s
All yis was bistowid vpon ye Auditor & receiuer & for
ther plesure bothe for yat ye Auditor was for my lord of
warwick then / & Also ye receiuer did help hus to our   10
mony at my lord wardens had at yat tyme

1586-7
Chamberlains' Accounts 1   KCRO: WMB/K
f 20   *(Wine and Other Expenses)*   15
...

pd ye iij of Iune for ye waites cotes   xxvij s
...

f 20v   *(30 September 1587+)*   20
...

pd to ye waytes at ye election diner   viij d
...

f 21v*   *(Additional Payments)*   25
...

pd to mr potter yat he paid to ye plaiers of my lord of
sussex & my lord of essex   ij s
...

                                                                                  30

1587-8
Chamberlains' Accounts 3   KCRO: WMB/K
f [16]*   *(Payments)*
...

pd to waites in reward   xij d   35
...

pd to garnet for plaieng on ye drome   vj d
...

6/ mr dickson: *Henry Dickson*
27/ mr potter: *Edward Potter or Thomas Potter (alderman 1584-5)*
37/ garnet: *Edward Garnett (2)*

f [16v]*

…

pd for A pot of Ale when ye playe was at mr wilsons   x d

…

pd to garnet for plaieng on ye drome   iiij d   5

…

pd for ye diners of mr doctor mr Ingall for ye curat &
clarke & peter Alansons at ye elections diner   iij s vij d
pd more in od mony at yat tyme   xiij d
pd to ye minstrels & for ye seriantes   xvj d   10

…

pd to ye waites at mr Alderman diner   xij d

…

pd for candles when mr Ingall play was   iiij d

…   15

1589–90
Chamberlains' Accounts 4   KCRO: WMB/K
f [11]*   *(Payments)*

…   20

pd to Iohn collen for his lofte for ye playe   iiij s

…

f [10v]*

…   25

pd to ye menstrells at ye dener at christofer foxes   xij d
more for the [⟨..⟩] clarkes & outhers   viij s viij d

…

1591–2   30
Chamberlains' Accounts 5   KCRO: WMB/K
f [15v]*   *(Extraordinary Payments)*

…

paid to ye waytes when mr ˰⌈docktor⌉ robinson was here   viij d

…   35

pd for x quartes of wyne when mr robinson was here to
him & his company   v s x d

…

5/ garnet: *Edward Garnett (2)*   12/ mr Alderman: *Henry Fleming*
7/ mr doctor: *Ambrose Hetherington*

1592–3
Chamberlains' Accounts 6   KCRO: WMB/K
f [12]*   *(Extraordinary Payments)*
...

pd to Iarvis dickson wif for ij pottes of Ale more at ye   5
maske   xx d
...

pd for ij q*uar*tes wine at ye maske   xiiij d
...

pd to mr dawson for ye charges of ye banket at ye maske   xiij s iiij d   10
...

f [12v]*

pd to ye plaiers in ye newe hall   v s   15
...

pd to mr dawson for ye waites cotes   xxxiij s
...

pd to ye quenes players y*is* som*er*   xx s
...   20

pd for charges at ye din*er* at ye election & for wine & to ye
waites   x s iiij d
...

1593–4   25
Chamberlains' Accounts 7   KCRO: WMB/K
f [22]*   *(Extraordinary Payments)*
...

It*em* pd to cudbert pearsone y*at* he layd forth to ye
players at ye dragon the last yeare   ij s vj d   30
It*em* pd to cudbert y*at* he pd to garnat ffor playing on the
drome on the crownatyon daye   iiij d
...

f [22v]   *(7 June–28 July)*   35
...

It*em* pd by the Apointment of mr Alderman for the

10,17/ mr dawson: *Roger Dawson*
30/ at ye dragon] at mydlames *WD/AG/Box 5 f [18]*
31/ garnat: *Edward Garnett (2)*
37/ mr Alderman: *William Wilson*

Charges of the Staig of Sir potters playe   viij s
...

f [23]   *(28 July*⁺ *)*

...   5
Item pd to Sir potter by cuthbert   xx s
...
Item pd Iames Aryey wyff for xxxvj mens dinners of the
election day   xviij s
Item pd for the ij Sargents dinners the same daie   viij d   10
...
Item pd mr Swaynson for A gallanne of Claried wine & A
quart seck on the election daie   ij s viij d
pd Cudbert yat he pd ye waytes on ye elecktyon day   xij d
...   15

1594-5
Chamberlains' Accounts 8   KCRO: WMB/K
f [17]*   *(Extraordinary Payments)*
...   20
Item to william Iudsons wyfe for the dinners of ix messe
and one person at the election dinner   xv s vj d
...
Item to the pypers which Iames Ayraye layd forth at ye
election dinner   xij d   25

1595-6
Chamberlains' Accounts 9   KCRO: WMB/K
f [17v]   *(28 November–29 December) (Extraordinary Payments)*
...   30
I*tem* to mr fleminge for iij yards and a half of blv to the
wets cots   xxxij s
...

f [18]*   *(3–24 July)*   35
...

6/ ye 10 awgust *added WD/AG/Box 5 f [19v]*
8/ Iames Aryey: *James Ayrey*
12/ mr Swaynson: *William Swaynson*
12-13/ to Iames ayrays hovse *added WD/AG/Box 5 f [20]*
14/ Cudbert: *Cuthbert Pearson*   31/ mr fleminge: *Henry Fleming*

Item to the drvmer at bvrning of bekens   iiij d

...

(24 July–28 September)

...

Item to Row*land* michell for goinge to perit at bvrnings of   5
bekens   ij s
Layd out for chesse to go to perit at the burnings of the
beking and bred   viij s iij d
Item to edward the cariar of it   ij s
Item to the weats and drvmer   vj d   10
Item for drinke that time   iiij d

...

Item to Richard selle for letther to a par of hampers y*at*
went to Carlill at the bvrning of the bekinngs   xij d

...   15

f [18v]
Item payed at the eleckcion dener for vij meas and on man
at vj d pes   xiiij s vj d
...   20
Item to the menstrills at dener   xij d

...

1596–7
Chamberlains' Accounts 10   KCRO: WMB/K   25
f [18v]*   *(Extraordinary Payments)*

...

Item pd to one playing on the drom*me* ye Q*uene*s daye   xij d

...
                                                                  30

f [8]   col a*

...

°mor at hwnts to the whaytts   xij d

...

mor to whayets at my m*aste*rs°   xij d   35

...

9/ edward: *perhaps Edward Archer or Edward Garnett (2)*

1597–8
Chamberlains' Accounts 12   KCRO: WMB/K
f [29]*   *(Extraordinary Payments)*
...

Item pd to Iames Ayreye wyffe for the leete courte   5
dynn*er* mychelmas 1597   ix s vj d
Item to the mynstrells at a dynner at Iames Ayreyes   xij d
Item payd to Edmu*n*d Hunt wyffe at the dynn*er* of mr
Iames willsons election   xxiiij s 8 d
...   10
Item pd in reward to the l*ord* Montegles players   x s
Item pd in reward to Therle of derbys players   x s
...

1598–9   15
Chamberlains' Accounts 13   KCRO: WMB/K
f [18v]*   *(Extraordinary Payments)*
...

payed vnto ye mvisioneres in kendall Churche for
playeng thar by Mr Aldrmanes Appoyntment   20
payed them 6 s 8 d   [vj s] ⌈vij s⌉ ⟨.....⟩
...

1599–1600
Chamberlains' Accounts 14   KCRO: WMB/K   25
f [19v]   *(28 May–20 July) (Extraordinary Payments)*
...

paid to my lorde quarton playeres   vj s viij d
...
                                                                           30

f [20]   *(19 September–10 October 1600)*

At the election of Mr Twhaite Alderman / paid to Willia*m*
denison Wife for a dinner   xj s x d
more for iij quartes of wine w*hic*h was feched to the   35
diners   ij s ij d
more to the wettes   xij d
...

20/ Mr Aldermanes: *Edward Wilkinson*   33/ Mr Twhaite: *John Thwaite*

1600–1
Chamberlains' Accounts 15   KCRO: WMB/K
f [21]*   *(Extraordinary Payments)*
...

paid the 28th off october to Christoffor Eskrige ffor ix   5
yardes off grey ffrese ffor the pipers Cottes   ix s
...

(21 March–12 June)
paid Christoffor hodgson when beakenes brunt ffor
going to peareth   ij s vj d   10
paid Robert Ayre ffor playing off drum at same time   vj d
...
paid mr Alderman ffor otes that he bestowed off a horse
when beakenes brunte   vj d   15
paid to Richard scales that he paid ffo v tarbareles when
beakenes brunte   ij s vj d
paid to a lad ffor plainge on the drum when wach was sett   vj d
...
                                                                          20
f [21v]   *(1 August–17 September)*
...
paid ffor wine off the play daie   iij s
...
                                                                          25
(17 September–11 October)
paid to Iohn Robinson wiffe ffor xxvij menes dinneres
sam daie Mr Alderman was chosen   xiij s vi d
...
°pd pipers for theyr fee same daye mr alderman was chosen   xij d   30
...
pd piper the 11 of ottutober for playinge at mr aldermans
diner   vj d
...
                                                                          35
f [22]
...
pd Gowen Caslaye for paven of stret whear playe was°   xij d
...

14/ mr Alderman: *John Thwaite*
28/ Mr Alderman: *John Smythe*

1601–2
Chamberlains' Accounts 16   KCRO: WMB/K
f [20v]   *(Extraordinary Payments)*
...

pd in Reward to ye new waytes at they*r* first Coming   5
7.nov   xij d
...

pd to edward archer for playing on drum quens day   vj d
...
                                                                                          10

f [21]
...

pd mor to Iohn robinson w*hich* he layd ovt abovt the play
by appoyntment   xxx s
...   15
pd more to Iohn Robinson wif for vij mease on the
election day ˍ⌈14 s⌉ wyne 20 d & waytes 12 d   xvj s viij d
...

1602–3   20
Chamberlains' Accounts 17   KCRO: WMB/K
f [16]
...

Item payd to Edward Artcher for playinge of th*e* drume
vpon the queens daie   xij d   25

f [17]*   *(April)*
...

Item payd to mr Robert Wilkinsonne as his note dothe
Appeare   30
...

Item 31 of same viij^th yeardes of blake ffreyse   xij s
Item ffor ffasinge button and bayse ffor the Waytes
Cottes   iiij s
...   35

1603–4
Chamberlains' Accounts 18   KCRO: WMB/K
f [19]*   *(before 22 October) (Extraordinary Payments)*
...   40
pd to Robert hodgshone shold have beine the wait   vj d
...

(4 March–7 April)
pd for 6 quarters of brod Read to the wayte 7 s   x s vj d
...

f [19v]   5

...
pd 5 August 1604 to drumer & mynstrells   xij d
pd 11 same for mending drume to watr backus   ij s
...
                                                                                          10

1604–5
Chamberlains' Accounts 19   KCRO: WMB/K
f [15]*   *(Extraordinary Payments)*
...
pd the 12 of Aprill to Iames Ayray for the Leete Coarte   15
dynner   ix s x d
pd the same daye [f] to Robert holme wif for Chardges for
the Commissoneres About the play   iiij s
paid to Iames Ayraye wyfe the same daye for the
Commissinares   xij s   20
...

f [15v]   *(12 April–9 May)*

More pd to hughe Iackson wyf for the Chardges of the
Commissinores   ix s   25
pd to hir for wyne the same tyme   ij s iiij d
...
pd to Iames Ayraye the 10 of Iune which was paid for A
Iorneye to yorck   xl s
...   30
(25 June–2 September)
pd more for mr tyrares seckond Iorneye to yorck for
Chardges   iiij li
...
pd the 4 of september for Chardges About mr Tyrar &   35
mr Ingalle   iij li xij d
...

7/ 5 August: *Gowrie's Day; see p 155 endnote to CA/4/139 f 53*

1607–8
Chamberlains' Accounts 21   KCRO: WMB/K
f [14v]   *(15 October 1608⁺) (Extraordinary Payments)*
…

pd when we wente to the play   ij s   5
…

1608–9
Chamberlains' Accounts 22   KCRO: WMB/K
f [13]*   *(26 November–8 December) (Extraordinary Payments)*   10
…

pd to Edward Archer for playeinge vpon the Drvme at ye
queenes departure   v s iiij d
…
                                                                                    15

f [13v]*
…
pd to william warriner ye 18 of march that his m*aster* gave
to ye Earle of da˄⌈r⌉byes men   v s
…   20
(8 June–29 July)
pd to ye earle of Lincolne his men   ij s vj d
…

1610–11   25
Chamberlains' Accounts 23   KCRO: WMB/K
f [8]   *(15 September) (Extraordinary Payments)*
…

pd p*er* the aponyment of mr alderman to my lord
mounteagell playres   00–02–06   30
…

1611–12
Chamberlains' Accounts 24   KCRO: WMB/K
f [3]   *(24 September⁺) (Monies Disbursed)*   35
…

pd to the Players   ij s vj d
…

18/ his m*aster*: *Michael Rowlandson, alderman*   29/ mr alderman: *Thomas Green*

1612–13
Chamberlains' Accounts 25   KCRO: WMB/K
f [5v]   *(Paid for the Chamber)*
…

pd mor to mr ffisher which was for the waittes Cottes   o 8 8   5

1613–14
Chamberlains' Accounts 26   KCRO: WMB/K
f [16v]   *(13 August)*
…   10
payd Bryan Preston ffor the waytes [cottes] Clokes   iiij li v s vj d
…

f [17]*   *(26 September)*
…   15
payd the waytes ffor playinge   xij d
payd ffor the Elekxtion diner   xxvj d
payd for wyne same tyme   iij s vj d
…
(3 October 1614)   20
pd ffor the Leet Courte dinner   xvj s vj d
payd ffor drinke & Bread to the Iurie   xviij d
payd ffor ij quartes of sake   ij s
payd ffor dresinge of A holbert to Iames Ienniges   iij d
payd William Warrinner for building the stage   iij s   25
…

1614–15
Chamberlains' Accounts 27   KCRO: WMB/K
f [13]   *(14 November) (Extraordinary Payments)*   30

payd mr willson Alderman which was bestowed in
Reward of the players belonging to the lord mounteagle   o 5 o
…

5/ mr ffisher: *Edward Fisher*
17/ xxvj d: *properly xxvj s to make up total of £1 10 s given for the month of September, f [17]*
25/ for buildinge the stage *added after payment entered*
32/ mr willson Alderman: *Thomas Wilson*
32/ w *of which* written *over* s

f [13v]   *(31 May)*

…

pd mr Alderman w*hic*h was geiu*en* to the pl*a*yers 5 s …

…

                                                                         5

f [14]   *(August)*

…

pd ffor xj yerds yerds off Cloth to the wayts Clokes &
Iacketts att 7 s 6 d yerd   4   2   6

…   10

pd to w*illia*m waryner wif.…   1   1   6
pd hir more for the diner att the Chusing of the Alderman
vizd for xiij mease att 6 d pece   1   6   0
pd ffor ⌜aples &⌝ nuts after diner att mr Alderman table   0   1   0
pd for drink after   0   1   0   15
pd to the waytes for Reward   0   1   6

…

1615–16
Chamberlains' Accounts 28   KCRO: WMB/K   20
f [11v]   *(Extraordinary Payments)*

…

Payed to Will*ia*m Warriner the first of November y*a*t was
given to the quens players   0–10–0

…   25

f [12]

…

pd to the quens men the 13 of Awgust for playing   0–10–0

…   30

1616–17
Chamberlains' Accounts 29   KCRO: WMB/K
f [14v]*   *(16–18 January) (Extraordinary Payments)*

                                                                         35

°payd p*er* mr Aldermans Consent and mr wilkinsons w*i*th

3/ mr Alderman: *Thomas Wilson*   8/ yerds yerds: *dittography*
12,14/ Alderman: *James Dixon (1)*   15/ *final* o *written over* 5
36/ mr Aldermans: *John Robinson*
36/ mr wilkinsons: *Edward Wilkinson or Robert Wilkinson*

the rest of of ye companye vnto one Symcock and
frannerton two of his ma*jes*tis vshurs of the gard when
they cam to the towne for looking for housses to
intertayne ye king   2–0–0
pd more ffor ther Charges in meat and drink one night &   5
one daye   00–08–0
more for 2 q*uar*tes of sack to theme   0–02–0°
...

(30 April)

payd for wine att the leet Court   0–3–⟨.⟩   10
payd to the kinges harbinger The Same tyme   0–3–0
...

Chamberlains' Accounts 29A   KCRO: WMB/K
f [2v]*   *(Assessment)*   15

                          august this .6. 1617
payd vnto mr Sledall ffor a pursse   01–05–00
...
put mor in to the kinges pursse   33–00–00   20
payd to the groumes of the Stable of estat   03–06–08
payd to The litter men   00–10–00
payd to mr harres   26–02–00
payd to the trumpeters   00–06–08
payd ffor proclaying the p*ro*clama*ci*on   00–10–00   25
payd to mr wilson ffor nacies   07–06–03
...

f [1]
                          october this .16. 1617   30
...
payd vnto the Quense players   0–11–0
...

1/ of of: *dittography*
10/ ⟨.⟩ *digit altered several times; possibly* 8
18/ mr Sledall: *Thomas Sledall*
26/ mr wilson: *Thomas Wilson*
26/ nacies *for* necessaries

Chamberlains' Accounts 29B   KCRO: WMB/K
f [1]*
...

pd for glass & othr things when the king was heere att mr
Aldrmans Comandment which he promist me to [p]
Allow me   viij s   5
...

Chamberlains' Accounts 29   KCRO: WMB/K
f [15]   *(15 September)*   10

pd more ... to ye minsterels at ye venyson ffeast   0–1–0
pd william Chamber wiff the same daye ffor the venyson
diner being 14 mease   01–14–0
...   15

1617–18
Chamberlains' Accounts 30   KCRO: WMB/K
f [22]   *(Extraordinary Payments)*
...   20
pd to William Chamber the 12th of november that was
given to the earle of Sussex players   00–05–00
...

f [22v]   25
...
pd more the 22th of march that was given to the queens
players in gould   00–11–00
...
pd more the 17th of Aprill 1618 to william Chamber wif   30
for the Leit Court diner beinge/5/mease & three [f]
men/8d/a peece   00–15–04
pd more for [meat] ⌈bread⌉ & drink yat was sent to Ieurie   00–01–06
pd more to Iasper [garnet] hey & his man for musack   00–01–00
...   35

4–5/ mr Aldrmans: *John Robinson*
34/ [garnet]: *Jasper Garnett; see pp 237–8, endnote to STAC/8/34/4 f 18*

(17–25 April)
pd more to Mr Alderman...   00–01–06
pd more to him which he had given to other towe poor
men the one was a Trumpater...   00–01–00

f [23]

...

pd to walter Beck the 20th of August for a peece of
broadcloth xij yeardes for the waites Cloakes   03–17–00
...

f [23v]

...

pd more the 30th of August to the yonge princes players   00–11–00
...

1618–19
Chamberlains' Accounts 31   KCRO: WMB/K
f [12v]   *(5 April) (Monies laid forth)*
...
pd the waitts at leet Court dinner   00.02.00
...
pd Bartholomew Shiphard ffor a meass which dined at
Court leet dinner   01.00.00
pd ffor Beare and Bread to the Iurie   00.02.00
...

f [14]

pd the 22th Iulie 1619 ffor ix yardes 1/4 Brode Read
delivered accordinge to mr Aldermans Appointment ffor
the waites Cloackes at 7.2.   03.06.03
...

f [24]   *(1618)*

...
pd more the 7th of October to Bartholomew Shipperd wif
for the leit Court diner being Seven mease & twoe men   00–15–00
pd more for bread & drinke that was sent to the leit Iuerie 00–01–10
pd more the sam day to our Waites for musacck at diner   00–02–00
...

2/ Mr Alderman: *Richard Pearson*   30/ mr Aldermans: *Thomas Sledall*

1619–20
Chamberlains' Accounts 32   KCRO: WMB/K
f [20]

...

m*ore* pd to mr Alderman that he payed vnto a company of   5
players   00–05–0

...

f [20v]

...   10
m*ore* pd to the Queens of bohemia players p*er* mr
Alderman   00–10–0
m*ore* pd for 9 yardes of brood clooth for the wayts
clookes   03 00 00
...   15
(1620)
m*ore* pd to the kings players the 21th of October p*er* mr
Alderman dawson appoyntment   00–10–0

...

m*ore* pd to mr Alderman that he disbursed to the princes   20
players as apears p*er* his note   00–10–0
...

1620–1
Chamberlains' Accounts 33   KCRO: WMB/K   25
f [17v]*   *(Monies Paid)*

...

Pd to the players   00 10 0

...
(17 September)   30
Pd to mr Steven Nuby...   01 16 4

...

Pd him more at same time for the princes players in the
old account   00 05 0
...   35
(27 September)
Pd for the wattes Cloakes   03 02 10

...

5,11–12/ mr Alderman: *Steven Nuby*
17–18, 20/ mr Alderman dawson: *Rowland Dawson*
33–4/ the princes players in the old account: *see above, ll.20–1*

1621–2
Chamberlains' Accounts 34   KCRO: WMB/K
f [20]   *(Extraordinary Payments)*
…
pd to mr Alderman which he gave to the kinges players   00–10–0   5
…

f [20v]*
…
pd the waytes at leete court dinner   00–02–6   10
…

Star Chamber Records   PRO: STAC/8/34/4
f 55*   *(5 December) (Kendal Stage Play: Bill of Plaintiff)*

15

…And to make the said Lordes the more odious to the people, Soe
it is further if it maie please yor moste excellent Majestie that the said
Confederates haue alsoe stirred and raysed vp one Richard Helm,
Henry warde, Thomas Duckett and diuers others whose names are as
yett vnknowne to yor said Attorney but humbly desireth that hee maie   20
incerte the same when they shalbee discouered they beinge Players and
Actors in a stage playe publickelie to personate & represent the persons
of the said Lordes of Mannors in theire said playe, and accordingelie
the said Helme, warde, and duckett and the said other vnknowne
persons on or aboute the moneth of Iulie last in the Nineteenth yeare   25
of yor Majestes Raigne did publickly act a stage plaie at kendale Castle
in the said County and did therein make a representacion of Hell and
in the same did personate and acte manie Lordes of the Mannors of
the said Countie which they did libellouslie and disgracefullie then and
there represent to bee in hell to the greate abuse of the said Lordes,   30
by which they were prouoked to haue fallen into outrage and to haue
broken yor Majestes peace and haue sought private Revenge of suche
disgracefull iniuries, had not they beene restrained by the due respecte
of the obeydience to yor majestes lawes Edict and proclamacion In
tender Consideracion whereof … It maie therefore please yor most   35
excelent Majestie to graunt vnto yor said Attorney yor most gracious
Writtes of Subpena to be directed to the said [persons including]
Richard Helme Henry Ward and Thomas duckett … Commaunding
them and euery of them … to be and appeare before yor highnes and
yor majestes most Honorable Councell in yor Majestes High Courte   40
of Starcham⟨…⟩ …

5/ mr Alderman: *Walter Becke*   41/ ⟨…⟩: ⟨ber⟩

f 49*

> The Ioynt and severall Answares of ...
> Rychard Helme [and other defendants named] ...
> to the Informacion of Sir Thomas Coventrey
> knight his majesties Attorney generall /   5

...

... And the defendant Richard Helme Confesseth that he was by the
perswasion of one Iasper Garnett (who was the Authore of the play)
ˏ⌈in the information mentioned /⌉ an actor in the ˏ [play] ⌈same etc⌉
acted at ⟨...⟩dall Castell about the tyme in the Informacion mencioned   10
But denyeth that he did in any sorte Represent or Act the part of any
Landlord or tenante in the same as in ⌈the⌉ said Informacion is
supposed And saith that the said play was penned by the said Iasper
Garnet aboue fower yeares agoe he being a Scholemaister in Lancashire
And drawn into fower large bookes And was seene and lyked by some   15
landlord and divers men in the barrony of kendall before the same was
acted....

f 51   *(Interrogatories to be put to the defendants)*
...   20

11 Itim whether doe you know that Richard Helme Henrie ward Thomas
Duckett or any of them in or a bout the month of Iulij last 1621 did
ackt or plaie a staige plaie att Kendall Castle in the said Countie of
westmerland whether weere you priuie afore hand yat the sayd plaie
was then to be plaied whether weare you pressent att the then actinge   25
of the said plaie whether was ther then in the same any representacion
of Hell & whether was any thinge then Acted or mencioned of any
landlordes of westmerland to bee seane there in hell, wherefore weare
they the said landlordes represented soe to bee in hell, what was the
Conscite or morallitie there of, weare you priuie to the Inuentinge   30
makinge or settinge forth of the said plaie who was the Inuentor or
maker ther of and by whose meanes or abettment or procurment was
the same soe inuented & maid & enacted accordinglie declaire yor
knowledge therein & how you know the same to be true://
...   35

f 14*   *(16 February) (Examination of defendant)*

> Samuell Knipe of ffairbancke in the Countie
> of Westmerland gentleman sworne etc   40

...

7/ And *written in large heavily stroked script*

f 15v

...

11.   Hee saieth that hee knoweth not that Richard Helme Henrie Ward,
Tomas Duckett or anie of them did in or about the moneth of Iulie
last 1621. act or play anie Stage play at Kendall Castell in the said   5
Countie of Westmerland. neither was hee this defendant privie that
anie such play would bee there plaied, nor was present at the acting
therof. And therefore cannot depose whether there was in the same
anie representacion of hell, or the mencion of anee of the Landlords
of Westmerland to bee [in] seene in hell or not. neither doth hee. this   10
Defendant know what the conceipt or moralitie of the said play
was. neither was hee this defendant privie to the inventing, setting
fourth or making of the same. nor knoweth who was the Inventor or
maker therof, nor by whose meanes, abettment or procurement the
same was invented, made, or acted.   15

f 54   (29 April 1622) (Examination of defendants)

...

        Thomas Prickett of Audland in the said
        Countie of westmrland gentleman aged   20
        xxxviij yeares or thereaboutes sworne &
        examined

...

11   To the xj th Interr he Cannot depose otherwise then that he did heare
that there was such a play acted at kendall aforesaid as in the said Interr   25
is mencioned. /

...

f 54v*

...   30

        Richard Helme of whinfell in the said
        Countie of westmerland aged lij yeares or
        thereaboutes sworne & examined

...

11   To the xj th Interr he saith that about the time in the Interr mencioned   35
there was a stage play acted at kendall Castell, & that he this Examinat
was an actor in the said plaie, haueinge a parte Called Raymond, &
that Thomas duckett Henry ward with others to the number of twentie
or thereaboutes were actores allso in the said plaie, but denieth that
in the said play there was anie representacion of hell or of anie land-   40
lordes within the said Barronie to be in hell, saue onely there was a ieast
betweene thomas Duckett and Henry ward who acted the partes of

towe Clownes in the said plaie deliuered by thone of them to thother
in these wordes vizt, Rauens quotha no, thou art farr byth square, ites
false landlordes makes all that Croakinge there, & those sheepe wee
poore men, whose right these by their skill, would take awaie, & make
vs tennantes at will, & when our ancient liberties are gone, theile puke   5
& poole & peele vs to the bare bone. the which speeches passed
betweene the the said Clownes vpon former speeches vsed betweene
them of hell, And allso saith that the said plaie was made by one Iasper
Garnett borne in the Barronie of kendall Schoolemaister at Lancaster
at the time of the makeinge of the said plaie, And at the time of the   10
said Actinge thereof resident within the said Barronie of kendall./

ff 40–40v*   *(Interrogatories to be put to witnesses against the
defendants)*

...

22   Item whether did the said defe⟨................⟩of them & which and   15
howe many of them by name styrrvp or procure any players & acters
in a Stage playe pvblickelie to personate & represent the persons of
the Lordes of Mannors in their said playe which were oppressors of
the said Custome of Tenant right howe & in what maner were the said
Lordes represented /| 20
23   Item did the said defendant Helme one Ward & one Duckett together
with other Actors and Stage players on or about the moneth of Iuly
in the nynteenth yeare of his Majestes Raigne acte a Stage playe at
Kendall Castle in the said Countye of Westmerland & which & howe
many of them by name did act or reprsent the persons or accions of   25
any the lordes of Mannors within the said Countye & was the same
playe acted in disgrace or contempt of the lordes of Mannors there
declare yor knowledge herein at large.

...

30

f 26v*   *(Interrogatories to be put to witnesses for the defendants)*
...
31:    Item whethether doe you knowe that the defendantes did [effe⟨...⟩]
publikely act a stage play and there in did personate and present the
persons of the Lordes of the Mannors within the Countie of   35
Westmerland in the moneth of Iuly in Anno domini 1621. in Kendall
Castell And whether did the said defendantes in the said Stage play

7/ the the: *dittography*
15/ ⟨................⟩ *faded*; ⟨...........⟩ all or anie *f 29*
33/ Item: *large and heavily stroked letters*
33/ whethether: *haplography*
33/ [effe⟨...⟩]: *fading at edge of folio*

make a representacion of Hell And in the same did personate and Act
manie Lordes of the said Mannors which they did lybellouslye and
disgracefully then and there represent to be in hell yea or noe, yf yea
then which or how manie of the defendantes did soe make a
representacion of Hell and did personate and represent the said   5
landlordes to be in hell, or which or how manie of the said Land Lordes
was so personated by anie of the defendantes or how manie of the said
defendantes did act the said stage play or what part or partes did anie
of them act therein or what wordes can you declare which was spoken
in anie part or partes which the defendantes or anie of them did act   10
or how manie of the defendantes were at the actinge of the said play
declare the trueth vpon your oath./

32:        Item who was the Author or Composer of the play which was acted
at Kendall Castell, and hath not Sir ffrauncis duckett knight seene and
redd the said play or some part thereof and liked allowede or   15
Commended the same before the actinge thereof, And was not Iames
Duckett which is grand sonne to the said Sir ffrancis Duckett one of
the actors in the said play at Kendall Castell and his bayliffe and
Tennantes actors therein and whether did he or they act the same by
the privitie or consent of the said Sir ffrancis Duckett, And whoe did   20
speake anie wordes in nameinge of Hell in the said play or make anie
representacion thereof.

33:        Item doe you knowe that these defendantes haue Raised vp anie
players or actors in anie stage play or playes to act and personate anie
of the Lordes of the Mannors of the Countie of westmerland, And to   25
represent the said Lordes or anie of them to be in hell and to make
a representacion of Hell and the Land Lordes therein, yea or noe, yf
yea declare whoe what where when and the circumstances thereof and
how you knowe the same to be true./.
        ...   30

f 33*   (10 September) (Depositions of witnesses for the defendants)

        Ierom Garnet of Ouerleuens in the Countie
        of westmerland about the age of xxviij yeares   35
        sworne and examined
        ...

31   To the xxxj th Interrogatory he deposeth and saith that about the time
        in the Interrogatory mencioned there was a Stage plaie publikly acted
        at kendall Castle wherein Richard Helme one of the defendantes and   40
        Thomas ducket and one ward in the Informacion named were amongst

13,23/ Item: *large and heavily stroked letters*

others actores, And further saith That he hath heard That in the same
plaie there was a representacion of Hell and that landlordes were
reprsented to be in hell but this he doth not knowe of his owne
knowledge, because he was not present at the Actinge of that parte
of the said plaie if anie such was./   5

32   To the xxxij th Interrogatory he cannot certainly depose otherwise then
     formerlie to the xxxj th he hath deposed./
33   To the xxxiij th Interrogatory he deposeth and saith That he doth not
     knowe nor now remember of any act done by these defendantes or
     anie of them in the said stage plaie by personateinge of the lordes of   10
     the Mannor of the Countie of westmerland or reprsentacion of hell
     otherwise or in anie other sort then in his answere to the xxxj th
     Interrogatory he hath deposed,/
     ...
                                                                                      15

f 35
...

          Anthonie Ducket of Grayrigge in the
          Countie of westmerland esquire about the
          age of 36 yeares sworne & examined   20

...

f 35v
...

31   To the xxxj th Interrogatory he deposeth & saith That Richard Helme   25
     one of the defendantes & Thomas ducket and Henrie Ward who as
     he thinketh were named in the Informacion were Actores in a Stage
     Play which was Acted at kendall Castle about the time in the
     Interrogatory mencioned, And that he this deponent was present at
     a parte of the said plaie wherein hell was reprsented, And in which   30
     Thomas Ducket & Henry Ward did Act the partes of towe fooles or
     Clownes & demaunded of a Boy who did looke into the said
     represented hell who ˌ ⌐he⌐ did see there which boy declared vnto the
     [⟨.⟩] Clownes & they to the people that they did see Land lordes &
     puritanes & Sheriffe Bailiffes & other Sortes of people whom they   35
     would haue made odious and gaue this reason (as he now remembreth)
     why the Landlordes were there in regard they did seeke to make their
     tennantes, tennantes at will, & in this or the like manner to this
     Examinates now remembrance was that parte of the said plaie acted./
32   To the 32 th Interrogatory he deposeth and saith That he doth not   40
     knowe who was the Author or Composer of the said plaie neither doth

34/ [⟨.⟩]: blot possibly over m

he knowe that Sir ffrancis Ducket knight this deponentes father Did read
Comend allowe or like the said plaie before the Actinge thereof neither
as he thinketh did [allowe] [knowe] thereof in particuler or otherwise
then by Common report that in generall there would be a plaie, And he
further saith That Iames Ducket sonne to this deponent beinge then about
the age of Seauen yeares was then an actor in the said plaie by the priuitie
and Consent both of this deponent and the said Sir ffrancis Duckett this
deponentes father, he the said Iames Duckett beinge a younge Scholler,
& therefore they willinge that he should be an actor in a play, But denieth
that he this deponent knewe what the said play   1
was or would be in particuler or anie parte thereof, which if he had
knowne he would neuer haue suffered his Sonne to haue beene an Actor
therein, And he further saith that the said Henrie ward beinge then
Bailiffe and tennant to this deponentes father and the said Richard Helme
being Tennant to the said deponentes father were actores in   1
the said plaie. /
...

1622–3
Chamberlains' Accounts 35   KCRO: WMB/K   2
f [23]   *(Payments)*
...

pd for mr Alderman and his Companie the 22th of
february to the kings majestie his players   00.10.00
                                                                                   2

f [23v]
...

pd to the waytes at the leet Court diner the 22th of Aperill
1623   00.02.6
pd to the prince his players by the appointment of mr   3
alderman the 27th of aperill 1623   00.10.00

...

pd to william Chamber wiffe for 3 mease at the leet Court
diner after Easter   00.08.00
pd the same tyme for Seven measse   00.14.00   3
pd for Bread and drinke to the Iury   00.02.00
...

f [24]   *(10–13 September)*   4

pd to the waytes at the venison feast   00.01.00

23,30–31/ mr Alderman: *Michael Gibson*

pd to peeter huggon for 18 quartes of wine at the feast   00.12.00

...

(24 September–3 October 1623)
pd to will*i*am Chambers wiffe for 17th measses at the
venison feast   01.14.00   5

...

pd to the waytes at the leet Court dinner at mychalmas
1623   00. 2. 6

Star Chamber Records   PRO: STAC/8/34/4   10
f 18*   *(19 November) (Deposition of witness for the defendants)*

Iasp*er* Garnett of [Penroethe] Penrothe [of]
in the County of Cumberland gent*leman* of
the age of 36. y*eares* or thereaboutes sworne   15
& *examined* /

...

2   To the 2. inter*rogatory* this [def*endant*] ⌐depon*ent*¬ sa he doth know
     of the actinge of a Stage play at Kendall Castle in the moneth of Iuly
     1621 & confesseth that this depon*ent* was auther & Composor of the   20
     s*aid* playe & noe other & sa that there were not any of the def*endantes*
     ⌐Actors [actors]¬ [be] in the Stage play saving the def*endant* Rich*ard*
     Helme ₍⌐[whoe acted the ... p*arte*]¬₍⌐whoe acted the p*arte*
     but denieth¬ that the s*aid* H[ell] def*endant* Helme[prsented] did make
     any rep*resentacion* of Hell but there were two other actors in the s*aid*   25
     play called by the Names of Tho*mas* duckett & one Hen*ry* Warde that
     in their actinge the represented a supposed hell vnder the stage but
     ₍⌐[whether]¬ there were not any of the def*endantes* ₍⌐presente¬ att the
     actinge of the s*aid* playe to this def*endantes* knowledge ₍⌐only¬ savinge
     the def*endant* Helme whoe was an actor in the same play neithr   30
     were any of the def*endantes* to his knowledge acquainted nor privy
     to the same before the same was [acq] acted savinge the def*endant*
     Helmes whoe was drawn by this def*endant* to play his p*arte* in the s*aid*
     playe.
3   To the 3. inter this depon*ent* sa that S*ir* ffranc*is* duckett kn*ight* &   35
     Anthony Duckett his sonne did move & intreate Mr Rowland dawson
     in this inter*rogatory* menc*ioned* that the s*aid* playe might be acted att
     Kendall & [vpon] ⌐by¬ there [p inter] meanes the saide [was played
     there] Mr Dawson gave way vnto the [acted] acting of the same, at
     wh*i*ch tyme [of] the s*aid* S*ir* ffranc*is* duckett & his son*ne* moved   40
     [⟨.....⟩f] the s*aid* Mr Dawson this defend*ent* was present & at the first
     movinge of the s*aid* mr Dawson the s*aid* mr Dawson seemed to be
     [vnwillg] vnwillinge to give way vnto by reason the whole

Corporacion of kendall had bene formerly questioned for suffering of
a play to be played there 1605 wherevnto this [defendant] deponent
answered the said mr Dawson that [the Clerk of t] mr George Warde
clerke of the peace both for the Countrie & towne of kendall had seene
& perushed the said play bookes & had libertie to correct [&] any   5
thinge that was offensive in the said play bookes which [th] Mr
Dawson acknowledged to be true [& that] sayinge that ˏ⌐neither⌐mr
warde [coulde & h.] nor he coulde fynde any thing contayned in the
said play bookes which were not to be allowed to be played, therevpon
mr Anthoney duckett replyed he sawe noe reason whye mr Dawson   10
or any othrs should lett the said playes to be acted alledginge that it
woulde bringe a greate Concourse of people to the towne & woulde
cause much money to be spent there & therevpon the said mr Dawson
gave way therevnto condiconally that there should be noe more added
to the playe then that which they had perused   15

f 18v*

4   To the 4. inter he saith he [neuer] had conferance & speeche with the
said Sir ffr Duckett & Anthony his sonne concerning the said play in   20
desiringe their helpe & furthrance that the same might be acted but
whether they had seene the said play bookes or any parte thereof
before the same was played this deponent knowth not but by ˏ⌐the⌐
relacion of one Thomas ducket whoe was an acter in the said playe
tolde this [defendant] ⌐deponent⌐ that the said Sir ffrancis Ducket had 25
seene parte of the said plea. & this deponent furthr sa that Iames
duckett is grand sonne to the said Sir ffrancis Duckett ˏ⌐&⌐ was one
of the Actors in the said plea at Kendall castle & ˏ⌐the said Sir ffr⌐ his
Balive & [te] some of his tennantes were actors therein & played their
partes in the said play with the privity & consent of the said Sir ffrancis 30
Duckett for any thing this deponent did know or hearde to the
Contrary & [furth] to the rest of the questions in this interrogatory
mencioned this [defendant] deponent hath before set downe saving
that the said playebookes were [⟨..⟩] made 7. yeares or thereaboutes
before the same ˏ⌐were⌐ acted but there was not any intent of hurt or   35
disgrace intended against the landlordes of the County of westmerland
[then] but [what] that the same concerned all in generall & furthr
deposeth not /
5   To the 5 inter this deponent sa there was not any of the defendantes
nor any other players that acted any of the stage playes wherein they   40
reprsented or personated any of the lordes of the Mannors within the

11/ lett *in sense of forbid*   26,39/ sa *for saith*

County of Westmrlande [nor] neithr were any of them personated to
be in Hell but what was then acted [..]was a reprsentacion of ravens
feeing of poore sheepe [which whoe] ⌈in Hell⌉ which ravens were
compared to [lan] greedy landlordes & the sheepe to ˄⌈their⌉ poore
tennantes whoe oppressed them & fedd vpon their [Carcasses]   5
Carkesses but the same was not intended more against any of the
County of westmrlande then against other counties & all in generall

6   To the 6. inter he saith that the Actors of the said pleas which were
acted at Kendall castle [the] had [their a]˄⌈[all] the best &⌉ the greatest
parte of their apparrell & playing Clothes lent them by & from the   10
howses of Sir Iames Bellingham knight & Sir ffrancis duckettes whoe
were the furthrers. of the acting of the said pleas & there were [so
divers] att the acting of the said pleas ˄⌈which were⌉ of Sir Iames
Bellinghams howse Mr Allen Bellingham & Sir ffrancis duckettes
howse the Lady duckett Mr Anthony duckett & his wife with divers   15
others & furthr he cannot depose

7   To the 7. inter this [defendant] deponent saith that [Ier. m. Ga] Ierom
Garnett this[defendant] deponentes brother [writ] & servant to Sir
Iames Bellingham writ alettere to this[defendant] deponent that he
should keepe out of the way alledgeing [tha] by his letteres that the   20
defendant Samuel Knipe had a proces to serve on him but he knew
not for what cause the same was but as he [supposed] ⌈thought⌉ it was
for a libell supposed to be made against him the said Samuel Knipe
by this[defendant] deponent, & the ˄⌈said⌉ Ierom Garnett by his lettere
advised this [defendant] Deponent to come over vnto Leavens to where   25
Sir Iames Bellingham then dwelt, & then the said Ierom Garnett &
this deponent would consider furthr cocerning the busines or word
to that effect & sa, vpon ˄⌈receipt of⌉ the said lettere he absented him
self & send worde vnto the defendant knipe by divers persons
concerning the said supposed writt which the said Ierom had written   30
vnto him thereof & that he should send this [defendant]deponent an
answere there ˄⌈of⌉ wherevpon this deponent received answer from the
said Knipe that he had | a writt of suppena to serve on him to testifie
the truth in this he⌈⟨..⟩⌉ Cort ˄⌈on the defendantes behalfe⌉ Concerning
the said plays & for noe othr cause & this deponent thought he was   35
in Conscience bounde to testife the truth on the behalfe of the
defendant, & this deponent saith that after [the] he [h] received
informacion from the defendant knipe this deponent met with his
brothr Ierom att Ascham in the County of westmerland where his
brothr Ierom seemed to be offended because this deponent had   40

8/ were written over was   27/ cocerning for concerning
17/ d of deponent written over s   28/ sa for saith

diclosed the secrettes of his *lette*res to such as had [infored] informed the
def*endan*t knipe thereof alledging that the def*endan*t knipe woulde
informe ag*ains*t the s*ai*d Ierom vpon ˹the˺ writing of the s*ai*d *lette*re, &
this dep*onen*t was likewise angrie w*i*th his brother for writing vntruly
vnto this dep*onen*t knowing as this dep*onen*t was *per*swaded to the   5
Contrarie [& furthr depo]

f 19

…

8   To the 8 inter this dep*onen*t sa [he sa] there were not any of the   10
def*endan*tes made acquainted nor [knewe] of the makinge of the s*ai*d
playes [vnto] neithr did any of them to his knowledge see or heare
reade [any of the s*ai*d playes] ˹the same˺ [for that that] savinge the
def*endan*t Helmes for that this [def*endan*t] dep*onen*t was not then
acquainted w*i*th them neithr had any of the s*ai*d def*endan*tes any hand   15
in the Contrivinge & composinge thereof before the same was acted
as in this inter is questioned & further he cannot depose /

1623–4
Chamberlains' Accounts 36   KCRO: WMB/K   20
f [23]   *(Extraordinary Payments)*
…

paid to will*ia*m Chamber wife ffor the Leet dynner att
micheallmas for 12 measse and A halff whereof 3 measse
were 8 d apece and the Rest 6 d ape*ce*   01 07 00   25
paid for bread and drink to the Iury   00 01 10

f [23v]*

Paid to mr Alderman Bank the 26th of march 1624 for 9   30
yeardes & A half of broad Cloth for the waites   02 17 00
…
pd S*i*r ffrancis keep*er* when he brought venyson w*h*ich
was Eaten att will*ia*m Chambeṙs   00 02 06
…   35
paid will*ia*m Chamber wife for 13 meass att the Leet
dynner att Easter where of 3 mease was 8 d ape*ce* and the
Rest 6   01 08 00
pd in bread and drink to the Iury   00 02 00
…   40

10/ sa [he sa] *for* saith [he saith]   30/ mr Alderman Bank: *William Bank*

more which was fetch to william Chamber att the
venyson feast 1 quart sack   00 01 04
more when mr Alderman was Chosen 1 gallon Clarett
and 1 quart Sack   00 04 00
more for wyne and Sack att his house att the venyson feast 00 09 00   5
more for five measse att the venyson feast   00 10 00

...

pd the waites att Easter att Leet dynner   00 02 6

...
                                                                              10

f [24]*

...

pd william Chamber wife att venyson ffeast for 9 measse
att 6: apece   00 18 00
pd the waites att thatt tyme   00 01 00   15
pd william Chamber wife att the Ellection dynner for 17
measse whereof 3 measse was 8 d apece and the Rest 6   01 16 00
paid the waites the same tyme   00 02 06

...
                                                                              20

1624–5
Chamberlains' Accounts 37   KCRO: WMB/K
f [24]*

...

more a gallon of Clarett wine to the election dinner   00 02 08   25
more 2 quarts of sack same tyme   00 02 08

...

payd Ned Ienninges wife at the election dinner for 16.
mease [at] whereof 3. mease at 8 d. and the rest at 6 d. a
peece   01 14 00   30
given the Wayts then   00 02 06

1625–6
Chamberlains' Accounts 38   KCRO: WMB/K
f [21]   *(Extraordinary Payments)*   35

...

paid to Edward Ienings wyf for 14. mease at leet Cort
dinner at mighallmas wheareof 3 mease was at 8 d a pece

3/ mr Alderman: *James Cock*
25,28/ election dinner: *Michaelmas 1625*
28,37/ Edward Ienings: *see p 238, endnote to WMB/K [Book 37] f [24]*

and and the rest at vj d a pec*e*   I IO O
paid waites for playing same tyme   O   2 6
...
paid Petter Hugon for a leuen quartes of wyne and a pynt
was had at the leet dnner at mighalmas   O   7 8   5
...

f [21v]
...
paid the waites for theire atendance at the leet dinner at   10
easter   O   2 6
...
paid to the kings plaies by the apoyntment of mr
Alderman   O IO O
...   15
paid to Petter huggon for 9 quartes of wyne and a pynt to
the leet Cort dinner at easter   O   6 4
...
paid Edward Ienings wyf for 12. mease at the lete court
dinner at Easter wheareof 3. mease were at 8 d apece, and   20
the rest 6 d apec   I   6 0
for drinke and bread to the Iuri   O   2 0
paid mor for drinke after dinner   O   I 0
...
                                                                                                   25

f [22]
...
paid the waites for playinge at the venyson ffeast, and the
election diner   O   3 6
...   30
paid to Mr Becke ffor the waites Clockes and wine had at
Sundeir tymes as by his note doth apeare   5 IO O
paid to Edward Ienings wyf for the Election dinner, for
tenn mease wheareof 3 of them was at 8 d apece and the
other at vj d a pece   I   2 0   35
...

1/ and and: *dittography*
13–14/ mr Alderman: *James Dixon (2)*
31/ Mr Becke: *Walter Becke*

paid at Petter hugons ffor venyson ffeast   4 16 4
...
paid to him which browght the venyson ffrom Greyrige   o 6 o
paid to him which browght the venysoun ffrom Leuens   o 6 o
...   5

1625–6
Diocese of Chester: Consistory Court Paper   CRO: EDC5/1625/13
single sheet *(22 October)*
                                                                                      10
Responsa personalia Willelmi Miller parochie de Kendall presentacioni
contra eum date et exemplificate per gardianos de Kendall capta
Octobris xxij do 1625 vi Iuramenti prout sequitur

That vpon a Saturday this respondent was one yat Consented vnto   15
and brought in a [⟨....⟩] ˏ ⌈showe before⌉ a sommer rodd or Maypole
all inhabite   diuers beinge disguysed some in Mens apparell and others in Womens
within   apparell as namely Iohn Sale a boye henry sonne of Richard Peareson
Kendall towne   Anthony sonne of William Wilkinson and Roland Chambers. were
attyred lyke women Iohn Phillipson Iames Iackson & Iohn Nuby   20
were in Mens apparell and sayth the sayd Anthonie Wilkinson Carried
a booke in his hand butt ˏ ⌈denieth⌉ yat he was in the habite or shape
of a devill as is obiected or yat there was anie intent ⟨..⟩ purpose to
deprave or scoffe att religion
                        Signum   dicti Miller   25

1626–7
Chamberlains' Accounts 39   KCRO: WMB/K
f [21v]*   *(Extraordinary Payments)*   30

Payd Iohn Troughton wyfe for 14 mease at Court leete
dynner at michaelmas whereof 3 mease at 8 d a peece and
the Rest at 6 d   o1 10 o
payd for breade and drinke to the Iury   oo 02 o   35
Payd to Robert wylkinson for 13 quarts of wyne for the
court leete dynner at 7 d the quart   oo–o7 7
Payd The Waytes for Theyre Atendance That day   oo–o2 6

4/ Leuens: *Sir James Bellingham of Levens, Westmld*
16/ [⟨....⟩]: *word heavily smudged over in ink; possibly* church
25/ *Miller signed with his personal mark between* Signum *and* dicti

Payd The first of November to my Lord Whartons
players by mr Aldermans apoyntment   00 05 0

...

Payd the 23th of November to the kyngs players by mr
Aldermans apoyntment   00–10 0   5

...

f [22]*

...

payd To wylliam Chambers the 4th of aprill 1627 for 13   10
mease at Court leete dynner whereof 3 mease at 8 d a peece
And the Rest at 6 d and for drinke and breade to the Iury   01 10 6
payd The waytes for theyre Attendance   00 02 6

...

payd by mr Aldermans apoyntment which was given to   15
The kyngs players The 4th of August   00 10–0

...

Payd to wylliam Chambers wyfe for The Ellection
dynner   02 07 6
payd The waytes for theyre atendance   00 02 6   20

1627–8
Chamberlains' Accounts 40   KCRO: WMB/K
f [18v]   *(Extraordinary Payments)*

25

pd william Chamber wife for 16 mease at leet Court diner
whereof 3 mease at 8 d the peece and the rest at 6 d and for
drinke and bread to the Iury   1. 14. 0
pd the waites for their allowance that day   0. 2. 6

...   30

pd to mr bankes the 11th of march 1627 for sarientes
Coates, waites coates, and beadle coat as may apeare by
his noate of parcelles   4. 18: 0

...

2,4–5,15/ mr Aldermans: *Henry Parke*
26/ leet Court: *Michaelmas 1627*
27–8/ and for drinke: *see p 239, endnote to WMB/K [Book 39] f [22]*
31/ mr bankes: *William Bank*

f [19]*

…

pd to will*ia*m Chamber wife for 7 mease & 3 forkes at leet
court diner whereof 3 mease at 8 d peece   0. 17. 6
pd for drinke after diner   0. 2. 0   5
pd for drinke that went to the Iury   0. 1. 6
pd fo the waites at leet coort diner   0. 2. 6

…

given to my lord Morley his seruant that brought halfe a
bucke, to the Companie   0. 5. 0   10

…

pd will*ia*m Chamber wife for 8 mease where of 3 mease of
the 12 at 8 d peece   0. 18. 0

…
                                                                            15

f [19v]*

…

pd to mr Alderman that he gave the waites at the venison
feast 18 d…

…   20

pd to will*ia*m Chamber wife for 16 mease at the venison
feast at 6 d peece   1. 12. 0
pd for drinke afterward   0. 3. 4
pd for tobacco & pips   0. 1. 5
pd for 16 mease want one bodie at the ellect*io*n diner   25
whereof 3 mease of the 12 at 8 d peece & therest 6 d peece 1. 13. 6
pd for drinke afterwardes   0. 1. 0
pd for tobacco & pips   0. 1. 5
pd to the fidlers for playinge at 2 feastes   0. 2. 6

…   30

pd to the waites for playinge at the mr Alderma*n*s at the
sweareinge diner   0. 2. 6

…

given to S*ir* ffrancis keper vj s…

…   35

3/ forkes *for* folkes   18/ mr Alderman: *James Rowlandson*
3–4/ leet court: *Easter 1628*   26/ 12 *in error for* 16
13/ 12 *in error for* 8   31/ mr Alderma*n*s: *Laurence Parke*

pd peter huggon for 8 quartes of wine at 2 venison feastes   0. 5. 4
pd to the players in August by mr fisher for agratuitie   0. 10. 0
…

1628–9   5
Chamberlains' Accounts 41   KCRO: WMB/K
f [20v]   *(Extraordinary Payments)*

pd will Chamber wyffe the leettes Courte dyner vizett 14
mease wherof 3 mease at 8 d apece and the Reste at 6 d   10
pece   01–10–00
pd waytes at lett Court dyner   00–02–06
…
pd ffor drinke & breat [to] the Iury at leete Courte   00–01–06
pd ffor tobaco & pipes   00–00–06   15
pd mr becke ffor v q*uartes* of Clartt and one q*uart* of
sacke at leett Court dyner   00–04–10
…
pd will Chambr wyffe the Court leete dyner for 3 mease
at 8 d pec*e* & 12 measse at vj d pece   01–12–00   20
pd ffor drinke & bread at Court leete Iurry   00–01–06
pd to waytes at that dyner   00–02–06
pd ffor tobaco & pips   00–01–02
pd ffor drinke after dyner   00–02–00
…   25

f [21]
…
pd to the earle of darbie his players by Aldrman deections 00–05–00
…   30
pd my lord wharton playrs by mr aldrman derections   00–05–00

f [21v]   *(1629)*
…
pd to will Chambr wyffe 29 sept ffor ffor election dyner   35
vizett ⌈3⌉ ⟨.⟩ measse at 8 d pec*e* .8 s. 17 measse & 2 folkes
at 6 d pec*e*. 35 s. all   02–03–00
pd to the waytes same tyme   00–02–06

2/ mr fisher: *Edward Fisher*   19/ Court leete: *Easter 1629*
9/ leettes Courte: *Michaelmas 1628*   29,31/ Aldrman: *Laurence Parke*
16/ mr becke: *Walter Becke*   35/ ffor ffor: *dittography*

pd ffor 3 qu*artes* of sacke same tyme   00–04–00
pd ffor v qu*artes* Clarrett 8 d qu*art*   00–03–04
pd ffor vj qu*artes* of wt wyne   00–04–00
pd ffor tobaco & pipes   00–00–10
pd ffor drinke afterwardes   00–01–00   5

...

1629–30
Chamberlains' Accounts 42   KCRO: WMB/K
f [21v]   *(Extraordinary Payments)*   10

Paid this 7^t of Ocktober to will*iam* Chamber wife for :14:
mese and a halfe [of] at leete Cort diner .3. mese at :8:d
apece and the rest vj d a pece and for drinke and bread to
Iurie   I 10 6   15
paid the waites for theire allowence for mewsike at diner   0 2 6

...

f [22]
                                                                                 20
This 24th of martch paid to mr Becke for sargentes Cotes
and waites Clokes as apeareth by his note of prjzes   4 17 0

...

This :8:th of aprell paid will*iam* Chambr wife for :9 mese
at leete Corte diner 3 mease at :8: pece the rest at vj d a   25
pece   I 0 0
paid for drinke & bread to Iurie   0 1 6
paid for drinke before diner and after extrordinarie   0 2 0
paid for A ounce of tobaco & pipes at that time   0 1 6
paid waites for thaire alow alowence for musike then   0 2 ⟨6⟩ 6   30

...

f [22v]
...
paid will*iam* Chamber wife for :16: mease and a halfe at   35
the elecktion diner whereof :4: mease at viij d a pece and
the rest at vj d a pece   I 15 8
paid hir for drinke had extrordanrie   0 4 4

...

3/ wt *for* whit   30/ alow alowence: *dittography*
21/ mr Becke: *Walter Becke*

paid the waites theire alowence for [playinge] ⸢atendance⸣
at the elecktion diner   0 2 6

...

paid Ed*ward* Turner for two ounces of tobaco had at the
elecktion diner & halfe pond of sugor had by allan
nickalson to mr sledals & a duson of pipes *with* tobaco   0 3 6

1630–1
Chamberlains' Accounts 43   KCRO: WMB/K
f [19v]   *(Extraordinary Payments)*

Payd Will*iam* Chambrs wife the *(blank)* of October
for 3 mease at mr Aldermans Table   00: 08: 00.
pd more for 9 mease & 3 *persons*   00: 19: 06.
pd more for drinke   00: 03: 06.
pd more for bread & drinke for the Leete Iurie   00: 01: 06.
pd mr Becke for 8 q*uartes* Clarett   00: 04: 00.
pd him more for j q*uart* Sacke   00: 01: 04.

...

(October–5 November)
pd waytes their wages, for the Leete Court dinner   00: 02: 06.

...

f [20]   *(30 March–6 May)*
...

pd at Leete Court dinner for 3 mease at mr Aldermans
Table   00: 08: 00.
pd for 7 mease, & 2 *persons* more at 6 d a peece   00: 15: 00.
pd more for drinke   00: 02: 08.
pd for Tobacco, & pypes   00: 01: 00.
pd for bread & drinke for Leete Iury   00: 01: 06.
pd for wage for mouthall Table   00: 00: 00.½.
pd the waytes their wages   00: 02: 06.

...

(10 August–23 September)
pd for 3 measse at mr Aldermans Table at venison feast   00: 08: 00.
pd for 13 measse, & di. more same night   01: 07: 00.
pd for 3 measse next daie   00: 06: 00.
pd for drinke for all   00: 06: 00.

6/ mr sledals: *Thomas Sledall*   17/ mr Becke: *Walter Becke*
13,26,36/ mr Aldermans: *Edward Fisher*

pd for Tobacco, & pypes in all   00: 02: 04.
pd the Waytes   00: 02: 06.

f [20v]

...   5
pd since the 13th of August, per mr mr Aldermans
note ...   00: 09: 00.
pd him more, which he spent of the Gentlemen, at
Tauerne, when feast was   00: 03: 00.
pd to Lord Morley his Keeper   00: 10: 00.   10
pd to Sir ffrancis duckett keeper   00: 06: 00.

...
pd William Chambrs wife, at the Eleccion dinner for 3
measse at mr Aldermans Table   00: 08: 00.
pd more for 15 measse, & 3 persons   01: 11: 06.   15
pd more for drinke   00: 07: 00.
pd for Tobacco, & pypes   00: 01: 10.
pd Waytes the same tyme   00: 02: 06.

...
(29 September 1631 [+])   20
pd mr Becke ... since Michelmas ...   02: 17: 00.
pd him more, according to his note, for sacke, & other
wyne, when the venison ffeast was at mr Adermans   01: 14: 11.

1631–2   25
Chamberlains' Accounts 44   KCRO: WMB/K
f [23]*

Paid William Chamber Wife the 5th of October 1631
ffor 13 measse and a bodie at Leete Courte dinner   30
whearof 3 measse at 2 s 8 d measse and the Rest at 2 s per
measse   01: 08: 06
paid her ffor Beare which was drunck befor and after
dynner   00: 04: 00
paid ffor bread and beare to Iurie   00: 01: 06   35
paid the waites ffor ther attendance ther ffee   00: 02: 06
...

6/ mr mr: *dittography*   21/ mr Becke: *Walter Becke*
6/ mr Aldermans: *Edward Fisher*   23/ mr Adermans: *Edward Fisher*
14/ mr Aldermans: *James Bateman*

(*November*)
paid mr Aldrman the 26th which he bestowd on the
lord Wharton men beinge players   00: 05: 00

…

paid ffor 1 oz Christo*pher* tobaco & half oz varino and
half dozen pipes to leete Courte dinner   00: 01: 05

…

paid Allan Nicholson Wif the 11th of Aprill 1632 ffor
14 Measse at Leete Courte dinner wherof 3 measse 2 s
8 d measse & the Rest 2 s measse   01: 10: 00

paid her ffor Beare which was drunk befor and after
dinner   00: 06: 06
paid ffor beare and Bread to Iurie   00: 01: 06
paid ffor 1 oz Christo*pher* Tobaco and almost an oz of
varino and a dozen of pipes   00: 02: 00
paid the Waites ffor ther attendance ther ffee   00: 02: 06

…

f [23v]

…

paid Willi*am* Chamber Wiffe the 31th of Iuly 1632 ffor
18 Measse at the venison ffeast wherof 4 Measse 2 s
8 d and the Rest 2 s   01: 18: 08
paid ffor Beare which was drunke befor & after dyner   00: 03: 00
paid ffor Cherisse which mr Aldrman bestowd on the
wines   00: 00: 06
paid Henery Beck ffidler ffor his paines   00: 01: 00
paid ffor Tobaccho and pipes   00: 01: 09

…

In Varino Tobaco and pipes to mr Aldrmans at the
venison ffeast Septembr 1th   00: 01: 07
paid the m*aste*r of ffence the 26th *per* mr Aldrman his
derecktions   00: 05: 00

…

paid ffor Tobacco and pipes   00: 02: 00
paid the waites ffor thear attendance thear ffee   00: 02: 06

…

paid Edward Turner the 4th Octobr 1632 ffor
Sargantes Coates the waites Cloakes and other Wares
ffor Chambr vse as *per* his note of *p*arcelles appearethe   05: 11: 04

…

2,25,30,32/ mr Aldrman: *James Bateman*

paid mr aldrman which he [had] bestowed on the Lord
Morlay keeper which he brought [Venison] venison   00: 10: 00
...

1632–3   5
Chamberlains' Accounts 45   KCRO: WMB/K
f [25]*

Imprms to william Chamber wife at the leet courte
dinner for 13 mease and 3 folkes 4 Mease where of at 8 d   10
peece   1. 10.   2
paid for beare and tobacco for all compaines before and
affter dinner   0.   5. 10
1 douzen of best tobacco pipes   0.   0. 6
for bread and drinke to the iurie   0.   1. 6   15

...

pd the waites the 21th of october 1632 for theire
attendance at Leet court dinner   0.   2. 6

...

pd to Brian Warrinner which was pd to mr waite to   20
make vp his stipend   1. 14. 3

...

pd to mr Alderman which he had disbursed to lorde
dudleyes players   0.   5. 0

                                                                    25

f [25v]
...

pd at leete courte dinner for 3 Mease at 8 d peece   0.   8. 0
for 9 Mease and 3 folkes at 6 d peece   0. 19. 6
pd for beare and tobacco and pipes before and affter   30
dinner   0.   5. 6
pd for bread and drinke to'th Iury   0.   1. 6
pd the waites for theire attendance   0.   2. 6
...

                                                                    35

f [26]
...

pd william Chamber wife the 22th of September at the
Election dinner for 3 Mease and 3 folkes at 8 d peece 0. 10. 0
11 Mease and 3 folkes at 2 s mease   1.   3. 6   40

1/ mr aldrman: *James Bateman*   23/ mr Alderman: *Richard Forth*

for drinke tobacco and pipes before and after dinner in
all   0. 5. 8

...

pd to'th waites for theire Attendance at the Election
dinner   0. 2. 6   5

...

pd to Richard Prisor for ... half a doozen of pipes at the
Election dinner   0. 0. 3

...

pd more to Peeter Huggon for 1 quart of wine sent for   10
to'th election dinner   0. 0. 6

1633–4
Chamberlains' Accounts 46   KCRO: WMB/K
f [31v]*   *(Payments)*   15

...

pd to william Chamber wife for 13 maase [of] and
one body at the Leete dinner the 7th of October
1633   01–10–00–00
More for drinke after dinner 4 s and for drinke &   20
bread to the Iurie 18 d for tobacco and pipes 18 d to
the waites 2 s 6 d for wyne vj s in all   00–15–06–00

...

f [30v]   *(17–20 February)*   25

...

for the Waites Cloakes to Richard Priesoe   03–08–08–00

...

f [26v]   30

...

°Paid to William Chamber wife for dinners and drinke att
the Chuseing of the Alderman   01 16 00
Paid ⌈more⌉ the same tyme for tabacco and pipes   00 01 06
Paid more to the waytes the same daie   00 02 06°   35

...

17–19/ *either* 13 maase ... and one body *or* 01–10–00–00 *in error*
33/ the Alderman: *Thomas Sledall*

1634–5
Chamberlains' Accounts 47   KCRO: WMB/K
f [21v]*   *(Extraordinary Payments)*

Imprimis   Paid William Chamber wife the 8th daie of October 1634:   5
ffor 14 mease and halfe att Leet Court dinner wherof 3
mease & halfe att 2 s. 8 d. the mease and the rest att 2 s. per
mease   01 11 04
Paid her for beare before and after dinner   00 05 02
Paid for bread & beare to the Iurie   00 01 06   10
Paid mr Becke for 4 quartes of sack & 9 quart in white &
Clarett to the Court Leet dinner   00 09 09
Paid the waytes   00 02 06
Paid Thomas Towson for Tabacco and pipes as appeares
by his note   00 *(blank)*   15
...

f [21]
...
Paid William Chamber wife the 8th of April 1635 / for 14.   20
mease and one person att the Court Leet dinner wherof 3.
mease att 2 s. 8 d. and the rest att 2 s. a mease   01 10 06
Paid ˌ⌜her⌝ for drinke before and after dinner   00 05 00
Paid her more for bread [to the] ⌜and⌝ beare to the Iurie   00 01 06
Paid for Tabacco and pipes as appeares by [their]   25
ˌ⌜Thomas Towson⌝ note   00 *(blank)*
Paid Waytes same daie   00 02 06
Paid mr Becke for 12 quartes and a pinte of wine att 7 d a
quart   00 07 03
...   30

f [20v]   *(28 September)*
...
Paid William Chamber wife for 16 mease & three persons
whereof 3 Mease & 3 persons after 2 s. 8 d. the Mease and   35
the rest after 2 s. a mease att the Election dinner   01 16 00
Paid drinke before & after dinner   00 05 ⌜10⌝ [04]
...

11,28/ mr Becke: *Walter Becke*   20/ 1635 *underlined* MS

Paid Waytes   00 02 06

...

1635-6
Chamberlains' Accounts 48   KCRO: WMB/K   5
f [19]   *(28 October)*

pd will Chamber wife for the leet Court dinner 3 measse
⟨.⟩s 8 d & 12 measse ⌐& 1 person⌐ att 6 d a peece more to 3
poore people 4 d a peece 33 s 6 d   01 13 06.   10
pd for drinke before & after dinner   00 07 5.
pd for Ale & bread to [Iury] Iurye   00 01 6.
pd the waites their fee for attend*ance*   02 6.
pd for 4 oz varona tobacco   00 04 00.
pd for 3 oz virginia 4 d p*er* oz   00 01 00.   15
pd for 1 oz Chr*istopher* 3 d & 26 pipes 13 d   00 01 4.
pd for ij oz varina & 3 d pipes at the dinnr when mr
Aldrm*an* was sworn   0 02 3.
...

20

f [19v]   *(23 November)*
...
bestowed on th earle of derbyes playrs   0 10 0.
...

25

f [20]   *(27 April)*

pd will Chambr wife at leet Court din*n*er for 3 mease att
8 d p*er* peece & 11 mease & 2 men att 6 d & 3 poore 4 d a
peece in all   01 12 00.
pd for beare before & after din*n*er   00 08 00   30
pd for bred & beare to Iurye   00 01 6
pd for tobacco 3 oz varina   00 03 00
for 3 oz & di. virginia 4 d & 20 pipes ⌐10 d⌐   00 02 0.
pd the waytes their fee   00 02 6.
...   35
(27 April–2 June)
pd Iohn Archer for 3 Clokes for the waytes   03 07 00.
...

9/ ⟨.⟩s *cancelled or blotted; correctly 3 mease at 8 d apiece to make up payment of £1 13 s 6 d*
17–18/ mr Aldrm*an*: *Rowland Dawson*

f [20v]*   (11 October 1636)

...

pd the waytes thr fee at dinner when mr Alderman vse to
be sworne 2 s 6 d   00 02 6.

...   5

(25 October 1636⁺)
pd mr Maior per Bryam warriner he bestowed on my lord
strange his players   00 10 00.

1636–7   10
Chamberlains' Accounts 49   KCRO: WMB/K
f [20v]   (4 September) (Disbursements)

Paid William Chamber bye thapointment of mr Maior for
ₐ⌐the⌐ kinges plaiors   01 00 00   15

...

1637–8
Chamberlains' Accounts 50   KCRO: WMB/K
f [23]   (7–21 November) (Disbursements)   20

...

Paid to ₐ⌐the⌐ waytes for playing att the light Court dinner
in mony   00–02–6

...
                                                                                   25

f [24v]   (30 June–7 July)

...

Paid to Iohn Becke for Clothe and baize for the waytes
Cloakes   03–15–0

...   30

1638–9
Thomas Crosfield's Diary   Queen's College, Oxford: MS 390
f 84*   (2 December)

...   35

2.   whether Corpus Christi play long since acted in Kendall, was tolerable
     by Gods law because it seemes to be a kind of preaching or setting out
     of ye scripture to edification worse was that about Clifton, one priest
     Sir Humfrey Close suffring a play to be acted in ye Church. as mr Airay
     hath the story./   40

...

4/ 2 s 6 d *added after payment entered*   7,14/ mr Maior: *Thomas Sledall*

1639–40
Chamberlains' Accounts 52   KCRO: WMB/K
f [24v]   *(30 March) (Disbursements)*

...

Payd for 9 yrdes di quarter of broode for Waytes Clookes 03 06 04   5

...

WINDERMERE

1537–8   10
State Papers Domestic   PRO: SP1/134, No 1370
single sheet*   *(James Leyburn to Thomas Cromwell)*

Iames labrones lettere to know yor pleysur toching Isaac dykson
being in prison for desyreinge a mynstrall to sing a song a genst yor   15
lordshyp
Ryght Honorable my Dewtie vnto youre Lordshippe remembride /
Pleassith yow to be aduerteshede I haue Sente yow herin clossede
certayn artikilles which is of truthe both worde & dede to knowe
your lordshipe pleassure ther in And I haue the vngracius &   20
myscheuus fellow ysaac dikson in the tooll buthe in kendall and hath
chargid the bailly deputes of the same with the sewre custody &
kepyng of hym afor Richard Ducket Iustice of peace within the countie
of westmorlande / vnto Such tyme I knowe ffurthere of yor lordshipe
pleassure .... and some of thes persones which gaue me informacion   25
of the premyss dide stayger & deny theyr wordes which maid me tary
the longer .... And as concernyng the mynstrall which is a rynner
abrod from place to place I haue hym at my howsse & shall be
aboutward to keipe hym to I know mor of yor lordshipe pleassure And
also I haue sent a copy of the artikilles herin closed to the kynges   30
honorable consaill establishede in the north parties accordyng to my
dewtye .... ffrom conyswik the xiij^th day of Iulye

...

State Papers Domestic   PRO: SP1/134, No 1346   35
single sheet

Memorandum ix^th Day of Iulye in The xxx^th yere of The Reigne of
our Soueraigne lorde kyng henry the viij^th / Alexandre stotson lat of
cartmell in the countye of Lancastre mynstrall Saieth the last day of   40

14–16/ *endorsement*

Iune Last past on ysaac dikson of wyndandermer in the countie of
westmorland A bout Sexe of the clock at afternone of the same day
come in to the howsse of on william willan in wynster in
wyndandermer aforsaid where the said Alexandre was playing on a
fedill & makyng mery with certayn honest persones   5
¶ Item the said ysaac commandit the said minstrall to Syng on Song he
had song At on ffayrbank howsse in crostwat in the said countye of
westmorland in the tyme of the Rebellion which songe was called
crummok / which was not conuenyent which the said mynstrall vtterly
Denyede /   10
¶ Item the said ysaac commandit the said mynstrall agayn in violente
maner to synge on song called crumwell & the said mynstrall said he
wold syng none such & then the said ysaac pulled the mynstrall by
the armes & smot hym about the hed with a pomell of a dager & hurt
the mynstrall in the hande & the said songe the mynstrall wold not 15
syng to Dye fore
¶ Item the Thrid tyme the said ysaac commaundit the said mynstrall to
syng the same songe / which then the mynstrall saide it wold turn tham
both to Angre / & wold syng no such / And then the said ysaac callid
for A cuppe of aill & bad the mynstrall syng agayn which he alwayes   20
denyed / & then the said ysaac tuk the said mynstrall by the Birde &
dasshet the cupe of aill in his fface
Item the said ysaac further more drewe his dager and hurt the said
william willan beyng the host of the said howsse sore & grevuslye in
the thight in rescuyng of the said mynstrall only for that matter   25
Item the said ysaac after the day goying in violent maner followede
& sought further for the said mynstrall to on Nicollus brokbank
howsse in the said wyndandermer which was iij quartteres of a myll
fro the said william willan howsse
¶ Thes witnesse of the premyss Robert phelipson of wyndandermer   30
aforsaid william belman of the same & wylliam dremylmyer of
wynster
...

Households

CLIFFORD

1616–17
Household Accounts Clifford   CH: Bolton Abbey MS 97
f 106v*   *(13 July) (Rewards)*

...

Item given this day in Reward to S*ir w*ill*iam* Constable   5
his Coachman whoe Came to knowe what daye he should
be readee w*ith* his Coach to Carree Doctor Campion
from Londsbrough to Browham. ij s–and to mr
Stewardes boy whoe brought a letter to Doctor Campion
from mr Io*hn* Tailor–vj d.   ij s. vj d   10

...

f 200v*   *(18 July) (Extraordinary)*

...

Item paied this day to a man of Hull, w*hich* was sent for   15
to Londsbrough to play on the lute at Browham, by Mr
George Mason, but was sent backe, there being noe
occasion to vse him   vj s

...

                                                                                             20
Francis Clifford's Letter to his son Henry
Whitaker: *History and Antiquities of Craven*, vol 2
p 369
...
Sonn,   25
    I have till now expected y*our* lett*er*es, according to your promis
at y*our* departure; so did George Minson y*our* directions touching
the musick, whereupon he mought the better have writt to doctor
Campion. He is now gone to my Lord President's, and will be ready
to do as he heares from y*ou*.   30
    For my own opinion, albeit I will not dislyke y*our* device, I fynde
plainly, upon better consideration, the charge for that entertaynment

will grow very great, besyde the musick; and that, instead of lessening, my charge in generall encreaseth, and newe paiments come on, which, without better providence hereafter, cannot be performed.

...

1616–17
Diary of the Lady Anne Clifford   KAO: U269 F48/2
nf*   *(23 November)*

...

Upon the 23.^d Baker Hookfeild Harry the Caterer &
Tom Fool went from hence towards London.†

...

Upon the 23^d, I went to Mr Blentre's House in
Cumberland ⌈whereI⌉ [I] staid an Hour or two & heard
Musick & saw all the House & Gardens.

...

LOWTHER OF LOWTHER

1640–1
Estate Accounts   CCRO: D/Lons/L3/1/5
f [28v]   *(2–15 February)*

...

pd to a piper   000 00 03

...

f [29]   *(24 February–5 March)*

...

pd to Penrith waites   00 01 00

...

f [30]   *(10–17 April)*

...

pd to the waites of Midlam...   00 01 00

...

1641–2
Estate Accounts   CCRO: D/Lons/L3/1/5
f [41]   *(24 December–4 January) (Disbursements)*

...

Pd to Players   000 10 00

...

29/ 01: 1 *written over* 0

APPENDIX 1
Undated Documents

Bampton, State Papers Domestic   PRO: SP14/86, No 34
single sheet*

...

men now become bould to abvse ye churche in tyme of diuine service,
as at christemas last, at bampton in westmorland, where ye tenantes,   5
and servantes of ye lord *William* assisted with others of ye parishe,
did erect a christemas lord, and resorting to ye church, did most
grossely disturb ye minister in tyme of prayer, ye minister him selfe
grantinge a kind of toleration for that, he for ye most part livethe with
ye lord *william* at his table, but never praye together. these christemas   10
misrule men, drunke to ye minister readinge an homilie in ye pulpitt,
others stept into ye pulpitt, and exhorted ye parishioners to an
offeringe for mayntenance of there sport, ye minister contynuinge still
his service, others of ye lord *william* owne servantes came in savage
manner disguised into ye churche, in ye tyme of prayer, others with   15
shootinge of gunnes, others with flagges, and banners borne entered
ye churche, others sported them selves in ye churche with pies, and
puddinges, vsinge them as bowles in ye churche allies, others tooke
dogges counterfeitinge ye shepherdes part when he fees his shepe, and
all there in ye tyme of diuine service.   20

...

Kendal Play   Weever: *Ancient Funerall Monuments*
p 405*

...   25

®*R. Marlow*
Lord Maior.

*Orate pro animabus Richardi Marloi quondam venerabilis Maioris
Ciuitatis London, & Agnetis consortis sue. Qui⟨.. ... ..⟩ ob ⟨.... ..⟩*
    This *Marlow* was Lord Maior in the yeare 1409. in whose Maioraltie
there was a Play at Skinners Hall, which lasted eight dayes (saith *Stow*)

®*Corpus Christi*
play.

to heare which, most of the greatest Estates of England were present.   30
The Subiect of the play was the sacred Scriptures, from the creation of

the world: They call this, *Corpus Christi* Play in my countrey, which
I haue seene acted at Preston, and Lancaster, and last of all at Kendall,
in the beginning of the raigne of King *Iames*; for which the
Townesmen were sore troubled; and vpon good reasons the play
finally supprest, not onely there, but in all other Townes of the   5
kingdome.

...

Kendal Play   BL: Add. MS 4460
ff 7–7v*   10

...I went to *Cartmell*, about the later end of April 1644, and about
the begining of May following, my wife came to me to Cartmell: where
I found a very large spacious Church, scarce any seats in it, a people
very ignorant, yet willing to learne; so as I had frequently some   15
thousands of hearers: I seeing my work great: a large feild & looking
something white towards harvest, & knowing my stay must be but
short, & finding also 4 chapels in the parish, I preached & catechised
often, seven or 8 times in one week; I preached and catechised in season
& out of season at every one of the chappells, and usually ye Churches   20
were so throng by 9 a clock in ye morning, yat I had muchadoe to
get to the pulpit, I also preached at other Churches round about in
ye weekday. One day an old man (about 60) sensible enough in other
things, & living in the parish of Cartmel, but in the chapelry of
Cartmel-fell, coming to me about some business, I told him, yat he   25
belonged to my care & charge, & I desired to be informed in his
knowledge of Religion; I asked him, How many Gods there were? he
said, he knew not: I informing him, asked him again: how he tho't
to be saved? he answered, he could not tell, yet tho't that was a hard
question than the other, I told him, yat the way to Salvation was by   30
| Iesus Christ God-man, who as he was man shed his blood for us on
the crosse etc Oh, Sir (said he) I think I heard of that man you speake
of, once in a play at *Kendall*, called *Corpus-Christi play*, where there
was a man on a tree, & blood ran downe etc And after, he professed,
that tho he was a good Churchman, yat is, he constantly went to   35
Common-prayer, at their chappel, yet he could not remember thatever
he heard of Salvation by Iesus + but in that play, This very discourse
made me ye more vigorously go thro the chappelrye, & both publikly
& from house to house, catechise both old & young....

...   40

APPENDIX 2
Kendal Tradesmen

Where a reasonable certainty exists, persons named in KCRO: WMB/K Chamberlains' Accounts are identified by occupation or office by reference to the manuscript and to Richard S. Ferguson (ed), *A Boke off Recorde* (BR), which lists corporation members, civic officers, and members of the trades 1575–[1642]. Each member of the corporation started as one of the 24 assistants (from whose ranks the chamberlains were normally drawn) before elevation to burgess and possibly alderman/mayor. In the list that follows, primary identification is by surname as it appears in the transcription (in its most common form if cited several times), but with modern capitalization and Christian names. Possessive forms that occur in the text (eg, Aldermans, Chambers) have been given in the singular (Alderman, Chamber) in this appendix.

Alanson, Peter p 173; sworn clerk of courts 1575, listed under Scriveners (BR, pp 30, 80).

Archer, Edward p 181, Edward Artcher p 179; sworn to Wrights 1607 (BR, p 76).

Archer, John p 212; sworn to Mercers 1635 (BR, p 60), chamberlain 1640–1 (WMB/K Chamberlains' Accounts, Book 53 f[1]), mayor 1648–9 (BR, p 24).

Armer, John the ... Alderman p 170; sworn to Shearmen 1581, alderman 1585–6 and 1587–8, dying of plague before second term completed (BR, pp 50, 23).

Ayrey, James Iames Aryey p 175, Iames Ayray p 180, Iames Ayraye pp 175, 180, Iames Ayreye p 177; listed as searcher under Tailors, sworn sergeant-at-arms 1589 (BR, pp 62, 30).

Bank, William Mr Alderman Bank p 198, mr bankes p 202; sworn to Mercers 1605, chamberlain 1613–14, burgess 1620, alderman 1623–4, mayor 1639–40 (BR, pp 36, 23–4).

Bateman, James Mr Alderman
pp 207–9; chamberlain 1625–6
(WMB/K Chamberlains'
Accounts, Book 38 f [1]),
burgess 1629, alderman 1631–2
(*BR*, pp 37, 24).

Becke, John p 213; sworn to
Mercers 1629, chamberlain
1634–5, one of the 20 burgesses
(displaced 1650), mayor 1665–6
(*BR*, pp 60, 38, 19, 25).

Becke, Walter Walter Beck
p 186, Mr Alderman p 188, Mr
Becke pp 200, 204–7, 211; sworn
to Mercers 1611 (*BR*, p 59),
chamberlain 1618–19 (WMB/K
Chamberlains' Accounts, Book
31 f [1]), burgess 1618, alderman
1621–2, mayor 1637–8 (*BR*,
pp 36, 23–4).

Caslaye, Gowan p 178; listed
under Wrights, sworn sergeant-
at-mace 1601 (*BR*, pp 30, 76).

Chamber, William pp 185,
194–5, 198–9, 202–5, 207–13,
William Chambr pp 204–8, 212;
sworn to Shearmen 1616,
sergeant-at-mace n.d. (*BR*, pp 55,
30).

Cock, James Mr Alderman
p 199; mercer, chamberlain
1622–3, alderman 1624–5 (*BR*,
pp 37, 23).

Dawson, Roger Mr Dawson
p 174; draper, chamberlain
1582–3, alderman 1590–1,

1599–1600 (*BR*, pp 28, 23).

Dawson, Rowland Mr
Alderman Dawson p 187, Mr
Alderman pp 187, 212; clothier,
chamberlain 1614–15, burgess
1619, mercer, alderman 1620–1,
1635–6, mayor 1640–1 (*BR*, pp
36, 23–4).

Denison, William p 177; listed
under Innkeepers (*BR*, p 75).

Dickson, Henry Mr Dickson
p 172; mercer, alderman 1582–3
and 1596–7 (*BR*, pp 22–3 and 27).

Dickson, Jarvis Iarvis dickson
p 174; sworn to Mercers 1593
(*BR*, p 58).

Dixon, James (1) the Alderman
p 183, Mr Alderman p 183,
chapman, alderman 1606–7 and
1615–16 'bis' (*BR*, p 23); but
WMB/K Chamberlains'
Accounts, Book 28 f [1], 1615–
16, gives James Wilson as
alderman.

Dixon, James (2) Mr Alderman
p 200; shearman dyer, alderman
1625–6 (*BR*, p 24).

Eskrige, Christopher
Christoffor Eskrige, p 178;
sworn to Shearmen 1582, chamberlain 1597–8 (*BR*, pp 50, 34).

Fisher, Edward Mr ffisher
p 182, Mr Fisher p 204; Mr
Alderman pp 206–7; chapman,

chamberlain 1610–11 (WMB/K, Book 23 f [1]), alderman 1611–12 and 1630–1, mayor 1638–9 (BR, pp 23–4).

Fleminge, Henry Mr Alderman p 173, Mr Fleminge p 175; Henry Fleminge senior, mercer, chamberlain 1580, burgess 1581, alderman 1588–9 (BR, pp 31, 22).

Forth, Richard Mr Alderman p 209; pewterer, sworn to Wrights 1619, alderman 1632–3 (BR, pp 77, 24).

Fox, Christopher Christofer Fox p 173; son and heir of Miles Fox who was seised at his death in 1581 of property in Kendal including 'duas tavernas sive salacia' (Court of Wards Inq. p.m., 4 November, 30 Elizabeth I, cited in James F. Curwen (ed), *Records relating to the Barony of Kendale*, vol 1, pp 97–8).

Fox, William p 172; listed under Innkeepers, named an assistant in charter of 1575, chamberlain 1585–6, died 1592 (BR, pp 75, 31). His inn, 'the head hostelrie of the town,' was in the old Soutergate, on the east side of the present Highgate (John Whitwell, *The Old Houses of Kendal*, p 15).

Garnett, Edward (1) p 170; mercer, chamberlain 1587–8, burgess 1592, died 1597 (BR, pp 33, 28).

Garnett, Edward (2) garnet pp 172–3, garnat p 174; same as Edward Garnett 'cobler' (WMB/K Chamberlains' Accounts, Book 8 f [17]).

Gibson, Michael Mr Alderman p 194; sworn to Mercers 1607, chamberlain 1619–20, burgess 1620, alderman 1622–3 (BR, pp 59, 36, 23).

Green, Thomas Mr Alderman p 181; shearman, chamberlain 1600–1, burgess 1607, alderman 1610–11 (BR, pp 34, 29, 23).

Holme, Robert Robert holme p 180; sworn to Shearmen (before 1587), sworn sergeant-at-mace 1596 and 1601 (BR, pp 52, 30), 'Robartt holme tabovurne,' (WMB/K Chamberlains' Accounts, Book 13 f [18v], 1598–9).

Huggon, Peter pp 195, 200, 204, 210, Petter Hugon p 200–1; sworn to Innkeepers 1646 (BR, p 75).

Jenniges, James p 182; sworn to Armourers 1594 (BR, p 72).

Judson, William p 175; listed under Innkeepers (BR, p 75).

Michell, Rowland p 176; casual employee of corporation – hauling stones (WMB/K Chamberlains' Accounts, Book 4 f [11]) and timber (Book 7 f [22]), working on dam and 'watching one week' (Book 10 f [19]).

Nickalson, Allan p 206, Allan Nicholson p 208; sworn to Shearmen 1617 (BR, p 55).

Nuby, Steven p 187, Mr Alderman p 187; sworn to Cardmakers 1607, chamberlain 1609–10, burgess 1617, alderman 1619–20 (BR, pp 35, 23).

Parke, Henry Mr Alderman p 202; sworn to Mercers 1613 (BR, p 59), chamberlain 1621–2 (WMB/K Chamberlains' Accounts, Book 34 f [1]), burgess 1623, alderman 1626–7 (BR, pp 36, 24).

Parke, Laurence Mr Alderman pp 203–4; sworn to Mercers 1613, chamberlain 1622–3, alderman 1628–9, mayor 1641–2 (BR, pp 37, 24).

Pearson, Richard Mr Alderman p 186; chapman, chamberlain 1610–11 (WMB/K Chamberlains' Accounts, Book 23 f [1]), alderman 1617–18 (BR, p 23).

Pearsone, Cuthbert Cudbert Pearsone p 174, Cudbert pp 174–5; Cuthbert p 175; sworn sergeant-at-mace 1582 (BR, p 30).

Potter, Edward p 170, Mr Potter (?) p 172; mercer, alderman 1581–2 (after death of Edward Swainson), and 1595–6 (BR, p 22).

Preston, Brian Bryan Preston p 182; sworn to Mercers 1612, chamberlain 1619–20 (BR, pp 59, 36).

Prisor, Richard p 210, Richard Priesoe p 210; sworn to Mercers 1624, chamberlain 1630, one of the 12 aldermen 1641, mayor 1645–6 (BR, pp 60, 38, 18, 24).

Robinson, John pp 178–9, Mr Alderman pp 183, 185; shearman, chamberlain 1601, burgess 1614, dyer, alderman 1616–17 (BR, pp 34, 29, 23).

Rowlandson, James Mr Alderman p 203; sworn to Shearmen 1608–10, shearman dyer, chamberlain 1620–1, alderman 1627–8 (BR, pp 55, 36, 24).

Rowlandson, Michael his master p 181; sworn to Tanners 1594, chamberlain 1604–5, elected alderman 1608 and died August 1609 – remainder of term served by Edward Wilkinson (BR, pp 68, 35, 23).

Scales, Richard p 178; sworn to Shearmen 1590 (BR, p 54).

Selle, Richard p 176; sworn to Saddlers, chamberlain 1594–5, burgess 1600, alderman 1604–5 (*BR*, pp 69, 33, 23).

Shipperd, Bartholomew p 186, Shiphard p 186; sworn to Tanners 1616 (*BR*, p 68); supplied wine for receivers in November 1620 (WMB/K Chamberlains' Accounts, Book 33 f [18v]).

Sledall, Thomas Mr Sledall p 184, Mr Alderman p 186, Mr sledal p 206, the Alderman p 210, Mr Maior p 213; gentleman, chamberlain (WMB/K Chamberlains' Accounts, Book 28 f [1]), alderman 1618–19 (Book 31 f [1] collated with *BR*, p 23, where the names of Sledall and Richard Pearson, originally in the wrong order, are corrected to their proper aldermanic years) and 1634–5, attorney-at-law, first mayor 1636–7 (*BR*, p 24).

Smythe, John Mr Alderman p 178; chapman, chamberlain 1589–90, burgess 1591, alderman 1594–5, 1601–2, 1612–13 (*BR*, pp 33, 23).

Swaynson, William Mr Swaynson p 175; cordwainer, chamberlain 1583–4, burgess 1586 (*BR*, p 32); same as vintner, burgess 1586 (*BR*, p 28) and vintner, alderman 1591–2 (*BR*, p 23).

Thwaite, John Mr Twhaite Alderman p 177, Mr Alderman

p 178; sworn to Shearmen 1581, chamberlain 1582–3, displaced (as burgess) but reappointed 1588, alderman 1592–3 and 1600–1 (*BR*, 50, 32, 23).

Towson, Thomas p 211 chamberlain 1635–6; perhaps same as Thomas Tolson, a tobacco dealer, who in 1638 built Tolson Hall in Burneside, just outside Kendal (Whitwell, *The Old Houses of Kendal* p 14).

Turner, Edward pp 206, 208; sworn to Mercers 1624 (*BR*, p 24), chamberlain 1631–2 (WMB/K Chamberlains' Accounts, Book 44 f [1]), sworn one of the 12 aldermen 1637, mayor 1652–3 (*BR*, pp 18, 25).

Warriner, William pp 181, 183 William Warrinner p 182, William Waryner p 183, William Warriner Jr, shearman, chamberlain 1585–6, burgess 1591, sworn sergeant-at-mace 1606 (*BR*, pp 32, 30).

Warrinner, Brian p 209, Bryam Warriner p 213; salter, sworn to Chapmen 1612, chamberlain 1628–9, sergeant-at-mace n.d. (*BR*, pp 49, 37, 30).

Wilkinson, Edward Mr Alderman p 177, Mr Wilkinson, p 183(?); mercer, chamberlain 1581–2, burgess 1581, alderman 1589–90, 1598–9 and 1609 (after death of Michael Rowlandson) (*BR*, pp 28, 32).

Wilkinson, Robert Mr Robert Wilkinsonne p 179, Mr Wilkinson, p 183(?), Robert wylkinson p 201; sworn to Mercers 1593, chamberlain 1594–5, burgess 1597, alderman 1602–3 (*BR*, pp 58, 33, 23).

Wilson, Henry the Alderman p 168; chapman, Alderman 1575–6, displaced (as burgess) 1579 (*BR*, pp 22, 26).

Wilson, James Mr Iames

Willson p 177; butcher, chamberlain 1583–4, alderman 1587–8 and after the death of John Armer in the 1597–8 term (*BR*, pp 32, 27, 23).

Wilson, Thomas Mr Willson Alderman p 182, Mr Alderman p 183, Mr Wilson p 184; mercer, chamberlain 1604, burgess 1612, alderman 1614–15 (*BR*, pp 23, 29, 35).

Wilson, William Mr Alderman p 174; chapman, alderman 1583–4, 1593–4, J.P. 1591 (*BR*, p 27).

Translations

KENDAL

1625–6
Diocese of Chester: Consistory Court Paper   CRO: EDC5/1625/13
single sheet   *(22 October)*

Personal responses, taken under oath on the twenty-second of October
1625, of William Miller of the parish of Kendal to the presentment given
against him and exemplified by the churchwardens of Kendal, as follows:
(English)

Endnotes

168   Boke off Recorde   f 219

This ordinance is one of a series laid down on 2 February 1575/6 for the purpose of regulating the number of persons attending wedding dinners and drinkings, churchings, and other events. The bidden dinner or drinking was a local Westmorland custom whereby people were invited, often by a messenger on horseback ranging over a wide area, to celebrate at a particular home. The sum intent of the regulations, however, seems to be aimed less at genuine private functions of this kind than at commercialized events, specifically laid on 'for money offor'; the preamble to the series recites the wastefulness of victuals and money involved. Excepted from the ordinance transcribed are those functions relative to the public or formal life of the borough; numbers attending corporation dinners, for instance, far exceed the limit of twelve persons set down here for private events. 'Shotinges in long bowes' is probably a reference to the annual shooting at the butts, for whose construction there are regular entries in the chamberlains' accounts each spring. 'Merye nyghtes' drew informal groups of people together for drinking, music, and dancing. 'Nutcastes' and 'aplecastes' were means of fortune-telling, the former described in Robert Burns' poem, 'Halloween,' as one of the many ways in which the young sought to divine their marital fate:

> The auld Guidwife's weel-hoordet nits
>   Are round an' round divided,
> An' monie lads' an' lasses fates
>   Are there that night decided:
> Some kindle, couthie, side by side,
>   An' burn thegither trimly;
> Some start awa, wi' saucy pride,
>   An' jump out-owre the chimlie ...

168   Boke off Recorde   f 224v

Folio 224v originally ended (1576) with the words, 'dwellinge howse, And also,' continuing f 225 'in like maner,' etc. 'And also' was subsequently deleted here together with those lines that followed, indicated as 'vac*at*' (and enclosed in a marginal brace) p 169, ll. 34–6. The penalty that originally concluded the vacated passage was then inserted as the last complete line of f 224v.

169–70   Boke off Recorde   f 225

The sense and timing of deletions in ordinances transcribed here may be briefly summarized. In 1578 sections of the ordinance dated 14 June 1576 were repealed (p 169, ll.8,14), with the result that for corporation members the wearing of caps was abolished whatever the occasion, and the wearing of special gowns was restricted to Christmas, Easter, and Whitsun, and to fair- and play-days. The ordinance of 25 April 1586, passed with the intent of clarifying the meaning of the 1578 deletions, was entered immediately below at the bottom of f 225 (p 170, ll. 33–8). Thus in 1586 the existence of the play itself was not in question, as is also evident from the ordinance of 22 September 1586 that dealt with its proper licensing. Deletion of references to the wearing of gowns on fair- and play-days, taken out subsequent to 1586 (from the ordinances of 14 June 1576 (p 169, ll. 34–6), and 25 April 1586, f 225 (p 170, ll.36–7), cannot be dated with certainty. It may well have occurred in or after 1605, with the suppression of the play, though other references – to the Corpus Christi pageants, 2 February 1575/6, to 'custom' for the play, 18 May 1581, and to its licensing, 22 September 1586 – were never removed.

172   WMB/K [Book 1]   f [16]

The annual Martinmas audit was on this occasion marked by more than the customary drinking. The auditor was 'for my lord of Warwick then' – a cryptic allusion, but suggesting that the earl had an interest in the accounting procedures. Ambrose Dudley, earl of Warwick, had been granted (23 Elizabeth I) part of the demesne lands of Kendal Castle, comprising the park of Kendal with appurtenant buildings and tenements (Nicolson and Burn, vol 1, p 50). This grant may have brought conflict with the corporation, since that body had taken over the revenues of the old Marquis fee of the barony of Kendal (from which the earl's grant was allotted) in virtue of its charter of incorporation, 1575. The chamberlains' account for 1582–3 makes reimbursement for money 'layd out at easter terme for our sute with my lord of Warwick for milne...' (Book 1, f 5v, 15 September) and similar payments are made in the two succeeding fiscal years. A dispute over the operation and profits of the castle mill may have been the cause of the auditor's acting for the earl at the Martinmas audit of 1585.

   The entertainment was also laid on in tribute to special help given by the receivers. Henry, Lord Scrope, warden of the West March and captain of Carlisle (1563–92) intermittently borrowed sums of money from the corporation, varying from £10 to £20, and was not entirely scrupulous about their repayment (Book 1 ff 5v, 12v, 13v – record of debts) in spite of assurances: 'Lent to my lord warden dewe & promisid to be paid to ye receiuers or to his at martinmas next' (f 24v). The audit festivities of 1585 celebrated the receivers' success in extracting repayment of debt: receipts for this year acknowledge payment of £40 by 'ye receiueres at martinmas 85 for yat was lent to my lord wardon before' (Book 2, f [20]).

172   WMB/K [Book 1]   f 21v

'Pd other paimentes sence more as followes,' f 21v, is the title of this section. The two previous accounts, for wine, etc, and for the mill, end respectively in September and August; 'paimentes sence' constitute the final entries prior to the chamberlains' retirement in early October; their successors (1587–8) head their payments account from 4 October (Book 3, f [16], account title.)

172   WMB/K [Book 3]   f [16]
An immediately preceding payment for ringing suggests that the waits and drummer are here rewarded for celebrating Queen's Day on 17 November.

173   WMB/K [Book 3]   f [16v]
Excluding gentry and persons of professional status, 'Mr' is a term the accounts reserve for those who have served as aldermen. Three men qualified for the title 'mr wilson' (l. 3) on these grounds in 1587–8: James Wilson, butcher, the incumbent alderman, who would, however, have therefore been referred to as 'Mr Alderman' in the account; William Wilson, chapman, alderman 1583–4 (and subsequently in 1593–4); Henry Wilson, chapman, Kendal's first alderman 1575–6, (BR, pp 22–3, 26). The latter had a house on the east side of Stricklandgate, which is still standing, known as Black Hall (J. Whitwell, *The Old Houses of Kendal* (Kendal, 1866), p 20). The alderman (l. 12) was elected on the Monday before Michaelmas Day (1595, BR, p 154) and sworn in on the following Monday (charter of Elizabeth 1, 1575, BR, p 293); the alderman's dinner – the only dinner made the subject of an ordinance – was named in 1583 'at his furste and principall ffeaste' (BR, p 123) and held on the first Sunday after his oath-taking, or almost two weeks after the actual election. With very few exceptions, however, the only dinner mentioned in the chamberlains' accounts during this season appears to have taken place on election day itself; at least it is normally referred to as 'the election dinner,' and in some cases explicitly occurs at the time of the election (Book 6, f [12v], 1593; Book 14, f [20], 1600; Book 27, f [14], 1615; Book 36, f [24], 1624; Book 46, f [26v], 1634).

References to the alderman's dinner, on the other hand, are few. In 1588 (Book 3, f [16v]) it is mentioned as an event separate from the election dinner, as also in 1601 when the date is given as 11 October, evidence that enables us to reconstruct for this year an electoral pattern that abides by the rules: Monday, 28 September would have been election day (for which a dinner is noted), the oath-taking would have occurred on the following Monday, 5 October; hence the alderman's dinner is properly placed (according to the 1583 ordinance) on Sunday, 11 October. Two subsequent entries are less straightforward: for 1603 there is 'the Alderman's dinner at the Election' (Book 17, f [16v], not transcribed), and for 1628 a payment for waits 'at the mr Aldermans at the swearinge dinner' (in addition to payments for the election dinner, Book 40, f [19v]). Similarly in 1636 (when the office of mayor replaced that of alderman) an entry for 11 October refers to the dinner 'when mr Alderman vse to be sworne' (Book 48, f [20v]); the date does not correspond with either the proper date for the oath-taking or for the alderman's dinner.

The expense of provisioning, and in most cases of the entertainment, was presumably borne at his dinner by the alderman himself, a fact that may explain the dearth of explicit references to the event in the chamberlains' accounts. It is possible that the dinner was abandoned after 1601, either because of the personal expense involved, a telling factor in Kendal life, or because of the congestion (?indigestion) around Michaelmas, as election, aldermanic, and court leet dinners followed hard upon each other. This lapse may well have gone hand in hand with a development in which the aldermanic/mayoral election assimilated the elements of oath-taking and alderman's dinner, so that normally one date (the Monday before Michaelmas Day) provided the occasion for all three. Certainly the few details of attendance to be gleaned from the accounts show that the vicar and schoolmaster, for example, named in the 1583 ordinance as guests invited to the alderman's dinner, were also invited to the election dinner.

Items transcribed in the text are from an account headed 'Paymentes made by the ... Chamberlayns,' for the year beginning 4 October 1597 (f [16]). A separate untitled list of payments occurs on f [17] where several items are repeated, each preceded by a small circle in the left margin; f [17] makes the payment for candles (l. 14) to 'mr potter' (Edward Potter or Thomas Potter; see p 172 footnote to l. 27).

173   WMB/K [Book 4]   f [11]
The identification of 'Iohn collen' is uncertain: John Collynges is listed as paying 40 s under Inhabitants Free, Soutergate, East side (1575); and John Collings, to whom an apprentice was bound in 1587, appears under Tanners (c. 1575–92) (BR, pp 2, 68, 260). Completely insoluble is the question as to whether the loft was used for a performance or for storage of properties.

173   WMB/K [Book 4]   f [10v]
The lower half of f [10v] is a continuation of f [11] as indicated by a sign at the foot of the left margin, f [11], and repeated to the left of the 'menstrells' entry. Mention of 'the clarkes & outhers' suggests that the occasion was an election dinner, either that of Edward Wilkinson (alderman 1589–90) or of William Swainson (1590–1).

173   WMB/K [Book 5]   f [15v]
In 1581 Henry Robinson was elected provost of Queen's College, Oxford, which had traditional links with Cumberland and Westmorland; he was consecrated bishop of Carlisle 23 July 1598, and died of the plague on 19 June 1616 (John Le Neve, *Fasti Ecclesiae Anglicanae*, vol 3 (Oxford, 1854), pp 552, 242; Henry Barnes, 'Visitation of the Plague in Cumberland and Westmorland,' CWAAS O.S. 11 (1889), 184). Robinson's successor as provost, Henry Airey, 1598–1616, (Le Neve, vol 3, p 553) was also entertained by the corporation, Book 14, f [20], 1599–1600. Several local bequests were later made in aid of Kendal scholars attending the college, 1627–31 (BR, pp 234–53).

174   WMB/K [Book 6]   ff [12–12v]
The occasion of the banquet and masque must remain conjectural. But a contemporaneous event significant in the life of the town was the building of the New Hall, or Moot Hall, on a site at the southwest corner of the present Market Place. WMB/K [Book 5], f [1], 1591–2 notes that the hall was 'in most part builded ... this yeare' and a separate account for work done on it is found here, f [16v], and in WMB/K [Book 6], f [13v], 1592–3. The completion of the building may have been celebrated with an opening banquet and masque; possibly the 'plaiers in ye newe hall,' l. 15, had a part in the same festivities. For the visit of players this year see also ll. 29–30.

174   WMB/K [Book 7]   f [22]
Collation notes, providing additional information, are from the Extraordinary Payments

section of a duplicate Chamberlains' Account Book 1593–4 (WD/AG/Box 5, ff [18–20v]).

The play at the 'dragon' (l. 30) was evidently performed in the summer of 1593. The site of the inn is uncertain. It was still in business 1616–18 when 'Elsabeth Senistere' was 'wif of dragon' (Book 29, f [15v], and Book 30, f [23]). John Whitwell (*The Old Houses of Kendal*, p 18), writing in 1866, says that an old inn, 'The Green Dragon,' once stood on the northerly site adjoining what was in his time 'The Elephant Inn'; 'The Green Dragon' was demolished to make way for a house built 1798–9 that Whitwell knew as the location of the Lancaster Bank. The site of 'The Green Dragon' lies on the west side of Stricklandgate, just north of the present 'Woolpack Inn' and a stone's throw from the old Moot Hall.

175   WMB/K [Book 8]   f [17]
The 'mease' or 'messe,' (l. 21) a local term, denotes a portion serving four persons. It is used in the accounts as the basic unit in totalling expenses at municipal dinners. Detailed calculations are not given here, but see example on p 176, l. 19, where 14 s 6 d is the payment for (7 x 4 + 1) 29 persons, at 6 d per head.

175   WMB/K [Book 9]   f [18]
These entries exemplify a turn-out of border service, normally summoned in time of Scottish incursion. Its performance was later to complicate the issue of tenant right, the subject of the Kendal Stage Play of 1621 (see p 235 endnote to STAC 8/34/4, f 55) A survey of 16 Elizabeth 1, which included lands and tenements in Kendal, found that those tenants who were liable,

> from the age of 16 years till 60, hath been always accustomed, and so still
> owe to be, at all times, in their most defensible array for the wars, ready
> to serve their prince, on horseback and on foot, at the west borders of
> England for anent Scotland, on their own proper costs and charges, and
> so to be ready night and day, at the commandment of the lord warden of
> the said west marches, being warned thereunto by beacon, fire, post, or
> proclamation (Nicolson and Burn, vol 1, p 49).

Carlisle, the seat of the warden, fired its beacon on the High Tower of the castle, and thence communicated with Kendal by way of beacons at Penrith and Orton, and Whinfell, a few miles to the northeast of the town (J.F. Curwen, *The Castles and Fortified Towers of Cumberland, Westmorland* (Kendal, 1913), pp 332–7). The celebrated border brigand, Willie Armstrong (Kinmont Willie), was captured in the spring of 1596 and imprisoned in Carlisle Castle. His subsequent rescue on the night of 12 April may have been the occasion for Kendal's response to the beacon-alert. There is no indication of the number who set out from the town; the 8s 3d spent on bread and cheese was probably supplemented by individual provisions.

176   WMB/K [Book 10]   f [18v]
A number of payments in Book 10 are duplicated in Book 11, which comprises receipts for the same year. In each book individual payments are preceded by a small circle in the left margin. Since entries in Book 11 are fuller than in 10, we may presume that Book 11 represents the first record, from which entries were for the most part transferred to 10, the final form

of the year's accounts. In Book 11, f [18v], a payment is recorded for 17 November 1596 'to one that playd the drume thrught the towne being the quenes day.' Normally the bells were rung on this occasion, but for 1596–7 the record is confused. Book 11, f [23] notes for 7 September 1597 a payment to the alderman 'which was bestowed of the Ringars at the Church of quenes day'; that is, he apparently waited almost a year before collecting a sum he had dispensed on 17 November 1596. In Book 10, f [19], however, the payment is recorded as made 'to the ryngers at the church /7/ september 97,' apparently a distortion of material entered in Book 11.

176–7 WMB/K [Book 10] f [8]; WMB/K [Book 12] f [29]
Although from two separate accounts, these items (for waits and dinner) are both for the election dinner held at Edmund Hunt's. The main body of payments in Book 10 ends, f [19], with one of the last items dated 7 September. Those transcribed from f [8], in a different hand, are among twenty-seven crammed in one and a half columns on a sheet about 105mm x 150mm pinned to the lower part of the folio, written recto only, and headed 'payed by me as ffoleth.' Sporadic internal dating 15 October–6 November, with the reference to 'hwnts,' where the election dinner was held, suggests that this list was made up after the main body was entered. The period covered by f [8] thus overlaps the next chamberlains' year, since Book 12, f [29] starts with payments for the election and leet dinners (ie, October 1597).

The title of the Chamberlains' Book 1597–8, Book 12, f [1], names John Armer as alderman. According to the *Boke off Recorde* (p 23), Armer died of plague while in office and the remainder of his term was served by James Wilson. Andrew B. Appleby, 'Disease or Famine?', pp 414–24, interprets high mortality figures for Kendal and the northwest in the period 1596–8 as indicative of plague only in the summer and autumn of 1598, towards the end of Armer's term. In the account itself (p 177, ll. 8–9) the chamberlains erroneously ascribe the Michaelmas 1597 election to Wilson, rather than (correctly) to Armer.

'At my masters' (ie, at the alderman's house, p 176, l. 35) may refer to the occasion of the newly elected alderman's dinner (see endnote to p 173, WMB/K [Book 3], f [16v]).

177 WMB/K [Book 13] f [18v]
In general this account shows a chronological sequence of intermittently dated items. Those dated variously June–August, f [18v], show some slight irregularity, but the entry for musicians occurs roughly at the end of July: 'vij s' is written above the end of the original entry; 'payed them vj s viij d' is added on the next line, with the 'viij d' subsequently lost in the stitching of the book; '6s 8d' is added after 'them.'

178 WMB/K [Book 15] f [21]
The occasion of this beacon-alert was probably Scottish raids carried out on the night of 20 March 1600. Among those places that suffered were Scotby township in the area of Penrith where buildings were burned and men and livestock carried off, and Ricardgate, a suburb of Carlisle, where the raiders forced the citizens 'in their defencyve arrayes, for to repayre to the walls, and the beacon to be sett in fyre, for the warning of the wardenry' (J. Bain (ed), *Calendar of Letters and Papers relating to ... the Borders of England and Scotland*, vol 2 (London, 1894), pp 736–7, no 1342).

179   WMB/K [Book 17]   f [17]
A sign after 'as his note dothe Appeare' denotes that lines 2–3 are intended as a title for the
remaining items in the account, evidently copied straight from Robert Wilkinson's bill; the
first of these is dated in April. It is almost certain that not only the facing, buttons, and baize
but also the eight yards of black frieze were brought for the waits' coats (cf the purchase in
1600 of nine yards of grey frieze for their use, p 178, ll. 5–6).

179   WMB/K [Book 18]   f [19]
The name, Robert Hodgshone (l. 41), or variations, appeared under Armourers, Innkeepers,
Pewterers, and Wrights, Wheelers (BR, pp 72, 75, 80, 76). Edward Archer, the town drummer,
was sworn to the last-named association in January 1607, while Robert Hodgson entered in
the following September; one Milo Atkinson, 'musitian,' was also sworn in 1619 (BR, pp 76,
77).
   The sum of 10s 6d (p 180, l. 2) represents payment for six quarter-yards (1½ yards) at 7s
per yard. Even for one wait, however, the yardage was skimpy; the account does not name
the garment that was produced from it.

180   WMB/K [Book 19]   f [15]
All the material excerpted from the 1604–5 account was probably connected with the suppression of the Kendal play in 1605. Timing of payments for the commissioners' inquiry into the
play suggests that it coincided with the Easter session of the Kendal leet court, perhaps in order
to make use of the jurors assembled on that occasion. Journeys to York indicate that the inquiry
was of an ecclesiastical kind, possibly carried out by the high commission that sat at York.
William Ingall was a parish curate and master of the Kendal Free Grammar School – 'mr Ingall
play' was performed 1587–8 (p 173, l. 14). Ralph Tyrer ('mr Tyrar'), who went twice to York,
was vicar of Kendal 1592–1627; at his death his possessions included a pair of virginals (Edward
M. Wilson, 'Ralph Tyrer, B.D., Vicar of Kendal 1592–1627,' CWAAS Trans., N.S., 78 (1978),
p 72). William Addison's journey to Chester, the seat of the diocese, is also recorded for this
year (ff [15v], [16]), though at least part of his business concerned the removal of seats in the
parish church. See p 195, l. 42–p 196, l. 2, for another contemporary reference to this 1605
episode.

181   WMB/K [Book 22]   f [13]
The occasion of this payment is baffling. There is no evidence that Anne of Denmark, consort
of James 1, was in the region of Kendal at this time.

181   WMB/K [Book 22]   f [13v]
Entries are frequently dated internally in this account; five items surrounding the payment
to the earl of Lincoln's men are not sequential – the end-dates of this group are given as the
payment-period.

182   WMB/K [Book 25]   f [17]
The first four payments (ll. 21–4) are connected with the Michaelmas leet court and subsequent
dinner. Since all five are associated with one date (3 October) it is probable that the item 'for

buildinge the stage' concerns the same occasion: perhaps a dais (for the justices' bench, for example), or a stage for entertainment for which details are not entered.

183   WMB/K [Book 29]   f [14v]
The record of the king's ushers' visit is entered in a different hand from that in the rest of the account. The search for royal lodgings ended, according to tradition, in the choice of what was later known as Brownsword House on the west side of Stricklandgate, now the site of the Carnegie Library (A. Wainwright, *Kendal in the Nineteenth Century* (Kendal, n.d.), no 105). The coincidence of payments for 30 April suggests that the forthcoming royal visit was formally proclaimed at the Easter leet court.

184   WMB/K [Book 29A]   f [2v]
A single sheet, folded once, ff [1–2v], records a special 'Sessment,' levied in the summer on each of Kendal's thirteen wards and on particular individuals. The assessment was evidently levied to meet the expenses of the royal visit, but various routine corporation expenditures are also debited to it. Monies received are listed ff [2–1v], 26 June–6 August, in all £96 8s 8d; on the reverse side of the sheet is a list of expenditures, ff [2v–1], 6 August–16 October, for a total of £91 6s 9d; Reginald Lickbarrow, one of the chamberlains 1616–17, accounts for the surplus of £4 9s 11d on 17 November, ie, at the Martinmas audit. According to John Nichols in *The Progresses...of King James the First*, vol 3, (London, 1828), p 389, the king came to Kendal on 9 August, a feasible date on the basis of evidence discussed below (see endnote to p 216, Bolton Abbey MS 97). The date, 6 August, heading Assessment expenditures probably pin-points the first entries, eg, for the king's purse – grooms, trumpeters, and others being paid later when the king was in the town.

185   WMB/K [Book 29B]   f [1]
This is one of five items listed on a loose sheet of paper in Book 27 between ff [9–10]. It is evidently a receipt for reimbursement of monies laid out by 'Ro: Dawson' (Rowland Dawson, alderman 1620–1); a note acknowledging discharge, with signature, appears at the bottom, probably given at the Martinmas audit.

187   WMB/K [Book 33]   f [17v]
Entitled 'Monies payd for the milnes and kilnes,' this account is effectually a group of Extra-ordinary Payments; it is written ff [18v–17v], ie, from the back of the book, upside down. Month and date are given marginally for many items November–August; ff [18–17v], how-ever, bear dates in non-chronological sequence, November, March, February, April, ran-domly placed in the margin. Where editorially noted, dates should be treated with caution.

188   WMB/K [Book 34]   f [20v]
The date of the dinner at which the waits entertained is difficult to pin down, especially since payments made at or near Michaelmas, when the new chamberlains entered office, may be divided between old and new accounts. One of the following leet court dinners may have pro-vided the occasion: Michaelmas 1621, for which there are catering payments to Thomas Readman's wife, ff [20] and [20v]; Easter 1622 (similar payments to William Chamber's wife, f [20]; Michaelmas 1622 (payments to Thomas Readman's wife, Book 35, f [24]).

188   STAC/8/34/4   f 55

Folio 48 is a draft of the same document (cursive hand, final formulaic clauses abbreviated).

The Kendal Stage Play of July 1621 was one of a series of incidents that marked tenant unrest in the barony of Kendal and adjacent border areas at this time. It was becoming increasingly difficult for customary tenants to defend their rights, since both king and landlords claimed a link between such 'tenant right' and the performance of border service (see p 176, ll. 1–14, and p 178, ll. 10–18). The latter had been in a long process of decay, hastened by the union of the Scottish and English thrones in 1603 and the theoretical extinction of possibilities of conflict between the two nations. In November 1616, upon composition, Charles, prince of Wales had confirmed to his tenants in the Marquis and Richmond fees of the barony their customary heritable estate and right to fine certain; tenants of other landlords were eager to gain similar confirmation. A meeting at Staveley Chapel in January 1619/20 led to the presentation of a bill in the House of Commons on the tenants' behalf, which was soon thrown out, and a petition to the king. The reaction of James I – a proclamation in July 1620 urging landlords to convert customary tenancies to leasehold – provoked further protest: first, a tenants' remonstrance, characterized by the landlords as a libel; and second, the performance of the Kendal Stage Play in July 1621, a pointed comment on those who sought to extinguish tenant right. The landlords thereupon initiated an action in Star Chamber, prosecuted by Sir Thomas Coventry, appointed attorney-general in January 1620-1. By statute (3 Henry VII c. 1) the competence of Star Chamber extended to riot and unlawful assembly. Summons to the court involved the preparation of lists of interrogatories from information initially laid before the authorities; these lists in turn served as a basis for the sworn examination of those persons named as defendants and the gathering of information from others (deponents), a process carried out locally.

STAC/8/34/4 is primarily the record of examination and depositions taken at Kendal in 1622. The authorities seem to have suspected that the incidents dealt with in the interrogatories were part of a conspiracy in which all the defendants were ultimately linked. Nevertheless, of the defendants named in the file, Samuel Knipe, James Smith, Thomas Prickett, and John Cartmell were principally charged in connection with 'riotous assembly' at Staveley Chapel; Anthony Wetherall, vicar of Kirkby Stephen, Westmorland, with the making of the libel; and Richard Helme with taking part in the Kendal Play.

Other persons are named in interrogatories or depositions in connection with the play. Among these Sir Francis Ducket of Grayrigg and Sir James Bellingham of Levens seem to have played a focal role. Thomas Ducket (not identified in the documents), an actor in the play, was probably a tenant of Sir Francis, possibly a relation. Certainly Helme, the defendant in this incident, and Henry Ward, bailiff of Sir Francis, were expressly named among the tenants alleged to have taken part, together with James, the young grandson of Sir Francis. Among those attending the play was Lady Ducket (Marian, second wife of Sir Francis and sister of Sir James Bellingham), the recusant wife of a conformist husband (J.A. Hilton, 'The Cumbrian Catholics,' *Northern History*, 16 (1980), 46, 49). Sir Francis himself, with his son Anthony, pressured the Kendal authorities to allow the play to be staged. Both the Ducket and Bellingham households provided clothing for the actors; Allan Bellingham, son of Sir James, attended the performance; and Jerome Garnett, brother of Jasper Garnett, the author of the play, was servant or agent of Sir James and of Sir Henry Bellingham, Sir James' son and heir.

The play itself, a comment on the rapacity of landlords, depicted the exploitation of tenants in exceedingly graphic terms. It is not easy to see why local gentry should have lent their support to this vehicle of tenant protest. It must be assumed that the Duckets and Bellinghams were representative of a party of local landlords whose close ties to the area alerted them to the dangers inherent in a protracted and bitter dispute. Their hope must have been that the airing of grievances would hasten the process of settlement. In fact the whole tenor of those interrogatories concerned with incidents other than the play suggests that the royal government was sceptical about the circumstances of the Star Chamber suit itself, evidently suspecting an agreement between the parties designed to thwart the intent of the royal proclamation and to force a speedy but equitable decision from the court on the whole issue of tenant right.

In 1625 Star Chamber postponed indefinitely consideration of all criminal offences, at the same time removing from the dispute all question of border service. The court confirmed to the tenants their heritable estate, with the hope that the parties would come to some agreement about fine certain. Sir James Bellingham and Sir Henry, his son, were two of the three landlords then present before the court, Samuel Knipe and John Cartmell attending on behalf of all the tenants (Nicolson and Burn, vol 1, p 57).

Kendal Castle (l. 26) dates from the thirteenth century. Situated on a high natural mound, the castle and its demesne lands were separated from the township of Kendal to the west by the river Kent. The castle was the childhood home of Katherine Parr, Henry VIII's last wife. Her brother William, marquess of Northampton, disgraced by implication in the plot to secure the throne for Lady Jane Grey, lost his estates in the barony of Kendal (the so-called Marquis fee) by escheat to the crown. These were restored to him in Mary's reign, but by his widow's exchange of properties with Elizabeth I the castle and its lands once more came to the crown. Part of the demesne, the park of Kendal, was granted to the earl of Warwick (see endnote to p 172, WMB/K [Book 1], f 16); thereafter, according to Nicolson and Burn, nothing is known of the ownership of the castle until the reign of Charles II. It is evident, however, that by 1572, just before passing into royal hands, the castle itself was already approaching ruin; a survey describes what remained: 'The out walls embatteled 40 foot square. And within the same no building left; saving only on the north side is situate the front of the gate-house, the hall, with an ascent of stairs to the same, with a buttery and pantry at the end thereof; one great chamber, and two or three lesser chambers and rooms of ease adjoining to the same: being all in decay, both in glass and slate, and in all other reparations needful. Under the hall are two or three small rooms of cellars' (Nicolson and Burn, vol 1, p 46). The domestic buildings were apparently never subsequently inhabited or restored, and the play acted 'at' Kendal Castle was therefore almost certainly staged outdoors in the castle precincts, possibly on land in which the corporation had acquired an interest at the time the charter was granted (1575).

189   STAC/8/34/4   f 49

The sequence of folios 49–54 is confused. The 'Ioynt' answer, f 49, incorporates various material from defendants Smith, Prickett, Cartmell, Thomas Lucas, and Helme. The 'severall Answares' of the title apparently continue as individual examinations of these defendants, based on twenty-one interrogatories, on ff 50–50v (Cartmell), f 52 (Smith), f 54 (Smith and Prickett), and f 54v (Lucas and Helme) – not necessarily originally in that order: f 52 is headed as the examinations of the five defendants (named) to the information of the attorney-general, with the date 29 April 20 James I (1622); f 50v, among other endorsements, has 'The

aunsweres and Deposicions of ... Thomas Prickett ... & others def*endantes* to the Inform*acion*
of S*ir* Thomas Coventry ....' Thus ff 49–50, 52, and 54 probably constituted an original dos-
sier, into which ff 51 and 53, together listing (recto only) the twenty-one interrogatories for
these five defendants, were mistakenly interpolated. The left side of the folio is intermittently
torn with portions of margin and script missing. A small triangular tear at l. 10 here is part
of a larger damaged area measuring from the foot of the folio 180mm vertically and penetrating
to a maximum of 9 letters horizontally.

189 STAC/8/34/4 f 14
A separate list of interrogatories was prepared for Samuel Knipe, f 17; the eleventh of these,
however, is identical with the eleventh interrogatory (f 51), transcribed on p 189, with the
exception of some slight spelling variants and the interlineation of the clause, 'wherefore weare
they the said landlordes represented soe to bee in hell,' incorporated in the text on f 51. Samuel
Knipe of Fairbank-in-Staveley was chosen 'agent' by those who assembled at Staveley Chapel
in 1619/20; he died and was buried in Crosthwaite Church 6 November 1645 (Nicolson and
Burn, vol 1, p 53; *Local Chronology,* p 111).

190 STAC/8/34/4 f 54v
Anthony Ducket deposed that Richard Helme (l. 31) was tenant of his father, Sir Francis
Ducket (p 194, ll. 14–15). At his death in 1635 Sir Francis was seised of a messuage or tenement
in Whinfell, in the tenure of the relict of Henry Holme (Inq. p.m. 24 May 12 Charles 1, 1636,
cited in J.F. Curwen (ed), *Records relating to the Barony of Kendale,* vol 4, p 219). 'Helme'
is occasionally spelt 'Holme' in the Star Chamber record.

191 STAC/8/34/4 ff 40–40v
Illegible words, f 40, are supplied from f 29, a second, on the whole less legible version, apparently identical in substance. The sole deposition recorded in STAC/8/34/4 keyed to this
list of interrogatories (thirty-three in all) is that of James Anderson the younger of Clayton,
Westmorland, taken on 23 April 1623 (f 30); he answers only the first and seventh interrogatories, evidently knowing nothing of the play.

191 STAC/8/34/4 f 26v
A draft version (with abbreviated formulaic clauses and minor variations in spelling but none
in substance) of these interrogatories, numbering thirty-five in all, is on f 24.

192 STAC/8/34/4 f 33
Jerome Garnett was named by Jasper Garnett as his brother (f 19, answer to seventh interrogatory). Jerome described himself as a servant of the Bellinghams, 'employed sometimes
(amongst other services) to looke to such Causes as the said S*ir* Iames Bellingham ... or S*ir*
Henrie Bellingham have in Suite at London' (f 33, reply to sixteenth interrogatory). In answer
to the first interrogatory he admitted that he knew all the defendants named in the suit (f 33).

195 STAC/8/34/4 f 18
The eight interrogatories to which this deposition replies are not preserved in STAC/8/34/4.
They were probably prepared specifically for Jasper Garnett as author of the suspect play.

The record, in an untidy hand with frequent emendations, is sometimes confused as to whether Garnett is properly defendant or deponent. Normally however, 'defendant' is corrected to 'deponent', and certainly Garnett is not named elsewhere in the file as one of the defendants in the case. Richard Helme (answer to the eleventh interrogatory, p 190) stated that Jasper Garnett, resident in the barony of Kendal where he had been born, was a schoolmaster in Lancashire at the time of writing the four books that comprised the play. Elsewhere (p 189), Helme asserts that the play was written 'aboue fower yeares agoe,' that is, about or before 1617. In 1616, however, Garnett was master of the Free Grammar School in Kendal: a memorandum entered in his own hand in Book 29, WMB/K, f[13v], dated 5 March, acknowledges receipt of one half-years wages; this is followed by other entries dated 30 October for 'mr garnett the scoollmaster.' It is therefore feasible that the play was conceived while Garnett was resident in Kendal. Helme's omission of the fact that Garnett had been the local schoolmaster may have been a deliberate attempt to play down his Kendal connection and to forestall any further inquiry into this period of Garnett's career and his association with local residents.

196   STAC/8/34/4   f 18v
A somewhat garbled response to the seventh interrogatory starts on p 197, l. 17. In essence it appears that Samuel Knipe, in his own defence, sought to subpoena Jasper Garnett in order to obtain his evidence about the play and thus prove that Knipe himself was not involved in that particular incident. Jerome Garnett, informing his brother of the writ but not its intent, hoped to counsel him first on how to respond. However, Jasper, communicating the contents of Jerome's letter to Knipe and learning that his evidence was necessary to the latter's defence, determined to tell the truth. Jerome understandably was angered and dismayed, both at the possible consequences for Jasper and his own employers, Sir James and Sir Henry Bellingham, and at the disclosure of his own attempt to interfere with the due process of law.

198–9   WMB/K [Book 36]   ff [23v–4]
Entries for the Easter leet court dinner, the venison feast, and the election dinner at Michaelmas 1624 (all occasions when the waits performed) are haphazardly entered. They may be grouped as follows: Easter leet court dinner, p 198, ll. 36–9; p 199, l. 8; venison feast, p 198, ll. 33–4; p 199, ll. 1–2, 5, 13–15; election dinner, p 199, ll. 3–4, 16–18.

199   WMB/K [Book 37]   f [24]
'Ned Ienninges' (l. 28) may conceivably be Edward Jennings, listed under Tanners, sworn 1594, but is more probably Edward Jennynge, sworn 1622 to the same trade (BR, p 68). According to his will dated 1 March 1642/3, Edward Jennings, tanner, held houses in the Market Place and Finkle Street, Kendal, and in Kirkland (Curwen, *Records relating to the Barony of Kendale*, vol 4, p 111).

201   WMB/K [Book 39]   f [21v]
The name, John Troughton (l. 32), occurs under Cordiners, sworn 1594, and Mercers, sworn 1599; and also under Glovers, sworn 1620 (BR, pp 64, 59, 70). The latter was probably the same John Troughton who served as chamberlain in 1624 (BR, p 37), and who, we may suspect, being close to the corporation, secured the provisioning of the Michaelmas leet dinner in that year.

202   WMB/K [Book 39]   f [22]
The last eight words ('and for drinke and breade to the Iury,' l. 12) were added to the item
as a fifth line after four lines detailing the '13 mease' were bracketed; the bracket was extended
to encompass this addition, and payment then entered for the whole sum.

203   WMB/K [Book 40]   ff [19–19v]
The order of items is confusing, as are varying references to venison feast(s). Two gifts of venison were certainly received, from Sir Francis Ducket (p 203, l. 34) and from Henry, Lord
Morley and Monteagle, (p 203, ll. 9–10), perhaps from Hornby Castle, Lanc, or from either
of his two manors of Farleton, Lanc and Farleton, Westmld. Fiddlers are paid for attendance
at two feasts, (p 203, l. 29) and Peter Huggon supplies wine on these occasions, (p 204,
l. 1). William Chamber's wife prepares and the waits attend only one venison feast (p 203,
ll. 18–19); the latter also attend the election (swearing) dinner, (p 203, ll. 31–2), as well as
the Michaelmas 1627 and Easter 1628 leet dinners, (p 202, l. 29, p 203, l. 7). This account contains the first record of smoking at a corporation dinner. Detailed accounts (until 1636) reveal
that the habit rapidly became popular at all principal dinners.

207   WMB/K [Book 44]   f [23]
The first 'Christopher' tobacco, from what is now St Kitts in the Caribbean, reached England
in 1626 (W.N. Sainsbury (ed), *Calendar of State Papers, Colonial*, vol 1 (London, 1860),
pp 83, 94, 124). At 3 d per oz, it was the cheapest of the tobaccos purchased by the corporation;
'Varinas,' from Venezuela, was a Spanish import, highly priced at 1 s per oz (see p 212, l. 17).

209   WMB/K [Book 45]   f [25]
I have been unable to trace any Waite (p 209, l. 20), Thwaite or similarly named person of
this date who might have received a stipend from the corporation. '(The) ma*ster* waite' may
be the sense of this entry, though there is no record of a Kendal wait receiving money other
than in the form of a gratuity at the time of playing. It is also possible that a 'Mr Waite' was
master of the Free Grammar School in Kendal at this period; the term 'stipend' was used earlier
in the chamberlains' accounts in connection with this post (Mr Ingall's 'stipend,' Book 3,
f [17], and Book 10, f [18v]).

210   WMB/K [Book 46]   f [31v]
The title, 'An account what is paid by vs this year 1633,' heads payments written upside down
from the back of the book ff [31v–26].

211   WMB/K [Book 47]   f [21v]
The Payments account is written ff [21v–20v], upside down (ff [7–8] from the back of the
book).

213   WMB/K [Book 48]   f [20v]
Kendal received a new charter of incorporation from Charles I. The chamberlains' account
shows that the first mayor, as appointed under the charter, replaced the alderman at Michaelmas 1636 (ll. 3–4).

213   MS 390 f 84

This is the second of four 'questions moued,' all enclosed in a marginal brace. Dealing with points of canonical significance, the questions presumably formed the basis of a discussion or more formal college debate in which Crosfield took part. Evidently the format of the Kendal Corpus Christi play, still remembered by local men, remained a matter of some academic interest even thirty years after its suppression.

214   SP1/134, No 1370

The material transcribed here illustrates the continued resentment and unrest that characterized northern areas in the aftermath of the Pilgrimage of Grace. From the letter's inscription it is evident that the rebel song, named variously 'crummok' or 'crumwell' in the articles that follow, libelled Thomas Cromwell, the chief and much hated architect of Henry VIII's Reformation; the letter is addressed to him as Lord Privy Seal, the office he had assumed in 1536. Sir James Leyburn, the writer of the letter, held the manor of Cunswick in the environs of Kendal and was a justice of the peace. In April 1537 the bailiff of Kendal, William Colyns, examined in the Tower of London, gave information concerning the rebellion and its aftermath in the Kendal area; his evidence reveals the existence of both religious and economic grievances among the population. The Kendal townsmen with the surrounding countryside had joined the rebels in the autumn of 1536; their number included some of the local gentry, even ultimately Sir James Leyburn himself and Richard Ducket, the other justice of the peace named in the letter. The royal pardon, proclaimed in Kendal in late December by Clarencieux Herald, was unwillingly accepted. Two subsequent incidents in the parish church, in which first the vicar and then a curate 'bid the beads' for the pope, indicate continued open hostility towards the liturgical changes called for by the Reformation. Early in 1537, at Cartmel in Lancashire, claimed by Leyburn as the former abode of the minstrel Alexander Stotson, complaints about the king's farmers had quickly culminated in the execution of four of the priory's brethren and eight yeomen (J. Gairdner (ed), *Calendar of Letters and Papers ... Henry VIII*, vol 12, pt 1 (London, 1890), no 914, pp 414–17). Leyburn's zeal in reporting the relatively minor incident described in the articles perhaps stems from his own dubious past performance.

216   Bolton Abbey MS 97, ff 106v, 200v

The relevance of these items to the entertainment given by Francis Clifford, fourth earl of Cumberland, for James I at Brougham Castle in 1617 is fully discussed by Ian Spink, 'Campion's Entertainment at Brougham Castle 1617,' (John H. Long (comp), *Music in English Renaissance Drama* (Lexington, 1968), pp 57–74). Spink suggests that the earl's son conceived the entertainment, but that Campion prepared the text and supervised the performance at the castle. The text of the songs (published in London in 1618), which George Mason, a musician in the earl's household, set to music, indicates that the event took place during the nights of 6–7 August, the king departing on 8 August. The first night probably saw complimentary table music with speeches, the second an anti-masque followed by a main masque celebrating the king's virtues. Spink discusses the possible influence of this work on Jonson's 'Gipsies Metamorphosed' of 1622. As he notes (p 60), the suggested length of the king's stay at Brougham contradicts John Nichols, *The Progresses ... of King James the First*, vol 3 (London, 1828), p 393, who states that the king left the castle on 7 August.

Nichols' statement that the king went on to stay at Appleby, another Clifford castle, is also in doubt. The Clifford household accounts show that well before the arrival of the king the earl left Skipton for Brougham by way of Wharton, and then continued to Carlisle where, as lord lieutenant of the county, he was to greet the king (Bolton Abbey MS 97, f 172, 30 July), later returning from Brougham to Londesborough (ibid, f 172v, 13–16 August). An account for 7 July 1617–27 September 1618 shows that £99 6s 8d was spent on provisioning the king's visit to Brougham (Bolton Abbey MS 166, f [4]); for Appleby, expenses totalling £10 14s 11d are given only for 18 January–21 March 1617/18, thus affording no evidence that the king was there in August 1617. Discounting a visit to Appleby, we may still accept the fact that the king stayed at nearby Wharton Hall on the night of 8 August (Nichols, vol 3, p 393) before proceeding to Kendal.

217   U269 F48/2 nf
Lady Anne came to Brougham Castle shortly after her mother died there, in July 1616, and attended the burial at Appleby. She set out for London on 9 December and did not return north again until 1643.

218   SP14/86 No 34   single sheet
Bampton provided the parish church for tenants on the Howard estate of Thornthwaite in Westmorland (see endnote to p 138, Howard C706 [Book 3] f 38v). Lord William Howard's Catholicism – he entered the church in 1584 – combined with his powerful border interests, made him a prime target of broad government suspicion, for which in fact he seems to have given no reasonable grounds. The material transcribed here, part of a document alleging his recusancy, comprises about a dozen articles naming other recusants with whom he is supposed to have had contact and detailing activities of a dubious nature. The whole, endorsed '1616 Mr Saundersones Note,' supplies insufficient detail for the precise dating of the alleged event; since the calendar year ended in March, either Christmas 1615 or Christmas 1616 may have provided the occasion for the misrule episode, depending on whether the document was drawn up before or after 25 December 1616. There is also a second version of the whole document (SP14/40, No 11) in which this and the other accusations are repeated – the enlivening of the Bampton Christmas service in substantially the same detail (and thus not collated here), but with other charges somewhat differently worded or condensed. Calendared (with query) under February 1608 (*Calendar of State Papers, Domestic Series...James I*, vol 8, 1603–10, p 479) the document itself is undated, and Ornsby (*Household Books*, pp 423–5) transcribes it as such. Indeed SP14/40, No 11 has the mark of a final version of the charges (both as to wording and to script), suggesting that it was based on SP14/86, No 34, whose rushed and almost illegible hand probably represents a preliminary draft. The latter is transcribed here, both as representing the earlier version, and also as providing an alternative reading to that given by Ornsby. In any case the bulk of both versions seems to be a taradiddle of hearsay and innuendo, probably intended to be kept in reserve as ammunition against a powerful border magnate should the need arise.

218   *Ancient Funerall Monuments* p 405
Weever's comment on the Corpus Christi play is interpolated in his discussion of monuments found in St Michael's Church, Queen-Hithe, in the diocese of London.

219   Add. MS 4460   ff 7–7v

Certain words are underlined throughout the manuscript: in this passage, 'Cartmell,' 'Cartmel-fell,' 'Kendall,' and 'Corpus-Christi play' (ll. 12,25,33).

The Civil War was well advanced when John Shaw, the manuscript's author, while living in Manchester, was approached by a deputation from the parish of Cartmel, asking him to spend seven or eight weeks preaching and instructing the people there. Shaw agreed to do so, provided that an 'able man' temporarily filled his own post. He does not elaborate on why Cartmel was without its own pastor, though presumably the circumstances of the war were a contributory factor. Shaw records an abrupt end to his mission after eight weeks (towards the end of June). His own flight into Yorkshire, and his wife's escape by sea, were occasioned by the passage through the vicinity of royalist troops commanded by Prince Rupert, on their way to raise the siege of York. The prince's forces were in fact defeated at the ensuing battle of Marston Moor on 2 July.

GLOUCESTERSHIRE

Acknowledgments

This edition could not have been produced without the considerable resources and assistance provided by the Records of Early English Drama office; I owe a great debt of gratitude to my colleagues there. First of all, I must thank Alexandra Johnston, general editor of the project, for her willingness to take a chance on an unproven graduate student and for her continuing guidance and encouragement. REED associate editor Sally-Beth MacLean sifted through my text with a keen eye for inconsistencies and confusion, coordinated the work of many people at the REED office and in England, settled matters of dispute reasonably and diplomatically, and generally brought a sense of calm orderliness to the whole endeavour. I am grateful to Abigail Young for correcting my meagre Latin, for providing the Latin glossary, and especially for engaging in a protracted struggle with Christopher Windle's awkward and verbose Latin; Appendix 3 could not have appeared without her efforts. Anne Quick did most of the paleographical checking and provided the English glossary. REED's bibliographers – Theodore De Welles, William Cooke, Mary Blackstone, and Ian Lancashire – furnished many valuable leads and checked the accuracy of all references in the final text. Elza Tiner helped prepare the patrons' list and Donna Best and William Rowcliffe typeset the text. Many others at the REED office contributed to the production of the edition and to my peace of mind, including Sheena Levitt, Darlene Money, Heather Phillips, and Nancy Rovers-Goheen. Penny Cole checked the translation of Appendix 3.

I am most grateful to the following libraries and owners for permission to quote extracts from documents in their possession: the Gloucestershire Record Office, the Corporation of Gloucester, the Bishop of Gloucester, the Dean and Chapter of Gloucester Cathedral, the Gloucestershire County Library, the Marquess of Bath, the Trustees of the Berkeley Estate, the Vicar of Tewkesbury, the Staffordshire Record Office, the Hereford Cathedral Library, the British Library, and the Public Record Office. Crown copyright material in the Public Record Office appears by permission of the Controller of Her Majesty's Stationery Office. I wish to thank the staffs of all these institutions for their assistance and concern; in particular, my thanks go to those at the Gloucestershire Record Office who made my work there pleasurable as well as productive: Victoria Thorpe, Tom Bowers, Heather Martin, Nicholas Kingsley,

Graham Whitehead, Margaret Richards, and Julie Craig. Special thanks are due to Mr. D.J.H. Smith, the county archivist, for his considerable efforts on my behalf regarding the Berkeley Castle muniments in addition to the record office's holdings. Canon David Welander was very helpful with the documents in his care as Gloucester Cathedral Librarian, while Neville Chapman speeded my researches at the county library. I am also grateful to R.H. Harcourt Williams, Librarian and Archivist to the Marquess of Salisbury, for his help. Brian Frith of Gloucester was not only an unfailing source of knowledge about the history and records of Gloucestershire, but a genial and entertaining companion as well.

A number of people kindly checked transcriptions and other details in England: David Klausner, J.A.B. Somerset, Alexandra Johnston, and Annette Jacob. Valuable advice on both editing and the interpretation of records came from John Wasson, William Streitberger, Peter Meredith, Peter Happé, Otto Reinert, and David Fowler. Peter Clark made useful suggestions about Gloucester's history for the introduction. I particularly wish to acknowledge the aid of John Coldewey, who supervised the dissertation that developed as an offshoot of this edition. He recognized that editing dramatic records suited my interests and temperament, masterminded my application for a grant, shepherded me through the extensive preparatory study needed for research of this kind, and gave acute and sensitive criticism of the results.

Having acknowledged my gratitude to all those who have helped to make this edition as accurate as possible, I take full responsibility for any errors of commission or omission that may remain.

My research in England was made possible by a REED grant funded by the National Endowment for the Humanities and administered by Stanley J. Kahrl and the Center for Medieval and Renaissance Studies at Ohio State University. A major editorial project grant from the Social Sciences and Humanities Research Council of Canada supported other research and publication costs of this volume.

Finally, I wish to thank my wife, Karen, whose enthusiasm for this project never waned, even when mine threatened to after days of empty page-turning in the record office. She searched indexes and proofread, and gave constant support throughout the preparation of this edition.

PHG/University of Puget Sound   1984

Introduction

The Boundaries

This edition delimits Gloucestershire according to pre-1642 boundaries, which followed largely the same lines as they did in this century, prior to the creation, in 1974, of the new county of Avon. The only major differences from modern Gloucestershire occurred in the north-east corner of the county, where the boundaries with Worcestershire and Warwickshire were complicated by the scattered holdings of the bishop of Worcester.[1] Bristol, although often associated geographically with Gloucestershire, became a county in its own right in 1373, and as such, its records will appear in a separate volume.

The dissolution of the monasteries in 1541 altered the boundaries of ecclesiastical administration for Gloucestershire and its environs. Bristol's northern suburbs became part of the new Bristol diocese. Administration of lands formerly controlled by the dioceses of Worcester and Hereford became the responsibility of the newly created diocese of Gloucester, with the exception of some areas along the Herefordshire border, which remained within the jurisdiction of the Hereford diocese. Reapportioning of ecclesiastical control notwithstanding, all these areas were administered civilly by Gloucestershire and are thus included in this collection.

Historical and Geographical Perspectives

Gloucestershire is traditionally divided into three distinct topographical areas. The Severn Vale, a relatively flat agricultural region, stretches from Bristol in the south to Tewkesbury in the north and includes most of the places with extensive surviving records of dramatic activity. Gloucester itself lies on the east bank of the Severn, as do the castles at Berkeley and Thornbury further south. To the east of the river valley are the Cotswold Hills which rise sharply, to as much as a thousand feet, along the Cotswold Edge, before sloping gently off to the south-east, toward the Thames. Wool production dominated the economy in this region, which was dotted with villages but possessed only a single substantial town, Cirencester. The Forest of Dean occupies the south-western corner of the county between the Severn and the Wye, and is hilly country, ill-suited to agriculture. Before the Industrial Revolution only a few villages existed in the area, surviving principally on forestry and coal-mining. The forest itself was a royal preserve, but nearly disappeared in the late sixteenth century, when it was heavily logged to build the ships that opposed the Spanish Armada.

Before the mid-sixteenth century, only Gloucester's position as the seat of the assizes and quarter sessions served to unify three areas of such disparate character, over which the Crown, the nobles, the bishops of Worcester and Hereford, the abbots of Gloucester, Tewkesbury, Cirencester, and Winchcombe all exercised varied and sometimes conflicting degrees of control. With the creation of a see at Gloucester and the city's growth as a commercial centre, the county became linked by both civil and ecclesiastical administration, and by patterns of trade into a somewhat less arbitrary unit.

Drama, Music, and Ceremony

Gloucester

DRAMA

Gloucester's heyday occurred under the early Norman kings, when it was the site of the Christmas court, the place where William I supposedly ordered the compiling of the Domesday Book, and where Matilda collected her forces to march against Stephen. By the time of Henry III, however, midwinter no longer found the court at Gloucester and the occasional parliaments still held there became briefer and less frequent; the last two recorded, in 1407 and 1420, lasted only two weeks before removing to Westminster.[2] Gloucester's political importance meant that it anticipated Bristol in such constitutional developments as obtaining a borough charter (in 1155) and a guild merchant (by 1200).[3] However, as Gloucester's political significance waned in the late Middle Ages, it was increasingly overshadowed by Bristol with its more advantageous position as a port. The variety of problems which caused a general decline in the population and prosperity of towns throughout England in the fifteenth century affected Gloucester as well: competition from rural industry (especially the Cotswold woollen mills), the rising cost of urban residence, and repeated epidemics.[4] Still, Gloucester remained an important cloth-making and metal-working town with a flourishing regional market. It also had a tourist trade with pilgrims coming to the shrine of Edward II in St Peter's Abbey. When the burgesses petitioned the king for remission of part of the fee-farm in 1487, they complained of 'the great ruyne and decay ... of the said town, within fewe yeris decaied to the nombre of ccc. dwellyng place,' but exaggerated complaints were the standard rhetoric of such petitions.[5]

Unfortunately, few civic records of the types likely to contain references to entertainment survive from before 1500 and only a single reference exists to dramatic performance in the city earlier than that year. An alms roll of Edward I indicates that in December 1283 the king rewarded clerks at Gloucester for performing the miracles of St Nicholas and for their boy-bishop. While the roll does not identify these clerks, the reference is a valuable one, for it is not only the earliest record of drama anywhere in Gloucestershire, but also an important addition to the scanty evidence for a St Nicholas play tradition in England.

The extant records of Gloucester become much fuller after 1483, when the city received a new charter, granting it additional privileges; among them was the jurisdiction over two hundreds of the county, the so-called county 'inshire' of the city of Gloucester. The wealth of these lands and of monastic lands acquired at the Dissolution benefited the city, as did the influx of people on business with the newly created diocese and the general increase of inland trade under the Tudor peace. In 1580, Queen Elizabeth made Gloucester a customs port, giving the city control of trade on a major part of the Severn.[6] The population increased from just under 4000 in the 1530s to slightly more than 5000 in the early seventeenth century.[7] A growth in dramatic activity, and in music and public ceremonial as well, appears to have accompanied this population increase; even when we allow for the fact that there are many more extant documents from the second half of the sixteenth century, we can still find a pattern of growth over the years covered by those records.

The chamberlains' accounts, which provide the greatest number of references, survive from 1550, and reveal an impressive increase in the number of professional playing companies visiting the city from that year to the last two decades of the century. The average number of rewards given to players in a year during the 1550s was less than one; in the 1560s it rose to nearly two, and in the 1570s to almost three companies a year. The peak period for the touring professionals was the 1580s and '90s, when the average number of troupes visiting Gloucester increased to four a year, and as many as seven different companies appeared in a single year, in 1584–5.

The growth of dramatic activity was entirely in the form of these visits by professional players. No evidence of a Corpus Christi cycle can be found in the borough custumnal or in early guild ordinances – the types of records which provide information about guild involvement in the drama at York and Chester.[8] Nor do the churchwardens' accounts of Gloucester parishes contain references to parish plays, like those at Tewkesbury.[9] The records do, however, yield considerable evidence concerning the professional players. By combining the chamberlains' accounts with civic ordinances regulating players and the well-known eyewitness description of a performance at Gloucester by R. Willis, we can reconstruct a detailed picture of the conditions faced by touring players when they came to the city.

Before they could perform, players had to obtain permission from the mayor, a condition which had become national law in 1559. Many troupes must have ignored the law when they came to Gloucester, however, since in 1580 the common council passed an ordinance which expressly required visiting companies to seek a license from the mayor. Then, as Willis tells us, 'if the Mayor like the Actors, or would shew respect to their Lord and Master, he appoints them to play their first play before himselfe and the Aldermen and common Counsell of the City; and that is called the Mayors play, where every one that will comes in without money, the Mayor giving the players a reward as hee thinks fit to shew respect unto them.'[10] It is these rewards that we find recorded in the chamberlains' accounts.

Players could give performances which were not 'Mayor's plays,' subject to the following limitations imposed by the 1580 ordinance. The total number of performances permitted to a company depended on the stature of its patron: the queen's players were allowed to perform three plays in three days or less; the players of a baron or a noble of greater rank could play twice in two days; while players whose patron was beneath the rank of baron could perform only once. An unwritten and somewhat less rigid scale appears to have applied to the amounts of the rewards given by the city. The queen's men consistently received larger rewards than other companies. Even when the lord admiral's men came to Gloucester in 1590–1, led by the great Edward Alleyn, they got only the same 30s given to the queen's players that year. The main exceptions to this practice were Lord Chandos' and Lord Berkeley's players, who sometimes received rewards larger than those given to companies of patrons of equal rank because both nobles had great local holdings which made their favour especially important to the city.

The chamberlains' accounts indicate that the mayor's plays were invariably given in the Bothall, and all licensed performances likely took place there, since the 1580 ordinance prohibited private performances in the homes and establishments, especially inns, of the burgesses. The Bothall stood in Westgate Street and served as the city's wool market, the site of the assizes, and for a variety of other civic functions.[11] According to Willis, the audience sat on benches and the players acted on some form of stage. Expenses for constructing these stages appear frequently in the chamberlains' accounts, although unfortunately without the sort of detail which would permit a complete reconstruction. The city usually employed a carpenter named John Batty to build these stages and the pageant scaffolds required for Queen Elizabeth's 1574 visit to the city.

The chamberlains' accounts from 1596–7 to 1634–5 have not survived, with the exception of a single year's accounts for 1628–9. By the time the accounts resume, the decline in provincial touring that occurred in the early seventeenth century is evident. Only two actual performances have been recorded between 1635–6 and 1642, although players were occasionally paid not to perform because of fear of spreading plague. The fact that the city rewarded players at all in those years is somewhat surprising. The city had suffered economically from the decay of its cloth industry in the late sixteenth century, from repeated outbreaks of plague, and from disputes with county gentry over the inshire. Tension between the wealthy few who ran the city and the growing number of urban poor led to the tightening of control by a magistracy already strongly puritan, and confirmed in its antagonism toward the king as a result of the Crown's heavy financial and military demands in the 1620s and 1630s.[12] Yet, unlike Worcester and Bristol, where paying players to go away without performing was the rule in the 1630s, Gloucester seems to have adopted this practice only when plague genuinely threatened.[13] As late as 1640–1, we have evidence of the mayor and justices attending a performance and giving the players a reward.

MUSIC

The earliest surviving references to professional entertainers at Gloucester concern minstrels who came to entertain while the assizes were in session. Five minstrels or groups of minstrels visited the city in 1393–4 and six in 1409–10, including those of Richard II, Henry IV, the countess of Stafford, and Lord Berkeley.

The chamberlains' accounts record occasional rewards to itinerant minstrels during the latter half of the sixteenth century, but the important musical development of those years was Gloucester's establishment of an official, salaried position of civic musician. When Queen Elizabeth visited the city in 1574, Gloucester had to hire the waits of Shrewsbury to furnish music, but in 1578 Garret Barnes began to receive a yearly fee of 20s for being 'the musicion.' In 1595–6, when no payment had been made to Barnes for two years, a civic ordinance adopted 'Iames (blank) musitians' as the city waits. The ordinance required them to play their recorders at four o'clock each morning in the chief streets of the city, and 'at the solempne vsuall assemblies.' For this service, each of the four received 20s for their fee and another 20s to buy the livery cloaks that marked them as retainers of the city. The near-monopoly their position gave them enabled them to augment their income by providing music at special Cathedral functions and at feasts given by the craft guilds. The Tanners, for example, employed the waits for this purpose as many as three times a year.

Gloucester's waits did not suffer as a result of the growth of puritanism. In 1632, when dramatic entertainment had declined greatly, the number of waits was increased from four to six, and their yearly fee doubled. Unlike Worcester, which suppressed its waits in 1642, Gloucester continued to employ its waits right through the Commonwealth period.[14]

CEREMONY

When Henry VII made his coronation progress from York to London in 1486, Hereford and Bristol greeted the king with elaborate pageantry, but at Gloucester 'ther was no pageaunt nor speche ordeynede.' It was not until the sixteenth century that civic ceremony became more frequent and elaborate. Entries in the corporation custumnal describe how Princess Mary (in 1525) and Henry VIII (in 1535) were welcomed by the mayor and conducted through the town by the scarlet-clad civic officials. Not, however, until Elizabeth's visit in 1574, did Gloucester make use of quasi-dramatic pageantry as a means of demonstrating affection for, and allegiance to, the sovereign. While no narrative description of the queen's entry exists, the chamberlains' accounts record, in great detail, the preparations the city made. Scaffolds were built to serve as pageant stages at the Outer Northgate, the High Cross, and an open area just outside the Southgate known as the 'Meadow.' Several groups of musicians were paid for playing at the gates and in the streets. The major civic buildings were painted and decorated for the occasion, and 'beastes', including an antelope, unicorns, and a dragon, were constructed, probably for some sort of tableau.

The annual watches on Midsummer's eve and St Peter's eve (28 June) also came to include pageantry. The watches may have originated in genuine attempts to protect the city, but later developed into a ceremonial procession of the mayor through the city. The 1541 ordinances of the Tanners' company reveal the part the guildsmen played in the watches:

Item it ys ordayned that euery brother of the said crafte shall be in redynes withe the maister and wardens at there commen haule euery yere on the eve of Saynte Iohn Baptiste at eighte of the clocke at nyght and on Sayncte peturs eve at eighte of the clock at nyght in theire best apparell withe bendes and badges on theire shulders towchynge theyre facultie to awayte on the mayer and Sheryffes on bothe nyghtes in the kynges watche withe the said towne And not to departe from the watche vntyll suche tyme it be done and haue broughte the maister and wardens to theire commen haule the which master and wardens shall make to the bretherne of the said crafte there assembled euery of these twoo nyghtes an honest drynchynge....[15]

The chamberlains' accounts are filled with payments for the firing of guns and the purchase of fireworks to be used on these occasions, but less explosive forms of entertainment appear infrequently. In 1570–1, the city rewarded 'the vssher of the fenche Schole for his paines in playenge before the watche.' Only a single entry has survived to suggest that civic pageantry accompanied the watches: the chamberlains paid 10s at Midsummer 1595 to Thomas Bubbe 'for a wagon in the pageant for the turke.'

Tewkesbury

By the second half of the sixteenth century, which furnishes all the surviving evidence of dramatic activity, Tewkesbury had become a reasonably prosperous market and a minor port on the Severn. The town received a charter of incorporation in 1575, making official the status of corporate borough which it had already essentially achieved. Its population at that time has been estimated at 1600 communicants from 400 households, or roughly a third that of Gloucester.[16]

The earliest references in the churchwardens' accounts of St Mary the Virgin, Tewkesbury, to renting of the parish 'players gere' reveal an established dramatic tradition but give no indication of its antiquity. Fifteen rentals are recorded in the seventeen years separating the first rental, in 1567–8, from the last, in 1584–5; the amounts received range from 18d to 8s 2d, with 3s 4d (a half-noble) being the most common figure. Inventories of the 'players geare', taken in 1576–7 and 1584–5, and the expenses for repairing and enlarging it in 1577–8, yield some picture of the costumes and properties available to the parish for producing plays. A sheepskin garment for Christ, wigs and beards for the apostles, and a mask for the devil suggest drama on New Testament subjects, while the varied array of caps, gowns, and jerkins could serve in almost any kind of performance. At least once, in 1578–80, one of Tewkesbury's own parishioners paid to use the wardrobe, but it was frequently rented to nearby villages, particularly at Christmas and Midsummer.

The churchwardens' accounts record only two performances of plays at Tewkesbury itself. The earlier instance, in 1575–6, got into the accounts only because a pew was broken during the performance and the churchwardens paid to have it mended. The parish seems neither to have spent anything on mounting the play, nor to have made any money from it. In 1600–1, however, plays were put on with the express purpose of helping to finance a new battlement on the church tower. In anticipation of a large expenditure (the total cost of constructing the battlement came to more than £45), the churchwardens proposed to brew ale from grain donated to the parish, and sell the ale at dramatic performances given at Whitsuntide. The borough council, however, fearing the abuses commonly associated with church ales, refused to permit the churchwardens to sell their wheat and malt, except as grain. A play was performed on each of the first three days in Whitsun week, and musicians and trumpeters performed. The entertainment made an effective advertisement for the grain sale, since the project as a whole made enough to cover two-thirds of the cost of the new battlement, although the plays themselves made only a meagre profit.

Both the churchwardens' accounts and the minutes of the borough council for 1600 agree that the plays were performed 'within the abbey,' making them a very late instance of plays performed inside a church in England. Indeed, they are one of the latest occurrences of parish drama, a fact which probably explains why they were a one-time revival of the parish's dramatic tradition, despite their financial success. No specific attack on these plays occurs in the extant diocesan records, but fear of the abuses which attended such performances elsewhere and the tinge of papistry which clung to local religious drama prevented them from becoming a regular practice again. By 1607, diocese-wide articles of visitation prohibited plays and church ales in the church or churchyard.

Other Parishes

Records of dramatic activity in other towns and villages in Gloucestershire are disappointingly scarce. Of the many towns which had some of the features of a borough, only Tewkesbury joined Gloucester in achieving full corporate borough status before 1642.[17] Even Cirencester, the trading centre of the Cotswolds, possesses few surviving records, perhaps because of the tyrannical control which the abbots of Cirencester Abbey exercised over the town until the sixteenth century, stunting its development as a borough.[18] Churchwardens' accounts are often the main source of evidence about local dramatic activity in smaller towns, but Tewkesbury's are among the few extant churchwardens' accounts that date from before 1630, and among the even fewer which are itemized. The records of the court of quarter sessions and those of the archidiaconal court, which have proved fruitful sources of evidence about dramatic activity outside the large towns elsewhere, have not survived for Gloucestershire.

Cheltenham, a relatively small manorial town at this time, provides a hint at how players may have operated in such places. In 1611, Richard Clerke, Guido Dobbins, and their fellows marched through the streets of the town, banging on a drum and proclaiming that they would perform a play at the sign of the Crown. The bailiff, citing fear of spreading plague as his reason, prohibited them from performing, and when they attempted to play anyway, they were arrested and fined by the manor court.

The traces of dramatic activity among the rural folk in Gloucestershire are faint indeed and consist mainly of general prohibitions. Extant printed articles from visitations of Gloucester diocese reveal the increasing strength of puritan animosity toward such activity. An article of 1607 prohibited the holding of plays, feasts, church ales, and drinkings in the church or churchyard. By 1622, the articles prohibited anywhere in the parish on the Sabbath 'Lords of misrule, dauncers, players, or any other disguised person...stage-playes, beare-baitings, bul-baitings, or other such vnlawfull and prophane exercises....sports, or any that doe sit in the Tauerne, or Alehouse, or streetes....' Only on the rare occasions when a cleric was accused of participating in a prohibited or questionable activity do we learn about it from the extant depositions sworn before the consistory court of Gloucester diocese. The most interesting of these cases concerns one Christopher Windle, vicar of the Cotswold village of Bisley. Several of his parishioners testified to the court of their distress at his encouragement of maypole dancing, which ran to the extent of making his own son lord of the maypole. In 1618 Windle sent James I a Latin commentary on the recently issued *Kings Maiesties Declaration to His Subiects Concerning lawfull Sports to be vsed*, in which the king defended against puritan opposition his subjects' right to participate in sports, games, and other pastimes – including maypole dancing – on Sundays. Windle endorses the king's pragmatic reasoning and adds an original rebuttal to the puritans' theological objections: he argues that God wants men to celebrate Him with their bodies as well as their minds, and that physical activities after Sunday service best accomplish this form of devotion. He also discusses the local impact of the controversy over Sunday sports and notes in the margin that maypoles have been pulled down at Gloucester and Berkeley.

At the same time that puritan pressure was increasing against sports, dancing, playing, church ales, and other such folk activities, a member of the Gloucestershire gentry was reviving and institutionalizing them in what became known as Robert Dover's Cotswold Games. The village of Weston Subedge, near Dover's estate in the northeast corner of the county, had long held an ale and revelry each year at Whitsuntide. As a protest against puritanism, Dover transformed this local festival, c 1604, by dressing it in the costume and spirit of Greece, in imitation of the Olympics, and making it into an entertainment for his gentle friends. Athletic contests dominated the celebration, but music and dancing were included. Dover himself played the king of the Games, wearing cast-off garments given to him by James I and directing proceedings from a wooden castle constructed as a centre-piece for the games. Unfortunately, no detailed records of the Cotswold Games exist; all we know of them comes from

Annalia Dubrensia (1636), a collection of poems dedicated to Dover.[19]

Households

BERKELEY

From the fourteenth to the sixteenth century, Gloucestershire ranked among the ten wealthiest counties in England and the lands not held by the monasteries were concentrated in the hands of a few families.[20] The Berkeleys, whose history in Gloucestershire goes back to Norman times, owned not only Berkeley Castle and environs, but also a great deal of agricultural land in the Severn Vale and wool-producing land in the southern Cotswolds, from Dursley and Wotton under Edge to Yate, near the southern boundary of the county. The earliest evidence of patronage of drama and music by the Gloucestershire nobility occurs in a household account book, for 1420–1, of Elizabeth Berkeley, countess of Warwick. The accounts for the Christmas holidays record expenditures on 'diu*ersis* disgisingez,' and rewards for playing given to groups from nearby Slimbridge and Wotton under Edge. Minstrels visited Berkeley Castle at Christmas and several other times during the year.

Elizabeth Berkeley was also involved in the beginning of a battle over title to the family estates which was not ultimately resolved until 1609. Because of this dispute, the Berkeleys did not live at Berkeley Castle for much of the intervening period. When Henry Berkeley succeeded to the title in the mid-sixteenth century he had to make Caludon Castle near Coventry his principal residence. Thus, the only instances of his extensive patronage of entertainers to appear in this study are the references to Lord Berkeley's players in the Gloucester chamberlains' accounts and the rewards given to musicians at Cirencester and Tortworth Park when he made a progress to view his Gloucestershire estates in 1603.

STAFFORD

The Staffords owned a huge estate around Thornbury in the lower end of the Severn Vale, as well as manors scattered about the county. However, they did not reside in Gloucestershire until Edward Stafford, third duke of Buckingham, made Thornbury Castle his seat in 1498. In 1476 Henry vii had reversed the attainder against Buckingham's father, the second duke, restoring Buckingham to his estates and making him the wealthiest and most powerful of the nobles. Buckingham then centralized administration of his lands at Thornbury and began a construction program designed to make the castle a monument to his greatness.[21] His magnificent life-style, which aroused Henry viii's envy and mistrust, often found expression in patronage of the arts. A household book for 1507–8 gives some indication of the magnitude of Buckingham's entertaining, especially during the Christmas season. On the feast of Epiphany, 519 people, of ranks ranging from knight to tenant farmer, gathered at

Thornbury Castle, consumed prodigious amounts of food and drink, and enjoyed performances by minstrels, trumpeters, the Bristol waits, and the players of Writtle,
Essex.[22] As at Berkeley Castle, minstrels turned up at irregular intervals throughout
the year. Even in 1520–1, Buckingham managed to ignore both the king's suspicions
(he was to be arrested in April 1521) and his own debts, and gave Christmastide fitting
celebration. The Bristol waits again provided music, a 'yong maide' performed tumb-
ling feats, and a troupe of French players, including two women, acted what Buckingham's accountant enigmatically recorded as 'the passion of oure lorde by a vise.'

An account of 1503–4 shows that, in addition to receiving visits from itinerant performers, the duke employed minstrels as members of his household. (Of the company
of players under his patronage that played at Greenwich in 1509, there is no trace in
the extant Thornbury records.[23]) The household wardrobe also contributed to the entertainment: an inventory of 1515–16 lists six ells of canvas for constructing a pageant
used in an interlude; one from 1516–17 reveals that morris dancing was popular at
Thornbury, because buckram, canvas, and bells were purchased to make costumes
for the morris dancers.

BRYDGES

Buckingham's lands passed to the Crown at the time of his execution for treason, and
with the Berkeleys residing at Caludon, the way was open for the Lords Chandos
to become Gloucestershire's most important patrons of the drama from the 1550s to
the early seventeenth century. John Brydges had been a groom of the privy chamber
under Henry VIII and later lieutenant of the Tower under Mary. In 1554, she created
him the first Baron Chandos and granted him Sudeley Castle and its estates around
Winchcombe, which had belonged to the executed Thomas Seymour. Lord Chandos'
players first appeared at Gloucester in 1558, and his heirs continued as patrons of a
provincial company until at least 1610.[24]

While no records of visits by professional performers to Sudeley have survived, the
entertainments presented during Queen Elizabeth's stay there in 1592 are important
to the history of drama in Gloucestershire, since they are the only dramatic performances given in the county for which we possess the texts. Though called 'speeches'
by the man who first printed them, these entertainments contain stage directions and
were clearly intended to be enacted, rather than merely spoken. Still, they remain more
similar to civic pageants or masques than to contemporary plays. All three entertainments have a compliment to the sovereign as their central purpose; the second day's,
for example, shows sympathy for Elizabeth's determination not to marry, by
dramatizing Daphne's successful resistance to Apollo's advances. The pastoral convention so popular with the Elizabethan aristocracy made especially fitting material
for entertainments at Sudeley, in its Cotswold setting. The performances occurred
outdoors, where one's eyes would naturally be led from the play-acting shepherds
to the real shepherds and their flocks on the surrounding hills. The text for the third

day of the queen's visit is particularly appropriate, based as it is on the king game of the folk: a cake was cut and distributed among the shepherds, with those whose pieces contained tokens becoming king and queen for the duration of the festival. At Sudeley in 1592, of course, the game-queen took precedence over the king.

Under James I, patronage of the drama by Gloucestershire nobles waned. The new king's visits to the county were less frequent than Elizabeth's, affording less opportunity for the nobles to display their loyalty and generosity through entertainment. In 1604, parliament's revision of the vagabondage laws withdrew the right of anyone but a member of the royal family to license a company to travel in his name.[25] Dissemination of this change in the law to the provinces was slow, and many companies relied on this fact to continue performing (both Lord Berkeley's and Lord Chandos' players are mentioned in civic accounts until 1610), but fewer and fewer were willing to risk arrest as vagabonds.

The Documents

Boroughs and Parishes

BISLEY

Gloucester Diocese Consistory Court Deposition Books
Gloucester, Gloucestershire Record Office, GDR 114; May 1611–April 1613; Latin and English; paper; 191 leaves; 289mm x 185mm (text area variable); unfoliated; original vellum cover, but most of front cover missing.

A book of depositions taken in consistory court cases dealing with offenses such as libel, fornication, and failure to observe the Sabbath. The depositions were recorded separately from the charges and dispositions of the cases, so that the charges often must be inferred from the answers given by the witnesses and the results of the cases are rarely known. The legal formulae and description of witnesses are in Latin, but the depositions themselves are taken down in English.

CHELTENHAM

Manor and Hundred Court Book
Gloucester, Gloucestershire Record Office, D855/M8; 1607–15; Latin and English; paper; i + 186 + ii; 300mm × 200mm (290mm × 150mm), average 46 long lines; original ink foliation; original vellum cover.

This court book is the main record of official acts in the manor and hundred of Cheltenham. In addition to presentments, fines, and court orders, it contains grants, essoins, and lists of free-, burgage-, and copy-holders.

CHURCHDOWN

A DIVINE TRAGEDIE | LATELY ACTED, | OR, |
A Collection of sundrie memorable ex- | amples of Gods judgements upon Sabbath-breakers, |

and other like Libertines, in their unlawfull Sports, hap- | ning within the Realme of *England*, in the compasse one- | ly of few yeers last past, since the Book was published, worthy | to be known and considered of all men, especially such, | who are guilty of the sin or Arch- | patrons thereof. | By that worthy Divine Mr. *Henry Burton*. | [within a rectangular block, an oval portrait of the author with 'Ætatis Suae 63' at left] | Printed in the yeer 1641. Colophon on f 4v, p 38: *LONDON*: | Printed for *John Wright junior*, and for *Tho. Bates*, and / are to be sold at their shops in the Old Baylie. | 1642. Quarto; A4 - F4; roman and italic; A1 (title page), A4, B4, C4, D4, E4, F4 unsigned; ornamental rectangular block begins 'To the Reader' and 'Examples of Gods Iudgements'; ornamental capitals, A2 and B2. Wing: B6161.

GLOUCESTER

Civic Records

The Gloucestershire Record Office is currently renumbering the borough records. The numbers which appear in parentheses in the document descriptions for the Corporation Custumnal, the Corporation Common Council Minute Books, the Borough Bailiffs' Accounts, and the Corporation Chamberlains' Accounts are the former numbers, based on W.H. Stevenson's *Calendar of the Records of the Corporation of Gloucester*.

Corporation Custumnal
Gloucester, Gloucestershire Record Office, GBR B 2/1 (1375/1450); 1486–c 1600; English and Latin; paper; x + 236 + iv; 290mm × 215mm (text area variable), average 33 long lines; modern arabic foliation corrects original roman numeral foliation; little ornamentation; first 13 and last 11 leaves laminated in plastic; 19th c. red leather-covered cardboard binding.

This book, begun during the reign of Henry VII as a custumnal, was used to preserve copies of the new borough charter granted by Henry VIII, acts regulating the practices of various crafts (none of which contain references to dramatic activity), and descriptions of important events, such as the visits of Princess Mary in 1525 and of Henry VIII with Anne Boleyn in 1535 – presumably recorded in order to preserve the accepted ceremonial forms. It also includes lists of city aldermen, of rents due on city land, of assessments to furnish soldiers, and of soldiers sent to various campaigns; copies of letters to and from the sovereigns regarding musters; and copies of documents concerning a land dispute between the city and the abbot of St Peter's Abbey, Gloucester.

Corporation Common Council Minute Books
Gloucester, Gloucestershire Record Office, GBR B 3/1 (1376/1451); 1565–1632; English with some Latin; paper; xii + 411 + vi; 360mm × 240mm (330mm × 170mm), average 38 long lines; original foliation (8 unfoliated leaves between 9 and 10, foliation jumps from 275 to 436,

240–75 also numbered 400–35 but crossed out, 220–39 also numbered 300–19 but crossed out); first 15 leaves laminated; 19th c. red leather-covered cardboard binding, title on spine.

Gloucester, Gloucestershire Record Office, GBR B 3/2 (1377/1452); 1632–56; English with some Latin headings; paper; x + 470 (last 22 index) + iv; 365mm × 210mm (330mm × 160mm), average 38 long lines; original pagination; first 20 pages laminated; 19th c. red leather-covered cardboard binding, title on spine.

These books contain the texts of acts and ordinances of the city council, arranged by mayoral year. Among the acts regulating various crafts are ordinances concerning the visits of professional players. Other acts of the council created new civic offices or redefined old ones, including the office of civic wait. After 1600, the books are increasingly devoted to copies of leases, orders to survey land, and repairs to civic buildings.

Corporation Clerks' Memoranda Books
Gloucester, Gloucestershire Record Office, GBR 1453/1542; 1609–35; English; paper; iii + 175 + iii; 395mm × 145mm (370mm × 130mm), average 43 long lines; modern foliation; 19th c. dark-brown leather-covered cardboard binding, title on spine.

Gloucester, Gloucestershire Record Office, GBR 1454/1543; 1636–70; English; paper; iii + 194 + iii; 395mm × 145mm (350mm × 130mm), average 35 long lines; modern foliation; 19th c. dark-brown leather-covered cardboard binding, title on spine.

The city clerks' memoranda books record arrests and punishments for vagabondage, bindings over to quarter sessions for more serious crimes, precautionary measures against plague, and loans to and by the city.

Borough Bailiffs' Accounts
Gloucester, Gloucestershire Record Office, GBR F 3/2 (1302/1357); 1393–4; Latin; parchment, single membrane; 300mm × 265mm (220mm × 210mm), 31 long lines (about 5 lines lost near top); stained and faded so that a good deal of the roll is illegible even under UV, a section of varying height running across entire membrane missing; parchment glued to heavy paper backing.

Gloucester, Gloucestershire Record Office, GBR F 3/4 (1304/1358b); 1409–10; Latin; parchment; single membrane; 290mm × 210mm (270mm × 200mm), 35 long lines (about 5 lines missing in middle of membrane); stained and faded, large section missing across entire roll; parchment glued to heavy paper backing.

These accounts, running from Michaelmas to Michaelmas, do not deal with the day-to-day operation of Gloucester, but with the bailiffs' expenses in entertaining the nobles who visited the city while the assizes were in session. Only two of the account rolls have survived, but both contain several payments to companies of minstrels. In addition, entries record expenses to the duke of York, the purchase of wine for the king's justices of the assize, and a gift to the king's harbinger. No details are given, and many of the patrons' names and the amounts paid are missing or illegible.

Corporation Chamberlains' Accounts
Gloucester, Gloucestershire Record Office, GBR F 4/3 (1394/1500); 1550–96; English; paper; x + 324 + iv; 385mm × 270mm (350mm × 210mm), average 45 long lines; original foliation; ff 2–96 laminated, ff 320–4 loose; 19th c. red leather-covered cardboard binding, title on spine.

Gloucester, Gloucestershire Record Office, GBR F 4/4 (1395/1500b); 1628–9; English; paper; vi + 43 + vi; 310mm × 190mm (270mm × 150mm), average 36 long lines; modern foliation (both sides of pages 1–46, then each leaf 47–51, remaining leaves unfoliated); 19th c. red leather-covered cardboard binding, title on spine.

Gloucester, Gloucestershire Record Office, GBR F 4/5 (1396/1501); 1635–53; English; paper; x + 503 + iv; 350mm × 225mm (300mm × 190mm), average 39 long lines; modern foliation; leaves 3–6, 35 laminated; 19th c. red leather-covered cardboard binding.

The Chamberlains' Accounts run from Michaelmas to Michaelmas and record all the city's financial dealings. City treasury receipts include rents, fines levied on new burgesses, and sales of city property. Disbursements are divided into several categories: rents, fees and wages of city officials (including the civic waits), costs of repairs to buildings and roads, gifts and rewards, and general payments. Payments to players occur in the last three of these categories, most commonly under 'Gifts and Rewards,' along with rewards to servants of the king and nobles, and holiday gifts of sugar and wine to the local nobility. Expenses for constructing stages and other preparations for performances are usually found under 'General Payments.'

The earliest extant volume, begun in 1550, may be the first account book in this form kept by the city, as it begins with a lengthy inventory of city land and other property not found in later volumes. The marginal headings and the first word of each entry – usually 'also' or 'geuen' – are large and heavily inked. One or more volumes containing the accounts for 1596–7 to 1634–5 have been lost, with only the accounts for the single year 1628–9 having survived.

Guild Records

Bakers' Company Minutes and Accounts
Gloucester, Gloucestershire County Library, 29334; 1558–1654; English; paper; i + 125; 320mm × 205mm (300mm × 170mm), average 34 long lines; unfoliated; original cover lost; first and last few leaves badly torn and frayed, some leaves at ends may have been lost.

Tanners' Company Orders and Accounts
Gloucester, Gloucestershire County Library, 28652/18; 1598–1724; English; paper; 261 leaves; 290mm × 195mm (260mm × 140mm), average 38 long lines; unfoliated; original vellum cover, titles on front and back of cover.

These guild books are quite similar in form and content. They begin with ordinances of the company and the oaths to be taken by company officers, followed by the accounts, within which occasional memoranda and lists of enrolled apprentices are interspersed. The receipts are primarily from initiation fees paid to join the company or from fines levied for offenses against the ordinances. The payments include no references to plays or processions, but are made up mostly of expenses incurred at celebratory meals, gifts to impoverished members, and rents for the meeting-halls. The meal expenses often include payments to the waits for entertaining. Before the seventeenth century, the Bakers' accounts are not as detailed as the Tanners' and even then some expenses for entertainment may be hidden in summarized expenses for meals. The Tanners' accounting year runs from one St Clement's Day to the next (St Clement being their patron saint), while the Bakers' accounts run from Michaelmas to Michaelmas.

Monastic and Ecclesiastical Records

Statutes of St Peter's Abbey
Hereford, Hereford Cathedral Library, No. 1826; 10 October 1301; Latin; parchment; single membrane; 550mm × 394mm (427mm × 374mm), 68 long lines; no heading.

These sixteen statutes were drawn up by John de Gamages, abbot of St Peter's, and twelve other monks, in response to the archbishop of Canterbury's demand that the abbey reform a number of abuses.

Cathedral Treasurers' Accounts
Gloucester, Gloucestershire Record Office, D 936 A 1/1; 1609–34; English and Latin; paper; i + 147 + i; 295mm × 200mm (280mm × 175mm), average 21 long lines; modern pencil pagination; title page illuminated with armorial bearings of the dean and chapter in silver and chartreuse, endpapers are leaves from a printed Latin Bible; 17th c. brown leather-covered cardboard binding, no title.

Gloucester, Gloucestershire Record Office, D 936 A 1/2; 1635–64 (no accounts for 1642–61); English with some Latin; paper; iii + 193 + i; 320mm × 210mm (255mm × 175mm), average 34 long lines; modern pencil pagination; p iii illuminated with armorial bearings of the dean and chapter; brown leather-covered cardboard contemporary binding, title on front cover.

The Cathedral Treasurers' Accounts record receipts from rents of lands owned by the dean and chapter. Disbursements include payments for salaries, repairs of the fabric, and gifts to the needy; and extraordinary payments for bell-ringing, supplies, and entertainment. While entries for liturgical music have not been transcribed here, the extraordinary payments occasionally contain payments to the civic waits for supplementing the cathedral's musical forces, and to a few poor musicians who received gifts.

Gloucester Diocese Consistory Court Deposition Books
Gloucester, Gloucestershire Record Office, GDR 89; June 1601–March 1604; Latin and English; paper; 248 leaves; 290mm × 185mm (text area variable); unfoliated; original vellum cover, no title.

Similar to GDR 114 (see under Bisley, p 261).

Miscellaneous Records

Account of Alms, Edward I
London, Public Record Office, E 101/351/15; 20 November 1283–19 November 1284; Latin; parchment; 1 mb (in roll of 4 mbs); 720mm × 378mm (520mm × 357mm); good condition.

The roll records alms and oblations given by Edward I while on progress during the last weeks of 1283 and the early part of 1284. The daily and weekly payments are set down in approximate chronological order and grouped in paragraphs covering two-week periods, with the name of the place where the court found itself at the beginning of each fortnight indicated in the left-hand margin.

A Divine Tragedie Lately Acted
See Churchdown, pp 261–2.

First Provincial Progress of Henry VII
London, British Library, Cotton Julius B XII; 15th–17th c.; English, Latin, Anglo-Norman; paper, ff 67–82 parchment; iii + 316 + iii; 279mm × 207mm (180mm × 122mm), collation impossible, now single leaves separately mounted; modern pencil foliation; some flourished initials, painted coats of arms (ff 3–4), some marginalia in red ink (ff 58–63); brown half morocco binding, gold lettering.

This account of the progress of Henry VII in 1486, apparently written by a herald in the king's train, describes the elaborate pageants given before the king in York, Bristol, and elsewhere.

Journal of Sir Simonds D'Ewes
London, British Library, MS Harley 162; 7 November 1640–24 February 1641; English; paper; iii + 421 + iii; 310mm × 190mm; original foliation (modern foliation of first four folios, last folio, and several insertions); good condition; 19th c. binding of leather-covered board,

title on spine, Harley crest on front and back cover, gold tooling around edges of covers and spine.

D'Ewes' journal records the proceedings of parliament in late 1640 and early 1641. Among the subjects of controversy at that time were *The King's Book of Sports* and the support of royalist ecclesiastics for Sunday entertainments.

HARESCOMBE

Gloucester Diocese Consistory Court Deposition Books
See Bisley, p 261.

HENBURY

Bristol Diocese Bishop's Cause Book
Bristol, Bristol Record Office; EP/J/1/11; 1597–1601; Latin and English; paper; 540 + v; original foliation; 290mm × 202mm (text area variable); cover of brown leather over board with leather hinges, no title.

Similar to GDR 90 (below).

LITTLEDEAN

Gloucester Diocese Consistory Court Cause Book
Gloucester, Gloucestershire Record Office, GDR 90; March 1601–June 1603; Latin and English; paper; 392 (1–3 lost) leaves; 300mm × 195mm (text area variable); original foliation; original vellum cover, modern pencil title on front.

GDR 90 is a book of office causes before the consistory court; most entries, arranged by parishes, give only the names of the accused and the charges on a particular date. Many cases deal with fornication, not receiving communion at Easter, libel, and refusal to pay parish rates. Detection for working or keeping shop on the sabbath is frequent, but the 1602 Littledean presentments for dancing and playing instruments at service time are the only such ones in the book.

MITCHELDEAN

Letter to the Queen from Anthony Bridgeman
London, Public Record Office, SP 12/222/no. 70. 1.; January 1589; English; paper; single sheet; 299mm × 414mm (277mm × 191mm); 43 long lines; bound into *State Papers Domestic: Elizabeth*, vol 222.

Anthony Bridgeman of Mitcheldean, Gloucestershire, wrote to Queen Elizabeth with a list of puritan-inspired reforms, ranging from the restraint of minstrelsy and bear-baiting on the sabbath, to the restriction of clerics to a single benefice.

TEWKESBURY

Letter from John Veysey, Bishop of Exeter, and Others to Wolsey
London, British Library, Cotton Vespasian F xiii, #187 (f 240, formerly f 134); 27 November 1525; English; parchment; single sheet bound into book; 270mm × 190mm (60mm × 17mm); direction on dorse: 'To the moost Reuerende fader in god I the lorde Cardynal his good grace.'

The letter is undated, but the 1525 date, given in *Letters and Papers, Henry VIII* (vol IV, p 792), is borne out by the fact that on her way north Mary passed through Gloucester on 12 September of that year (GBR B 2/1, ff 116–16v).

Borough Minute Book
Gloucester, Gloucestershire Record Office, TBR A 1/1; 1575–1736; Latin and English; paper; ii + 223 + ii; 340mm × 230mm (300mm × 170mm), average 38 long lines; original ink foliation begins from both ends with some duplication of numbers, modern foliation in pencil; leaves at either end damaged and repaired, some fading but text generally legible; brown leather-covered cardboard binding (original) with leather straps and brass clasp, no title.

The Tewkesbury Borough Minute Book appears to have been used to record many different kinds of information important to the borough government. It contains ordinances, lists of freemen and apprentices, subsidies, oaths to be taken by town officials, copies of wills, and copies of letters concerning musters. The bailiffs' accounts are generally given in summary form, but in one of the rare years (1584) when the accounts were itemized to some extent, there is a reference to players.

Church of St Mary the Virgin Churchwardens' Accounts
Gloucester, Gloucestershire Record Office, P 329 CW 2/1; 1563–1703; English; paper; vi + 296 + v; 410mm × 145mm (370mm × 120mm), average 51 long lines; original pagination to 530 then foliation to end (559); early leaves repaired with cheesecloth, occasional loss of text at edges; references to players often marked by antiquarians, either with pencilled arrows or ·✗· marked in purple pencil; red-brown leather-covered cardboard binding, title on spine.

This book of churchwardens' accounts records amounts received by the churchwardens from seat money, burial charges, land rents, and occasionally from renting out the parish stock of costumes and properties (the 'players gere'). The expenditures include repairs to the church fabric and bells, repairs and improvements to the 'players gere,' and expenses at visitations. The receipts and expenses in connection with the plays and grain sale, held in 1600 to finance a battlement on the church tower, occur in a separate section of accounts, following the ordinary accounts for 1600. The churchwardens' terms of office varied in duration, ranging from ten months to more than three years; each section of accounts reflects the period during which each particular pair of churchwardens served.

Gloucester Diocese Consistory Court Cause Book
See Littledean, p 267.

TORTWORTH

Gloucester Diocese Consistory Court Deposition Books
See Gloucester, p 266.

WESTON SUBEDGE

Gloucester Diocese Consistory Court Deposition Books
Gloucester, Gloucestershire Record Office, GDR 32; November 1573–June 1575; Latin and English; paper; 170 leaves; 307mm × 215mm (text area variable); irregular 16th c. foliation, modern pagination; original vellum cover, title on front cover obliterated.

Similar to GDR 114 (see under Bisley, p 261).

Diocese of Gloucester

VISITATION ARTICLES

ARTICLES, | TO BE ENQVIRED | of within the Dioces of Glocester, in the | first generall Visitation of the Reuerend | Father in God, Henry Lorde | Bishop of Glocester. || HOLDEN || In the yeare of our Lord God, 1607 | In the fift yeare of the Raigne of our most gra- | cious Soueraigne Lord Iames, by the grace of | God King of great Brittaine, France, | and Ireland, defender of the faith, &c. Imprinted at London by William [Iag]gard, for Clement Knight. 1607. | A⁴, B⁴, C². Bound into GRO: GDR 102 at beginning. No colophon. Catchwords. STC: 10209.3

ARTICLES | To be inquired of, in the | first Metropoliticall visitation, of the most | Reuerend Father, GEORGE, by Gods pro- | uidence, Arch-Bishop of Canterbury, and Primate of all Eng- | land; in, and for the Dioces of Glocester, in the yeare of | our Lord God, 1612. and in the second yeare of his | Graces Translation. || LONDON | Printed by William Iaggard. | A⁴, B⁴. Bound into GRO: GDR 115. STC: 10209.5

ARTICLES | ECCLESIASTICALL | TO BE ENQVIRED OF BY | THE CHVRCH-WAR-DENS | AND SWORNE-MEN WITH- | IN THE DIOCES OF GLOVCESTER. ||

In the Visitation of the Right Reuerend, | Father in GOD, MYLES, Lord Bishop of the | said Dioces, this present yeere. | 1622 ‖ And in the twentieth yeere of the Raigne of our most | dread Soueraigne Lord King IAMES. ‖ LONDON | Printed by IOHN LEGATT. | 1622. | A⁴, B². Bound into GRO: GDR 146. Modern pencil pagination. Catchwords. STC: 10209.7

ARTICLES | TO BE ENQVIRED | OF, IN THE GENERAL | VISITATION OF THE ARCH- | DEACON of the Diocesse of Glocester: | Holden in the yeare of our Lord GOD, 1624. | In the 21. yeare of the Raigne of our most gracious | Soueraigne Lord IAMES, by the grace of God, King of Great Britaine, France and Ireland, | Defender of the Faith, &c. | [McKerrow 343 woodcut 67mm × 55mm] | LONDON: | ¶ Printed for *Nathaniel Butter*. | 1624. | [within foliated border-frame]; A⁴, B⁴. No colophon. STC: 10213.8.

The clergy, churchwardens, and selected parishioners from all the parishes in the diocese were examined over these articles of visitation to determine if they were in compliance with church policy regarding a wide variety of practices. The 1607, 1612, and 1624 articles mention dramatic activity only to ask if plays have been permitted in the church or churchyard. The effect of puritan sabbatarianism can be seen in the 1622 articles, which also ask whether any plays, dances, lords of misrule, bull- or bear-baitings have been allowed anywhere on the sabbath.

Households

BEAUCHAMP

Household Account Book of Richard Beauchamp, Earl of Warwick
Longleat House, Warminster, Wilts., collection of the marquess of Bath, Ms. Misc. IX; 1420–1; Latin; paper; i + 141 + ii; 410mm × 285mm (342mm × 270mm), average 33 long lines; modern pencil foliation (two f 138s); 19th c. red leather-covered cardboard binding, title on spine.

Actually, the accounts are of the household of Elizabeth Berkeley, countess of Warwick, as her husband was at war in France during most of the relevant period. The only child of Lord Thomas Berkeley, she inherited the estate on her father's death in 1417 and had to remain in residence at the castle during Warwick's absence to protect her right to it against the claims of Lord Thomas' closest male relative, his nephew James Berkeley. The book begins with undated accounts: payments for large purchases, to creditors, for the upkeep of the stable and kennel, and to various persons, including minstrels, as rewards. The largest part of the book is given to day-by-day accounts of the expenditures of the household departments – the pantry, buttery, and wardrobe – from Michaelmas 1420 to Michaelmas 1421. A list of visitors present at the castle precedes each day's accounts. Expenses during the Christmas season for entertainment are not recorded daily, but are lumped together.

BERKELEY

Lord Henry Berkeley's House Steward's Book
Berkeley Castle, Glouc, Muniment Room, General Series Bound Book #109; October
1600–July 1605; English, paper; ii + 132 + ii; 310mm × 205mm (260mm × 140mm), average
31 long lines; unfoliated; modern cream-coloured paper over cardboard binding, titles on label
on front cover and spine.

This household book is primarily concerned with the receipts and expenditures of
Lord Henry Berkeley's household at Caludon Castle near Coventry. It also includes
expenses incurred in visiting the lord's Gloucestershire estates, with occasional payments to musicians for entertaining him on progress.

BRYDGES

SPEECHES | DELIVERED TO | HER MAIESTIE AT THE | LAST PROGRESSE, AT
THE | Right Honorable the Lady Rvssels, at | Bissam, the Right Honorable the Lorde |
CHANDOS at Sudley at the Right | Honorable the Lord NORRIS, at | Ricorte. | [McKerrow
336] | At Oxforde, Printed by Ioseph Barnes. | 1592. | A⁴,B⁴,C⁷. No colophon. *STC*: 7600.

STAFFORD

Household Accounts of Edward Stafford, Duke of Buckingham
Stafford, Staffordshire Record Office, D 641/1/3/7a; 31 March 1503–31 March 1504; Latin;
parchment; 5 membranes, written serially mbs 1–5, inventory written on dorse, mbs 1d–5d;
530mm × 287mm (425mm × 233mm), average 72 long lines.

Stafford, Staffordshire Record Office, D (W) 1721/1/5; 5 November 1507–22 March 1508;
Latin; paper; xi + 128 (with 127 blank leaves interleaved) + ix; 400mm × 267mm (330mm
× 189mm), average 43 long lines; modern pagination; original leaves have been glued to modern paper with every other modern leaf left blank; tan leather-covered cardboard binding, title
on spine.

London, Public Record Office, E. 101. 631/20; 1514–15; Latin with some English; paper;
26 membranes, attached serially; 383mm × 290mm (383mm × 210mm), average 40 long
lines; written mb 1d, mbs 1–26.

Stafford, Staffordshire Record Office, D 641/1/3/9; 31 March 1516–31 March 1517; Latin;
paper; 38 membranes, attached serially, written mbs 1d–10d, 1–38; 419mm × 344mm (380mm
× 240mm), average 47 long lines.

London, Public Record Office, E. 36/220; September 1520–April 1521; English; paper; iv
+ 17 + iv; 342mm × 264mm (170mm × 142mm), average 30 long lines; modern pencil

foliation and pagination, and modern ink-stamped pagination, which has been followed; modern patterned paper-covered cardboard binding, spine and corners reinforced with leather, title on paper glued to spine.

These accounts refer to the finances of the household of Edward Stafford, duke of Buckingham, while he was in residence at Thornbury Castle in southern Gloucestershire. The earliest set of accounts, for 1503–4, does not explicitly indicate the location concerned, but the extensive expenditures for building repairs suggest that the accounts refer to Thornbury. Buckingham had made the castle his principal residence in 1498 and embarked on major repair and refurbishing prior to the massive building campaign begun in 1507–8. (An unnamed scholar working for the Historical Manuscripts Commission made a transcription of these accounts in the mid-nineteenth century which is still tied up with the original roll. The transcriber also identified the accounts as being from Thornbury.)

The 1507–8 household book consists of accounts of each day's expenditure for provisions (foodstuffs, candles, stable supplies) with a list of guests present at dinner and supper in the left-hand margin, including players and musicians. The household's location is given at the top of each page; the winter months generally found it at Thornbury.

The accounts of 1515–16 and 1516–17 inventory materials used for new clothes and other special purposes by the duke's department of the wardrobe; they do not record daily expenses. The canvas used in making a pageant in 1515–16 is listed under the rubric, 'Dona.' The bells and buckram for morris dancers' costumes occur in a section of the 1516–17 account primarily devoted to hunting and hawking accessories.

The account book for 1520–1 also does not deal with everyday supplies and services, but only with rewards to entertainers, to servants of other nobles, and with the duke's oblations.

Editorial Procedures

Principles of Selection

The intent of this edition has been to include every reference to dramatic and musical activity in Gloucestershire before 1642. In addition, material adjacent to these items has been transcribed when it provides the context for a play or musical performance, as in the Gloucester Tanners' accounts, where payments to the waits follow other expenses at guild dinners. Some caution has had to be exercised, however, against the temptation to include anything which even remotely suggests drama, music, or ceremonial in an effort to fill the many gaps in our knowledge about these activities left by the surviving records.

References to church drama appear here, such as the St Nicholas play performed before Edward I at Gloucester in 1283, but church music and ceremonial have been omitted. Thus, entirely liturgical practices like the sepulchre watchings recorded by Minchinhampton and Gloucester parishes have not been included. Payments found in the Cathedral Treasurers' Accounts for the purchase and repair of musical instruments, and to musicians for playing at services, have not been transcribed. Only those entries which seem to refer to non-liturgical performance are included – a payment for music at a feast at the bishop's residence, for instance. The reference to a boy-bishop at Gloucester in 1283 is given, but not the text of a sermon preached by a boy-bishop there on the feast of the Holy Innocents, 1558: the sermon itself is serious as well as appropriate to the day, the entertainment being provided solely by the youth of the preacher.[26] Sixteenth-century registers of the abbots of St Peter's, Gloucester, make several intriguing mentions of the 'communes ludos,' translated in the registers themselves as 'common plays.' Unfortunately, further examination has revealed that these plays are not dramatic performances, but rather periods of recreation when the monastic rule was relaxed and they are therefore omitted.

Church ales may well have provided the occasion for parish plays in Gloucestershire, as they did elsewhere, but the only surviving evidence comes from Tewkesbury, where the borough council refused to allow the parish to hold an ale in conjunction with plays in 1600. Occasional mentions of ales in churchwardens' accounts, court records, and the papers of John Smyth of Nibley have not been included, as they are not accompanied by any indication of dramatic activity.

Ceremonial practices appear here only when they involve music or quasi-dramatic activity. Payments for entertainment at Gloucester's Midsummer watch have been transcribed, but the annual expenses for gunpowder and matches, and for beating the drum at Midsummer have not. Descriptions of royal entries have been included, although those of Henry VII in 1486 and Princess Mary in 1525 yield only negative evidence. The city's expenses in entertaining royalty during their visits to Gloucester are also given, but payments for bell-ringing, street-cleaning, and the like at these times are not. Similarly, references to civic and guild feasts have been excluded, unless accompanied by music or other entertainment.

Finally, one incident beyond the chronological limit set by REED must be mentioned, for it shows that the desire for drama persisted in Gloucester under the Commonwealth. In 1657, Thomas Wright appeared before the city council to ask permission for a troop of 'poppet players' to perform at his inn. The council forbade it, but Wright defied them, and was left to face the quarter sessions alone when the players slipped out of town.[27]

Dating the Documents

The documents in the original are dated according to a year that began on 25 March rather than 1 January (following the Julian calendar in use in England until the eighteenth century). In addition, some dates are given by regnal year, and some by saints' days or movable feasts. I have converted all dates to conform to modern practice, except that I have adopted a chronology which starts a new year at Michaelmas (29 September) and employs double-year dates. Thus, for example, 15 September 1550 would convert to 15 September 1549–50, while 15 October 1550 would become 15 October 1550–1.

This system of dating is suggested by the documents themselves. Many of the documents – borough minute books, civil and ecclesiastical court books, even some of the household accounts – date each entry separately. Most of the accounts, however, simply list all the receipts and payments within a given accounting year without indicating specific dates for individual entries. Even in the rare cases when, for instance, the Gloucester city chamberlains record in their accounts for 1582–3 that 13s 4d was 'Geven to my lorde Barckleyes players the xxx[th] of November,' we cannot be absolutely certain that 30 November was the date of performance: the recorded date may refer to a payment made to the players a few days after the actual performance, or even – as appears to have happened occasionally – to the reimbursement of some civic official who had rewarded players out of his own pocket, perhaps as much as several months earlier. Since the most common evidence in this collection is from the accounts, and the only dates that can be fixed with any confidence for the payments in these accounts are the beginning and end of the accounting year, I have chosen to base the chronology on the accounting year most commonly employed, one which ran from 29 September to the following 28 September. The Michaelmas to Michaelmas accounting year was used in the important Gloucester bailiffs' and chamberlains' accounts, in the accounts of the Gloucester Bakers' company, and in some of the household accounts of Elizabeth Berkeley and of Edward Stafford, duke of Buckingham (though the household accounts also give specific dates).

A few sets of accounts present difficulties for this arrangement. The Tanners' company observed an accounting year that began on St Clement's Day (23 November). The only events mentioned in the Tanners' accounts which we can consistently date are the dinners given by each new master when he took office on the St Clement's Day which opened the accounting year. In order to place the only precisely datable entries in the correct year, I have located each set of accounts under the year which began on the previous Michaelmas (rather than in the year the account was rendered). This arrangement has the added advantage that only the section of each account covering the two months from Michaelmas to St Clement's Day appears under the wrong year.

The Tewkesbury churchwardens rendered their accounts at irregular intervals, generally about a year apart, but ranging from eight months (3 September 1577 to 3 May 1578) to nearly two years (4 May 1572 to 20 April 1574). In some cases, the manuscript tells only the date the account was rendered and we can only assume that it covers the entire period between that date and the rendering of the previous account. The treasurers of Gloucester Cathedral used an accounting year beginning on Lady Day (25 March), a half-year out of phase with the system employed in this collection, and none of the entries can be dated any more precisely. The same is true of two household accounts of the duke of Buckingham (Staffordshire Record Office: D 641/1/3/7a and 9), which began their accounting year on 31 March. All these accounts have been placed under the years in which they were rendered with the inclusive dates covered given in the entry headings in parentheses.

Notes

1 H.C. Darby, 'Gloucestershire,' *The Domesday Geography of Midland England*, 2nd ed, H.C. Darby and I.B. Terrett (eds) (Cambridge, 1971), pp 1–2.
2 Thomas Rudge, *The History and Antiquities of Gloucester, from the Earliest Period to the Present Time* (Gloucester, 1811), pp 15–21, 25.
3 William Page (ed), *The Victoria History of the County of Gloucester*, vol 2 (London, 1907), p 151.
4 Charles Phythian-Adams, 'Urban Decay in Late Medieval England,' *Towns in Societies: Essays in Economic History and Historical Sociology*, Philip Abrams and E.A. Wrigley (eds) (Cambridge, 1978), pp 163–4, 174, 179–80.
5 W.H. Stevenson (ed), 'The Records of the Corporation of Gloucester,' *Historical Manuscripts Commission*, 12th Report, Appendix, Part 9 (London, 1891), pp 406–7; M.D. Lobel and J. Tann, 'Gloucester,' *Historic Towns*, vol 1, M.D. Lobel (ed) (London, 1969), p 9; Peter Clark, '"The Ramoth-Gilead of the Good": Urban Change and Political Radicalism at Gloucester 1540–1640,' *The English Commonwealth 1547–1640: Essays in Politics and Society Presented to Joel Hurstfield*, Peter Clark, Alan G.R. Smith, and Nicholas Tyacke (Leicester, 1979), pp 168–70.
6 Stevenson, pp 403–4; Lobel and Tann, p 12.
7 Clark, p 168.
8 The Borough Custumnal (GRO: GBR B 2/1) includes some guild ordinances; the ordinances of the Tanners' company adopted in 1541 survive separately (Gloucestershire County Library #28652/4). The records of York and Chester guilds can be found in Alexandra F. Johnston and Margaret Rogerson (eds), *York*, Records of Early English Drama (Toronto, 1979) and Lawrence M. Clopper (ed), *Chester*, Records of Early English Drama (Toronto, 1979).
9 Itemized sixteenth-century churchwardens' accounts survive from St Michael's, St Aldgate's, and St Mary de Crypt.
10 R.W[illis], *Mount Tabor. or Private Exercises of a Penitent Sinner* (London, 1639), p 110. STC: 25752.
11 The uses of the Bothall are enumerated in an indenture between the city and Robert Ingram, 26 August 1569 (GBR B 2/3, ff 138–9v).

12 Clark, pp 168–86.

13 The plague reached Worcester in 1637 and Gloucester then enacted severe restrictions on entry by any strangers, not only players (GBR 1454/1543, ff 10v–12).

14 David Klausner transcribes the Worcester ordinance in 'Research in Progress [Hereford and Worcester],' REEDN, 1979:1, 22.

15 Gloucestershire County Library #28652/4.

16 C.R. Elrington (ed), *The Victoria History of the County of Gloucester*, vol 8 (London, 1968), pp 110–11, 120.

17 William Bradford Willcox, *Gloucestershire: A Study in Local Government, 1590–1640*, p 204, n 1.

18 Colin Platt, *The English Medieval Town* (London, 1976), p 140.

19 Christopher Whitfield, *Robert Dover and the Cotswold Games* (London, 1962), p 20; VCH *Glouc*, vol 2, p 306.

20 Roger S. Scofield, 'The Geographical Distribution of Wealth in England, 1334–1649,' *Economic History Review*, 2nd ser, 18 (1965), 483–510.

21 Carole Rawcliffe, *The Staffords, Earls of Stafford and Dukes of Buckingham, 1394–1521* (Cambridge, 1978), pp 86–7; A.D.K. Hawkyard, 'Thornbury Castle,' TBGAS, 95 (1977), 51–8.

22 See Appendix 1 for a complete day's entry from this household book.

23 John Payne Collier, *The History of English Dramatic Poetry to the Time of Shakespeare: and Annals of the Stage to the Restoration*, vol 1 (London, 1831), p 49.

24 John Tucker Murray, *English Dramatic Companies, 1558–1642*, vol 2, pp 29–30.

25 Glynne Wickham, *Early English Stages, 1300 to 1660*, vol 2, pt 1, p 91.

26 John Gough Nichols (ed), 'Two Sermons preached by the Boy Bishop at St. Paul's, temp. Henry VIII., and at Gloucester, temp. Mary,' with an introduction giving an account of the festival of the boy bishop in England by Edward F. Rimbault, *The Camden Miscellany*, vol 7 (1875), Camden Society, new ser, p 14.

27 GRO: 1454/1543, f 80v.

Select Bibliography

This short list includes books and articles with first-hand transcriptions of primary documents, together with a few essential reference works. No attempt has been made to list all works cited in the Introduction, textual footnotes and Endnotes.

Bennett, James. *The History of Tewkesbury* (Tewkesbury, 1830; rpt Dursley, Glouc, 1976).

Blair, Lawrence. *English Church Ales: As Seen in English Churchwardens' Accounts and Other Archival Sources of the Fifteenth and Sixteenth Centuries with a Note on Church Fairs* (Ann Arbor, Michigan, 1940).

Boas, F.S. 'Play in Ancient Abbey,' *Observer*, 15 January 1933, p 8, col 4.

– 'Tewkesbury Abbey's Theatrical Gear,' *Times Literary Supplement*, 16 March 1933, p 184.

Brewer, J.S. (ed). *Letters and Papers, Foreign and Domestic, of the Reign of Henry VIII*, vol 3, pts 1 and 2; vol 4, pt 1 (London, 1867–70).

Chambers, E.K. *The Elizabethan Stage*, 4 vols (Oxford, 1923).

– *The Mediaeval Stage*, 2 vols (London, 1903).

Finnegan, Robert E. 'Research in Progress: Gloucestershire and Bristol,' REEDN, 1977:1, 9–10.

Hannam-Clark, Theodore. *Drama in Gloucestershire (The Cotswold County): Some account of its development from the earliest times till to-day* (Gloucester and London, 1928).

Hart, William Henry (ed). *Historia et Cartularium Monasterii Sancti Petri Gloucestriae*, 3 vols. Rolls Series, 33 (London, 1863–7).

The Historical Manuscripts Commission. W.H. Stevenson (ed). 'The Records of the Corporation of Gloucester,' *The 12th Report of the Manuscripts Commission*, Appendix, Part 9 (London, 1891), 400–529.

'A Letter from John Gage, Esq. Director, to Sir Henry Ellis, Secretary, Accompanying Extracts from the Household Book of Edward Stafford, Duke of Buckingham,' *Archaeologia*, 25 (1834), 311–41.

Murray, John Tucker. *English Dramatic Companies: 1558–1642*, 2 vols (London, 1910).

Nichols, John. *The Progresses and Public Processions of Queen Elizabeth*, 3 vols (London, 1823).

Notestein, Wallace (ed). *The Journal of Sir Simonds D'Ewes from the Beginning of the Long Parliament to the Opening of the Trial of the Earl of Strafford* (New Haven, 1923).

Ross, C.D. 'The Household Accounts of Elizabeth Berkeley, Countess of Warwick,' *TBGAS*, 70 (1951), 81–105.

Smith, Brian S. and Elizabeth Ralph. *A History of Bristol and Gloucestershire* (Beaconsfield, 1972).

Southern, Richard. *The Staging of Plays before Shakespeare* (London, 1973).

Stevenson, W.H. (comp). *Calendar of the Records of the Corporation of Gloucester* (Gloucester, 1893).

Taylor, Arnold. 'Royal Alms and Oblations in the Later 13th Century: An Analysis of the Alms Roll of 12 Edward I (1283–4),' *Tribute to an Antiquary: Essays Presented to Marc Fitch by Some of his Friends*. Frederick Emmison and Roy Stephens (eds) (London, 1976), pp 93–125.

Wickham, Glynne. *Early English Stages: 1300 to 1660*. 2 vols in 3 pts (London, 1963–72).

Willcox, William Bradford. *Gloucestershire: A Study in Local Government, 1590–1640* (New Haven, 1940).

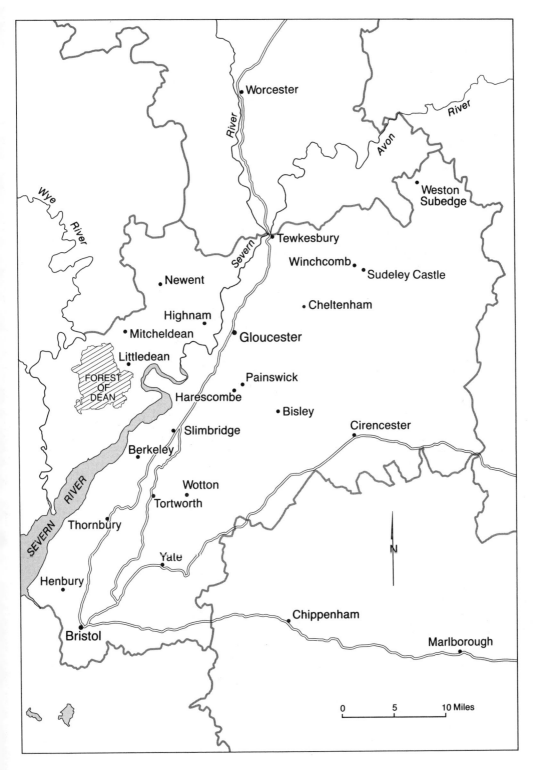

Gloucestershire with principal renaissance routes

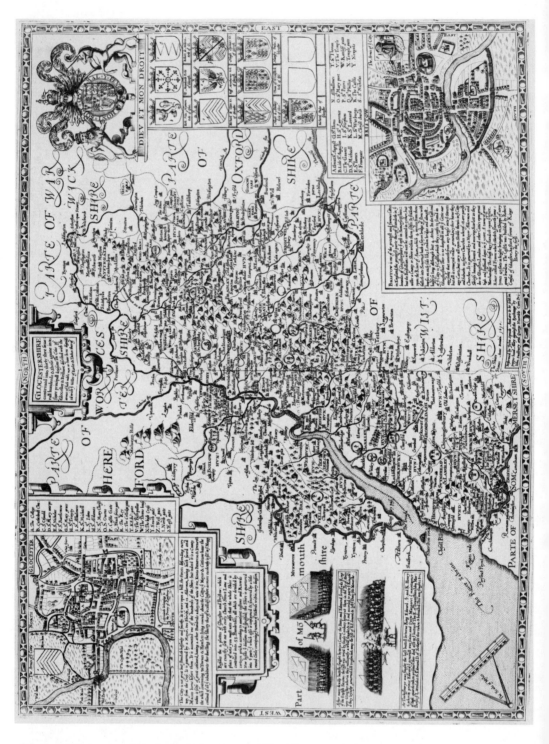

Map of Gloucestershire from John Speed, *The Theatre of the Empire of Great Britaine*, by courtesy of the Huntington Library

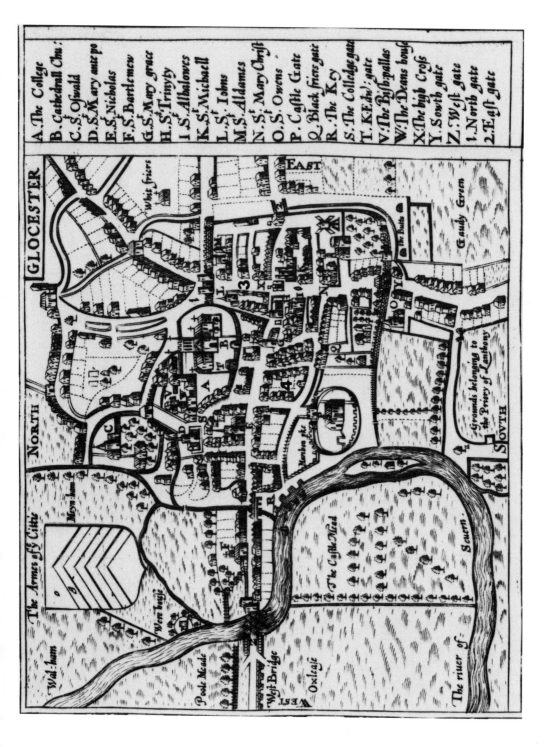

Map of Gloucestershire from John Speed, *The Theatre of the Empire of Great Britaine*, by
courtesy of the Huntington Library   3   New Inn   4   Boothall

Boroughs and Parishes

BISLEY

1610–11
Gloucester Diocese Consistory Court Deposition Books
GRO: GDR 114
ff [4–4v]* *(21 May)*

5

       Die p*redicto* super articu*lis* p*redictis*
Garrettus Band de Beisley in Com*itatu* Glouce*strie* tucker vbi
moram fecit per spatiu*m* quinq*ue* Ann⟨..⟩ et vltra natus apud
Estington in Com*itatu* p*redicto* aetatis quadraginta quatuor
Annor*um* aut eo circiter testis &c.

10

Ad d*ictos* Articu*los* ar*ticu*lorum predictor*um* Depo*nit* et Dicit that at
Whitsontide in Anno D*omini* 1610 there was a maye pole sett vpp
neare vnto the parish ⸠ᴛchurchᴛ of Bieslye & [pipe⟨..⟩g] pipeing &
Daunceinge at the same pole by the youth of the parish there & all
of the same was Done as this Depo*nent* hath very credibley heard at

15

the appointe[d]m*ent* & abettinge of mr chr*istoph*re windle ye viccar
there: & he saieth that he Doth verely believe in his conscience that
the sayd reporte is true because that vppon the Munday in the same
whitson weeke the sayd chr*istoph*re windle Did in a sermon that he
then preached before the congregac*ion* most prohanely & erroniously

20

Defend averre and affirme that pipeinge & Daunceinge at a Maye
poule; & keepinge of Somerale was as lawfull to be vsed & ke[e]pte
by the people as it was lawfull for them to here the word of god
sincerely preached: wh*ich* assertion of the sayd windle the sayd
congregac*ion* Did very much [at that tyme] mislike being–as most of

25

them [aff] affirmed very contrary to the worde of Allmightye god And
he this Depo*nent* saieth further that the sayd mr Windle is very much
subiecte to the like phantasicall & idle speeches in his sermons. for he

---

12/ 1610 *underlined* MS   20/ prohanely *for* prophanely

sayeth that the sayd windle did on[⟨.⟩] a Sabaoth Daye between
Allhollantyde & Cristmas last paste preach on a parte of [scp] scripture
out of the [Gos] 18th chapter of St Mathew, & expoundinge the same
before the congregacion he sayed and [af] Did most idley & ˌ⌜in⌝ most
vnfitte & prophane Manner averre & say that the sayed texte of   5
screpture was Arithmatike & not the logicall Divinitye. yet sayed he
nunber are necessary. for [2 hosen to] two feete two shooes 2. slops
2 sleeves 4. quarters of a ierken. yf the taylor cutteth five he stealeth
one. 24. buttons twenty fowre butten holes seven churches of Asia.
[p] tenn commandementes & keepe neuer and with many other idle   10
& prophane and senceles speeches as they seemed to the congregacion
Et aliter ad Dictos articulos nescit vt dicit Deponere/
Henricus Aisgill   Signum
                                    Garetti Band|

                                                                        15
               Die predicto super articulis predictis/
        Willelmus Hopton de Barkley in Comitatu Gloucestrie yeoman
        vbi moram fecit per sex hebdomodas et antea apud Bieslye in
        Comitatu predicto ætatis .32. Annorum aut eo circiter ibidem
        ortus [ætatis] testis &c.   20
        Ad Dictos articulos Deponit et Dicit that at Whitsontyde last was
        twelve ˌ⌜moneth⌝ there was a May pole sett vppe & pipeinge &
        Daunceinge kepte in the parish of Bieslye [and that] with the consent
        of the churchwardens (as they themselues haue affermed but onely as
        this Deponent hath credibly heard) at the appointement of mr   25
        christophre Windle the viccar there who [es] as this Deponent hath
        likewise heard [was] ⌜caused his sonne to be⌝ Lord of the same pole.
        And saieth that the sayd mr windle Did on the sabaoth before
        Whitsontide aforesayed preach before the congregacion in the parish
        church of Bieslye aforesaid & in his sermon he the sayed christophre 30
        Windle Did then & there afferme & Defend that pipeinge &
        Daunceinge at a Maypole were by the word of god lawfull to be
        kepte....

ff [8–8v]*   (31 May)   35
...
        officium Domini promotum per Richardum Hall contra
        christopherum Windle†
        Super articulis ex parte promotoris in hoc negotio Datis./
        Iohannes Clissold de Beisely in Comitatu Gloucestrie yeoman vbi 40

14/ Band signed with a cross (personal mark)

moram fecit plerumq*ue* a nativitate sua ib*ide*m ortus aetatis
quinquaginta Annor*um* aut eo circiter testis &c.

Ad D*i*ctos ar*ticu*los Depon*it* et dicit that in the yeare of o*ur* Lord god
1610 last past he this Depon*ent* [was] & one christophre Bidmead   5
weare churchwardens of the parish of Beisley in the countye of
Glouc*ester*: & did exequute the same office of churchwardenship the
same yeare. & saieth that ˎ⌐at Whitsontide⌐ in the same yeare mr
chr*istoph*re Windle ar*ticu*late without the consent & privity of him this
depon*ent* & his sayd fellow churchwarden & against the goodwill of   10
the honest and relligiouse desposed people of the same parish erecte
& sett vpp a May pole or somner pole and caused ⌐& mainteynde⌐
pipeinge and Daunceinge to be kepte & vsed at the same tyme./ & for
the better countenanceinge of that pr*o*phane buisines suffered his
sonne ar*late to be lord of the sayd May pole: And after he the sayd   15
chr*istoph*re Windle | was by [this] the well Desposed people of the same
p*a*rish reprov⟨..⟩ for that his pr*o*phane action and [⟨.⟩] toyes ˎ⌐ar⌐ not
ˎ⌐thaught⌐ fitt for a ⟨...⟩ of his callinge & pr*o*fession and intreated to
Desiste from further vseinge the same. he the sayd chr*istoph*re Did (as
th⟨.⟩ Depon*ent* hath credibly heard) in a sermon Defend & mayntayne   20
that the erectinge of Maypoles pipeing & Daunceing about the same
& keepinge of somer ale was by the Word of god lawfull: to be kepte
to the greate interruption & Discontentm*ent* of the consiences of the
whole parish as this Depon*ent* hath heard most of the p*a*rishion*ers*
since saye....   25

Die pr*edicto* sup*er* ar*ticu*lis pr*edictis*
Christoferus Bidmeade De Beisley in Com*itatu* Gloucestrie yeoman
vbi moram fecit [plerumq*ue*] quatuor Annos elapsos natus apud
Ellc⟨...⟩ in Com*itatu* pr*edi*cto aetatis sexaginta Annor*um* aut eo   30
circiter. testis &c.
Ad D*i*ctos ar*ticu*los depon*it* et dicit that [the ar*late] ⌐in⌐ the yeare of
o*ur* lord god 1610 Iohn Clissold & [chr*istoph*re Bi] this depon*ent* wear
churchwardens of Bieslye ar*ticu*late & [⟨..⟩] at Whitsontide in the same
yeare a maye pole was sett vppe, pipeing & Daunceinge kepte &   35
somorale or churchale [l] made & sold in the p*a*rish of Biesley
aforesa*id*. & [⟨.⟩] chr*istoph*re Windle [⟨.⟩] sonne of the [sayd]
⌐ar*ticu*late⌐ chr*istoph*re Windle clarke was lord of the sayd Maypole
But whether the sayd Maypole was erect⟨..⟩ by the meanes &

5,33/ 1610 *underlined* MS   12/ somner *for* sommer
15,32/ ar*late *for* ar*ticu*late: *brevigraph omitted*

instigacion of the sayd viccar or whether h⟨.⟩ was the aughter therof
or defended the same to be lawfu⟨..⟩ this Deponent knoweth not
neyther hath credibily heard|

CHELTENHAM

1611
Manor and Hundred Court Book   GRO: D855/M8
f 90v*

          M*isericordia* lusor*um*   10

⟨.⟩xx s

x s

⟨.⟩ s   Affir*mantur* provt pat*et* super
⟨.⟩ s   dep*ositionibus* capit*ulorum.*/†

x s   15

⟨.⟩ s

⟨.⟩ s

...

Item *present*ant *super* sacram*entis* s*uis* provt sequitur in his Anglican*is*
verb*is* viz. that vpon thursday the xvij^th daie of Ianuary last past Guido   20
dobbins sounded his drume vp & downe the towne of Cheltenham
in the tyme of m*arkett* accompanied with Richard Clerke & divers
other younge fellowes being artificers & laborers, and the said Richard
Clerke following the said dobbins sounding his drume with a
trunchion or short staffe in his hand in the maner of a lyvten*ant* or   25
marshall man in very disorderly & rude maner caused proclam*acion*
to be made in divers places of the said towne publicquely proclayming,
that whosoever would heere a play should com*m*e to the signe of the
crowne such an howre, where they intended to play, whervpon the
Bayliffe of the lib*er*tie & towne of Cheltenham, taking notice therof,   30
much disliked therat, the rather for that the neighbor townes, namely
Tredington & Presbury were then infected with the plague, & the
towne of Cheltenham it self much suspected & greatly doubted that
th'infection was there also And thervpon required the said dobbins
Clerke & the rest that they should desist & forbeare to sounde the   35
drum*m*e & to make any further p*ro*clam*acion*. And did also send vnto
Thomas Milton keeping the signe of the Crowne to will him not to
suffer the said p*er*sons to play there, whervpon the said Clerke dobbins
& the rest in murmuring maner dep*ar*ted, but not satisfied did endevor
to play notwithstanding at the house of one david Powell a victualler   40

11–17/ *some numbers missing where page has frayed; note in* MS *opposite p 289, ll.7–14.*

likewise in Cheltenham, and some of them caused the drumme to
be sounded againe about viij of the clocke in the night of the said daie
which the Bayliffe hearing sent Iohn holdy vnder bayliffe there to will
them to forbeare from playing & drawing company together so
contemptuously especially in so dangerous a tyme, otherwise he the   5
said Bayliffe would come himselfe & suppresse them, which message
being deliuerid to the said Clerke & to the rest his consortes, &
companions he the said Clerke ⌜xx s⌝ dobbins ⌜v s⌝ Thomas Clerke ⌜v
s⌝ Richard ffortey ⌜v s⌝ Edmund Trinder ⌜v s⌝ Walter Milton ⌜v s⌝ &
Robert Cliveley ⌜v s⌝ with many others then assembled of their   10
company much insulted & revyled against the said holdy & also the
said chiefe Bayliffe with many rayling & opprobrious termes saying
that they respected neither of them both in contempt of all aucthority
& good governement, whervpon the said cheife Bayliffe vnderstanding
their insolent course went himselfe to suppresse them & to punish   15
them accordingly, which they vnderstanding departed & went away
before the comming of the said Bayliffe Ideo ipse in misericordia &c.

CHURCHDOWN

20

1633–5
Judgment upon Sabbath-breakers   Burton: *Divine Tragedie*
pp 10–11
...

A Miller at Churchdown, neer Glocester, would needs (contrary to   25
the admonitions both of his Minister in private, and generally in
publike, yea and that very day, and of other Christian friends) keep
a solemn Whitson ale, for which he had made large preparation and
provision, even of threescore dozen of cheesecakes, with other things
proportionable, in the Church-house, half a mile from his Mil, his   30
musicall instruments were set forth on | the side of the Church-house,
where the Minister and people were to passe to the Church to Evening
Prayer. When Prayer and Sermon were ended, the Drumme is struck
up, the peeces discharged, the Musicians play, and the rowt fall a
dauncing, till the evening; where they all with the Miller resort to his 35
Mill; where that evening before they had supt, about nine of the clock
on Whitsunday, a fire took suddenly in his house over their heads,
and was so brief and quick, that it burnt down his house and mill, and
devoured with all the greatest of all his other provision and
housholdstuffe. This is confirmed by sundry good testimonies.   40
...

8/ Clerke *underlined* MS

GLOUCESTER

1283–4
Account of Alms, Edward I   PRO: E 101/351/15
mb 1*   5

...

...In oblationibus Regis, apud Winchecumbe in ecclesia maiori per
manus dicti. H. vij.s.vij.d. Item in elemosina Regis data. xviij. infirmis
de manu Regis benedicentis in diuersis locis per illam ebdomadam.
xviij.d. Item Priori & Conuentui de Newent ad vnam pietanciam per   10
manus dicti H. de elemosina Regis. xx.s. Item clericis ludentibus
miracula sancti Nicholai & eorum Episcopo de elemosina Regis xxvj
s. viij d. Item fratribus sancti Iohannis de Crikelade de elemosina Regis
per manus dicti .H. xl.s.
                              Summa xvi. li. xv. s. vi. d.   15

Gloucestria
Die dominica v^{to} die Decembris in uigilia sancti Nicholai in pascendo
.xl. pauperes in honore sancte Trinitatis de statuta elemosina Regis per
manus dicti H. v. s. Die Lune sequenti in festo sancti Nicholai in
pascendo .L. pauperes de communi elemosina Regis per manus dicti
.H. vj.s.iiij.d. Eodem die in pascendo .C. pauperes in honore sancti   20
Nicholai de elemosina Regis .xij.s.vj.d. Die martis sequenti in
pascendo L pauperes in honore sancti Thome martyris de consueta
elemosina Regis .vj.s.iiij.d. in oblationibus Regis apud Gloucestriam
die sancti Nicholai predicto per manus dicti .H. vij s....

25

1301–2
Statutes of St Peter's Abbey   Hereford Cathedral Library: No 1826
single mb*   *(10 October)*

...

Nono Ne camera iuxta ordinaciones domini Cantuarie. pro ffratrum   30
necessariis deputata / aliis exaccionibus indebite oneretur / ordinatum
est/quod dominus Abbas / decem marcas quas de Camera percepit
porcionem etiam / quam soluunt Priores forinseci pro fratrum suorum
indumentis pro suo tempore tantum percipiat Ita quod alteri succedenti
eidem nichil contribuatur predictorum / sed dicta pecunia Camerario   35
totaliter assignetur vt fratribus valeat in vestibus vberius prouidere /
nec liceat Abbati cuicumque succedenti / Citharedas / aut ministrallos
alios tamquam de familia continue sustentare habeat autem Abbas
vnum esquierium in consilio discretum / & circumspectum qui in
monasterii necessitatibus valeat deseruire / et cum ad excercendum   40
visitacionis officium circuit Prioratus occacione statuti dicti Cantuarie

de non dandis pecunia & iocalib*us* in obedi*encia* aliq*u*a puta Camera
vel sac*ri*staria. siue Prioratu mora*m* no*n* trahat nisi sicut *tr*ahere
consueu*er*at ab antiquo

...

5

1393–4
Borough Bailiffs' Accounts   GRO: GBR F 3/2
single mb*

...

Item sol*uti* p*ro* diu*er*sis ministrall*is* & Nuncijs d*o*mini reg*is*   ⟨...⟩   10
Item sol*uti* ministrall' d*o*mini Ducis Glou*ce*strie   ⟨...⟩
Item sol*uti* ministrall' com*itis* marchie per iij⟨....⟩   ⟨...⟩
Item sol*uti* ministrall' & cuidam Nuncio com*itis* W⟨.....⟩   ⟨...⟩
Item sol*uti* ministrall' d*o*mini Dess⟨...⟩ij   ⟨...⟩

15

1409–10
Borough Bailiffs' Accounts   GRO: GBR F 3/4
single mb*

...

I⟨...⟩ sol*uti* Ministrall*is* d*o*mini Reg*is* hoc A*n*no   xiij⟨....⟩   20
Item in costag*ijs* fac*tis* sup*er* ministrall*os* d*o*mini Principis & donis
ip*s*is   xxxix vij⟨.⟩

...

Item in donis & expens*is* fac*tis* sup*er* ministrall' d*o*mini de codemore
& Ioh*annis* greynder   vij s v d   25

...

Item sol*uti* ministrall' d*o*mine comitisse stafford   ⟨...⟩

...

Item sol*uti* ministrall' d*o*mini de Berkeley d*imidia* mar⟨..⟩

...

30

1485–6
First Provincial Progress of Henry VII   BL: Cotton Julius B XII
ff 18–18v*

...

35

...Than the ffriday next folowing the king Roode & Remeved to
gloucester wher iij myles wit*h*oute the towne the mair wit*h* his brether
And Shriffes In Scarlet gownes And other people in great nomber in
Rede gownes al on horse bakk*es* Welcom*m*ed the king And

1/ occacione *for* occasione

wi*th*out the gate betwixte both brigges The *p*rocession of the freres
And also the *p*rocession of the town of Al the pariche chirches
Receyuede the king And in that towne ther was no pageaunt nor speche
ordeynede Thabbot And his Monk*es* Receyued the king wi*th*
*p*rocession | At thabbey Chirche doore wher the king Abode Satirday   5
And Sonday al day whiche was the trinytie Sonday And thabbot
mitred sange the high masse And in *p*rocession The Bisshop of
Worcest*er* prechide shewing the pop*es* Bull*es* touching as afor And on
the Monday the king Remeved to Bristow warde & lay at thabbey of
king*es* Woode And on tewsday dynyd at Acton wi*th* Sir Robert   10
poynez Shryef of gloucestershire....

...

1524–5
Corporation Custumnal   GRO: GBR B 2/1   15
ff 116–16v*   *(12 September)*

...

How the *p*rinces of Englond °ˏˡLady Maryˡ° was Receyved by the
Meire & Burgessez of the Towne of Glouce*ter* the xij^th day of
Septembre yn the xvij^th yere of the Reigne of o*ur* Soueraigne lord kyng   20
henry the viij^th yn the tyme of Iohn Rawlens Meyre ˏˡofˡ the same
Towne William Mathew and hen*re* ffrensche Shreff*es* there/ ffirst the
Meire Aldermen & Shreff*es* yn Scarlett & C. Burgesses [yn] Rode to
Quoddisleys Grene wi*th*yn the libertye of the seid Towne there
kepyng array tyll the seid *p*rinces came & then there obeysaunce on   25
horsebak showyng oon of the mases of the Towne/
Then by thadvyse of ther Counsell M*r* Meire & all his brederne yn
Scarlett settyng forward on horsebak ij & ij the *ser*iaunt*es* ledyng the
wey formust & knyght*es* squyars & gentyltylmen yn the myddes and
the Meire next byfore her g*ra*ce rydyng wi*th* the *ser*iaunt at Armys   30
barehede & oon of the sergeaunt*es* mases yn his hand
Then all the ladyes & gentilwomen folowyng her g*ra*ce on horsebak
After them all her *ser*ua*u*ntes yn a lyue*r*ey & her officers
And after them other of the Stywarde*s* & Burgesses of the Town ij &
ij so rydyng to the Town ende Where all the Clerge Were yn Copys   35
Crosses Carpett*es* & Cusshyns and her g*ra*ce lovyngly there kyssynge
the Crosse on horsebak/|
And then Rode forthe eu*er*y man After the seid man*er* throwȝe the

24/ Quoddisleys Grene: *Quedgeley Green, two miles south of Gloucester*
29/ gentyltylmen: *dittography*
37/ verte foliu*m* (*turn the page*) *written slightly below end of line*

Towne bryngyng her grace into the Abbey throwȝe Seynt Edwardes
gate The Abbott & his brederne then beyng yn the Abbey porche with
Copys Crosse Carpettes & Cusshyns receyvyng her grace And so she
dyd a lyght of horse & kyssed the Crosse/ And then went vp to the
high Awter Mr Meyre & all his brederne yn Skarlett goyng byfore her   5
grace & there she offered A pece of gold & then proceded to her
loggyng Mr Meire & his seid brederne byfore her/
The Gyfte and present gevyn by the Meire & his breþern to þe princes
ffirst ij fatte oxen of the best that myght be gotton
Item x fatte Wethurs of the best þat myght be gotton/   10

1534–5
Corporation Custumnal   GRO: GBR B 2/1
ff 117v–19*   (*31 July–7 August*)

                                                                            15

Howe owre most dreade Soueraign lorde Kyng henry the viij^th
by the grace of god of England & of ffraunce Kyng defender of
the ffaith lorde of Ireland & in erthe Supreme hedde of the
Churche of England & his most dere & entierly beloued lawfull
Wiff quene Anne at ther ffirst commyng to Glouceter after his   20
graces Coronacion was resceyued by the maire Aldermen Shriffes
& Burgessez of the seid towne of Glouceter commyng from
Tewkysbury toward Glouceter the Saturday the last day of Iuly
in the xxvij^th yere of [the reign] his most Riall reign in the tyme
of Iohn ffawconer then beyng Maire of the towne of Glouceter   25
Thomas Payne & Richard Edwardes Shriffes there as hereafter
ensuyth//
ffirst the maire Aldermen Shriffes & Shriffes peres in ther Skarlett
gownes & velfett typpettes with an .C. of other Burgessez or ther
abowtes in Cootes of Musterdevilles all. And rode ffourth of the towne   30
toward Tewkysbury till they came to the grene at the hether ende of
the lane athisside Brickehamptons brigge within the libertie of the seid
towne? Then & there metyng the kynges grace & the quene and did
ther obeysaunce all on horsebacke gevyng his grace the right hande/
And then the maire rode vnto his grace (seyng these wordes) thankes   35
be to god of your graces helth & good prosperite. Whiche god long
Contynue. And therwith the maire beyng still on horsebacke with oon
of ˄'the' towne masez in his hand kissed the same Mase & did his
Obeysaunce. & delyuered it vp vnto his grace (seyng these wordes)
[thankes to be to god of your graces] that all suche liberties privelages   40
Customes & grauntes as your grace & other your noble progenytours
˄'here' tofore haue gevyn vnto the Maire & Burgessez of this your

towne of Glouceter. We delyuer [haue] vp vnto your grace. trustyng
that your grace wilbe as good & graciouce lord vnto vs nowe as ye
haue byn here to ffore? And ferthermore I here presente my selff vnto
your grace as maire of your seid towne of Glouceter certyfying you
that all your burgessez there be in a redynes & obedyent at your graces   5
Commaundement & hartely thankes your grace for suche liberties
priveleges & grauntes that your grace hathe gevyn vnto vs/ besechyng
you of your graciouuce aide & [assiss] assistaunce herafter in the
execucon therof in doyng Iustice/. And so the kynges grace resceyved
the | same mase. Wheruppon his grace immediately delyuered it ayen   10
vnto the maire with all such liberties priveleges Customes & grauntes
as were byfore tyme graunted. And then rode foreward in maner &
forme folowyng/. That is to wit first & foremost rode all the burgesses
in a ray ij & ij next them the Skarlett gownes. then all Gentilmen
Esquyers knyghtes lordes & other greate men and then the maire opyn   15
hedde with the mase still in his hand & the kyng of arrodes with hym.
then rode next the kyng he that bare the Swirde & on euery side of
hym a sergeaunt at armys with ther masys. And then folowid the
kynges grace & the quene with all the lades & gentilwomen folowyng
them. & after them the Garde & other Sondry persons folowyng the   20
Courte/ till they came byfore the White ffrires without the vtter north
yate/. Wher all the Clergie were in Coopys & the lorde Suffryngam
mytourde with Crosse Carpettes & Cusshynges. And his grace & the
quene bothe beyng on horsebacke lovyngly there kissed the Crosse.
And then rode forthe euery man after the seid maner throwght the   25
towne bryngyng his grace into the Abbey throwght Seynt Edwardes
lane. The abbott & his bretherne then beyng in the abbey Churche
porche with Coopys Crosse Carpettes & Cusshynges receyvyng his
grace. And so lighted of his horsebacke & the quene also & kneled
downe bothe & kissed the Crosse with greate Reueraunce. And then   30
went vp to the highe Alter. And so fromthens to there lodgynges. And
the maire Alwey byfore his grace with the mase in his hande till he
came to his lodgyng &c/
Item the monday the second day after his graces comyng to Glouceter
abowte x of the Clocke his grace & the quene both beying rydyng   35
toward paynswicke to huntyng, the maire with certen of his bretherne
mett his grace in the abbey Churche yarde. & presented hym there
with tenne ffatte Oxen price xx li. for the whiche his grace gave vnto
them lovyng thankes. And the same day in the darke evenyng they
came from paynswicke. And at Aillesgate mett them Certen persons   40

41/ Aillesgate: *Gloucester's east gate*

to the noumbre of xv with torches light & browght there graces in to
the Abbey/ for the whiche they gave hartie thankes. & the quenes grace
gave them in reward iiij angellett nobles at that tyme//|
Item the tewesday the thirde day after his graces comyng he & the
quenes grace also beyng rydyng toward Coberley the seid Maire &   5
his bretherne mett the quene in the abbey Churche yarde and ther

xj li.v s   presented hir with a purse of gold price xij s & xxᵗⁱ rialles in golde
theryn whiche Amounted to xj li. v s. for whiche hir grace gave like
lovyng thankes as the kyng hadd don tofore/. And the same day the
kyng hunted at myserden in so moche it was nyght er his grace came   10

torches   to Aillysyate. where mett hym xl burgessez in there best apparell with
torches light as they did byfore & browght his grace into the abbey
for the whiche he gave hartie thankes & ffyve markes in gold for there
reward in soe doyng &c/

15
Howe our seid Soueraign lorde the kyng & the quene also departed
from Glouceter the vijᵗʰ Day of august then next folowyng at after
none. & that nyght laye at leonard Stanley & on the morowe from
thens toward Barkeley. And the maner & forme howe is grace rode
forth till he came to quoddesleys grene/   20

ffirst the maire & his brethern with suche burgesses as were byfore
appoynted prepared them selffes in like apparell as they were yn at his
graces resceyvyng on horsebacke at the Abbey Churche dore & there
gave attendaunce till his grace came ffourthe & was on horsebacke.   25
And then rode fforthe euery man in there degree after the maner &
forme as they did at his graces resceyving into the towne/. throwght
the towne forthe at the Sowthe yate. And so rode accordyngly till they
came into quoddesley grene/ where all the townes men sate on
horsebacke in a raunge gevyng his grace the right hande And there did 30
the kyng take the maire by the hande & so departed. And soe both
the kynges grace & the quene passid by the seid townes men. And gave
them all thankes. That don the maire with the aldermen Shriffes & all
other [of] burgessez returned all to gethers homeward & rode with the
maire to his dore ij & ij to gethers in a ray in like maner & forme as   35
they rode forthe. And then at the maires dore euery man departed and
went home &c//.|

5/ Coberley: *eight miles east of Gloucester in the Cotswold Hills*
10/ myserden: *Miserden, ten miles southeast of Gloucester in the Cotswolds*
18/ leonard Stanley: *eight miles south of Gloucester*
20/ quoddesleys grene: *Quedgeley Green, two miles south of Gloucester*

The giftes gevyn by the Maire & Burgessez of the towne of
Glouceter vnto the kynges grace the quene with there officers &
servauntes at there ffirst beyng at Glouceter after the Coronacon
as before is mencioned as hereafter ensuyth

5

In primis to the kynges grace tenne ffatte	
oxen price	xx li
Item to the quenes grace A purce of golde price	
xij s. with xxᵗⁱ rialles of gold theryn conteynyng xj li. v s	
Summa	xj li. xvij s 10
Item for gese capons & chekyn gevyn to	
Maister Secutorys	[xv] xj s v d
Item in reward gevyn to oon of the kynges	
seruauntes whiche made proclamacon ayenst	
his graces ffirst comyng	xiij s iiij d 15
Item to the kynges ffotemen at his graces	
departure	xij s vj d
Item to quenes ffotemen	v s.
Item to the kynges Trompettors	xij s vj d
Item to the seruauntes of the kynges boterye	iij s ix d 20
Item to the seruauntes of the kynges pantrye	iij s ix d
Item in reward gevyn to the blacke garde	viij s
Item geven to the kynges Amners seruaunt	xij d
Item to the arrode of arremes	xxvij s. vj d.
Summa totalis	xxxiij li. ix s j d 25

1550–1
Corporation Chamberlains' Accounts   GRO: GBR F 4/3
f 23v*   *(Gifts and necessary expenses)*

30

...Also in reward gevyn to maister kyngestons abbott of Mysrule
Commyng to the Citie of Glouceter in the Cristemas tyme by the
Commaundement of the maior x s. Also in reward gevyn to the pleyers
of the seid maister kyngeston by the Commaundement of the maior
by the tyme of this present accompte v s....

35

1551–2
Corporation Chamberlains' Accounts   GRO: GBR F 4/3
f 30*   *(Gifts and necessary expenses)*

40

...Also in money paied & gevyn to the pleyers of Sir Anthony
kyngeston by the Commaundement of the maior & his brethern the
tyme of this present accompte x s ...

1552–3
Corporation Chamberlains' Accounts   GRO: GBR F 4/3
f 37v*   *(Gifts and necessary expenses)*

...Also in money gevyn in reward to Sir Anthony Kyngestons   5
pleyars the tyme of this present accompte by the Commaundement
of the maire vj s. viij d. And in money likewise gevyn in reward to
a geister of the kynges maiesties & an other Commyng with hym by
the Commaundement of maister maire v s.... Also in money gevyn
to the Gentilman that browght the proclamacon for the   10
Quenes grace that nowe is by the Commaundement of maister maire
& his brethern att the newe Inne lx s. And in money gevyn the same
tyme to Sir Iohn A Bridges Trompetor by like Commaundement x s....
Also in reward gevyn to maister Arnoldes seruauntes on may day at
the bryngyng in of may by the Commaundement of the maire   15
xx s. Also in reward gevyn the same tyme to William Tele & his
Company by like Commaundement vj s. viij d. And more to those
persons that daunsed the moorys daunse the same tyme by like
Commaundement v s.
...   20

1553–4
Corporation Chamberlains' Accounts   GRO: GBR F 4/3
f 44*   *(Gifts and expenses)*
                                                                              25
...Also in money gevyn in reward to the pleyers of the Citie by
mr maires Commaundement vj s viij d ...
...

1554–5   30
Corporation Chamberlains' Accounts   GRO: GBR F 4/3
f 50   *(Gifts and necessary expenses)*

...Also in reward gevyn to the Quenes Geister by the
Commaundement of maister maire iij s iiij d ...   35

1555–6
Corporation Chamberlains' Accounts   GRO: GBR F 4/3
f 56v   *(Gifts and necessary expenses)*
                                                                              40
...Also in money gevyn to the Quenes pleyars by the tyme of this
accompte by like commaundement of the seid maior vj s viij d...
...

1558–9
Corporation Chamberlains' Accounts   GRO: GBR F 4/3
f 73   *(Gifts and necessary expenses)*

...Also in moneye payed & gevyn by the tyme of this accompte by
Mr. mayor*es* com*m*aundement to my Lord Chaundos player*es* vj s
viij d...

...

1559–60
Corporation Chamberlains' Accounts   GRO: GBR F 4/3
f 78*   *(Payments)*

...

...Also in money payed for an hundred of bordenayles to make a
Scaffolde in the Bothall for Quenes ma*iestes* players – j d Also payed
to Iohn battye carpinter & his fellowe for the makinge of the seide
Scaffolde – iiij d ...

f 79*   *(Gifts and necessary expenses)*

...Also paid at the com*m*aundeme*n*t of Mr Maier & other the aldermen
of the Citie to the Quenes ma*iestes* players playeng openly in the
bothall in the tyme of this accompte x s Also paide in money for a
banket the same day by the said maire & aldermen at the taverne upon
the saide plaiers v s vij d Also in money paide by the afor seide
Accom*m*ptaunt*es* to the Lord ambrose dudleies plaiers by the
com*m*aundement of mr mayre playeng openly in the bothall in the
tyme of this accompte vj s viij d ...

1560–1
Corporation Chamberlains' Accounts   GRO: GBR F 4/3
ff 83v–4*   *(Gifts and necessary expenses)*

...

...Also geven in Rewarde to the lorde Roberte dudleyes playor*es* at
mr mayor*es* com*m*aundemente in Redye moneye vj s. viij d. Also
geven in rewarde to Sir Androwe ffortescues players at mr mayor*es*
com*m*aundemente in redye moneye by Iohn Smythe iiij s. Also geven
in p*r*esente to the lorde p*r*esidente of the m*er*ches at his late | beinge
here in Glouceter one hoggeshedde of Clarrett wyne w*hi*ch coste xlix
s. viij d....Also geven in rewarde to my lord*es* Trumpettor in redye
moneye ij s. Also geven in rewarde to Iustyce Trogm*er*ton his
mynstrell*es* in redye moneye ij s....

...

1561-2

Corporation Chamberlains' Accounts   GRO: GBR F 4/3

f 89*   *(Gifts and necessary expenses)*

...

Also the same Accomptaunt*es* aske allowaunce in moneye payed &   5
geven in Rewarde to the Quenes ma*i*esties players this yere x s. Also
bestowed & spente vpon the same players at the taverne iiij s. Also
payed to Mr Ingram for a pounde of candell*es* at the same playe
iij d....Also in Reward*es* geven to the Erle of warwick*es* players at Mr
mayor*es* Com*m*aundemente in redye monye x s. Also payed for a   10
bankett made to the seid players & for makynge of a [S⟨..⟩ f] Scaffold
in the bothall iiij s. ij d. ob....Also geven in Rewarde to the lorde
Roberte dudleye his *s*ervaunt*es* & players by the ⟨...⟩
com*m*aundemente of Mr mayor in Redy moneye xiij s. iiij d. Also
spente vppon the seid players at the taverne and for makynge of the   15
scaffold in the bothall iiij s. viij d.

1562-3

Corporation Chamberlains' Accounts   GRO: GBR F 4/3

f 94v   *(Gifts and necessary expenses)*   20

Also the same accomptaunt*es* aske allowaunce of moneye payed &
geven in Rewarde to the duchesse of Suffolk*es* players by the
com*m*aundemente of Mr mayor x s. Also bestowed & spente vppon
the same players at the taverne xx d. Also payed for the makynge of   25
the skaffold at the Bothall & for nayles there iiij d....

1563-4

Corporation Chamberlains' Accounts   GRO: GBR F 4/3

f 100v⁺   *(Payments)*   30

...Also paid by the Com*m*aundement of Mr mayor to one that brought
golden som*m*es [to] p*a*rchment from the lord of misrule of hineham
xij d....

35

f 102   *(Gifts and necessary expenses)*

...Also geven Stanweye the Quenes Iugler for shewinge pastimes and
other f his Iuglinge feat*es* to Mr mayor and other of his bretherne this
yeare by the com*m*aundement of Mr mayor x s. Also geven to the Erle   40
of warwickes playor*es* by the com*m*aundement of Mr mayor this yeare
x s. Also vp*on* the same playor*es* at the wine taverne iij s. Also geven
in rewar⌈de⌉ this yeare likiwise by the Com*m*aundemente of Mr mayor

ₐ⌐to⌐ the lorde Cobhames player*es* v s....

1564–5
Corporation Chamberlains' Accounts   GRO: GBR F 4/3
f 107   *(Payments)*

...Also paid for the makinge of the scaffold in the bothall at the tyme
that the Quenes ma*i*esties player*es* did play*e* there befor mr mayor and
thaldermen ij d. Also in money paid for takinge of the same scaffold
awaye agayne ij d....

f 108   *(Gifts, rewards, and necessary expenses)*

Also the same accomptaunt*es* aske allowaunce of money paid and
geven*n* in rewarde to the Quenes m*a*iest*es* playor*es* by the
commaundement of mr mayor xvj s. viij d. Also in money paide &
geven in reward to the lorde stranges playores by the like
comaundement of mr mayor x s....

...

1565–6
Corporation Chamberlains' Accounts   GRO: GBR F 4/3
f 114   *(Gifts, rewards, and necessary expenses)*

Allso the same accomptaunt*es* aske allowaunce of money paied &
geven in reward*es* to the lorde hundsdons plaiars the makinge of the
scaffolde in the bothall & the drinckinge xij s. viij d....Allso geven to
the quenes plaior*es* playinge at the bothall by the commaundement of
mr maior xiij s. iiij d. Allso for wine & chirries spente vppon them
at Mr Swerdbearers ij s. viij d....

1567–8
Corporation Chamberlains' Accounts   GRO: GBR F 4/3
f 123v   *(Payments)*

...Alsoe pd to battie for C & iij quarter*es* of elme bourd*es* for a skaffold
for playors to play*e* one viij s. Alsoe pd to hime for a peece of tymber
to sett vnder the bourd*es* ij s....

f 124   *(Gifts, rewards, and necessary expenses)*
...

Also the same accomptaunce aske a lowaunce of money pd and geven
in rewarde to the erle of worcester his players and their drinkynge at
Mr swordberers by the commaundement of mr mayore xij s. vj d. alsoe

in money pd and geven to the quenes ma*iestes* players and their
drinkinge xvj s. ij d....

...

1568–9   5
Corporation Chamberlains' Accounts   GRO: GBR F 4/3
f 128v*   *(Gifts and rewards)*

...

ffirste thesame accomptaunt*es* aske allowaunce of money by them
geu*en* to mr ffoskeues plaiers at the Co*m*maundement of mr maior x   10
s. And for theire drinckling ij s. vj d. Allsoe geu*en* to the lorde mong*es*
plaiers at the Co*m*maundement of Mr maior iij s. iiij d....

f 129   *(Gifts and rewards)*
...Allsoe geu*en* to the erle of woorcesters plaiers xiij s. iiij d....   15

1569–70
Corporation Chamberlains' Accounts   GRO: GBR F 4/3
f 133v   *(Gifts and rewards)*

...   20
...Allsoe geu*en* in rewarde to the Quenes plaiers xiij s. iiij d....Allsoe
geven in rewarde to therle of lecesters players playing before Mr Maior
xiij s iiij d....Allsoe geu*en* to theirle of suxsex plaiers plainge before
Mr Maior x s. Allsoe spent on them ij s. vj d....

                                                                        25

1570–1
Corporation Chamberlains' Accounts   GRO: GBR F 4/3
f 138*   *(Payments)*
...Alsoe paicd to the vssher of the fenche Schole for his paines in
playenge before the watche one midsomer yeve and Sainte Peters yeve   30
xij d....

f 139   *(Gifts and rewards)*

...Alsoe geven to the Earle of worcesters plaiers for playinge before   35
Mr Maior and his bretherne the vj^{th} of februarie x s. Alsoe spente
vppon them at the taverne the same time ij s....Alsoe geven to thearle
of Leysetors plaiers for playinge before Mr Maior and his bretherne
the xxx^{th} of Aprill by the Co*m*mandemente of Mr Maior xiij s. iiij d.
Alsoe spente vppon them at the Taverne by the like co*m*mandemente   40
iij s. viij d. Alsoe geven in rewarde to the Quenes Ma*iestes* Berward
for baytinge of his bears before Mr Maior and his bretherne the
seconde of m⟨.⟩ie ⟨vj s.⟩ viij d....

f 139v

…Alsoe geven to the lifftenante of the tower his plaiers for playinge
before Mr maior and his bretherne the xx^th of September x s. Alsoe
spente vppon them at the Swordberers by the commandemente of Mr   5
Maior ij s. vj d.

1571–2
Corporation Chamberlains' Accounts   GRO: GBR F 4/3
f 146   *(Gifts and rewards)*   10
…
…geven to the Queenes ma*i*esties plaiers at the comaundment of
Master Maior alsoe Spente vppon them at the swoordbearars by Like
comaundmente iiij s. vj d. allsoe geven to Ladie Manches plaiers by
comaundmente of Master Maior x s. Allsoe for ˏ⌈their⌉ dringinge ij s.   15
viij d.…

1572–3
Corporation Chamberlains' Accounts   GRO: GBR F 4/3
f 153*   *(Gifts and rewards)*   20
…
Alsoe the same accomptantes aske allowance of money geuen in
rewarde as folowethe ffirste gevene to the Earle of Wosters plaiers the
firste daie of December Anno D*o*m*i*ni 1573 by Com*m*aundemente of
Maister Maior x s. Allsoe spente vppon them by like   25
Com*m*aundemente iij s. iiij d.…

f 153v

…Allsoe geven by like Com*m*aundement to the Earle of Sussex plaiers   30
the thirde of Aprell xiij s. iiij d. Allsoe spent vppon them at that time
v s. Allsoe geuen by like com*m*aundement to the Earle of Essexe plaiers
the tenthe of Iulie xiij s. iiij d. Allsoe spent vppon them iiij s. vj d.
Allsoe geuen to the Lorde Moongeis plaiers the laste of September by
like Com*m*aundemente then not plaienge before the Maior v s.…   35
…

1573–4
Corporation Chamberlains' Accounts   GRO: GBR F 4/3
f 159v*   *(Payments)*   40
…
Alsoe the same accomptauntes praie allowaunce of iiij s. by them paied

to Maister Semis for three staf torches Allsoe paied to Edward
ffleminnge for eighttenthe linkes to lighte in the Quenes Maiestie ix
s. Allsoe paied to him for tene staffe torches xvj s. viij d.....Allsoe paied
for benttes for Maister maior and Maister recorder to knele vpon at
the receauinge of the Quenes Maiestie ij d....   5

f 160   *(Gifts and rewards)*

...Allsoe geuen to the Earle of wosters plaiers x s. Allsoe spente one
them in charges iiij s....   10

f 160v*

°All Rewardes° Alsoe the same accomptantes praie allowaunce of money geuene in
gifftes as followethe./ffirste geuen to the Quenes Maiestie one Cuppe
doble gilte weienge threscore seuentene ounces and three quarters at   15
sixe shillinges tenne pence the ounce xxvj li. xj s. iiij d. Allsoe geuen
to her Maiestie in golde in the same Cuppe xl li. Allsoe geuene to the
kinge of heraldes *(blank)* Allsoe geuen to the Sergeauntes at armes xl s.
Allsoe geuen to her Maiesties footemen iij li. Allsoe geuen to her
Maiesties Tromppettors 1 s. Allsoe geuen to the Clarke of the markett   20
xl s. Allsoe geuen to the yeomene of the Bottelles xx s. Allsoe geuen
to the ordenarie massingers of the Quenes Chamber xl s. Allsoe geuen
to them that did kepe the Quenes Maiesties sworde and the mace xx
s. geuen to the Quenes musitianes xx s. Allsoe geuen to her maiesties
porters x s. Allsoe geuen to her maiesties Couchemen xxvj s. viij d. 25
Allsoe geuen vnto the blacke garde xx s. geuen to her maiesties Bakers
vj s. Allsoe geuen to the waie maister x s. Allsoe geuen to the officers
of the boylinge house v s. Paied to the Marshall for a proclamacion
xiij s. iiij d. paied for a Copie of the same proclamacion ij s. vj d. geuen
to the marshalls man vj s. viij d. geuen to the Clarke of the marketts   30
man vj s. viij d. Allsoe geuen to the waytts that came with the Quenes
footemen to dinner to maister maiors v s. Allsoe geuen to my Lorde
of Leycestors Trumppettors and musitianes vj s. viij d. Allsoe geuen
to the Lorde Treasorer one sugger loffe weyinge fiftie pounde at
sixtene pence the pounde xx s. Allsoe geuen to him twoe gallons of 35
secke and one gallande of clarrett wine vj s. viij d. Paied to him that
broughte the redde dere which the Quenes maiesties sente x s. Paied
to the waytes of Shresburie for plaienge aboute the Citie everie
moreninge as longe as the Quenes grace was here xxvj s. viij d....
                                                                                                              40

f 162*   *(Charges for repairs)*

Alsoe the same accomptauntes praie allowaunce of money by them

disbursed as folowethe ffirste for paintinge of the Tollsey xxx s. Allsoe
paied to Iohn Rise for trimenge of the kinges borde xxij s. Allsoe paied
to Gilden for makinge the beastes for the kinges boorde iij li. paied
to him for Coloringe of the Criste schole xij s paied to William Sannes
for hornes for the Antelap and vnicornes and the tonge for the Dragon   5
ij s. viij d. paied vnto Iohn windowe for the Cariedge of twoe loode
of birche to the medow viij d. and for one loode of sande to the kinges
borde viij d. and for the Carriage of twoe lode of grauell to the forren
bridge vj d. paied for pauinge aboute the crosse vj d. paied to fiftene
laborers for makinge of the highe waie with owte the Southegate   10
throught the pastures for the Quenes Maiestie vij s. vj d. paied to
William Dove for the hawlinge of fower draftes of plankes to make
bridges to the meadowe ij s. paied to sparkes and hickes for twoe daies
worke ij s. viij d. Paied for twoe loode of sande for the Castell lane
ende xx d. Paied for twoe loode of sande more hade into the Colledge   15
lane xx d. paied to harrison for dressinge the Bothall and the Tollsey
xx s. paied for packethred for the Scaffolde in the meadow vij d. paied
to Battie for takinge downe the scaffolde in the meadowe and settinge
vpp a paire of tesselles at the Crosse xv d. paied for the makinge cleane
of the Trinitie Crosse iiij d. paied for makinge cleane of the Streate   20
at the colledge gate xij d. paied to Roger Layton Iohn Shewell Iohn
Viner and Richard hickes for woorkinge in the meadowe xij d. paied
to William Cugley for tenne daies worke vj s. viij d. paied to Thomas
wheler for the hawlinge of one lode of birche and one lode of bordes
into the meadowe viij d. paied for sixetene lode of grauell bestowed   25
betwene the twoe northe gates xiij s. paied to Gildene for mendinge
the Quenes picture and the pinicle vj s. viij d. Allsoe they aske
allowaunce of money by them disbursed for dressinge and paintinge
the Crosse and the kinges borde viz. for stones bordes Timber Canvas
verdigrese allablaster worke manes hier and manie other necessarie   30
thinges as by the perticulers thereof shewed and examined plainlie maie
appere xlij li. xiij s. x d. Allsoe paied for paintinge of the fowere gates
x li. xiiij s. iiij d. Allsoe the aske allowaunce of money by them
disbursed for makinge of twoe Scaffoldes with the furniture of the
pagentes at the vtter northegate and at the highe Crosse viz. for timber   35
bordes Ivie mosse workemans hier and diuerse othere necessaries as
by the perticulers thereof shewed and examined plainlie appearethe
lxiiij li. ij s. v d. Allsoe paied to the musitians that plaied at the
Scaffoldes and the Gates x s. Allsoe paied to Maister henrie Shrieffe
for a greate powle for the skaffolde for the gate xij d. paied to Thomas   40

19/ tesselles *for* tresselles

wheler for hawlinge certaine peces of timber from the meadowe into
the Towne xij d. Allsoe paied to Iohn Battie and twoe laborers for
mendinge of the cradell and measuringe of bordes and timber iij s. vj d.
Allsoe paied to Iacson for twoe peces of timber xviij d.

     Su*mm*a Cxxviij l. iij s. iij d.   5

1574–5
Corporation Chamberlains' Accounts GRO: GBR F 4/3
f 169v *(Gifts and rewards)*

                     10

…Allsoe geven to the Lorde of Sussex plaiers xiij s. iiij d. and more
to them in wine and makinge a skaffolde xviij s. viij d. Allsoe geven
to Maister Comptrollers players iij s. iiij d. Allsoe geven to the Quenes
Berrardes iiij s.…. Allsoe geven to the Erle of Essex players by Mayster
Maiors Com*m*aundement xiij s. And more in wine to them bestowed 15
v s. Item geven to the Lorde of Leycesters bearrade vj s. viij d.…

1575–6
Corporation Chamberlains' Accounts GRO: GBR F 4/3
f 184v *(Payments)*   20

…payed Batty for plankes for the scaffould at the Boothall and
workmanshipp iiij s. vij d.…

…

                     25

f 185 *(Gifts and rewards)*

…Allso geeven to the Lorde of Sussex players xx s. Allso geeven vnto
the Lorde Comptons players xxiij s. iiij d.

…   30

1577–8
Corporation Chamberlains' Accounts GRO: GBR F 4/3
f 195v* *(Gifts and rewards)*

                     35

…Geven to my lorde Sheffields players x s. Geven to the lorde
mountyoes xiij s. iiij d. *Item* and for a drinkinge and for a drinkinge
for them iiij s. viij d. and so in the holl xviij s. Geven to my lord
wourcesters players xiij s. iiij d.…. Geven to my lorde Barkleyes players

---

37/ and for a drinkinge and for a drinkinge: *dittography*

and spente on them xiiij s. vj d....Geven to the Earle of Bathes players
vj s. viij d....

...

1578–9   5
Corporation Chamberlains' Accounts   GRO: GBR F 4/3
f 198v*   *(Fees and wages)*
...
...Also paide to Garratt Barneys for his yeeres fee ended at
Michaellmas xx s....   10

f 199v*   *(Gifts and rewards)*

...Geuen to the Barons of kyndertons Players ⌐vj s. viij d. Also geuen
to the Countes of Essex players⌐ xx s. Also geuen to my *Lord* Ogles   15
Players vj s. viij d. Also geuen to the Lorde Barckleys Players vj s.
viij d....
...

1579–80   20
Corporation Chamberlains' Accounts   GRO: GBR F 4/3
f 202   *(Fees and wages)*
...
...Also paide to Garrett Barnys, for his yeerely fee ended at
Michaellmas xx s....   25

f 202v

Paymentes of   ...Paide vnto the Earle of Darbyes Players v s....
money   The same accomptauntes praye allowaunce of money by them   30
Gyftes and   disbursed for giftes and rewardes bestowed as followeth/ ffirste geuen
Rewards   the xxviij^th of *(blank)* 1579/ vnto my lorde Barkleys Players by Mr
                 Thomas Machen Maior xiij s. iiij d....Geuen the 20th of Iune/1580/
                 by Mr Mayors appoinctmente vnto the Lorde Sheffildes Players vj s.
                 viij d....   35

1580–1
Corporation Common Council Minute Book   GRO: GBR B 3/1
ff 71v–2*   *(3 November)*
...   40
°plaiers of   At the Counceill it was moued that some restreinte mighte be hadde
enterludes°   ageinst commen Players of Enterludes./ And for so much as daillie
°pg. 130:°   experience teacheth and delyuereth that the commen Players of

Enterludes and playes Drawe awey greate Sommes of money. from
diuerse persons. and allure seruauntes, apprentices and iorneyman &
other of the worst desposed persons to leudenes and lightnes of life.
besides the maintenaunce of idlenes and diuerse other inconveniences
which arise thereby. most necessarie to be redressed. It is therfore   5
at this Councell graunted, concluded and condiscended vnto/ by the
holle ˌ⸢company at this⸣ Councell assembled/ That Players of
Enterludes. and common Players shall not be suffred within this Citie
at any tyme herafter in any other sorte or manner, or otherwise than
°Queenes .iij.°   followeth and herinconteyned./. ffirst the Queenes maiestes Players   10
to be allowed to playe three interludes or playes within three dayes
or vnder. at euery one tyme of theire comminge to or beinge within
this Citie/ and no more/ nor oftener// And the players of any subiecte
| beinge a baron of the parliamente or of higher callinge or degree to
°Baron .ij.°   be allowed to playe ij playes or interludes in twoe dayes or vnder at   15
every ⸢one⸣ tyme of theire comminge to or within this Citie and noe
moore nor oftener./ And any other subiectes players vnder the degree
°others .j.°   of a Baron of the parliament and beinge allowed by the statutes and
Lawes of the Realme to keape or have players to be allowed to playe
but one playe or interlude in one daye at every one tyme of there   20
comminge to or beinge within this Citie and noe more nor oftener./
And that none of the players above mencioned be they her maiestes
players or others be suffered or allowed to playe in the nighte season
°time°   nor at any vnfeet tyme neither at any tyme withoute Warrante or
°licence°   Licence from Mr Maior of this Citie./ And it is lyke agreed and   25
ordeyned that noe Burges of this Citie shall at any tyme hereafter
°howse°   permitt or suffer any players to be played in his howse withoute
ˌ⸢expresse⸣ Licence of mr Maior nor otherwise then in other sorte then
is above declared vnder paine of discomininge/
...   30

Corporation Chamberlains' Accounts   GRO: GBR F 4/3
f 207   *(Fees and wages)*

...Allsoe paide vnto Garrett Barnes for his yerelie fee ended at   35
micklemas xx s....

f 208v   *(Gifts and rewards)*
...
The same accomptauntes doe aske and praie allowaunce of money by   40

1/ S *of* Sommes *written over illegible letter*   27/ players *for* playes
29/ discomininge: *part of second* n *missing*

them disbursed for gieftes and rewardes by them bestowed as
followeth/ ffirste paied vnto the lorde Strainges players by
thappointment of mr maior xiiij s. iiij d....

f 209   5

...Allsoe geven vnto the lorde Berckleis players vj s. viij d....

1581–2
Corporation Chamberlains' Accounts   GRO: GBR F 4/3   10
f 212   *(Fees and wages)*

...Also payde to Garrett Barneyes for his yeeres fee xx s....

f 214*   *(Gifts and rewards)*   15

...Geven by mr maiors comaundement to my lorde Barkleyes players
xiij s. iiij d....Geven to my lorde morleyes players the xviij^th of Iuly
1582 vj s. viij d. Geven to my lorde Staffordes players vj s. viij
d....Geven to my ⟨L⟩ *(blank)* players vj s. viij d. Geven to my lorde   20
Huntesdounes players xiij s. iiij d. Geven to her maiestes poppette
players the vij^th of december 1582 xx s....
...

1582–3   25
Corporation Chamberlains' Accounts   GRO: GBR F 4/3
f 218   *(Fees and wages)*
...
...Also paide to Garrette Barneyes the musicion for his holl yeeres fee
xx s....   30

f 218v   *(Gifts and rewards)*

...Geven by mr maiors appoinctement to my lorde Chaundos players
the vij^th of November 1582 xx s. Geven to my lorde Barckleyes players 35
the xxx^th of November xiij s. iiij d....Geven to [my] ˹the˺ Lorde
Staffordes players x s. Geven to the Earle of Oxonford players the
xxvj^th of may xvj s. viij d....Given to her maiestes players xxx s....
...

1583–4
Corporation Chamberlains' Accounts   GRO: GBR F 4/3
f 225   *(Fees and wages)*

...Also paide to Garrette Barneyes for his holl yeeres fee xx s....   5
...

f 226   *(Gifts and rewards)*
...
Also they aske allowaunce of diuerse sommes of money by them
disbursed for giftes and rewardes bestowed as followeth. viz. To the   10
players of the Master of the Revelles of the Queenes maiestes howse
xiij s. iiij d. To the Earle of woorcesters players the the two and
twentith of December vj s. viij d. Paid to the Lorde Chaundos players
the xj^th of Ianuarye x s. To the Earle of Oxefordes players vj s. viij
d....Given the seconde of Maye to the Lorde Staffordes players vj s.   15
viij d....

f 226v

...Given to the Earle of Essex players the fifth of October vj s. viij d.   20

1584–5
Corporation Chamberlains' Accounts   GRO: GBR F 4/3
ff 231–1v   *(Gifts and rewards)*
...   25
...geven by the appoinctement of mr maior to the Lord Barckleyes
players x s....geven by the appoinctement of mr maior to the Lorde
(blank) players vj s. viij d....geven by the appoinctement of Mr Maior
to the Earle of Essex players xiij s. iiij d....geven by the appoinctement
of mr maior to the Lorde Staffordes players vj s. viij d....| Geven by   30
the appoinctemente of mr Maior to the Earle of Oxfordes players x
s....Geven by the appoinctemente of mr maior to the Earle of Sussex
players xiij s iiij d Geven by the appoinctement of mr maior the Earle
of Leycesters players xx s....
...   35

12/ the the: *dittography*

1585–6
Corporation Chamberlains' Accounts   GRO: GBR F 4/3
f 237   *(Gifts and rewards)*

...To the Lord of Essex plaiers v s....To the Earle of Sussex plaiers   5
v s....

1586–7
Corporation Chamberlains' Accounts   GRO: GBR F 4/3
f 242v   *(Fees and wages)*   10

...Paid Garrett Barnes the musicion for his yeeres fee xx s.

f 243   *(Gifts and rewards)*

                                                                        15
...Geauen to the Earle of Essex plaiers xv s....Geauen to the Queenes
maiestes plaiers xxx s. Geauen to the Earle of Leycesters plaiers xx
s....Geauen to the Earle of Essex plaiers xiij s. iiij d....
...

                                                                        20

1587–8
Corporation Chamberlains' Accounts   GRO: GBR F 4/3
f 249   *(Gifts and rewards)*
...
And the same Accomptantes aske allowance of diverse sommes of   25
money by them layed out in Giftes and Rewardes as followeth: And
firste to my Lord of Leycesters Players the xvij^th of Iune by mr Mayors
appointement xx s....Geaven the xij^th of Iuly to the Queenes maiestes
Players xxxiij s. vj d....To the Earle of Sussex Players the xvij of
September vj s. viiij d....   30

f 249v   *(Fees and wages)*

...To Garret Barnes the musicion for his yeeres ffee xx s....

                                                                        35

1588–9
Corporation Chamberlains' Accounts   GRO: GBR F 4/3
f 255v   *(Fees and wages)*

...To Garrett Barnes the musicon for his yeeres fee xx s....   40 f 256   *(Gifts and rewards)*

And the same Accomptant*es* aske allowance for moneys by them laied
out in giftes and rewardes to diverse *per*sons as followeth And first
to the Queenes players the xvij^th of Aprill xx s....To the Earle of Sussex   5
players the secconde of September xx s....

1589–90
Corporation Chamberlains' Accounts   GRO: GBR F 4/3
f 262v   *(Fees and wages)*   10

...Paide to Garrett Barnes the musici*o*n for his yeeres fee xx s....

f 263   *(Gifts and rewards)*   15

...geven to the Lord Chandos players the xxviij^th of December xx
s....geven to the Lord Beacham*es* players the vj^th of Aprill xx s. geven
to the Lord Chandos poppett players the xxx^th of Iune x s....geven
to the Queenes players which played in the Colledge Churche yarde
xxx s. geven to the lorde Admiralls players the xvij^th of September   20
xx s....

1590–1
Corporation Common Council Minute Book   GRO: GBR B 3/1
f 130*   *(20 August)*   25
...
Item it is agreed that one former ordinance made at a com*m*on
Councell houlden iij° die Nouemb*ris* anno xxij^do R*egi*ne touchinge
pleyers of enterludes shall stande in force and that noe plaies be
suffered hereafter to be plaied vppon any sundaies nor any reward*es*   30
to be geven w*i*thout good occasion by the Mayor and Alldermen

Corporation Chamberlains' Accounts   GRO: GBR F 4/3
f 271   *(Fees and wages)*
...   35
...paid to Garrett Barnes the musici*o*n for his yeeres fee xx s....

ff 271v–2   *(Gifts and rewards)*
...
And the same accomptant*es* aske allowance for moneys by them layed   40
out in giftes and rewards to diu*er*se *per*sons as followeth geven to the
Earle of worc*est*ers players by mr Mayors appointm*en*t x s....geven

plaiers

⟨dat⟩.71.

to the Lord Bechams players xiij s. iiij d.... I to the Queenes players
xxx s. To the Queenes and the earle of Sussex players xxx s. to the
Children of powls xx s. to the Lord admiralls players xxx s....

...

1591–2
Corporation Chamberlains' Accounts   GRO: GBR F 4/3
f 278   *(Fees and wages)*

...Payed to Garret Barnes the musicion for his yeares fee xx s....

f 278v   *(Gifts and rewards)*
...

And the same accomptauntes aske allowance of moneyes by them
layed out in giftes and rewardes to diuerse persons as followeth.
Imprimis geuen to the Earle of Worcester his players xiij s. iiij d....To
the Queenes players xxx s. Payed for a breakfast for them at Mrs
Powelles ix s. v d....

f 279*

...To the Queenes trumpetters by the appoyntmente of Mr Mayor xl s
....Gaue the Lord Straunge his players x s....Gyuen to the Lorde
Chandos in money for gratificacion against the receauing of the
Queenes Maiesty at Sudely in progresse vj li. xiij s. iiij d....
...

1592–3
Corporation Chamberlains' Accounts   GRO: GBR F 4/3
f 284v

ffees and wages   ...Paid to mr Garret the Musicion for his fee for three quarters of a
yere xv s....

Guiftes and
rewardes   ...To my lord Morl⟨.i⟩es players in money and j pottle of wine and
sugar by mr Maiors and mr Seamys appointment the xxviij^{th} of Iune
xj s. viij d....

1593–4
Corporation Chamberlains' Accounts   GRO: GBR F 4/3
f 293   *(Gifts and rewards)*
...

...Gaue the lord Ogles players viij s. iiij d....Item gaue to the Queenes
maiestes Players xl s....

1594–5
Corporation Chamberlains' Accounts   GRO: GBR F 4/3
f 305* *(Gifts and rewards)*

...

...geven to the blind harp*er* for the wine w*hi*ch he gave mr maior   5
xij d....geven to Anthonie Cooke and his companie at midsom*m*er one
gallon of wine & suger iij s. paied Thomas Bubbe for a wagon in the
pageant for the turke x s....

f 305v   10

...To the L*or*d Chandois man that brought venison v s. and to my
Lordes players v s. Geven to the Queenes players xxx s. geven to the
L*or*d Ogles players v s....

Corporation Common Council Minute Book   GRO: GBR B 3/1   15
f 157v   *(19 December)*

...

Musitians/40 s   It is allso agreed that °Iames° *(blank)* musitians, [plaieng] having plaied
on the Rcorder as the Waites for this quarter of yere passed [shall
therefore] at iiij of the clock in the mornin*ges* in the Chief stree*tes* of   20
this city shall therefore, and in recompence of their s*er*vice at the
solempne vsuall assemblies, ˬ⌐this yere⌐ have xx s for a Reward and
xx s for their liu*er*eys to be paied by the steward*es* of this City/

...

25

1595–6
Corporation Chamberlains' Accounts   GRO: GBR F 4/3
f 311v   *(Fees and wages)*

...

...Paied to Iames the musition and his men towards their liverie of   30
stamell cloakes and for their service xl s....

ff 312v–13   *(Gifts and rewards)*

...Geven to my L Staffor*des* plaiers vj s. viij d. geven to my L Chandois   35
plaiers by mr maiors appoinctme*nt* geven to the queenes plaiers for

18/ h *of* that *written over* t
18/*(blank): remainder of the line left blank for the names of the musicians*
19/ Rcorder *for* Recorder   22/ caret *written over* paied

their play xxx s. geven to the Earle of Darbies plaiers xxx s. geven to
my L Oagles plaiers iii s. iiij d. geven to my L Admiralls plaiers
xx s.... | Geven to the Queenes plaiers in wine and suger iij s. ij d. geven
for wine and suger for my Lord Admiralls players xx d.

...   5

1602–3
Tanners' Company Orders and Accounts   GCL: 28652/18
f [43v]   *(23 November–22 November)*

...   10
And to the musicions   vj d
...

Gloucester Diocese Consistory Court Deposition Books
GRO: GDR 89   15
f [116v]*   *(22 October)*

Super articulis contra wylmott

wayt et howell   Thomas Hyll Ciuitatis Gloucestrie yoman vbi moram fecit plerumque
contra wylmott   a natuitate sua ibidem ortus etatis xxxv. annorum aut circiter libere vt   20
dicit condicionis testis &c.
Ad primum articulum dicit eundem esse verum

Ad iiij deponit that twelue monethes now past or there aboutes this
deponent was at a stage play in the Botholl in the Cytty of Gloucester
in the Company of tharticulate Iohn wylmott, at which tyme the said   25
mr Iohn wylmott [did] ⌈offered to⌉ present himself vppon the said
stage, and sayd to this deponent that he could play better then any of
those stage players, and offered to goe vppon the same stage and to
take one of the same players instrumentes out of their handes to haue
played vppon yt himself. And this deponent perceauinge the said mr   30
wylmot to be very earnest to haue gon vppon the said stage and fearing
that he would haue then [haue] discredyted himself did pull him and
hold him back and did not suffer him to goe vpp to the same stage/
And this deponent dyd Iudge the said mr Iohn wylmot to be overtaken
with drynck at that tyme, and so did others then there   35
present/ et aliter nescit deponere
Super reliquis articulis non est examinatus
...

36/ et ... deponere *added later*

f [117]*

Iohannes fflemyng de Ciuitate Gloucestrie Barbor vbi moram fecit
plerunque a natiuitate sua ibidem ortus etatis xxxvj annorum et amplius
libere vt dicit condicionis testis &c./   5
Ad primum articulum dicit eundem esse verum
Ad ij et iij nescit deponere
Ad iiij deponit that twelue monethes last past or there aboutes this
deponent was at a stage play at the Botholl in the Cytty of Gloucester
in the Company of the articulate mr Iohn wylmot at which tyme the   10
sayd mr Iohn wylmot did offer to haue gon [vpp] vppon the said stage,
And then this deponent [then] asked Thomas hill his precontest what
the matter was, and the said Thomas hill tould this deponent that mr
wylmot said he would haue gon vppon the stage to play vppon one
of the players Instrumentes, And at the tyme this deponent did   15
perceaue the said mr wylmot to be very pleasa⟨nt⟩ and merry but
whey⟨t⟩her he was then druncken or not this deponent cannot depose,
but doth Iudge that he had ben dryncking hard before that [tyme] day,
and doth thinck that excepte he had ben moued by drynck that [⟨..⟩]
he the said mr wylmot would not haue offered to doe soe/ et aliter   20
nescit deponere
...

1603–4
Tanners' Company Orders and Accounts   GCL: 28652/18   25
f [44v]   *(23 November–22 November)*
...
Alsoe for wyne and sugar at the masters howse at
St Clementes tyde   viij s./
Alsoe for money geeven to the musicions.   vj d./   30
...

1607–8
Tanners' Company Orders and Accounts   GCL: 28652/18
f [48]   *(23 November–20 November)*   35
...
The said Accomptant prayeth to bee allowed of diuerse
sommes of money by him layed oute within the tyme of
his accompte, viz: payed for musick at Iohn Morganes   v s. x d./

4/ plerunque *for* plerumque: *minim missing*

xij d./ geeven in money to Richard Lye ij s./ ffor wyne at
his comnge in master ij s. x d. in all
...

1608–9   5
Tanners' Company Orders and Accounts   GCL: 28652/18
f [52v]*   *(23 November–22 November)*
...

Alsoe hee prayeth allowance for wyne and sugar and
museck at his dynner   *(blank)*   10
...

1609–10
Bakers' Company Minutes and Accounts   GCL: 29334
f [84]   15
...

Item for the oddes of moneye at o*u*r Breakefast in
the haule   j s–viij d
[Item p*ai*d to Iohn Atking*es* for j s loaffe   j s 0–0]
Ite*m* p*ai*d for j vj d loaffe to Abell Aungell & for j pottell   20
of Secke   ij s–[vi] j d–0
Ite*m* p*ai*d for the wayght*es*   ij s–iiij d
...

1611–12   25
Tanners' Company Orders and Accounts   GCL: 28652/18
f [54]   *(23 November–22 November)*
...

Allso he prayeth Alowance of xij s x d w*hi*ch he laide
out for wine att mr Smithes dinner   xij s x d   30
Allso he prayeth Allowance of v s w*hi*ch he laid out for
musicke att the same dinner   v s

f [54v]
...   35
Allso he prayeth Allowance for wine & sugar and
musicke att his dinner   xiiij s x d
...

2/ comnge *for* cominge: *minim missing*

1612–13
Tanners' Company Orders and Accounts   GCL: 28652/18
f [55v]*   *(23 November–22 November)*

...

Alsoe payed for a supper at the Newyne and for wyne   5
and museck there   Liij s

...

Alsoe he prayeth allowance for wyne and sugar.
and museck. at his dynner   xix s viij d
...   10

1613–14
Tanners' Company Orders and Accounts   GCL: 28652/18
f [58]   *(23 November–22 November)*

...   15
It this Accomptant craueth allowance for money laid
out for one supper att new Ine the xxvth day of Iune   xlvj s. iij d
It giuen to the wait players the same day by the
appoyntment of the Companie   v s.
                                                                       20

f [58v]
...
It Laid out for wine & sugar when I went forth maister
of the Companie   viij s.
It this same day to the waite plaiers   v s. 25
...

1614–15
Tanners' Company Orders and Accounts   GCL: 28652/18
f [59v]   *(23 November–22 November)*   30
...
It laid out for wine when I went forth maister of
the Companie   xj s.
It the same day to the waite plaiers   v s.
...   35

1615–16
Tanners' Company Orders and Accounts   GCL: 28652/18
f [61]   *(23 November–22 November)*
...   40
It laide out for wine when I went forth of the

Companie maister   x s.
It the same day to the waite player   v s

...

1616–17   5
Tanners' Company Orders and Accounts   GCL: 28652/18
f [62v]   *(23 November–22 November)*

...

...ffor wyne and sugar at Robert Reynoldes dynner   v s. x d.
To the musitions at thattyme   iij s iiij d... 10

...

Also he prayeth allowance of money by him layed out for
a supper at a meeting at the newyn*n*e   xlij s
ffor wyne at the same tyme   xxiij s [x d] j d
ffor musick at the same tyme   vj s   15

...

ffor wyne and sugar; at the masters dynner   xviij s. x d./
To the musick at the same tyme   v s.

1617–18   20
Tanners' Company Orders and Accounts   GCL: 28652/18
f [64v]   *(23 November–22 November)*

...

ffor wine and sugar att the maisters dinner   xviij s. x d.
ffor musicke att the same time   v s.   25

...

1618–19
Tanners' Company Orders and Accounts   GCL: 28652/18
f [67]   *(23 November–22 November)*   30

...

Payd for musicke att the maisters dinner   v s.

...

1619–20
Tanners' Company Orders and Accounts   GCL: 28652/18   35
ff [68v–9]   *(23 November–22 November)*

...

Item layd out for wine and sugar att w*illia*m Ieynes

14/ xxiij s: *second* x *converted from* v

his dinner   x s. viij d
Allso for musicke the same time   v s.

...

Item layd out for wine and sugar att Richard Luggs dinner xiiij s iiij d
Allso for musicke the same time   v s.   5

...

It iiij gallons of sacke. ij gallons of Clarett & j pottle of
Clarett & iij li. of sugar att our maisters dinner   xxiij s. |
Item for musicke   v s.

...   10

1621–2
Tanners' Company Orders and Accounts   GCL: 28652/18
f [71]   *(23 November–22 November)*

...   15

Allso for wine and sugar att Richard Nashes dimner   xx s. iij d.
ffor musicke   v s.

1623–4
Tanners' Company Orders and Accounts   GCL: 28652/18   20
f [74v]*   *(23 November–22 November)*

...

It att Iohn Nichols dinner att newe Inne in wine
sugar & musicke   j li. –xiiij s–iij d
...   25
It for vij pottles of sacke iiij pottles of Clarett
j pottle of white wine ij pounde of sugar att our
master his dinner   j li. –iij s–iiij d
⟨It⟩ for musicke   0–v s.–0   30
It for Linkes   0–[vii]–viij d

...

1624–5
Corporation Clerks' Memoranda Book   GRO: GBR 1453/1542   35
f 110v

...

xxvth of October 1624

At which tyme one Henry Sandes with three others brought a
commicon vnder Sir Henry Harberts hand & seale master of the revells 40

16/ dimner *for* dinner: *extra minim*

& requested mr mayor to let them play according to their com*m*icon,
w*h*ich com*m*icon was dated the xviijth day of Sept*ember* Anno R*egni*
R*egis* Iacobi xxijth directed to the sayd Henry Sandes [Allexdin]
Allexander Baker & Robert Smedley, & the sayd Allexander Baker
confessed his name ʌ⌈was⌉ Barker & not Baker & they had w*i*th them   5
one Iarvis Gennatt./a mynstrell./

...

Tanners' Company Orders and Accounts   GCL: 28652/18
f [76v]   *(23 November–22 November)*   10

...

Item spent in wine at the Maisters dinn*er* and suger   j li. – ⟨v⟩j s – iij d
Itm for wine   iij s iiij d
Itm for Musick   vj s viij d

...   15

1625–6
Tanners' Company Orders and Accounts   GCL: 28652/18
f [79v]   *(23 November–22 November)*

...   20

Allso layd out for wine sugar & musicke when Iames
Stevens keepte his dinner   j li. – iiij s – oo

...

f 80   25

...

It spent in wine & sugar att the maisters dinner   j li. – iij s – viij d
Item for musicke   oo – v s – oo

...   30

1626–7
Bakers' Company Minutes and Accounts   GCL: 29334
f [102v]

...

mor the .6. of November for beare and ffyer   0 – 0 – 9   35
more that Daye at o*u*r Dinner j galland of Clarrett and
one pottell of Secke   0 – 5 – 0

12/ iij d: ii *written over* oo

more then for Beare to make the musicians Drincke   0 – 0 – 5
...

Tanners' Company Orders and Accounts   GCL: 28652/18
f [81v]   *(23 November–22 November)*   5
...

Item spent in wine and sugar att the maisters dinner   xxiij s vj d
Item for musicke   v s./
...
                                                                                       10

1627–8
Tanners' Company Orders and Accounts   GCL: 28652/18
f [82v]   *(23 November–22 November)*
...

It when Anthony ffeeld came into *our* Companie in   15
methegline beare & Cakes   ij s – x d.
It att his dinner in wine & sugar   vj s – vj d
It att the same time for musicke   ij s – vj d
...

It when Robert Teyther keepe his dinner att his   20
Cominge into the Companie in wine & sugar   xix s
It for musicke   ij s – vj d
...

It in wine & sugar att the maisters dinner   xviij s – iiij d
It for musicke att *our* maisters dinner   00 – v s – 00   25
...

Cathedral Treasurers' Accounts   GRO: D 936 A1/1
p 111   *(25 March–24 March)*   *(Rewards)*
...   30
Item to Trowte a poore Musican   vj d
...

1628–9
Corporation Chamberlains' Accounts   GRO: GBR F 4/4   35
f 12   *(Fees and wages)*
...

Payd the Weight Players for their Wages from this
Cittie for their pay   xl s
...   40

f 35a   *(General payments)*

...

Payd the Drummers and Trumpetts vppon the
Proclayning of the prolimation for peace with ffraunce   ij s. vj d.

...   5

f 37*

Payd Mr Merowe at Cristie for their Mussicke
in the Colledg   v s.   10

...

Tanners' Company Orders and Accounts   GCL: 28652/18
f [83v]   *(23 November–22 November)*

...   15

It payd vnto the waightplayers att Lawrence Luggs &
Richard Williams dinner   v s.

...

It for wine and sugar att *our* maisters dinner   xxiiij s
It for musicke   v s.   20

1629–30
Tanners' Company Orders and Accounts   GCL: 28652/18
f [85v]   *(23 November–22 November)*

...   25

It for wine and sugar att *our* maisters dinner   j li. – j s – ij d
It for musicke   v s

...

Cathedral Treasurers' Accounts   GRO: D 936 A 1/1   30
p 153   *(25 March–24 March)*   *(Extraordinary payments)*

...

Repayed to Iohn Merro for a Rome which he rented of
Iohn Beames to teache the Children to playe vppon the
Vialls   10 s.   35

p 162   *(Rewards)*

...

To A poore Singingman at the intreaty of the
Quiremen   2 s.   40

...

To A poore Musicion sent by Mr Subdeane   6 d.

...

1/ Proclayning *for* Proclayming: *minim missing* MS; prolimation *for* proclimation

1630-1
Tanners' Company Orders and Accounts   GCL: 28652/18
f [86v]   *(23 November–22 November)*

...

It to the prisners as we went to william Packers   5
dinner   00 – 00 – vj d
It giuen to the musicke the same tyme   00 – ij s – vj d

...

f [87]   10

...

It ffor wine and sugar att *our* maisters dinner   j li. – v s – vj d
It the same tyme to the musicke   00 – v s – 00

...

                                                                                    15

1631-2
Corporation Common Council Minute Book   GRO: GBR B 3/2
p 3*   *(21 January)*   *(Livery allowance)*

...

It is also agreed at this house that the [bu] publike musici*o*ns of this   20
Cittie in regard their number is increased from ffower to Six beeing
avery able & sufficient consort shall haue yearly for their liveryes out
of the Chamber of this Cittie the Sume of ffower pound*es* During the
pleasure of this house to begin *presently*

...   25

Tanners' Company Orders and Accounts   GCL: 28652/18
f [89v]   *(23 November–22 November)*

...

It for musicke att Alexander Hores Dinner   00 – ij s – vj d
...   30
It he craueth allowance of forty shillings towards the
keeping of his maisters Dinner accordinge to the order
in that case made and *provided*   ij li. – 00 – 00
It for wine   j li. – 00 – 00
It the same tyme for musicke   00 – v s – 00   35

...

1632-3
Tanners' Company Orders and Accounts   GCL: 28652/18
f [91]   *(23 November–22 November)*   40

...

Item the 29th of Nouember att W*illia*m Luggs dinner

spent in wine and sugar	00 – x s – 00
Item the same tyme by the consent of the maister	
wardens and the rest of the companie spent more	
in wine & sugar	00 – viij s – 00
Item for musicke the same tyme	00 – v s – 00

...

Item he craueth allowance for fortye shillinges	
towardes the keepeinge of his maisters dinner	
accordinge to the order in that case made &	
provided	ij li – 00 – 00
Item the same tyme spent in wine	j li. – 00 – 00
Item for sugar	00 – iij s – 00
Item for musicke	00 – v s – 00

1633–4
Tanners' Company Orders and Accounts   GCL: 28652/18
f [94]   *(23 November–22 November)*
...

It spent in wine and sugar when I keepe my	
maisters dinner	j li. – viij s – vj d
It payd for musicke	00 – v s – 00

...

It for musicke att Iohn Luggs dinner	00 – ij s – vj d

...

Cathedral Treasurers' Accounts   GRO: D 936 A 1/1
p 256   *(25 March–24 March)*   *(Rewards)*
...

To some of the Waytes for playinge in the Quire per	
Consensum Magistri Decani	0 5. 0.

...

1634–5
Tanners' Company Orders and Accounts   GCL: 28652/18
ff [95–5v]   *(23 November–22 November)*
...

It spent in wine & sugar when I kept my masters	
dinner	j li.–j s–viij d
It payd for musicke	00 – v s – 00

...

Cathedral Treasurers' Accounts   GRO: D 936 A 1/1
p 272* *(25 March–24 March) (Extraordinary payments)*
...
Given to the Waites at Ablods Court.   o.   2.   6.
...

Judgment upon Sabbath-breakers   Burton: *Divine Tragedie*
ff 24v–5
...
Vpon May Eve Thomas Tree of Glocester, Carpenter in the Parish 10
of S. Michael, some coming unto him, and asking him, whether he
would go with them to fetch the May-pole, he swore by the Lords
wounds, that he I would, though he never went more. Now whiles
he was working on the May-pole on May day morning, before he had
finished his work, the Lord smote him with such a lamenesse and   15
swelling in all his limbs, that he could neither go, nor lift his hands
to his mouth, to feed himself, but kept his bed for half a yeer together,
and stil goes lame to this day; May 4, 1636.
...

1635–6
Corporation Chamberlains' Accounts   GRO: GBR F 4/5
f 8   *(Fees and wages)*
...
Item payd the Wayte players for their wages for   25
the whole yeare   4–0–0
...

Tanners' Company Orders and Accounts   GCL: 28652/18
f [96v]   *(23 November–22 November)*   30
...
It att my [mais] keeping of our maisters dinner spent in
wine & sugar   j li – vj s – oo
It for musicke   oo – v s – oo
                                                                   35

1636–7
Corporation Chamberlains' Accounts   GRO: GBR F 4/5
f 38 *(Fees and wages)*
...
Item payd the wayte players for theire wages for the   40

whole yeare   4–0–0
...

f 40*   *(Gifts and rewards)*
...   5
Item payd vnto Vincente that Caries Sightes
and shewes with dauncing on the Ropp wch was by
order of the Iustices   1–6–8
Item payd vnto William Daniell one of the Kings
Reuells because he should not playe beeing in the   10
contagious tyme by order of the Iustices   1–6–8
...
Item payd more vnto Vincent at his Retorning to
towne in that the tyme of contagious sicknes
might prove dangerous by the order of   15
the Iustices —   0–13–4
...

Tanners' Company Orders and Accounts   GCL: 28652/18
f [98]   *(23 November–22 November)*   20
...
It att my keepinge of o*u*r maisters dinner in wine
and sugar   j li. – 00 – 00
It for musicke   00 – v s – 00
...   25

1637–8
Corporation Chamberlains' Accounts   GRO: GBR F 4/5
f 66v   *(Fees and wages)*
...   30
Item payd the Waightplayers theyr wages for the
whole yeare   4–0–0
...

f 67v   *(Gifts and rewards)*   35
...
Item payd the Quiristers at Cristemas by Mr Mayor
and Iustices order   0–2–0
...

Tanners' Company Orders and Accounts   GCL: 28652/18
f [99v]   *(23 November–22 November)*
...

Item at my keeping of our masters dinner in wine
and suger   j li. – ix s – viij d   5
Item spent by consent of the company afterwards   viij s vij d
Item for musicke   v s
...

Cathedral Treasurers' Accounts   GRO: D 936 A 1/2   10
p 58   *(25 March–24 March)* *(Extraordinary payments)*

To Richard Brodgate Iun*ior* for playinge on the
Sagbott the whole yeare.   3: 0: 0.
...   15

1638–9
Corporation Chamberlains' Accounts   GRO: GBR F 4/5
f 97v   *(Annuities, fees, and wages)*
...   20
Item Payd the Waytplayers theyr wages for the
whole yeare   iiij li.

Cathedral Treasurers' Accounts   GRO: D 936 A 1/2
p 81*   *(25 March–24 March)* *(Extraordinary payments)*   25
...
To Richard Bradgate Iun*ior* for playing on the
Sagbutt the whole yeare   3   0   0

1639–40   30
Corporation Chamberlains' Accounts   GRO: GBR F 4/5
f 128   *(Annuities, fees, and wages)*
...
Item payd the Wayte players theyr Wages for the
whole yeare   iiij li.   35
...

f 129   *(Gifts and rewards)*
...
Item given to Stage playars by the appoyntem*en*te   40
of Mr Mayor and the Iustices in regard they

should not acte any play at that tyme in this City   XX S.
...

Cathedral Treasurers' Accounts   GRO: D 936 A 1/2
p 103   *(25 March–24 March) (Extraordinary payments)*   5
...
To Henry Vizard for playing on the Sagbutt the
whole yeare   3 . 0 . 0

p 104   10
...
ffor amending the Saggbutt   0 . 0 . 6
...
To the Oxford musicke for playing on their Cornet*tes*
att the Summer Assizes by the appointment of the   15
Prebendaryes   0 . 10 . 0
...

1640–1
Corporation Chamberlains' Accounts   GRO: GBR F 4/5   20
f 152   *(Annuities, fees, and wages)*
...
Item payd the Wayt players theyr Wages for j
whole yeare   iiij li.
...   25

f 153v   *(Gifts and rewards)*
...
Item payd to the Stage players by the Mayor & Iustices
order when they went to see the Accte   XX S   30
...

Cathedral Treasurers' Accounts   GRO: D 936 A 1/2
pp 125–6   *(25 March–24 March) (Extraordinary payments)*
...   35
To Henry ⟨.⟩yssen for playing on the Saggbutt the
whole yeare   03 :00 :00
To Mr Machins man for bringing the Saggbutt w*hich*
was his M*asteres* his gift to ye churche   00 :05 :00l

12/ he *of the written over another letter*   36/ ⟨.⟩yssen: *probably* vyssen *(Vizard)*

To [the] Thomas Smyth for playing on the Cornett two
yeares granted by peticion   02 :00 :00
...

Journal of Sir Simonds D'Ewes   BL: Harley 162   5
f 219a   (*12 February*)
...

The petition of the Mayor & citizens of Gloster was read that they
have ther eleven churches & [in] but one preaching minister. That at
ther owne coste they maintained on Mr Workman a godlie divine: 10
but hee was called into the high commission and censured, & silenced.
That after the citizens of Gloster allowing him some maintenance
weere likewise troubled in the high Commission Court. That Dr.
Goodman the Bishopp of Gloster was an enemie to all preaching &
godlines: maintaining fidlers in his howse on the sunday, & dancing   15
in the cittie. It was after divers motions ordered to bee referred to the
Committee touching Dr. Peirce Bishopp of Bath & Wells.
...

1641–2   20
Corporation Chamberlains' Accounts   GRO: GBR F 4/5
f 174   (*Annuities, fees, and wages*)
...

Item. payd the Wayte players theyr wages for the
whole yeare   04 li.–00–00   25
...

Cathedral Treasurers' Accounts   GRO: D 936 A 1/2
p 148   (*25 March–24 March*) (*Extraordinary payments*)

                                                                          30
To Henry Vizard for playing on the Saggbutt the
whole yeare   3–0–0
...

1642–3   35
Corporation Chamberlains' Accounts   GRO: GBR F 4/5
f 207   (*Annuities, fees, and wages*)
...

Item: paid the Wayte players their wages for the
whole yeare   04–00–00   40
...

HARESCOMBE

1611–12
Gloucester Diocese Consistory Court Deposition Books
GRO: GDR 114   5
f [87] *(16 March)*
...

        decimo sexto die Martij Anno d*om*ini 1611
Katherina Haselton vx*or* Wille*lm*i   Sup*er* lib*ello* ex p*ar*te d*i*cte
Haselton *versus* Doratheam   Katherinæ Haselton in hac causa 10
Dorney vx*or* Ri*car*di Dorney   dat*o* et exhibit*o*
sen*ioris* in *cau*sa diff*amacio*nis

    Alicia Arthure de Harsfield in com*itatu* Glou*cestrie* Spinster vbi
    mora*m* fecit p*er* spacium duoru*m* annoru*m* vltra elaps*orum* aut 15
    eo circit*er* nata apud Painswick in com*itatu* pred*icto* ætatis viginti et
    vniius annoru*m* aut eo circit*er* testis pro duct*a* Iurat*a* et exa*m*inat*a*/
    ...
    Ad secundu*m* arti*cu*lum libe*lli* pred*icti* deponit et dicit That vpon a 20
    Saboath day in Harvest last aboute a Moneth before Mich*aelm*as last
    or thereaboute*s* the tyme more certaine this Depon*ent* remembreth
    ₐ⌜not⌝ shee this Depon*ent* did goe to the dwelling howse of Richard
    Dorney thelder scituate in harsfield arti*cu*late husband of Dorathy
    Dorney arti*cu*late to carry achilde of [the sai⟨.⟩] Richard Dorney the 25
    younger, whoe then dwelled in howse wi*th* his father (he the said
    Richard Dorney the yonger havng before that tyme marryed one Iane
    Arthure this Depon*entes* sister And the same day assoone as this
    Depon*ent* came to the dwellg howse of the said Richard Dorney
    thelder as aforesaid Dorathy Dorney arti*cu*late came to this Depon*ent* 30
    standing at the doore vnto whome this Depon*ent* [diff] did offer the
    child that it might be there kept because the said Ric*h*ard Dorney the
    younger would not come nere the childe nor give his wife any
    maintena*n*ce at all for to keepe it and then the same tyme the said
    Dorathy Dorney beganne to fall out wi*th* this Depon*ent* and called 35
    her many ill names as Iade [⟨..⟩] ₐ⌜⟨Qune⟩⌝ such other like termes And
    also the said Dorathy saied to this Depon*ent* the same tyme, thy
    mother mea*n*ing katheryne Haselton arti*cu*late hath said that I am a

8/ 1611 *underlined* MS   14/ c *of* Alicia *written over another letter*
15/ p *of* per *written over* s   17/ pro ducta *for* producta
29/ dwellg *for* dwelling   31/ [diff] *corrected to* did

whoore)) but I am not such a whore as shee is for thy mother mean*i*ng
katheryne Hasleton ar*ticu*late was naught at Harsecombe vpon a Bedd
and that one Bond a Musitian did play at the bed*es* feete in the meane
tyme, [All w*hi*ch] meaning thereby as this Depon*ent* conceived that
some one man or another had had the carnall knowledge of (the body   5
of the said katheryne Haselton ar*ticu*late....

HENBURY

1599   10
Bristol Diocese Bishop's Cause Book   BRO: EP/J/1/11
f 269v

...

contra Robertu*m* Stoak*es*	Siimil*i*ter Comp*ar*uit Stoak*es* et ̦ ⌐fassus
p*a*roch*ie* de henburie	est p*re*sentacioni⌐ [negat p*re*sentacio⟨..⟩ esse 15
ar*ticu*latu*r* by report for	veru*m* vnde Domin*us*] vnde Domin*us*
kepeinge of musicke &	iniunxit ei p*e*nit*e*nti*am* sequent*em* vi*de*licet
Dansinge in his howse	that he hath [on the] ̦⌐to⌐ morrowe
at the time of eue*n*iinge	[followenge] in the p*a*rishe church of
praier	henburie sig⟨.⟩nifye publiquelye vnto the 20
	whole congregacon that he hath offended
	the lawe in keepinge of musique & dancinge
	in his howse in time of Devine service &c et
	ad certificand*um*

...   25

LITTLEDEAN

1601–2
Gloucester Diocese Consistory Court Cause Book   30
GRO: GDR 90
ff 178–8v*   *(10 March)*
...

Will*el*m*us* hopkins	detected for playeing at tabber & pipe at
de ead*em*	[s*er*vis] tymes. inconvenient./ 35
[excom*m*unicat*us*]	
	Citat*us* in ecclesia

Comp*ar*uit et d*omin*us iniunxit ei ad fatend*um* culpam vestib*us*
assuetis die d*omin*ica prox*ima* et ad cert*ific*and*um* in prox*ima*/
peregit   40

Welthiana ˌ⌐harte alias¬   detected for dancing at prayer tyme
higeve ⌐vidua¬ de eadem
excommunicata:

                  citata in ecclesia:/

5

Comparuit et dominus detectione predicta inunxit ei ad fatendum
culpam die dominica proxima [suis] genibus flexis etc et ad
Certificandum in proxima.
excommunicata: 24° Martij 1601

10

Blanchia Iones et Maria
Iones de eadem   pro eodem
excommunicate:

                  citate in ecclesia

15

Comparuit Catherina Iones [et] mater dicit. et suscepit |

Deane parva   Ioanna Eston   detected for dauncing at servis tyme/
de eadem

                  Citata in ecclesia/   20

excommunicationem
ema⟨t⟩
...
Ioanna Turnor   detected for dauncinge
de eadem   25

                  citata in ecclesia

Maria Buffrey   pro eodem   Comparuit et dominus iniunxit ei ad
de eadem   fatendum culpam postea cum
                              monicione dimisit &c.   30

Margeria fflewellin   pro eodem
et soror de eadem

                 citate in ecclesia

    abijt ex diocesis   35
    Gloucestrie
...
Andreas Philpott   detected for playing at tabber & pype at
de eadem   servis tyme/

6/ inunxit for iniunxit: minim missing MS   22/ ema⟨t⟩ for emittat
35/ diocesis for diocese

                    Citatus in ecclesia
        refertur ministro et gardianis

Persivall &
Iohannes Tilar   detected for dauncing with young Women at   5
de eadem   inconvenient tyme/.

                    citati in ecclesia
        Comparuit et Dominus iniunxit ei ad fatendum culpam die
        dominica proxima et ad certificandum in proxima   10
        Comparuit et certificauit quod peregit

        Richardus harte   pro eodem
        de eadem
                                  citatus in ecclesia   15

        Comparuit mater
        ...
        Anna Lewis   ffor dauncinge
        de eadem   20
            Comparuit et dominus iniunxit ei ad fatendum culpam vestibus
            assuetis &c/ et ad certificandum in proxima
        peregit penitenciam

MITCHELDEAN   25

1588–9
Letter to the Queen from Anthony Bridgeman of Mitcheldean
PRO: SP 12/222/no. 70. I.
single sheet   *(January)*   30

        To the Quenes most excelent maiestie his Soueraigne Lady
        and most greate mistres, the perfect frucion of all grace and
        happines.
Sacred and most gracious Quene may it please your maiestie to accept   35
as a new yeares gifte at the handes of me your most humble poore
subiect these thirteene branches to the dozen to be planted in this your
highnes garden of England, if it seeme vnto your grace to be convenient
and necessary, whose nature and vertue I omitte to speake of, both
for that I would not be tedious, and also for that the rarenes and   40

4/ Persivall & *added in same hand after* Iohannes Tilar *written*

excellencie of your highnes witt can consider and examine advisedlie,
and iudge [and] easilie of the same.

the first.
branche.

A restraint of the profaning of the Saboth day especiallie with
minstrelcie, baiting of beares and other beastes, and such like.   5

2.   That it be felonie in hym that will haue hencefoorth two wiues lyving
     and felony in her that will haue hencefoorth two husbandes lyving.

3.   A restraint of publishing profane poetrie bookes of profane songes
     sonnettes pamphlettes and such like, otherwise then to be sold out
     of your highnes dominions.   10

4.   That there be no booke pamphlett sonnet ballad or libell printed or
     written of purpose either to be sold or openlie [b] published without
     your maiestes licence.

5.   The psalmes of the prophett David being now in english meeter to
     be printed in folio in such sort as prophane ballades now are.   15

6.   To prohibite euery spirituall person to haue any more then one
     benifice, and that they be resident vppon the same except six weekes
     in the yeare.

7.   That there be not any admitted into the ministery but at such time
     as there shalbe a place voide of a Curate, And that such as can preache   20
     the word be thervnto preferred rather then others.

8.   To nominate and sett downe euery suspicion of papistrie and to punish
     the offendors by fyne or otherwise for the first second and third
     offence.

9.   That euery papist and recusant be exempted out of euery Iury and   25
     inquisicion and to be barred of his othe if challenge be made against
     hym.

10. That the inhabitantes of euery parish suffering any scholemaister to
     teache publkely within their parishe without licence of the Lord
     Bishop of the same dioces do forfaite vnto your maiestie for euery   30
     weeke so teaching x li. And euery person keping in his howse any
     scholemaister teaching privatlie vnlicenced as is aforsaide to forfaite
     for euery day so kepte x li. The righte honorable the Lordes of your
     maiestes privy Counsaill and such as shall please your highnes to be
     excepted.   35

11. That euery person arested within the County of Middlesex recouer
     his treble costes if after his apparance the plaintiff doth not declare
     within three daies next after and prosequuteth with effect,

12. That no spirituall person do make or write any manner of evidences
     but onlie testamentes and last wills.   40

13. The thirteenth, and if it please your maiestie, is the bodie & service
     of my self your most humble poore subiect and dailie Orator to

commaunde at your highnes pleasure.

Anthonye Bridgeman
of Mychell Deane
in the County of Gl⟨...⟩

5

TEWKESBURY

1525–6
Letter from John Veysey, Bishop of Exeter, and Others to Wolsey
BL: Cotton Vespasian F XIII #187   10
f 240*   *(27 November)*

Please it youre grace for the great repaire of strangiers supposed vnto
the pryncesse honorable householde this solempne fest of Cristmas.
we humbly beseche the same/ to let vs knowe youre gracious pleasure/   15
concernyng aswell a ship of siluer for the Almes Disshe requysite for
her high estate/ and spice plates/ as also for trumpettes and a Rebek
to be sent/ and whither we shall appoynte any lord of mysrule for the
said honorable householde/provide for enterludes Disgysynges or
pleyes in the said fest/ or for banket on twelf nyght/ And in likewise   20
whither the pryncesse shall sende any newe yeres giftes to the kynge
the quene youre grace and the frensshe quene/ and of the value &
Devise of the same Besechyng your grace also to pardon oure busy
and Importunate sutes to the same in suche bihalf made/ Thus oure
right syngler good lorde we pray the holy trynyte haue you in his   25
holy preseruacion/ At Teoxbury the xxvij Day of nouember/
                    youre humble orators
                        (signed)   Iohn Exoniensis
                                                Ieiliz Grevile
To the most reuerent ffather in god   pcter burnell   30
the lord Cardinall his good grace./   Iohn Salter
                                                G. Bromley
                                                Thomas Audeley

1567–8   35
St Mary the Virgin's Churchwardens' Accounts   GRO: P 329 CW 2/1
p 21   *(4 May 1567–16 May 1568)*
...
Item Recevid for the hier of the players gere   xviij d
...   40

4/ Gl⟨...⟩: *probably* Gloucester; *page torn*

1572–4
St Mary the Virgin's Churchwardens' Accounts   GRO: P 329 CW 2/1
p 41   *(4 May 1572–20 April 1574)*
...
Res*eved* ffore the Lone off the players aperell   iij s iiij d   5
...

1575–6
St Mary the Virgin's Churchwardens' Accounts   GRO: P 329 CW 2/1
p 51   *(July – July)*   10
...
p*ai*d for mendinge ye newe seate beinge brokene Downe
at Aplaye   ij d
p*ai*d for naylles to Doo ye same   j d
...   15

1576–7
St Mary the Virgin's Churchwardens' Accounts   GRO: P 329 CW 2/1
p 55   *(July – July)*
...
Item R*ece*ved for the hyer of players gere   iij s viij d   20
...

p 57
...
It*em* R*ece*ved of Thom*as* Wheler for hier of the players   25
geare   iiij s
...

p 60
...   30
ffurther we haue loned out some players geare to Thoms
& Iohn Wheler the note wherof we receued by theyr hand
wrytyng & they [s] most paye for hyer of it on myd somer
yeve & then delyu*er* it agayne   iiij s

Areregis there is due to be Receued & to be chargyd to the next   35
Churchwardens as followeth
...
[of Thomas & Iohn Wheler – iiij s]
...

p 62   *(July–July)*

…

    The charge of the nowe churchwardens Iohn
    Bubbe & Ric*hard* ffield anno 1577.
ffirst de*livere*d to them in lead – xxiij.^{C} 5
twentie three hundred poundes
Item in brasse half hundred lacking ij. li
Item five Corslettes ˏ⌐furnished⌐ tenn Calivers/
sixteene murrens/ fower pickes/
Ite*m* in yron one barr/ one highe Candlestick.   10
one Casement/ ij chaynes
Item one riche Coape/ five players gownes/ iiij Iacketts/ iiij beardes/
twoo heades/
Ite*m* tenn towel [⟨..⟩]s/ vij albes or sirplisses/ xj other pieces of lynnen./
Item ij curtynns up at the hand*es* of Mr Gailetiewood by Ric*hard* ffield   15
& Iohn Bubbe then churche wardens/

1577–8
St Mary the Virgin's Churchwardens' Accounts   GRO: P 329 CW 2/1
p 63   *(3 September 1577–3 May 1578)*   20

…

Item Rece*ue*d of Richarde Donne for ye hyer of ye
players Apparell   iij s iiij d

…

p 65   25

…

More that is by vs/ p*ai*de vnto those whose names
are vnderwritt for ye players geare as followeth
Item to Roberte Collens for payntinge   iiij s vj d
Ite*m* to Roger Mylwarde for makinge of garment*es*   iiij s viij d   30
Item to Ric*hard* Westone for makinge A Ierkine   xiij d
Item for vj sheepe skyns for Christ*es* garment*es*   iij s
Item to W*illia*m ffyelde for buckeram for capes   viij d
Item for two kippe skines for ye thunder head*es*   xvj d

…   35

1578–80
St Mary the Virgin's Churchwardens' Accounts   GRO: P 329 CW 2/1
p 66*   *(13 July – ?)*
…   40
Item Rece*ue*d for the hyer of the players apparell   vj s viij d

…

Itim Rece*u*ed of Roger wiette for the hire of the
players apparell   iij s

...

1582-3   5
St Mary the Virgin's Churchwardens' Accounts   GRO: P 329 CW 2/1
p 74*   *(Account rendered 7 August 1583)*

...

Item Rece*u*ed of luke hurst for ˏ⌐hyer of⌐ ye players
app*a*rell   ij s vij d   10

...

Item Rece*u*ed for ye hyer of the players beard*es*   vj d

...

p 75

...   15

Item Rece*u*ed for the players capes   vj d

...

p 79   *(Arrears)*

...   20

Item of Ric*h*ard mathew*es* & salsburie for the hyer of the
players geere   iij s iiij d

...

1583-4   25
St Mary the Virgin's Churchwardens' Accounts   GRO: P 329 CW 2/1
p 80   *(24 May 1584)*

...

*I*tem Reseuyd off Wyllya*m* salsbery & Rychard mathews
for the hyer off ye players Rament   iij s iiij d   30

...

p 81

...

Item Reseuyd for the lonne off ye Reparell at   35
Chrystymas   viij s ij d
Item We haue Reseuyd off Rychard Wood / & /
Iohn farley off mathen for ye hyer off ye Reparell   v s

...

9–12/ *entries marked with asterisk (in later hand)?*
38/ mathen: *Mathon, Worc, eleven miles from Tewkesbury*

1584
Borough Minute Book   GRO: TBR A 1/1
f 15*

...

bailiff*es* accom*pt* m*emorandum* iij° novembris 1584 as in the last yeere aforesaid the   5
abouesaid bailiff*es* and Tho*mas* Cru*m*p accomptinge before W*illia*m
hill & W*illia*m willis then bailiff*es* the abouenamed bailiff*es* having
receaved in to their hand*es* vj li. xiij s iiij d they accompted laid out
by them vnto players, in wyne to the Iustices, rent for their m*ar*ket
standing, to the clarck of the m*ar*ket & tenshall money – iij li. xv s.   10
viij d.

...

1584–5
St Mary the Virgin's Churchwardens' Accounts   GRO: P 329 CW 2/1   15
p 86   *(24 May 1584–3 May 1585)*

...

Item receavid of certen men of Mathon for the vse of
the pleyers apparrell   v s.
...   20
Item receavid of the person of hyllchurche for the
vse of the plaiers apparrell at Cristmas last   iij s vj d

...

p 88   *(Church goods delivered to new churchwardens)*   25
...

players Apparrell Item viij^t gownes and clokes
                  Item vij Iirkyns
                  Item iiij capps of green sylke.
                  Item viij heades of heare for the apostles and   30
                  .x. beard*es*
                  Item a face or vysor for the devyll

...

1600   35
Borough Minute Book   GRO: TBR A 1/1
f 24

...

⟨.⟩attelm*ent* on   The Churchewardens this yeere after mich*ae*lmas intendinge of them

---

9/ Mathon: *Mathon, Worc, eleven miles from Tewkesbury*
12/ hyllchurche: *unidentified (many villages in the Tewkesbury area have* hill *as an element
in their names)*

⟨..⟩e steeple selves to build a battlem*ent* vppon the toppe of the churche tower
offred to do the same by contracting martes w*i*thout any com*m*on
charge: and to that p*ur*pose did sett furthe iij stage playes shewed in
the abby at Whitsontide following, and making further mocion for a
churchale, the same could not be gra*n*ted but vnder some condicons   5
of abuses accustomed to be reforned and abouts midsom⟨..⟩ following
⟨didd⟩ that battlem*ent* wh*i*ch cost vppon the accompt – lxvj li.
...

1600–1   10
St Mary the Virgin's Churchwardens' Accounts   GRO: P 329 CW 2/1
pp 130–1*   *(July–July)*

Also these Churchewardens vndertooke to sett a battlem*ent* of stone
vppon the topp of the tower as now it standeth where before was none,   15
but stoode as it was at the fall of the spier of leade, wh*i*ch happened
on Easterdeye in the first yeere of the Quenes ma*ie*stis raigne on wh*i*ch
was a beautifull woodden battlem*ent*.

This battlem*ent* of stone they adventured vppon themselves by   20
makinge of martes w*i*th suche as would take of them, only was licensed
them for that yeere to devise some meetinges to be had w*i*thin the
towne for their helpe therein wh*i*ch they after practised by settinge
furthe iij severall stage playes w*i*thin the abbey on the iij first dyes of
whitsonweeke anno Do*m*ini . 1600. havinge begun that woorck in lent   25
before of wh*i*ch charge they acquainte the bailiffes & p*ar*ishe as
followeth;
Imprimis they accompt to have gotten by gifte w*i*thin the towne &
countrey [a] neere aboute in wheate & malte / *videlicet* wheate xvj
b*u*shels at iij s iiij d a b*u*shel and of malte xxxj b*u*shels at ij s vj d rated   30
vj li. x s. x d. of wh*i*ch they gained by vtteraunce of the same at their
playes so muche as made the the same amounte to   xij li. ij s. x d.

Item rece*v*ed for the gaine of the iij playes   xij li. vij s. ij d
Item rece*v*ed of free gifte aboue martes   xv s.   35
Item rece*v*ed for lead that was spared from the topp
of the tower   xviij li. xv s.
Item rece*v*ed for spare tymber   xxij s.
                        Sum*m*a – xlv li. ij s.

6/ reforned *for* reformed: *minim missing* MS   25/ 1600 *underlined* MS
28/ Imprimis *in extra large, heavily inked letters*

Expended aboute the same battlementes and playes as followeth;
Imprimis for making a whele to drawe vp stone to
the tower   xlj s.
Item for takinge vp the lead & wyniige the tymber
woorck   xxij s iij d.   5
Item for wynding vp stones to the masons   iij li. xj s.
Item for baskettes, cradles & necessaries   viij s viij d.
Item for xix lodes of stone from coscombe quarr   v li. iiij s.
Item for hallinge over stones from Stanwey hill   iiij li.
Item for sand, hallinge it & lyme and timber & morter   xliiij s ij d.| 10
Item paidd to the masons   xxxj li. xij d.
Item paid Bradburye to attend them   xiiij s
Item for yron woorck for bothe battlementes &
pyinacles   xliij s iiij d
Item for carpenters woorck & nayles to laye the lead   15
on the tower   xij s
Item for castinge gutters laying & soldringe   xxxij s iij d
               Summa liiij li. xiij s. vij d.

                    laid out aboute the playes.   20
Imprimis for the place to playe in   xiij s iiij d.
Item for attendantes & other thinges   xj s x d.
Item to T.B. for his charges   xxx s.
Item for hier of apparell   xx s.
Item for iij trumpetters   xv s.   25
Item for musicions all the tyme   xxxiij s iiij d.
Item for [i] j butte[s] [⌜& halfe⌝] of beare and
brewing our malte   xl s.
Item for fruites & spices   xvij s.
Item for coockery   xij s viij d. 30
Item for meate for the players   xxx s vj d.
Item for wayters in the seller & cuppes   ix s
All the receiptes towardes the makinge of the
battlementes   xlv li. ij s.
The whole charges vppon the battlementes   35
and playes   [lxx] lxvj li. vj s iij d.
By which accompt appeareth that the
Churchewardens have in this woorcke expended
more then they gained by there playes the sum of   xxj li. iiij s.

1/ Expended in large, heavily inked letters   10/ & morter added after entry complete
4/ wyniige for wyninge: minim missing

This xxj li iiij s is to be compared with the martes which they adventured

Gloucester Diocese Consistory Court Cause Book
GRO: GDR 90   5
f 52   (*12 June*)
...

Tewxbury

Robertus Ieynes   Ad *respondendum* articulis
de eade*m*   comp*a*ruit d*i*ctus Ieynes et vigore iuramenti
affirmavit that aboute*s* christmas laste was 3 yeeres Thomas Deacons   10
called to this deponent Robert Ieynes then co*m*minge from the play
and [told him that] requested him to goe alonge with him to Richard
Brushes howse and there he should fynde Iohn [Hodges] hazard &
Margery Hodges in an vpper chamber togeather which he did
accordingly and when they came thither they found there [the said Io.]   15
ᵗʰᵉ Constable & divers others to the nomber of xx^ty persons or
thereaboute*s* and the matter beinge then called in question the said
Iohn hazard did as it did then appeare lament his falte and the said
Margery Hodges as one Iohn Cooke told this deponent offered to giue
him v li or three poundes & a gold ringe to saue her honestye &   20
to conceale this matter &c/
...

TORTWORTH   25

1602–3
Gloucester Diocese Consistory Court Deposition Books
GRO: GDR 89
f [106]*   (*13 October*)   30
...

Will*e*lmus Lawrence de Torthworth in Com*itatu* Glouc*e*strie
husbandman vbi moram fecit *per* dudicim aut circiter ortus in
Chavenidge infra *p*arochiam de Horseley in Com*itatu* pred*i*cto etatis
xxxij. annor*um* aut circiter libere vt dicit condicionis testis &c.   35
Ad primu*m* dicit that mr wylmot ar*ti*cu*l*ate ys a mi*n*ister in holy orders
as he beleeveth and *p*arson of Tortworth and so comonly accompted
and taken/

33/ dudicim *for* duodecim   34/ Chavenidge: *Chavenage, Glouc, in the parish of Horseley*

Ad iij. deponit that vppon the sunday before St. Thomas day last past
at a wedding and in the Church howse of Tortworth after Candellighting
this deponent did see mr wylmot ar*ticu*late amongest diuers others of his
parishioners dance and lay a Cushion on the ground and kneele downe
vppon ˏ⸢it⸣ and kysse[d] a woman that then daunced w*i*th him, as all the   5
rest that then daunced w*i*th him (being [⟨..⟩] v. or vj. or more) also
did/ and ymedyatly after, this deponent did heare the said mr wylmott
say thus in effecte/ viz. Bycause my Lo*rd* Byshopp of Glou*ce*ster will
not geue me leaue to preach, I will studdy noe more on my booke and
nowe I will studdy knauery. And there were then present this   10
depo*n*ent Gyles Daunt and diuers others et al*it*er nescit deponere./
...

[f 106v]*

                                                                              15

Egidius Dawnte p*arochi*e de Osellworth in Com*itatu* Glouce*stri*e
gen*er*osus vbi moram fecit p*er* duodec*em* annos vl*tra* elapss etatis xlvj
annor*um* aut eo circiter testis productus et iuratus Dicit et deponit vt
sequitur.
Ad primum credit eundem esse verum.   20
Ad secundum nescit deponere./
Ad tertium dicit that the sundaye before Sainte Thomas daye last past
ˏ⸢(as this depo*n*ent remembreth) he⸣ this deponent accompanyed w*i*th
others came into the Churchhouse att Tortworth about vij or viij a
clock in the Eveninge and there founde divers of that p*ari*she and other   25
straingers dawnceinge and amongest the rest thar*ticu*late mr willm⟨ott⟩
and beinge well acquainted w*i*th him mr willmott came vnto this
deponent and asked him if he wolde dawnce to whome this deponent
replyed yea if he (meaneinge the saide mr willmott) wolde beginn and
leade a dawnce, and mr willmott saide faith that I will, for nowe the   30
Bishopp hath suspended me ˏ⸢from preacheinge⸣ I will practise and
studdye all knaveries and therew*i*thall he begann, and ledd the Cushin
dawnce w*i*th a Cushin on his sholder and kneeled downe as the order
of the dawnce is, and kissed one goodwife Hickes [there pr*e*sente] there
beinge pr*e*sente Thomas Taute and others whome this deponent doth   35
not nowe verie well remember. Et al*it*er nescit deponere.
...

17/ elapss *for* elapsos
25/ that *converted from* the

WESTON SUBEDGE

1574
Gloucester Diocese Consistory Court Deposition Books
GRO: GDR 32
p 178*   *(7 July)*

Responsiones personales Michaelis Hyndemer clerici facte contentis
in quibusdam presentibuss articulis ad voluntariam promocionem
Iohannis Castler parochiani sui versus eum Dat⟨.⟩ sequuntur.'
The the first article He aunsweareth yat in a Christmas Hollydayes
he went a masking & yat ther was ann egge brok
...

7ᵐᵒ Die Iulij
1574 repetit/

9/ *presentib*uss *for* presentibus   11/ The the: *dittography*

Diocese of Gloucester

1607
Visitation Articles   GRO: GDR 102
sigs B3–B3v
    Articles concerning the parishioners, and other of the Laity
...   5

17 Whether haue you or your predecessors, Churchwardens there
suffered since the last pardon, any playes, feasts, banquenttes,
Churchales, Drinkinges or any other prophane vsages, to bee kept in
your Church, chappels, or Churchyard, or bels to be rung
superstitiously vpon holy daies or Eues abrogated by the booke of 10
Common Prayer, contrary to the 68. Canon?
...

1612
Visitation Articles   GRO: GDR 115   15
sig B3
...
1   Touching the Church-wardens and Side-men.
Whether you and the Church-wardens, Quest-men, or Side-men,
from time to time, doe and haue done their diligences, in not suffering 20
any idle person to abide either in the Church-yard, or Church-porch,
in Seruice or Sermon time, but causing them either to come into the
Church to heare Diuine Seruice, or to depart, and not disturbe such
as be hearers there? And whether haue they, and doe you diligently
see the Parishioners duely resort to the Church euery Sunday and 25
Holliday, and there to remaine during Diuine seruice and sermon?
And whether you or your predecessors, Churchwardens there, suffer
any Plaies, Feasts, Drinkings, or any other prophane vsages, to be kept
in your Church, Chappell, or Church-yards, or haue suffered to your
and their vttermost power and endeuour, any person person or 30

30/ person person: *typographical error*

persons, to be tipling or drinking in any Inne or Victualing house in
your Parish, during the time of Diuine Seruice or Sermon, on Sundaies
and Holydaies.

...

1622
Visitation Articles   GRO: GDR 146

P 7

...

28 Whether haue any Lords of misrule, dauncers, players, or any other
disguised person, beene suffered to dance or play vpon the Sabbath
day, or to enter into the church or chappell, with games or daunces,
to the prophaning of Gods house, or into the church-yarde in time
of Diuine seruice: and if they haue, what bee the names of such
disordered persons.
29 Whether there be any stage-playes, beare-baitings, bul-baitings, or
other such vnlawfull and prophane exercises vsed vpon the Sabbath
day: and who gaue them Licence. Whether there be any common
drinkings in the Church, and who were present at such drinkings: or
sports, or any that doe sit in the Tauerne, or Alehouse, or streetes
vpon Sundayes or Holidayes, in time of morning or euening prayer.

...

1624
Visitation Articles   Folger Shakespeare Library: #10213.8

sig B2

...

17 Whether haue you or your predecessors, churchwardens, there
suffered (since the last pardon) any playes, feasts, banquets, chuchales,
drinkings, or any other prophane vsages, to be kept in your Church,
chappell, or churchyard, or bels to be rung superstitiously vpon
holidayes or Eues, abrogated by the Booke of Common Prayer,
contrary to the 68. canon.

...

29/ chuchales *for* churchales

Households

BEAUCHAMP

1420–1
Household Account Book of Richard Beauchamp, Earl of Warwick
Longleat House: Ms Misc. IX
f 30v* *(External expenses to date)*

...   5

...Et in expensis .ij. minstrallis domini de Wallia venientibus usque
Berkeley ad loquendum cum domina & existentibus in hostelaria
eiusdem Iohannis. Shephurde. per .vj. noctes dicta mense. viij d

f 43   *(6 November) (Guests)*   10

...

Ad prandium   ...Item I. mynstrallus domine. de Staffordia....

...

f 56   *(23 December) (Guests)*   15

Ad prandium   ...Item .iij. Trumpettes domini. Item .ij. harpers....

f 57*   *(24 December–6 January) (External expenses)*

                                                                       20

...In. diuersis disgisingez. factis hoc. festo .x. d. Et dato cuidam
mynstrallo domini de Clarense. existenti in hospicio per I diem et I
noctem [hos] hoc. festo. vj. s. viij. d. Et dato vj. ludentibus coram
domina. hoc festo de Slymbrugge per preceptum domine .iij. s. iiij.
d. Et dato .iiij. ludentibus de Wotton. pro consilio. ex precepto domine   25
.xx. d. Et dato .ij. minstrallis [de] domine de Bergeveny. existentibus
in hospicio videlicet in festo Epiphanie. vj. s. viij. d...

24/ Slymbrugge: *Slimbridge, Glouc*   25/ Wotton: *Wotton under Edge, Glouc*
26/ Bergeveny: *Abergavenny*

f 58v   *(10 January)* *(Guests)*

...

Ad prand*ium*   ...Item ij harpers de Wallia....

...

f 68   *(12 February)* *(Guests)*

Ad prand*ium*   ...Item .ij. mynstrall*is* do*m*i*n*e de Bergeveny....

...

BERKELEY

1602–3
Lord Henry Berkeley's House Steward's Book
Berkeley Castle Muniment Room: General Series Bound Book #109
f [67]*   *(8 July)* *(Rewards)*

...

Reward   Item geven the viij^th of Iulie to the kee*per* of Tortworth p*ar*ke for a
buck. – x s

Reward   Item geu*en* the same day to the Weigh*tes* – ij s

...

1603–4
Lord Henry Berkeley's House Steward's Book
Berkeley Castle Muniment Room: General Series Bound Book #109
f [72]   *(October)*

my Lords diet   ...
at Cirencester
Item paid for y*our* lo*r*dshi*p*s diet at Cirencester...   xj li. v s. x d.
Reward   Item geu*en* to the musi*c*i*o*ns there   ij s

...

Reward.   Item to the musi*c*i*o*ns at Sir Io*hn* Hungerford*es*   ij s. vj d

...

BRYDGES

1592
Speeches Delivered to Her Maiestie...at Sudley...   STC: 7600
sigs B.j.–C

At her Maiesties entrance into the Castle,
an olde Shepheard spake this saying.

Vouchsafe to heare, a simple Shephard, shephards and simplicity
cannot part, your highnes is come into Cotshold, an vneuen country,
but a people, that carry their thoughtes leuell with their fortunes, lowe
spirites, but true harts, vsing plaine dealinge, once counted a Iewell
nowe beggery, these hills afoorde nothing but cottages, and nothing   5
can we present to your highnes, but shephards. The country healthy,
and harmeles, a fresh aier, where there are noe dampes, and where a
black sheepe is a perilous beast, no monsters, we carry our harts, at
our tongues ends, being as farre from dissembling, as our sheepe from
fiercenesse, and if in anything, we shall chance to discouer our leudnes, 10
it wilbe in ouer boldnesse, in gazinge at you, who fils our harts with
ioye, and our eies with wonder, as for the honorable Lord and Lady
of the Castle, what happines they conceiue, I would it were possible
for them selues to expresse, then should your Maiestie see, that al
outwarde enterteinment, were but a smoake rising from their inward   15
affections, which as they cannot be seene, being in the hart, so can they
not be smoothred, appearing in their countenance, this lock of wooll
Cotsholdes best fruite, and my poore gift, I offer to your highnes, in
which nothing is to be esteemed, but the whitenes, virginities colour,
nor to be expected but duetye, shepards religion.   20

> Sunday, Apollo running after Daphne, a
> Shepheard followed vttering this.

> Nescis temeraria; nescis,   25
> Quem fugias; dieque fugis.

A short tale, but a sorrowfull, a iust complaint, but remedelesse, I
loued, (for shephardes haue their Saints) l long I loued (for beauty
bindeth prentices) a Nymph most faire & as chast as faire, yet not more 30
faire, then I vnhappy, Apollo who calleth him selfe a god (a title among
men, when they will commit iniuries) tearme themselues gods,
pursued my Daphne with bootelesse loue, and me, with endlesse hate,
her he woed; with fair wordes, the flatteries of men, with great gifts,
the sorceries of gods, with cruell threates, the terrefiing of weake   35
damosels Nec prece nec pretio néc mouet ille minis. me; he terrified
with a monstrous word metamorphosing, saying that he would turne
me into a woolfe and of a shepheard make me a sheepe-biter, or into

---

25-6/ You do not know, rash girl, you do not know whom you flee: you flee from the day:
Ovid, *Metamorphoses*, I. 514
36/ Neither by entreaty, nor by reward, nor by threats does he move (her).

a Cockatrice and cause mine eies which gazed on her, to blind hers which made mine dazell, or to a molde that I should heare his flattering speech, but neuer behold her faire face, tantæné animis calestibus iræ? sometimes would he allure her with sweete musicke, but harmony is harsh when it is lusts broaker, often with promise of immortality, but   5 chastetye is of it selfe immortall, euer pursuing her with swiftnes, but vertue tying wings to the thoughts of Virgins, swiftnes becommeth surbated; thus liued he twixt loue and ielousy; I twixt loue and danger; she twixt feare and vertue. At last and alas, this day I feare of all my ioyes the last, I cannot as a Poet (who describing the morning, and   10 before he tell what it is, make it night,) stand on the time, loue coyneth no circumloquutions, but by the sunne, a Shepheardes Diall, which goeth as true as our harts, it was four of the clock, when she flying from his treason was turned into a tree; which made me stand, as though I had bene turned into a stone, and Apollo so enchanted as   15 wounded with her losse, or his owne crueltye, the fingers which were wonte to play on the Lute, found no other instrument then his owne face, the goulden haire the pride of his heade pulde off in lockes and stampt at his feete, his sweete voice, turned to howling; and there sitteth he, (long maie he sorrowe,) wondring, and weeping, and kissing   20 the lawrell, his late loue, and mine euer. Pleaseth your Maiestye to viewe the melancholy of Apollo, my distresse, and I Daphnes mischance, it may be the sight of so rare perfection, will make him die for griefe, which I wish, or Daphne returne to her olde shape, which must be your wounder; if neither, it shal content me that I haue   25 reuealed my griefes, and that you may beholde his.

This speech ended, her Maiesty sawe Apollo
with the tree, hauing on the one side
one that sung, on the other one   30
that plaide.

Sing you, plaie you, but sing and play my truth,
This tree my Lute, these sighes my notes of ruth:
The Lawrell leafe for euer shall bee greene,   35
And chastety shalbe Apolloes Queene.
If gods maye dye, here shall my tombe be plaste,
And this engrauen, fonde Phoebus, Daphne chaste.

3/ (Can) such great wrath (lie hidden) in heavenly hearts?: Virgil, *Aeneid* I. 11; calestibus *for* caelestibus

After these verses, the song.

My hart and tongue were twinnes, at once conceaued,
The eldest was my hart, borne dumbe by destenie,
The last my tongue, of all sweete thoughts bereaued,   5
Yet strung and tunde, to play harts harmonie.
Both knit in one, and yet asunder placed,
What hart would speake, the tongue doeth still discouer,
What tongue doth speake, is of the hart embraced,
And both are one to make a new found louer: 10
New founde, and onely founde in Gods and Kings,
Whose words are deedes, but deedes nor words regarded:
Chaste thoughts doe mount and flie with swiftest wings,
My loue with paine, my paine with losse rewarded:
Engraue vpon this tree, Daphnes perfection,   15
That neither men nor gods, can force affection.|

The song ended, the tree riued, and Daphne
issued out, Apollo ranne after, with
these words.   20

Nimpha mane, per me concordant carmina neruis.
Faire Daphne staye, too chaste because too faire,
Yet fairer in mine eies, because so chaste,
And yet because so chaste, must I despaire?   25
And to despaire, I yeelded haue at last.
Shepheard possesse thy loue, for me too cruell,
Possesse thy loue, thou knowest not how to measure,
A dunghill cock doeth often finde a Iewell,
Enioying that, he knowes not to be treasure.   30
When broomy bearde, to sweepe thy lips presume,
When on thy necke, his rough hewen armes shall moue,
And gloate on thee with eies that drizell reume,
When that his toothlesse mouth shall call thee loue,
Noght will I saie of him, but pittie thee,   35
That beauty might, but would no wiser bee.

Daphne running to her Maiestie
vttred this.

22/ Nymph, remain: it is through me that songs blend with stringed instruments: Ovid,
   Metamorphoses, I. 518

I stay, for whether should chastety fly for succour, but to the Queene
of chastety, by thee was I enterred in a tree, that by crafte, way might
be made to lust, by your highnes restored, that by vertue, there might
be assurance in honor: these tables, to set downe your prayses long
since Sibillas prophesies I humbly present to your Maiesty, not   5
thinking that your vertues can be deciphered in so slight a volume, but
noted; the whole world is drawen in a small mappe, Homers Illiades
in a nutshel, and the riches of a Monarch, in a few cyphers, and so
much ods, betwext explaining of your perfections, and the touching,
as is betvvixt painting and thinking, the one, running ouer a little table   10
I in a vvhole day, the other ouer the whole world in a minute, vvith
this vouchsafe a poore virgins wish, that often wish for good husbands,
mine, only for the endlesse prosperity of my soueraigne.

                    The verses, written in the tables which   15
                        were giuen to her Maiesty.

            Let fame describe your rare perfection,
            Let nature paint your beuties glory,
            Let loue engraue your true affection,   20
            Let wonder write your vertues story,
            By them and Gods must you be blazed,
            Sufficeth men they stand amazed.

                The thirde day shoulde haue beene presen-   25
                ted to her Maiestie, the high Constable of
                Cotsholde but the weather so vnfit, that it
                was not. But this it should haue beene,
                one clothed all in sheepes-skins, face
                & all spake this by his interpreter.   30

May it please your highnes, this is the great Constable and
commandadore of Cotsholde, he speaks no language, but the
Rammish tongue, such sheepishe gouernours there are, that can say
no more to a messenger then he, (Bea), this therfore, as signifying his   35
duety to your Maiestye, and al our desires, I am commanded to be
his interpreter, or shepheards starre, pointing directly to Cotshold,
and in Cotshold, to Sudley, made vs expect some wonder, and of the
eldest, aske some counsel, it was resolued by the ancientst, that such
a one should come, by whome all the shepheards should haue their   40

37/ or *for* our

flocks in safety, & their owne liues, all the country quietnes, & the
whole world astonish-|ment: our Constable commaunds this day to
be kept holliday, all our shepheards are assembled, and if shepheards
pastimes may please, how ioyful would they be if it would please you
to see them; which if you vouchsafe not, as pastimes too meane for 5
your Maiestie, they meane to call this day the shepheards blacke day;
in all humilitie we entreat, that you would cast an eie to their rude
deuices, and an eare to their harshe wordes, and if nothing happen to
be pleasing, the amends is, nothing shalbe tedious.

10

    After this speech her Maiesty was to be
    brought amonge the shepheards amonge
     whome was a King and a Queene
      to be chosen and thus they
       beganne.   15

   Melibaus. Nisa. Cutter of Cootsholde.

Mel. Cvt the Cake, who hath the beane; shalbe King, and where the
peaze is, shee shalbe Queene.   20
Nis. I haue the peaze, and must be Queene.
Mel. I the beane and King, I must cammaunde.
Nis. Not so, the Queene, shall and must commaunde, for I haue
often heard of a King that coulde not commaunde his subiects, and
of a Queene that hath commaunded Kings.   25
Mel. I yeeld, yet it is within compasse of my authoritie to aske
questions and first I will beginne with you in loue, I meane
Shepheardes loue, for I will not meddle with Gentlefolkes loue, which
is most constant, the man or the woman?
Nis. It is no question, no more then if you should aske whether on 30
a steepe hill, a square stone, or a globe stoode most steddye.
Mel. Both louing, which is most louing?
Nis. The woman if she haue her right, the man, if he be his owne
Indge.
Mel. Why doth the man euer vvoe the vvoman, the woman neuer 35
the man?
Nis. Because men are most amorous and least chaste, women
carelesse of fonde affections, and vvhen they embrace them, fearefull.
But vnlesse your questions were vviser, I commaunde you to silence.
You sirra, that sit as though your wits were a vvoole-gathering vvill 40

34/ Indge *for* Iudge

you haue a question, or a commaundement?
Cut.   No question of a Queene, for they are harde to be answered,
but anie commaundement, for that must be obeyed.
Nis.   Then sing, and you sir, a question, or commaundment?
Do.   A commaundment I, and glad that I am?   5
Nis.   Then play: Do. I haue plaide so long with my fingers that I
haue beaten out of play al my good fortunes

The Song.

Hearbes, wordes, and stones, all maladies haue cured,   10
    Hearbes, wordes, and stones, I vsed when I loued.
Hearbes, smels, words, winde, stones hardnes haue procured,
    By stones, nor wordes, nor hearbes her minde was moued;
I askt the cause, this was a womans reason,
    Mongst hearbes are weedes, and thereby are refused,   15
Deceite, as well as truth speakes wordes in season,
    False stones by foiles haue many one abused,
I sight, and then shee saide my fancie smoaked,
I gaz'd, shee saide my lookes were follies glauncing,
I sounded deade, shee saide my loue was choaked,   20
I started vp, shee saide my thoughtes were dauncing,
O sacred loue if thou haue any Godhead,
        Teach other rules to winne a maidenheade.

Mel.   Well song, & wel plaide, seldome so well amonge shepheards,   25
but call me the Cutter of Cotsholde, that I lookes as though he onlie
knew his leripoope, amorous he is, and vvise, carying a sheepes eie
in a calfs heade.
Nis.   Will you 3 questions, or 3 commaundments?
Cut.   Halfe a dozen of eache. My wits worke like new beare, and they   30
will breake my head, vnlesse it vent at the mouthe.
Nis.   Sing.
Cut.   I haue forsworne that since cuckow-time, for I heard, one sing
all the sommer, and in the winter was all balde.
Nis.   Play on the Lute.   35
Cut.   Taylers crafte, a knocke on the knuckles, wil make one faste
a fortnight, my belly and back shall not be retainers to my fingers.
Nis.   What question shall I aske?
Cut.   Any so it be of loue.
Nis.   Are youe amorous?   40
Cut.   No, but fantasticall.
Nis.   But what is loue?

Cut. A single   Ioy   Sorrow
Accidens. In   Hope   all tole-   Anger   all intole-
loue there are Truth   rable.   Ielousie   rable.
eight partes.   Constancy   Dispaire
These containe all, till you come to the rules, and then in loue,   5
there are three concords.

1   The first, betwixt a Bacheler, and a maide,
2   The seconde, betwixt a man and his wife,
3   The thirde, betwixt any he and she, that loueth stragling.

Nis.   The foole bleeds, it is time to stopp his vaine, for hauing wet his   10
foote, he careth not how deepe he wades. Let vs attend that, which
we most expect, the starr, that directs vs hither, vvho hath in
Almanacke?

Cut.   What meane you, a starmonger, the quipper of the firmament,
here is one. I euer carrie it, to knowe the hye vvaies, to euerie good   15
tovvne, the faires, and the faire weather.|

Mel.   Let me see it. The seuenth of September, happines was borne
into the world, it may be the eleuenth is some wonder. The moone
at the ful, tis true, for Cynthia neuer shined so bright, the twelfth the
weather inclined to moisture & shepheards deuises to dryenes, the   20
thirteenth, sommer, goeth from hence, the signe in virgo, viuat
clarissima virgo. The diseases shalbe melancholies, some proceeding
of necessitie, some of superfluity, many shalbe studying how to spend
what they haue, more, beating their braines to get what they want.
Malice shalbe more infectious then the pestilence, and Drones more   25
fauoured then Ants, as for Bees, they shal haue but their laboure for
their paines, and when their combes be full, they shalbe stilde; the
warre shal be, twixt hemlocke and honie. At foure of the clocke this
day, shal appeare the worldes wonder that leades England into euery
land, and brings all lands into England.   30

                Then espying her Maiesty, he & al the shep-
                heards kneeling, concluded thus.

This is the day, this the houre, this the starre, pardon dread   35
Soueraigne, poore shepheards pastimes, and bolde shepheards
presumptions. We call our selues Kings and Queenes to make mirth,
but when we see a King or Queene, we stand amazed. The sunne
warmes the earth, yet looseth no brightnes; but sheweth more force,
& Kings names that fall vpon shepheards, loose no dignity, but breede   40

12/ in for an   21–2/ May the most bright virgin (ie, the queen) live forever!

more feare. Their pictures are drawen in colours, and in brasse their
portraytures engrauen. At chests, there are Kings, and Queenes, &
they of wood. Shepheards are no more, nor no lesse, woodde*n*. In
Theaters, artificers haue plaide Emperours, yet the next day forgotte*n*,
neither their dueties nor occupations. For our boldenes in borrowing   5
their names, and in not seeing your Maiesty for our blindnes, we offer
these shepheards weedes, which, if your Maiestye vouchsafe at any
time to weare, it shall bring to our hearts comfort, and happines to
our labours.

STAFFORD   10

1503–4
Household Accounts of Edward Stafford, Duke of Buckingham
SRO: D 641/1/3/7a   15
unnumbered mb   *(31 March – 30 March)*
...

Regarda extranior*um* seruient*ium* d*o*mini ministrallor*um* seruient*ium*
vltra vada &c.†
...Et in consimili*bus* regard*is* p*er* eunde*m* mandatu*m* solut*is* tam   20
diu*er*s*is* ministrall*is* & trumpett*is* extranijs q*u*am ministrall*is* d*o*mini ad
diu*er*s*as* vices infra temp*us* predict*um* vt p*ar*ticularit*er* p*at*et in libro
de p*ar*ticula*ri*b*us* supradic*to*   vj. li. xvij s iiij d...
...

1507–8   25
Household Accounts of Edward Stafford, Duke of Buckingham
SRO: D (W) 1721/1/5
p 7   *(15 November)*
...   30
Presentes prand*io*...ij Trumpett*es*/...
...

p 42   *(21 December)*
...   35
Cen*a*...ij minstrell*es*...
...

p 43   *(22 December)*
...   40
Presentes prand*io*...ij mynstrell*es*...
...

p 44* *(23 December)*
…
Presentes prandio…vj Trumpette*s*/ ij. mynstrelle*s*/…
Cena…Et xv Cant*atores* Capelle…
…   5

p 45 *(24 December)*
…
Presentes prandio…xviij Cantatore*s* Capelle/ ix pueri/ vj famil*iares*
Cantatore*s*/ vj. Trumpette*s*/ ij Lez/ mynstrelle*s*/…   10
…

p 46 *(25 December)*
…
Presentes prandio…ij le Mynstrelle*s*/ vj Trunpette*s* iiij^{or} lusore*s* d*omini* 15
de Writell/…
…

p 53 *(2 January)*
…   20
Presentes prandio…ij le minstralle*s* vj Trompette*s* iiij lusores/…

p 54 *(3 January)*
…
Presentes prandio…ij le mynistr*alles* vj Trompette*s* iiij^{or} lusores…   25

p 55 *(4 January)*
…
Presentes prandio…ij lez ministrall/ vj trompette*s*/ iiij^{or} lusores/…
Cena…iiij le wayte*s* de Bristoll   30

p 56* *(5 January)*
…
Presentes prandio…ij le minstr*alles* vj Trompette*s*/ iiij^{or} le Waite*s* de
Bristoll/ iiij^{or} lusores de Writhill/…   35

p 58 *(6 January)*
…
Presentes prandio…ij le ministrall vj lez Trompette*s* iiij le Waite*s* de

16/ Writell: *Writtle, Essex*   35/ Writhill: *Writtle, Essex*

Bristoll iiij^or lusores de Writhill...

...

p 60   *(7 January)*

...

Presentes prand*io*...ij le minstral*les*/ vj lez Trompett*es* iiij^or luso*res*...

p 61   *(8 January)*

...

Presentes prand*io*...vj le Tompett*es*/ ij le ministral*les*/...

p 75   *(22 January)*

...

Presentes prand*io*...vj Trompett*es*...

1515–16
Household Accounts of Edward Stafford, Duke of Buckingham
PRO: E. 101. 631/20
mb 20   *(31 December)*

dona

...

do*m*ino Regi & diu*ercis* generosis. seruient*ibus* tam hospic*ii* q*uam*
fforinc*ecis* do*m*ini ducis†
do*m*ino Regi &.
Diuersis seruient*ibus*.hospicij. d*icti* do*m*ini
ducis ad h*abendum* ex. dono ipsius ducis.
vid*elicet* vj vlne Canvas.pro ffactur*a* vnius lez.   Canvas – vj vlne
pagent. & ostens*ione* in I lez enterlude. coram
p*refa*to do*m*ino duce in ffesto Nat*ali* do*m*ini....   30
...

1516–17
Household Accounts of Edward Stafford, Duke of Buckingham
SRO: D 641/1/3/9
unnumbered mb   *(31 March – 30 March)*

...

Ad vsum   ...x. dd. moresbell*es*. vj. virg*e*.   moresbelles   x.^dd.

1/ Writhill: *Writtle, Essex*   28/ vj vlne *underlined* MS

Gardrobe   iij q*uart*er*ia* nig*ri* bokeram &   Bokeram nig*er* vj virg*e* iij q*uart*er*ia*
lector*um*   di. virg*e* rub*ri* bokeram p*r*o ij   Bokeram rub*er* di. virg*e*
ipsius ducis Tunicis p*r*o le moresdaunce. &   Canvas   iij virg*e*
              iij virg*e* Canvas pro linura vni*us*   ...
              d*i*ctar*um* Tunicar*um*....   5

1520–1
Household Accounts of Edward Stafford, Duke of Buckingham
PRO: E. 36/220
p 12* *(1 January)*   10
...

Liberacion*es* et   Item in Rewarde geven by the said Duk*es* coimmaundement
soluc*iones* dict*i* vnto certain frenshe men and ij frenshe women playing afore
mens*is* Ianuarij   the said Duc the passion of oure lorde by a vise and also to a   xl s.
                      yong maide a Tumbeller by Reaport of Iohn kyrk being   15
                      present maist*er* poley

p 13   *(6 January)*
...
Item the same day in Reward geven by the said Duk*es*   20
commaundement vnto the wait*es* of bristowe [th] by Reaport of Iohn
kyrk   vj s viij d
...

12/ coimmaundement: *extra minim* MS

APPENDIX 1
Christmas at Thornbury Castle

1507–8
Household Book of the Duke of Buckingham   SRO: D(W) 1721/1/5
p 46 col 1

Thornbury   5

	Generosi	iiij^{xx} xv
Prandium	valetti	Cvij
	garciones	iiij^{xx} xvij

ij^{C} iiij^{xx} xiiij^{e} 10

	generosi	iiij^{xx} iiij
Cena	valetti	Cxiiij
	garciones	iiij^{xx} xij

Presentes Prandio Dominam Annam se xiiij^{a} Abbatem de kaynsham
se vij^{mo} W Walwyn se iij^{cio} I Seyntgeorge se ij^{do} Robertum P'ticile   15
se ij^{do} Cancell*arium* se v^{to} H Blunt se ij^{do} Iohannem Burrell se ij^{do} /
balliu*um* de Hatfield se ij^{do} / ball*iuum* de okeham se ij^{do} / balliu*um*
de Navisby se ⟨*illegible*⟩ / balliuum de Rowell se ij^{do} Q. Barth se ij^{do} /
ij al*ios seruientes* de Penshurst / Henr*icum* Dunston / ij le mynstrell*es* /
vj Trunpett*es* / iiij^{or} lusor*es domini* de Writell / H Boughey se ij^{do} /   20
Recept*atorem* de Nuport se ij^{do} / T Morgan se iij^{cio} / ij al*ios seruientes*
domini de Nuport cum I famul*iare* / viij seru*ientes domini* Brechon
cum x famul*iaribus domini* Iohannis Burton / xviij Clericos Capelle
& ix pu*eros* eiusd*em* Capelle / iij Cissor*es* iiij Penulator*es* I natiu*um*
ij de lez Hardwaremen xxij de vill*a* xxxij de P*atria* / ij cocos de Bristol   25
&c
Cena vt in p*randio* preter vj

Extranei ad Prandium C iiij^{xx} ij
Cenam Clxxvj

col 2*

®ffestum
Natalis
Domini

Die Sabbati xxv^{to}. die Decembris Panetrie expense iiij^C iiij^{xx} xj panes iij
quarterii [iij quarterii] ij Manchet frumenti precij xiij s viij d ob. vnde
Iantaculo xv panes dimidium & I manchet vt in diebus precedentibus
ac Thesaurario I panis Abbati de Kaynsham I panis I manchet
generosis Capelle viij panes generosis extraneis xij panes / in ffercul'
ij^c iiij^{xx} xiiij panes Sissor' xxxiiij panes Regardator' lxx Salt' vj panes
Coquine pro operibus x panes / Chaundelar' v panes le vrs' ij panes
Elemosinar' ij panes Potacionibus xv panes dimidium / scilicet
Extraneis / [prep...] / liberacioni xv panes iij quarterii   Sellarie
expense xj sextarii iij quarte vini gasconiensis precii xiij s I picherius
dimidium vini de Royn' precii xv d ac dimidium picherii de Maluesey
precii vj d vnde Iantaculo dimidium picherii / in ffercul' I sextarius I
picherius vini gasconiensis & I picherius vini de Royn' pro Waller
nutrice dimidium picherii magna camera I sextarius aula iiij^{or} sextarii
ij picherii per arnoldum Dietis dimidium picherii vini gasconiensis I
quarta vini de Royn' & I quarta de Maluesey Coquine pro operibus
iij picherii ad hostium ij sextarii iij picherii Liberacioni ij picherii I
quarta vini gasconiensis ac I quarta de Maluesey   Buttrie expense in
Ceruisia Clxxj lagene I quarta precii xiij. s vij d q. vnde Iantaculo xvij
lagene iij quarte / in ffercul' / lxxiij lagene dimidium Regardator' xxxix
lagene Coquine pro operibus v lagene / Potacionibus vj lagene iij quarte
ad hostium xx lagene / Liberacioni ix lagene I quarta /   Coquine
expense de stauro domini I carcosium & vij Rondes Carnis bouis precij
xx s ix casea multonis precii xvj s iiij porci viij s ac I vitulus dimidium
precii iiij s /   Achatoris expense videlicet in iij Signis precii xij s iiij^{or}
aucis ij s v porcellis xx d xiiij Caponibus viij s xviij pullis gallinariis precii
xviij d xxi Cuniculis iij s vj d I Pavone ij s iiij Malardes viij d v Wigions
x d xij Teles xij d viij Castrimargis viij d xxij Snytes xij volucribus
grandibus iij d iiij^C ouis gallinariis iij s iiij d xx Discis butiri xx d x
Lagenis Lactis x d I Lagena dimidium quaice vj d ij Lagenis frumenti
cocti iiij d ac herbis precii j d   Chaundrie expense de Candellis
pariciensibus xxxvj lb precii ij s x d Sises lxiiij precii xvij d quariars ij
precii ij d ac Prikettes iiij precij iij d ob   Aule & camere expense
de focali vj Carecte vj s ac vj quarte Carbonis Siluestris precij ij s
Totalis Dieta

15/ Sellarie for Cellarie

Willis' Description of a Play at Gloucester

This description of a play at Gloucester's Bothall by R. Willis is well known and has been printed in numerous histories of the theatre as a generalized example of provincial performance during the latter half of the sixteenth century. The description appears here in its particular local context. The entire meditation has been transcribed, because the conclusion Willis draws gives us reason to trust his remarkably detailed account, despite the fact that it was written many years after the performance took place. Willis argues that great care must be taken in educating the young, 'for that their young memories are like faire writing tables' (p 113), and says of his own experience that the play 'tooke such impression in me, that when I came towards mans estate, it was as fresh in my memory, as if I had seen it newly acted' (p 113).

The performance described cannot be precisely dated, yet as Willis himself tells us that he stood between the legs of his sitting father to watch the play, he must have been fairly young, and yet old enough to remember what he saw. The title page of *Mount Tabor* proclaims the author to have been seventy-five in the year of publication, 1639, so it seems likely that the performance took place during the 1570s, when Willis was between six and fifteen years of age.

> ***Mount Tabor. or Private Exercises of a Penitent Sinner.*** By R.W. Esquire. (London: Printed by R.B. for P. Stephens and C. Meredith, at the gilded Lion in S. Paul's Church-yard, 1639.)   STC: 25752 pp 110–14

5

> Upon a Stage-play Which I saw
> when I was a child.

> IN the City of Gloucester the manner is (as I think it is in other like corporations) that when Players of Enterludes come to towne, they   10 first attend the Mayor to enforme him what noble-mans servants they are, and so to get licence for their publike playing; and if the Mayor like the Actors, or would shew respect to their Lord and Master, he appoints them to play their first play before himselfe and the Aldermen

and common Counsell of the City; and that is called the Mayors play,
where every one that will comes in without money, the Mayor giving
the players a reward as hee thinks fit to shew respect unto them. At
such a play, my father tooke me with him and made mee stand
betweene his leggs, as he sate upon one of the ben-Iches where wee   5
saw and heard very well. The play was called (the Cradle of security,)
wherin was personated a King or some great Prince with his Courtiers
of severall kinds, amongst which three Ladies were in speciall grace
with him; and they keeping him in delights and pleasures, drew him
from his graver Counsellors, hearing of Sermons, and listning to good   10
counsell, and admonitions, that in the end they got him to lye downe
in a cradle upon the stage, where these three Ladies joyning in a sweet
song rocked him asleepe, that he snorted againe, and in the meane time
closely conveyed under the cloaths where withall he was covered, a
vizard like a swines snout upon his face, with three wire chaines fastned 15
thereunto, the other end whereof being holden severally by those three
Ladies, who fall to singing againe, and then discovered his face, that
the spectators might see how they had transformed him, going on with
their singing, whilst I all this was acting, there came forth of another
doore at the farthest end of the stage, two old men, the one in blew   20
with a Serjeant at Armes, his mace on his shoulder, the other in red
with a drawn sword in his hand, and leaning with the other hand upon
the others shoulder, and so they two went along in a soft pace round
about by the skirt of the Stage, till at last they came to the Cradle, when
all the Court was in greatest jollity, and then the foremost old man   25
with his Mace stroke a fearfull blow upon the Cradle; whereat all the
Courtiers with the three Ladies and the vizard all vanished; and the
desolate Prince starting up bare faced, and finding himselfe thus sent
for to judgement, made a lamentable complaint of his miserable case,
and so was carried away by wicked spirits. This Prince did personate   30
in the morall, the wicked of the world; the three Ladies, Pride,
Covetousnesse, and Luxury, the two old men, the end of I the world,
and the last judgement. This sight tooke such impression in me, that
when I came towards mans estate, it was as fresh in my memory, as
if I had seen it newly acted. From whence I observe out of mine owne   35
experience, what great care should bee had in the education of
children, to keepe them from seeing of spectacles of ill examples, and
hearing of lascivious or scurrilous words: for that their young
memories are like faire writing tables, wherein if the faire sentences
or lessons of grace bee written, they may (by Gods blessing) keepe   40
them from many vicious blots of life, wherewithall they may otherwise
bee tainted; especially considering the generall corruption of our

nature, whose very memories are apter to receive evill then good, and
that the well seasoning of the new Caske at the first, keepes it the better
and sweeter ever after, and withall wee may observe, how farre unlike
the Plaies | and harmlesse morals of former times, are to those which
have succeeded, many of which, (by report of others,) may bee termed   5
schoolmasters of vice, and provocations to corruptions: which our
deprived nature is too prone unto: nature and grace being contraries.
...

A Commentary on The King's Book of Sports

In 1618 Christopher Windle, vicar of Bisley, addressed to James I a slim, handwritten volume entitled A Book, for a Buck with a Parke or, for a good Bishopricke or, for a fatt Benefice at least. (BL: Royal Ms. 12 A. LXX). Windle hoped to win a royal pardon from the debts for which he had been imprisoned in Gloucester jail and perhaps further royal preferment on his release. According to the letter of petition with which he opens the volume, Windle was then fifty-eight or fifty-nine years of age, and had held the Bisley living for thirty-one years (since 1587). He claims to have publicly supported James from the moment of his accession and to have consistently opposed the king's Puritan detractors. In fact, his antagonism toward Puritan attitudes had previously caused him trouble; in 1611, his own parishioners attacked him before the consistory court of Gloucester diocese for encouraging maypole-dancing and preaching against numerological interpretation of the Bible (see entries under Bisley, pp 285–8). Windle even blames his incarceration on the over-zealous enforcement of the debt laws by officials hostile to his royalist views rather than on the poverty of the living.

In addition to the petition asking for the king's intervention and a number of commendatory verses, Windle included in his book this commentary in Latin on *The Kings Maiesties Declaration to His Subiects, Concerning lawfull Sports to be vsed* (London: Bonham Norton and John Bill, 1618), pp 1–9. *The Book of Sports*, as it came to be known, responded to the growing power of Puritan Sabbatarianism, which attacked the practice of holding folk games, sports, and other pastimes on Sundays and holy days. Since most of the people in agricultural communities were not free to participate in or attend sports and games during the work-week, restraints against having them on Sundays theatened to stamp out these folk pastimes altogether. In 1617 petitioners from Lancashire complained to the king that they were barred from all recreations after divine service on Sunday (James Tait, 'The Declaration of Sports for Lancashire (1617),' *EHR* 32 (1917), 561–8). James first granted the desired licence to the inhabitants of Lancashire and then expanded its provisions to apply to the entire country by issuing *The Book of Sports* on 24 May 1618. The entire text of the declaration has been printed here, since in the second half of his commentary Windle discusses it point by point, providing key phrases as references in the left margin.

...

Whereas vpon Our returne the last yeere out of Scotland, Wee did publish Our pleasure touching the recreations of Our people in those parts vnder Our hand: For some causes Vs thereunto moouing, We haue thought good to command these Our directions then giuen in 5 Lancashire with a few words thereunto added, and most appliable to these parts of Our Realmes, to be published to all Our Subiects.

Whereas We did iustly in Our Progresse through Lancashire, re-|buke some Puritanes & precise people, and tooke order that the like vnlawfull cariage should not bee vsed by any of them hereafter, 10 in the prohibiting and vnlawfull punishing of Our good people for vsing their lawfull Recreations, and honest exercises vpon Sundayes and other Holy dayes, after the afternoone Sermon or Seruice: Wee now find that two sorts of people wherewith that Countrey is much infested, (Wee meane Papists and Puritanes) have maliciously traduced 15 and calumniated those Our iust and honourable proceedings. And therefore lest Our reputation might vpon the one side (though innocently) haue some aspersion layd vpon it, and that vpon the other part Our good people in that Countrey bee misled by the mistaking and misinterpretation of Our meaning: We | haue therefore thought 20 good hereby to cleare and make Our pleasure to bee manifested to all Our good People in those parts.

It is true that at Our first entry to this Crowne, and Kingdome, Wee were informed, and that too truely, that Our County of Lancashire abounded more in Popish Recusants then any Countie of England, and 25 thus hath still continued since to Our great regreet, with litle amendment, saue that now of late, in Our last riding through Our said County, Wee find both by the report of the Iudges, and of the Bishop of that diocesse that there is some amendment now daily beginning, which is no small contentment to Vs. 30

The report of this growing amendment amongst them, made Vs the more sory, when with Our owne Eares Wee | heard the generall complaint of Our people, that they were barred from all lawfull Recreation, and exercise vpon the Sundayes afternoone, after the ending of all Diuine Seruice, which cannot but produce two euils: The 35 one, the hindering of the conuersion of many, whom their Priests will take occasion hereby to vexe, perswading them that no honest mirth or recreation is lawfull or tollerable in Our Religion, which cannot but breed a great discontentment in Our peoples hearts, especially of such as are peraduenture vpon the point of turning; The other 40 inconuenience is, that this prohibition barreth the common and meaner sort of people from vsing such exercises as may make their

bodies more able for Warre, when Wee or Our Successors shall haue
occasion to vse them. And in place | thereof sets vp filthy tiplings and
drunkennesse, and breeds a number of idle and discontented speaches
in their Alehouses. For when shal the common people haue leaue to
exercise, if not vpon the Sundayes and Holydayes, seeing they must   5
apply their labour, and winne their liuing in all working dayes?

   Our expresse pleasure therefore is, that the Lawes of Our
Kingdome, and Canons of Our Church bee aswell obserued in that
County, as in all other places of this Our Kingdome. And on the other
part, that no lawfull Recreation shall bee barred to Our good People,   10
which shall not tend to the breach of Our aforesaid Lawes, and Canons
of Our Church: which to expresse more particularly, Our pleasure is,
That the Bishop, and all other inferiour Churchmen, and Churchwar-
|dens, shall for their parts bee carefull and diligent, both to instruct
the ignorant, and conuince & reforme them that are misled in religion,   15
presenting them that will not conforme themselues, but obstinately
stand out to Our Iudges and Iustices: Whom We likewise command
to put the Law in due execution against them.

   Our pleasure likewise is, That the Bishop of that Diocesse take the
like straight order with all the Puritans and Precisians within the same,   20
either constraining them to conforme themselues, or to leaue the
Countrey according to the Lawes of Our Kingdome, and Canons of
Our Church, and so to strike equally on both hands, against the
contemners of Our Authoritie, and aduersaries of Our Church. And
as for Our good peoples lawfull Recreation, | Our pleasure likewise   25
is, That after the end of Diuine Seruice, Our good people be not
disturbed, letted, or discouraged from any lawfull Recreation; Such
as dauncing, either men or women, Archerie for men, leaping,
vaulting, or any other such harmelesse Recreation, nor from hauing
of May-Games, Whitson Ales, and Morris-dances, and the setting vp   30
of Maypoles and other sports therewith vsed, so as the same be had
in due and conuenient time, without impediment or neglect of diuine
Seruice: And that women shall haue leaue to carry rushes to the
Church for the decoring of it, according to their old custome. But
withall We doe here accompt still as prohibited all vnlawfull games to   35
bee vsed vpon Sundayes onely, as Beare and Bullbaitings, Interludes,
and at all times in | the meaner sort of People by Law prohibited,
Bowling.

   And likewise Wee barre from this benefite and libertie, all such
knowne Recusants, either men or Women, as will abstaine from   40
comming to Church or diuine Seruice, being therefore vnworthy of
any lawfull recreation after the said Seruice, that will not first come

to the Church and serue God: Prohibiting in like sort the said
Recreations to any that, though conforme in Religion, are not present
in the Church at the Seruice of God, before their going to the said
Recreations. Our pleasure likewise is, That they to whom it belongeth
in Office, shall present and sharply punish all such as in abuse of this   5
Our libertie, will vse these exercises before the ends of all diuine
Seruices for that day. And We likewise straightly | command, that
euery person shall resort to his owne Parish Church to heare diuine
Seruice, and each Parish by it selfe to vse the said Recreation after
diuine Seruice. Prohibiting likewise any Offensiue weapons to be   10
caried or vsed in the said times of Recreations And Our pleasure is,
That this Our Declaration shalbe published by order from the Bishop
of the Diocesse, through all the Parish Churches, and that both Our
Iudges of Our Circuit, and Our Iustices of Our Peace be informed
thereof.   15
...

 The Puritans remained unconvinced, and some vicars lost their livings because
they refused to read *The Book of Sports* to their congregations as directed (L.A.
Govett, *The King's Book of Sports* (London, 1890), p 37). On the other hand,   20
compliance in this matter became grounds for removal under the Commonwealth
(Christopher Whitfield, *Robert Dover and the Cotswold Games* (London, 1962),
p 17). In his commentary, Windle praises the king's political and pragmatic
reasoning, but makes his own contribution in the form of a theological answer to
the Puritans.   25

A Book, for a Buck with a Parke... BL: Royal Ms. 12 A. LXX
pp 5–21*

In hanc Regiam eximiam et Dulcissimam Declarationem Christophori   30
  Windlei variè mixtus commentarius, *vel* copiosa Oratio.
Hanc Regiam tum eximiam tum dulcissimam Declarationem de Ludis
et Lusibus, Iocis et recreationibus, honestis, ingenuis, licitis ac
legitimis, populo suo quàm optimo, charissimis Subditis exhibitam,
propositam, concessam, legenti mihi primùm (Lector Charissime; seu   35
Rex Ipse, vt Serenissime, potentissime, edoctissime, Pientissime; sic
Subditorum Amantissime, cupientissime, Studiosissime, Inclytissime
quidem Ipse, dilectissime, et quid non? seu Minister, Populusve,
cuiuscunque Ordinis, sortis, allectionis; vt qui vel Indolis bonæ
conditionisque es, vel optimarum conditionum esse debes) et inter   40
Legendum primo temporis articulo, dixit Minister quidam
Gloucestriensis, et dixit quàm gravatus et ingemiscens, se sibi valdè

timere, metuere, formidare, ne multum doloris, damni, præiudicij, detrimenti, multis Ecclesiæ Ministris, hæc licentia, libertas, lenis concessio facesseret, progigneret, vndequaque pareret. Cui tum ego Respondi; Quid ita, quæso? Satisne sani sumus? vel nunquid insani atque inscij? vt quid nobis et nostræ plebi sit bonum et commodum,   5 nesciamus. Esfne periculum aliquod timendum, tentandúmve; si consentimus Declarationi? Vel autem nunquid est præiudicij in Ipsa Declaratione? Tum Ille: Iubemur reminisci, vt sanctè Sabbatum agamus et colamus; et non partem tantùm, sed totum Sabbatum sanctificare debemus. Ludere verò, iocari, ridere, saltare, recreare   10 corporali actione animos, est Sabbatum violare, polluere, prophanare, contaminare; si vel tantillum è viginti quatuor horis Illîus diei à sanctificatione sanctimoniáque discerpatur. Siccine doctus es, inquam ego; vel Iudaicum colendi Sabbati ritum nobis imponere; vel in Ludicris et recreationibus corporeis contaminationem eius ponere?   15 Certè si Iudaeos imitari vel placeat, vel liceat; in lætis exultationibus, Iubilationibus, Choreis, tripudijs, saltationibus id fieri potest, et debet potiùs, quàm in præcisâ perstrictáque temporum, dierum, locorum, ceremoniarum, circumstantiarum observatione. Istud tamen, quoad dierum seu temporum rationem respectúmque ausim affirmare;   20 nullum vnquam vel diem, vel tempus, choreis, saltibus, corporeis gestibus, rebus ioculatijs, ingenuis gaudendi modis, quàm Sabbata, Solis, ferias, festósque ac Dominicos dies magis convenisse, potiùs satiùs competisse. Sabbata verò solennésque ferias sic istis convenîsse; vt neque his praeteritis ritè coli transigíque possint; neque vlli vnquam   25 tales dies absque istis ritibus ˌ ⌜absolutè⌝ transigantur. Atque hoc quidem (perquàm Charissimi fratres) in apricum proferre, planum, perspicuum, apertum facere statuo, et statim huc me converto et recipio, quò nihil talis sit timoris, nihil metus, nil formidinis; quin omne potiùs periculum, omne præiudicium eximatur; omni simul   30 detrimento, displicentiâ doloréque quisque vestrûm liberetur. |
Principiò peterem equidem, non Principium, mali causâ Syllogismi; sed principalem et præcipuam causam nostri tum creandi, tum instaurandi. Respondebitis procul-dubio, Gloriam Dei, seu creationis seu Redemptionis, sive rerum aliarum omnium, finem vltimam et   35 finalem esse causam. Atqui verò Gloria Dei, quomodo, quibúsque in rebus explicatur, illustratur, apparere cogitur? Habesne fidem? inquit Apostolus. Apud teipsum habeto coram Deo. quasi diceret homines non possunt corporeis oculis fidem videre. Vt è platone de

Ro. 14.
22.

11/ prophanare *for* profanare   27/ Charissimi *for* Carissimi

Sapientia Cicero: Hæc si oculis cerneretur, mirabiles amores excitaret

Iaco. 2.
18.

sui. Sic itidem D. Iacobus: ostende mihi fidem tuam ex operibus tuis;
et ego tibi fidem meam per opera mea demonstrabo. Deus ergò
manifestatur inter homines, Dei Gloria micat, nitet, elucescit; quum

phil. 4.
8.

interioris hominis vultum pium, mentis ingenium perquàm ingenuum, 5
secreti cordis veram fidem, synceram voluntatem, exterius actionibus
honestis, probis, sacrosanctis declaremus. At num tripudia, choreæ,
saltationes, gestus corporei agiles et versatiles sunt ista opera, actiones
istæ externæ, videor mihi vos dicentes audire? Quid ni sint eorum bona
magnáque pars, inquam ego? Nam et corporibus semper gaudemus; 10
et aliquid semper agendum est; et plurima sæpè facimus, quæ sunt
istis minus vtilia, magis servilia; eáque sine correptione, sine

Ro. 14.
23.

exceptione facimus. Nihil tamen absque fide faciendum, nihil invtile,
nihil servile, ei sanè quod vtile, quódque liberum sit, est præferendum.
Corpora nobis esse, non opus est vlla probatione; vt neque semper 15
agendum esse aliquid; et agi quodammodo, tametsi dormiamus. Iam
verò quoad vtilitatem minorem, maiorem fortasse vilitatem; quid vili-

Io. 5.
6–10–
Lu. 14.
3.4.5.

us, precor, quàm vel cibos coquere, et alijs edendos parare, morbosis
medicari, vrinam reddere, stercus eijcere, boves, oves, vel asinos è
puteis extrahere? Quid invtilius, praeter vilitatem, quàm sacrificare, 20

Io. 7.
22–

circumcidere, pecora occidere, præputium concidere? quæ omnia
ferijs in vsu fuêre. Sin autem priorum commoditatem, posteriorum
verò sanctitatem, instatis, vrgetis, contenditis non esse minimam:
tamen quanto sunt commodiora, præfatis exercitijs cibos concoquere,
salubriter eos digerere, morbis mederi, vel potiùs prævenire, 25
incolumem ab aegritudine sanitatem, tutam ab hostibus sospitatem
procurare; amicitias inire, promovere, confirmare? Sanctiora verò

Ro. 12.
1.2–

seipsos sacrificare, corda sua circumcidere, Deo plaudere, in Deo
lætari, coram Deo præ nimio gaudio salire, saltare, exultare? Vos
autem: Quasi verò hæc ita sunt. Salaces scilicet adolescentes cum 30
lascivis puellis choreas ducentes, tanquam cum prurientibus capris
salientes hædos, ea de causâ circumcisos, sacrosanctos, et quasi
suijpsorum sacrificos evadere. Quasi verò, et Ipse quoque dico, vel |
vel Rex serenissimus, fidei Defensor constantissimus, Evangelij Iesu
Christi synceræque Religionis professor et propugnator veracissimus, 35
pientissimus potentissimus; vel quisquam alius alicuius notæ, quantum
ad Ecclesiæ rempublicam et animarum salutem attinet; choreas vllas
alias, gestus, saltus, aut gymnasia, vel postulat, vel permittit, nedum

---

3/ fidem: *part of* f *missing*
6/ synceram *for* sinceram
9/ externæ: ex *written over something else*

9/ Quid ni *for* Quidni
33–4/ vel vel: *dittography*
35/ synceræque *for* sinceraeque

Luc.
15.23.
25.31.

præscribit, aut plusquàm tolerans perfert; quàm quæ Christianam
iuventutem deceant, illorum gaudia, læticiam, exultationem in
Domino, summam et singularem gratitudinem adversus Deum,
conditorem, Redemptorem, conservatorem suum repræsentent et
demonstrent. Nam quod huiusmodi gymnasia, talia exercitia, vel 5
eximiæ pietatis et σημεῖον et πρᾶξιν exhibere possint in populo Dei,
docent et probant, infallibilitérque confirmant hæc exempla cum
reliquis Scripturæ testimonijs, et Ecclesiæ consuetudine. Ac primùm
quòd vel in Paradiso rerumque principio, cum illa quiete laborumque
cessatione, conceditur, vel iniungitur magis, esus arboris vitæ; eiúsque 10
vescendi copia, quasi sacramenti cuiusdam fœderis operum (et is status
valdè perfectus erat) quid illud nobis potiùs intimare queat, quàm nunc
dierum sub fœdere gratiæ, in mysterijs Christi consulendum esse vitæ,
dum carnem Eius comedimus etiam, sanguinem verò bibimus et
epotamus? At ista comestio, dicitis, et potatio spiritualis est; quid hoc 15
ad tripudia, res iocularias, et tales gesticulationes? Sed estne Christi
caro spirituale quiddam? Nunquid non fuit Christus verus homo?
Noṅne gavisus est carne et cruore? Annon est duplex genus
comedendi, praeter illa phantastica et imaginaria, capernaiticum
scilicet, pontificium, seu papisticum, sive quod est aliud? Annon et 20
nos cum animis corporibus quoque gaudemus: carnem cum spiritu,
quoad humanam naturam et substantiam habemus. Annon corpus
comedit sacramentaliter, vt manducat anima spiritualiter? Annon
Cyprianus ait, et alij, corpora fidelium, vt è terris resurrectura, sic in
cælum cum animis ascensura, quàm certissimum hoc argumentum 25
esse, quòd sacramentum accipiunt corporis Christi corpora nostra,
sicuti animæ nostræ gratiam illîus; vtraque suo modo Christi σάρκα
sanguinemque? Vt mystικῶς typicωs, Metaphysicῶs ac πνευματικῶς
isthæc potissimum intelligantur; Annon ergò fuit christus inquam,
verus homo? Annon Eundem Christum, qui conceptus è Spiritu 30
sancto, natus est ex virgine Maria, crucifixus, mortuus et sepultus, et
ita deinceps, edimus, bibimus, in eoque recreati coalescimus? Certè
non est alius verus Christus, verus Dei hominisque filius; Hunc
vtcunque vsurpamus. Iam officium, quod nostra interest
ampliùspræstare; an non agimus, peragimus, perficimusque psallendo, 35
canendo, gaudendo, exultando? At vos: Non autem saliendo,
saltando, gestiendo, ludendo, ridendo, ducendo | choreas, et iocando.

1 Cor
11.22.

Et ego; Sic neque manducando nimis, aut multum epotando. Nam,
annon habetis domos, ait Apostolus, in quibus edatis et bibatis, vt
Ecclesiam contemptui sic habeatis? Reliqui proinde gestus et gesta locis 40
alijs convenientibus usurpanda, peragenda, perficiendáque sunt. Sunt
autem vt vtrique vitæ quàm necessaria, tam corporis, quàm animæ,

tum spirituali, tum naturali, non penitùs omittenda, negligendáve; sed
locis idoneis, aptis temporibus adhibenda, præbenda quidem et
præstanda. Neque sanè imponenda est pœnitentia nobis à lapsu
primorum parentum eâ tantùm Significatione, vt semper sit dolor,
tristicia, contritio, asperitas, amaritudo, sub nomine scilicet pij   5
gemitus, mæroris, planctûs, eiulatûs. Et gaudia simul requiruntur,
alacritas, hilaritas, læticia, delectatio. Et dies gaudijs, læticiæ, lusibus,
oblectamentisque sunt indicti atque assignati. Nunquam enim data fuit
et tributa tanta talis causa lætandi, gaudendi, iocandi, ridendi, saltandi,
exultandi, ne Adamo quidem in statu suo perfectissimo, nempe   10
innocentiæ quidem et integritatis eximiæ, nedum Abrahamo, præ

Ro 4.
1.2.

operibus suis in se lætanti; qualis quanta nobis in Adamo secundo,
Christo nimirum, Abrahamo promisso semine benedicto; sicut in
Izhac vocatum iri semen eius, præ ostensum, præsignificatum et
præmonstratum fuit. Qui quidem Izhac, quod ad vocabuli   15

gen. 17.
17.et
18.12–
15.ps.
65.14.
126.2.

significatum, et appellationis rationem spectat, tum quòd parentes,
quùm promissus esset, vtrique risêre, tum quòd occasionem summam,
causam ridendi maximam exhibuit, risum denotat; in risum reddendo
convertitur, risum linguâ canaanæa præsignat, designat, consignátque.
Ecquid aliud est, quod sic efferri gaudio; effundi læticiâ, risu diffluere,   20
cor dilatare, mentem exhilarare valeat; atque Dei gratia, divini favoris
fœderisque in Christo, ad salutem vsque et vitam æternam, hoc est,

ps.103.

ad remissionem peccatorum et cælestem sempiternam hæreditatem,
beneficium? Aut certè hoc ineffabile quidem, inæstimabile,
incompræhensibile beneficium minimè dignum est, quo lætemur et   25
gaudeamus? Sed videamus vlteriùs, quid olim fecerint Israelitæ; quid
primitùs, et hucvsque fideles continuò Christiani; quid semper à
populo Dei vehementius fuerit exactum; quid nunc temporis à nobis
constanter exigatur. Sit Iubal pater et Author eorum omnium, qui
nablijs, citharis, tubis, tibijs, fidibus, tympanis psallendo sunt vsi,   30
alijsque similibus organis et instrumentis: Sed Moses et Miriam ad

Exodi
15.1–
20–

vsum adhibent, vsum fructum capiunt; vsura, piâ, licitâ, sacrosanctâ,
quid valeant, experiuntur. Etenim his Deum collaudaverunt Optimum
Maximum ob egregiam super hostes, populum scilicet Ægyptiacum
cum crudelissimo suo Tyranno victoriam. Per alias novi ac memini   35
multò secus evenîsse. Quippe trigesimo-secundo capite, versibus 6–
19. describit eorum Idololatriam, mentionem vnà faciens edendi, |
bibendi, cantandi, saliendi. Neque sum oblitus, quid in novo
testament⟨.⟩ ⟨.⟩abetur eadem de re, nimirum priore ad Corinthios

13/ grammatically necessary 'eo quod' omitted after in
14/ præ ostensum for præostensum
39/ testament⟨.⟩ ⟨.⟩abetur: ie, testamento habetur

epistola ͺ ⌜10 ca*pite*⌝ versu septimo, quasi comestio, potatio, ductio
chorearum, et saltatio, vel ipsa Idololatria; vel ipsius aliquæ pars esset;
quum tamen hi gestus, lusus et gymnasia non simpliciter odio
habentur, vitio vertuntur, sive culpæ criminíq*ue* dantur: sed vsus mali,
malæ applicationis ratione, Ipsius Idololatriæ respectu, sicuti videre   5
est præfati capitis Exodi v*er*su decimo-nono, cuius hæc sunt aliquæ
verba: Quum primum ad exercitum appropinquavit Moses, vitulum
vidit et saltationem. Vitulus igitur et vituli adoratio in causâ sunt, quòd
Moses ita rixat*us* est, et obiurgavit Aaronem. Et vitulum illum aureum
postèa rep*er*it, in ignem posuit, prorsus combussit, in cineres redegit,   10
in pulvere quasi molitum convertit, super aquas stravit, aquas illas
ebibere coegit Israelitas. De saltatione ne verbum vlteriùs vnum
quide*m*. Porrò video non solùm in illo pentateucho constitutum
Sabbatum observandum; verùm etiam multas alias ferias et festivos
dies, paschæ scilicet et panis azimi, pentecostes vel hebdomadarum,   15
Tabernaculor*um*, it*em* et alior*um* nonnullorum. Sed quomodo feria,
quî festivi sunt? Aliáne ratione, more, modové; quàm quiescendo
servilibus ab operibus; pijs, sanctis, probis, honestis, festivis, ingenuis,
et vel divinis actionibus atq*ue* exercitijs dies illos omnes, tum

Exod.
35.3.

Sabbatorum, tum etiam festos et feriales insumere, impendere,   20
præterire? Sed neq*ue* ignem accendere Sabbato licuit. Quid ni liceret
alijs modis licitis, seipsos, vt decuit, et oportuit, calefacere? Iam quid
hoc est, quòd in his festis lætari, gaudere sic, atq*ue* exultare iubet, deu.
16. non semel, at sæpiùs; et quâ viâ, quo modo gaudebunt, lætabuntùr,
exhilarabuntur? Nam vt symphoniam illam Ecclesiasticam,   25
psalmorum, hymnorum, laudum in Templo cautionem permittentes
concedatis; quid illud ad plebem et populum gregarium seorsum
agentem apud se, quod illis convenit et consentaneum est? Annon in
ipsis psalmis Ipse psalmista, quid in hac causa deceat, edocuit? Anno*n*
id omnes et singulos quàm sæpissimè, iuxta canones à seipso iam ant*ea*   30
co*n*stitutos? Quo tempore quàm sanctissimus David etiam ipse
psalmographus fecit, in vsu praxiq*ue* posuit, quod vel alijs imposuit,
vel pro alijs composuit, vel licitum esse demonstravit .1. Chron.15.
et 25. et 29. ps. 28.8.33.1.2.3.68.25.57.7.108.1.2.95–98–100–
107.149.et 150. Obijciet fortasse quispiam ex prophetis, vt Isa.24.8–   35
11.Am.6.4.5.6. culpari multùm condemnariq*ue* eiusmodi omnia
exercitia, gymnasia, iocularia. Sed enim annon apparet facilè, non
vsu*m* rectum, sed pravissimos abusus vitio verti, condemnari,
abominari? Quod idem observandum Iudicum 21.21.22.23. Mat'.14.6.
et siqua sunt plura loca similia. Nam quòd Math.9.23. Tibicines cum   40
citha, et cum cantante, clama*n*te, vociferantéq*ue* multitudine
Chri*stus* è mortui domo discedere cogens extrudit; tantùm abest, vt

contra nos sit, aut faciat in hoc negotio; vt nihil ferè magis aptum
appositúmque dici possit. Nuptijs non inter sunt modò gaudia, lusus
et Musica: | sed exequijs etiam et funeribus. cuiusnam rei, quaeso,
causa? quâ significatione? Nimirum cælestia gaudia, cælicam læticiam,
sanctorum in cælis exultationem repræsentare, asserere, affirmare,   5
confirmare, stabilire. Quò spectant, quæ in Apocalipsi Divi Iohannis
de citharis Dei, præstantissimis, quàm eximijs, excellentissimis
Organis cæli narrantur et declarantur. Capitibus videlicet 5.14. et 15.
& cætera. Itidem quæ apud Divum Paulum habentur 1.Cor.13.1. et
14.7.8. Eph.5.19. Col. 3.16. et phil.4.4. præcipuè Domini Christi   10

mat'.
9.15.

delineatio apud lucam Evangelistam capite 15. versibus 23.25.31
necnon septimo decimóque. Vt rectè lugere ieiuni dicantur præ Sponsi
defectu et absentiâ, qui præsentiâ gaudere nolunt, lætóque præsentis
sponsi vultu lætari recusant. Id quod à Nostratibus sic effertur: Panis
et Butyrum est esca quàm optima; dolor autem sit Eius amantibus,   15
cupientibus, expetentibus vt qui tam dolosi, quàm dolorosi, ipsi
desipiunt, séque ipsos defraudant meritò atque decipiunt. At non
Alcithoe Mineies orgia censet Attribuenda Deo. Scilicet vt à
debacchantibus offerantur Ethnico Baccho, quæ Deo Optimo Maximo
soli omninò debentur; illis interim per auras et æra sonantibus: Io   20

Hos.2.
Hab.1.
Zeph.1.
Ezek.16.
15–17–
19–

comites, veneremur Iacchum. Non aliter quàm egisse, séque impiè
gessisse, videre est apud Hoseam, Habacucum, Zephaniam et alios,
Idololatricos Israelitas. Ea tamen in Iehovam piè contulisse, quæ
nefariè sic Idolis suis et prophanis atque impijs exposûere procis,
nunquam offenderet Dominum, [offenderet] vitio nunquam   25
verteretur. Rex autem noster, et pastor Agamemnon, sive magis
Davidicus Salomon, sentit et censet, per legitimos Mystas et Tyresias
Christicolas, litandum esse divinæ Maiestati ac Numini, tum

[a]By the
King

animabus, tum corporibus suis à iuventute Christianâ.[a] Videte proinde
nunquid maiorem rationem quasi præsentis sponsi Rex habeat,   30
Domini Iesu Christi scilicet, in verbo suo, in Evangelio, in Ministris,
in populo suo, per spiritum sanctum semper instantis ad mundi finem
vsque, Mat.28.20. quàm eorum quisquam, vel vniversi quidem isti; qui
præ nimio zeli synceri, sanctimoniæ vel purissimæ prætextu; nullum in
Sabbato corporale prorsus excercitium, præsertim quod recreationem,   35
alacritatémque quandam resipiat et præ se ferat; ferre, sinere,
sustinere; nedum perferre, permittere, patienter tolerare, vt

---

9/ cætera for cetera
18/ Mineies for Mineides; second e of Mineies written over another letter
24/ prophanis for profanis   34/ synceri for sinceri

maximum, probare possunt. Ego verò summu*m* quoddam
Argume*n*tum et certissimam demonstrationem hinc colligo Regiæ
noticiæ sanæ, certæ*que* scientiæ Christi Ipsîus et Evangelij sui veræ
naturæ, *proposi*ti, sensus intimi, proprietatis. Similem itidem
æquiparámq*ue* colligo notam ac significationem Eius amoris   5
dulcissimi, Charissimi favoris, Regiæ, paternæ, pientissimǽq*ue* curæ
in Subditos suos quàm dilectissimos, populum Ipsîus amantissimum,
cupientissimum, studiosissimum, vt et fidelissimu*m*, co*n*stantissimu*m*
integerrimum. Que*m* | Quem quidem haud semel aut secundò, sed
quàm sæpissimè populum suum, populum quàm optimum, in paucis   10
his paginis nominat. Our People; Our good people plusquam decies
certe. vt vel decies repetita semper placeant. Vtrùm autem maiorem
benevolentiam benignitatémq*ue* testificetur; vel quòd eiusmodi
recreationes concedit Regia Maiestas; vel quòd easdem excudit suâ
quasi Ipsîus propria manu; non est in *p*romptu, non in proclivi   15
patefacere. Neq*ue* minùs est difficile, quantum amorem, quàm
æqualem, perinde et æquam benevolentiam, paternam curam,
episcopalem, seu potiùs Apostolicam vigilantiam, in vtramq*ue* huius
Insulae Regionisq*ue* Inclytissimæ partem, cum Aquilonis, tum
Australem, ínque *omne*s et singulos comitatus, collaudandas quasq*ue*   20
Civitates societatesq*ue*, gerat, ferat, amplectatur, ostendere,
Describere, manifestare. Proinde adiunxi huic tractatui meam Ipsîus
Regiae Maiestatis Reditûs è Boreæ finibus gratiosissimi
exoptatissimíq*ue* gratulationem. Quam tametsi rude*m* valdè
imperitámq*ue*; Amoris tamen incontinentis, animíq*ue* non   25
mediocriter benevoli gratiâ, non potui non meorum Oxoniensium
egregijs gymnasijs, Aræq*ue* sacrasanctæ simul affigere. b Iam vos
interrogo (fratres, præsertim siqui sunt inter vos puritani) quid op*us* est
esse præcisos, puritátem, pietatem, sanctimoniam in rebus externis
prætexere? An non est Deus spiritus? An non spiritu et veritate,   30
venerandus, adorandus et colendus? Præcisi potestis esse conscientiâ,
vt verbis nihil sciatur, sed operibus. Externa et corporalia, ceu parùm
prosunt, parùm proferunt, nihil ferè conducunt ad pietatem: sic in
potestate non sunt sita, non collocata vestrâ, proinde de lanâ caprina
ˏ⸢de Asini vmbra⸣ de rebus nihili contenditis, et vos stultos esse   35
declaratis, de non pertinentibus, non proficuis. Subinde præsumentes,
arrogantes, insolentes habemini, otiosi, negotiosi, conte*n*tiosi,
Puritani. Odiosum sanè nomen, et iam olim plùs min*us*

b Reb*uking*
some
purit*anes*
& precis*ians*

6/ Charissimi *for* carissimi   27/ sacrasanctæ *for* sacrosanctae
9/ Quem | Quem: *dittography*

abominandum. Vobis enim ominatum est, vel omen vestrum. Sed
vestrâ culpâ, vestro crimine. Quî namque vocentur, quo nomine
gaudere vel debent, vel possunt, ex loco coniugatorum Aristotelico;
qui sibi puritatem arrogant, se puros videri haberique volunt; nisi vel
purorum, vel puritanorum? At puri non estis. Ergò non purorum. Sed   5
factis impuri potius, maximè puritatem scilicet, pietatem, sanctitatem
ad nauseam vsque prætendentes et prætexentes, vt præfati sumus.
Ergò Puritani. Neque tamen vel gratum, vel non grave mihi potest esse
(fratres dulcissimi) Si qui sunt alioqui viri verè pij peritique, qui
nihilominùs sensu suo nimium abundantes, vt Hieronymi verbis vtar,   10
nimis arctè præconceptis opinionibus, in rebus vel indifferentibus, vel
nugatorijs ferè, vel etiam extra communem optionem positis,
præiudicatis et præfractis | affectibus, respectibus, et sententijs
adhærent. Id quod Rex Ipse serenissimus non omisit in eximio suo ac
verè aureo opusculo, quod βασιλικὸν Δῶρον dicitur, suam mentem   15
esse declarare. Ne vicio vertatis igitur, quòd ita nominamini, nisi
culpatis vosmet etiam ipsos, quod sic operamini. Num Philosophum
meministis, qui demonstrans Ostentum; En, inquit, magnos fures,
fures pusillos ad crucem ducentes, adigentesque suspendendos ad

Aspersions
c Misin-
terpretation
of our
meaning

patibulum? Vos itidem in magnis lædentes, vt vel læsae Maiestatis rei   20
ferè; parvulos tamen incusatis, maximoperè criminamini, pessimarum
noxarum reos agitis? c Id autem minimè mirum; quum Rex Ipse
quidem vestras acerbas criminationes, vafras Aspersiones et
traductiones amaras, vt est innocentissimus, pientissimus,
benevolentissimus, evitare nequeat. Quos enim pertentare, irritare,   25
sollicitare, traducere, lædere, nocere, necare non audetis; qui Regem
Ipsum, tam Evangelicum, Orthodoxum, Angelicum, et Sanctissimum,
mordere, molestare, traducere, per auras, aures et ora mortalium
trahere, sugillare, blasphemare, quàm audacissimi cœpitis, arripitis,
irruitis? Interest Eius Serenæ Maiestatis, Nomen Numeńque suum   30
Christianum, gloriosum et cælicum, à vestrarum macularum
aspersione vindicare; Ius suum Imperiale, supremam Authoritatem,
meritum honorem vindicare; quinimò cur non vobis fœdas culparum
criminúmque notas, mendarum et noxarum, præsertim petulantium
et pestilentium vociferationum conflatas labes, quas demeruistis, quas   35
aduocatis accercitisque, inferre, imponere, infligere? Medius-fidius
non agit vobiscum Regia clementia secundum merita vestra. Imò ver⟨.⟩
venientem in memoriam Æsopicam quandam vt moralem, ita
memorabilem fabulam, non possum ex animo eijcere, neque me
continere, quin enarrem; quomodo scilicet olim Ranæ rogatum   40
habuerunt Iovem, vt illis concederet et daret Regem. Cessit Iupiter,

et dedit ingentem trabem *pro* Rege. Cuius vt casu quatefacta fuit terra;
sic conspectu terrefactæ Ranæ. Proinde certis diebus delituêre .
*Tem*poris intervallo Latebris egressi ˏ ⌈ad⌉ Regem appropinquabant.
Vident quietum, tranquillum, pacatum, sedatum, non moventem.
Tra*n*scendunt, transiliunt, insiliunt, resiliunt; spernunt, co*n*temnu*n*t,   5
despiciunt, reijciunt. Iovem rursum accedunt; Hunc soporis, desidiæ,
ignaviæ, pigritiæ damnant; alium postulant. Audit eos iterum Iupiter,
et Ciconiam in Regem assignavit. Hæc Ranam vllam quoties
intueretur, statim arripuit et devoravit. Hinc sunt Ranæ rursus
vniversæ conquestæ, se crudelissimè à ciconia dilaniari, excruciari,   10
absorberi. Sed incassùm et frustrá. Essent enim contenti et grati | de
superiore, tam omnis acerbitatis immuni ac libero . Videtis
adumbratum in hâc hypotyposi, quid siet, Regem pacificum,
beneficum, mitissimum, Christianum nolle, negare, recusare, reijcere.
Audite nunc aliam veram et nupera*m* historiam; Quum hæc   15
scripserim, et eodem temporis momento, dum pinxerim, erectus est
polus æstivalis in Ipsius custodiæ (Castelli nempe Gloucestriensis)
horto seu fundo adiacente, quo solent alternis vicibus incarcerati
deambulare, confabulari, seipsos paulisper recreare. Id multi
vitup*erant* factum, eiusmodi res ludicras eò loci exerceri, in vsu ibi   20
poni, vbi tot sunt potiùs lachrymarum et Lamentationis, quàm
Lusuum et Musicæ ostenta et indicia. Verùm in hoc q*uoque* quid ego
dicam, perpendíte. Si Regis edicto, si regimine discreto, si mente boni
conscia plaudere, psallere, salire po*ssunt* in carceribus et custodijs, in
ergastulis et angustijs, nimiru*m* homunciones captivi; quid nequeant,   25
non audeant ij, qui in immunibus civitatibus libère agunt, et
voluntarié? Insuper illud simul aspicio, vel in ijs tenebrosis latibulis
plærosque secum Baccho ac Veneri facere et litare; quum his g*y*mnasijs
aliquo vel casu, vel causâ prohibentur, interdicuntur, deprivantur.
Accipite simul et aliud simile. In Civitate præfatæ Glocestriæ, me   30
prædicto tempore in Castello diversante, sicut fit inter cætera similia,
quidam Sicarius ad vxorem vicini accessit; idq*ue* multoties et sæpe-
numero. Re*m* habere cum eâ petijt, expetijt, et impetrare visus est;
intereà foeminam dum tacturus quassit, venit subitò Maritus, qui tale
quiddam videns, exclamavit, contine, contine, hold, hold. Quæ Verba   35
ab alijs audita, iam ab omnibus quotidie parabolæ proverbíve vice
recitantur. At Polis quibusdam et pyramidibus ib*i*dem elevatis
oblatrant nonnulli obganniúntq*ue*, quum eorum ratione co*mmun*iter

9/ d *of* devoravit *written over* v
28/ plærosque *for* plerosque
30/ Glocestriæ *for* Gloucestriae

31/ cætera *for* cetera
34/ foeminam *for* feminam

Iuventus à carnalibus incitamentis, incantamentis, lenocinijs, compotationibus, ebrietate, scortationibus avocantur tamen. Vos igitur, vt immunes liberíque Regis misericordiâ perquàm ineffabili evaditis; at quaeso, permittite, si hoc a vobis petere; expetere, impetrare, potirique licitum, par, fas, et æquum sit; permittite,   5
inquam, et perpetimini quieti sedati, modesti; vt falsæ pravæque expositionis evitandæ gratiâ, sensus suos eximios, Regale placitum et propositum explicet, enodet, explanet. Quòd Lancastria tantoperè recusantibus Papistis abundavit, id me malè habet, vt decet, et doleo multùm (etenim tum Rex Ipse mirificè dolet idem; tum ego puer   10
[quatt⟨...⟩] decennius in eâ Diocœsi per tres vt minimum annos scholam petij Grammaticam et studui) Quòd verò reformari homines, mores emendari conformarique, Regiæ Maiestati significent Magnates, id benè quidem habet, vt præfatas ob causas oportet; méque multâ perfundit læticiâ, magno gaudio afficit.[d] Verum enimverò   15
quomodocunque abundavit cacolicis | Papistis Comitatus Ille Lancastrensis, pro certo, comperto, exploratóque habemus hoc, totum terrarum Orbem Regiæ Ditionis, et Regium vniversum superabundanter exundare Puritanis. Quibus (quanquam veræ puritatis avidi, synceræ pietatis cupidi cultores non sunt hoc nomine   20
gravandi, vt qui soli sunt habendi appellandique christiani; tamen abiecta omni vafra, callida, perniciosa adulatione) non sunt Schismaticis istis homunciones vlli peiores, praviores, pestilentiores, periculosiores. Hi profectò sunt dolendi; imò sanè penitus delendi; proinde verò præcavendi. Vsurpant hi potestatem, Authoritatem,   25
Dominationem, Imperium in ijs rebus, in quibus absolutè contracta est, et ab ijs quoad partem alteram abstracta libertas. Dominantur, et principatum tenent ac gerunt, vimque alienis conscientijs faciunt peremptori⟨.⟩ Religionem ac cultum Dei vel statuunt in ijs rebus, in quibus aut nulla est; aut si vlla, in earum vsu recto, non neglectu   30
perspicitur: vel collocant in Iudaico quodam colendi Sabbati more, hoc est ipsorum suo; quasi nullo prorsus modo aliter quàm Isti præscribunt et profitentur, dies ille prætereundus, ritus cultúsque eius

d
countie
of Lan-
cashire-

e
Barred
from all
recreationes

6/ perpetimini: pe *somewhat smeared, apparently written over other letters*
11/ [quatt⟨...⟩: *ie,* [quattuor]
11/ Diocœsi *for* Diœcesi
14m/ e *written over* d
20/ synceræ *for* sincerae
24/ delendi: endi *written over erasure*
29/ peremptori⟨.⟩: *final letter obscured by binding*

obseruandus.[f] Non obseruant Isti cum sacrosancto Rege
sapientissimo, quàm multa solent incommoda, pessimáque effecta de
suo iure praxique insequi ac ingruescere. Non cernunt, non curant,
quantum obstaculum præbent é pontificiorum sectâ catholicáque
superstitione conversuris, vel infirmis etiam protestantibus, cum   5
quibus agunt sacerdotes pontificij; quum isthinc obijcere possint isti
nebulones histrionici, nostram Religionem nullam admittere
iucunditatem, nullam iubilationem; proinde non esse probam, non
veram, certam, piam, non æquæ mentis consciam[g]. Non perpendunt,

non considerant, non cogitant, quantum præiudicium, et   10
nocumentum horum gymnasiorum interdictio rebus sit martijs, dum
perquam apposite, præ nimio rerum prœliarum neglectu, in scænam,
arenam, vel tanquam campum introducti iuvenes conscendunt,
discendunt, facies altervtri vultusque invicem conspiciunt, agiles fiunt,
bellicosi, et perquàm strenui milites. Israelitæ, nostis, vt omittam   15
Lacedæmonios et eiusmodi quosdam alios, exercebant iuventutem
suam in bellicis negotijs, in exercitamentis ad Martem, Minervam, et
prœlia pertinentibus. Christiana fortasse religio non adeò rigidè
desiderat, efflagitátve bellicos apparatus. Eò satiùs tolerat et postulat
mitiora mansuetioráque exercitamenta. Quanquam si peropus et   20
necesse fuerit, non prohibet, vel omninò, vel Sabbato depugnanda
prœlia, Domini Nostri Iesu Christi Evangelium contra communes
Illîus hostes, sævos, barbaros, immanes, crudeliter irruentes Inimicos.
Id quod multis sacrarum literarum locis demonstrari potest; quæ nunc
non est enumerandi locus, ex = | expediendóque nullus vsus. Neque   25
hoc Enunciatum ab alijs quàm ab huius ætatis acerbissimis
Anabaptistis denegatur. Istis autem in hoc Argumento satis supérque
à multis est responsum; vt meâ non iam egeat defensione.[h] Cæteroquin

quum ab ijs, quarum iam sæpiùs mentionem fecimus, exercitationibus
humanioribus et ingenuis ingeniosisque recreationibus cohibentur   30
Adolescentes; Deus bone, quanta subinde Tabernarum frequentia?
quanta domibus inhiatio cervisiarijs? quantæ et quam fœtidae
comessationes, epotationes, ebrietates, ebibitiones; ineptæ, absurdæ,
obcœnæ sermocinationes, confabulationes, contumeliæ,
obtrectationes, lites, dissidia, iurgia, rixæ, pugnæ, contentiones?   35
Cúmque his quot fœdæ fornicationes? quot turpia stupra, execranda
adulteria, incestus horrendi, abominanda Lenocinia? Pudet nominare
quæ fiunt ab istis in tenebris; imò qualia non pudet istos sub sole

25/ ex = | expediendóque: *dittography*   34/ obcœnæ *for* obscenae
28/ Cæteroquin *for* ceteroquin

Eph. 5
3–12.
1.Cor.
5.1–
ps.16.
4.

p*er*petrare, designare, in propatulo committere; quæ ne nomin⟨.⟩ntur
quidem apud obcœnas et Idololatricas gentes. Patet id vndique et in
aprico iacet, cunctisq*ue* patefactum ex multitudine spuriorum in
vniverso superexvndantium. Sed de his videntur habere Praecisi,
reverâ nihil habent omninò pensi. Tantummodo iudicant eiusmodi   5
notabiles peccatores reprobos esse, deinde relinqunt eos in errore, in
periculo. Nunquid hoc notum est Regiæ Maiestati, notatúmq*ue* tam
accuratè, nos autem tanquam ignotum inscij penitùs præterlabimur?
certè sumus quàm fidi subiecti, seduli officiarij, Reip*ublicae*, et

I If not
vpon
Sund*ays*,
& holy
days.

Ecclesiæ charissimi commodissimiq*ue* Amici; aut fallor miré.[I]   10
Veruntamen audire me videor, nonnullos effantes, infantes tamen:
Alijs diebus septimanæ possunt homines se recreare, istiusmodi ludos
vsurpare, iocis vti, gesta, gestus, res ludicras exercere; vt dieb*us*
d*o*m*i*nicis non inferant, ingerant obtrudant, imponant. Quasi verò dies
hebdomadis alij, ijdem op*er*ibus ac laboribus addicti, talibus humanis   15
mansuetisq*ue* ludis et recreationibus aptiores essent, appositi magis,
accommodatiq*ue*, quàm dies festi ab alijs negotijs tum servilibus tum
necessarijs liberi, immunes et q*ui*eti. Annon egregiè ridiculum
immenséq*ue* absurdum hoc est, vel ab agricultura Rusticos, vel a
scrobibus fossores, vel à popinis coquos, vel calcearios à scamnulis,   20
sive sutores à sedibus, vel vpiliones à caulis, vel a capris et hædis
caprarios pastores, vel bubulcos à stabulis ⌐ ⌐vel laniones à macellis,⌐
vel à molendinis molitores, vel a Textrinâ Textores, vel etiam à Lanâ
ac tela pedissequas, à lacte mulgendo, premendo, tundendo, multrices
ancillas mox in plateas exilire, ibidem in pannis laceratis, vestib*us*   25
defœdatis, corporibus adipe deturpatis, saltare, exultare; insultare,
insanire ferè tantùm non furere ac furare? Quemadmodum enim |
deutero*no*m 5 vers*ibus* 14. 15. non conceditur modò, sed et requiritur,
iniungitur, et demandatur, vt et servi quiescant à laboribus, sese
oblectamentis recreantes, memóribus interim Israelitis, semetipsos   30

Exod. 12.
26 –
Iosh. 4.
6–

servos et mancipia fuisse in Ægypto: sic impræsentiarum hac ætate
docendi sunt Iuvenes in sermonibus Dominicalibus qua ratione,
quibus moribus se gerant in exercitijs, quibus etiam finibus se recreent,
iocentur et ludant. Non id agendum, quod à nostris vbiq*ue* factitatu*m*
est, vt Doctrinæ loco de recto rerum externarum atq*ue* indiffer*entium*   35
vsu, res ipsas à Deo Ipso Opt*imo* Max*imo* creatas, constitutas,
ordinatas, subtrahant, abigant, prorsus tollant. Miror equidem quam
responsionem facient, quam rationem reddent olim Domino, de

1/ nomin⟨.⟩ntur: *ie*, nominantur

2/ obcœnas *for* obscenas

6/ relinqunt *for* relinquunt

10/ charissimi *for* carissimi

27/ ac *written over something else*; furare *for* furari

31/ impræsentiarum *for* in praesentiarum

Ordinationis Ei⟨..⟩contemptu, de benignitatis Eius in his
oblectamentis et recreationibus abiectione. Quid enim aliud agunt isti,
quàm vt Deum Ipsum doceant, qui dies quieti atque lusibus, qui
laboribus atque alijs vsibus maximè sunt appositi; quando simul
operari, quando verò recreare seipsos debent? Ecquis prætereà nescit,   5
ecquis ignorat, vel Musicam ex Artibus ingenuis, è scientijs liberalibus
unam esse; vel sine vsu, lusu, choreis, applausu, gaudio, læticiâ,
delectatione, nihili ac nullîus esse?ᵏ Hæc cum, quasi nesciant ipsi,
neminem instruunt, neminem scire volunt, digni sunt et demeriti, qui
in his, cum reliquis suis enormibus, deformibus, absurdissimis erratis,   10
à Dominis Episcopis, et quàm honoratis Magistratibus castigentur,
corripiantur, reconformentur. Verum enimverò non parum videtur
mihi metuendum, à Iusticiarijs, Iudicibus, Episcopis etiam ipsis
nonnullis, ac si non æque se gererent in his Conformitatibus, in his
reformationibus. Etenim nisi sibi in animum inducerent, se certò   15
persuasos haberent, Istis, quos puritanes nominari solet et decet,
summè pios in omnibus, puros, sanctos esse; quî fieri omninò posset,
Vt regi facesserent vndique tantum assiduè negotium? quomodò esset
tanta vbique Regionis Multitudô. Novimus istorum iactantiam,
novimus ostentationem, se suis xenijs et muneribus cum potentibus   20
ad placitum vsque promovere posse. Interim conformes vel præsentes
ipsi, vel effrœnes et refractarios præsentantes, negliguntur, non
animantur, nedum corroburantur; imò verò benè cum illis est, si non
obiurgantur, exanimantur, repelluntur; idque cum contumeliosissimis
vociferationibus, Thou, Thou, Sirra, Thou, I'll make ye bee quiet   25
yfayth, Sir. & cætera. Sic boni isti ordinarij ad Ministros ordinatos et
conformes, de vel pro præfatis illis præfractis et inordinatis. Sed spero
iam hinc inde divinâ gratia, Regiæ Maiestatis eximiâ curâ, imposterum
omnia emendatum iri, futura meliora. Mihi autem quod meâ refert,
condonent ista, propter meum ipsîus experimentum. | Vel si nolent   30
ignoscere, neque placet hæc conditio, si lubet magis, vlteriùs faciant
periculum, et quid in hac re sit verum experiantur. Me nanque illorum
tractatus in hâc causâ et huiusmodi, prorsus pessundedit; nec peius
agere, plusve nocere vel opus est, vel omnino possunt. At verò cur non
potiùs sermonem meum converto ad Polos Æstivos et Maias   35
Pyramides, in ⟨e⟩a invectus et vociferans, quæ tanquam essent Idola

1/ Ei⟨..⟩: *ie*, Eius; *final letters lost in binding*
22/ effrœnes *for* effrenes
26/ cætera *for* cetera
29/ Mihi: *first* i *written over another letter*
31/ lubet *written over erasure*

32/ nanque *for* namque
33/ pessundedit: n *written over* d(?)
34/ omnino: om *written over erasure*
36/ ⟨e⟩a: *partly obscured by blot*

surda, muta, mortua, nihil vacent respondere? Vt nihil respondea*n*t,
obijcitur tamen esse ea Diabolica Idola, cultúsq*ue* Diabolicos esse
simul omnes illos Ludos Maios, Allas Whitsonias, Mauritii choreas,
varia tripudia, ioca quam plurima, Ludorum genera penè infinita,
cæterùm ego respondeo, neq*ue* tale quippiam esse, necesse posse; si,   5
quod piè requiritur, locis et temporib*us* æquis et aptis sine divini cultus
vel impedimento, vel incuria fieri docea*n*tur: At choreas ducunt circa
polos; populus circumstans et vndiq*ue* collecta multitudo in polum
conijciunt oculos, in fidicines tibicines, citharædos, in Musica
instrumenta, in saltatores, collusores, colluctatores, in Ludicra omnia   10
ioculariáq*ue*. Sic et qui templum adeunt, Ecclesiam frequentant, et
sacros cœtus petunt crebriùs, Lumina conijciunt, circu*m*spiciunt,
aspectant pulpita, biblia, concionatores; Conciones et cantiones suas,
mores, conditiones atq*ue* gestiunculas planè stupent et admirant*ur*.
Quæ quidem ista vt doctrinâ recta fieri atq*ue* integra queunt ac debent;   15
sic illa reformari. Imò sanè dilige*n*ter docendo quæ in recto vsu sunt
necessaria, si perveniri ad rectum perfectúmq*ue* no*n* pot*est*; certe recta
paulatim et co*m*mendata cum imperfectis et nonnecessarijs
intolerandisq*ue* siqua sunt istiusmodi absq*ue* repr*ae*hensione viribus
suis et voluntate simul irrecuperabiliter corru*nt*. Memini, quod refert   20
facundus Aschamus, Dominam Ianam a Matre tam rigidè vrgeri, sic
arceri ad a⟨r⟩ctè æquiparéq*ue* saltandu*m* in tripudijs, ad singulas
me*n*suras in quibusvis choreis, ad tam innumeras repeditationes et
gestiunculas observandas adigi; vt prorsus habuit odio saltationem
omnem, et ad linguas, cùm latinam, tum græca*m*, ediscendas, ad   25
Authores veteres edoctissimos versandos, legendos, perlegendos,
relegendos, terendos, trahendos, discerpendos, se penitùs convertere
et recipere delegit. Rectus *ergo* Ludorum vsus intimandus et
instillandus est potius, quàm tum in abvsus, tum in lusus ipsos
invehendu*m*; quòd ita vel se reformabunt et ad rectum recipient; vel   30
vsum om*n*em pro abvsuum periculo ac scandalo p*r*otenus et penitùs
reijci*n*t. Sopore*m* aut somnu*m* quis desiderat | in ægritudine. non
autem potest dormire præ multis phantasmatis recurrentibus,
pragmatibusq*ue* tum peioribus, tum potioribus, cerebrum eius
versantibus, circumvolitantibus sollicitantibus. Precetur seriò, fundat   35
vota Deo; mox obrepet sopor, et suaviter dormiet, altùm dormitabit.
Dicetis fortassis: Istud agit Diabolus, qui nolet homines precari, pia
vota fundere, sanctè quovismodo se gerere. Quasi verò multum

3/ Mauritii: tii *written over erased as*
4/ genera: ra *written over erasure*
5/ cæterùm *for* ceterum

11/ templum: um *partly obscured by blot*
22/ a⟨r⟩cte: r *partly obscured by blot*
33/ phantasmatis *for* phantasmatibus

nonnullis sit pensi curǽve, quis eorum Author sit conceptuum, modò
Deum prætexant, et suas vias, voluntates, consilia concessa sibi
habeant, et ad placitum gaudeant. Experto crede Roberto, inquiunt.
Hæc enim tum domi, tum foris verissima reperi. Descripsi namque
diligenter vsus et abvsus rerum indifferentium, eorúmq*ue* rationem et   5
differentiam. Rectum vsum in vsu tantummodò praxíq*ue*, esse debere
graviter et gnaviter institi. Mox evanuerunt omnia simul. Proinde
longè mecum aliter agitur, quàm cum morosis istis fratribus, in
q*uorum* Paroechijs excitantur poli, simúlq*ue* turbæ commoventur,
magis opponendi vociferanti Ministro gratiâ, quàm sibi placendi in   10
rebus Ludicris, vel Regi parendi in exercitijs et recreationibus. Et in
custodia Gloucestriensi, vbi me*n*ses quosdam iam ferè co*n*sumpsi,
Deus immortalis, quàm disertè, discretè, laudabiliter geruntur om*n*ia?
Est ibi quasi pyramis elevata, polus Æstivus collocatus, vt a*n*teà dictum
est. Genera Ludorum præfata statuunt exercere. Rebus ego, id est,   15
exercitijs et recreationibus haud contradico, nedum interdico. At
rectu*m* vsu*m* ostendo; quomodo se gerere recrearéq*ue* debent, edoceo.
Hâc etia*m* occasione, statuta quædam et Ordinationes Ædi Illi ac
custodiæ maximè convenientes edidimus, Omnium et singuloru*m*
incarceratorum manibus et cordibus, scilicet consensu subscribi   20
fecimus. Exinde, Deus bone, quàm modestè, quàm honestè, quàm piè,
sanctè vivitur, quàm degitur christiané? Vt ia*m* Exemplum possit esse
pietatis et Modestiæ carcer Iste seu custodia pl*a*erisq*ue* alijs, sive
custodijs, sive societatibus, vel carcerib*us* vel civitatibus ferè. Vt est
hoc pernotum tam vrbes quà*m* Rura sua omnia mancipia membráve   25
depravata et vitiosa in eiusmodi carceres et custodias, quasi loca
domósq*ue* correptionis co*n*ijcere atq*ue* obtrudere, quò Dominicis
Castigationibus emendari reformariq*ue* possint. Sunt autem hæc
statuta vel Ordinatio*n*es huiusmodi, ea de causâ hoc loco inserta, quò
nostru*m* consilium factiq*ue* nostri rationem, faciliùs quisqua*m*, cuius   30
intererit, colligere q*ue*at.
¶ Certein Orders meet and necessarie to be observed and kept of all and
    every the Prisoners in the Castle of Glouc*ester*, to ye Glorie of God,
    ye king*es*, honour and their owne welfare, and subscribed vnto by their
    owne hand*es* 1618. R*egni* R*egis* Iac*obi* Dei gratiâ nunc & cætera   35
    decimo-sexto, et quinquagesimo-secundo, Iul*ij* |
¶ Imprimis whosoever come not vnto, and are not present at the service
    of God in the Chapel or Gallerie of the sayd Castle on the Sabbaoth
    daies and all and everie other festival daies, and Wensdaies and ffridaies

1/ modò: *grammatically necessary* ut *omitted after this word*
9/ Paroechijs *for* Paroecijs *or* Parochijs

on the forenoon, & that so, as they bee present thereat within one
quarter of an houre after nine of the clock of the forenoone, and after
3. of the clock on the afternoon, not departing till within a quarter
of an houre at the most of Eleven of the clock on the forenoon, and
five a Clock on the after-noon, without a reasonable Cause declared   5
vnto, and alowed of the Arbitrators to that purpose appoynted: Hee
or Shee shall paie for euerie such defalt xij d or be left in the Stockes
sixe houres. And whosoever shal walk, or talk, or stand aloof at
prayer, or sermon time, or vse anye meanes of disturbaunce of the
Minister and service of God, hee shal forfeyt vj d or be stocked 3.   10
houres Item whosoever shal vse anie vnlawfull game at anie time, or
the lawful games otherwise than the Kinges Maiesty hath declared and
required, shal forfeyt lykwise for [feyte lykewyse] ⌜e⌝verie such
defalt – xij d to the vse of the poor Prisoners of the common or maign
Gaole of or in the sayd castle, to be disposed by the Arbitrators, or   15
some of them. or els shall sitt in the stockes sixe houres.
Item whosoever shal falselie or rashlie sweare, or tell a false lie, or bee
druncken, or committ fornication, or Adulterie, or shall have anie
Ribaldish talke, or shall abuse anie by nicknames, and by brabling and
brawling, they shalbee at the lyke forfeyture and penaltie.   20
Item whosoever shal purloin, steal, beguile of, or take awaie anothers
money, vittayles or apparell, or anie thing els; They shalbee at the lyke;
besyde Restiticion, and aunswere to the lawes of the Realme, for so
doing, at the pursuit of the Robbed and beguyled.
¶ Atque hoc modo ac ratione certiores fieri facilè queunt omnes de Regiæ   25
Maiestatis mente ac consilio, quoad prædicta gymnasia Olympiaca
quasi, libera exercitia et recreationes. De fidelium omnium itidem
subiectorum ingenuo consensu, obsequio submisso, rectâ
constructione, officijs atque obedientia quàm prompta, quàm
paratissimâ. Puritani valeant, qui corporalia Dominicalium dierum   30
exercitia prorsus abnegant. Valeant et Papistæ, qui à nostra Religione
deterrentur, quòd nullam putant approbare, nullam admittere
christianam recreationem. Vtrosque sanè prohibet nisi prius unà
conveniunt in sacris coetibus ad divina concelebranda. Quod quidem
vtrique recusant agere; papistæ nempe schismaticum esse credentes,   35
Puritani Pontificium et impium. Ambo sub uno iugo contrahentes, sub
vno vexillo commilitantes cum meris prophanis histrionibus,
Nebulonibus, et vel negligentibus, vel praefractis reprobis, qui
communibus precibus, votis fidelium vsitatis, pientissimis
Christianorum orationibus interesse, non possunt omninò sustinere.   40

1/ & written over as   37/ prophanis for profanis

Sed iam satis superque de his omnibus anteá. Tantùm ad hæc pauca
proba ex meâ ipsîus experientia. Fui quodam die cirencestriæ (iam
Anni sunt plus minus duo) ad mensam cum Magistro Archi[.]diacono
ac Eius decanatus Ministris et contionatoribus. Intraverunt ad nos in
illud conclave cœnobiale Musici quidam | Lyrici, Myntyi dicti quidem   5
illi, spondentes nobis Musicæ nonnihil illorum harmoniæ,
symphoniæ, melodiæ. Mox quidam è Ministris (quem eò nominandum
censeo, ne cæteris ingenuis, liberis et inculpatis aspersionem alicuius
mendæ maculæve, notamque vllam inferam) Alderus nomine, abeant,
inquit, abeant; quid hîc agerent? sunt enim per Statutum vagabundi;   10
atque inter plebem et populum multorum malorum caput et causa. Hi
statim abituri, ne mutire quidem audentes, quantum ego tum
auscultavi, à nemine revocantur. Tandem ego: Maucte, maucte, vos,
boni viri; commoramini parumper, fortasse libenter audiemus. Ad
criminantem me converto, aio; Quid quæso, abirent? Annon sponte   15
veniunt, si non ab aliquibus accersiti? Annon amantes nos et
venerantes accedunt? Annon in hoc, vt in alijs elucet Divina
providentia? Annon æquè Musica, atque mensæ et convivia, nobis
conceditur? (nisi fortè sumus illis similes, qui Mulierum interesse
gratiarum-actioni post puerperium præ papistica superstitione, quam   20
fingunt, pernegantes, epulis tamen et bellarijs comessationibus et
epotationibus inter illas adsunt quàm lubentissime) Annon est Musica
è Liberalibus scientijs vna? Grammatica loquitur, Dialectica vera
docet, Rhetorica verba colorat, Musica canit, Arithmetica numerat,
Geometria ponderat, Astronomia colit Astra. Annon, vt nos, sic illi   25
lubenter ⌜vsum⌝ fructum caperent, læticiam cum vtilitate meterent è
sua scientiâ, facultate, professione? Eheu, quàm multos dies, noctes,
septimanas, menses, annos, vt ne miseram totam vitam dicam,
impendunt, impertiunt, consumunt ieiuni miseruli, vt peritiam
aliquam cantandi, psallendi, chordas vel plectro percutiendi, vel digitis 30
graciliter tangendi nanciscantur; quò nobis magis placeant, mirè
delectent, exhilarent, gratulentur? Nos verò tali more, præfatis modis,
contumælijs scilicet et convitijs eos recipimus, tractamus,
gratificamur? Taceamus nos, et eos potiùs humaniter tractemus.
Nunquid Davidem illum sanctissimum meminimus in psalmis et alias,   35
quid pro psalmodiâ, symphoniâ, musica harmonia fusissimè dicat, et
quàm planè plenéque describat? Illo tamen hoc temporis omisso, vt
in hac causa cunctis notissimo; locum illum sacrarum litterarum de
propheta Elisha commemoremus, in 2° libro regum Iudaicorum, capite

servi Domini
Graij
Domini
S Chandos

Verso .15.

8/ cæteris for ceteris   13/ Maucte for Macte
12/ abituri: r corrected from t   33/ contumælijs for contumelijs

3°. Adducite, inquit, citharædum seu Musicum aliquem. Lyricus autem, seu Tibicen, dum psallit et cecinit, manus Dei fuit super Eum et prophetavit. Nunquid hîc videtis (confratres mei Dilectissimi) quòd Propheta sit musica Melodia magis ad prophetandum excitatus? Itidem et nos fortasse post Istorum musicam harmoniam magis apposite   5
gratias agemus Deo Optimo Maximo propter hæc et innumera alia Eius in nos collata beneficia. Magister Archidiaconus Magister Suttonus, reliqui omnes, quantum, scio, suavissima concordia concedunt; accedunt Musici propiùs, psallunt, ludunt, cum Instrumentis sonant, boant, tinniunt; Nobis placent, et delectant. Ego, non dico, subtilis 10
emungo, sed facilè collatam et contributam accipio vniuscuiusque ministri drachmam vice cuiusdam symboli; musicis recipio quosdam
| hinc conflatos solidos; ij placantur et grati discedunt. Quare mihi est opus alicui, nulla causa data, cur Regiam dicat Maiestatem agere summo iure, proinde iniuria; Qui si vulpis Aures cornua vocitet, aures 15
pro cornibus sunt habendæ. Tantummodo vocat Aures Aures, cornua cornua, viros viros, Asinos Asinos; et pro libito habet et placitis Leges ipsas christianas et constitutior pias. Deo gratiæ. Vivat Rex æternúm.

f 10 col 2 (*insertion*)   20

Remember at ye pulling down of 2. poles in Barkley so 1. in St. Nicolas parish in Gloucester. some say at ye Iudges commandment.at ye Instigation of ye Maior & prior that puritan Minister. & thomas cherics a precisian.   25

12/ symboli *for* symbole   18/ constitutior *for* constitutiones

Translations

BISLEY

1610–11
Gloucester Diocese Consistory Court Deposition Books   GRO: GDR 114
ff [4–4v]   (*21 May*)

On the aforesaid day upon the aforesaid articles
Garret Band, tucker, of Bisley in the county of Gloucester where he
has dwelt for the space of five years and more, born at Eastington in
the aforesaid county, forty-four years of age or thereabouts, a witness,
etc. To the said articles of the aforesaid articles he deposes and says
(*English*). And he does not know how to depose otherwise to the said
articles, as he says.|

On the aforesaid day upon the aforesaid articles /
William Hopton, yeoman, of Berkeley in the county of Gloucester
where he has dwelt for six weeks, and formerly (he used to dwell) at
Bisley in the aforesaid county, thirty-two years of age or thereabouts,
born at the same place, a witness, etc.
To the said articles he deposes and says (*English*).

ff [8–8v]*   (*31 May*)
...
The office of the lord (bishop) promoted by Richard Hall against
Christopher Windle.†
Upon the articles given on behalf of the promoter in this business. John
Clissold, yeoman, of Bisley in the county of Gloucester where he has
dwelt for the most part from his birth, born at the same place, fifty
years of age or thereabouts, a witness, etc.
To the said articles he deposes and says (*English*).|

On the aforesaid day upon the aforesaid articles
Christopher Bidmeade, yeoman, of Bisley in the county of Gloucester

where he has dwelt for four years past, born at Ellc⟨...⟩ in the aforesaid
county, sixty years of age or thereabouts, a witness, etc.
To the said articles he deposes and says (*English*).

CHELTENHAM

1611
Manor and Hundred Court Book   GRO: D855/M8
f 90v*

(These sums) are established as is set out upon
the depositions of the articles.†

Amercement of
the players

Also they present upon their oaths as follows in these English words
(*English*). Therefore he himself (is) in amercement, etc.

GLOUCESTER

1283
Account of Alms, Edward I   PRO: E 101/351/15
mb 1*

...

...7s 7d (were given) in the king's offerings at Winchcombe in the larger
church by the hand of the said H. Likewise, 18d in alms of the king
(were) given to eighteen sick (persons) from the hand of the king (who
was) conferring his blessing in various places throughout the week.
Likewise, 20s (were given) to the prior and convent of Newent for one
pittance by the hand of the said H. from the alms of the king. Likewise,
26s 8d (were given) to the clerics playing the miracles of St Nicholas
and to their (?boy-) bishop from the alms of the king. Likewise, 40s
(were given) to the brothers of St John of Cricklade from the alms of
the king by the hand of the said H.

Total: £16 15s 6d

Gloucester

On Sunday the fifth day of December on St Nicholas' Eve, 5s (were
given) to feed forty poor (persons) in honour of the Holy Trinity from
the set alms of the king by the hand of the said H. On the following
Monday, the feast of St Nicholas, 6s 3d (were given) to feed fifty poor
(persons) from the common alms of the king by the hand of the said
H. On the same day, 12s 6d (were given) to feed one hundred poor
(persons) in honour of St Nicholas from the alms of the king. On the

following Tuesday, 6s 3d (were given) to feed fifty poor (persons) in
honour of St Thomas the martyr (ie, Thomas of Canterbury) from the
customary alms of the king. 7s (were given) in the king's offerings at
Gloucester on St Nicholas' Day aforesaid by the hand of the said H....

1301
Statutes of St Peter's Abbey   Hereford Cathedral Library: No 1826
single mb*   *(10 October)*

...

Ninth: Lest the treasury designated by the orders of the lord
(archbishop) of Canterbury for the brothers' necessities be burdened
improperly with other demands, it is ordered that the lord abbot shall
levy only the ten marks which he has indeed levied from the treasury
as the portion which the external priors pay for their brothers' clothing
during their term; (this is) so that nothing of the aforesaid (sums?) be
contributed to another (abbot) succeeding the same, but the said
money shall be completely assigned to the treasurer to provide the
brothers with clothing more adequately. Nor shall any abbot be
permitted to maintain continuously other persons as harpers or
minstrels as if (they were) of the household; however, the abbot shall
have a squire (who is) discreet in judgement and circumspect, who may
be able to be of service in the necessities of the monastery. And when
he (the abbot) goes about the priories to exercise the duty of visitation,
he should not stay (at those priories) unless he had been accustomed
to stay (in them) of old on account of the statute of the said
(archbishop) of Canterbury against spending the money and valuables
derived from monastic revenues(?), whether (they are held) in a
treasury, or a sacristy, or a priory.

...

1393-4
Borough Bailiffs' Accounts   GRO: GBR F 3/2
single mb*

...

Also paid for various minstrels and grooms of the lord king	⟨...⟩
Also paid to minstrel/s of the lord duke of Gloucester	⟨...⟩
Also paid to minstrel/s of the earl of March for 3 ⟨....⟩	⟨...⟩
Also paid to minstrel/s and a groom of the earl of W⟨.....⟩	⟨...⟩
Also paid to the minstrel/s of Lord Dess⟨....⟩	⟨...⟩

1409–10
Borough Bailiffs' Accounts   GRO: GBR F 3/4
single mb*

...

(Also) paid to minstrels of the lord king this year	13⟨....⟩
Also on costs incurred with respect to minstrels of the lord prince and upon gifts to them	39(s) 7⟨.⟩

...

Also on gifts and expenses incurred with respect to minstrel/s of Lord Codnor and of John Greynder	7s 5d

...

Also paid to the minstrel/s of the lady Countess Stafford	⟨...⟩

...

Also paid to the minstrel/s of Lord Berkeley	one-half mark

...

1602–3
Gloucester Diocese Consistory Court Deposition Books   GRO: GDR 89
f [116v]*   *(22 October)*

On the articles against Wylmott

Wayt and
Howell
against
Wylmott

Thomas Hyll, yeoman, of the city of Gloucester where he has dwelt for the most part from his birth, born in the same place, thirty-five years of age or thereabouts, of a free status as he says, a witness, etc. To the first article he says that the same is true. To the fourth he deposes (*English*) and otherwise he does not know how to depose.

On the rest of the articles he was not examined.

...

f [117]*

John Flemyng, barber, of the city of Gloucester where he has dwelt for the most part from his birth, born in the same place, thirty-six years of age and more, of a free status as he says, a witness, etc. To the first article he says that the same is true. To the second and third he does not know how to depose. To the fourth he deposes (*English*) and otherwise he does not know how to depose.

...

HARESCOMBE

1611–12
Gloucester Diocese Consistory Court Deposition Books   GRO: GDR 114
f [87]   *(16 March)*

The sixteenth day of March in the year of the Lord 1611

Katherine Haselton, the wife of William Haselton, against Dorothy Dorney, the wife of Richard Dorney, senior, in a case of defamation.

Upon the bill of complaint issued and exhibited on behalf of the said Katherine Haselton in this case.

Alice Arthure, spinster, of Haresfield in the county of Gloucester where she has dwelt for the space of two years (and) more past or thereabouts, born at Painswick in the aforesaid county, twenty-one years of age or thereabouts, produced, sworn, and examined as a witness.

...

To the second article of the aforesaid bill of complaint, she deposes and says *(English)*...

HENBURY

1599
Bristol Diocese Bishop's Cause Book   BRO: EP/J/1/11
f 269v

...

Against Robert Stoakes of the parish of Henbury. He is named in the articles *(English)*

Likewise Stoakes appeared and ˄⸢confessed to the presentment⸣, [denied that the presentment was the truth, whereupon the lord (bishop)] whereupon the lord (bishop) enjoined upon him the following penance, namely *(English)* and (enjoined him) to certify (the performance of the same).

...

LITTLEDEAN

1601–2
Gloucester Diocese Consistory Court Cause Book   GRO: GDR 90
ff 178–8v*   *(10 March)*

William Hopkins   *(English)*
of the same
[excommunicated]
                              Cited in church
He appeared and the lord enjoined him to confess his guilt in the
customary clothes on the next Sunday and to certify (his compliance)
on the next (court day).
He complied.

Welthiana ˏ ⌈harte al*ias*⌉ higeve ⌈widow⌉   *(English)*
of the same
excommunicated:
                              Cited in church
She appeared and the lord enjoined her by the aforesaid detection to
confess her guilt the next Sunday on bended knees etc, and to certify
(her compliance) on the next (court day).
excommunicated on the 24th of March 1601.

Blanche Jones and   for the same (charge)
Mary Jones of the same
excommunicated:
                              Cited in church
Catherine Jones (their) mother appeared. She speaks (for them) and
undertook (that penance would be performed).|

Littledean   Joanna Eston   *(English)*
             of the same
                              Cited in church
(The lord) shall send out the excommunication.
             …
Joanna Turnor   *(English)*
of the same   Cited in church
                           for the same (charge). She appeared and
Mary Buffrey   the lord enjoined her to confess her guilt.
of the same   Afterwards he dismissed her with a
                           warning, etc.

Margery Flewellin   for the same (charge)
and her sister of the
same
                         Cited in church
She has left the diocese of Gloucester
...

Andrew Philpott   (English)
of the same
                         Cited in church
It is referred to the minister and churchwardens.
...

Percival &   (English)
John Tilar
of the same
                         Cited in church
He appeared and the lord enjoined him to confess his guilt the next
Sunday and to certify (his compliance) on the next (court day).
He appeared and certified that he has complied.

Richard Harte   for the same (charge)
of the same
                         Cited in church
His mother appeared.
...

Anna Lewis   (English)
of the same
She appeared and the lord enjoined her to confess her guilt in the
customary clothes, etc, and to certify (her compliance) on the next
(court day).
She carried out (her) penance.

TEWKESBURY

1600–1
Gloucester Diocese Consistory Court Cause Book   GRO: GDR 90
f 52   (*12 June*)

Tewkesbury   Robert Jeynes   To respond to the articles, the said Jeynes
              of the same   appeared and he affirmed under oath
                                               (*English*)...

              ...

TORTWORTH

1602–3
Gloucester Diocese Consistory Court Deposition Books GRO: GDR 89
f [106]*   *(13 October)*

...

William Lawrence, husbandman, of Tortworth in the county of
Gloucester where he has dwelt for twelve (years) or thereabouts, born
in Chavenage within the parish of Horseley in the aforesaid county,
thirty-two years of age or thereabouts, of a free status as he says, a
witness, etc.
To the first (article), he says *(English)*....
To the third (article), he deposes *(English)*...and otherwise he does not
know how to depose....

...

f [106v]*

Giles Dawnte, gentleman, of the parish of Ozleworth in the county
of Gloucester where he has dwelt for beyond twelve years past, forty-
six years of age or thereabouts, produced and sworn as a witness, says
and deposes as follows.
To the first (article), he believes that the same is true.
To the second he does not know how to depose.
To the third he says *(English)*....And otherwise he does not know how
to depose.

...

WESTON SUBEDGE

1574
Gloucester Diocese Consistory Court Deposition Books GRO: GDR 32
p 178*   *(7 July)*

7th day of July 1574. It (? court session) resumes†
Personal responses of Michael Hyndemer, cleric, made to the things
contained in some present articles issued at the voluntary promotion
of John Castler, his parishioner, against him. They follow. *(English)*

...

BEAUCHAMP

1420–1
Household Account Book of Richard Beauchamp, Earl of Warwick
Longleat House: Ms Misc. IX
f 30v* *(External expenses to date)*
...
...And in expenses incurred for two of the lord of Wales' minstrels coming to Berkeley to speak with the lady and staying in the guest-house (?inn) of the same John Shephurde for six nights in the said month, 8d.

f 43   *(6 November) (Guests)*
...
At dinner   ...Also one minstrel of Lady Stafford....

f 56   *(23 December) (Guests)*

At dinner   ...Also three trumpeters of the lord. Also two harpers....

f 57*   *(24 December–6 January) (External expenses)*

...On various disguisings done on this feast 10d. And as a gift to a minstrel of Lord Clarence staying in the guest-house (?inn) for one day and one night on this feast, 6s 8d. And as a gift to six (persons) from Slimbridge playing before the lady on this feast by the lady's orders, 3s 4d. And as a gift to four (persons) from Wotton playing for the council (?) by the lady's order, 20d. And as a gift to two minstrels of Lady Abergavenny, staying in the guest-house (?inn), namely on the feast of Epiphany 6s 8d...

f 58v   *(10 January) (Guests)*
...
At dinner   ...Also two harpers from Wales....
...

f 68   *(12 February) (Guests)*

At dinner   ...Also two minstrels of Lady Abergavenny....

STAFFORD

1503-4
Household Accounts of Edward Stafford, Duke of Buckingham
SRO: D 641/1/3/7a
unnumbered mb   *(31 March–30 March)*

Rewards of external servants of the lord, of minstrels, of servants beyond wages, etc†
...And in similar rewards paid by the same order to various external minstrels and trumpeters as well as to the lord's minstrels at various times within the aforesaid period as is made clear in detail in the above-mentioned book of particulars £6 17s 4d...
...

1507-8
Household Accounts of Edward Stafford, Duke of Buckingham
SRO: D (W) 1721/1/5
p 7   *(15 November)*
...
Present at dinner...two trumpeters...
...

p 42   *(21 December)*
...
(Present at) supper...two minstrels...
...

p 43   *(22 December)*
...
Present at dinner...two minstrels...
...

p 44   *(23 December)*
...
Present at dinner...six trumpeters, two minstrels...
(Present at) supper...And fifteen singers of the chapel...
...

p 45 *(24 December)*

...

Present at dinner...eighteen singers of the chapel, nine boys, six household singers, six trumpeters, the two minstrels...

...

p 46 *(25 December)*

...

Present at dinner...the two minstrels, six trumpeters, four players of
the lord of Writtle...

...

p 53 *(2 January)*

...

Present at dinner...the two minstrels, six trumpeters, four players...

p 54 *(3 January)*

...

Present at dinner...the two minstrels, six trumpeters, four players...

p 55 *(4 January)*

...

Present at dinner...the two minstrels, six trumpeters, four players...
(Present at) supper...the four waits of Bristol.

p 56* *(5 January)*

...

Present at dinner...the two minstrels, six trumpeters, the four waits
of Bristol, four players of Writtle...

p 58 *(6 January)*

...

Present at dinner...the two minstrels, the six trumpeters, the four waits
of Bristol, four players of Writtle...

...

p 60 *(7 January)*

...

Present at dinner...the two minstrels, the six trumpeters, four
players...

p 61   *(8 January)*
...

Present at dinner...the six trumpeters, the two minstrels...

p 75   *(22 January)*
...

Present at dinner...six trumpeters...

1515–16
Household Accounts of Edward Stafford, Duke of Buckingham
PRO: E.101. 631/20
mb 20   *(31 December)*

Gifts

...

To the lord king and various gentlemen, to servants of the lord duke, both of the household and external†
To the lord king &.
To various servants of the household of the
said lord duke to have as a gift of the duke
himself, namely six ells of canvas for the   Canvas –
making of the one pageant and (its) showing   six ells
in the one interlude before the aforesaid lord   ...
duke on Christmas....

...

1516–17
Household Accounts of Edward Stafford, Duke of Buckingham
SRO: D 641/1/3/9
unnumbered mb   *(31 March–30 March)*

...

To the use
of the petty
wardrobe of
the duke himself

...ten dozen morris bells. six   Morris bells – ten dozen
(and) three-quarter yards of   Black buckram – six (and)
black buckram and half a yard   three-quarter yards
of red buckram for two tunics   Red Buckram – half a yard
for the morris dance. And three   Canvas – three yards
yards of canvas for the lining of   ...
one of the said tunics....

1520–1
Household Accounts of Edward Stafford, Duke of Buckingham
PRO: E.36/220
p 12* *(1 January)*

Deliveries & payments for the said month of January†
(English)

APPENDIX 1

Thornbury

Dinner	Gentlemen	95	
	Yeomen	107	
	Grooms	97	
			294
Supper	Gentlemen	84	
	Yeomen	114	
	Grooms	92	

Present at dinner: the Lady Anne, herself (being) fourteenth(?); the abbot of Keynsham, himself (being) seventh(?); W. Walwyn, himself (being) third(?); I. Seyntgeorge, himself (being) second(?); Robert P'ticile, himself (being) second(?); the chancellor, himself (being) fifth(?); H. Blunt, himself being second(?); John Burrell, himself (being) second(?); the bailiff of Hatfield, himself (being) second(?); the bailiff of Oakham, himself (being) second(?); the bailiff of Navesby, himself (being) ⟨…⟩; the bailiff of Rowell, himself (being) second; Q(?) Barth(?) himself (being) second(?); two others, servants from Penshurst; Henry Dunston; two minstrels; six trumpeters; four players of the lord of Writtle; H. Boughey, himself (being) second(?); the receiver of Newport, himself (being) second(?); T. Morgan, himself (being) third(?); two others, servants of the lord of Newport with one attendant; eight serving the lord of Brecon with ten attendants of the lord; John Burton; eighteen clerks of the chapel and nine boys of the same chapel; three tailors (? or carvers); three furriers; one villein; two 'hardwaremen'; twenty-two from the town; thirty-two from the country; two cooks from Bristol; &c.

Supper as at dinner, except six.

Strangers at	Dinner	182
	Supper	176

13/ *it is not clear what the expressions translated 'herself (being) fourteenth,' 'himself (being) seventh,' or 'fifth,' or 'third,' or 'second' mean. The only way these expressions make grammatical sense, however, is as ablatives of attendant circumstance, and the translation given is a literal one of that idiom. Perhaps it means that the Lady Anne, for instance, was fourteenth of her party, so that she was accompanied by thirteen servants.*

Saturday the 25th of December. Expenses of the pantry: 491¾ loaves, 2 manchets of grain, price 13s 8½d. From this: for breakfast, 15½ loaves and one manchet, as on preceding days; and to the treasurer one loaf; to the abbot of Keynsham one loaf, one manchet; to the gentlemen of the chapel 8 loaves; to gentlemen strangers 12 loaves; in dishes(?) 294 loaves; to the tailor/s (? or carver/s) 34 loaves; to the regarder/s 70 (loaves); to the salter/s (? or tumbler/s) 6 loaves; to the kitchen for works (?cooking) 10 loaves; the chandler/s 5 loaves; the bearward 2 loaves; the almoner/s 2 loaves; for drinkings 15½ loaves, that is, to strangers, for livery 15¾ loaves. Expenses of the cellar: 11 sesters and 3 quarts of Gascon wine, price 13s; 1½ pitchers of Rhenish wine, price 15d, and half a pitcher of Malvoisie, price 6d. From this: for breakfast half a pitcher; in dishes(?) one sester, one pitcher of Gascon wine and one pitcher of Rhenish wine; for Waller the nurse half a pitcher; for the great chamber one sester; for the hall 4 sesters, 2 pitchers (delivered) by Arnold; for daily allowances half a pitcher of Gascon wine, one quart of Rhenish wine, and one quart of Malvoisie; for the kitchen for works (? cooking) 3 pitchers; at the door (?) 2 sesters, 3 pitchers; for livery 2 pitchers, one quart of Gascon wine, and one quart of Malvoisie. Expenses of the buttery in beer: 171 gallons, one quart, price 13s 7¼d. From this: for breakfast 17 gallons, 3 quarts; in dishes(?) 73½ gallons; to the regarder/s 39 gallons; to the kitchen for works (? cooking) 5 gallons; for drinkings 6 gallons, 3 quarts; at the door(?) 20 gallons; for livery 9 gallons, one quart. Expenses of the kitchen from the lord's store: one carcass and 7 strips of beef, price 20s; 9 sheep's-milk cheeses, price 16s; 4 pigs, 8s; and 1½ calves, price 4s. Expenses of the caterer: namely on 4 swans, price 12s; 4 geese 2s; 5 small pigs, 20d; 14 capons, 8s; 18 chickens, price 18d; 21 rabbits, 3s 6d; one peacock 2s; 3 mallards, 8d; 5 widgeon, 10d; 12 teal, 12d; 8 woodcock, 8d; 22 snipe(?), 12d; 12 large birds, 3d; 400 hen's eggs, 3s 4d; 20 dishes of butter, 20d; 10 gallons of milk, 10d; 1½ gallons of 'quaice,' 6d; 2 gallons of frumenty, 4d; and on herbs, price 1d. Expenses of the chandlery: for Paris candles, 36 lb (of wax), price 2s 10d; 64 small candles, price 17d; 2 large square candles, price 2d; and 4 tapers, price 3½d. Expenses of the hall and chamber: for fuel, 6 cart-loads, 6s, and 6 quarters of charcoal, price 2s. The whole provision for the day.

5–6/ in dishes(?): *perhaps this expression means 'at dinner' since it is associated with three of the other standard daily meals: breakfast, drinkings, and livery; or perhaps '294 loaves as trenchers' is meant.*

APPENDIX 3

The variously mixed Commentary, or copious Oration, of
Christopher Windle upon this royal, exceptional, and very pleasant
declaration.

O very dear reader – whether you be the king himself, (who is) most
serene, most powerful, most learned, most pious, as well as most lov-
ing of his subjects, most well-disposed, most eager, indeed most celebrated himself, most loved – and why not? –, or (whether you be) a
minister or layman of whatever order, sort, (or) station or (whether
you be) one who is of the best natural character and condition, or one
who ought to be in the best circumstances – a minister from
Gloucestershire spoke to me as I was reading this royal, exceptional,
and very pleasant declaration for the first time, and just as I was reading
the first article, concerning honourable, liberal, permissible, and lawful sports and public amusements, jests, and pastimes, (which declaration has been) shown forth, proposed, (and) granted to his very fine
people (and) to his most dear subjects. And he – how troubled he was
and sobbing! – said that he was extremely afraid, frightened, (and) terrified on his own behalf lest this permission, freedom, (and) lenient
grant might make, produce, (and) bring forth on every side much pain,
condemnation, prejudice, and loss for many ministers of the church.
I then answered him: Why so, pray tell? Have we not good enough
judgement? Or have we poor judgement and so little knowledge that
we do not know what is good and useful for us and for our people?
Is there any danger to be feared or experienced, if we agree to the declaration? Or is there anything prejudicial in the declaration itself?
Thereupon he (said): We are ordered to be mindful that we keep and
observe the Sabbath in a holy way; we ought to keep holy not simply
part, but all, of the Sabbath. But to play, jest, laugh, dance, (and) refresh the spirit by physical activity is to violate, pollute, profane, (and)
contaminate the Sabbath, if even an iota of the twenty-four hours of
that day were taken away from holiness and sanctity. I said: Were you
then taught in such a way to impose the Jewish practice of Sabbath
observance on us, or to place its condemnation upon fun and physical
activities? Even if it were pleasant and permissible to imitate the Jews,
it can and must be done in happy rejoicings, jubilations, round dances,
ritual dances, (and) set dances rather than in precise and restricted observance of times, days, places, ceremonies, (and) circumstances. I
would go so far as to say that, with respect to days and times, no day
or time whatever has been more befitting or appropriate for round
dances, dances, physical actions, jests, (and) liberal ways of rejoicing

than Sabbaths, Sundays, holidays, feast days, and Lord's Days. Indeed, Sabbaths and solemn feasts have been so appropriate to such things that they could neither be observed and spent properly without these (activities), nor should any such days ever be spent wholly without these observances. Most dear brothers, I resolve to bring this (fact) to the light, to make it plain, clear, and obvious. And I am at once turning my attention to it, and undertaking that there might be no such fear, fright, (or) terror, but rather that all danger (and) all prejudice may be wiped out (and) each one of you may be freed altogether from harm, discomfort, and distress.|

To begin with, I should seek not the beginning, for the sake of a bad syllogism, but the principal and especial cause both of our being created and of our being restored. You will reply no doubt that the glory of God is the ultimate end and final cause of creation or redemption or of anything else. But how and in what matters is the

Rom.14.22   glory of God unfolded, illustrated, forced to appear? Have you faith? says the Apostle. Have it within yourself before God, as if to say, men cannot see faith with the eyes of the body. As Cicero says about wisdom, (borrowing) from Plato: if this (wisdom) were discerned by the

James 2.18   eyes, it would arouse a wonderful love of itself. So too St James: Show me your faith from your works and I shall show you my faith by my works. Therefore God is manifested among men (and) the glory of God gleams, shines, (and) stands out when we declare externally the pious aspect of the inner man, the innate genius of the mind, the true

Phil.4.8   faith of the inmost heart, (and) the sincere will by honourable, honest, (and) holy actions. But surely ritual dances, round dances, set dances, (and) nimble and versatile physical actions are not such works, such external actions, I seem to hear you say! Why should they not be a great and good part of those (works), I ask? For we always rejoice in (our) bodies and there is always something to be done by them. And we often do many things which are less useful and more servile than those (actions), and we do such things without correction or reserva-

Rom.14.23   tion. Nevertheless, nothing should be done apart from faith; nothing useless (or) servile should be preferred to what is useful and free.

There is no need to prove that we have bodies, as (there is no need to prove) that there is always something for them to do and that they are always in action, even when we sleep. But as for (the idea that)

Jo.5.6–10   the less the usefulness, the more perhaps the baseness: what, I ask, is
Luke 14.3,   more base than to cook meals, and prepare them to be eaten by others;
4,5   to treat the sick; to urinate; to muck out (stalls); to pull oxen, sheep, or asses from wells? What more useless, leaving baseness aside, than

Jo.7.22   to sacrifice (and) to circumcise, to kill cattle and to cut the foreskin? All these things were done on holidays. But even if you insist, urge,

(and) contend that the benefit of the former (and) the holiness of the
latter are not slight, then how much more useful (it is) by means of
the aforesaid exercises to cook meals together; to digest them healthily;
to cure, or rather to prevent sickness; to acquire (both) health
untroubled by disease (and) safety free from foes; to enter into, pro-
mote, (and) strengthen friendships? (How much) more holy to sacrifice oneself; to circumcise one's own heart; to praise God; to rejoice
in God; to leap, dance, (and) exult before God from an excess of joy?
But, you (reply), as if these (exercises) are of that kind! Lustful youths
leading round dances with unrestrained girls, just like he-goats mounting wanton she-goats, thereby exceed those (ways of rejoicing which
are) circumcised, holy, and as it were self-sacrificed. As if truly, and
I also say it, either the most serene king, the most constant defender
of the faith, the most powerful, pious, (and) truthful professor and
champion of the gospel of Jesus Christ and of true religion, or anyone
else of any importance as pertains to the commonwealth of the church
and the salvation of souls, either demands or permits, let alone pre-
scribes or does more than tolerate, any round dances, actions, dances,
or gymnastics other than those which become Christian youth (and)
represent and show their joy, happiness, (and) exultation in the Lord
(and) their great and singular gratitude toward God, their creator, redeemer, and preserver!

For these examples, together with the remaining testimonies of
Scripture and the custom of the church, teach and prove and infallibly
confirm that gymnastics of this kind (and) such exercises can even
show forth the sign and practice of exceptional piety amongst the
people of God. And in the first instance, given that even in paradise
and at the beginning of the universe – and that state was most perfect –
together with that rest from and stopping of work, the eating of the
tree of life and the opportunity of eating it as it were a sacrament of
the covenant of works is given or rather enjoined, what else can this
suggest to us other than that nowadays under the covenant of grace
we must take care for life in the mysteries of Christ, while we indeed
eat his flesh and drink and swallow his blood? But, you say, that eating
and drinking is spiritual: what (has) this (to do) with ritual dances,
jests, and such mimings? But is the flesh of Christ something spiritual?
Was not Christ a true man? Did he not rejoice in flesh and blood? Is
it not a twofold kind of eating, leaving those fantastic and imaginary
(sorts) aside; (one which is) Capernaitic, popish or papistic, or (one)
which is different? Do we not rejoice in minds as well as bodies, (having) flesh together with spirit so long as we have human nature and
substance? Does not the body eat sacramentally as the soul eats spiritually? Does not Cyprian say – and others – that the most certain

Rom. 12.1.2

Luke 15.23
25.31

argument possible that the bodies of the faithful will ascend with (their) souls into heaven just as they will rise (with them) from the earth is that our bodies receive the sacrament of Christ's body, just as our souls receive its grace, each (receiving) the body and blood of Christ in its own way? (The result of all this is) that these things may be best understood mystically, typologically, metaphysically, and spiritually.

Was not Christ, I say, true man? Do we not eat, drink, and, having been re-created in him, become united to the same Christ who was conceived of the Holy Ghost, born of the Virgin Mary, crucified, dead, and buried, and so on? Certainly there is no other true Christ, the true son of God and man, no matter how we perceive him. Do we not now do, perform, and complete the obligations which it rather behoves us to exceed by harping (*or* chanting), singing, rejoicing, exulting? But you (respond): Not, in any case, by leaping, dancing, gesturing/miming; playing, laughing, leading | round dances, and jesting. And I (rejoin): Therefore by neither eating too much nor drinking

1 Cor.11.22

a lot. For, as the Apostle says, have you not homes in which you may eat and drink that you thus hold the church in contempt? In the same way, the other actions and deeds must be performed, carried out, and completed in other suitable places. Moreover, these things are not to be omitted or neglected, as necessary to both lives, both spiritual and natural, of the body as well as of the soul, but must be introduced, offered, and presented in appropriate places at suitable times.

Nor ought penance to be imposed upon us because of the fall of (our) first parents only by means of this interpretation which requires that there always be sorrow, sadness, contrition, harshness, (and) bitterness under the name, that is, of pious groaning, mourning, lamentation, (and) wailing. At the same time, rejoicing, zeal, cheerfulness, happiness, (and) delight are required. Days also have been designated and assigned for rejoicing, amusement(s), and delights. For never has such a great cause for enjoying, rejoicing, jesting, laughing, dancing, (and) exulting been given and granted, not even to Adam in his most perfect state of innocence and exceptional integrity, nor yet to

Rom.4.12

Abraham rejoicing in himself because of his works, such as (has been given) to us in the second Adam, Christ, the blessed seed promised in Abraham, just as it was foreshadowed, foreshown, and foretold that

Gen.17.17
and 18.12–13
Ps.65.14,
126.2

this son would be called Isaac. This (name) 'Isaac' means 'Laughter,' which applies (both) to the meaning of the word and the reason for the name, both because his parents both laughed when he was promised and because he provided the supreme occasion (and) greatest cause for laughter (*ie*, for joy). He is translated, by rendering (? his name), into laughter: in the Canaanite language, (Isaac) foretells, denotes, and attests laughter. Is there anything else which can be so expressed with joy, burst forth (so) with happiness, pour forth (so) in laughter, (so) swell the heart and cheer the mind, other than the grace of God, of divine favour, and of a covenant in Christ for salvation and life eternal, that is, for the remission of sins (and) the eternal heavenly inheritance and favour? Or is this ineffable, inestimable, (and) incomprehensible benefit not at all worthy of our happiness and rejoicing?

But let us examine further what the Israelites once did, what faithful Christians (did) in the beginning and still (do) to this day, what has always been strictly required of the people of God, (and) what is now consistently required of us. Jubal may be the father and author of all those who play harps, stringed instruments, trumpets, reed-pipes, lyres, drums, and other similar devices and instruments, but Moses and Miriam put (them) to use (and) profited (by them): they learned what they (ie, the instruments) can (do) by a pious, licit, (and) holy use. For with these (instruments) they together praised God the best and greatest for outstanding victory over (their) enemies, that is, the Egyptian people and their evil king. I know and remember that (matters) turned out very differently at other times. In the thirty-second chapter, verses 6 to 19, for example, he describes their (the Israelites') idolatry, mentioning at the same time eating, | drinking, singing, (and) dancing. Nor have I forgotten what is in the New Testament on the same point, in the first letter to the Corinthians, the tenth chapter, verse seven, as if eating, drinking, round dancing, and set dances were either idolatry itself or a part of it, when nonetheless these actions, public amusements, and gymnastics are not simply being hated, treated as faults, or imputed as blame or crimes but by reason of bad usage (and) wrong application, with respect to that idolatry, just as is seen in the previous chapter of Exodus, verse nineteen, whose words are: When Moses first approached the host, he saw the calf and the dancing. Therefore the calf and the adoration of the calf were the reason why Moses was so angry and rebuked Aaron. And afterwards he found that golden calf, put (it) in the fire, burned (it) up, reduced (it) to ashes, turned (it) into dust as if (it had been) milled, strewed (it) upon the waters, (and) forced the Israelites to drink that water. (There is) not even one further word about the dancing.

Moreover, I see in that Pentateuch not only the Sabbath established for observance but also many other feasts and festivals, for instance, (the feast) of the Passover and the unleavened bread, Pentecost or (the feast) of Weeks, (the feast) of Tabernacles, and many others. But how are they feasts, in what way festivals? (Is it) by any other reason, means, or way than by resting from servile works to spend, devote, (and) pass all those days, Sabbaths as well as feasts and festivals, in

Ps 103

Exodus
15.1–20

Exod.
35.3

pious, holy, honest, honourable, festive, worthy, and even divine
activities and exercises? But it is not even permitted to light a fire on
the Sabbath. Why would they not be allowed to warm themselves as
was fitting and necessary by other licit means? Why is it that
Deuteronomy 16 orders them to be happy on these feasts, to rejoice,
and exult not once, but often? And in what way (and) how will they
rejoice, be happy, (and) be cheered? For even if you should concede
that ecclesiastic performance, allowing the exception of psalms,
hymns, (and) praises in the temple, what (has) that which is fitting and
appropriate to them (ie, to the psalms, etc?) (to do) with the mob and
the common people acting apart among themselves? Did not the
psalmist himself teach in the psalms what is suitable in this circumstance? (Did he) not (teach) it to each and every one as often as
possible, according to canons (which had been) already laid down by
him beforehand? At the time when the most holy David the psalmist
himself composed (the psalms), he put into use or practice what he
imposed upon some or composed for others or demonstrated to have
been permitted in 1 Chron. 15 and 25 and 29; Pss. 28:8; 31:1,2,3;
68:25; 57:7; 108:1,2; 95; 98; 100, 107; 149; and 150. Perhaps someone
will object from the prophets, as from Isa. 24:8–11 (or) Amos 6:4,5,6,
that all exercises, gymnastics, (and) jests of this kind are blameworthy
and greatly to be condemned. But is it not readily apparent that it is
not a right use but a most depraved abuse (which is) treated as a fault,
condemned, (and) abhorred? The same thing ought to be observed of
Judges 21:21,22,23; (and) Matt. 14:6, and many other similar passages.

The text of Matt. 9:23, (in which) Christ threw out the pipers along
with the players of stringed instruments and the singing, shouting,
noisy crowd, forcing (them) to leave the house of the dead (child), is
so far from being or acting against us in this matter, that almost nothing
can be said more apt or fitting (ie, to our case). Rejoicing, amusements,
and music belong not only to weddings, | but also to burials and fun-
erals. What (is) the cause of this fact, pray tell; what (is its) meaning?
Undoubtedly to represent, assert, affirm, confirm, and establish celes-
tial joys, heavenly happiness, (and) the exultation of the saints in
heaven. The things which are described and declared in the Apocalypse
of St John in chapters 5, 14, and 15, etc, about the harps of God (and)
the most outstanding, very remarkable, (and) most excellent instruments of heaven; similarly, what is in 1 Cor. 13:1 and 14:7, 8; Eph.
5:19; Col. 3:16; and Phil 4:4 according to St Paul; (and) especially the
description of the lord Christ according to Luke the evangelist in chapter 15, verses 23, 25, (and) 31, also (chapter) 17, (all) point to the conclusion that those are rightly said to mourn (and) fast for the lack and

Matt.
9.15

absence of the Bridegroom who are not willing to rejoice in (his) presence and refuse to be happy in the joyful countenance of the present Bridegroom. Thus that which is said among our countrymen: Bread and butter is the finest food possible. Moreover, may there be (such) sorrow for (them as they) love, desire, (and) await him (the Bridegroom) as is natural for those who, deceitful as well as sorrowful, are themselves without reason and defraud and deceive themselves as they deserve!

But Alcithoe daughter of Minyas did not think the secret rites should be attributed to God, on the grounds that (the rites) which were owed only to God the best and greatest were being offered by the bacchantes to heathen Bacchus, while they (the bacchantes) cried out through the breezes and the air: Io! Comrades, let us worship Iacchus! According to Hosea, Habakkuk, Zephaniah, and others, one sees that the idolatrous Israelites (did) not (behave) any differently than to act and bear themselves impiously; nevertheless, (one sees) that to confer piously upon the Lord what they (formerly) offered wrongfully to their idols and to profane and impious elders/ancestors would never offend the Lord, never be regarded as a fault.

Now our king and shepherd, (our) Agamemnon, or rather our Davidic Solomon, decides and recommends through lawful priests and Christian seers that Christian youth must make offerings to the divine majesty and godhead both in spirit and body[a]. Behold accordingly how great a reason the king has, as it were (that) of the present bridegroom, the Lord Jesus Christ, present always in his word, in the gospels, in (his) ministers, (and) in his people by the Holy Spirit until the end of the world, (as is written in) Matt. 28.20. How each one of them – or indeed all of them – who from too great a pretext of sincere zeal or most pure holiness cannot bear, allow, (or) endure any bodily exercise on the Sabbath, especially that which savours of and displays refreshment and liveliness, is far less able to brook, permit, patiently bear, (and) most especially approve (of this)! But I am gathering together from these points the most complete argument for and surest demonstration of the sensible royal knowledge and the certain understanding of the true nature, plan, inner sense, (and) meaning of Christ himself and his gospel.

I am also gathering the similar and like indication and meaning of his (the king's) most sweet love, dearest favour, (and) royal, fatherly, and most dutiful care toward his most beloved subjects, his most loving, desirous, (and) eager people, as (they are) also most faithful, most constant, (and) most upright. | Indeed, he names them, not once or twice but very often, his people, his best people, in these few pages,

Hos.2
Hab.1
Zeph.1
Ezek.16.15,
17,19

a. By the king

(calling them) Our people, Our good people more than ten times, (in such a way) that even a tenfold repetition is always acceptable. It is not within (my) capacity, (it is) not easy (for me) to reveal whether the fact that the royal majesty allows recreations of this kind, or that (the royal majesty) fashions the same (recreations) with his own as it were proper hands, testifies to a greater goodwill and kindness. Nor is it less difficult to show, describe, (and) make known how great, how equal the love; and the goodwill equal to it; the fatherly care; the episcopal, or rather the apostolic watchfulness (with which) he bears, has, (and) embraces both parts of this island and most famous clime, both north and south, and each and every county and praiseworthy city and community. On account of this I have joined to this treatise my thanksgiving for his royal majesty's most gracious and hoped-for return from the northern regions. I could not fail to add this, although rude and unskilful, to the famous exercises and holy altar of my Oxford (confrères), out of (my) unrestrained affection and no less benevolent mind.

b. Rebuking some puritans and precisians

b. Now I ask you, brethren, especially if some among you are puritans, why the precisians need allege purity, piety, (and) holiness in external matters. Is not God a spirit? Is he not to be venerated, adored, (and) worshipped in spirit and in truth? You can be precisians in conscience, (claiming) that nothing is known by words, but by deeds. (But) external and physical (acts), in the same way as they profit little, advance little (and) conduce practically in no way to piety: thus they are not placed, not located in your power. Wherefore you are contending about trifles, the ghost of an ass, things of no value, and you declare yourselves to be stupid about things (which are) irrelevant and profitless. Therefore you are held (to be) presumptuous, arrogant, insolent, (and) useless busybodies; contentious puritans.

(That) name (is) odious, and (has been) more or less abominated for some time now. For it was a foretelling of you or an omen of you (or) rather of your blame, your crime. For how may they be called, in what name ought or can they rejoice, according to the Aristotelian passage on etymologically related names, who arrogate purity to themselves, (and) wish themselves to be seen and held (as) pure except (by the name) of pure ones or of puritans? But you are not pure. Therefore, not (the name) of pure ones. But rather (that of) impure ones by (your) deeds, pretending and dissimulating especially purity, piety, (and) holiness to the point of nausea, as we have said before. Therefore, (you are called) puritans. Nevertheless, dearest brethren, it is neither here nor there to me if there are men otherwise truly pious and practised who, nonetheless, too rich in their own judgement – to use the words

of Jerome – (and) (having) opinions too narrowly preconceived,
adhere to prejudiced and harsh likes and dislikes, considerations, and
opinions in matters (which are) either indifferent or trivial or at least
placed outside ordinary choice. | Such the most serene king himself
has not failed to declare his opinion to be in his own truly golden work
called the *Basilikon Dōron*. Therefore, do not treat it as a fault that
you are referred to in this way, unless you blame yourselves for
behaving in that way.

You don't remember the philosopher (?Aristotle) who said as a
demonstration (of his point): 'Behold strong thieves leading weak
thieves to the gallows, driving those (who) should be hanged to the
gibbet!' do you? Don't you accuse the little ones at the same time as
you offend in great things, and are guilty even of *lèse-majesté*; do you
not accuse (them) grievously (and) accuse them as of the worst
offences? c. But this is less remarkable since even the king himself,
although he (is) most innocent, pious, (and) benevolent, cannot escape
your bitter charges, harsh aspersions, and sharp accusations. For
whom do you not dare to try, annoy, bother, scorn, hurt, injure, (and)
slay, you who have begun, started, (and) commenced to hurt; molest;
scorn; drag through the air, the ears, and the mouths of men; whisper
against (and) blaspheme most boldly the king himself, so evangelical,
orthodox, angelic, and holy? It concerns his serene majesty to vindicate his name and Christian, glorious, and heavenly authority from
the sprinkling of your filthy charges, to lay claim to his imperial right,
supreme authority, (and) deserved honour: why then does he not put
upon you, impose, and inflict the foul brands of (your) faults and
crimes, of your defects and offences, especially the assembled stains
of your very petulant and pestilent tirades, which you have deserved
(and) which you summon up and bring upon yourselves? So help me
God, the royal mercy does not deal with you according to your
deserts!

I cannot get out of my mind or keep from telling a fable from Æesop
(which is) both moral and memorable (and) (which) comes to mind,
how once the frogs asked Jupiter to grant and give them a king. Jupiter
agreed and gave them a huge log for a king. When it fell there was an
earthquake. The frogs (were) so terrified by the sight that they hid for
several days; after a space of time, leaving their hiding-places, they approached the king. They saw it quiet, peaceful, subdued, sedate, (and)
not moving; they climbed across (it), leaped across (it), leaped on it,
(and) leaped back; they spurned (it), held (it) in contempt, despised
it, rejected it. They approached Jupiter again; they condemned it for
torpor, sloth, laziness, (and) lassitude; they sought another. Jupiter

Aspersions
c. Misinterpre-
tation of our
meaning

heard them again and gave them a stork as a king. This (stork) snatched up and devoured immediately any frog it saw. Thereupon all the frogs complained again that they were being most cruelly slaughtered, tormented, (and) eaten by the stork. But in vain and to no avail. Would that they had been content and pleased | with the former (king), so safe and free from all harshness. You see foreshadowed in this model what it would be to refuse, deny, object to, (and) reject a peaceful, kind, very gentle, (and) Christian king.

Hear now another true and recent story. When I had written these things, and at the same point of time as I had ornamented (them) (? rhetorically), a summer pole was put up in the adjacent garden or farm of this very prison, Gloucester Castle, where the inmates are accustomed to walk, talk, and refresh themselves somewhat in turn. Many carp at this happening, that fun is there, is happening in that place where there are so many examples and signs of tears and laments rather than of plays and music.

But pay attention also to what I am going to say. If by means of the king's edict, a strict rule, (and) a mind aware of (what is) good, mere prisoners are able to rejoice, make music, (and) dance in prisons and jails, in workhouses, and in confinement, what could they not (do), what should they not dare who live freely and voluntarily in unrestricted cities? Moreover I am also aware that even in their dark holes many drink and make love and fight when they are kept from, forbidden, or deprived of these exercises whether by accident or design. Take this other similar (example). In the aforesaid city of Gloucester, while I was spending (my) aforesaid time in the castle, just as happens in other similar (situations), a murderer approached the wife of (his) neighbour, many, many times. He asked, sought, and was seen to insist on having an affair with her; while he was threatening to touch her, (her) husband suddenly arrived who, seeing what sort of thing (was happening), yelled: Hold! hold! These words, having been heard by others, are now repeated daily by everyone as a parable or proverb. But when some (summer) poles and pyramids had been put up, a good many snarled and muttered, although (it is) by reason of these (poles) (that) young people are wooed away from carnal inducements, spells, brothels, drinking matches, drunkenness, (and) whoring.

Therefore I pray you, as those who escape safely and freely by the king's most ineffable mercy, permit, if it be allowed, fair, right, and just to ask, seek, obtain, and get this of you: permit, I say, and endure quietly, sedately, and modestly that the royal will and plan might explain, set out, and explicate his own exceptional intentions for the sake of avoiding (your own) false and depraved exposition. I take it ill, as

d. county of
Lancashire

indeed I should, that Lancashire abounded in recusant papists, and I grieve greatly, both (because) the king himself is wonderfully grieved by the same fact, and (because) when I (was) a ten-year-old boy I went to school in that county for at least three years and studied grammar. (I) take it well, as indeed (I) should for the aforesaid reasons that (now) the magnates (?magistrates) may inform (his) royal majesty that the people are reformed, that (their) customs are amended and conform;

e. Barred from
all recreations

it fills me with great pleasure, it affects me with great joy. d. But indeed however Lancashire abounded with Catholic | papists, we have it as certain, proved, and established that the entire world of the royal dominion and the royal universe overflows abundantly with puritans. There are no creatures worse, more depraved, pestilent, (and) dangerous than these schismatics: although worshippers desirous of a sincere piety (and) greedy for true purity ought not to burdened with this name (of puritans), as ones who should be held and called only Christians, having nevertheless rejected all artful, shrewd, (and) destructive flattery.

These men ought to be grieved over, nay, rather, to be destroyed; certainly one must beware of them. They usurp power, authority, dominion, (and) rule over those matters in which freedom has been completely restricted and from which it (has been) removed to another field. They have mastery and keep and exercise rule, and peremptorily attack the consciences of others. They either legislate religion and the worship of God in these activities in which either there is no religion or, if (there is) any, it concerns the right use of those things and not their neglect; or they devote (themselves) to a Jewish way of keeping the Sabbath, that is, their very own (way), as if the day could be spent or its ritual and worship observed in no other way than (that which) they prescribe and profess.

f. produce
two evils.

f. They do not observe, with the very wise (and) holy king, how many inconveniences and ill effects follow and grow up from their law and practice. They do not see, they do not care, how great an obstacle they present to those converting from the popish sect and Catholic superstition, or even to weak Protestants with whom popish priests deal, when those histrionic rogues can offer as an objection there that our religion admits no happiness, no rejoicing, wherefore it is not

g. more able
for war

tried, true, sure, pious, (or) partaking of patience. g. They do not think, do not consider, do not realize how great a prejudice and harm to military science the interdiction of these gymnastics is, while (thereby) youths introduced onto the stage, into the arena, or as it were the camp, very appropriately, in view of the very great neglect of battle-related affairs, climb up, descend, gaze at one another's faces and expressions in turn, (and) become agile, warlike, and very strong soldiers. The Israelites, you know – to say nothing of the Spartans and others of this sort – used to drill their youth in warlike business, in exercises belonging to war, strategy, and battles. Perhaps the Christian religion does not desire or demand warlike gear so relentlessly. It rather tolerates and demands softer and gentler exercises. But if there is need and necessity the gospel of our Lord Jesus Christ does not forbid battles to be fought, either entirely or on the Sabbath, against his common enemies, savage, barbarous, terrible, (and) cruelly attacking foes. This can be proved by many passages of Holy Writ, which this is not the place to enumerate | nor (is there) any need to explain (them). Nor is this statement denied by any, except the anabaptists, the most foul beings of this age. Many have made a sufficient answer and more to them on this point: it needs no defense from me.

h. filthy tipplings

h. Moreover, when youths are forbidden these more humane exercises and liberal and ingenious amusements of which we have often made mention – Good God! What a great frequenting of taverns ensues! How much gulping at alehouses! How many and how disgusting the feasts, drinkings, and drunkenness (and) quaffings! How inept, absurd, (and) obscene the discussions, conversations, insults, imprecations, quarrels, disagreements, discords, brawls, fights, (and) contentions! And along with (all) this, how many foul fornications! How many base rapes, execrable adulteries, horrible incests, abominable whorings! (I am) ashamed to name what they do in darkness, but they are not ashamed to perpetrate in daylight, do, (or) commit openly things which are not even named by obscene and idolatrous heathens. This is completely clear, certain, and plain to all from the multitude of bastards springing forth everywhere. But the precisians seem to hold and actually do hold these people unimportant. They only judge notorious sinners of this kind to be reprobates, then abandon them in error (and) in danger! Is this not known to the royal majesty, and known very accurately? Shall we pass over this as unknown, as if (we were) ignorant? (No; for) surely we are very faithful subjects, sedulous servants, very dear and useful friends of the state and the church or I am much mistaken.

Eph. 5.3–12
1 Cor. 5.1
Ps. 16.4

j. If not upon Sunday, and holy days.

j. But I seem to hear some saying – although (they are) speaking foolishly – people can refresh themselves on the other days of the week, play, joke, (and) practise deeds, gestures, (and) playful activities of these kinds so that they do not interfere with, intrude, obtrude, (or) impose upon Lord's Days. As if the other days of the week, the same (days) set aside for work and labour, were more suitable, apposite, and apt for such humane and mild sports and recreations than holidays free

of, immune from, and quit of other business both servile and necessary. Is it not very laughable and immensely absurd for peasants to
run from their farming, or diggers from their ditches, or cooks from
their kitchens, or cobblers from their benches, or tailors from their
seats, or herdsmen from their folds, or goatherds from their goats and
kids, or cowherds from their stalls, [or butchers from their markets],
or millers from their mills, or weavers from their shops, or even maid-
servants from their wool and loom, (and) milkmaids from their milk-
ing, cheese-pressing, and churning, into the streets; (and) to dance and
exult in torn cloth, dirty clothing, (and) disfigured bodies; to leap
about, run wild almost, if not to go mad and pillage? Just as | in
Deuteronomy 5, verses 14 and 15, servants are not only allowed, but
even required, enjoined, and ordered to rest from their labours, re-
freshing themselves with amusements, when the Israelites are mindful
that they themselves had been slaves and chattels in Egypt, so now in
these days youths ought to be taught in Sunday sermons by what
reason (and) in what ways to behave in exercises and within what limits
to relax, jest, and play. What these people of whom we are speaking
used to do everywhere, removing, driving away, and taking away external and (morally) indifferent activities created, established, and ordained by God himself the best and greatest, instead of (developing)
a doctrine of the right practice of those very activities, ought not to
be done. I wonder myself what answer they can give, what excuse they
can make to the Lord in the future, for (their) contempt of his ordinance, (their) disparagement of his kindness in these pleasures and recreations.

For what else are they doing except teaching God himself what days
are quit of games, what days are especially suited to labour and other
employments, when they ought to work together, (and) when they
ought to refresh themselves? Does anyone not know, is anyone ignorant either that music is one of the liberal arts, part of a liberal education,
or that it is to no purpose and of no value without practice, playing,
round dances, applause, rejoicing, happiness, (and) delight?

K. When they, as if they were ignorant of these things, instruct no
one in them (and) wish no one to understand them, they are worthy
of (being) and deserve to be chastised, corrected, (and) strengthened
anew in these matters as in the rest of their enormous, odious, (and)
most absurd errors by the lord bishops and very honourable magis-
trates. But indeed it seems to me that the justices, judges, and even
some bishops have no small cause to fear that they might not act fairly
in their corrections and reformations. For unless they were to keep
in mind (what) we have said about the true nature of the puritans) for

Exodus 12.26
Joshua 4.6

Our Judges &
Justices –
Bishop of
the Diocese

A pole (was)
cast down in
St Nicholas'
parish,
Gloucester, on

July 10, 1618;
similarly in
a second case,
a little before
at Berkeley.

their own good, they would certainly be persuaded by those who are
usually and properly called puritans that such folk are extremely pious,
pure, (and) holy in all things. How (then) could they possibly carry
out assiduously for the king business as great as the size of (their) district is vast? We know that their (ie, the puritans') bragging (and)
showing off can through gifts and presents advance them with the
powerful in their pleading. Then those (who are) obedient (magis-
trates), whether presiding themselves or presenting (the puritans) as
disobedient or refractory, are neglected, not supported, not even cor-
roborated: indeed it goes well with them if they are not charged,
examined, (and) rejected; and that with most contemptuous expressions *(English)* etc. Thus these good officers towards ordained and
obedient ministers concerning or on behalf of those inflexible and disorderly (puritans)!

But I hope on this point that by God's grace (and) the outstanding
care of the royal majesty all this will be amended in future (and) be
better. But let them (ie, the loyal and obedient bishops and judges)
grant me these points because it is a matter of concern to me because
of my own experience. I Or if they should not wish to make allowances
and this proposal does not please (them), then let them hazard further
danger if it pleases (them) and let them find out by experience what
is true in this respect (ie, with respect to puritans' court appearances).
For their (ie, the puritans' and their fellow-travellers') treatment
thoroughly ruined me in this respect and in this way: it is neither necessary or possible for them to do worse or harm (me) more.

But why do I not rather turn my discourse to summer poles and
May pyramids, inveighing and clamouring against things which would
not be free to answer, as if they were dumb, mute, dead idols? Even
if they answer nothing, they are still charged with being diabolic idols;
all those May games, Whitsun ales, morris dances, various ritual
dances, many jests, the all but infinite varieties of games are likewise
charged with being forms of devil worship. But I answer that that is
not, need not be, cannot be, the situation if, as is piously requested,
(young people) are taught that (these games) should happen (only) in
proper and suitable places, at proper and suitable times, (and) without
either hindrance or neglect of divine worship.

In fact, they do dance round dances around the poles. The people
standing about and the crowd (which has) collected from every side
cast their eyes upon the pole; upon the lyrists, pipers, harpists; upon
the musical instruments; upon the dancers, their fellow players, their
fellow wrestlers; upon all the fun and jests. So also those who come
to the sanctuary, frequent the church, and often attend sacred

assemblies cast their eyes upon, look about at, gaze at the pulpits, the
Bibles, the preachers; they are awed and wonder at their sermons and
their chanting, customs, positions, and gestures. These things can and
should be wholesome and be made morally right in conformity with
doctrine; in this way they can and should be reformed.

Nay, rather, if it is not possible to achieve what is morally right and
perfect by diligently teaching what things are necessary for right use,
then things (which are) right and suitable will surely be irrecoverably
ruined gradually together with things (which are) imperfect, unnecessary, and intolerable – if there are any of that sort – without censure,
(without) their opposition, and (without) a choice. I recall what the
learned Ascham relates, that the lady Jane was so forcefully urged (and)
controlled by her mother, (so) compelled to dance strictly and with
equal steps in ritual dances, to observe each measure in every round
dance, to observe such countless steps and gesticulations, that she regarded all dancing with loathing and preferred to turn her attention
to and undertake to learn languages, both Greek and Latin, to ponder,
read, read thoroughly, reread, waste time over, slog through, (and)
pick apart the very learned ancient authors. Therefore the right use
of games ought to be taught and instilled (in people) rather than inveighing against abuses and the games themselves, because they will
either reform themselves in that way and be restored to a right use (of
games) or else they will reject all use (of games) automatically and completely for fear of the danger and scandal of abuses.

Let anyone who wants relaxation or sleep I during an illness but cannot sleep for the many recurring fantasies and the subjects, some
worse, some better, (which) whirl round, fly about, (and) trouble his
mind pray earnestly (and) pour forth prayers to God; soon drowsiness
will creep in and he will sleep sweetly, drowse deeply. Perhaps you
will say: The devil, who would not wish human beings to pray, to pour
forth pious prayers, to behave in any way holy, does that. As if it were
a great object of thought or concern to some who the originator of
these notions may be, so long as they pretend (it is) God and have their
own ways, wills, (and) plans allowed them and rejoice as they please.

'Trust in Bert, he's an expert,' as the saying goes. For I have found
these (observations) to be very true both at home and abroad. I have
seriously and diligently described the uses and abuses of (morally) indifferent activities, (and) the reason for and difference between these
(ie, use and abuse). I set to work with great urgency, in order that right
use only should be in use and practice. In time everything (abusive)
lost force altogether. Accordingly my situation is very different from
that of those peevish brethren in whose parishes crowds gather as soon

as the poles are raised, more to oppose the clamouring minister than
to give themselves pleasure in playful activities or to obey the king in
exercises and recreations.

And in Gloucester jail, where I have already spent some months,
everlasting God! How clearly, properly, praiseworthily everything is
going! There a pyramid has been erected, as it were; a summer pole
has been put up, as was said before. They have decided to practise the
aforesaid varieties of games. I do not gainsay nor yet forbid these activities, that is, exercises and recreations. But I demonstrate a proper
use: I teach how they should behave and take recreation. On this occasion I have established some statutes and ordinances especially suitable for the chapel and jail and I have caused them to be signed with
the hands and hearts – that is, the consent – of each and every inmate.
Good God! How modestly, honestly, piously one lives thereby! In
what a Christian way one spends the time! In order that this prison
or jail might be an example of piety and modesty to many others,
whether jails or societies, whether prisons or cities – as it is well
known that both towns and rural districts cast out and push off all
(their) depraved and vicious servants and members into prisons and
jails of this kind, as if to places and houses of correction where they
can be amended and reformed by the corrections of authority – these
statutes and ordinances of this kind have been inserted for this reason
here where anyone who is interested can gather my plan and the reason
for my deeds more easily.

(*English*)

And in this way and with this explanation all can easily inform themselves of the mind and plan of the royal majesty in so far as (it pertains)
to the aforesaid as it were Olympic games, liberal exercises, and recreations (and) at the same time of the frank consent, dutiful submission, right construction, services, and obedience, both prompt and
very ready, of all faithful subjects. Off with the puritans, who deny
bodily exercises on Lord's Day! Off with the papists, who are deterred
from our religion because they think that no (religion) approves, no
(religion) admits Christian recreation!

To both sides (the king) forbids (recreation) unless they first come
together in sacred assemblies to celebrate divine service together. This
both refuse to do: the papists think it schismatic (and) the puritans
(think it) popish and impious, both pulling together under one yoke,
fighting together under one banner with nothing short of profane men,
actors, rogues, and reprobates, whether wild or hardened, who cannot
in any way bear to be involved in common prayers, the customary petitions of the faithful, the most pious supplications of Christians – but

(I have said) enough and more already before about these matters. (Now I shall add) to these matters a few facts from my own experience.

One day about two years ago, more or less, I was at Cirencester for dinner with Mr Archdeacon and the ministers and preachers of his deanery. While we were in that monastic conclave, some musicians came to us, lyrists, those called *Myntyi*, promising us some of their music, harmony, and melody. Soon one of the ministers – I have decided he should be named lest I bring any aspersion of some fault or flaw and any notice upon the rest, (who were) generous, liberal, and innocent – Alder by name, said: Be off with them! Be off! What are they doing here? They are vagabonds under the Act and the head and cause of many evils among the people and populace. They, immediately intending to go, not even daring to murmur as far as I could hear, were called back by no one. Finally I (said): Well done, gentlemen, well done! Stay a bit, perhaps we will listen willingly. I turned to (Alder who was) denouncing me. I said: Why should they go, pray tell? Do they not come willingly, if in fact they (have) not been sent for? Do they not come with affection and respect for us? Is not divine providence revealed in this as in other events? Is not music allowed us just as much as tables and dinner parties (are)? Or are we like those (ministers) who completely refuse to take part in the churching of women after childbirth, alleging that is a papist superstition, but are very pleasurably present along with the women for the delicacies and dainties (ie, served afterwards?), the eating and drinking?

Is not music one of the liberal arts? 'Grammar speaks, dialectic teaches what is true, rhetoric adorns words, music sings, arithmetic counts, geometry weighs, astronomy studies the stars.' Might not those men gladly have the fruits (and) reap happiness as well as utility from their art, skill, (and) profession, as we do? Alas, how many days, nights, weeks, months, years, not to say (their) whole miserable life, have these wretches spent, passed, (and) used up, starving, in order to acquire some skill in singing, playing a stringed instrument, striking strings either by using the pick or touching them gracefully with the fingers so as to please, wonderfully delight, exhilarate, (and) gratify us the more? Do we receive them, treat them, act kindly toward them in such a way by the aforesaid means, that is, by contumely and insults?

Let us be silent and rather treat them with humanity. Do we not remember what that most holy David says most profusely in the psalms and elsewhere in favour of psalmody, music, (and) musical har-

6/ harmony *translates both* harmonia *and* symphonia

Servants of Lord Grey, Lord Chandos

mony, and how plainly and fully he describes them? Leaving this or that occasion aside as well known to all in this regard, let us be mindful Verse 15 of the passage in Holy Writ about the prophet Elisha, in the third chapter of the second book of Kings: Bring in, he says, the singer accompanying himself upon the lyre or some musician. For while a lyrist or a piper played and sang, the hand of God was upon him and he prophesied. Do you not see here, my beloved brethren, that the prophet was roused to prophesy to a greater degree by melodious music? Pehaps in the same way we, after the harmonious music of these men, will give thanks more appositely to God the best (and) greatest for these and his innumerable other benefits conferred upon us. Mr Archdeacon, Mr Sutton, (and) all the rest as far as I know agreed with the sweetest concord; the musicians came nearer, harped, played, sounded (their) instruments, made a loud noise, (and) jingled: they pleased and delighted us. I, being refined, do not say I actually extorted, but I did easily collect a penny given and contributed by each of the ministers in lieu of a dinner charge: I received several shillings thus collected for the musicians. They were appeased (for our bad behaviour) and went away thankful.

Therefore, for my part, there is no need that, no reason given why, anyone should say that the royal majesty is acting strictly, therefore injuriously, whereby, if he should call foxes' ears horns, ears must be held to be horns. He is only calling ears, ears; horns, horns; men, men; (and) asses, asses; and willingly and at (his) pleasure he observes the Christian laws and pious decrees.

Thanks be to God. May the king live forever.

Endnotes

285–8 GDR 114 ff [4], [4v], [8], [8v]
The defendant in this case is Christopher Windle, vicar of Bisley. In 1618, Windle wrote a commentary on King James' *Book of Sports*, in which he justified his encouragement of maypoles and other games on the sabbath. The text of this commentary is printed in Appendix 3.

Each of the depositions continues as does Band's, with a description of Windle's sermon on numeration. The diamond brackets in f [8v] indicate words written near the right-hand margin which were obliterated when the gatherings were sewn together.

288–9 D855/M8 f 90v
The left-hand edge of the page is frayed. Only two of the amounts of the defendants' fines given in the left-hand margin appear to be complete. These both read x s so the fines were probably raised from the amounts first given in the text, which were 5s for all but Richard Clerke. The marginal amounts would thus all be 10s except the first, which would be 40s if doubled like the marginal amounts we can read.

Hannam-Clark, p 67, offers what appears to be a verbatim quotation of the first part of the entry, but actually condenses it somewhat. He also incorrectly identifies the year as 1612.

290 E 101/351/15 mb 1
The reference to playing the miracles of St Nicholas is not specifically located, but they were almost certainly performed at Gloucester. The payments recorded in this alms roll are given in approximate chronological order and grouped into paragraphs covering two weeks each, with the name of the place where the court happened to be at the beginning of the period noted in the left-hand margin. The St Nicholas play entry occurs in the paragraph begun at Worcester and follows payments made at Winchcombe and Newent, but precedes one made at Cricklade (the last entry in the paragraph). The next paragraph is headed Gloucester, and the date of the first entry is Sunday, 5 December, the vigil of St Nicholas. A later entry records the king's oblations on St Nicholas' day as being given 'apud Glouce*striam*.' While it is unclear why the accountant should have placed the St Nicholas play and Cricklade entries in the earlier paragraph, the progress of Edward I's entourage south from Worcester to Winchcombe and Newent in northern Gloucestershire would have naturally brought it next to Gloucester. (Cricklade, on the Gloucestershire-Wiltshire border, would not have been reached for several days, and it is this entry which is obviously out of place.) In addition, St Nicholas plays were

normally performed on the saint's day; most of the extant texts conclude with the *Te Deum*, the antiphon *O Christi pietas*, or some other link with the office of St Nicholas' day (Karl Young, *The Drama of the Medieval Church* (Oxford, 1933) 2, 308–9, 321–3, 333–4).

'eor*um* Ep*iscopo*' undoubtedly refers to a boy-bishop, as the festival of the boy-bishop was associated with St Nicholas' day in many places, rather than with the feast of the Holy Innocents. In fact, the boy-bishop is sometimes known as the 'episcopus sancti Nicolai' or the 'episcopus Nicholatensis' (Chambers, *Mediaeval Stage*, vol 1, 369).

A question remains as to who actually performed the St Nicholas play and boy-bishop ceremonies. St Peter's Abbey seems the most likely place for a major celebration attending the visit of the king, but it would be most unusual for 'clericis' to mean the Benedictine monks. Gloucester offers no obvious solutions to this problem, such as the existence of a college of secular canons in the town. However, Llanthony Priory, just west of Gloucester, was a major house of Augustinian canons, who could be referred to as 'clerici.' Any such identification must of course remain conjectural.

290–1   No 1826   single mb
That there must have been abuses of the monastic rule at St Peter's Abbey in the years preceding the drafting of these statutes can only be inferred from the statutes themselves; no records of such abuses have survived. Abbot John de Gamages and the convent actually drew up these statutes in the form of a petition to Archbishop Winchelsey of Canterbury. After his metropolitical visitation of 1301, Winchelsey returned to the abbey a set of injunctions (*Historia et Cartularium Monasterii Sancti Petri Gloucestriae*, William Henry Hart (ed), vol 1, pp lxxxiv–xcii) which in large part confirmed the statutes, adding a few new regulations, but did not include the prohibition against the abbot's maintaining harpers or minstrels at community expense.

291   GBR F 3/2   single mb
The right edge of the roll has deteriorated badly and a section from the middle of the page is missing. The roll has also faded so that some letters are legible only under ultraviolet light and others not at all. The diamond brackets indicate both letters lost to deterioration and letters illegible due to fading.

'Ministrall'' has been left unexpanded because there is no way to determine whether it is singular or plural, except in the first entry.

291   GBR F 3/4   single mb
The right-hand edge of the roll has deteriorated and some other letters have been lost due to tears and fading. 'Ministrall'' has been left unexpanded because there is no way to determine whether it is singular or plural.

291–2   Cotton Julius B xii   ff 18–18v
After his coronation, Henry vii made a tour of the provinces. At York he was received with elaborate pageants and speeches; he then turned south and west to Worcester and Hereford, where the pageantry was on a smaller scale. Next, he made his way to Gloucester and finally to Bristol, with overnight stops at Kingswood Abbey near Wotton under Edge and at the manor of Sir Robert Poynz (or Poyntz) at Iron Acton, a few miles north of Bristol.

292–3   GBR B 2/1   ff 116–16v
Mary Tudor was made princess of Wales in 1525 and sent to reside in the Marches with her
own council. She set out for her headquarters at Ludlow late in the summer, stopping first
at Thornbury, then at Gloucester, Tewkesbury, and Coventry (Carolyn Erickson, *Bloody
Mary* (Garden City, N.Y., 1978), p 60).

   Marginalia in a seventeenth-century hand have been added throughout this Corporation
Custumnal.

293–6   GBR B 2/1   ff 117v–19
The progress which brought Henry VIII and Anne Boleyn to Gloucester and the west occurred
shortly after the executions of Fisher (12 June) and More (6 July). However, the king's activities
during his visit to Gloucester appear to have been purely recreational rather than political.

296   GBR F 4/3   f 23v
Sir Anthony Kingston, son of the Sir William Kingston who was comptroller of the royal
household under Henry VIII (*DNB*, 11, p 185), lived at Painswick, six miles south of Gloucester.

296   GBR F 4/3   f 30
This entry is incorrectly assigned to 1550–1 by Murray (vol 2, p 276) and Hannam-Clark
(p 40).

297   GBR F 4/3   f 37v
'maist*er* Arnold' is Sir Nicholas Arnold, who resided at Highnam Court, two miles west of
Gloucester. His lord of misrule is mentioned in the accounts for 1563–4 (GBR F 4/3, f 100v).

   Sir John Brydges had been a groom of the privy chamber under Henry VIII, then lieutenant
of the Tower under Mary, for which she created him the first Baron Chandos in 1554 and
granted him Sudeley Castle and the lands around it, which had belonged to the executed
Thomas Seymour (*DNB*, 3, p 163). Although not yet Lord Chandos in 1553, Brydges was a
Gloucestershire man by birth, making it appropriate for his trumpeter to be sent to accompany
the announcement of Mary's accession.

   For the New Inn see p 423, endnote to GBR F 4/3, ff 78, 79.

297   GBR F 4/3   f 44
This payment is the sole record of players of the city of Gloucester.

298   GBR F 4/3   ff 78, 79
The Bothall (from 'booth hall') appears to have been the usual place for players to perform
when they were rewarded by the city; the chamberlains' accounts mention the Bothall frequently, but record a different performance site only once, when the queen's men played in
the cathedral churchyard in 1589–90 (GBR F 4/3, f 263). An indenture of 26 August 1569
between the city and Robert Ingram (GBR B 2/3, ff 138–9v) gives some indication of the shape
and uses of the Bothall, which stood in Westgate Street on the site of the modern Shire Hall.
It contained one large hall, a smaller one sometimes called the 'shreeve hall,' and at the top
of the stairs the election chamber, reserved by the mayor and aldermen for their meetings.
Performances could conceivably have been given in any of these rooms, even in the election

chamber, for at Worcester an ordinance was made prohibiting plays in the council chamber and restricting them to the lower end of the hall (Murray, vol 2, p 409). However, the kind of public performance attended by R. Willis and described in his *Mount Tabor* (see pp 362–4), 'where every one that will comes in without money,' would have required the large hall. The usual daily function of this hall was as the town market, especially for the weighing and selling of wool. It also served as the customary seat of the assizes when they were in session, and could be used for other large meetings. Although the Bothall was being used several times a year for dramatic performances when the Ingram indenture was made, this use is not among the many mentioned in the indenture.

Photographs of the New Inn in Northgate Street, Gloucester have often been included in histories of the theatre because it possesses the best-preserved example of the inn-yard which some believe to have influenced the shape and décor of the London public theatres. The extant records, however, contain no evidence that players ever performed in the yard of the New Inn. While it may have been the scene of performances not sponsored by the city, which would not show up in the chamberlains' accounts, the only entertainments known to have taken place at the New Inn occurred when the civic waits furnished music for the feasts occasionally held there by the Tanners' guild, and these certainly happened indoors, not in the yard (GCL 28652 [18], f 55v, *passim*).

298   GBR F 4/3   ff 83v–4
The trumpeter mentioned here is the lord president of the marches' trumpeter. The ellipses represent several gifts given to the lord president which have not been transcribed.

299   GBR F 4/3   f 89
'Mr Ingram' is Robert Ingram, lessee of the Bothall, where the players performed. The tavern where the players were sometimes fêted after a performance was probably the one in the Bothall itself. (The existence of this tavern is attested to by a rental of 1445, *Rental of all the houses in Gloucester, from a roll in the possession of the corporation of Gloucester, compiled by Robert Cole*, W.H. Stevenson (ed) (Gloucester, 1890)).

299   GBR F 4/3   f 100v
Highnam Court was the residence of Sir Nicholas Arnold.

301   GBR F 4/3   f 128v
The transcribed entries appear on the second of two folios designated f 128v.

301   GBR F 4/3   f 138
I am unable to identify the 'fenche Schole' with either of the two schools in Gloucester at this time: the Crypt or Christ's School in the parish of St Mary de Crypt, or the King's School connected to the cathedral.

302   GBR F 4/3   f 153
The 1 December 1573 date of the first entry is probably an error. While the accounts were written down at the end of the accounting year from temporary bills, and may not always have been set down in chronological order, the payments to players in the 1572–3 account

would be in chronological order if the 1 December payment to the earl of Worcester's players was made in December of 1572.

302–5   GBR F 4/3   ff 159v, 160v, 162

In the accounts for this year, each of the usual sections ('Gifts and Rewards,' 'Payments of Money') is followed by another group of accounts which are given the same marginal heading, but include only expenses related to Queen Elizabeth's visit to the city. (For instance, the second section headed 'Divers Rep*aracons*' does not deal with normal repair and maintenance of roads and civic structures, but only with repairs and new construction done in preparation to receive the queen.)

Queen Elizabeth came to Gloucester in early August of 1574. According to Walsingham's journal, the queen was at Sudeley Castle on 4 August ('The Journal of Sir Francis Walsingham, from Dec. 1570 to April 1583,' Charles Trice Martin (ed), *The Camden Miscellany*, vol 6, Camden Society, 104 (London, 1871), p 20. On the seventh, Walsingham arrived in Gloucester, but it is not certain that Elizabeth also arrived on that day, as Walsingham's itinerary differed from hers somewhat. She spent the night of 10 August at George Huntley's house at Frocester, an easy day's ride from Gloucester (GRO: P 153 IN 1/1). It seems likely that the queen arrived in Gloucester on or about the seventh of August and left on the tenth. The fourteenth brought her to Bristol, where she was greeted with the extensive speeches and pageants devised by Thomas Churchyard.

Unfortunately, no narrative description of Elizabeth's visits to Gloucester exists to compare with those of Mary Tudor's visit in 1525 and Henry VIII's in 1535. Still, a general picture of the reception Gloucester gave her can be pieced together from the chamberlains' accounts. As she had come from Sudeley, she would have entered Gloucester by the Outer Northgate, where musicians played and a scaffold had been erected for the presentation of some sort of pageant (GBR F 4/3, f 162). Another pageant scaffold awaited her at the High Cross in the centre of the city. Both of the buildings where the mayor and council conducted business had been 'dressed' for the occasion: the Tollsey, near the Cross, and the Bothall in Westgate Street. It must have been at one of these that the mayor and recorder received the queen, by kneeling on the benches mentioned in the accounts (f 159v).

At some point during her stay, Elizabeth must have paused at the King's Board in Westgate Street. While many of the civic structures had been mended and painted for the occasion, the King's Board was decorated with 'beastes' made by a man named Gilden, and presumably included the antelope and unicorns for which William Sannes was paid for providing horns, and the dragon for which he made a tongue (f 162). The King's Board was a decagonal structure about fifteen feet across with open arches on five sides which may originally have been used for public masses but had been turned to the sale of butter and cheese (M.H. Medland, 'The So-Called King's Board at Tibberton Court, near Gloucester', *TBGAS* 26 (1903), 339–41). The beasts may simply have formed a decorative tableau, although the low roof of the King's Board could also have been used as a pageant stage in the same way as were the water conduits in London (Wickham, *EES*, vol 1, pp 54–5).

A third scaffold was set up in the 'meadowe,' an open area just outside Gloucester's Southgate. Since the queen proceeded south towards Frocester on leaving the city, this scaffold may have provided the setting for a farewell pageant. The Southgate itself, however, would have been the more common location for such a pageant and Churchyard's description of his Bristol entertainments suggests another possibility (*The First Parte of Churchyardes Chippes* (London, Thomas Marsh, 1575; *STC*: 5232), ff 101v–2). Bristol greeted Queen Elizabeth with speeches by personified figures (Fame, Salutation, Gratulation, Obedient Good Will) at the city gate and High Cross. On the following three days, the entertainment moved outside the city walls to a place known as 'The Marsh,' a site similar to the 'meadowe' mentioned in the Gloucester accounts. This more open location allowed for pageantry on a scale impossible in the cramped city streets, involving mock battles around a fort and even including the arrival of three ships sailing up the Avon to bring aid to the besieged fort. The scaffold in Gloucester's 'meadowe,' then, may have been the site of a more extensive pageant on one of the days Elizabeth remained in Gloucester, though certainly less lavish than the Bristol pageantry, which cost that city nearly £1000 (David M. Bergeron, *English Civic Pageantry*, 1558–1642 (Columbia, S.C., 1971), p 26), in contrast to Gloucester's expenditure of about £130 (GBR F 4/3, f 162).

305–6   GBR F 4/3   f 195v
Murray (vol 2, p 281) gives the amount paid to Lord Berkeley's players as 13s 6d, perhaps thinking of the common figure of 13s 4d.

306   GBR F 4/3   f 198v
Although Garret Barnes is not identified as 'the musici*o*n' until the accounts for 1582–3 (f 218), his annual fee of 20s is first recorded in this entry.

306   GBR F 4/3   f 199v
Murray (vol 2, p 281) does not transcribe the interlineation, which not only records the payment to the Countess of Essex's players but also changes the amount given to Baron Kinderton's players.

306–7   GBR B 3/1   ff 71v–2
The marginal note 'pg. 130:' refers to the page containing an ordinance of 1591 which reaffirms and amends the 1580 ordinance regulating players.

308   GBR F 4/3   f 214
The payment to the queen's puppet players on the seventh of December may have been incorrectly ascribed to 1582. Since, however, the entry is the last one listed regarding players, it is more likely that the chamberlains were quite late rendering their accounts in 1582 and included under 1581–2 a reward which was given well after Michaelmas and thus properly belonged to the 1582–3 accounting year.

311   GBR B 3/1   f 130
The marginal notation '⟨dat⟩.71.' refers to the page on which the 'one former ordinance' regulating players appears (GBR B 3/1, ff 71v–2).

312   GBR F 4/3   f 279
The queen's 1592 progress through Gloucestershire took her to a number of the county's great

houses, including Sherborne House, home of the Duttons, Sir Richard Berkeley's manor at Rendcombe, and Sudeley Castle, where Lord Chandos received her with the pageant entertainments printed under Brydges 1591–2. Unlike her 1574 progress, this one did not stop at Gloucester, so the city fathers made a gift of £6 13s 4d to Lord Chandos 'for gratificacion against the receauing of the Queenes Maiesty at Sudely.' (They may well have been grateful to escape the expense and disruption of normal city operations caused by the queen's visit in 1574.)

313   GBR F 4/3   f 305
It is not clear what 'Anthonie Cooke and his companie' did at Midsummer to earn their reward. This entry has been included in order to link the following one with the Midsummer date. The choice of prepositions in the entry concerning Thomas Bubbe and his wagon is interesting: the wagon is not to be used 'for' the pageant, which would indicate that 'pageant' here meant the stage for a performance, but rather 'in' the pageant, suggesting that 'pageant' means the performance itself. Such a pageant might have included other wagons, and performers mounted and on foot. The phrase, 'for the turke' could thus apply only to Bubbe's wagon, or to the pageant as a whole.

314–15   GDR 89   ff [116v], [117]
John Wylmott, rector of Tortworth parish in southern Gloucestershire, was presented before the consistory court of Gloucester diocese on a variety of charges ranging from drunkenness and gambling to using witchcraft to poach the lord's deer and conies. (Cf Tortworth 1602 for depositions which give a fascinating description of the 'Cushin dawnce' performed by Wylmott and some of his parishioners.) Some of the accusations are quite incredible and may indeed have been trumped up. Several of the witnesses testified that Wylmott and the man who had appointed him to the Tortworth living, Sir Thomas Throckmorton, had been 'at varryaunce' for some time. As the witnesses against Wylmott were all servants, tenants, or relatives of Throckmorton's, it could be that the local lord exerted a good deal of pressure on them to help rid him of a troublesome minister. Still, the description of a play given in these depositions must have had enough truth in it to make the witnesses' stories plausible.

316   28652/18   f [52v]
The accounts of the Tanners' company were rendered by each master within a few days of leaving office. The master's own dinner, at which music was often provided, took place when he assumed office on St Clement's day (Tanners' company ordinances, 1541, GCL: 28652/4). The master's dinner mentioned in this year's accounts, which were rendered on or about the 23rd of November 1609, therefore happened on 23 November 1608. (The expenses for the master's dinner were frequently entered near the end of the year's accounts, but this was the result of convention, rather than an attempt to put the accounts in chronological order.)

317   28652/18   f [55v]
The Tanners had a hall of their own, but occasionally held their dinners at the New Inn, which still stands in Northgate Street.

322   GBR F 4/4   f 37
John Merowe (or Merro) appears to have been responsible for teaching music to the students at Christ's School ('Cristie,' also known as the Crypt School).

323   GBR B 3/2 p 3
The new annual wage of £4 doubled the waits' previous wage of 40s, although their number had only been increased from four to six. From later accounts it appears that each man received 10s as his wage, with the remaining £1 going for their liveries. In 1643–4, the fee dropped to £3, but it was restored in 1647–8, the entry explaining:

> Paid to mr Alderman William Singleton towards the charge of the Waytes
> Liveryes their wages yearely being formerly iij li per annum but by
> custome that yeare they haue their Liveryes to pay them 04–00–00 (GBR
> F 4/5, f 364v)

Thereafter the fee alternated between £3 and £4 until after the Restoration, indicating that the waits received an allowance for their livery every second year.

325   D 936 A 1/1 p 272
Abloads Court was a residence of the bishop of Gloucester, situated about a mile north of the city. The waits likely played as the entertainment at a dinner or other festive occasion.

326   GBR F 4/5   f 40
While plague had become a convenient excuse for getting rid of unwanted entertainers during the 1620s and 30s, Gloucester's fear of plague in 1636–7 was surely genuine. The epidemic raged in London that year, and when it spread to Worcester in the spring of 1637, the mayor and aldermen ordered a watch set at Gloucester's gates. At first the watch simply questioned any suspicious persons, but when Worcester's troubles increased, it began to turn away all strangers (GBR 1454/1543, ff 10v–12). The city's vigilance had some success in preventing the spread of the disease, but by 1638, the council had to excuse the mayor and sheriffs from providing their traditional installation banquet because of plague (GBR B 3/2, pp 95–6).

335   Cotton Vespasian F xiii #187   f 240
Mary Tudor was made princess of Wales in 1525 and sent to reside in the Marches, headquartered at Ludlow Castle. She set out for Ludlow in the late summer, travelling through Thornbury, Gloucester, and Tewkesbury. The signatories to the letter were all members of the princess' entourage. John Veysey, bishop of Exeter, was president of her council; Giles Grevile, her comptroller; Peter Burnell, her almoner (Carolyn Erickson, *Bloody Mary* (Garden City, N.Y., 1978), pp 61–2). John Salter, George Bromley, and Thomas Audeley were all lawyers attached to her council (Frederick Madden (ed), *Privy Purse Expenses of the Princess Mary* (London, 1831), p xxxix).

337–8   P 329 CW 2/1 p 66
An entry regarding seat money later in the same year's accounts reveals that Roger Wiette was a resident of Tewkesbury parish, the only one of those who rented the 'players apparell' who can definitely be identified as a parishioner.

338   P 329 CW 2/1 p 74

These accounts were rendered 7 August 1583 and, as the previous accounts were rendered in 1580, this set may cover a three-year period. The Tewkesbury churchwardens made up their accounts when they left office, which occurred at irregular intervals. A three-year tenure would have been unusual, but not so much so as to indicate that some accounts have been lost or unrecorded, especially as these accounts are relatively lengthy.

339   TBR A 1/1   f 15

The 'tenshall money' paid out by the bailiffs probably refers to the fee charged a *tenser*: 'an inhabitant of a city or borough who was not a citizen or freeman, but paid a rate for permission to reside or trade' (*OED*). The word occurs several times in records connected with Tewkesbury, variously spelled *tenshall, tensell*, and *tensiall* (C.R. Elrington (ed), *VCH Glouc*, vol 8 (London, 1968), p 147.)

340–2   P 329 CW 2/1 pp 130–1

These receipts and expenditures connected with the construction of a battlement on the church tower appear in a special section of accounts following the regular accounts rendered in 1600.

Parishes in southern England frequently put on plays with ales to raise money, so the churchwardens may have been reviving a parish tradition. The accounts, however, make no explicit connection between plays and ales before the entry in 1600. Ales during Whitsun had been a much more lucrative source of income than renting out the parish wardrobe: in 1566–7, an ale brought in £11 10s (P 329 CW 2/1, p 14). The latest receipts from a church ale at Tewkesbury were recorded in the accounts for 1571–2, although the churchwardens may have disguised receipts from later ales due to growing opposition to ales from the church hierarchy.

The expenditures on the plays alone totalled £11 12s 9d, while the receipts amounted to only £12 7s 2d, for a meagre profit of 14s 5d. Yet the plays appear to have had an important part in the relative success of the whole venture, since the summary statement at the end of the accounts labels the total receipts from all sources as the amount 'they gained by there plays.' The contribution of the plays was undoubtedly to create a festive atmosphere in which grain valued at a little over six pounds could be sold for better than twelve. With the addition of £19 12s from the sale of lead and timber from the old spire, the total receipts of £45 2s left a deficit of only £21 4s to be made up in the following years from the total expenses for both the battlements and the plays of £66 6s 3d.

The plays may well have been performed in the nave of Tewkesbury Abbey, which had served as the parish church of the town's single large parish until the Dissolution. When the Royal Ministers declared the choir superfluous, along with the chapter house, cloisters, and other monastic buildings, the town managed to purchase the condemned section of the abbey from the Crown, for the estimated value of the bells and lead from the roof – £483. The parish then appears to have moved into the choir and the nave appears to have been neglected (James Bennett, *The History of Tewkesbury* (Tewkesbury, 1830; rpt Dursley, Glouc., 1976), pp 125–7; H.J.L.J. Massé, *The Abbey Church of Tewkesbury, with Some Account of the Priory Church of Deerhurst, Gloucestershire* (London, 1900), pp 14–16). Wherever the plays were located inside the abbey, the payment of 13s 4d 'for the place to playe in' is a curious one. Was the parish paying itself rent for the use of the church? Both the churchwardens' accounts and the borough minutes call the plays 'stage plays,' so perhaps 'place' is being used in the sense of a delineated space in which to perform, a stage constructed inside the abbey.

The 30s paid to 'T.B. for his charges' is an unusually large sum for a single individual. A possible explanation may be found in the records of Chelmsford and several other south-eastern towns, which contain references to 'property players.' The property player was a professional man of the theatre, brought in (probably from London) to organize and direct local productions. His services included supervising the construction of stages, marshalling of costumes and props, direction of the players, and perhaps himself acting important roles (John C. Coldewey, 'That Enterprising Property Player: Semi-Professional Drama in Sixteenth-Century England,' *Theatre Notebook*, 31 (1977), p 6). Such a man would have been invaluable to Tewkesbury, which remembered its dramatic tradition, but was no longer familiar enough with the practicalities of performance to mount the sort of spectacle which would bring in a profit.

342–3   GDR 89   ff [106], [106v]
Cf endnote p 427 to pp 314–15, GDR 89, ff [116v], [117].

344   GDR 32 p 178
Michael Hyndemer was instituted rector of Weston Subedge in 1567 (GDR 16, p 22). Hyndemer had been accused before the consistory court by one Agnes Tise of calling her whore, but the other witnesses answered only that they believe the first article (regarding masking) to be true, which Hyndemer himself here admits.

The phrase 'ann egge brok' might be a name, Anne Edgebrook, but it can also bear the meanings 'an egg broken,' 'a sword broken.' It is impossible to be more precise; Hyndemer's answer to the first article is printed here in its entirety, and neither it nor the document as a whole provides any clues to the meaning of the phrase.

347   Ms. Misc. IX   f 30v
The entry occurs in a group of undated foreign payments listed at the beginning of the household book.

The 'lady' mentioned here is Elizabeth Berkeley, countess of Warwick. Richard Beauchamp, the earl of Warwick, was fighting in France with Henry V during most of the period covered by the household book.

347   Ms. Misc. IX   f 57
The accounts for the Christmas holidays, 24 December to 6 January, have been lumped together and no guest list is provided for this period.

The six from Slimbridge and four from Wotton who were rewarded for playing ('ludent*ibus*') were probably tenants hoping to gain favour with the landlord by entertaining Lady Berkeley at Christmas. Slimbridge, a village four miles north of Berkeley Castle, was on the Berkeley estate, and the Berkeleys maintained a favourite residence at Wotton under Edge, five miles south-east of the castle.

The 'hostelar*ia*' and 'hospicio' mentioned in these accounts probably refer to an inn in the town of Berkeley, which adjoins the castle. They may, however, indicate the existence of a guesthouse within the castle itself.

348   General Series Bound Book # 109   f 67
Tortworth park was on the estate of Sir Thomas Throckmorton.

357   D(W) 1721/1/5 p 44
The 'Cantatores Capelle' are the singers of the duke's own chapel at Thornbury.

357   D(W) 1721/1/5 p 56
The manuscript incorrectly gives the date for this day's accounts as 5 December rather than
5 January.

359   E 36/220 p 12
John Kyrk was a gentleman of Buckingham's household (Carole Rawcliffe, *The Staffords,
Earls of Stafford, and Dukes of Buckingham, 1394–1521* (Cambridge, 1978), p 241). George
Poley was Buckingham's treasurer from 1515 to 1520 (Rawcliffe, p 230).

361   D(W) 1721/1/5 p 46 col 2
The word 'vrs" (l. 13) probably represents a form of Latin 'ursarius', bearward. The 'le' which
here precedes it is usually used, within a Latin text, to signal the presence of a vernacular word,
but there is no English word beginning 'urs-' or 'vrs-' that makes sense in context and 'vrs"
occurs later in the accounts without the preceding 'le.'

368–86   A Book, for a Buck with a Parke ... pp 5–21
Windle's abbreviated forms of biblical book titles have not been fully expanded, as they would
normally be, because there is no consistent way of doing so. Windle uses some forms which
are clearly abbreviations of the Latin names of books of the Bible, some which are abbreviations
of the English names, and some which could be either. The titles have been left unexpanded,
to avoid imposing a false consistency.

PATRONS AND TRAVELLING COMPANIES, GLOSSARIES, AND INDEX

Patrons and Travelling Companies

The following list has two sections. The first gives companies alphabetically by patron, according to the principal title under which their playing companies and entertainers appear, with cross-references from other titles if they are also so named in the records. The second section lists companies identified by place of origin, including counties for locations wherever identification is certain.

The biographical information supplied here has come entirely from printed sources, the chief of which are the following: S.T. Bindoff (ed), *The History of Parliament: The House of Commons 1509–1558*, 3 vols (London, 1982); *Calendar of Patent Rolls* (edited through 1576); *Calendar of State Papers*; G[eorge] E[dward] C[okayne], *The Complete Peerage...*; *The Dictionary of National Biography*; James E. Doyle, *The Official Baronage of England Showing the Succession, Dignities, and Offices of Every Peer from 1066 to 1885*, 3 vols (London, 1886); P.W. Hasler (ed), *The History of Parliament: The House of Commons 1558–1603*, 3 vols (London, 1981); and F. Maurice Powicke and E.B. Fryde (eds), *Handbook of British Chronology*. All dates are given in accordance with the style in the sources used. The authorities sometimes disagree over the dates of birth, death, creation, succession, and office tenure. Where this evidence conflicts, the *Calendar of State Papers*, *Calendar of Patent Rolls*, and similar collections are preferred: for example, *List of Sheriffs for England and Wales from the Earliest Times to A.D. 1831*, Public Record Office, Lists and Indexes, no 9 (London, 1898); J.H. Gleason, *The Justices of the Peace in England: 1558 to 1640* (Oxford, 1969); and J.C. Sainty, 'Lieutenants of Counties, 1585–1642,' *Bulletin of the Institute of Historical Research*, Special Supplement no 8 (May, 1970).

Normally each patron entry is divided into four sections. The first lists relevant personal data and titles of nobility with dates. Succession numbers are given only for the most important titles held by a person, as well as for those titles by which he or she is named in the records. These numbers follow the absolute sequence given in *The Complete Peerage* rather than the relative ones that begin afresh with each new creation. Knighthood dates are included only for minor gentry not possessing higher titles. The second section lists titles of jobs showing local connections and includes those known to have been used as titles of playing companies. Purely expeditionary military titles have been largely omitted, along with most minor Scottish and Irish landed titles. Where possible, the date of an appointment is taken from the date of a document assigning that position. If the appointment is stated in the document to be 'for life,' then these words follow the job title. If the original document has not been edited and a secondary source is used that states 'until death,' then this form appears. Otherwise dates of appointment and termination are given, if available. If the length of time an office is held is not known, then only the date of appointment is given. Alternatively, if the only evidence comes from a source dated some time during the period of tenure, then the word 'by' plus date appears. If only the date of termination is known, 'until' is used. Finally, if no dates at all are available, 'nd' follows the title of the job. The third section, for which information is often incomplete or unavailable, contains the names and locations of the patron's principal seats, and locations of other properties he or she is known to have held. Extensive property lists have been condensed. The fourth section is an annotated index by date of the appearances of each patron's company or companies in the records. Following the date are the page numbers in parentheses where the citations occur. If a patron's company appears under a title other than the usual or principal one, this other title is in parentheses next to the designation of the company.

The reader may also wish to refer to the Index for additional references to some of the patrons and to various unnamed companies and their players. When it has been possible to identify a patron of an unnamed company, the reference has been included here; otherwise the only references to such are in the Index.

Abbreviations

acc	acceded	JP	Justice of the Peace
adm	admiral	jt	joint
bapt	baptized	KG	Knight of the Garter
bet	between	kt	knight
br	brother	lieut	lieutenant
capt	captain	MP	Member of Parliament
co	county	nd	no date
comm	commissioner	Parl	Parliament
cr	created	PC	Privy Councillor
custos rot	custos rotulorum	pres	president
d	died	succ	succeeded
gen	general	summ	summoned
gov	governor	Univ	University

Companies Named by Patron

Abergavenny (Lady)
Joan Fitz Alan (1375–14 Nov 1435), married William Beauchamp, Lord Abergavenny (d 8 May 1411); held castle and honour of Abergavenny, Monmouthshire, Wales, in dower until death.

or

Isabel Le Despenser (26 Jul 1400–27 Dec 1439), married Richard Beauchamp, 2nd Lord Abergavenny (d 18 Mar 1421/2), 27 Jul 1411, and Richard de Beauchamp, 13th earl of Warwick, 26 Nov 1423.

minstrels	Glouc	Berkeley	1420–1 (347, 348)

Admiral
Charles Howard (c 1536–14 Dec 1624), succ as Baron Howard, 11 or 12 Jan 1572/3; cr 10th earl of Nottingham, 22 Oct 1597. Keeper of Oatlands Park, Surr, 1562; MP, Surr, 1563 and 1572; JP, Surr, by 1573, and Kent and Somers, 1608; lord lieut, Surr, sole, 1573 and 3 Jul 1585, and jt, 27 Jul 1621 until death and Suss, sole, 3 Jul 1585 and jt, 2 Sept 1586; lieut of musters, Surr, 1579; chamberlain of the Household, 1 Jan 1583/4– Jul 1585; PC, by 5 Mar 1583/4 until death; lord high adm, 8 Jul 1585– 27 Jan 1618/19; high steward, Guildford, Surr, from 1585; constable of Windsor Castle, 5 Dec 1588 and high steward of Windsor, 15 Jan 1592/3, both until death; keeper of Hampton Court, Midd, and bailiff and steward of several manors in Surr, 24 Mar 1593; chief justice in eyre south of Trent, 15 Jun 1597 until death; lord steward of the Household, 24 Oct 1597–Nov 1615; queen's lieut and capt gen in the south of England, 10 Aug 1599 and 14 Feb 1600/1. Seat at Effingham, Surr; manor of Haling, near Croydon, Surr, granted 3 Mar 1611/12; held many manors in Surr.

players	Glouc	Gloucester	1589–90 (311)
			1590–1 (312)
			1595–6 (314)

Albany see Charles Stuart under King

Bath
William Bourchier (1557–12 Jul 1623), succ as 4th earl of Bath, 10 Feb 1560/1. JP, Devon, 1584 or 1585 and Somers, 1584 and 1608; vice-adm, 1586, lord lieut, 12 Sept 1586 until death, recorder of Barnstaple by 1589, and eccles comm, Exeter, 11 Sept 1604, all in Devon. Seat at Tawstock; family residence at Bampton; owned manor of Ilfracombe; house near Barnstaple, all in Devon.

players	Glouc	Gloucester	1577–8 (306)

Beauchamp
Sir Edward Seymour (12 Oct 1537–6 Apr 1621), styled earl of Hertford, 1547 until his father's attainder, 12 Apr 1552; restored 1553 or 1554; cr Baron Beauchamp and earl of Hertford, 13 Jan 1558/9; imprisoned 1561; released after 27 Jan 1567/8. Jt comm of musters, Wilts, 1579; lord lieut, Somers and Wilts, 24 Apr 1601 until death; custos rot, Wilts, Jun 1603; JP, Hants, Linc, Midd, Somers, and Wilts, 10 Jan 1611. Seat at Elvetham, Hants.

or

Edward Seymour (21 or 24 Sept 1561–c 13 Jul 1612), son of Sir Edward, above, styled Lord Beauchamp.

players	Glouc	Gloucester	1589–90 (311)
			1590–1 (312)

Berkeley
Thomas de Berkeley (5 Jan 1352/3–13 Jul 1417), succ as 5th Lord Berkeley, 8 Jun 1368; styled Lord Lisle from 28 Jun 1382. Comm of array, Glouc, 1367, 1377, 1380–1, 1392, 1399, and 1403 and Bristol and Glouc, 1415; JP, Glouc, 1374–5, 1380, 1397–1401, 1404, 1406–8, and 1413–16; comm of oyer and terminer, Glouc, 1382, 1402, and 1413, Bristol, 1400, and Dors, Somers, Southants, and Wilts, 1401; PC, Feb 1395; adm of the South and West and capt, Brecknock Castle, Brecknockshire, Wales, 1403; jt warden of the Welsh Marches, 23 Jul 1403; regent of the Kingdom, Apr 1416. Lands in Essex, Glouc, Somers, Wilts, and the city of Bristol; inherited estates of the baronies of Lisle and Tyes through marriage and manors in Berks, Bucks, Cornw, Devon, Northants, Oxf, and Wilts, 1382; principal seat at Berkeley Castle, Glouc.

minstrels	Glouc	Gloucester	1409–10 (291)

Henry Berkeley (26 Nov 1534–26 Nov 1613), succ as 7th Lord Berkeley at birth. Keeper of Kingswood Forest, Glouc and Filwood, Somers, for life, 26 Jun 1559; JP, Glouc, 1562 and 1564; comm of oyer and terminer, Berks, Glouc, Heref, Oxf, Shrops, Staff, Worc, and Monmouthshire, Wales, 1564; jt comm of musters, Glouc, 1569; lord lieut, 14 Aug 1603 and vice adm, Glouc, 14 Nov 1603 until death. Principal residences at Yate Court, Glouc and Caludon Castle near Coventry, Warw; lands included manors in Glouc, Leic, Somers, Suss, and Warw.

players	Glouc	Gloucester	1577–8 (305)
			1578–9 (306)
			1579–80 (306)
			1580–1 (308)
			1581–2 (308)
			1582–3 (308)
			1584–5 (309)

Buckingham

Edward Stafford (3 Feb 1477/8–17 May 1521), restored as 3rd duke of Buckingham, earl of Stafford, 7th earl of Buckingham, and Lord Stafford, Nov 1485. PC, 1509; JP, Bucks, 1503–4, 1507, 1509–10, 1512, and 1514, Glouc, 1500–6, 1508, 1510–11, 1513–15, and 1520, Heref, 1503, 1505, 1507, 1509–10, 1513–15, and 1521, Kent, 1498–1506, 1509–10, 1512, 1514–15, and 1517, Shrops, 1503–4, 1510–11 and 1513–14, Somers, 1503, 1505, 1506–8, 1509, 1512–15, and 1521, Staff, 1503–4, 1508, 1509–11, 1514, and 1520, Surr, 1499–1506, 1511–12, 1514–15, 1518, and 1520, Warw, 1503, 1506–7, 1509–11, and 1514–15, and Yorks, ER, 1503, 1506–7, 1509–11 and 1514; beheaded 17 May 1521. Seats at Thornbury, Glouc and Brecknock Castle, Brecknockshire, Wales; manor at Penshurst, Kent.

minstrels	Glouc	Thornbury	1503–4 (356)
			1507–8 (356, 357, 358, 360)
players	Glouc	Thornbury	1507–8 (357, 358)
players (lord of Writtle)	Glouc	Thornbury	1507–8 (357, 360)
trumpeters	Glouc	Thornbury	1507–8 (356, 357, 358, 360)

Chandos

John Brydges (9 Mar 1491/2–12 Apr 1557), cr 1st Baron Chandos, 8 Apr 1554. Comm of musters, Glouc, 1522 and Wilts, 1 Mar 1539 and 1 Oct 1542; comm for subsidy, Glouc, 30 Aug 1523–4; JP, Glouc, 1528, 1531–2, 1537, 1539–40, 1542, 1544–5, 1547, and 1554, Heref, 1540, and 1543–4, Wilts, 1531–2, 1537, 1543–4, 1547, and 1554, and Berks, Oxf, Shrops, Staff, and Worc, 1540; MP, Glouc, 1529–36; jt keeper of the manor and park of Langley and of Cornbury Park, Oxf, 10 Jun 1536; comm of jail delivery, Gloucester Castle, 16 Oct 1537; sheriff, Wilts, 14 Nov 1537–8 and Glouc, 12 Nov 1549–50; constable of Sudeley Castle, sole, 21 Mar 1538–42 and jt, 15 Oct 1542 until death; comm of oyer and terminer, Berks, Heref, Oxf, Shrops, and Staff, 1539, 1541, and 1543–5, Glouc, 1540 and 1543–5, and Monmouthshire, Wales, 1543–5; jt steward, Winchcomb and hundreds of Greston, Holford, and Kiftsgate, all in Glouc, 15 Oct 1542 until death; comm of relief, Glouc and Wilts, 1550; comm of goods of churches and fraternities, Glouc, 1553; lieut of the Tower, Aug 1553–Jun 1554. Principal seat at Sudeley Castle, Glouc; held manor at Coberley, Glouc and many manors in Wilts.

| trumpeter | Glouc | Gloucester | 1552–3 (297) |

Edmund Brydges (by 1520–11 Mar 1572/3), son of John, 1st Baron Chandos, qv, succ as 2nd Baron Chandos, 12 Apr 1557. Jt constable, Sudeley Castle and jt steward, Winchcomb and hundreds of Greston, Holford, and Kiftsgate, all in Glouc, 15 Oct 1542–57, and sole, 1557 until death; MP, Wootton Bassett, Wilts, 1545 and Glouc,

Oct 1553; JP, Glouc, 1547, and Glouc and Wilts, 1554, 1562, and 1564 until death; comm of relief, Glouc, 16 Dec 1550; comm of musters, Glouc, 1557–8, 22 Jul 1569–80; steward and keeper of various manors in Wilts, 22 May 1557 until death and of the hundred of Slaughter, Glouc, 25 Oct 1567 until death; lord lieut, Glouc, 10 May 1559 and 20 Nov 1569; vice-adm, Glouc, 22 Jul 1561; steward, manor of Hailes, Glouc, 4 Jun 1563; comm of jail delivery, Berks, Glouc, Heref, Oxf, Shrops, Staff, Worc, and Monmouthshire, Wales, 1 Feb 1564. Principal seat at Sudeley Castle, Glouc; owned manors in Glouc, Wilts, and Worc.

| players | Glouc | Gloucester | 1558–9 (298) |

Giles Brydges (c 1548–21 Feb 1593/4), son of Edmund, 2nd Baron Chandos, qv, succ as 3rd Baron Chandos, 11 Mar 1572/3. JP, Glouc, 1570–1; MP, Cricklade, Wilts, 1571 and Glouc, 1572; chief steward of the manor of Hailes and of the hundreds of Greston, Holford, and Kiftsgate, all in Glouc, and steward of the hundred of Slaughter, Glouc and various manors in Wilts, all for life, 19 Jun 1573; lord lieut, Glouc, 17 Nov 1586 until death; member, Council in the Marches of Wales, 16 Dec 1590. Seat at Sudeley Castle, Glouc.

players	Glouc	Gloucester	1582–3 (308)
			1583–4 (309)
			1589–90 (311)
puppet players	Glouc	Gloucester	1589–90 (311)

William Brydges (after 1548–18 Nov 1602), br of Giles, 3rd Baron Chandos, qv, succ as 4th Baron Chandos, 21 Feb 1593/4. MP, Cricklade, Wilts, 1572 and Glouc, 1584 and 1586; steward of Cricklade, 1594; member, Council in the Marches of Wales, May 1594; lord lieut, Glouc, 9 Sept 1595 until death. Seat at Sudeley Castle, Glouc.

| players | Glouc | Gloucester | 1594–5 (313) |
| | | | 1595–6 (313) |

Grey Brydges (c 1579–10 Aug 1621), son of William, qv, succ as 5th Baron Chandos, 18 Nov 1602. MP, Cricklade, Wilts, 1597; imprisoned in the Fleet 14 Feb–31 Mar 1601; JP, Glouc and Wilts, 1603; keeper of Ditton Park, Bucks, for life, 2 Jul 1609; lord lieut, Glouc, jt, Aug 1603 and sole, 23 Dec 1613 until death; custos rot, Glouc, Mar 1614; member, Council in the Marches of Wales, 1617. Seat at Sudeley Castle, Glouc.

| musicians | Glouc | Cirencester | c 1616 (385) |

Clarence

Thomas, styled 'of Lancaster' (29 Sept 1389–22 Mar 1420/1), second son of Henry IV, qv, cr 2nd duke of Clarence and earl of Aumale, 9 Jul 1412. Seneschal of England, 4 Oct 1399; JP, Yorks, ER, 1400–1, 1405, 1407, 1409, 1411–12, 1416, and WR, 1414; chief gov of Ireland, 27 Jun 1401–13; lord high adm, 20 Feb 1405–28 Apr 1406; lieut of Ireland, 1 Mar 1406; pres of the Council, 1411; jt keeper of the castles, manors, and lands of the earldom of Somerset, 16 Jul 1412; high steward, Chester,

Ches and constable, Hawarden and Mohaut Castles, both in Flintshire, Wales, 27 Apr 1415.

| minstrel | Glouc | Berkeley | 1420–1 (347) |

Cobham

William Brooke (1 Nov 1527–6 Mar 1596/7), succ as 10th Lord Cobham, 29 Sept 1558. MP, Hythe, 1547 and Rochester, 1555, both in Kent; JP, Kent, 1558–9, 1562, and 1564 until death; lord warden of the Cinque Ports and constable of Dover Castle, both in Kent, for life, 28 Apr 1559; lord lieut, Kent, 26 May 1559 until death; comm, Rochester Bridge, 1571; PC, 19 Feb 1585/6 and keeper of Eltham Palace and Park, Kent, 1592, both until death; lord chamberlain of the Household, 8 Aug 1596 until death. Seat at Cobham Hall, Kent.

| players | Glouc | Gloucester | 1563–4 (300) |

Codnor

Sir Richard Grey (c 1371–1 Aug 1418), succ as 4th Lord Grey, 14 Dec 1392. JP, Derb, 1399, 1401, 1404, 1406–8, 1410, 1413, and 1415, Essex, 1402, 1404, 1405–7, 1410–14, and 1416, Kent, 1404, 1406–7, 1411, 1413–14, and 1416, and Leic, 1404, 1406–8, and 1412–14; gov, Roxburgh Castle, Roxburgh, Scotland, 1400; adm of the fleet from the mouth of the Thames to the North, 20 Apr 1401; keeper, Brecknock Castle, Brecknockshire, Wales and Horston Castle, Derb, 1405; lieut at Brecknock and in Heref and adjacent Marches, Oct 1405; constable of Nottingham Castle, Nott, 1 Nov 1406; lieut of South Wales, 2 Dec 1405–1 Feb 1406; justice of South Wales during pleasure, 28 Nov 1403 and 6 Sept 1407; jt warden of the East and West Marches, 1415. Seat at Codnor, Derb; granted lordships of Knighton, Cnwclas, and Cefn Llys, all in Radnorshire, Wales, 27 Jan 1405/6; held manors in Derb, Essex, Hants, Kent, Northants, and Nott, and through marriage, portions of manors in Leic, Linc, Rut, and Staff.

| minstrels | Glouc | Gloucester | 1409–10 (291) |

Compton

Henry Compton (14 Jul 1544–bef 22 Nov 1589), summ to Parl as 1st Lord Compton, 8 May 1572. MP, Old Sarum, Wilts, 1563; sheriff, Warw, 14 Nov 1571; JP, Northants, 1584. Seats at Compton Wynyates, Warw and Tottenham, Midd.

| players | Glouc | Gloucester | 1575–6 (305) |

Comptroller

James Croft (1517/18–4 Sept 1590), kt 24 Nov 1547. MP, Heref, 1542, 1563, 1571–2, 1584, 1586, and 1589; capt, Haddington, Linc, by Jun–Sept 1549; member, 1550 and vice-pres, 1550–1, Council in the Marches of Wales; lord deputy of Ireland, 29 Apr 1551–Apr 1553; deputy constable of the Tower of London, 1 May?–8 Jul 1553; imprisoned in the Tower, 21 Feb 1554–18 Jan 1555; member, Council of the North,

1557; restored in blood, 3 Mar 1559; JP, Heref, 1559, 1562, and 1564, and in most Marcher and Welsh cos, 1573, all until death; seneschal of Hereford, Heref, 1559; gov, Berwick upon Tweed, Northumb, 14 Apr 1559–21 Aug 1560; comm of musters, Heref, 1569; steward, Heref, by 1570; comptroller of the Household, steward, Kedewen, Kerry, and Montgomery, all in Montgomeryshire, and constable, Aberystwyth Castle, Cardiganshire, and Montgomery Castle, all in Wales, 1570; PC, 24 May 1570; steward, Leominster, Heref, by 1571; custos rot, Heref, c 1573; imprisoned Aug 1588–18 Dec 1589. Seats at Croft Castle and Shobdon, both in Heref; granted lands in Heref and Kent, 3 Mar 1559.

| players | Glouc | Gloucester | 1574–5 (305) |

Cumberland

Francis Clifford (1559–21 Jan 1641), succ as 4th earl of Cumberland and hereditary sheriff of Westmld, 19 Oct 1605. MP, Westmld, 1584, 1586, and Yorks, 1604; JP, Yorks, ER and WR, 1592; sheriff, Yorks, 24 Nov 1600–1; jt constable and steward, Knaresborough, Yorks, WR, 1604; keeper, Carlisle Castle, Cumb, 1605 and Carlisle Gaol, 1606; custos rot, Cumb, 1606–39; lord lieut, Cumb, Newcastle upon Tyne, Northumb, and Westmld, jt, 27 Oct 1607–11, 11 Feb 1614–39, and sole, 1 Jul 1611–14, and Westmld, jt, 31 Aug 1639 until death; member, Council of the North, 1619. Estates in Cumb, Westmld, and Yorks, including Londesborough, Yorks, ER, castles of Appleby, Brougham, and Brough, all in Westmld, and of Skipton, Yorks, NR.

| waits | Cumb | Carlisle | 1613–14 (76) |

Curwen

Henry Curwen (d bet Mar 1623–Mar 1624), kt 28 Aug 1570. Sheriff, Cumb, 9 Nov 1619; MP, Cumb, 1620–1. Seat at Workington Hall, Workington, Cumb.

waits	Cumb	Naworth	1612–13 (135)
musicians	Cumb	Carlisle	1613–14 (75,76)
			1620–1 (99)

Dalston

John Dalston (1556–after 1621), kt 1603. JP, Cumb 1573 and Westmld, from 1601; sheriff, Cumb, 25 Nov 1583, 14 Nov 1586, 21 Nov 1594, and 5 Nov 1604; steward, barony of Burgh, by 1582; MP, Carlisle, 1589; capt, Carlisle Castle for life, 13 Nov 1589; eccles comm, Yorks, 1599; deputy warden of the West March, Jan 1603. Seat at Dalston Hall, Little Dalston, Cumb; inherited manors in Cumb, Westmld, and Yorks.

| musicians | Cumb | Carlisle | 1617–18 (87) |

Derby

Henry Stanley (Sept 1531–25 Sept 1593), styled Lord Strange until summ to Parl as

Lord Strange of Knockin, Shrops, 23 Jan 1558/9; succ as 13th earl of Derby and lord
of the Isle of Man, 24 Oct 1572. High steward, Ormskirk, Lanc, 6 Dec 1550; jt comm
of musters, Lancaster, 1569; lord lieut, 24 Oct 1572 until death and vice-adm, Lanc
and Ches, May 1574–87; eccles comm, York, 17 Jun 1577; PC, by 20 May 1585; lord
steward of the Household, after 4 Sept 1588–93; chamberlain of Chester, 5 Nov 1588–
93; member, Council of the North. Estates at Lathom and Knowsley, both in Lanc.

players (Lord Strange)	Glouc	Gloucester	1564–5 (300)
players	Glouc	Gloucester	1579–80 (306)

Ferdinando Stanley (c 1559–16 Apr 1594), son of Henry, 13th earl of Derby, qv,
styled Lord Strange from 1572; summ to Parl as Lord Strange, 28 Jan 1588/9; succ
as 14th earl of Derby and lord of the Isle of Man, 25 Sept 1593. Deputy lieut, 1585
and lord lieut, 25 Sept 1593 until death, Lanc and Ches; mayor of Liverpool, Lanc,
1588; vice-adm, Lanc and Ches, 1594.

players (Lord Strange)	Glouc	Gloucester	1580–1 (308)
			1591–2 (312)

William Stanley (c 1561–29 Sept 1642), succ as 15th earl of Derby, 16 Apr 1594;
confirmed in the lordship of the Isle of Man, 7 Jul 1609. PC, Mar–May 1603;
chamberlain, co palatine of Chester, 30 Oct 1603 and jt, with James Stanley, qv, for
life, 23 Oct 1626; lord lieut, Lanc and Ches, 22 Dec 1607, and jt with James for life,
12 Dec 1626; member, Council in the Marches of Wales, by 1617; vice-adm, Lanc
and Ches, 1619–38; jt steward of Furness, Lanc, 30 Nov 1627. Seats at Lathom and
Knowsley, Lanc; granted manor of Ormskirk and others in Lanc, 21 Jul 1603.

players	Glouc	Gloucester	1595–6 (314)
	Westmld	Kendal	1597–8 (177)
			1608–9 (181)
	Cumb	Workington	1628–9 (129)
	Westmld	Kendal	1628–9 (204)
			1635–6 (212)

James Stanley (31 Jan 1607–15 Oct 1651), son of William, 15th earl of Derby, qv,
summ to Parl as Lord Strange, 7 Mar 1627/8–3 Nov 1639; succ as 16th earl of Derby
and lord of the Isle of Man, 29 Sept 1642. MP, Liverpool, Lanc, 1625; lord lieut, Lanc
and Ches for life, jt, 12 Dec 1626 and sole, Chester, from 28 Feb 1642 and Lanc, from
29 Sept 1642; chamberlain of Chester for life, jt, 23 Oct 1626 and sole from 29 Sept
1642; jt steward of Furness, Lanc, 30 Nov 1627; lord lieut, North Wales, by 1642;
eccles comm in the North, 1629; jt high steward of Blackburn, Hidenowe, Rochdale,
and Tottington, all in Lanc, 8 Jun 1636; chief comm of array, Lanc, 11 Jun 1642;
alderman of Chester until 27 Oct 1646; capt gen, Ches, Lanc, Staff, Worc, and North

Wales, Aug 1651; custos rot, Lanc, nd; beheaded 15 Oct 1651.

players (Lord	Westmld	Kendal	1635–6 (213)
Strange)	Cumb	Workington	1636–7 (133)

Dudley

Edward Sutton or Dudley (bapt 17 Sept 1567–23 Jun 1643), succ as 5th Lord Dudley by 12 Aug 1586. MP, Staff, 1584; JP, Staff, by 1585 and Worc, 1608, 1626, and 1636; high steward, Norwich Cathedral, 1631–5. Seat at Dudley Castle, Staff.

players	Cumb	Carlisle	1619–20 (93)
			1626–7 (107)
	Westmld	Kendal	1632–3 (209)

Dudley (Lord Ambrose) *see* Warwick

Dudley (Mr)
Possibly

Edmund Dudley (nd), sheriff, Cumb, 7 Dec 1602 and 11 May 1623. Seat at Yanwath Hall, Yanwath, Westmld.

or

Thomas Dudley, son of Edmund, *qv*, sheriff, Cumb, 7 Nov 1622. Seat at Yanwath Hall, Yanwath, Westmld.

musician	Cumb	Carlisle	1608–9 (69)

Essex
Walter Devereux (16 Sept 1539–22 Sept 1576), succ as Viscount Hereford and Lord Ferrers, 27 Sept 1558 and as Lord Bourchier, 28 Jan 1570/1; cr 18th earl of Essex, 4 May 1572. Steward of Tamworth, Staff and of Welsh courts in Cardiganshire and in Widigada and Elfed, both in Carmarthenshire, steward and receiver of the lordship of Builth, Brecknockshire, Wales, and steward, surveyor, and receiver of Talley, Carmarthenshire, 8 Nov 1558; JP, Staff and Cardiganshire and Pembrokeshire, Wales, 1564; chief comm of musters, Staff, Jun 1569; lord lieut, Staff and city of Lichfield, Staff, 18 Nov 1569; constable, Carmarthen Castle, Carmarthenshire and chief steward and bailiff of the lordships of Arustley and Cavylocke, both in Montgomeryshire, Wales, for life, 17 May 1570; gov and capt gen of Ireland, 24 Jul 1573; earl marshal of Ireland, Mar 1574/5; member, Council in the Marches of Wales, Jun 1574; chief justice and chamberlain in South Wales, by 16 Jul 1574. Houses at Chartley, Staff and Llamphey, Pembrokeshire; granted manor of Marks Hall, Essex, 1571; sold lands in Cornw, Essex, Staff, Wilts, and Yorks, 1576; granted land in co Monaghan, Ireland, 9 May 1576.

players	Glouc	Gloucester	1572–3 (302)
			1574–5 (305)

Robert Devereux (19 Nov 1566–25 Feb 1600/1), styled Viscount Hereford until he succ as 19th earl of Essex, Lord Ferrers, and Lord Bourchier, 22 Sept 1576. PC, 25 Feb 1592/3; lord lieut, Staff, 1594, chancellor of Cambridge Univ and Univ of Dublin, 1598, and high steward of Yarmouth, Isle of Wight, 1598, all until death; lord lieut, Ireland, Mar–Nov 1599; beheaded 25 Feb 1600/1. Houses at Chartley, Staff and Lamphey, Pembrokeshire, Wales; manor of Keyston, Hunts, sold May 1590.

players	Glouc	Gloucester	1583–4 (309)
			1584–5 (309)
			1585–6 (310)
			1586–7 (310)
	Westmld	Kendal	1586–7 (172)

Essex (countess of)
Lettice Knollys (1539 or 1540–25 Dec 1634), married Walter Devereux, 18th earl of Essex, qv, bet 1560 and 1565, and Robert Dudley, 14th earl of Leicester, qv, 21 Sept 1578, and Sir Christopher Blount (d 18 Mar 1600/1), before Aug 1589.

players	Glouc	Gloucester	1578–9 (306)

Eure
Ralph Eure (24 Sept 1558–1 Apr 1617), succ as 3rd Baron Eure, 12 Feb 1593/4. JP, Yorks, NR, from c 1583 and Durham, c 1593; warden of the Middle Marches, 1595–8; sheriff, Yorks, 26 Nov 1593; member, 14 Aug 1594 until death and vice-pres, 1600, Council of the North; custos rot, Northumb, 1596; lord pres, Council in the Marches of Wales and lord lieut, Heref, Shrops, Worc, and Wales, 12 Sept 1607–17. Seats at Ingleby, Greenhow, Malton, and Stokesley, all in Yorks, NR.

players	Cumb	Carlisle	1602–3 (66)

Fortescue
Sir Andrew Fortescue. Not identified.

players	Glouc	Gloucester	1560–1 (298)

Mr Fortescue. Not identified.

players	Glouc	Gloucester	1568–9 (301)

Gloucester
Thomas of Woodstock (7 Jan 1354/5–8 or 9 Sept 1397), son of Edward III, cr earl of Buckingham, 16 Jul 1377, earl of Essex, 26 Oct 1380, and 1st duke of Gloucester, 6 Aug 1385. Guardian of the Kingdom during the king's absence, Jul 1355–May

1360; JP, Essex, 1376, 1386–7, 1390, and 1394, Glouc, 1376, and 1394, and Heref, 1376, 1385, and 1394; comm of array, Essex, 29 Apr 1377; keeper of the castles of Brecknock and Hay, Brecknockshire, Caldicot, Monmouthshire, and Newton, Pembrokeshire, all in Wales, and Huntingdon, Hunts, 24 May 1377; on various commissions in Essex, Glouc, and Heref, May 1381; chief comm of oyer and terminer, Camb, 1381; justice of Chester and North Wales, 8 Jun 1388–30 Mar 1394; constable of Gloucester Castle for life, 14 Feb 1389; sheriff, Rut, 6 May 1390; lieut of Ireland, 29 Apr–Jul 1392; imprisoned 10 Jul 1397. Seat at Pleshey, Essex; held custody of several manors in Essex, Glouc, Linc, Oxf, and Wilts; granted St Briavel's Castle, Glouc, 17 May 1384 and Castle Rising, Norf, 17 May 1386; secured reversions of Brustwick, Holderness, Yorks, ER and castle of Oakham, Rut, 6 May 1390.

minstrels   Glouc   Gloucester   1393–4 (291)

Grey

Charles Grey (c 1545–28 Sept 1623), succ as 17th earl of Kent and 10th Lord Grey, 31 Jan 1614/15. Lord lieut, Beds, sole, 25 Feb 1614/15 and jt, 27 Jul 1621. House in the Barbican, London and manor house at Blunham, Beds.

musicians   Glouc   Cirencester   c 1616 (385)

Greyndour

John Greyndour (c 1356–by 30 Oct 1416), kt by 1398. Constable of St Briavel's Castle and the forest of Dean, both in Glouc, 8 Nov 1385; granted custody of the lands of the late William Blount, during minority of his heir, 12 Oct 1399; comm in Wales, 16 May 1401, 23 Aug 1405, 28 Oct and 28 Nov 1412, 12 Jun 1413, and 16 Jun 1415; keeper of castle and lordship of Radnor and villages of Presteigne and Norton, all in Radnorshire, Wales, and villages of Kingsland and Pembridge, both in Heref, during pleasure, 24 Sept 1402; JP, Glouc, 1406–8, Heref, 1404–8 and 1413; comm to keep and govern castle, town, and lordship of Chepstow, Monmouthshire, Wales, 11 Jun 1405; comm of oyer and terminer, Glouc and Heref, 1405; sheriff, Glouc, 22 Nov 1405 and 10 Dec 1411; on various commissions in Glouc and Heref, Jan 1406; steward of the lordships of Usk and Caerleon, both in Monmouthshire, 29 Mar 1406. Enfeoffed of part of the manor of Little Dean, Glouc, 10 Mar 1383; granted lands in the lordship of Newport, Monmouthshire, 22 May 1408; held other lands in Glouc.

minstrels   Glouc   Gloucester   1409–10 (291)

Home

Alexander Home (c 1566–5 Apr 1619), restored as 6th Lord Home, 25 Jul 1578; cr earl of Home and Lord Dunglas, 4 Mar 1604/5. Warden of the East Marches, 1582–99; imprisoned, 1583–20 Jan 1584/5; sheriff, Berwickshire, Scotland, 1592; justiciary over the West, Middle, and East Marches, 7 Jul 1603; PC, 1603. Seat at Home Castle,

Berwickshire; granted priory of Coldingham, Berwickshire, 1592.

or

James Home (c 1607–13 Feb 1633), son of Alexander, 1st earl of Home, *qv*, styled Lord Dunglas until he succ as 2nd earl of Home and Dunglas, and 7th Lord Home, 5 Apr 1619.

fool	Cumb	Carlisle	1619–20 (95)

Hunsdon

Henry Carey (4 Mar 1525/6–23 Jul 1596), cr 1st Baron Hunsdon, 13 Jan 1558/9. MP, Buckingham, Bucks, 1547, Apr and Nov 1554, and 1555; JP, Essex, Herts, and Kent, 1562, 1564, and 1584, Beds, 1564, and Yorks, NR, 1584; gov of Berwick upon Tweed, Northumb, 25 Aug 1568–87; warden of the East Marches towards Scotland, 23 Oct 1571; PC, 16 Nov 1577; lord chamberlain of the Household, Jul 1585, lord lieut, Norf and Suff, 3 Jul 1585, and chief justice in eyre south of Trent, 1589, all until death; recorder of Cambridge and high steward of Ipswich, Suff and of Doncaster, Yorks, WR, 1590; chief justice itinerant of the royal forests south of Trent, 20 Dec 1591 until death; high steward of Oxford for life, 2 Mar 1591/2. Seats at Buckingham and Hunsdon, Herts; lands in Bucks, Derb, Essex, Hants, Herts, Kent, Wilts, and Yorks.

players	Glouc	Gloucester	1565–6 (300)
			1581–2 (308)

Kinderton

Thomas Venables (by 1513–19 Jul 1580), styled Baron Kinderton; kt 11 May 1544. Chamberlain, Middlewich, Ches, 1540–72; JP, Ches, 1543–6, 1547, 1562, and 1564 until death; sheriff, Ches, 1544–5 and 13 Nov 1556; comm of musters, Ches, by 1545; MP, Ches, Mar 1553 and 1563. Seat at Kinderton and lands in Bradwell, Eccleston, and Middlewich, all in Ches.

players	Glouc	Gloucester	1578–9 (306)

King

Richard Plantagenet (6 Jan 1367–14 Feb 1400), son of Edward, prince of Wales, and Joan, daughter of Edmund, earl of Kent; cr prince of Wales, 20 Nov 1376; acc as Richard II, 21 Jun 1377, crowned 16 Jul 1377. Abdicated 29 Sept 1399.

minstrels	Glouc	Gloucester	1393–4 (291)

Henry of Bolingbroke (Apr 1366–20 Mar 1413), son of John of Gaunt and Blanche of Lancaster; declared Henry IV by Parl, 30 Sept 1399; crowned 13 Oct 1399.

minstrels	Glouc	Gloucester	1409–10 (291)

Henry of Monmouth (9 Aug 1387–31 Aug 1422), son of Henry IV, *qv*, and Mary de
Bohun; cr prince of Wales, 15 Oct 1399; acc as Henry V, 20 Mar 1413; crowned
9 Apr 1413.

| minstrels (prince) | Glouc | Gloucester | 1409–10 (291) |

Henry Tudor (28 Jun 1491–28 Jan 1547), son of Henry VII and Elizabeth of York;
cr prince of Wales, 18 Feb 1503; acc as Henry VIII, 22 Apr 1509; crowned 24 Jun 1509.

| trumpeters | Glouc | Gloucester | 1534–5 (296) |

Edward Tudor (12 Oct 1537–6 Jul 1553), son of Henry VIII, *qv*, and Jane Seymour;
acc as Edward VI, 21 Jan 1547, crowned 20 Feb 1547. Edward Seymour, duke of
Somerset, designated his Protector.

| jester | Glouc | Gloucester | 1552–3 (297) |

James Stuart (19 Jun 1566–27 Mar 1625), son of Henry, Lord Darnley and Mary
Stuart, Queen of Scots, acc as James VI of Scotland, 24 Jul 1567 and as James I of
England, 24 Mar 1603; crowned 25 Jul 1603.

players	Cumb	Carlisle	1618–19 (91)
	Westmld	Kendal	1619–20 (187)
	Cumb	Carlisle	1620–1 (97, 99)
			1621–2 (101)
	Westmld	Kendal	1621–2 (188)
	Cumb	Carlisle	1622–3 (102)
	Westmld	Kendal	1622–3 (194)
juggler	Cumb	Carlisle	1621–2 (100)

Charles Stuart (19 Nov 1600–30 Jan 1649), son of James I, *qv*, and Anne of Denmark,
qv; cr duke of Albany, 23 Dec 1600; duke of York, 6 Jan 1605; succ as duke of
Cornwall, 6 Nov 1612; cr earl of Chester and prince of Wales, 4 Nov 1616; acc as
Charles I, 27 Mar 1625; crowned, 2 Feb 1625; executed, 30 Jan 1649.

players (duke of Albany)	Cumb	Carlisle	1610–11 (72)
players (prince)	Cumb	Naworth	1617–18 (136)
	Westmld	Kendal	1617–18 (186)
			1619–20 (187)
	Cumb	Carlisle	1620–1 (97)
		Naworth	1620–1 (138)
	Westmld	Kendal	1620–1 (187)
	Cumb	Carlisle	1622–3 (102)
	Westmld	Kendal	1622–3 (194)
players	Cumb	Carlisle	1624–5 (104)

	Westmld	Kendal	1625–6 (200)
			1626–7 (202)
	Cumb	Carlisle	1626–7 (107)
	Westmld	Kendal	1636–7 (213)
King's Revels	Cumb	Carlisle	1627–8 (109)
Company			

Kingston

Anthony Kingston (by 1512–14 Apr 1556), kt 2 May 1540. Keeper, town and castle of St Briavel's, Glouc, 1547; steward, castle and lordship of Berkeley, Glouc, 1531 and duchy of Lancaster, Glouc, and Heref, 5 Feb 1541, all until death, and various manors in Glouc and Worc, 28 Jun 1541; sheriff, Glouc, 17 Nov 1533 and 11 Nov 1550; JP, Glouc, 1537, 1539–40, 1542–5, 1547, and 1554 until death; MP, Glouc, 1539, 1542?, 1545, 1547, Mar 1553, and 1555; comm of musters, Glouc, 31 Mar 1539, 1 Oct 1542, and 20 Jan 1546; comm of oyer and terminer, Glouc, 1540; chief steward, town and hundred of Tewkesbury, 28 Jun 1541 and former lands of Cirencester Abbey, by 1547–9, both in Glouc; custos rot, Glouc, by 1546; comm for the survey of chantries, Glouc, including cities of Gloucester and Bristol, 14 Feb 1546; member, Council in the Marches of Wales, 1551. Seats at Chudleigh, Devon and Painswick, Glouc; held manors of Chudleigh and Honiton, Devon, through marriage; granted Flaxley Abbey and lands, 21 Mar 1537, priory of Stanley and lands, 22 Oct 1544, manor of Quenington, 25 Sept 1545, and Miserden, 4 Nov 1546, all in Glouc.

abbot of misrule	Glouc	Gloucester	1550–1 (296)
players	Glouc	Gloucester	1550–1 (296)
			1551–2 (296)
			1552–3 (297)

Lady Elizabeth *see* Princess

Lawson

Wilfred Lawson (1545–16 Apr 1632), kt 1604. Sheriff, Cumb, 5 Dec 1582, 25 Nov 1597, 17 Nov 1606, and 6 Nov 1612; JP, Cumb, by 1587; lieut, honour of Cockermouth and capt, Cockermouth Castle, Cumb, c 1591; MP, Cumb, 1593, 1604, and 1614; border comm, 1605. Seat at Isell Hall, Isell, Cumb.

musicians	Cumb	Carlisle	1618–19 (90)
fool	Cumb	Carlisle	1619–20 (93)

Leicester

Robert Dudley (24 Jun 1532 or 1533–4 Sept 1588), cr baron of Denbigh, Denbighshire, Wales, 28 Sept, and 14th earl of Leicester, 29 Sept 1564; imprisoned Jul 1553, attainted 22 Jan 1553/4, pardoned 18 Oct 1554, and restored in blood,

7 Mar 1557/8. MP, Norf, 1547, Mar 1553, and 1559; jt steward and constable, Castle Rising, Norf, 13 Dec 1550; comm of relief, Norf, 16 Dec 1551; jt comm of lieutenancy, Norf, 16 May 1552–3; comm of church goods, Norf, 3 Mar 1553; PC, 23 Apr 1559; lord lieut, Warw, 10 May 1559, Berks, 1560?, Worc, 20 Nov 1569–15 Nov 1570, and Essex and Herts, 3 Jul 1585 until death; lieut of forest and castle of Windsor, Berks, 24 Nov 1559; JP, Heref, Warw, and Worc, 1562, 1564, and 1584, Northants, 1584; constable of Windsor Castle, 23 Feb 1562 and high steward of Cambridge Univ, 15 Jul 1563, both until death; high steward, Windsor, 9 Sept 1563, bishopric of Ely, Camb, 1565, Reading, by 1566, Abingdon, 1566, and Wallingford, 1569, all in Berks, Bristol, Glouc, 20 Apr 1570 until death, Grafton, Northants, 14 Dec 1571, King's Lynn and Great Yarmouth, both in Norf, 1572 until death, Andover, Hants, 1574, and St Albans, Herts, by 1584; high steward and receiver of the honour of Pickering Lythe and constable of Pickering Castle, Yorks, NR, 4 Nov 1564; chancellor of Oxford Univ, 31 Dec 1564 and chamberlain of Chester, 2 Jul 1565, both until death; custos rot, Warw, 1568; high steward, Norwich Cathedral, 1574 until death; chancellor and chamberlain of Anglesey, Caernarvonshire, and Merioneth, all in Wales, 26 Sept 1578; lord steward of the Household, 1 Nov 1584–8; warden and chief justice in eyre south of Trent, 25 Nov 1585 until death; lieut and capt gen at Tilbury, Essex, 1 Jul 1588. Seat at Kenilworth, Warw, from 29 Sept 1564; estate at Drayton Basset, Staff; house at Cornbury, Oxf; granted Hemsby Manor near Great Yarmouth, Norf, 4 Feb 1553, lands in Leic and Northants, 1553, lordship of Beverley, Yorks, ER, 1561, lordship of Denbighshire, including Denbigh Castle and borough of Chirk, 1563, and other lands in various parts of England and Wales, from 1563.

players	Glouc	Gloucester	1560–1 (298)
			1561–2 (299)
			1569–70 (301)
			1570–1 (301)
			1584–5 (309)
			1586–7 (310)
			1587–8 (310)
musicians	Glouc	Gloucester	1573–4 (303)
trumpeters	Glouc	Gloucester	1573–4 (303)
bearward	Glouc	Gloucester	1574–5 (305)

Lieutenant of the Tower

Owen Hopton (c 1519–bet 22 Jul and 20 Dec 1595), kt 1561. JP, Suff, 1544–5, 1554, 1562, and 1564, Midd, 1569, 1570–1, and 1591–2; MP, Suff, 1559, 1571, Midd, 1572, 1584, and Arundel, Suss, 1589; comm of oyer and terminer, Beds, Bucks, Camb, Hunts, Norf, Suff, and city of Norwich, 1564; sheriff of Norf and Suff, 9 Nov 1564; comm for ports, 10 Nov 1565, comm of sewers, 8 May 1566, and comm of musters, by 29 Jun 1569, all in Suff; lieut of Tower of London, by Nov 1569–90; comm *post mortem*, Midd, 10 Jul 1576. Seats at Cockfield Hall, Yoxford and Blythburgh, Suff; lands in Somers and Suff.

players	Glouc	Gloucester	1570–1 (302)

Lincoln

Henry Clinton or Fiennes (after 1539–29 Sept 1616), styled Lord Clinton, 1572 until he succ as 17th earl of Lincoln and Lord Clinton, 16 Jan 1584/5. MP, Launceston, Cornw, 1559 and Linc, 1571; comm of sewers, Linc, 14 Jun 1564, 14 Jun 1570, and 9 Nov 1570; jt comm of musters, Linc, 1569; JP, Linc, 1570–1; vice-adm, York, by 1572 and Linc, by 1574; comm *post mortem*, Linc, 12 Feb 1573 and 12 Oct 1576; high steward of Boston, Linc, 1574; PC, Mar–May 1603; steward and keeper, manor of Kirton, Linc 10 Jul 1608. Seat at Tattershall, Linc; lands in Derby, Essex, Leic, Linc, Nott, Suff, Suss, Yorks, and Montgomeryshire, Wales.

players	Cumb	Carlisle	1608–9 (70)
	Westmld	Kendal	1608–9 (181)

Lord President of the Marches of Wales

Henry Sidney (20 Jul 1529–5 May 1586), kt 1551 and KG 14 May 1564. MP, Brackley, Northants, 1547 and Kent, Mar 1553, 1563, 1571, and 1572; high steward, honour of Oxford and Knole Park, Kent, 1553; vice-treasurer and receiver-gen of Ireland, 27 Apr 1556–9; lord justice of Ireland, jt, 5 Dec 1557 and sole, 18 Jan 1558; lord pres, Council in the Marches of Wales, 1559 until death; JP, Chester, 1562 and 1564, Heref, 1562 and 1564, Kent and Shrops, 1561/2, Worc, 1562 and 1564, Brecknockshire and Monmouthshire, both in Wales, 1562 and 1564, and various Welsh cos, from 13 Jun 1562, and English cos, from *c* 1573; lord deputy of Ireland, by 22 Jun 1565–71 and 31 Jul 1575–Jul 1580; PC, 31 Jul 1575. Seat at Penshurst, Kent; inherited lordship of Kingston on Hull and manor of Myton, both in Yorks, ER, and manors of Southwell, Nott and Tyburn, Midd; granted manor and borough of Wootton Bassett, Wilts, 2 Jul 1553; residence at Ludlow Castle, Shrops; lands in Glouc, Kent, Linc, Nott, Surr, Suss, and Yorks.

trumpeter	Glouc	Gloucester	1560–1 (298)

Manche (Lady)

Probably Lady Mountjoy.

Katherine Leigh (nd–25 Jun 1576), married James Blount, 6th Lord Mountjoy, *qv*, 1558.

players	Glouc	Gloucester	1571–2 (302)

March

Roger de Mortimer (11 Apr 1374–20 Jul 1398), succ as 4th earl of March, earl of Ulster, and Lord Mortimer, 27 Dec 1381; hereditary constable of Brimpsfield Castle,

Glouc and of Trim Castle, co Meath, Ireland; lieut of Ireland, 24 Jan 1381/2–3, 23 Jul 1392, and 24 Apr 1397–1400; ambassador to Scotland, 16 Feb–30 Mar 1394; lieut in cos Connaught, Meath, and Ulster, Ireland, 25 Apr 1396–29 Sept 1397. Lands in many counties, including Dors, Somers, and Worc.

| minstrels | Glouc | Gloucester | 1393–4 (291) |

Master of the Revels
Edmund Tilney (nd–20 Aug 1610), MP, Gatton, Surr, 1572; master of the revels to the Household, 24 Jul 1579 until death; subsidy comm, Surr, 1593–4. Seat at Leatherhead, Surr; held property in Midd and Surr; residence at Clerkenwell, Midd, from 1586.

| players | Glouc | Gloucester | 1583–4 (309) |

Metcalfe
Thomas Metcalfe (c 1579–Jul 1650 or 1655), kt May 1603. Seat at Nappa Hall, Wensleydale, Yorks, NR.

| musicians | Cumb | Carlisle | 1614–15 (81) |
| players | Cumb | Carlisle | 1626–7 (107) |

Monteagle
William Parker (c 1575–1 Jul 1622), son of Edward, 12th Lord Morley, qv, succ as 5th Lord Monteagle, 12 Jun 1585 and as 13th Lord Morley, 1 Apr 1618. Seat at Hornby Castle, Lanc; houses at Shinglehall, Epping and Great Hallingbury, both in Essex; granted manor of Martok, Somers, 1605.

players	Westmld	Kendal	1597–8 (177)
			1610–11 (181)
			1614–15 (182)

Morley
Edward Parker (c 1551–1 Apr 1618), succ as 12th Lord Morley, 22 Oct 1577. Imprisoned, Apr 1573; (?)deputy comm, Essex, 6 Nov 1580; JP, Norf, 1584, Somers, 1584 and 1608, and Yorks, NR, 1584. Obtained manor of Belhouse, North Tuddenham, Norf, 1 Mar 1578.

players	Glouc	Gloucester	1581–2 (308)
	Westmld	Kendal	1585–6 (172)
	Glouc	Gloucester	1592–3 (312)
	Cumb	Carlisle	1602–3 (66)

Mountjoy
James Blount (c 1533–20 Oct 1581), succ as 6th Lord Mountjoy, 10 Oct 1544. Lord lieut, Dors, 26 May 1559; JP, Dors and Wilts, 1562 and 1564; comm of oyer and

terminer, Cornw, Devon, Dors, Somers, Southants, and Wilts, 1564; shareholder in the company of Mines Royal, Cornw, Cumb, Devon, Glouc, Lanc, Westmld, Worc, and Wales, 28 May 1568. Country seat at Apethorpe, Northants.

players	Cumb	Keswick	1568–9 (126)
	Glouc	Gloucester	1568–9 (301)
			1572–3 (302)
			1577–8 (305)

Neville
Possibly

Edmund Neville (bef 1555–c 1618), styled himself 5th Lord Latimer after 27 May 1590 and claimed title of 7th earl of Westmorland, 1601; claim rejected, 29 Sept 1604. Imprisoned in the Tower, 1584–8 Feb 1598 and in the Fleet until 31 Dec 1598.

| musicians | Cumb | Carlisle | 1619–20 (92) |

Ogle
Cuthbert Ogle (c 1540–20 Nov 1597), succ as 7th Lord Ogle, 1 Aug 1562. Member, Council of the North, Oct 1572–97; comm to survey forts and castles, East and Middle Marches, 1580–8; JP, Yorks, NR, 1584.

players	Glouc	Gloucester	1578–9 (306)
			1593–4 (312)
			1594–5 (313)
			1595–6 (314)

Oxford
Edward de Vere (12 Apr 1550–24 Jun 1604), styled Lord Bolbec until he succ as 17th earl of Oxford and lord great chamberlain of England, 3 Aug 1562. Chief comm of musters, Essex, 1579. Seat at Hedingham Castle, Essex; sold estate of Earls Colne, Essex, Sept 1583; granted Earls Colne Priory, Essex, 8 Jun 1588; sold it in 1592; lived at Hackney, Midd, 1596 until death.

players	Glouc	Gloucester	1582–3 (308)
			1583–4 (309)
			1584–5 (309)

Prince see Henry of Monmouth and Charles Stuart under King

Princess
Elizabeth Stuart (mid Aug 1596–13 Feb 1662), daughter of James VI of Scotland and I of England, qv, and Anne of Denmark, qv; married, 14 Feb 1613, Frederick V, then elector palatine; became queen of Bohemia, 7 Nov 1619.

| players (Lady | Cumb | Carlisle | 1617–18 (89) |
| Elizabeth) | | | 1619–20 (95) |

| players (queen of Bohemia) | Westmld | Kendal | 1619–20 (187) |

Queen

Mary Tudor (18 Feb 1516–17 Nov 1558), daughter of Henry VIII, *qv*, and Catherine of Aragon, acc as Mary I of England, 19 Jul 1553; crowned, 1 Oct 1553; married, 25 Jul 1554, Philip, king of Naples and Jerusalem, and king of Spain from 16 Jul 1556.

| jester | Glouc | Gloucester | 1554–5 (297) |
| players | Glouc | Gloucester | 1555–6 (297) |

Elizabeth Tudor (7 Sept 1533–24 Mar 1603), daughter of Henry VIII, *qv*, and Anne Boleyn; acc as Elizabeth I, 17 Nov 1558; crowned, 15 Jan 1559.

players	Glouc	Gloucester	1559–60 (298)
			1561–2 (299)
			1564–5 (300)
			1565–6 (300)
			1567–8 (301)
			1569–70 (301)
			1571–2 (302)
			1580–1 (307)
			1582–3 (308)
			1586–7 (310)
			1587–8 (310)
			1588–9 (311)
	Cumb	Carlisle	1588–9 (65)
	Glouc	Gloucester	1589–90 (311)
			1590–1 (312)
			1591–2 (312)
	Westmld	Kendal	1592–3 (174)
	Glouc	Gloucester	1593–4 (312)
			1594–5 (313)
			1595–6 (313)
juggler	Glouc	Gloucester	1563–4 (299)
bearwards	Glouc	Gloucester	1570–1 (301)
	Glouc	Gloucester	1574–5 (305)
musicians	Glouc	Gloucester	1573–4 (303)
trumpeters	Glouc	Gloucester	1573–4 (303)
			1591–2 (312)
puppet players	Glouc	Gloucester	1581–2 (308)

Anne of Denmark (12 Dec 1574–2 Mar 1619), married James VI of Scotland (later James I of England), *qv*, 20 Aug 1589; crowned queen of England, 25 Jul 1603. Her acting company continued in her name for several years after her death.

players	Westmld	Kendal	1615–16 (183)
			1616–17 (184)
	Cumb	Carlisle	1617–18 (87)
	Westmld	Kendal	1617–18 (185)
	Cumb	Carlisle	1619–20 (94)

Queen of Bohemia *see* Princess

Savile
John Savile (1556–31 Aug 1630), cr Baron Savile (of Pontefract, Yorks, WR), 21 Jul 1628. MP, Lincoln City, 1586 and Yorks, 1597, 1604, 1614, 1624, and 1626; steward, honour of Wakefield, Yorks, WR, 1588; JP, Lindsey, Linc and Yorks, WR, from *c* 1591; custos rot, Yorks, WR, from *c* 1594–9 Dec 1615 and Jul 1626–8; member, northern high commission, 1599; member, Jul 1603 until death, and vice-pres, 1626–8, Council of the North; PC, 8 Nov 1626; mayor, Leeds, Yorks, WR, Jul 1626; comptroller of the Household, by 1627 until death; high steward of the honour of Pontefract, nd. Seats at Doddington, Linc and Howley Hall, Batley, Yorks, WR; estates at Barkston, Linc and in Yorks, WR.

| musicians | Cumb | Carlisle | 1617–18 (89) |

Scrope
Henry Scrope (*c* 1534–13 Jun 1592), succ as 9th Lord Scrope, 22 Jun 1549. Member, Council of the North, before 20 Jan 1561 until death; warden of the West Marches and capt of Carlisle, Cumb, 6 Apr 1563 until death; JP, Yorks, ER and NR, 1562 and 1564 and Cumb, Durham, Northumb, Westmld, Yorks, Berwick upon Tweed and Newcastle upon Tyne, both in Northumb, and Kingston on Hull, Yorks, ER, 1564; comm *post mortem*, Cumb, 7 Jul 1568 and 21 Jun 1571; comm to assess fines in northern cos, Mar 1570; bailiff and steward, Richmond and constable and keeper of Richmond and Middleham Castles, all in Yorks, 23 Nov 1570. Seat at Bolton Castle, Wensleydale, Yorks, NR; lands in Derby, Devon, Essex, Linc, Notts, Southants, Wilts, and Yorks, and in Cardiganshire and Merioneth, Wales.

| players | Cumb | Keswick | 1573–4 (127) |

Sheffield
Edmund Sheffield (7 Dec 1565–Oct 1646), succ as 3rd Baron Sheffield (of Butterwick, in the Isle of Axholme, Linc), 10 Dec 1568; cr earl of Mulgrave, 5 Feb 1625/6. Lord lieut, Yorks, 1 Aug 1603–19; lord pres, by 22 Jul 1603–by 11 Feb 1618/19 and member, 21 May 1625, Council of the North; JP, Yorks, NR, 1608, 1626, and 1636;

vice adm, Yorks, 1616 until death. Granted manor of Mulgrave, Yorks, NR, Apr 1591; seat at King's Manor, Yorks.

players	Glouc	Gloucester	1577–8 (305)
			1579–80 (306)

Stafford
Edward Stafford (17 Jan 1535/6–18 Oct 1603), succ as 12th Baron Stafford, 1 Jan 1565/6. MP, Banbury, Oxf, Nov 1554 and Staff, 1558 and 1559; lord lieut, Staff, 1559?; lieut and justice in eyre, Needwood Forest and parks in the duchy of Lancaster, 13 May 1559; justice and ranger, forest of Cannock, Staff, 24 Sept 1560; jt comm of musters, Staff, by 8 Aug 1569; JP, Glouc, Shrops, and Staff, by 1573/4, and Montgomeryshire, Wales, by 1591; vice-adm, Glouc, 1587; member, Council in the Marches of Wales, Aug 1601. Seat at Stafford Castle, Staff.

players	Glouc	Gloucester	1581–2 (308)
			1582–3 (308)
			1583–4 (309)
			1584–5 (309)
			1595–6 (313)

Edward Stafford (bapt 20 Sept 1572–25 Sept 1625), son of Edward, 12th Baron Stafford, qv, succ as 13th Baron Stafford, 18 Oct 1603. Imprisoned in the Fleet, Mar 1605. Seat at Stafford Castle, Staff; granted manor of Islingham, Kent, 1604; obtained manor of Thornbury and other lands in Glouc, 20 Jun 1615.

players	Cumb	Carlisle	1608–9 (69)
			1613–14 (76)
			1614–15 (80)

Stafford (countess of)
Anne (c 1380–c 16 Oct 1438), daughter and sole heir of Thomas of Woodstock, 1st duke of Gloucester, qv, married Thomas de Stafford, 3rd earl of Stafford (d 4 Jul 1392), 1392, his brother Edmund, 5th earl of Stafford (d 21 Jul 1403), 1398, and William Bourgchier, count of Eu, Normandy, 1404.

minstrels	Glouc	Gloucester	1409–10 (291)
		Berkeley	1420–1 (347)

Strange see under Derby

Suffolk (duchess of)
Katherine Willoughby (22 Mar 1518/19–19 Sept 1580), de jure suo jure Baroness Willoughby de Eresby (of Eresby, Linc); married c 7 Sept 1533 Charles Brandon, 4th duke of Suffolk (d 22 Aug 1545), and Richard Bertie, probably early 1553; fled England, 5 Feb 1554/5; returned, summer 1559. Residence at Westhorpe, Suff, from

c 1528; principal seats at Grimsthorpe and Tattershall Castle, Linc, with associated lands, from *c* 1536; all lands seized by the Crown, 1557; returned, Aug 1559.

players	Glouc	Gloucester	1562–3 (299)

Sussex

Thomas Radcliffe (1525 or 1526–9 Jun 1583), styled Lord FitzWalter, 27 Nov 1542–53; succ as 8th earl of Sussex and Viscount and Baron FitzWalter, 17 Feb 1556/7. Warden and capt of Portsmouth, Hants, 24 Nov 1549–Apr 1551; MP, Norf, Mar 1553; JP, Essex and Norf, 1554, 1562, and 1564 and Suff, 1562 and 1564; lord deputy of Ireland, 27 Apr 1556–60; chief justice in eyre south of Trent, 3 Jul 1557 until death; lord lieut of Ireland, 6 May 1560–13 Oct 1565; lord pres, Council of the North, Jul 1568–Oct 1572; lord lieut of the North, 15 Nov 1569; PC, 30 Dec 1570; steward, New Hall, Beaulieu, Jul 1572 and Maldon, at death, both in Essex; lord chamberlain of the Household, 13 Jul 1572 until death; chief comm of array, sole, Beds, Cambs, Hunts, Kent, Midd, Norf, and Suff and jt, Essex and Herts, 1579. Seat at New Hall, granted 23 May 1574 and at Woodham Walther, Essex; house at Bermondsey, Surr and manors in Essex; granted forts of cos Leix and Offaly, Ireland and castles in several Irish cos, 1558.

players	Glouc	Gloucester	1569–70 (301)
			1572–3 (302)
			1574–5 (305)
			1575–6 (305)

Henry Radcliffe (by 1533–14 Dec 1593), son of Thomas, 8th earl of Sussex, *qv*; succ as 9th earl of Sussex and Viscount and Baron FitzWalter, 9 Jun 1583. MP, Maldon, Essex, 1555, Chichester, Suss, 1559, Carlingford, co Louth, Ireland, 1560, Hants, 1571, and Portsmouth, Hants, 1572; PC, Ireland, by 25 Feb 1556/7; lieut, cos Leix and Offaly, Ireland, 1557–29 Oct 1564; comm, cos Dublin, Kildare, and others in Ireland during the absence of the lord deputy, 8 Aug 1557; lieut, Maryborough Castle and Fort, Ross and Cromarty, Scotland, 1558–9; constable, Porchester Castle and lieut, Southbere Forest, Southampton, both in Hants, for life, 14 Jun 1560; jt steward, crown possessions in Essex, 1561; warden and capt, 4 May 1571 and high steward, 9 Sept 1590, Portsmouth, both until death; JP, Hants, 1573/4 and Norf, 1584; comm of musters, Hants sole, by 1576 and jt, 16 Mar 1579/80; jt lord lieut, Hants and Winchester and Southampton, both in Hants, 3 Jul 1585 until death. Seat at New Hall, Boreham, Essex.

players	Glouc	Gloucester	1584–5 (309)
			1585–6 (310)
	Westmld	Kendal	1586–7 (172)
	Glouc	Gloucester	1587–8 (310)
			1588–9 (311)
			1590–1 (312)

Robert Radcliffe (12 Jun 1573–22 Sept 1629), son of Henry, 9th earl of Sussex, *qv*, styled Lord FitzWalter until he succ as 10th earl of Sussex and Viscount and Lord FitzWalter, 14 Dec 1593. Lord lieut, Essex, 26 Aug 1603–25, jt, 8 Sept 1625–6, and sole, 11 Sept 1626–9; gov, Harwich, Essex and Landguard Fort, Suff, Sept 1626–Mar 1628. Sold ancestral estate of New Hall, Boreham, Essex, Jul 1622; family estate at Attleborough, Norf.

players	Cumb	Carlisle	1617–18 (86)
	Westmld	Kendal	1617–18 (185)

Throckmorton

John Throckmorton (by 1524–22 May 1580), kt 1565. MP, Leicester, Leic, 1545, Camelford, Cornw, 1547, Warw, Mar 1553, Old Sarum, Wilts, Oct 1553, and Coventry, Warw, Nov 1554, 1555, 1558, and 1559; attorney, 1550–4, member, 1558 until death, and vice-pres, 1565–9, Council in the Marches of Wales; steward, manor of Feckenham, Worc, 1552 until death; recorder, Coventry, 1553 and Worc, from 1559, both until death and Ludlow and Shrewsbury, both in Shrops, by 1560; JP, Warw, from 1554 and Welsh and Marcher cos, from 1558/9; under-steward of Westminster, 1557; justice of Chester and of Denbighshire and Montgomeryshire, both in Wales, 1558–79; eccles comm, diocese of Chester, 1562; comm for piracy, Ches, 1565. Seat at Feckenham; residence at Congleton, Ches.

minstrels	Glouc	Gloucester	1560–1 (298)

Vavasour

Maior Vavasour (b before 1563), of Weston, Yorks, WR.

musicians	Cumb	Carlisle	1608–9 (69)

Wales (lord of)
Not identified.

minstrels	Glouc	Berkeley	1420–1 (347)

Warwick

Ambrose Dudley (c 1528–21 Feb 1589/90), styled Lord Ambrose Dudley from Oct 1551; cr Baron Lisle, 25 Dec, and 21st earl of Warwick, 26 Dec 1561; imprisoned and attainted 1553, pardoned 22 Jan 1554/5, and restored in blood, 7 Mar 1557/8. Constable of Kenilworth Castle, Warw, 20 Dec 1549; JP, Linc and Warw, 1562 and 1564; lord pres of the North, by 22 Feb 1564; comm of musters, jt, London, 1569 and chief, Warw, 1569, 1579, and 16 Mar 1580 and Berks, Bucks, Northants, Oxf, and Staff, 1579 and 16 Mar 1580; lord lieut, Warw and city of Coventry, Warw, Nov 1569–Nov 1570 and by 9 Oct 1587 until death; PC, 5 Sept 1573; high steward of St Albans, Herts, 1589 and of the honour of Grafton, 10 May 1589; chancellor and chamberlain, Anglesey, Caernarvonshire, and Merioneth, all in Wales, 20 May 1589.

Seat at Warwick Castle; owned park of Wedgnock, Warw; inherited lordship of
Halesowen, Worc, 1555; granted manor of Kibworth Beauchamp, Leic, 28 Mar 1559.

players (Lord Ambrose Dudley)	Glouc	Gloucester	1559–60 (298)
players	Glouc	Gloucester	1561–2 (299)
			1563–4 (299)

Wharton

Philip Wharton (23 Jun 1555–26 Mar 1625), succ as 3rd Baron Wharton, 14 Jun or
Jul 1572. JP, Cumb, Northumb, Westmld, and Yorks, by 1578; jt high comm,
province of York, 24 Nov 1599; jt border comm, 23 Jan 1617/18 and 1619. Seat at
Wharton Hall, Westmld.

players	Westmld	Kendal	1599–1600 (177)
	Cumb	Carlisle	1610–11 (71)
			1613–14 (75)
			1614–15 (80)
			1617–18 (86)
			1618–19 (90)
			1621–2 (100)
			1622–3 (102)

Philip Wharton (8 Apr 1613–4 or 5 Feb 1695/6), grandson of Philip, 3rd Baron
Wharton, qv, succ as 4th Baron Wharton, 26 Mar 1625. Lord lieut, Lanc, 5 Mar 1642,
Bucks, 24 Jun 1642, and Westmld, 11 Sept 1644; custos rot, Cumb and Westmld and
JP, Cumb, Westmld, and Yorks, WR and NR, all by 1650; PC, 14 Feb 1688/9. Held
lands in Beds, Bucks, Cumb, Westmld, Yorks, and Ireland, including a house at
Woburn, Beds and lands in Healaugh, Yorks.

players	Westmld	Kendal	1626–7 (202)
	Cumb	Workington	1628–9 (129)
	Westmld	Kendal	1628–9 (204)
	Cumb	Workington	1629–30 (129)
	Westmld	Kendal	1631–2 (208)
	Cumb	Workington	1632–3 (131)
			1633–4 (132)
	Cumb	Carlisle	1638–9 (122)

Worcester

William Somerset (c 1527–21 Feb 1588/9), styled Lord Herbert until he succ as 8th
earl of Worcester, 26 Nov 1549. Capt and keeper of castles of Aberystwyth,
Cardiganshire and Carmarthen, Carmarthenshire, both in Wales, 17 May 1543;
member, Council in the Marches of Wales, Nov 1553 and from 1576; JP, Glouc, Heref,
Shrops, and Worc, 1554, Monmouthshire, Wales, 1562 and 1564, and Shrops, 1582;

comm of musters, Monmouthshire, 1579 and 16 Mar 1580 and Denbighshire, Wales, 12 Dec 1580. Seat at Raglan, Monmouthshire; residence at Hackney, Midd.

players	Glouc	Gloucester	1567–8 (300)
			1568–9 (301)
			1570–1 (301)
			1572–3 (302)
			1573–4 (303)
			1577–8 (305)
			1583–4 (309)

Edward Somerset (c 1550–3 Mar 1627/8), son of William, 8th earl of Worcester, qv, styled Lord Herbert until he succ as 9th earl of Worcester and Baron Herbert, 21 Feb 1588/9. Member, Council in the Marches of Wales, 16 Dec 1590; PC, 29 Jun 1601; lord lieut, Glamorgan and Monmouthshire, both in Wales, sole, 17 Jul 1602 and jt, 3 Dec 1626 until death; custos rot, Monmouthshire, Jun 1603; keeper of Nonsuch Great Park, Surr, 1 Dec 1606; steward, lordship and manor of Lewisham, Kent, 6 Feb 1613/14; keeper, manor of Plesaunce, East Greenwich, Kent and high steward, Greenwich, 19 May 1615; lord keeper of the Privy Seal, 2 Jan 1615/16 until death; JP, Kent, Norf, Northants, Somers, and Yorks, NR, 1626, and Worc, 1608 and 1626. Seat at Raglan, Monmouthshire; residence at Hackney, Midd.

players	Glouc	Gloucester	1590–1 (311)
			1591–2 (312)

Writtle see **Buckingham**

Companies Named by Location

Appleby, Westmld

waits	Cumb	Carlisle	1610–11 (71)
			1613–14 (76)
			1618–19 (90)

Aske

Possibly Aske Hall, Yorks, NR.

waits	Cumb	Carlisle	1619–20 (95)

Askrigg, Yorks, NR

waits	Cumb	Carlisle	1634–5 (116)
			1639–40 (124)

Atherton, Lanc

waits	Cumb	Carlisle	1613–14 (77)

Barnard Castle, Dur
players	Cumb	Carlisle	1613–14 (76)
waits	Cumb	Carlisle	1618–19 (90)

Barwick
Barwick in Elmet, Yorks, WR or Berwick upon Tweed, Northumb.
musicians	Cumb	Carlisle	1613–14 (77)
waits	Cumb	Carlisle	1616–17 (83)
			1621–2 (101)
			1634–5 (116)
			1636–7 (122)

Bedale, Yorks, NR
waits	Cumb	Carlisle	1617–18 (89)

Berwick
Berwick upon Tweed, Northumb or Barwick in Elmet, Yorks, WR.
waits	Cumb	Naworth	1621–2 (140)

Boston, Linc
waits	Cumb	Carlisle	1621–2 (100)

Bradford
waits	Cumb	Carlisle	1634–5 (116)

Brampton, Cumb
piper	Cumb	Brampton or Naworth	1626–7 (142)

Bristol, Glouc
waits	Glouc	Thornbury	1507–8 (357–8)
			1520–1 (359)
	Cumb	Carlisle	1613–14 (78)
			1614–15 (81)

Canterbury, Kent
waits	Cumb	Carlisle	1613–14 (76)

Carlisle, Cumb
waits	Cumb	Naworth	1612–13 (135)
			1618–19 (138)
			1624–5 (141)
			1627–8 (142)

Cockermouth, Cumb

waits	Cumb	Carlisle	1602–3 (66)
			1634–5 (116)
players	Cumb	Workington	1628–9 (129)
			1633–4 (132)

Darlington, Dur

| waits | Cumb | Naworth | 1633–4 (143) |

Darrington, Yorks, WR

waits	Cumb	Carlisle	1624–5 (104)
			1626–7 (107)
			1636–7 (122)

Doncaster, Yorks, WR

| waits | Cumb | Naworth | 1612–13 (135) |

Durham, Dur

waits	Cumb	Carlisle	1608–9 (69)
			1617–18 (87)
			1620–1 (98)
pipers (waits)	Cumb	Naworth	1633–4 (144)
waits	Cumb	Naworth	1633–4 (144)

Edinburgh, Scotland

| musicians | Cumb | Carlisle | 1620–1 (97) |

Halifax, Yorks, WR

waits	Cumb	Carlisle	1608–9 (69)
			1613–14 (77)
			1617–18 (88)
			1627–8 (109)
musicians	Cumb	Carlisle	1617–18 (89)

Kendal, Westmld

waits	Cumb	Carlisle	1604–5 (67)
			1608–9 (68)
			1614–15 (81)
			1617–18 (86)
			1618–19 (90)
			1619–20 (93, 94)
			1620–1 (99)
	Cumb	Naworth	1620–1 (139)
	Cumb	Carlisle	1621–2 (101)

			1624–5 (104)
			1626–7 (106)
			1627–8 (108)
			1635–6 (119)
			1636–7 (122)
			1638–9 (123)
			1639–40 (124)
players	Cumb	Carlisle	1613–14 (76)

Keswick, Cumb

waits	Cumb	Carlisle	1638–9 (123)

Kirkby Lonsdale, Westmld

waits	Cumb	Carlisle	1621–2 (100, 101)

Kirkby Stephen, Westmld

waits	Cumb	Carlisle	1614–15 (80)

Kirkby Thore, Westmld

waits	Cumb	Carlisle	1614–15 (80)

Knaresborough, Yorks, WR

waits	Cumb	Carlisle	1613–14 (78)
			1614–15 (81)

Lancaster, Lanc

waits	Cumb	Carlisle	1602–3 (66)
			1610–11 (71)
			1613–14 (76, 77)
			1614–15 (80, 81)
			1616–17 (84)
			1621–2 (101)
	Cumb	Naworth	1621–2 (140)
			1622–3 (141)
	Cumb	Carlisle	1626–7 (107)
minstrel	Westmld	Windermere	1537–8 (214–15)

Leeds, Yorks, WR or NR

waits	Cumb	Carlisle	1604–5 (67)
			1610–11 (72)

Leeming, Yorks, NR

waits	Cumb	Carlisle	1608–9 (69)

Lincoln, Linc

waits	Cumb	Carlisle	1610–11 (72)
			1614–15 (81)
			1616–17 (83)
			1617–18 (89)
			1619–20 (95)
			1621–2 (101)
			1624–5 (103, 104)

Middleham, Yorks, NR

waits	Cumb	Carlisle	1608–9 (69)
			1610–11 (71)
			1613–14 (77)
			1619–20 (95)
			1620–1 (98)
	Cumb	Naworth	1620–1 (139)
	Westmld	Lowther	1640–1 (217)

Millom, Cumb

waits	Cumb	Carlisle	1618–19 (90)
			1620–1 (99)
drummer/piper	Cumb	Carlisle	1619–20 (94)

Newcastle upon Tyne, Northumb

waits	Cumb	Carlisle	1608–9 (68)

Orton, Westmld

waits	Cumb	Carlisle	1634–5 (116)

Oxford, Oxf

musicians	Glouc	Gloucester	1639 (328)

Penrith, Cumb

players	Cumb	Carlisle	1602–3 (66)
	Cumb	Naworth	1622–3 (140)
waits	Cumb	Carlisle	1602–3 (66)
			1604–5 (67)
			1608–9 (68)
			1610–11 (70, 71, 72)
	Cumb	Naworth	1612–13 (135)
	Cumb	Carlisle	1613–14 (76)
			1614–15 (80)
			1617–18 (87)
			1618–19 (90)

			1619–20 (95)
			1620–1 (97)
	Cumb	Naworth	1620–1 (139)
	Cumb	Carlisle	1621–2 (101)
	Cumb	Carlisle	1624–5 (104)
	Cumb	Naworth	1624–5 (141)
			1625–6 (141)
	Cumb	Carlisle	1626–7 (107)
	Cumb	Naworth	1626–7 (142)
	Cumb	Carlisle	1627–8 (108)
	Cumb	Naworth	1633–4 (144)
	Cumb	Carlisle	1634–5 (116)
	Westmld	Lowther	1640–1 (217)
musicians	Cumb	Naworth	1618–19 (138)

Richmond, Yorks, WR

waits	Cumb	Carlisle	1604–5 (67)
			1608–9 (70)
	Cumb	Naworth	1620–1 (139)
pipers	Cumb	Naworth	1629–30 (142)

Ripon, Yorks, WR

waits	Cumb	Naworth	1612–13 (135)
	Cumb	Carlisle	1618–19 (90)
			1619–20 (95)
			1620–1 (98)
			1621–2 (101)
	Cumb	Naworth	1621–2 (139)
	Cumb	Carlisle	1624–5 (104)
			1626–7 (107)
			1627–8 (109)
			1636 7 (121)
			1638–9 (123)
			1639–40 (124)

Shrewsbury, Shrops

| waits | Glouc | Gloucester | 1573–4 (303) |

Slimbridge, Glouc

| players? | Glouc | Berkeley | 1420–1 (347) |

Thirsk, Yorks, NR

| waits | Cumb | Carlisle | 1616–17 (82) |

Wakefield, Yorks, WR

waits	Cumb	Carlisle	1604–5 (68)
			1608–9 (69)
			1610–11 (71)
	Cumb	Naworth	1612–13 (136)
	Cumb	Carlisle	1617–18 (88)
			1618–19 (90)
			1624–5 (104)

Warwick, Warw

players	Cumb	Naworth	1624–5 (141)

Wotton under Edge, Glouc

players?	Glouc	Berkeley	1420–1 (347)

Writtle, Essex

players	Glouc	Thornbury	1507–8 (357, 358)

York, Yorks

waits	Cumb	Carlisle	1608–9 (70)

Glossaries: Introduction

The purpose of the glossaries is to assist the reader in going through the records text; definitions are given only for those senses of a particular word which are used in the records printed in this this volume. The criteria for the selection of glossary entries are discussed below, under the headings Latin Glossary and English Glossary. The glossaries include both words found in records printed in the main text and words found in records printed or quoted in the appendixes and endnotes.

Only the three earliest occurrences of each word (and each form of each word) are listed; 'etc' following three page references means that there are more occurrences of that form. References are listed in page order, rather than chronological order. Glossed words from entries which appear twice, once within the records text and again in Appendix 1 of the Gloucestershire records, are given page and line references to records text occurrences only. Within the references, page and line numbers are separated by an oblique stroke. If words occur within marginalia, this is indicated by a lower-case 'm' following the page and line reference. Manuscript capitalization has been ignored, except where proper names are glossed.

Latin Glossary

Words are included in the Latin glossary if they are not to be found in the *Oxford Latin Dictionary* (OLD), now the standard reference work for classical Latin. Words listed in the OLD whose meaning has changed or become restricted in medieval or Renaissance usage are also glossed. If a word may be found in the OLD, but appears in the records text in an obscure spelling, or an unusual or anomalous inflectional form for which the dictionary provides no cross-reference, that word has been included and its standard lexical entry form indicated, without giving a definition. There are exceptions to this rule, where the spelling variations or anomalous inflectional forms have been treated as scribal errors and more correct forms given in textual notes. Forms thus noted are not repeated in the glossary.

Most of the Latin words used in the records are common classical words whose spelling has changed according to common medieval variations. The results of these common variations are not treated here either as new words or as forms which require cross-referencing. These variations are:

ML *c* for CL *t* before *i*
ML *cc* for CL *ct* before *i*
ML *d* for CL *t* in a final position
ML *e* for CL *ae* or *oe*
Neo-Latin over-correction of CL *e* to *ae* or *oe*
Neo-Latin over-correction of *ae* to *oe*
Neo-Latin over-correction of *oe* to *ae*
ML *ff* for CL *f*, common in an initial position
ML addition of *h*
ML omission of CL *h*
ML variation between *i* and *e* before another vowel
ML *n* for CL *m* before another nasal
Intrusion of ML *p* in the CL consonant cluster *mn* or *ms*
ML doubling of CL single consonants
ML singling of CL double consonants

No attempt has been made to 'correct' these spellings to classical norms; rather, scribal practice has been followed in such cases, as well as in the case of 'i/j' and 'u/v' variation. Where the same word occurs in spellings which differ according to the list above, the most common spelling is treated as standard and used for the headword.

The unusual inflectional forms which are listed are dealt with in one of two ways: they are listed separately and cross-referenced to the main entry or, if they follow the headword alphabetically, they are listed under that headword and set apart by boldface type.

Two anomalies are created by the inclusion of Latin texts written after the revival of Classical Latin in schools and universities. One is orthographic, the second is semantic. This semantic anomaly is caused by the difficulty of determining in such texts whether words are being used in the classical sense or in the modified senses which had been acquired in Anglo-Latin usage during the later Middle Ages. Therefore, in these cases we have fully indicated the range of possibilities under the appropriate lexical entry. This is in keeping with the new look of the glossary, in which unclear, technical, or archaic terms which have been given stock translation equivalents then receive in the glossary a fuller treatment than can be provided in the context of the translations. This can be seen especially in legal terms and those relating to performers, entertainers, and their activities.

The orthographic anomaly arises from the adoption of classical spelling with, however, some neo-Latin over- and mis-corrections in the sixteenth and seventeenth centuries. Glossed words only appearing in the records in sixteenth and seventeenth century texts and orthography will appear in classical Latin orthography in the glossary so that, for instance, we will spell the genitive singular of such words using the *ae* diphthong.

There are some Greek words in the text of Appendix 3 of the Gloucestershire records which are variously written in Greek letters, Roman letters, or a mixture of Greek and Roman letters. Where appropriate, ie, when their meaning is not that of Liddell, Scott, Jones, *A Greek-English Lexicon* (LSJ), they have been defined as part of the Latin glossary. The alphabetic characters used in the text have been preserved, even where this creates a mixture of alphabets in a single word.

In all cases, headwords are given in standard form: ie, nouns are listed by nominative, genitive, and gender; adjectives by the terminations of the nominative singular, or in the case of adjectives of one termination, by the nominative and genitive; verbs by their principal parts. The abbreviation *qv* is used to refer the reader to the definitions of words in the standard dictionaries, OLD for Latin and LSJ for Greek. It has not been used for internal cross-references, for which the expression *See* has been used.

English Glossary

The English glossary lists, for the most part, words which have not survived in modern English and words which, in the records, bear meanings which do not survive in modern use. All variant spellings of such words are listed. Forms of words interesting from a purely morphological or phonological point of view have generally not been included in the glossary, but unusual spellings of words which might not be easily identified (eg, 'iuerie' for 'jury') are listed. Words that look unusual because of the absence of an abbreviation mark (eg, 'pd' for 'paid') have not been glossed. It is assumed that the reader is familiar with such common spelling alternations as 'au/a,' 'c/s,' 'd/th,' 'e/a,' 'ey/i,' 'i/e,' 'i/y,' 'o/oo,' 's/z,' 'u/v,' 'y/þ' (eg, 'ye' for 'þe'), and 'e' or 'ea' for 'ai' and 'ay.' Combinations such as 'tharticulate' (for 'the articulate') and 'theile' (for 'they'll') have not been listed unless one of their elements is a word that requires glossing. When variant spellings of the same glossed word occur, the first spelling in alphabetical order has normally been chosen as headword. Spellings separated from their main entries by more than two intervening entries have been cross-referenced.

German Glossary

There is no German glossary, because the German text is so short and because comparatively few words in it require glossing. Those that do are glossed at the foot of the page on the German text pages.

Works consulted

Arndt, William F. and F. Wilbur Gingrich (eds). *A Greek-English Lexicon of the New Testament and Other Early Christian Literature: A Translation and Adaptation of the Fourth Revised and Augmented Edition of Walter Bauer's Griechisch-Deutsches Wörterbuch zu den Schriften des Neuen Testaments und der übrigen urchristlichen Literatur*. Revised and augmented 2nd edn by F. Wilbur Gingrich and Frederick W. Danker (Chicago and London, 1957; rpt 1979).
Cunnington, C. Willett and Phillis. *Handbook of English Costume in the Sixteenth Century* (London, 1964).
– *Handbook of English Costume in the Seventeenth Century* (London, 1965).

Glare, P.G.W. (ed). *Oxford Latin Dictionary* (Oxford, 1982).

Kurath, Hans and Sherman M. Kuhn. *Middle English Dictionary*. Fascicules A.1 – P.2 (Ann Arbor, 1952–82).

Latham, R.E. *Dictionary of Medieval Latin from British Sources*. Fascicules 1–2: A – C (London, 1975–81).

– *Revised Medieval Latin Word-List from British and Irish Sources* (London, 1965).

Liddell, Henry George, Robert Scott, Henry Stuart Jones, and Roderick McKenzie. *A Greek-English Lexicon*. 9th edn (Oxford, 1940; rpt with supplement, 1968).

Munrow, David. *[Musical] Instruments of the Middle Ages and Renaissance* (London, 1976).

The Oxford English Dictionary. Compact edition. 2 vols (New York, 1971).

Wright, Joseph (ed). *The English Dialect Dictionary*. 6 vols (Oxford, 1898–1905).

Abbreviations

adj	adjective	ML	Medieval Latin
adv	adverb	n	noun
art	article	nt	neuter
CL	Classical Latin	NT	New Testament
comm	common noun	OT	Old Testament
compar	comparative	pa	past tense
conj	conjunction	phr	phrase
EG	English Glossary	pl	plural
f	feminine	poss	possessive
Gk	Greek	pp	past participle
Gn	Genesis	pr	present tense
imper	imperative	prep	preposition
in	inches	pron	pronoun
inf	infinitive	prp	present participle
interj	interjection	sg	singular
intr	intransitive	sbst	substantive
Jn	John	subj	subjunctive
m	masculine	tr	transitive
mf	masculine/feminine	v	verb
Mk	Mark	vb	verbal

Latin Glossary

abbas, -atis *n m* abbot (the head of a
monastery) 290/32, 290/37, 290/38, etc

abiectio, -onis *n f* belittlement, scorn,
disparagement 381/2

achator, -oris *n m* caterer (officer responsible
for providing a household's food) 361/31

actio, -onis *n f* action, physical activity, here
used often to refer to activity suitable to
leisure or recreation or to a display of physical
skill or prowess 369/11, 370/6, 370/8, etc

aduincula *prep phr see* **uigilia**

adumbratus, -a, -um *adj* foreshadowed,
prefigured 377/13

aequiparus, -a, -um *adj* equal 375/5

aequipare *adv* equally 382/22

Aesopicus, -a, -um *adj* pertaining to the
Greek fabulist Aesop or to his works 376/38

aestiualis, -e *adj see* **polus**

aestiuus, -a, -um *adj see* **polus**

aetas, -atis *n f* age (ie, the length of one's life):
in idiom, eg, **aliquis aetatis 32 annorum**
someone 32 years old 285/9, 286/19, 287/1,
etc; era 379/26; **impraesentiarum aetate** at
the present time, nowadays 380/31

Agamemnon, -onis *n m* Agamemnon, king
of Mycenae and leader of the expedition
against Troy, here used as a complimentary
address for King James I, perhaps in reference
to Agamemnon's traditional wisdom in
judgement 374/26

alla, -ae *n f* ale-drinking, church-ale (a parish
festivity), *see* EG; **alla Whitsonia** a church-ale
held at Whitsuntide 382/3

allectio, -onis *n f* station in life, position
368/39

altum *adv* deeply 382/36

Anabaptista, -ae *n m* anabaptist, a member
of any one of a number of pietistic sects in
Europe, originating in the sixteenth century,
which held the doctrines of adult baptism and
re-baptism after conversion, and often those
of common ownership of property, the
illegality of oaths of any kind, and devotion
to a higher authority than the civil; hence held
to be revolutionary 379/27

angelicus, -a, -um *adj* pertaining to angels,
angelic, spiritual 376/27

Anglicanus, -a, -um *adj* pertaining to
England, English, here used of language
288/19

antiquus, -a, um *adj* ancient: **ab antiquo** of
old, from antiquity 291/3

Apocalypsis, -is *n f literally* revelation,
manifestation, here the Greek and Latin title
of the NT book Revelations, Apocalypse 374/6

apostolicus, -a, -um *adj* pertaining to or
worthy of the apostles or the apostolic age
375/18

apostolus, -i *n m* one of the first followers of
Jesus, an apostle: used absolutely, St Paul
369/38, 371/39

arbor, -oris *n f* tree: **arboris uitae** the Tree
of Life (Gn 2:9, 3:22) 371/10

archangelus, -i *n m see* **festum**

archidiaconus, -i *n m* archdeacon: in the
English church, a clergyman appointed by the

bishop to assist him principally in administering justice and in supervising the rural clergy 385/3, 386/7

arcte *adv* strictly, stringently 376/11, 382/22

Aristotelicus, -a, -um *adj* pertaining to the Greek philosopher Aristotle or his works 376/3

armiger, -gri *n m* (*here in form* ⟨...⟩**iger**) squire 64/22

articulo, -are, -aui, -atum *v tr* to name someone or something in an article, ie, a charge, before a court (here ecclesiastical) 331/16

articulum, -i *n nt* article, a charge laid against the accused party in court 64/15, 342/8, 344/9, etc; *see also* **libellus**; a section of a book or document 368/41

aspersio, -onis *n f* stain, blot 376/23, 376/32, 385/8

auca, -e *n f* goose 361/32

aula, -e *n f* hall: the centre of community life and the dining area in a noble household 361/20, 361/39; **aula communis** town hall 64/29

aurisfaber, -bri *n m* goldsmith 64/19

author, -oris *n m* founder, originator, creator 372/2, 383/1; author (of a book, etc) 382/26

authoritas, -atis *n f* (royal) authority 376/32, 378/25

azimus, -a, -um *adj see* **dies**

balliuus, -i *n m* bailiff: a civic official subordinate to the mayor 64/28, or the manager of an estate or manor 360/17(3)

Barklaea, -ae *n f* Berkeley 381/21m

benedico, -cere, -xi, -ctum *v tr* to bless 372/13; to distribute something in blessing or as a blessing 290/9

biblium, -ii *n nt* a Bible 382/13

blasphemo, -are, -aui, -atum *v tr* to blaspheme 376/29

butirum, -i *n nt for* **butyrum**, *qv* 361/35

buttria, -e *n f* buttery, a storeroom for beer and spirits, and by extension for other

provisions as well 361/24

cacolicus, -a, -um *adj for* catholicus (possibly a play on the Gk adj κακός, -ή, -όν, 'wicked,' or noun κάκκη, -ης, ἡ, 'excrement') 378/16; *see also* **catholicus**

caelicus, -a, -um *adj* pertaining to heaven, here used in a spiritual rather than a physical sense 374/4, 376/31

caeteroquin *adv* moreover 379/28

camera, -e *n f* treasury 290/30, 290/32, 291/1; room, chamber, suite; **magna camera** the lord's chamber in a noble household (?) 361/20

camerarius, -ii *n m* chamberlain, treasurer: here, of a monastery 290/35

Canaanaeus, -a, -um *adj* pertaining to Canaan or the Canaanites: by transference, pertaining to Israel or Israelites, here used of language 372/19

cancellarius, -ii *n m* chancellor, here, of a noble household 360/16

canon, -onis *n m* standard of reference, rule 373/30

Cantuaria, -e *n f* Canterbury 290/30, 290/41

capella, -e *n f* chapel 357/4, 357/9, 360/23, etc

Capernaiticus, -a, -um *adj* pertaining to Capernaum, a town in Galilee: by extension, with reference to Jn 6:24–59, of or pertaining to an adherent of transubstantiation, the Roman Catholic doctrine that the bread and wine of the eucharist are transformed in substance to the body and blood of Christ during their consecration, used disparagingly 371/19

caprarius, -a, -um *adj* pertaining to a goat: *hence* **caprarius pastor** a goatherd 380/22

capucium, -ii *n nt* hood 63/22(2), 64/25

caput, -itis *n nt* head: literally 63/21, 64/23, or metaphorically 385/11; chapter (of a book or other document) 372/36, 373/1, 373/6, etc

carcosium, -ii *n nt* carcass, here used of beef 361/29

carecta, -e *n f* cart-load 361/40

carnalis, -e *adj* pertaining to flesh, fleshly: by transference, bodily, carnal (as opposed to spiritual) 378/1

caro, -nis *n f* flesh: of animals, **caro bouis** beef 361/29; of men 371/21; also used with particular reference to that of Christ, referring to his human nature 371/17, 371/18, or his eucharistic presence 371/14

castellum, -i *n nt* castle (here as the location of a jail) 377/17, 377/31

castrimargus, -i *n m* woodcock 361/34

castrum, -i *n nt* (royal) castle (here as a fortification) 63/9, 64/5

catholicus, -a, -um *adj and sbst* Roman Catholic 379/4

cena, -e *n f* supper (the less important and later of the two main meals of the day) 356/36, 357/4, 360/12, etc

ceremonia, -e *n f* liturgical or religious rite, ritual 369/19

certifico, -are, -aui, -atum *v intr* to certify the performance of a penance imposed as a sentence by an ecclesiastical court 331/24, 331/39, 332/8, etc

ceruisia, -e *n f* beer 361/25

ceruisiarius, -a, -um *adj* pertaining to beer: *hence* **domus ceruisiaria** an alehouse, inn 379/32

chaundelarius, -ii *n m* chandler, candle-maker 361/13

chaundria, -e *n f* chandlery, originally a storeroom for candles, but later a household department, as it is here 361/37

chorea, -ae *n f* round dance, here apparently used to indicate folk or country dancing, including Maypole dancing 369/17, 369/21, 370/31, etc; **Mauritii chorea** a morris dance 382/3

Christianus, -a, -um *adj and sbst* Christian 371/1, 372/27, 374/29, etc

Christicola, -ae *n m* Christian 374/28

circiter *adv found alone* 314/20, 342/33, 342/35; *or in idiom* **eo circiter** 285/10, 286/19, 343/18, etc: thereabouts (of time)

circumcido, -dere, -di, -sum *v tr* to circumcise 370/21; by transference, to make pure or righteous 370/28

circumcisus, -a, -um *adj* circumcised, purified 370/32

Cirencestria, -ae *n f* Cirencester 385/2

cissor, -oris *n m* clothcutter, tailor, *or possibly* carver 360/24; **sissor** 361/12

cithara,- ae *n f literally*, lyre, but here probably harp 372/30, 374/7

cithareda, -e *n comm literally*, in CL, a female lyrist, but here probably harper (although there is evidence that the word could refer to one who played any plucked string instrument) 290/37, possibly 373/41; context suggests that in ML the word is to be treated as masculine and refers to a man

citharaedus, -i *n m literally*, lyrist, here probably harper 382/9, 386/1, possibly 373/41 *see also* **cithareda**

clericus, -i *n m* cleric, one in holy orders 63/17, 64/21, 290/11

colluctator, -oris *n m* fellow-wrestler 382/10

collusor, -oris *n m* fellow-player of a sport or game, or in some form of entertainment 382/10

comessatio, -onis *n f* feast, banquet 379/33, 385/21

comestio, -onis *n f* eating 371/15, 373/1

comitatus, -us *n m* county 342/32, 342/34, 343/16, etc

comes, -itis *n m* companion, comrade 374/21; earl 291/12, 291/13

comitissa, -e *n f* countess 291/27

comitiua, -e *n f* retinue, train of followers 64/5

commissio, -onis *n f* (royal) commission, usually of judicial inquiry or of the peace 63/8, 64/14, 64/15

communis, -e *adj* common, communal 379/22, 384/39; common, ordinary, usual 290/19, 376/12; pertaining to the community or town (*see* **aula**)

communitas, -atis *n f* community, commonalty, commons 63/10, 64/29

compareo, -ere, -ui, -- *v intr* to appear in

court or before judges 331/14, 331/38, 332/6, etc

concionator, -oris *n m* preacher 382/13, 385/4

concio, -onis *n f* sermon, homily 382/13

conclaue, -is *n nt* meeting, assembly 385/5

confabulatio, -onis *n f* conversation 379/34

conformis, -e *adj* obedient 381/21, 381/27

conformitas, -atis *n f* correction 381/14

confrater, -tris *n m* brother: *intensive form of* frater, here in extended sense, member of the same community or group 386/3

connoto, -are, -aui, -atum *v tr* to call together, to summon 64/28

conquestus, -us *n m* (Norman) conquest 63/6, 64/13

constructio, -onis *n f* interpretation 384/29

contritio, -onis *n f* sorrow for wrong-doing, contrition 372/5

conuentus, -us *n m* convent, a community of monks or nuns 290/10

coquina, -e *n f* kitchen 361/13, 361/22, 361/27, etc

Corinthius, -a, -um *adj and sbst* Corinthian: **prior ad Corinthios epistola** Paul's first epistle to the Corinthians 372/39–373/1

coronator, -oris *n m* coroner, a royal officer charged, among other responsibilities, with holding inquests into cases of accidental or violent death 64/2

costagium, -ii *n nt* cost, expense 291/21

curia, -e *n f* court of law 170/7m, 171/3m

custodia, -ae *n f* jail 377/17, 377/24, 383/12, etc

Dauidicus, -a, -um *adj* pertaining to David, king of Israel, Davidic 374/27

debacchans, -ntis *n comm* bacchante, one of the orgiastic votaries, usually but not exclusively female, of the god Bacchus 374/19

decanatus, -us *n m* deanery, the area over which a dean or rural dean has ecclesiastical jurisdiction, here used, by extension, of the area of authority of an archdeacon as

immediate supervisor of the rural deans 385/4

decanus, -i *n m* dean, here the head of a cathedral or collegiate chapter of clergy 324/30

declaratio, -onis *n f* (royal) proclamation 368/30, 368/32, 369/7

delineatio, -onis *n f* description, delineation 374/11

depono, -onere, -osui, -ositum *v tr* to depose, to make a statement of evidence 343/1, 343/11, 343/18

detectio, -onis *n f* detection, a formal report or allegation of wrong-doing made before an ecclesiastical court 332/6

diabolicus,-a, -um *adj* pertaining to or worthy of the devil, diabolic 382/2(2)

diabolus, -i *n m* the devil 382/37

dies, -ei *n m and f* day 285/6, 286/16, 361/7, etc; day of the week 380/12, 380/14: **dies dominica** *or* **dominicalis** Sunday 63/16, 64/20, 290/16, etc; **dies lune** Monday 63/5, 64/12, 290/18; **dies Martis** Tuesday 290/21; **dies Sabbati** Saturday 361/7; day (as opposed to night) 347/22, 385/27; day (as a unit of time) 369/12, 369/20, 369/21, etc; day set aside for a special purpose: a saint's day, eg, **dies sancti Nicholai** 290/24; **dies paschae** *or* **dies panis azimi** Passover, the feast of unleavened bread 373/15; **dies pentecostes** *or* **dies hebdomadarum** Pentecost, the feast of weeks 373/15; **dies tabernaculorum** Succoth, the feast of tabernacles 373/16: these three, named together in Appendix 3 of *Gloucestershire*, constitute the three great pilgrim festivals of Judaism, at which times personal attendance at the Temple was mandatory, but it is unclear why the author has singled them out.

dieta, -e *n f* daily allowance of provisions 361/21, 361/41

diffamacio, -onis *n f* defamation of character (a crime under the jurisdiction of the ecclesiastical courts) 330/12

diocesis, -is *n f* diocese (the area under the jurisdiction of a bishop) 332/35, 378/11

dissidium, -ii *n nt* disagreement 379/35

diuus, -a, -um *adj* holy: *hence*, as a title, saint 374/6, 374/9

doctrina, -ae *n f* church teaching, doctrine 380/35, 382/15

domina, -e *n f* lady (especially as title of a peeress or a peer's wife) 291/27, 347/7, 347/12, etc

dominicus, -a, -um *adj* pertaining to a lord or lordship, of or pertaining to authority 383/27; in a restricted sense, of or pertaining to the Lord (as a divine title); *see* **dies**

dominicalis, -e *adj see* **dies, sermo**

dominus, -i *n m* Lord (title of God) 285/12, 302/24, 340/25; lord, sir (title of royalty, peer, knight, bishop, priest, Benedictine choir monk) 63/7, 63/8, 63/19, etc

δῶρον, -ου, τὸ *n nt* Gk n here in phr Βασιλικὸν Δῶρον, Basilikon Doron, the title of a work of James I, a political treatise composed for his eldest son, Prince Henry, and strongly Protestant in tone 376/15

drachma, -ae *n f* penny 386/12

ductio, -onis *n f* leading, directing 373/1

dux, -cis *n m* duke 291/11, 358/24, 358/27, etc

ebibitio, -onis *n f* the act of drinking, quaffing 379/33

ecclesia, -e *n f* the church: as a community of believers 371/40; an institution 369/2, 370/37, 371/8; or a physical structure 290/7, 332/4, 332/14

ecclesiasticus, -a, -um *adj* of or pertaining to the church 373/25

elemosina, -e *n f* alms 290/8, 290/11, 290/12, etc

elemosinarius, -ii *n m* almoner (a household officer charged with the distribution of alms on behalf of his lord) 361/14

Epiphania, -e *n f see* **festum**

episcopalis, -e *adj* of or pertaining to a bishop 375/18

episcopus, -i *n m* bishop 63/19, 63/23, 64/3; boy-bishop (?) 290/12

epistola, -ae *n f* letter, here an epistle of St Paul 373/1

epotatio, -onis *n f* drinking, a party or gathering for the primary purpose of drinking (as opposed to **comessatio**, a gathering for the primary purpose of eating (?); *see also* **comessatio**) 379/33, 385/22

ergastulum, -i *n nt* workhouse 377/25

esquierius, -ii *n m* esquire, household attendant 290/39

ethnicus, -a, -um *adj* heathen, barbarian (the Latinized spelling of a Gk adj ἐθνικός, -ή, -όν, used in the Septuagint to refer to non-Jews) 374/19

euangelicus, -a, -um *adj* of, pertaining to, or worthy of the gospels or their teaching 376/27

euangelista, -ae *n m* evangelist, one of the authors or redactors of the gospels 374/11

euangelium, -ii *n nt literally*, good news, here used to refer to one of the four gospels 370/32, 374/31, 375/3, etc

excommunicatio, -onis *n f* excommunication, an ecclesiastical penalty under which the guilty party was punished by exclusion from the sacraments and especially the reception of communion; at various times, further disabilities were imposed as well, such as exclusion from all social intercourse with other members of the church 332/21

excommunicatus, -a, -um *adj* excommunicated, suffering from the penalty of excommunication 331/36, 332/3, 332/9, etc

exemplificatus, -a, -um *pp* having been exemplified, that is, having had a formal attested copy made 201/12

Exodus, -i *n f literally*, a leaving, going away; Exodus, the Greek and Latin name of the second book of the Pentateuch 373/6

Exoniensis, -e *adj* of or pertaining to Exeter, here designating the bishop of Exeter 335/28

factura, -e *n f* making, fashioning 358/28
familia, -e *n f* household 290/38
familiaris, -e *adj and sbst* of or pertaining to the household, *hence mf as sbst* member of a household 357/9; **famuliaris, -e** 360/22, 360/23
feria, -ae *n f* holiday, festival, holy day 369/23, 369/24, 370/22, etc
ferialis, -e *adj* of or pertaining to a holiday 373/20
festum, -i *n nt* religious festival 369/23, 373/20, 373/23; feast of the Christian church 347/21, 347/23, 347/24: **festum Epiphanie** Epiphany, 6 January 347/27; **festum Natale** *or* **Natalis domini** *see* natalis; **festum Sancti Michaelis** *or* **Sancti Michaelis Archangeli** Michaelmas, 29 September 63/5–6, 64/12–13; **festum Sancti Nicholai** St Nicholas' Day, 6 December 290/18
fides, -ei *n f* faith, belief, in a restricted sense Christian belief, either in an abstract sense or as a concrete body of dogmas 369/37, 369/39, 370/2, etc
fidelis, -e *adj and sbst* worthy of trust, faithful 375/8, 384/27; *m as sbst* a faithful Christian; *in pl* the faithful 371/24, 372/27, 384/39
focale, -is *n nt* fuel for fires or stoves 361/40
for, fari, fassus sum *v tr* to speak, to say, here used in restricted sense, to acknowledge, to confess the validity of a charge 331/14, 331/38, 332/6, etc
forinsecus, -a, -um *adj* external, alien, foreign 290/33, 358/24
forisfactura, -e *n f* forfeiture (eg, of a monetary fine) 169/28, 169/36
frater, -tris *n m* brother: literally, 64/25, or in an extended sense of fellow members of the same community or group 369/27, 375/28, 376/9, etc; a member of a religious order 290/13, 290/30, 290/33, etc

garcio, -onis *n m* groom, servant 360/9, 360/13
gardianus, -i *n m* churchwarden 201/12, 333/2
gardroba, -e *n f* wardrobe (department of a royal or noble household): *hence* **gardroba lectorum** petty wardrobe, the lord's personal clothing and effects 359/1–2m
gasconiensis, -e *adj see* uinum
generosus, -i *n m* gentleman 360/7, 360/11, 361/11, etc
gestio, -ire, -ii, -- *v intr* to exult; to gesture; to express oneself by gesture; *hence possibly* to represent mimetically: it is impossible to be sure exactly in what sense this word is being used here 371/37
gestiuncula, -ae *n f diminutive of* **gestus** 382/14, 382/24
gestus, -us *n m* physical movement; (dance) movement; gesture, sign (either accompanying or independent of speech); hence possibly mimetic action: it is impossible to be sure to which of these senses these occurrences, all in Appendix 3 of the Gloucestershire records, should be assigned 369/22, 370/8, 370/38
Gloucestria, -e *n f* Gloucester 290/16m, 290/23, 291/11, etc
Gloucestriensis, -e *adj* of or pertaining to Gloucester 368/42, 377/17, 381/15–16m, etc
gratia, -ae *n f* favour, good-will, used in a restricted sense: grace, a divine gift operating in man to sanctify, regenerate, and strengthen 371/13, 371/27, 372/21, etc; thanks 375/26, 386/18; *in accusative, with 'agere,'* to thank, to give thanks to 386/6; *in ablative, followed by genitive,* for the sake of 378/7, 383/10; **gratiarum actio post puerperium** service for the thanksgiving of women after childbirth (commonly known as the churching of women) 385/20

gratitudo, -inis *n f* thankfulness, gratitude 371/3

gymnasium, -ii *n nt* Gk *n* γυμνάσιον, -ου, τὸ *qv* 370/38, 371/5, 373/3

Habacucus, -i *n m* Habakkuk, one of the OT prophets, or the OT book called by his name 374/22

hebdoma, -ade *n f* week 290/9, 380/15; *see also* **dies**

histrio, -onis *n m* an entertainer: in CL, an actor of the better sort, in later Latin, one who performed in pornographic plays, in ML usage in England, apparently a generic term, often synonymous with **ministrallus** and 'mimus,' which often refers to a musician (here as in other instances it is impossible to be sure which sense is intended) 384/37

histrionicus, -a, -um *adj* of or pertaining to a histrio 379/7

homo, -inis *n m* person, human being 63/9, 64/5, 369/39, etc; Christ's human nature 371/17, 371/30; liege man, servant 63/19, 64/1, 64/8, etc; **interior homo** the inner man, the true self 370/5

Hosea, -ae *n m* Hosea, one of the OT prophets, or the OT book called by his name 374/22

hospicium, -ii *n nt* inn, guest-house 347/22, 347/27, 358/23, etc

hostelaria, -e *n f* hostelry, inn 347/7

hymnus, -i *n m* hymn 373/26

hypotyposis, -is *n f* Gk *n* ὑποτύπωσις, -εως, ἡ *qv* 377/13

iantaculum, -i *n nt* breakfast, earliest of the daily meals 361/9, 361/18

idola, -ae *n f* image of a (pagan) deity 374/24, 381/36, 382/2

idololatria, -ae *n f* worship offered to the images of (pagan) deities 372/37, 373/2, 373/5

idololatricus, -a, -um *adj* of or pertaining to the worship of images of (pagan) deities

374/23, 380/2

imperialis, -e *adj* of or pertaining to the exercise of royal authority 376/32

imposterum *adv* for the future, hereafter 381/28

imprimis *adv* in the first place, first 312/16, 340/28, 341/2, etc; **inprimis** 73/29, 82/9, 105/23

incarceratus, -i *n m* prisoner, one who has been put in jail 377/18, 383/20

indebite *adv* undeservedly, not in a proper or due manner 290/31

inprimis *adv see* **imprimis**

instrumentum, -i *n nt* (musical) instrument 372/31, 382/10, 386/9

iocor, -ari, -atus sum *v intr* to jest, joke; to play, engage in pleasant pastimes; *hence possibly* to take part in an entertaining performance: it is impossible to determine in which of these senses any one occurrence of the word is being used here 369/10, 371/37, 372/9, etc

iocularius, -a, -um *adj* of, pertaining to, or suitable for a iocus; playful, pleasant, entertaining 369/22, 371/16; *nt as sbst, synonym for* iocus 373/37, 382/11

iocus, -i *n m, nt in pl* in CL joke, jest; (verbal) witticism; in Anglo-Latin medieval usage, recreation (eg, sports, dancing); a play, an entertaining performance, a trick (eg, of a performing animal): it is impossible to know in what sense any one occurrence of this word is used here 368/33, 380/13, 382/4

irrecuperabiliter *adv* irrecoverably, irreversibly 382/20

Israelita, -ae *n m* Israelite, here used generally for Hebrew OT characters 372/26, 373/12, 374/23, etc

iubilatio, -onis *n f* rejoicing, celebration 369/17, 379/8

iurator, -oris *n m* juror 63/15, 64/20

iusticiarius, -i *n m* justice of the peace, judge 381/13

Kariolium, -i *n nt* Carlisle 63/5, 63/10(2), etc

lagena, -ae *n f* gallon (liquid measure) 361/25, 361/26(2), etc

Lancastrensis, -e *adj* of or pertaining to Lancaster, Lancastrian, *hence mf as sbst* Lancaster 378/17

Lancastria, -ae *n f* Lancaster 378/8

le, lez *vernacular art see* EG

libellus, -i *n m* formal accusation or set of charges laid against the accused party in a court (composed of individual charges or **articula**) 330/9, 330/20

liberacio, -onis *n f* delivery (of money or goods), *hence*, payment 359/12m; 'livery,' one of the five daily meals in a noble household 361/15, 361/23, 361/28

linura, -e *n f* lining (of clothing) 359/4

littera, -ae *n f* letter of the alphabet, *in pl* letters, literature: *hence* **sacrae litterae** sacred letters, ie, the Bible 379/24, 385/38

ludicrum, -cri *n nt* a synonym for **ludus** 369/15, 382/10; *probably derived from this noun is the adj* **ludicer, -cra, -crum** of, pertaining to, or suitable for a **ludus** 377/20, 380/13

ludo, -dere, -si, -sum *v tr* to perform (a play or some other form of entertainment) 64/21, 290/11, 347/23, etc: in Appendix 3 of the Gloucestershire records it is difficult to tell whether this meaning or one of the logically prior meanings, to take part in recreation or to play (a game, a sport, a game of chance), is intended 369/10, 371/37, 380/34; to play (music or a musical instrument) 386/9

ludus, -i *n m* play (as a form of performance), *a synonym of* **miraculum** 63/17, 63/25; in Appendix 3 of the Gloucestershire records it is sometimes hard to tell whether this meaning or one of the logically prior meanings, play, recreation, game, sport, is intended 368/32, 380/12, 380/16, etc; **ludi Maii** May games 382/3

lusor, -oris *n m* player in (unspecified)

entertainment or sport 357/15, 357/21, 357/25, etc

lusus, -us *n m* play (as a form of recreation), game, sport, game of chance; play (as a form of entertainment); it is difficult to distinguish which meaning is intended in a given context here 368/33, 372/7, 373/3, etc

lyricus, -i *n m* musician, *literally*, one who plays the lyre, here probably a harper 385/5, 386/1

magister, -tri *n m* master, Mr (as a title of respect) 385/3, 386/7(2), etc

magnas, -atis *n m* magnate, person of wealth or high political or ecclesiastical standing 378/13

maiestas, -atis *n f* majesty (as a royal or divine title) 374/28, 375/14, 375/23, etc; **laesa maiestas** lèse-majesté, treason 376/20

maior, -oris *n m* mayor 64/28, 64/30, 218/25

maior, -us *compar adj* greater (in size, dignity, or worth) 290/7, 370/17, 374/30, etc

Maius, -a, -um *adj see* **ludus, pyramis**

marca, -e *n m* mark (currency denomination equal in value to 13 s 4 d) 290/32, 291/29

Marchia, -e *n f* march, border district, *hence* **comes Marchie** earl of March 291/12

martyr, -is *n m* martyr, one who dies in defence of Christianity or moral principles 290/22

Mauritii *see* **chorea**

melodia, -ae *n f* music, melody: a Gk n taken over into Latin; both Gk usage and CL usage of related words have the connotation of song, but Anglo-Latin medieval usage is more ambiguous, and so seems to imply either instrumental music or song; hence it is difficult to know in what sense the word is used here 385/7, 386/4

metaphysicῶs *adv a Gk adv* μεταφυσικῶς metaphysically (a post-classical formation) 371/28

minister, -tri *n m literally*, servant, *hence*,

with reference to Mk 10:43–5, a minister, a clergyman 333/2, 368/41, 369/2, etc

ministrallus, -i *n m* minstrel, entertainer (one of the three most common terms, together with **histrio** and 'mimus,' for a performer; it seems to have been generic, although one called a **ministrallus** was sometimes a wait or musician 290/37, 291/10, 291/11, etc; **minstrallus** 347/6, 347/26; **mynstrallus** 347/12, 347/22, 348/8

miraculum, -i *n nt* an object of wonder, a miracle, *hence* a play, probably one about the miracles of the Bible or a saint 64/22, 290/12

misericordia, -e *n f* mercy, kindness 378/3; alms 288/10; amercement, fine 289/17

molendinum, -i *n nt* mill 380/23

monasterium, -ii *n nt* monastery 290/40

mora, -e *n f* interval or space of time 291/2; also in idiom **moram facere** to pass one's time, to stay or reside (in a place) 314/19, 315/3, 330/15, etc

multo, -onis *n m* mutton 361/30

multrix, -icis *n f* milkmaid 380/24

municio, -onis *n f* fortress, garrison, here in idiom **in municione** in munition, that is, among the standing garrison of a fortified town or castle 63/9

mynstrallus, -i *n m see* **ministrallus**

Myntyus, -i *n m* name of a kind of musician (?); this word may be a scribal error for some other but unknown term; it is unknown elsewhere 385/5

mysterium, -ii *n nt* religious mystery, doctrine, dogma 371/13

mystίϰῶς *Gk adv* μυστιϰῶς mystically 371/28

natalis, -e *adj literally,* of or pertaining to birth, here in idiom **festum Natale domini** 358/30 or *nt as sbst* **Natale domini** 361/8–9m: Christmas

natiuus, -i *n m* serf, villein 360/24

nimpha, -ae *n f for* **nympha** *qv* 351/22

nonnecessarium, -ii *n nt* that which is unnecessary, a non-essential 382/18

nuncius, -ii *n m* groom, servant, *or possibly* messenger 291/10, 291/13

oblatio, -onis *n f* offering, alms 290/7, 290/23

officiarius, -ii *n m* officer, official (of the crown, a city, a household, etc) 380/9

officium, -ii *n nt* office, position: the legal idiom **officium Domini contra aliquem** describes proceedings in an ecclesiastical court undertaken by the office of the court, in the person of the presiding judge or his representative, against a person, which are not the result of a suit by an injured party, although the office may be acting upon information received from a presentment or a promotion 286/37 (*see* **presentacio** and **promotio**); duty, obligation, responsibility 290/41, 371/34, 384/29

oratio, -onis *n f* discourse, treatise 368/31; prayer 384/40

ordinarius, -ii *n m* officer, official 381/26

ordinatio, -onis *n f* ordinance, regulation (issued by either civil or ecclesiastical authorities) 290/30, 381/1, 383/18

organum, -i *n nt* musical instrument, organ 372/31, 374/8

orthodoxus, -a, -um *adj* orthodox, doctrinally correct 376/27

Oxoniensis, -e *adj* of or pertaining to Oxford and its university 375/26

panetria, -e *n f* pantry, a storeroom for bread and other staples, *here possibly* a household department 361/7

papista, -ae *n m* papist, derogatory nickname for a Roman Catholic 378/9, 378/16, 384/31, etc

papisticus, -a, -um *adj* papistical, derogatory term for Roman Catholicism 371/20, 385/20

Paradisum, -i *n nt* paradise, the garden of Eden (Gn 2:8–3:24) 371/9

parisiensis, -e *adj* of or pertaining to Paris:

parisiensis candela Paris candle, a kind of large wax candle 361/37–8

parochia, -e *n f* parish, the smallest distinct unit of ecclesiastical jurisdiction and Christian ministry, each parish having its own church, priest, wardens, and tithes 331/15, 342/34, 343/16, etc

parochianus, -i *n m* parishioner, inhabitant of a parish 344/10

particulare, -is *n nt* detail, item, particular 356/23

particulariter *adv* in detail, item by item 356/22

pascha, -ae *n f see* **dies**

patria, -e *n f* local district, country 360/25

peccator, -oris *n m* sinner (one who commits offenses against God or divine law as embodied either in the Bible or ecclesiastical law) 380/6

peccatum, -i *n nt* sin, an offense against God or divine law as embodied in either the Bible or ecclesiastical law 372/23

penitencia, -e *n f* penance (the act of contrition or restitution imposed upon the penitent sinner by ecclesiastical or divine authority) 331/17, 333/23, 372/3

pentateuchum, -i *n nt* Pentateuch, the Greek and Latin name of the Torah, the five (Gk adj πέντε) books of Moses 373/13

pentecostes, -es *n f see* **dies**

penulator, -oris *n m* furrier 360/24

personalis, -e *adj* here found in idiom **responsio personalis** 344/8 or **responsum personale** 201/11: a reply or response to a charge delivered by the respondent in person

phantasma, -atis *n nt* fantasy, fancy; dream 382/33

phantasticus, -a, -um *adj* fantastic, fanciful 371/19

picherius, -ii *n m* pitcher (liquid measure) 361/16, 361/17, 361/18, etc

pietancia, -e *n f* pittance: allowance of alms 290/10

polus, -i *n m* pole: here apparently either a Maypole or a summer pole 381/13m, 382/8(2); **polus aestiualis** 377/17 or **aestiuus** 381/35, 383/14 summer pole; *see* **somner pole** *in* EG

pontificius, -a, -um *adj literally,* of or pertaining to a bishop, *hence* applied as a derogatory term to Roman Catholicism: of or pertaining to the pope, popish, Roman Catholic 371/20, 379/4, 379/6, etc

potacio, -onis *n f* drinking: used literally 371/15, 373/1; or as the name of one of the five daily meals in a noble household 361/14, 361/27

praeconceptus, -a, -um *adj* preconceived, thought out in advance 376/11

praeputium, -ii *n nt literally,* the foreskin: here in idiom **praeputium concidere** to circumcise 370/21

prandium, -ii *n nt* dinner, the earlier and more important of the two main daily meals 347/12m, 347/17m, 348/3m, etc

praxis, -is *n f Gk n* πρᾶξις, -εως, ἡ, *qv*: it occurs in Roman letters 373/32, 379/3, 383/6 and also entirely in Gk letters 371/6

presentacio, -onis *n f* presentment, a specific allegation or series of allegations of misconduct made against (a) named person(s) to an ecclesiastical official or court 201/11, 331/15(2); *see also* **officium, promocio**

presento, -are, -aui, -atum *v tr* to make presentment (*see* **presentacio**) 288/19

princeps, -ipis *n m* prince 291/21

prioratus, -us *n m* priory, a religious house under the jurisdiction of a prior 290/41, 291/2

prior, -is *n m* prior, an officer of a religious house subordinate to the abbot or the head of a religious house, itself occasionally dependent upon another house 290/10, 290/33

prior, prius *compar adj* earlier (in time) 370/22; first (of two) 372/39

professor, -oris *n m* one who avows or supports a position or belief 370/35

promocio, -onis *n f* promotion, the bringing of an allegation in an ecclesiastical court by one not authorized to make presentment; the promoter may be a lay person or an officer of the court 344/9; *see also* **officium, presentacio**

promotor, -oris *n m* promoter, one who brings an allegation before an ecclesiastical court 286/39; *see also* **promocio**

promotus, -a, -um *adj* having been promoted (of an allegation) 286/37; *see also* **promocio**

propheta, -ae *n m* prophet, one who speaks on behalf of God and with divine authority 373/35, 385/39, 386/4

propheto, -are, -aui, -- *v intr* to prophesy, to speak on behalf of God and with divine authority 386/3, 386/4

protestans, -ntis *n m* Protestant 379/5

psallo, -ere, -i, -- *v intr* to play on a stringed instrument, *hence*, to play music of any kind 371/35, 372/30, 377/24, etc

psalma, -ae *n m* psalm, a religious song: specifically one of the OT psalms 373/26, 373/29, 385/35

psalmista, -ae *n m* composer of psalms, ie, David 373/29

psalmodia, -ae *n f* psalmody, the musical arrangement or performance of psalms and other hymns 385/36

psalmographus, -i *n m* author of psalms, ie, David 373/32

puritanus, -i *n m* Puritan 375/28, 375/38, 376/5, etc

pyramis, -idis *n f literally*, a pyramid, here apparently used as a synonym for **polus**: pole, as in Maypole, summer pole 377/37, 381/36, 383/14

quarta, -e *n f* quart (liquid or solid measure) 361/16, 361/22(2), etc

quarterium, -ii *n nt* quarter, one-fourth 361/8(2), 361/15, etc

quum *conj for* **cum** *qv* 370/4, 372/17, 373/7, etc

recreatio, -onis *n f* recreation: fun, refreshment, relaxation, exercise 368/33, 369/15, 374/35, etc

recuso, -are, aui, -atum *v tr* to refuse, not consent to 374/14, 384/35; to oppose 377/14; *hence*, to refuse to attend services of the Church of England 378/9

redemptio, -onis *n f* redemption, the saving act of God in Christ to save man from the effects of sin 369/35

redemptor, -oris *n m* redeemer, a divine title or appellation 371/4

regardator, -oris *n m* regarder, an officer charged with the supervision of forests 361/12

regardum, -i *n nt* reward, gratuity, customary payment 356/18, 356/20

remissio, -onis *n f* here in idiom **remissio peccatorum** the remission or forgiveness of sins 372/23

repeditatio, -onis *n f* stepping or moving back and forth, steps (in a dance or other pattern) 382/23

responsio, -onis *n f* formal reply to charges or questioning 344/8, 380/38; *see* **personalis**

resurgo, -rgere, -rrexi, -rrectum *v intr* to rise up to life (from death) 371/24

sabbatum, -i *n nt* the Jewish sabbath 369/14, 373/14, 373/21, etc; Sunday 369/8, 369/9, 369/11, etc; *see also* **dies**

sacramentaliter *adv* as a sacrament 371/23

sacramentum, -i *n nt* an oath: **super sacramentum suum** on oath 63/15 (*here in form* **sacra⟨......⟩**), 64/20, 288/19; a sacrament of the Christian church, here used with special reference to the eucharist 371/11, 371/26

sacristaria, -e *n f* sacristy, the repository for the vestments, vessels, and other valuables of a church or religious house 291/2

salio, -ere, -ui, -um *v tr* to leap, jump; to mount (used of mating animals) 370/29, 370/32, 371/36, etc

saltatio, -onis *n f* dancing, a dance 369/17, 370/8, 373/2, etc

saltator, -oris *n m* in CL, dancer; here it is impossible to know whether this sense, or the more usual Anglo-Latin meaning, tumbler, is meant 382/10

salto, -are, -aui, -atum *v intr* to dance: in CL, this verb can imply dancing which was representational or mimetic in character, but it is impossible to say whether this connotation is intended in Appendix 3 of the Gloucestershire records, though it must have been known to the author 369/10, 370/29, 371/37, etc

saltus, -us *n m* leap, spring: by extension, step, dance-step 369/21, 370/38

sanctifico, -are, -aui, -atum *v tr* to make holy or sacred 369/10

sanctificatio, -onis *n f* the act of making holy or sacred 369/13

scandalum, -i *n nt* stumbling-block, an occasion or potential cause of sin or divisiveness 382/31

schismaticus, -a, -um *adj and sbst* of or pertaining to a schism, schismatic 384/35; *m as sbst* a member of a schism 378/23

Scriptura, -ae *n f* the Bible 371/8

secta, -ae *n f* sect, usually a religious subgroup having beliefs and practices different from those of the group as a whole 379/4

sellaria, -ie *n f* storeroom, cellar 361/15

septimana, -ae *n f* week 380/12, 385/28

sermo, -onis *n m* conversation, discourse 381/35; sermon: **sermo dominicalis** Sunday sermon 380/32

seruiens, -ntis *n m* servant, liege man 63/18, 63/23, 356/18, etc

seruus, -i *n m* servant 385/5m; *historically*, a slave 380/29, 380/31

sextarius, -ii *n m* sester, a dry and liquid measure whose equivalent is unknown

361/16, 361/18, 361/20, etc

siccine *adv for* **sicine** *qv* 369/13

siet *archaic pr subj of* **sum** *qv* 377/13

signus, -i *n m for* **cycnus** *qv* 361/31

siluestris, -e *adj literally* of or from the woods: here in idiom, **carbo siluestris** charcoal 361/40

sissor *n m see* **cissor**

spiritualis, -e *adj* spiritual, of or pertaining to the human or divine spirit 371/15, 371/17, 372/1

spiritualiter *adv* in a way pertaining or appropriate to the spirit or soul 371/23

spiritus, -us *n m* spirit, soul, mind 371/21, 375/30(2); **spiritus sanctus** Holy Spirit 371/30-1, 374/32

sponsus, -i *n m* bridegroom, here used to refer to Jesus on the basis of his parables of the bridegroom 374/12, 374/14, 374/30

Staffordia, -e *n f* Stafford 347/12

statutum, -i *n nt* statute, law 290/41, 383/18, 383/29, etc

statutus, -a, -um *adj* established, set 290/17

staurum, -i *n nt* store, storeroom 361/29

subditus, -i *n m* subject (of a king or other ruler) 368/34, 368/37, 375/7

subiectus, -i *n m* subject (of a king or other ruler) 380/9, 384/28

superabundanter *adv* in great abundance 378/19

superexundans, -ntis *adj* springing up to a great extent, greatly abounding 380/4

tabernaculum, -i *n nt see* **dies**

taberna, -ae *n f* tavern, drinking establishment 379/31

testamentum, -i *n nt* will, testament; here in idiom **testamentum nouum** New Testament 372/38-9

thesaurarius, -ii *n m* treasurer 361/10

tibia, -ae *n f* pipe, flute, reed pipe 372/30

tibicen, -inis *n m* piper, perhaps used generically for musician 373/40, 382/9, 386/2

totalis, -e *adj* entire, whole, total 296/25,

361/41

totaliter *adv* entirely 290/36

Trinitas, -atis *n f* the Trinity 290/17

tripudium, -ii *n nt* ritual dance, dance: it is unclear whether the connotation of ritual is intended by the author of Appendix 3 of the Gloucestershire records, but it must have been known to him 369/17, 370/7, 371/16, etc

trumpetta, -e *n f* trumpeter 356/21

typicos *adv Gk adv* τυπικῶς typologically, according to types (post-classical formation) 371/28

uaco, -are, -aui, -atum *v intr* to have time or leisure for, *hence*, to be able to (with infinitive) 382/1; to be null and void (of orders or ordinances) 169/35m

uagabundus, -i *n m* vagabond, itinerant laborer with no visible means of support, hence, **statutum vagabundi** a statute governing the movements of itinerant labourers 385/10

ualettus, -i *n m* esquire 360/8, 360/12

uersus, -us *n m* verse (as a division or subdivision of a text) 372/36, 373/1, 373/6, etc

uersus *prep* against 330/10, 344/10

uigilia, -e *n f* eve (of a saint's day or other church festival); **uigilia Sancti Nicholai** 5 December 290/16; **uigilia Sancti Petri ad uinculum** 31 July 63/16, 64/21

uilla, -e *n f* town, vill, township 360/25

uindico, -are, -aui, -atum *v tr* to lay claim to, arrogate (to oneself) 376/33; to defend, vindicate 376/32

uinum, -i *n nt* wine; **uinum gasconiense** Gascon wine 361/16, 361/19, 361/21, etc; **uinum de Royn'** Rhine wine 361/17, 361/19, 361/22

uirga, -e *n f* stick, staff, rod 63/21, 64/24; yard (as a unit of distance or length) 358/38, 359/1, 359/2, etc

uisitacio, -onis *n f* visitation, a formal inquiry, based upon specific articles, into the life of a religious house or a parish, carried out by the relevant ecclesiastical jurisdictional superior 290/41

ulna, -e *n f* ell, a unit of distance or length equivalent in English usage to 45 in 358/28(2)

undequaque *adv* on every side, all about 369/3

urs' *see endnote*

Whitsonius, -a, -um *adj see* **alla**

Zephania, -ae *n m* Zephaniah, one of the OT prophets, or the OT book called by his name 374/22

English Glossary

abbott *n* abbot or lord of misrule, one chosen to preside over Christmas games and revels 71/13; **abbott of misrule** 296/31; *see also* **lord of misrule, Christemas lord**

abettinge *vb n* urging, encouraging 285/16

abettment *n* encouragement, aid 189/32, 190/14

abode *v pa 3 sg* lodged, stayed 292/5

about *prep* (usually with reference to expenses) in connection with 115/29; 180/18; 180/35; **aboute** 341/1; 341/20; **abovt** 179/13

abouts *prep* about the time of 340/6

accidens *n* the rudiments or first principles of any subject (*hence*, **a single accidens**, 'a primer in itself' (?)) 355/1–2

accompt *n* account 339/5m, 340/7, 341/37; **accompte** 296/35, 296/43; 297/6, etc

accompt *v pr 1 pl* account, hold (to be) 367/35; **accompted** *pp* 342/37; **accompt** *pr 3 pl* count, reckon 340/28; **accompted** *pa 3 pl* 339/8; **accomptinge** *prp* accounting, rendering a reckoning 339/6

accomptant *n* one who renders an account 315/37, 317/16; **accomptantes** *pl* 302/22, 303/13; 310/25, etc; **accomptaunce** 300/41; **accomptauntes** 298/26; 299/5, 299/22, etc

accte *n* part of a play; performance, in a general sense (?) *or v inf* act, perform (with 'the' in error for 'them') (?) 328/30

aduerteshede *pp* notified, informed 214/18

adventured *v pa 3 pl* risked, dared to undertake 340/20, 342/2

afor *adv* before 292/8; **afor** *prep* before 214/23; **afore** 359/13; **afore hand** *prep phr* used as *adv* beforehand 189/24

after *prep* according to 292/38, 294/25, 295/26

against *prep* in preparation for 98/5, 115/28, 121/12, etc; **againste** 83/13, 84/28; **ayenst** 296/14

albes *n pl* albs, vestments of white cloth reaching to the feet 337/14

alderman *n* in Kendal, the elected head of the municipal corporation 168/7, 169/1; 169/15, etc; **aldrman** 208/2; 208/25, 208/32, etc; **adermans** *poss* 207/23; **aldermans** 168/23; 178/32; 183/36; etc; **aldrman** 204/29, 204/3; **aldrmanes** 177/20; **aldrmans** 185/5, 208/30; **aldermen** *n pl* in most English boroughs and cities, members of the governing corporation 292/23, 293/21, 293/28, etc

alehouse *n* a house where ale is retailed 346/20; **alehouses** *pl* 367/4

a leuen *adj* eleven 200/4

alhallow thursday *n phr* 'Allhallow Thursday,' the Thursday after Rogation Sunday, *ie*, Ascension Day (a moveable feast 94/12 **alhallowe thursday** 72/8, 83/32, 95/1; etc; **alhallowes thursdaye** 81/9–10; **Allathursdaye** 88/23; **allhallow thursday** 98/10; **allhallowe thursday** 82/6; **allhallowthursday** 98/12; *see also* **hallow thursdaie**

allhollantyde *n* 'All Hallows Tide,' the Feast of All Saints (1 November) 286/2

allowance *n* acceptance (by auditors) as

legitimate expenses 302/22, 311/2, 311/40, etc; **allowaunce** 299/5, 299/22, 300/14, etc; **alowance** 316/29; **a lowaunce** 300/41; **alowances** *pl* 84/27

allowe *v inf* approve of, sanction 194/2, 194/3; **allowede** *pa 3 sg* 192/15; **alowede** 85/4; **allowed** *pp* 114/32; **alowte** 118/38; **allowinge** *vb n* 171/12; **allowed of** *pp phr* permitted (by someone), *especially*, permitted to claim as expenses 315/37; **alowed of** 384/6

almanacke *n* book containing astronomical and astrological tables together with an ecclesiastical calendar and (sometimes) weather and astrological predictions 355/13

almes disshe *n phr* a vessel for the reception of alms, used in churches, in the houses of the rich, or carried by beggars 335/16

aloof *see* **stand aloof**

alowance, alowances *see* **allowance**

alowede, alowed of *see* **allowe**

amending *vb n* mending, repairing 93/1, 328/12

amners *n poss* of the almoner, a functionary who distributes alms for someone else 296/23

anempste *see* **to anempste**

angellett nobles *n phr pl* gold coins, each having half the value of the angel 295/3

ann egge brok *probably the name* Ann Edgebrook, *but perhaps a phrase,* an egg broken, *or,* a sword broken *(see endnote)* 344/12

antelap *n* antelope 304/5

apec *adv* apiece 200/21; *see also* **pece**

aplecastes *n pl* a method of telling fortunes *(see endnote)* 168/27

apointment *n* direction, order 174/37, **aponyment** 181/29; **apoyntment** 200/13, 202/5; 202/15; etc; **appoinctement** 308/34, 309/26, 309/27, etc; **appoinctemente** 309/31, 309/32; **appoinctment** 313/36; **appoinctmente**

306/34; **appointement** 285/16, 286/25, 310/28; **appointment** 78/33, 186/30, 194/30, etc; **appoyntemente** 327/40; **appoyntment** 177/20, 179/14, 187/18, etc; **appoyntmente** 312/22

appliable *adj* applicable, suitable, pertinent 366/6

appoynte *v inf* decree, direct 171/19, 171/20, 171/28; **appoints** *pr 3 sg* 362/14; **appointed** *pp* 146/4

aquarter *see* **quarter**

a ray *n* array, order 294/14, 295/35; **array** 292/25

areregis *n pl* arrears 336/35; **arrerages** 117/28

armes *n pl* hereditary heraldic insignia 83/18

arrode of arremes *n phr* herald of arms, an officer who makes royal proclamations, arranges state ceremonies, regulates the use of armorial bearings, etc 296/24; **kinge of heraldes** *n phr* King of Arms, the title of the three chief heralds of the College of Arms 303/18; **kyng of arrodes** 294/16

article *v inf* specify, state 92/2

article *n* article, a distinct charge or count in an accusation or indictment 344/11; **artikilles** *pl* 214/19; 214/30; **articles** separate clauses or provisions, of, *eg*, a statute or enactment 345/4

articulate *adj* charged or specified in the articles of an accusation or indictment 287/9, 287/34, 287/38, etc; **tharticulate** *art and n* 314/25, 343/26

assistauntes *n pl* in Kendal, the 24 persons who formed the lower rank of the governing coporation of the borough 169/2; 169/3

assize *n* periodic session, or sitting, of king's justices in each county for administration of civil and criminal justice 99/6; **assizes** *pl* 328/15; **assyeses** 162/16

atendance *n* escorting or accompanying (someone) in order to perform some service 200/10, 201/38, 202/20, etc; **attendance** 116/23, 202/13, 207/36, etc; **attendaunce** 295/25

athisside *adv* on this side (of) 293/32

⟨.⟩attelment *see* battlement

attend *v inf* escort or accompany (someone)
in order to perform some service 341/12;
attend *pr 3 pl* 'wait upon,' visit on a matter
of business 362/11

attendance, attendaunce *see* atendance

attendantes *n pl* servants, helpers 341/22

aughter *n* author, originator 288/1

awake *see* waike

awter *n* altar 293/5

ayen *adv* again 294/10

ayenst *see* against

bailiffe *n* the agent of a lord of the manor, who
collects his rents, etc 194/14; balive
196/29; bayliffe 192/18; balife chief public
administrative officer of a particular
district, 103/31; bayliffe 288/30, 289/3,
289/6, etc; bailly *poss* 214/22; bailiffes *n pl*
339/6, 339/7(2), etc; bailiffes *poss pl*
339/5m

baiting *vb n* setting dogs to bite and worry
(an animal, usually one confined for this
purpose) for sport 334/5; baytinge 301/42;
see also beare-baitings; bul-baitings

baize *n* a kind of woollen cloth, finer and
lighter than that now called baize 213/28;
bayse 179/33

ballad *n* popular song which sometimes
attacks persons or institutions 334/11;
ballades *pl* 334/15

band *n* neck-band, collar (of a shirt) 94/32

banket *n* banquet 172/4, 174/10, 298/24, etc;
bankett 299/11; banquenttes *pl* 345/7;
banquets 346/29

bar *n* a bar used in some trial of strength or
skill (?) 93/38, 115/33

barbor *n* barber-surgeon, one who does hair-
dressing, blood letting, and minor surgery
315/3

bare faced *adj phr* without a mask 363/28

barehede *adj* bareheaded 292/31

baron *n* nobleman, peer, lord of Parliament
307/15m; barons *poss* 306/14; baron of the

parliament *n phr* 307/18; baron of the
parliamente 307/14

barred of his othe *pp phr* prevented from
taking his oath (?) 334/26

barr monnye *n phr* in Carlisle, customary
payments claimed by the city's sergeants
118/37

barronie *n* estate, honour of a baron
190/41, 191/9, 191/11; barrony 189/16

battlement *n* an indented parapet at the top
of a wall 340/1; 340/7, 340/14; etc;
⟨.⟩attelment 339/39m; battlementes *pl*
341/1, 341/13, 341/35, etc

bayliffe *see* bailiffe

bayse *see* baize

baytinge *see* baiting

bea *interj* baa, the noise a sheep makes 352/35

beadell *n* beadle; a minor town official 65/22;
beadle *poss* 202/32; beadles *pl* 123/2;
beadles *poss* 100/38, 103/33; beedles 91/18

beakenes *see* beking

beare-baitings *n pl* form of entertainment in
which dogs are set on a chained bear
346/16; beare and bullbaitings 367/36; *see
also* baiting

bearrade *n* bearward; keeper of a bear, who
leads it about 305/16; bearwarde 91/4;
berward 301/41; berrardes *pl* 305/14

beedles *see* beadell

beggery *n* rubbish, beggarly stuff 349/5

beguile *v inf* deprive (of) by fraud, cheat out
(of) 384/21; beguyled *pp* 384/24

beking *n* beacon, signal-fire on a hill 176/8;
beakenes *pl* 178/10, 178/15, 178/17;
bekens 176/1, 176/6; bekinngs 176/14

belman *n* town-crier, one who goes around
a town and makes public announcements,
to which he attracts attention by ringing a
bell *(see endnote to p 65 CA/4/1 f [1v])*
65/22; belman *poss* 103/33; bellmans
91/22

belongeth in office *v phr* belongs as a duty
368/4–5

benevolence *n* gift or grant of money 99/30,
109/37, 112/37, etc

benifice *n* benefice, ecclesiastical living 334/17

benttes *n pl* benches 303/4

berrardes, berward *see* **bearrade**

bestowe *v inf* expend, lay out 76/30; **bestowd** *pa 3 sg* 208/2, 208/25 *(but meaning not certain here)*; **bestowed** 178/14, 209/1, 213/7; **bestowed** *pp* 74/36, 79/30, 82/9, etc; **bistowid** 172/8; **bestowed** *pp* placed 304/25; **bestowe ... in** *v inf phr* apply toward (?) 91/39–40

bidd *pp* bidden, invited 113/6

birde *n* beard 215/21

blacke garde *n phr* the lowest menials of the royal household 296/22, 303/26

blazed *pp* depicted, portrayed 352/22

blv *adj used as n* blue cloth 175/31

bodie *n* portion of food serving one person, (in contrast to a 'mess;' *see* **mease**) 203/25, 207/30; **body** 210/18

bokeram *n* buckram, a kind of coarse linen or woollen cloth stiffened with gum or paste 359/1(2); 359/2, etc; **buckeram** 337/33

boorde, borde *see* **kinges boorde**

boothall *n* town hall *(for further information see endnote to p 298 GBR F 4/3 ff 78, 79)* 305/22; **bothall** 298/15, 298/23, 298/27, etc; **botholl** 314/24, 315/9

bordenayles *n pl* some kind of nails, perhaps spikes or large brads 298/14

boroughe *n* a town or city holding privileges conveyed by charter 168/11, 168/16, 168/30, etc; **bourghe** 171/17, 171/21, 171/25, etc

boterye *n* buttery; place where provisions are stored and dispensed 296/20

bothall, botholl *see* **boothall**

bounder *n* boundary 73/30, 82/9, 85/16, etc

bowle *see* **runninge bowle**

bowling *vb n* an outdoor bowling game of some kind, probably skittles or what is now called lawn-bowling 367/38

boylinge house *see* **officers of the boylinge house**

brabling *vb n* quarrelling noisily, squabbling, brawling 384/19

breat *n* bread 204/14

breatch *n* breach, break (?) 90/9

breathren *n pl* 'brethren;' in Carlisle, members of the governing corporation 91/37; **brederne** 292/27, 293/2; 293/5; **brether** 291/37; **bretheren** 67/1, 100/8, 100/24, etc; **brethern** 295/22, 296/42, 297/12; **bretherne** 294/37, 295/6, 299/39, etc; **brethren** 74/36, 82/5, 83/36, etc

broad arrowes *n phr pl* arrows having two-pointed arrowheads 91/38

broad cloth *n phr* a fine woollen cloth of plain weave, two yards wide 198/3; **broadcloth** *n* 186/9; **brodclothe** 67/8; **brood clooth** *n phr* 187/13; *see also* **broode**

broaker *n* go-between, pimp, pander 350/5

brod *adj* broad, applied technically to certain fabrics distinguished by their width 103/32, 180/2; **brode** 100/37, 186/29

brok *see* **ann egge brok**

broode *adj used as n* broadcloth; a fine woollen cloth of plain weave, two yards wide 214/5; *see also* **broad cloth**

brother *n* member of a guild 117/19; **brothers** *poss* 99/22, 101/29

brotherhoode *n* members of the guild 113/33

brought in *v phr (v pa 2 sg)* caused to begin (*eg*, an event or a season) 77/30; **bryngyng in** *vb n phr* 297/15

brunt *v pa 3 pl* burned, blazed 178/10; **brunte** 178/15, 178/17

buckeram *see* **bokeram**

bul-baitings *n pl* form of entertainment in which dogs are set on a chained or tied bull 346/16; **bullbaitings** 367/36; *see also* **baiting**

bulles *n pl* papal edicts or mandates 292/8

burges *n* in Kendal, one of the twelve persons who, with the alderman and the 24 assistants, formed the governing corporation of the borough 307/26; **burgesses** *pl* 168/8, 168/35, 169/1, etc; **burgessez** 292/19, 293/29, 293/42, etc

busy *adj* earnest, eager, importunate 335/23

buthe *see* **tooll buthe**

butte *n* butt; cask for holding wine or ale, of a capacity not now known 341/27

byd *v inf* in Kendal, to invite (someone) to (a party or celebration at a particular house) 168/13, 168/25; **bydden** *pp* 168/7m, 168/14, 168/26

byth *see* **farr byth square**

calivers *n pl* a light kind of musket 337/6

Candlemas *n* the Feast of the Purification of the Virgin Mary, or the Presentation of Christ in the Temple (2 February) 111/28, 114/33

canon *n* a rule, law, or decree of the Church, especially a rule laid down by an ecclesiastical council 345/11, 346/33; **canons** *pl* 367/8, 367/11, 367/22

capes *n pl* caps 337/33, 338/16

capon *n* gelded rooster 109/35; **capons** *pl* 73/14, 74/1, 74/14, etc

careing *vb n* carrying 121/36

carfull *n pl* carts-full, cartloads 83/12

cariage *n* treatment of others 366/10

carsaie *n* kersey; a kind of coarse, narrow cloth, woven from long wool and usually ribbed 78/4; **carsay** 78/1; **carsey** 84/6; **kersay** 109/26; **kersaye** 88/1, 88/2, 88/5, etc

catechise *v inf* instruct in the elements of religion; question as to belief 219/39; **catechised** *pa 1 sg* 219/18, 219/19

certyfying *prp* assuring, making (someone) certain 294/4

chamber *n* room or chamber belonging to one of the city's trade guilds; also, the guild itself 73/29, 74/37, 77/26, etc; **chaber** (*error for* 'chamber') 85/17, 89/35, 96/18; **chambers** *pl* 72/9, 81/4, 83/33

chamberlaine *n* officer who accounts for civic receipts and expenditures 154/17; **chamberlane** 160/44; **chamberlayns** *pl* 87/38, 230/5–6; **chamberlens** 74/24, 154/39, 154/42; **chaberlens** (*error for* 'chamberlens') 113/29; **chamberlines**

111/7, 114/14, 118/13, etc

chapelry *n* the district attached to a chapel 219/24; **chappelrye** 219/38

charge *n* expense 84/38, 216/32, 217/2, etc; **chardges** *pl* 180/17, 180/24, 180/33, etc; **charges** 73/29, 174/10, 174/21, etc; **chargis** 85/5, 91/23, 112/23; **common charge** *n phr* generally shared expense 340/2–3

chekyn *n* chicken 296/11

cherisse *n* cherries 208/25

chesse *n* cheese 176/7

chests *n* chess 356/2

Christemas lord *n phr* lord of misrule, one chosen to preside over games and revels at Christmas 218/7; *see also* **abbott, lord of misrule**

christopher *n* a kind of tobacco imported from the island of St. Kitts, in the Caribbean (*see endnote to p 207, WMB/K 44, f [23]*) 212/16; *adj* 208/5, 208/14

churchale *n* periodical festive gathering held in connection with a church 287/36, 340/5; **churchales** *pl* 345/8; **chuchales** (*error for* 'churchales') 346/29; *see also* **somer ale, Whitson ale**

churchhouse *n* house belonging to a church, used for church purposes 343/24; **church-house** 289/30, 289/31; **church howse** *n phr* 343/2

clarck of the market *n phr* royal officer who attends fairs and markets to keep the standard of weights and measures 339/10; **clarke of the markett** 303/20; *poss* **clarke of the marketts** 303/30

clared *n and adj* claret, claret wine (in the 17th century, the period of most of these occurrences, the term 'claret' was applied to red wines in general) 68/9, 76/22, 103/13; **claret** 108/6; **clarett** 199/3, 199/25, 206/17, etc; **claried** 102/39, 175/12; **clarred** 106/10; **clarrede** 105/11; **clarrett** 205/2, 298/39, 303/36, etc; **clarrit** 77/36; **clartt** 204/16

clerke of the peace *n phr* an officer who

prepares indictments and keeps a record of
proceedings at sessions of the peace 196/4

cloackes *n pl* cloaks (of varying lengths,
hooded or hoodless, sometimes having
sleeves) 186/31; **cloakes** 133/39, 186/9,
187/37, etc; **clockes** 200/31; **clocks** 103/32;
clokes 88/6; 182/11, 183/8, etc; **clookes**
187/14, 214/5

cloath *n* woollen cloth 125/38; **cloth** 123/2,
183/8; **clothe** 65/22, 87/38, 169/7, etc

clossed, clossede *see* **herin clossed**

coape *n* ecclesiastical vestment resembling a
long cloak 337/12; **coopys** *pl* 294/22,
294/28; **copys** 292/35, 293/3

coarte *see* **leet cort**

coat *n* coat, sometimes a sleeveless close-
fitting garment coming no lower than the
waist, sometimes loose, with skirts and
sleeves 71/13, 71/16, 72/3, etc; **coatt**
66/12; **coote** 81/16; **cote** 91/23, 167/5; **cott**
88/7, 88/34; **cotte** 78/2, 78/11, 87/36, etc;
cootes *pl* 170/18, 293/30; **cotes** 100/37,
170/27, 172/17, etc; **cots** 175/32; **cottes**
178/6, 179/34, 182/5, etc; **cotts** 103/33

cockatrice *n* a fabulous serpent, said to kill by
its mere glance, and to be hatched from a
cock's egg 350/1

coloringe *n* painting (?) 304/4

combes *n pl* honeycombs 355/27

comffites *n pl* sweetmeats made of some fruit,
root, etc, preserved with sugar 172/6;
comfittes 68/11

commandadore *n* commendador,
commander (used chiefly as a Spanish or
Venetian title) 352/33

commicon *n* commission; warrant
authorizing someone to do something
319/40, 320/1, 320/2

commissinares *n pl* commissioners, members
of a commission established to investigate
(something) 180/20; **commissinores**
180/25; **commissoneres** 180/18

common charge *see* **charge**

common councell *n phr* in Gloucester, a
body composed of thirty or more of the

principal burgesses, from among whom
the mayor and aldermen were elected
311/27–8; **common counsell** 363/1

common welthe *n phr* public welfare,
common good 171/9

companie *n* trade guild 105/19, 317/19,
317/24, etc; **company** 99/31, 170/8, 327/6;
companye 105/23, 170/9; **comp** (*error for*
'company') 111/17; **companies** 116/13;
companyes 113/38; **companie** a party of
players or a band of musicians 130/19,
143/3, 143/5, etc; **company** 83/3, 114/36,
130/41, etc; **companye** 75/19; **companies**
pl 144/5

conceipt *n* notion, idea 190/11; **conseite**
189/30

conceived *v pa 3 sg* understood, apprehended
331/4

condiscended *pp* agreed, consented 307/6

conforme *v refl inf* to comply with the usages
of the Church of England 367/16, 367/21

conforme *adj* who has complied with the
usages of the Church of England 368/2

connyes *n pl* conies, rabbits 74/1; **cunnyes**
92/11, 96/3, 108/7, etc; **cunyes** 73/14,
102/26, 103/1, etc

consort *n* company of musicians 323/22;
consorts *pl* 136/34

constable *n* an officer of a parish or township
appointed to act as conservator of the peace
342/16; **high constable** *n phr* an officer of
a hundred or other large administrative
district, appointed to act as conservator of
the peace 352/26; **constable** (*with* 'high'
understood) 352/32, 353/2

contemners *n pl* despisers, scorners 367/24

contemptuously *adv* in the manner of those
setting legal authority at defiance 289/5

contracting martes *see* **martes**

conuenient *adj* decent, appropriate, suitable
367/32; **conuenyent** 215/9; **convanient**
92/2; **convenient** 333/38; **convenyente**
169/5

coocke *n* cook (?) *or*, proper name Cook (?)
145/12

coopys *see* coape

coote, cootes *see* coat

copys *see* coape

cornetor *n* one who plays a cornett *(see* cornett*)* 140/29; **cornetter** 137/21

cornett *n* cornett, a wooden wind instrument (not to be confused with the modern cornet) 329/1; **cornettes** *pl* 328/14

corporacion *n* a town possessing self-governing privileges; the name given to its governing body, empowered to act as a legal entity 170/11, 196/1; **corporations** *pl* 362/10

corslettes *n pl* pieces of defensive armour covering the body (as opposed to the limbs) 337/8

cote, cotes, cots, cott, cotte, cottes, cotts, *see* coat

counterfeete *n* imitator, actor (?) 100/27

counterfeitinge *prp* acting, imitating 218/19

course *n* reprehensible behaviour, 'goings on' 289/15; **course** race, horse-race 120/10; **courses** *pl* 116/17; **course of horse race** *n phr* a single race within a set of horse-races 114/1

cradell *n probably,* a suspended scaffolding or stage used by workmen on buildings 305/3; **cradles** *pl* 341/7

craueth *v pr 3 sg* asks, requests 317/16, 323/31, 324/7; **craved** *pp* 84/27

Cristie *n* Christ's School 322/9

crownatyon daye *n phr* Coronation Day, the anniversary of the accession of Queen Elizabeth I (17 Nov 1558) 174/32

cuckow-time *n phr* April, the time of the cuckoo's arrival in the British Isles 354/33

cunnyes, cunyes *see* connyes

cusshynges *n pl* cushions, 294/23, 294/28; **cusshyns** 292/36, 293/3

cutter *n* tailor (?) 353/17, 354/26

cyphers *n pl* numbers, numerals 352/8

damosels *n pl* damsels; young unmarried women 349/36

dampes *n pl* gases or vapours of a noxious kind 349/7

dasshet *v pa 3 sg* dashed, threw 215/22

dauncing pumpes, daunsing pumpes *see* pumpes

decoring *vb n* decorating, adorning 367/34

deections *see* derection

defend *v inf* uphold, maintain by speech or argument 285/21, 286/31, 287/20; **defended** *pa 3 sg* 288/2

deponent *n* one who makes a deposition under oath, one who gives written testimony to be used as evidence in a court of justice 193/29, 194/5, 194/7, etc; **deponentes** *poss* 194/1, 194/8, 194/14, etc

depose *v inf* testify, bear witness 190/8, 190/24, 193/6, etc; **deposeth** *pr 3 sg* 192/38, 193/8, 193/25, etc; **deposed** *pp* 193/7, 193/13

deprave *v inf* decry, disparage 201/24

derection *n* instruction, authoritative guidance 89/12; **derecktions** *pl* 208/33; **derections** 204/31; **deections** *(error for* 'derections' *(?))* 204/29; **directions** 216/27, 366/5

detected *pp* informed against, accused 331/34, 332/1, 332/18, etc

device *n* something devised or fancifully invented for dramatic representation 216/31; **deuices** *pl* 353/8; **deuises** 355/20; *see also* vise; **devise** design 335/23

di *n* one-half *(for Latin* 'dimidium'*)* 206/37, 212/33, 214/5, etc

diall *n* clock 350/12

diclosed *pp* declosed; disclosed, revealed 198/1

diet *n* food, board 348/27m, 348/28

diligences *n pl in v phr* **done their diligences** done their utmost endeavour, exerted themselves 345/20

directions *see* derection

discomininge *vb n* discommoning, depriving of citizenship 307/29

discouer *v inf* reveal, disclose 349/10, 351/8; **discouered** *pp* 188/21; **discovered** *v pa 3 sg* uncovered, bared 363/17

discredyted *pp* brought into discredit or disrepute 314/32

disgisingez *n pl* masques, masquerades 347/21; **disgysynges** 335/19

disguised *pp* dressed up as for a pageant or entertainment 218/15, 346/11; **disguysed** 201/17

diuers *adj* various, sundry 188/19, 201/17, 343/3, etc; **diuerse** 304/36, 307/2, 307/4, etc; **divers** 94/10, 189/16, 197/13, etc; **diverse** 310/25, 311/3; **dyveres** 117/9; **dyvers** 171/5

dli *error for* 'di. li.,' *ie, Latin* 'dimidium librae,' half a pound 76/22

doble gilte *adj phr* having two layers of gilding 303/15; **duble giltt** 84/32

dosan *n* dozen 113/36; **duson** 206/6

doubted *v pa 3 sg or pp* feared 288/33

draftes *n pl* loads 304/12

drawn *pp* written out 189/15

dresinge *vb n* cleaning, furbishing (?) 182/24; **dressinge** preparing, *perhaps also* decorating, adorning 105/27, 117/22, 304/16, etc

drinkinge *n* a convivial revel 305/37(2); **drinkynge** 300/42; **drinkinges** *pl* 345/8; **drinkings** 345/28, 346/19(2), etc; **drynkynges** 168/9m, 168/27; **drynkyns** 168/20

drumme *n poss* drummer's 100/38

drummercotte *n poss and n* drummer's coat 103/33

drynkynges, drynkyns *see* **drinkinge**

duble giltt *see* **doble gilte**

duble *adj* of twice the value 84/36

dulle sole *adj phr* double-soled; having soles made from material of double thickness, or in two layers 86/18

duson *see* **dosan**

dyes *n pl* days 340/24

dyveres, dyvers *see* **diuers**

earnest *adj* intent, zealous 314/31

egge *see* **ann egge brok**

eighttenthe *adj* eighteen 303/2

eleccion dinner *n phr* a dinner given on the day of the election of the alderman 207/13; **eleckcion dener** 176/18; **elecktion diner** 205/36, 206/2, 206/5; **election diner** 172/22, 200/29; **election dinner** 175/22, 175/25, 199/25, etc; **election dyner** 204/35; **elekxtion diner** 182/17; **ellection diner** 203/25; **ellection dynner** 199/16, 202/18–19; **elections diner** *n poss phr* 173/8

enterlude *n* play, especially of a light or humorous kind 358/29; **interlude** 307/20; **enterludes** *pl* 306/42m, 306/42, 307/1, etc; **interludes** 307/11, 307/15, 367/35

entertayninge *see* **intertayne**

entertaynment *n* public performance or exhibition designed to interest or amuse 216/32; **enterteinment** hospitable provision for the wants of a guest 349/15

er *conj* ere, before 295/10

erect *v inf* elevate to office 218/7

esquyers *n pl* men belonging to the order of gentry, and ranking immediately below knights 294/15

estat *see* **groumes of the stable of estat**

estates *n pl* orders or classes of society 218/30

euenday *see* **fasten euenday**

evidences *n pl* documents by means of which facts are established, especially title-deeds 334/39

examinat *n* person under examination, either as witness or as accused person 190/36; **examinates** *poss* 193/39

excepte *conj* unless 315/19

exercyse *n* formal recitation 100/10; **exercises** *pl* activities (especially sports and entertainments) 346/17

expect *v inf* await, wait for 355/12; **expected** *pp* 216/26

extraordinarij *adj* extra, additional, not routine 85/5; **extrordanrie** *adv* 205/38; **extrordinarie** 205/28

face *n* mask 339/32

fantasticall *adj* inclined to love (?) 354/41

farr byth square *adv phr* 'far by the square,'

'way out,' out of line (in an assumption, judgment) (?) 191/2

fasten euenday *n phr* Shrove Tuesday 123/9; **fasteneuenday** 123/12; **fasteneuen day** 123/18; **fastineven day** 102/20; **ffastineven day** 102/13

fedill *n* fiddle, violin 215/5

fees *v pr 3 sg* feeds, grazes 218/19; **feeing of** *prp phr* feeding off 197/3

fellowe *n* 'mate,' co-worker 298/16

fetch *pp* fetched 199/1

ffasinge *n* fabric used for facing garments 179/33

ffastineven day *see* **fasten euenday**

ffayne *n* 'fane;' flag, banner 83/19

ffence *see* **master of ffence**

ffo *prep* for 178/16; **fo** 203/7

ffoale *n* performing fool, jester, clown 93/1; **ffoall** 82/34; **ffoole** 78/35, 86/16m, 87/1m, etc; **ffowle** 82/30; **foal** 94/21; **foale** 93/3, 93/15, 93/18, etc; **foole** 67/37, 78/5, 78/7, etc; **foule** 86/16, 87/1; **fowle** 71/7; **ffooles** *poss* 91/23; **foall** 84/9; **foalls** *pl* 84/6; **fooles** 78/2, 78/11, 193/31; **foule** 87/10, 87/35, 88/34; **fowles** 72/40

ffoleth *v pr 3 sg* followeth, follows 232/15

ffolkes *n pl* people 168/19; **folkes** 204/36, 209/10, 209/39, etc; **forkes** 203/3

ffooll *n* fowl 103/1; **ffowle** 108/7, 109/35, 113/7; **foole** 73/14, 74/1, 92/11, etc; **fowle** 96/3

fforton *v inf* fortune, chance 168/11

ffowers *n pl* 'fours,' the group, consisting of four members of each trade guild, which assisted the mayor and 'brethren' of Carlisle with the annual audit and other matters 118/37

ffree *adv* freely, copiously (?) 112/21

ffreeman *n* guild or company member, one who possesses the freedom of a guild or company 170/8

ffreese *n* frieze, coarse woollen cloth with a heavy nap on one side 100/37; **ffrese** 178/6; **ffreyse** 179/32

ffrires *see* **White ffrires**

fo *see* **ffo**

foal, foale, foall, foalls *see* **ffoale**

foiles *n pl* thin leaves of metal placed under a transparent substance to give it the appearance of a precious stone 354/17

folkes *see* **ffolkes**

foole, fooles *see* **ffoale, ffoole**

forkes *see* **ffolkes**

foule, fowle, fowles *see* **ffoale**

fowle *see* **ffooll**

freres *n pl* friars, members of one of the four mendicant orders 292/1

fro *prep* from 215/29

furnished *pp* fitted up, prepared for use 337/8

furniture *n* accessories, *here probably* props and scenery 304/34

furthrance *n* aid, assistance 196/21

furthrers *n pl* supporters, promoters 197/12

galland *n* gallon 320/36; **gallande** 303/36

game *n* traditional sport or amusement 384/11; **gaimes** *pl* 108/27; **games** 69/3, 71/21, 77/23, etc; **gams** 93/34, 97/19

gard *see* **vshurs of the gard**

garde *see* **blacke garde**

geare *n* apparel, clothes 336/26, 336/31, 337/28, **geere** 338/22; **gere** 335/39, 336/20

geister *n* jester, professed maker of amusement, especially one maintained in a prince's court or a nobleman's household 297/8, 297/34; **ieaster** 100/27

gene *pp* given 113/36

gentilman vsher *n phr* official of the royal household 84/41

gentlefolkes *n poss* of persons of good position and family 353/28

gere *see* **geare**

giltinge *n* gelding (*hence,* **giltinge boule,** **giltinge bo⟨.⟩le** a prize for a race run by geldings (?)), *or pp* gilt, gilded (?) 98/20, 98/29

golden sommes *n poss* Goldenson's (?), *or n proper and pron* Golden some (?) (*see* **sommes**) 299/33

goodwife *n* a title, prefixed to surnames,

equivalent to Mrs. 343/34

gowen *n* a long, loose robe, usually open at the front, having hanging or puffed shoulder sleeves 169/7, 169/8; **gownes** *pl* 170/37, 291/38, 291/39, etc

gowres day *n phr* 'Gowrie Day,' 5 August, day of Thanksgiving for the deliverance of King James I from an alleged assassination attempt *(see endnote to p 84 CA/4/139 f 53)* 86/11; **gowryeidaye** 85/32; **Gowryes daye** 84/22

gratificacion *n* recompense 312/24

groumes of the stable of estat *n phr* grooms of the royal household 184/21

gunpowder daye *n phr* 5 November, Guy Fawkes Day, the anniversary of the Gunpowder Plot 100/8–9; **gunpowther day** 108/18

had *pp* delivered 172/11; **hade** 304/15; **had** consumed 200/5, 200/31, 205/38, etc

halbert *n* halberd, a weapon consisting of a sharp-edged blade ending in a point, and a spear-head, mounted on a handle 5 to 7 feet long 112/25; **holbert** 182/24; **halbertes** *pl* 122/2

halbyteers *n pl* halberdiers, soldiers armed with halberds 116/18

hallow thursdaie *n phr* 'All Hallow Thursday,' the Thursday following Rogation Sunday, *ie*, Ascension Day (a moveable feast) 67/37; **hallow thursday** 99/34–5; **hallow thursdaye** 92/23; 96/18, 117/18; **hallowe thursdaie** 67/1; **hallowe thursday** 92/26; **hallowe thursdaye** 74/37; 113/32, 120/20; **hallowthursdaye** 96/13; **halow thursdaie** 67/18; **halowe thursdaie** 68/11; **hall thursdaye** *(error for* 'hallow') 91/1; *see also* **alhallow thursday**

hand *n in prep phr* **vnder...hand** with the signature of 319/40; **vnder...hande** 84/40, 85/1–2

harbinger *see* **kinges harbinger**

hardwaremen *n pl* dealers in hardware 360/25

harne *n* harden, a course fabric made from the

hards of flax or hemp 78/3, 84/7

harvest *n* harvest-time, harvest-season 129/10, 129/35, 130/31, etc

hase *see* **plaie hase**

heades *n pl* wigs 337/13; **heades of heare** *n phr pl* 339/30

heather *adv* hither 65/10; **hether** 293/31

hedde *see* **opyn hedde**

heraldes *see* **kinge of heraldes**

herin clossed *pp phr* closed herein, here enclosed 214/30; **herin clossede** 214/18

herper *n* harper 144/18, 144/22

hether *see* **heather**

hex *n* abbreviated form of 'hexpenses', *ie*, expenses (?) 70/19

high constable *see* **constable**

highe *adj* tall 337/10

hird *n poss* herdsman's (in Carlisle, this civic official looked after the cattle on Kingmoor) 103/34; **hirdes** 91/19, 100/38

hoas *n pl* breeches and long tailored stockings sewn together to form a single garment; sometimes, after about 1550, used for breeches portion only 82/34; **hoisen** 75/30; **hose** 78/23, 86/17; **hosen** 286/7; **hosse** 81/17

hobbie horsse *n phr* a figure of a horse, made of wickerwork, etc, and worn by a performer 143/19

holbert *see* **halbert**

holden *pp* held 363/16; **houlden** 311/28

honest *adj* seemly, decent 366/12

horse nages *see* **naggs**

hose, hosen, hosse *see* **hoas**

house *n* a legislative or deliberative assembly 323/20, 323/24; **howsse** inn, tavern 215/3, 215/7(?), 215/24, etc

housholdstuffe *n* the goods belonging to a household 289/40

howse kepinge *vb n phr* housekeeping expenses 85/6

hus *pron* us 172/10

iacketts *n pl* jerkins, close-fitting, full-skirted men's garments worn over doublets 183/9,

337/12

iacobusies *n pl* 'Jacobuses,' the popular name of the twenty-shilling sovereigns struck in the reign of James I 85/27

iade *n* jade (as term of reprobation applied to a woman) 330/36

ialor *n* jailer 161/39; **ialor** *poss* 133/39

ieast *n* jest 190/41

ieaster *see* **geister**

ierken *n* jerkin, a close-fitting, full-skirted men's garment worn over a doublet 286/8; **ierkine** 337/31; **iirkyns** *pl* 339/28

ieurie *n* jury 185/33; **iuerie** 186/38; **iuri** 200/22; **iurie** 182/22, 186/25, 205/15, etc; **iurry** 204/21; **iury** 194/36, 198/26, 198/39, etc; **iurye** 212/12, 212/31

incerte *v inf* insert, add 188/21

inconveniences *n pl* improprieties, unseemly behaviour 307/4

inconvenient *adj* unsuitable 331/35, 333/6

incorporacion *n* corporation (*see* **corporacion**) 171/6

inhabite *pp* dwelling, settled 201/17m

inquisicion official investigation, inquest, or the record of an investigation or inquest 334/26

interlude, interludes *see* **enterlude**

interrogatory *n* a question formally put, or drawn up in writing to be put, to an accused person or witness 192/38, 192/39, 193/6, etc; **inter** *abbreviated form* 195/35, 196/19, 196/39, etc; **interr** 190/25; 190/35(2), etc

intertayne *v inf* receive as a guest, show hospitality to 184/4; **entertayninge** *vb n* 85/5

intruder *n error for* 'interluder,' player, especially, a player in an interlude (?) 81/9

inuented *pp* composed as a work of literary art 189/33; **invented** 190/15; **inuentinge** *vb n* 189/30; **inventing** 190/12

inuentor *n* composer, author 189/31; inventor 190/13

it *adv error for* 'item,' also 317/16, 317/18, 317/23, etc; **ite** 73/13, 73/14, 73/15, etc

ites *pron and v pr 3 sg* it is, it's 191/2

iudgler *n* juggler, one who entertains people by stories, songs, buffoonery, tricks, etc 82/27, 94/9, 95/19; **iugler** 88/18, 100/30, 137/16, etc

iuerie *see* **ieurie**

iuglinge feates *n phr* feats of legerdemain, sleight of hand or conjuring tricks 299/39

iuri, iurie, iurry, iury, iurye *see* **ieurie**

iustyce *n* a justice of the peace, or other inferior magistrate 298/41; **iustices** *pl* 326/8, 326/11, 326/16, etc; **iustices** *poss pl* 326/38, 328/29

kersay, kersaye *see* **carsaie**

keep *v inf* celebrate, observe as a special occasion 289/27; **keepe** 85/31; **keepe** *v pa 1 sg* 324/19; **kept** 324/37; **keepe** *v pa 3 sg* 321/20; **keepte** 320/22; **keepeinge** *vb n* 324/8; **keeping** 323/32, 325/32, 327/4; **keepinge** 285/22, 287/22, 326/22; **kept** *pp* 345/8, 345/28, 346/30, etc; **kepte** 285/22, 286/23, 286/33, etc; **keepe** *v inf* maintain, support, provide for the sustenance of 330/34; **kept** *pp* 330/32; **keeping** *prp* managing, carrying on (as a business) 288/37; **keepinge** *vb n* holding, having 331/22; **kepeinge** 331/17

keeper *n* gamekeeper, an officer who has the charge of forest, woods, or grounds 198/33, 207/10, 207/11, etc; **keper** 203/34

kepinge *see* **howse kepinge**

kinge of heraldes *see* **arrode of arremes**

kinges boorde *n phr* a stone structure used for displays of various kinds (*see endnote to pp 302–5 GBR F 4/3, ff 159v, 160v, 162*) 304/3; **kinges borde** 304/2, 304/7–8, 304/29

kinges harbinger *n phr* one sent ahead to make provision for a royal retinue 184/11

kippe *n used as adj* the hide of a young or small beast 337/34

kyng of arrodes *see* **arrode of arremes**

lace *n* ornamental braid used for trimming, a

trimming made of this 88/6

laye *v pa 3 pl* lodged, spent the night 295/18; **laid out** *v phr* spent 316/31; **laide out** 316/29–30; **layd ovt** 179/13; *pp phr* 317/16–17, 317/23, 317/32, etc; **laide out** 317/41; **laied out** 311/2–3; **layd out** 176/7, 318/38, 319/4, etc; **layed out** 310/26, 311/40–1, 312/15, etc; **layd forth** spent 174/29, 175/24

le *(from French 'le')* in Latin texts, this marker signals the appearance of a vernacular (here English) word 357/15, 357/21, 357/25, etc; **lez** 357/10, 357/29, 357/39, etc

leadder *n* leather 87/10

leadinge *vb n* driving 83/12

leet *n and adj* a court of record having manorial origin 182/21, 184/10, 186/21, etc; **leete** 177/5, 180/15, 188/10, etc; **leett** 204/17; **leit** 185/31, 186/37, 186/38, etc; **lete** 200/19; **lett** 204/12; **light** 213/22; **leettes** *poss* 204/9

leripoope *n* 'liripipe,' rôle, part 354/27

lett *v inf* prevent, hinder 196/11; **letted** *pp* 367/27

leudnes *n* ignorance, want of good breeding 349/10

leuen *see* **a leuen**

leuerye *n* livery, distinctive suit of clothing worn by an official or a servant 91/19; **leverey** 91/20, 91/21, 91/22, etc; **liverie** 313/30; **lyuerey** 292/33; **leueries** *pl* 91/17, 91/18; **leveres** 91/30, 100/38; **leveryes** 65/23; **liuereys** 313/23; **liveryes** 323/22, 428/12, 428/13

lez *see* **le**

libell *n* little book, short treatise 334/11

libertie *n* district subject to the control of the municipal authority 288/30, 293/32; **libertye** 292/24; **liberties** *pl* 168/11, 168/17; **libertie** permission, leave (to do something) 368/6

lifftenante *see* **lyvetenant**

light *see* **leet**

light *pp* lit 295/1, 295/12

lighted *v pa 3 sg* alighted, dismounted 294/29

like *adj* similar 169/34, 193/38, 285/28, etc; **lyke** 168/20, 169/26; **lyke** *adv* 307/25; **lyke** *adj used as n* 384/20

linkes *n pl* links, torches made of tow and pitch, used for lighting people along the streets 303/2, 319/31

litter men *n phr pl* men who carry a litter or moveable bed 184/22

liuereys, liueries, liverie, liveryes *see* **leuerye**

loffe *see* **sugger loffe**

long bowes *n phr pl* long-bows (as opposed to cross-bows), bows drawn by hand and discharging long feathered arrows 168/21

lorde presidente of the merches *n phr* Lord President of the Marches of Wales 298/38

lordes of mannors *n phr pl* persons holding rights, feudal in origin, to rents, services, and jurisdiction in respect of specific lands and tenants that constitute their manors 188/23, 191/18, 191/26, etc; **lordes of the mannor** 193/10–11; **lordes of the mannors** 188/28, 191/35, 192/2, etc

lord of misrule *n phr* one chosen to preside over Christmas games and revels 299/33; **lord of mysrule** 335/18; **lords of misrule** 346/10; *see also* **abbott**; **Christemas lord**

lord of the ... maypole *n phr* one chosen to preside over the sports and games associated with the maypole 287/15; **lord of the ... may pole** 287/38; **lord of the ... pole** 286/27

Lord President's *n phr poss probably,* the house of the President of the Council of the North 216/29

lord wardens *n phr poss* of the Warden of the West March *(see endnote)* 172/11

lowaunce *see* **allowance**

lute *n* stringed musical instrument 216/16, 350/17, 350/34, etc

lyke *see* **like**

lyuerey *see* **leuerye**

lyvetenant *n* lieutenant 288/25; **lifftenante of the tower** Lieutenant of the Tower of London (the acting commandant delegated by the Constable of the Tower) 302/3

maase *n (sg, but usually pl in sense)* 'mess,' a portion of food intended to serve four people 210/17; **meas** 176/18; **mease** 179/16, 183/13, 185/14, etc; **meass** 186/23, 198/36; **measse** 194/35, 198/24(2), etc; **mese** 205/13(2), 205/24; **messe** 175/21; **measses** *pl* 168/19, 195/4

mace *n* a heavy staff or club, of metal, or having a metal head, and often spiked 363/21, 363/26 *(but these instances may refer to the ceremonial mace; see next definition);* **mases** *pl* 292/31; **masys** 294/18; **mace** ceremonial sceptre 303/23; **mase** 294/10, 294/16, 294/32, etc; **mases** *pl* 292/31; **masez** 293/38

maide *n* maiden, young unmarried woman 355/7, 359/15

maintained *v pa 3 pl* provided with livelihood, bore the living expenses of (someone) 329/10; **mainteynde** *pa 3 sg* supported, gave countenance to 287/12; **maintaining** *prp* 329/15; **manteyning** *vb n* establishing (?) 92/1

maintenance *n* means of subsistence 329/12; **maintenaunce** maintaining, support 307/4; **mayntenance** 218/13

maioras *n* mayoress, wife of a mayor 96/33

maister *n* head, chief officer (of a trade guild) 317/23, 317/32, 318/1; **master** 316/2, 319/29; **maisters** *poss* 318/24, 318/32, 319/8, etc; **masteres** 328/39; **masters** 315/28, 318/17, 324/37, etc

makeinge *vb n* writing, composing (?) 103/39, 191/10; **making** 190/13; **makinge** 189/31, 198/11; **maid** *pp* 189/33; **makeinge** *vb n* organizing, making ready 106/30, 108/29, 121/11

maker *n* composer, author 189/32, 190/14

maluesey *n* malvoisie, malmsey, a kind of strong sweet wine 361/17, 361/22, 361/24

man *n* servant, employee, assistant 76/23, 185/34, 303/30, etc

manchet *n* a small loaf of the finest wheat bread 361/9, 361/10; **manchet** *pl* 361/8

mannor, mannors *see* **lordes of mannors**

manteyning *see* **maintained**

markes *n pl* monetary units, each equal to two thirds of a pound sterling 295/13

market standing *n phr* a place in the market for a booth, stall, etc 339/9–10

marshall *n* officer charged with the arrangement of ceremonies 303/27; **marshalls man** *n phr* marshal's man, one of a number of men belonging to the royal household, and going before the king in processions to clear the way 303/30; **marshall man** 288/26

martes *n pl* sales *(here*, of articles donated to make money for a good cause) 340/21, 340/35, 342/1; **contracting martes** *vb n phr here*, selling donated articles to make money for a good cause 340/2

Martinmas *n* the feast of St Martin, 11 November 172/5, 228/35, 228/37

mase, mases, masez *see* **mace**

maske *n* masque, court entertainment variously including dancing, dumb show, dialogue, and song 174/6, 174/8, 174/10

masking *prp* taking part in a masque or masquerade 344/12

massingers *n pl* messengers 303/22

master *see* **maister**

master of ffence *n phr* master of the art of fencing 208/32

Master of the Revelles *see* **Ravelles**

masys *see* **mace**

May-Games *n phr pl* merrymaking and sports associated with the first of May 367/30

mayntenance *see* **maintenance**

may pole *n phr* a high, decorated pole, set up in an open space, for merrymakers to dance around on May-day 286/22, 287/12, 287/15; **maye pole** 285/12, 287/35; **maye poule** 285/21–2; **maypole** *n* 201/16, 286/32, 287/38, etc; **may-pole** 325/12, 325/14; **maypoles** *pl* 287/21, 367/31; *see also* **pole, somner pole**

meane *adj* low, humble 353/5

meas, mease, meass, measse, measses *see* **maase**

meat *n* food (as opposed to drink) 184/5,
185/33; **meate** 341/31

meet *adj* suitable, fit, proper 383/32

meeting *n* gathering of people for
entertainment 318/13; **meetinges** *pl* 340/22

men *v inf* mend 87/10

men *n pl* 'men,' sometimes used to describe
a company of entertainers having a noble
patron 92/35, 132/19, 132/29, etc

menstrells, menstrills *see* minstrall

merches *see* lorde presidente of the merches

merye nyghtes *n phr pl* parties at which the
entertainments offered were drinking,
music, and dancing 168/27

mese, messe *see* maase

methegline *n* a spiced or medicated variety of
mead, originally peculiar to Wales 321/16

Michaellmas *n* Michaelmas, the feast of St
Michael, 29 September 306/10, 306/25;
Michaelmas 103/23, 109/8, 201/33, etc;
Micheallmas 198/24; **Michelmas** 207/21;
Micklemas 307/36; **Mighallmas** 199/38;
Mighalmas 200/5; **mychaelmes** 84/20,
84/21; **mychalmas** 195/7; **mychelmas**
177/6

midsomer *n and adj* Midsummer Day, 24
June 301/30; **midsommer** 313/6; **Midsom**
⟨..⟩ 340/6; **myd somer** 336/33

milne *n* mill 228/27; **milnes** *pl* 234/33

minstrall *n* a professional entertainer using
music, singing, story-telling, juggling, etc
215/6; **minstrell** 139/3; **mynstrall** 214/15,
214/27, 214/40, etc; **mynstrell** 320/6;
menstrells *pl* 173/26; **menstrills** 176/21;
minsterels 185/12; **minstralls** 74/5;
minstrells 73/15, 74/19, 137/24; **minstrels**
66/25, 173/10; **mynstrelles** 298/42,
356/41, 357/3, etc; **mynstrells** 177/7,
180/7

minstrelcie *n* the activities of a minstrel
especially playing and singing 334/5

misrule men *n phr pl* participants in
Christmas revels and games 218/11; *see
also* abbott; lord of misrule

mitred *pp* wearing a mitre, the head-dress

worn by bishops (and some abbots) 292/7;
mytourde 294/23

molde *n* mole (the animal) 350/2

moorys daunse *n phr* Morris-dance, a
grotesque dance performed by persons in
fancy costume 297/18; **moresdaunce**
359/3; **Morris-dances** *pl* 367/30

moralitie *n* moral interpretation 190/11;
morallitie 189/30

morall *n in prep phr* in the morall according
to the moral interpretation 363/31

morals *n pl* morality plays, plays in which
some lesson is inculcated, and in which the
chief characters are personifications of
abstract qualities 364/4

moresbelles *n pl* Morris bells, the many small
bells attached to the clothing of Morris
dancers 358/39(2)

moresdaunce, Morris-daunces *see* moorys
daunse

mought *v pa 3 sg* might 216/28

mouthall *n* moot-hall, town-hall 206/32

munisseners *n pl* musicians (?) 77/17

murmuring *prp adj* complaining in low
muttered tones 288/39

murrens *n pl* morions, soldiers' helmets of a
kind worn in the 16th and 17th centuries
337/9

musick *n* a company of musicians 318/18;
musicke 111/19, 112/12, 113/17, etc;
musike 110/9, 111/12, 114/21

musitioner *n* musician 98/25; **musitioners** *pl*
97/30; **mussishiners** 78/26; **mvisioneres**
177/19

musterdevilles *n* a kind of grey woollen cloth,
originally from the town now called
Montivilliers, in France 293/30

muuiissians *n pl* musicians 75/22; **muzistians**
75/7

mychaelmas, mychalmas, mychelmas *see*
Michaellmas

myd somer *see* midsomer

myll *n* mile 215/28

mynstrall, mynstrell, mynstrelles,
mynstrells *see* minstrall

mysrule *see* **abbott, lord of misrule; misrule men**

mytourde *see* **mitred**

naggs *n pl* small riding-horses or ponies 158/19; **horse nages** *n phr poss* of a small riding-horse 91/38

naturall ffoole *n phr* natural fool, one who is born simple-minded, though he may also be a performing fool 81/16

naught *adj* sexually immoral 331/2

neckes *n pl* neck, that part of a garment that covers the neck 88/6

newers *n poss* New Year's 80/32

nobles *see* **angellett nobles**

nutcastes *n pl* nut-casts, a method of telling fortunes *(see endnote)* 168/27

obeysaunce *n* act or gesture expressive of submission or respect, usually a bow 292/25, 293/34, 293/39

obiected *pp* charged, laid as an accusation 201/23

occupacion *n* trade-guild 146/4, 146/6; **occupation** 103/11, 110/5, 114/24; **occupacion** *poss* 73/13, 73/39, 112/32; **occupacions** 105/9, 109/32, 110/24, etc; **occupacons** 106/8, 108/4; **occupacions** *pl* 81/4, 90/10, 118/37, etc; **occupations** 67/18, 77/22, 83/32, etc; **ocupations** 98/13

od mony *n phr* surplus sum of low denomination 173/9; **oddes of moneye** 316/17

officers of the boylinge house *n phr pl* boilers of food (distinguished from cooks in some way not now clear), part of the kitchen staff of the royal household 303/27–8

offor *pp* offered 168/17, 168/28

oppressors *n pl* those who suppress or put down (a custom, etc) 191/18

opyn hedde *adj phr* bareheaded 294/15–16

orator *n* suppliant, petitioner 334/42; **orators** *pl* 335/27

ordenarie *adj* belonging to the regular staff 303/21; **ordnere** ordinary, usual (of

expenses) 100/8m, 100/36m

order *n* authoritative direction 168/35, 323/32, 324/9; **orders** *pl* 168/22, 171/19

packethred *n* stout thread or twine, often used for bundling 304/17; **packthred** 121/38

pageant *n* a wagon used as a stage; a play performed on such a wagon 313/8; **pageaunt** 292/3; **pagent** 358/29; **pagentes** *pl* 304/35; **pagiandes** 168/22

paisboard *n* pasteboard 119/13; **pastboard** 115/30; **paysbourd** 121/16

pamphlett *n* small, paper-bound treatise, on a topic of current interest 334/11; **pamphlettes** *pl* 334/9

pantrye *n* a room or apartment in which bread and other provisions are stored 296/21

papist *n* Roman Catholic *(used with derogatory sense)* 334/25

papistrie *n* Roman Catholicism *(used with derogatory sense)* 334/22

par *n* pair 176/13

parcelles *n pl* small sums of money 202/33, 208/40

parchment *n* roll of parchment, parchment document 299/33

parsons *n pl* persons, people *(the number which would be expected to follow this word has been omitted)* 101/30

particular *n* statement giving details (of some matter) 84/40; 85/1

parties *n pl* parts, regions 214/31

passengers *n pl* wayfarers, travellers 76/31

pastboard *see* **paisboard**

paven *vb n* paving 178/38

payn *n in phr* **vpon payn to** on pain of 168/29; **vpon payne to** 171/33

paysbourd *see* **paisboard**

peaces *n pl* 'pieces,' *ie*, pieces of gold (the exact value of these coins is not known; here they are equated with the twenty-shilling sovereigns struck in the reign of James I) 85/27; **peaces of goulde** *n phr pl*

84/36; **peeces** *n pl* pieces of artillery 289/34

peaze *n* pea 353/20, 353/21

pece *adv* a piece 183/13, 204/11, 204/20, etc; **peece** 203/4, 203/13, 203/22, etc; **pes** 176/19; **the peece** *art and n* 202/27; *see also* **apec**

peniston *n* a kind of coarse woollen cloth used for garments, linings, etc 88/3, 88/4

per *prep (Latin word used as English)* according to 181/29, 183/36, 187/11, etc

peraduenture *adv* perhaps, maybe 366/40

peres *see* **shriffes peres**

personate *v inf* impersonate 188/22, 188/28, 191/17, etc; **personated** *v pa 3 pl* 196/41; **personateinge** *vb n* 193/10; **personated** *pp* 192/7, 197/1, 363/7

pes *see* **pece**

pinicle *n* pinnacle, small ornamental turret 304/27; **pyinacles** *pl* 341/14

pips *n pl* tobacco pipes 203/24, 203/28, 204/23

pitts *n pl (but sg in sense?)* cockpit, pit or enclosed area in which gamecocks are set to fight for sport 108/29

plaiars *n pl* players, stage-players, actors 300/26; **plaiers** 72/37; 172/27, 174/15, etc; **plaies** 200/13; **plaiores** 300/28; **plaiors** 213/15; **plaires** 75/27; **playeres** 80/29, 90/34; 91/9, etc; **players** 65/7, 66/11, 66/13, etc; **playores** 298/34, 299/41, 299/42, etc; **playors** 300/36; **playres** 181/30; **playrs** 204/31, 212/23; **pleyars** 29//6, 297/41; **pleyers** 296/33, 296/41, 297/26, etc; *see also* **stage playars**

plaie hase *error for* 'plaie hade,' *ie*, entertainment presented 72/13

plat *n* plate, a prize consisting of a silver or gold cup (or something similar) given to the winner of a race 117/28; **plate** 114/25, 115/4, 115/6, etc

play bookes *n phr pl* books containing a play or plays 196/5, 196/6, 196/9, etc; **playebookes** 196/34

play daie *n phr* the day on which a play was performed 178/23; **play dayes** *pl* 169/35; **playdayes** 170/37

playeres, players *see* **plaiars**

playes *n pl* public sports and entertainments 123/12

playgames *n pl* games, sports *(perhaps the same as* **silver playgames**; *see* **siluer games)** 65/26

playores, playors, playres, playrs *see* **plaiars**

plea *n* play, dramatic representation 196/26, 196/28; **pleas** *pl* 197/8, 197/12, 197/13

pleasure *n* will, desire 366/3, 366/21, 367/7, etc

pleyars, pleyers *see* **plaiars**

pole *n* May-pole, a high, decorated pole, set up in an open space, for merrymakers to dance around on May-day 285/14, 286/27; **poles** *pl* 386/22; *see also* **May pole, somner pole**

pomell *n* the knob terminating the hilt of a sword or dagger 215/14

poole *v inf* pull 191/6

Popish *adj* 'Papist,' Roman Catholic *(used with derogatory sense)* 366/25

poppett players, poppette players *see* **puppie player**

potle *n* liquid measure equalling two quarts 68/9; **pottell** 316/20, 320/37; **pottle** 76/21, 76/22, 312/34, etc; **pottles** *pl* 319/26(2)

powder *n* gunpowder 72/14, 72/16, 72/18, etc; **powther** 119/33; **puder** 88/11

praye *v inf* ask, request 65/13; **pray** *pr 1 pl* 335/25; **prayeth** *pr 3 sg* 315/37, 316/9, 316/36 etc; **praie** *pr 3 pl* 302/42, 303/13, 303/42, etc; **praye** 306/30

prebendaryes *n pl* holders of prebends, benefices funded from the cathedral's revenues 328/16

precise *adj* precise or punctilious in religious observance 366/9

precisian *n* one who is precise in religious observance (in the 16th and 17th centuries synonymous with 'Puritan') 386/25; **precisians** *pl* 367/20, 375/29m

precontest *n* a former or previous fellow-witness 315/12

premyss *n and adj* aforesaid, aforementioned

214/26, 215/30

prentices *n pl* apprentices 349/30

present *v inf* to bring before a court, magistrate, or person in authority, for consideration or trial 368/2

presently *adv* immediately 114/32, 323/24; **presentlye** 85/29

prikettes *n pl* candles or tapers (originally, those stuck on pricket or spiked candlesticks) 361/39

priuie *adj* privately cognisant or aware (of, that) 189/24; **privie** 190/6; **priuie to** *adj phr* 189/30; **privie to** 190/12; **privy to** 195/31–2

priuitie *n* private knowledge (here probably implies consent also) 194/7; **privitie** 192/20; **privity** 196/30, 287/9

pro *prep (Latin word used as English)* for 103/31, 103/32, 103/39, etc

proces *n* process, the mandate, summons, or writ by which a person or thing is brought into court for litigation 197/21

procure *v inf* induce, persuade 191/16

procurement *n* causing, instigation, contrivance 190/14; **procurment** 189/32

prohanely *adv* error for 'prophanely,' ie, profanely 285/20

published *pp* made known, declared 368/12

puder *see* **powder**

puke *v inf* poke 191/5

pumpes *n pl* light, low-heeled, close-fitting shoes without any fastening, used especially for dancing 135/7, 138/22

puppie player *n phr* puppet-player, one who manages or exhibits puppet-plays 125/27; **poppett players** *pl* 311/18; **poppette players** 308/21–2; **puppie players** 94/3

pyinacles *see* **pinicle**

quaice *n pl* wheys (?) or *(in sg)* some other liquid used in cooking (perhaps the same as *OED* 'quacham,' the meaning of which is unknown) 361/36

quariars *n pl* quarriers, large square candles 361/38

quarter *n* one-quarter of a yard 78/35, 214/5; **aquarter** *art and n* 103/32; **quarters** *n pl* 180/2, 84/32 (?); **quartes** 67/8; **qurtrs** 88/4; **quarter** *n sg* one-quarter of a cask or barrel 105/26

queens daie *n phr* anniversary of the accession to the throne of Elizabeth I (17 November) 179/25; **quenes day** 232/5; **quens day** 179/8

querye *n* equerry, the stables belonging to a royal or princely household 84/42

quest-men *n pl* annually elected ward officials who enquire into abuses of various kinds 345/19

quipper *n* one who quips, makes witty or sarcastic remarks 355/14

quire *n* choir 324/29

quiremen *n pl* choir-men 322/40

quiristers *n pl* choristers 326/37

qune *n* quean, hussy 330/36

quotha *interj* indeed! 191/2

qurtrs *see* **quarter**

rather *adv* the more quickly, the sooner 288/31

raunge *n* row, line 295/30

Ravelles *n pl (but sg in sense)* the Revels, the office of the royal household responsible for organizing games and merry-making 109/22; **reuells** 326/10; **Master of the Revelles** *n phr* the person appointed to organize revels in the royal household 309/11; **Master of the Revells** 319/40

ray *see* **a ray**

read *adj used as n* red cloth 88/33, 103/32, 109/24, etc; **reed** 100/37

rebek *n* rebec, a pear-shaped stringed instrument, played with a bow, and having from one to five strings; *here perhaps* the player of a rebec 335/17

recorder *n* borough magistrate having jurisdiction defined under the charter of incorporation 85/24, 303/4, 313/19

recusant *n* one who refuses to submit to authority, especially a Roman Catholic

who refuses to attend the services of the
Church of England 334/25; **recusants** *pl*
366/25, 367/40

redde dere *n phr cervus elaphus* or red deer,
a species so called from its red-brown
colour 303/37

reed *see* **read**

remeved *v pa 3 sg* went away (from one place
to another) 291/36, 292/9

repaire *n* resort or going to a place 335/13

reparell *n* apparel 338/35, 338/38

repayer *v inf* go, make one's way 65/7

respondent *n* a defendant in a lawsuit 201/15

resting *prp* remaining 115/4

restraint *n* prohibition 334/4, 334/8;
restreinte means of checking or restraining
(someone's activities) 306/41

Reuells *see* **Ravelles**

reume *n* rheum, watery matter that drops
from the eyes, nose, etc 351/33

Revelles, revells *see* **Ravelles**

reward *n* remuneration 100/5m, 100/10m,
100/16m, etc; **rewarde** 83/16, 86/5m,
86/20m, etc; **rew** *(error for 'reward;'*
abbreviation sign missing) 86/10m,
87/18m, 87/34m, etc; **rewardes** *pl* 299/9,
300/26, 303/13m, etc

riall *adj* royal 293/24

rialles *n pl* gold coins originally of the value
of ten shillings, first issued by Edward IV
in 1465 295/7, 296/9

ribaldish *adj* abusive, scurrilous 384/19

rishes *n pl* rushes, plants used for strewing on
floors and making rush-lights 120/22

riued *pp* riven, split, broken in two 351/18

rondes *n pl* rands, strips or long slices of meat
(not to be confused with 'rounds') 361/29

rowem *n* 'room,' a place to which a person
is assigned 169/24

rowt *n* company or band of persons 289/34

runninge bowle *n phr* a bowl awarded as a
prize at the Carlisle horse race 114/8

ryding *vb n* riding along (a boundary, etc) for
the purpose of maintaining or reviving a
clear knowledge of it 74/30; **rydinge**

73/30, 79/26, 79/30, etc

sa *error for v pr 3 sg* 'saith,' says 195/18,
195/21, 195/35, etc

sack *n* a general name for a class of white
wines formerly imported from Spain and
the Canaries 76/21, 184/7, 199/2, etc;
sacke 81/6, 102/39, 105/11, etc; **sake**
182/23; **seck** 175/13; **secke** 68/9, 103/14,
303/36

sad *adj* dark, deep (in colour) 169/7

sagbott *n* sackbut, the ancestor of the modern
trombone 327/14; **sagbutt** 327/28, 328/7;
saggbutt 328/12, 328/36, 328/38, etc

Sainte Peters yeve *n phr* 28 June, the eve of
the Feast of St Peter and St Paul *(for further*
information see endnote to p 79, CA/4/2 ff
[13–14v]) 301/30; **St Peters euen** 79/14–15

sake *see* **sack**

saregantes, sargantes, sargentes, sargents,
sarientes *see* **sergiants**

saye *n* a woollen cloth of fine texture
resembling serge 78/35

scaffold *n* temporary raised platform or stage
for dramatic performances or exhibitions
299/11, 299/16, 300/7, etc; **scaffolde**
298/15, 298/17, 300/26, etc; **scaffould**
305/22; **skaffold** 299/26, 300/35; **skaffolde**
304/40, 305/12; **scaffoldes** *pl* 304/34,
304/39

scholler *n* one who is taught in a school
158/17, 194/9; **schollers** *pl* 93/25, 108/23;
scolleres 117/4; **scollers** 100/10; **skhollers**
121/21

scituate *pp* situated, located 330/24

scotes *adj* Scots, Scottish 66/25, 66/29, 75/10;
scotts 93/27

seck, secke *see* **sack**

secutorys *n pl* 'secretaries,' important
officials of the royal household, possibly
members of the Privy Council 296/12

seller *n* a store-room for provisions 341/32

send *v inf* send word 288/36

sergiants *n pl* serjeants-at-mace, low-ranking
municipal officers 123/2, 125/38; **seriantes**

118/38; 173/10; **seriauntes** 292/28;
saregantes *poss* 88/6; **sargantes** 208/39;
sargentes 205/21; **sargents** 175/10;
sarientes 202/31; **seargantes** 79/11;
sergeauntes 292/31; **seriantes** 91/17,
100/36; **sergeaunt at armys** *n phr* one of
a body of men of knightly rank, who were
required to be in immediate attendance on
the king's person 294/18; **seriaunt at
armys** 292/30; **serjeant at armes** 363/21;
sergeauntes at armes *pl* 303/18
servants *n pl* 'servants,' sometimes used to
describe the members of a company of
players or entertainers having a noble
patron 362/11
sessment *n* assessment 234/13
sett furthe *v inf phr* furnish, provide (as
entertainment) 340/3; **settinge forth** *vb n
phr* 189/31; **settinge furthe** 340/23–24;
setting fourth 190/12–13
setting *vb n* making (a table) ready (for a
meal), *especially*, by providing beer
101/31, 102/29, 105/9, etc; **settinge** 73/13,
73/39, 74/13, etc
seuerall *adj* separate, different 116/13,
168/15; **severall** 144/5, 168/22, 340/24, etc
sewger *n* sugar 74/3, 92/10, 96/1
sex *adj* six 102/25; **sexe** 215/2
shearman *n* shearer of woollen cloth 170/7;
shearmen *pl* 170/5, 170/9
shewes *see* **sightes and shewes**
shotinges in long bowes *n phr pl* archery
practice *(see endnote)* 168/21
Shraffe Tewsdaye *n phr* Shrove Tuesday, the
day before Ash Wednesday, on which Lent
begins 81/1–2; **Shroftuesday** 115/28,
116/24; **Shroufe Theusday** 97/18;
Shrough Tuesday 106/33;
Shroughtuesday 119/12, 121/12, 121/19;
Shrougtuesday 108/26; **Shrove Tewesday**
71/21, 93/34, 95/6; **Shrovetewesdaie**
65/26, 67/13; **Shrovetewesday** 69/4, 83/6,
93/40
shryef *n* sheriff, high-ranking county official
who represents royal authority in the

county 292/11; **shreffes** *n pl* town officials
of high rank, usually royally appointed
(but some towns had the privilege of
choosing their own) 292/22, 292/23;
shriffes 291/38, 293/21, 293/26, etc;
shriffes peres *n phr pl literally*, sheriffs'
peers, those equal in rank to sheriffs; *here
perhaps* the name of a group of high-
ranking corporation officials, including all
ex-sheriffs 293/28
side-men *n pl* sidesmen, churchwardens'
assistants 345/18, 345/19
sight *v pa 1 sg* sighed 354/18
sightes and shewes *n phr pl* displays and
exhibits 326/6–7
siluer games *n phr pl* games of some kind
(exact meaning unknown); in Carlisle,
they were held on Shrove Tuesday 115/28;
silver playgames 65/26; *see also*
playgames
singingman *n* singer; especially, one who
sings in an ecclesiastical choir 100/5,
322/39
sirplisses *n pl* surplices, loose white vestments
having wide sleeves 337/14
sirra *n* sirrah, a term of address used to men
or boys, expressing contempt, reprimand,
or assumption of authority on the part of
the speaker 353/40, 381/25
sises *n pl* sizes, small candles, used especially
in churches 361/38
skaffold, skaffolde *see* **scaffold**
skhollers *see* **scholler**
skirt *n* edge 363/24
slops *n pl* trouser-legs 286/7
smoothred *pp* smothered 349/17
snytes *n pl* snites, snipe (in some early
examples, however, the two words seem to
refer to different birds) 361/34
some *n* sum 117/20
somer ale *n phr* summer festival at which ale
was drunk 287/22; **somerale** *n* 285/22;
somorale 287/36; *see also* **churchale,
Whitson ale**
sommergames *n pl* traditional Carlisle games

(for further information see endnote to p 77 CA/4/2 f [6]) 90/8; **summergames** 80/34, 101/10

sommes *error for* 'somme,' some (?) 299/33; *see* **golden sommes**

somner pole *(error for* 'sommer pole') *n phr* a pole decked with flowers, erected during a spring/summer festival 287/12; **sommer rodd** 201/16; *see also* **May-pole, pole**

sonnet *n* short poem or piece of verse 334/11; **sonnettes** *pl* 334/9

sort *n* way, manner 193/12, 334/15; **sorte** 189/11, 307/9, 307/28

spared *pp* left over 340/36

speach play *n phr* recitation 93/25

spice plates *n pl* small plates or dishes used for holding spices 335/17

spirituall person *n phr* cleric, clergyman 334/16, 334/39

sportes *n pl* amusements, entertainments 87/39; **sports** 346/20

stable of estat *see* **groumes of the stable of estat**

staf torches *n phr pl* tall thick candles used for ceremonial purposes 303/1; **staffe torches** 303/3

stage plaie *n phr* dramatic performance 188/26, 192/39, 193/10; **stage-play** 362/6; **stage play** 190/5, 190/36, 191/34, etc; **stage playe** 188/22, 191/17, 191/23; **staige plaie** 189/23; **stage-playes** *pl* 346/16; **stage playes** 171/29, 196/40, 340/3, etc

stage playars *n pl* players, actors 327/40; **stage players** 314/28, 328/29; *see also* **plaiars**

stamell *adj* a fine woollen cloth, possibly a variety of kersey 67/8, 313/31

stand aloof *v inf phr* take no part in, hold back from 384/8

standing *see* **market standing**

stand on *v inf phr* dwell on, consider at length 350/11

starr *n* planet, or star in one of the constellations of the Zodiac 355/12; **starre** 352/37, 355/35

stayger *v inf* hesitate, waver (in speech) 214/26

St Clementes tyde *n phr* 23 November, the Feast of St Clement 315/29

stewardes *n poss probably* the possessive form of the proper name Stewart, *but possibly* of a steward, one who manages the affairs of an estate on behalf of his employer 216/9

stewardes *n pl* corporation officials of some kind 313/23; **stywardes** 292/34

St Iohn Euen *n phr* 23 June, the eve of the Feast of the Nativity of St John *(for further information see endnote)* 79/14

stock *n* a sum of money set aside to provide for certain expenses, a fund 91/38; **stocke** 114/23, 117/21

stocked *pp* placed in the stocks *(see* **stockes***)* as a punishment 384/10

stockes *n pl* instrument of punishment consisting of two planks, set edgewise one over the other and furnished at the edges with holes to receive the ankles of the person to be punished 384/7, 384/16

St Peters euen *see* **Sainte Peters yeve**

stragling *vb n* interloping, intruding (where one has no right) 355/9

straightly *adv* strictly 368/7

straingers *n pl* guests, visitors (technically, non-members of the guild) 103/10, 115/12; **strangers** 73/16, 74/2, 74/15, etc; **strangiers** 335/13

strangeres *adj or n pl* (someone) from out-of-town, not local 117/9

styrrvp *v phr* stir up 191/16

stywardes *see* **stewardes**

subdeane *n* an official immediately below a dean in rank, and acting as his deputy 322/42

subpena *see* **writt of suppena**

subscribed vnto *pp phr* attested to by signing 383/34

suffer *v inf* permit, allow 168/14, 168/26, 307/27, etc; **suffering** *prp* 334/28; **sufferinge** 78/14; **suffring** 213/39; **suffered** *pp* 194/12, 287/14, 307/23, etc;

suffred 307/8; **suffering** *vb n* 196/1, 345/20

suffragan *n* an assistant or subsidiary bishop 294/22m; **suffryngam** 294/22

sugger loffe *n phr* sugar-loaf, a moulded conical mass of hard refined sugar 303/34

summergames *see* **sommergames**

suppresse *v inf* put down by force 289/6, 289/15

surbated *pp* weary, foot-sore 350/8

sweareinge dinner *n phr* a dinner given on the day of the election of the alderman, the 'election dinner' (*see* **eleccion dinner**) 203/32

swerdbearers *n poss* of a municipal official who carries a sword of state before a magistrate on ceremonial occasions 300/30; **swoordbearars** 302/13; **swordberers** 300/43, 302/5

syngler *adj* 'singular,' superior, pre-eminent 335/25

tabber *n* tabor, a small kind of drum, used chiefly as an accompaniment to the pipe or trumpet 331/34, 332/38

table *n* a board or other flat surface on which a picture is painted 352/10

tables *n pl* writing-tablets 352/4, 352/15; *see also* **writing tables**

take ... order *v phr (v pr 3 subj sg)* make arrangements, take measures 367/19–20; **tooke order** *(v pa 3 sg)* 366/9

tarbareles *n pl* tar-barrels, which were used to make bonfires 178/16

teles *n pl* teal, a kind of duck 361/34

tenant right *n phr* a customary form of landholding, with fixed obligations, affording security of tenure 191/19

tennantes at will *n phr pl* tenants holding land 'at the will' of the lord, unprotected by custom 191/5, 193/38

tenshall money *n phr* the fee charged a 'tenser' (*see endnote*) 339/10

testamentes *n pl* wills; *originally*, documents in which personal (as opposed to real)

property was disposed of 334/40

tharticulate *see* **articulate**

the *pron* they 195/27

therewithall *adv* with that 343/32

thight *n* thigh 215/25

threre *adj* three 77/17

throng *adj* crowded 219/21

throught *prep* through 304/11; **throwght** 294/25; 294/26, 295/27

thunder heades *n pl* the clouds portending a thunderstorm 337/34

tipling *prp* drinking intoxicating liquor to excess, or selling strong drink by retail 346/1

tiplings *n pl* habitual indulgence in liquor 367/2, 379/30m

to *conj* till 214/29

to anempste *prep* towards (?) 169/27

tofore *adv* before 295/9

tolerable *adj* permitted, allowed of 213/36; **tollerable** 169/13, 366/38

tollsey *n* tolsel, a guildhall or court-house 304/1, 304/16

tooke order *see* **take ... order**

tooll buthe *n phr* a municipal building, part of which was used as a prison or jail 214/21

touching *prep* concerning, about 216/27, 292/8 (?) (*or here perhaps prp* speaking of, discoursing on), 345/18; **touchinge** 311/28; **touching** *vb n* touching on, mentioning briefly 352/9

to ... warde *prep* towards 292/9

toyes *n pl* antics, tricks, *or perhaps* amusements, entertainments 287/17

trimenge *vb n* making ready, preparing 304/2; **trinning** (*error for* 'trimming') 105/27

trompettes *n pl* trumpeters 357/21, 357/25, 357/29, etc; **tompettes** (*error for* 'trompettes') 358/10; **trumpettes** 347/17, 356/31, 357/3, etc; **trunpettes** 357/15, 360/20

tumbeller *n* tumbler, acrobat 359/15

Twelfth Day *n phr* the twelfth day after Christmas (6 January), on which the Feast of the Epiphany is celebrated 169/17

typpettes *n pl* short shoulder capes 293/29

varina *n and adj* an expensive kind of tobacco, imported from Venezuela *(see endnote to p 207 WMB/K 44, f [23], 13–14)* 212/17, 212/32; **varino** 208/5, 208/15, 208/30; **varona** 212/14

venison feast *n phr* customary autumn feast 194/41, 195/5, 203/18–19, etc; **venison ffeast** 207/23, 208/22, 208/31; **venyson feast** 199/2, 199/5, 199/6; **venyson ffeast** 185/12, 199/13, 200/28, etc; **venyson diner** 185/13–14; **venison feastes** *pl* 204/1

verdigrese *n* verdigris (acetate of copper), used as a pigment 304/30

vialls *n pl* viols, bowed instruments having five, six, or seven strings, and played in a sitting position 322/35

vicitacion *n* a visitation of sickness or plague *(see endnote)* 100/21

victualing house *n phr* an eating-house, inn, or tavern 346/1

victualler *n* one who makes a business of providing food and drink for payment; a keeper of an eating-house, inn, or tavern 288/40

virginia *n* a variety of tobacco grown in Virginia 212/15, 212/33

vise *n* device, something devised or fancifully invented for dramatic representation 359/14; *see also* **device**

vittayles *n pl* victuals, food or provisions 384/22

vizard *n* mask 363/15, 363/27; **vysor** 339/32

vizd *adv* Anglicised, *abbreviated form of Latin 'videlicet,'* that is, namely 183/13; **vizett** 204/9, 204/36; **vizt** 191/2

vnder ... hand, vnder ... hande *see* **hand**

vnfeet *adj* unfit, unsuitable 307/24

vngracius *adj* reprobate, wicked 214/20

voide *adj* (of a benefice or living) vacant, unoccupied 334/20

vouchsafe *v pr 2 sg imper* grant (something), be willing (to do something) 349/1, 352/12; **vouchsafe** *pr 2 sg subj* 353/5, 356/7;

vouchsafed *pa 3 sg* received graciously, deigned to accept 85/27

vrs' *meaning not certain; see endnote* 361/13

vsages *n pl* customs 171/7, 345/8, 345/28, etc

vse *v inf* engage in, practise 368/6, 368/9, 384/9, etc; **vsed** *pp* 366/10; **vsing** *prp* 349/4; **vsing** *vb n* 366/12, 366/42; **vsed** *pp* (of a rite or custom) observed, celebrated 168/21, 171/12, 171/29, etc

vse *n* usage, custom 146/5

vsher *see* **gentilman vsher**

vshurs of the gard *n phr pl* officers of the royal household 184/2

vssher *n* assistant to a head-teacher 301/29

vtter *adj* outer 294/21, 304/35

vtteraunce *n* sale 340/31

vysor *see* **vizard**

wage *n* rent 206/32

waie maister *n phr* 'weigh master,' official who monitored the weighing of commodities in the Bothall market 303/27

waike *n* wake; festivities often associated with saints' days 79/11(2), 155/26; **awake** *art and n* 96/31

wait *n* musician employed by the city government 82/28, 179/41; **waitt** 66/23; **waitte** 66/12; **wate** 80/23, 82/22; **wayte** 180/2; **waites** *pl* 76/18, 76/23, 76/30, etc; **waits** 68/28, 68/33, 68/36, etc; **waittes** 66/18, 66/32, 67/30, etc; **waitts** 103/29, 104/6, 104/14, etc; **waiytes** 76/13; **wates** 74/38, 79/20, 79/32, etc; **wats** 89/18; **wayghtes** 316/22; **waytes** 76/2, 77/12, 78/13, etc; **wayts** 199/31; **waytts** 122/16, 303/31; **weats** 176/10; **weightes** 348/20; **wettes** 177/37; **whaites** 76/34; **whaitts** 119/16, 121/19; **whayets** 176/35; **whaytts** 176/33; **waites** *poss pl* 170/18, 170/27, 172/17, etc; **waittes** 182/5; **waitts** 103/29; **wates** 81/13, 91/7; **wattes** 187/37; **waytes** 179/33, 182/11, 213/3, etc; **wayts** 183/8, 187/13; **wets** 175/32

waite player *n phr* musician employed by the city government 318/2; **waightplayers** *n pl*

322/16, 326/31; **wait players** *n phr pl*
317/18; **waite plaiers** 317/25, 317/34; **wayt
players** 328/23; **wayte players** 325/25,
325/40, 327/34, etc; **waytplayers** *n pl*
327/21; **weight players** *n phr pl* 321/38

want *adv* less, minus 203/25

warde *see* **to ... warde**

wardens *n pl* members of the governing body
of a guild 324/3

wardens *see* **lord wardens**

warne *v inf* call, give notice of (a meeting of
some kind) 168/13, 168/25; **warnyd** *pp*
168/15, 168/26

wasted *pp* used up, consumed 81/11

watche *n* in Gloucester, a civic celebration
held on St John's Eve and St Peter's Eve
301/30

watchers *n pl* those celebrating or observing
the eve of a festival 79/12

wate, wates *see* **wait**

wating of *vb n phr* attending, escorting 83/26

wats, wattes, wayghtes, wayte, waytes *see*
wait

wayt players, wayte players, waytplayers *see*
waite player

wayts, waytts *see* **wait**

weadoes *n pl* widows 103/11

weedes *n pl* 'weeds,' garments 356/7

weight players *see* **waite player**

weightes *see* **wait**

**wets, wettes, whaites, whaitts, whayets,
whaytts** *see* **wait**

where withall *adv* with which 363/14;
wherewithall 363/41

white ffrires *n phr pl* White Friars, friars of
the mendicant order of the Carmelites
294/21

Whitson ale *n phr* parish festival held at
Whitsuntide, marked by feasting, sports,
and merry-making 289/28; **Whitson Ales**
pl 367/30; *see also* **churchale, somer ale**

wif *n* wife 172/4, 174/5, 179/16, etc; **wife**
177/34, 197/15, 198/23, etc; **wiff** 185/13,
293/20; **wiffe** 178/27, 194/33, 195/4, etc;

wyf 180/24, 199/37, 200/19, etc; **wyfe**
175/21; 180/19, 201/32, etc; **wyff** 175/8;
wyffe 177/5, 177/8, 204/9, etc

wigions *n pl* widgeon, a kind of duck 361/33

will *v inf* enjoin, give order 288/37, 289/3

wit *n in phr* **that is to wit** that is to say,
namely 294/13

withall *adv* at the same time 65/13, 364/3

withall *see* **where withall**

without *prep* outside 292/1, 294/21;
withoute 291/37

woed *v pa 3 sg* wooed 349/34

wonte *pp* wont, accustomed 350/17

woorck *n* a particular piece of labour 341/5;
woorcke 341/38

worshipp *n* honour, credit 85/6

wounder *n* wonder 350/25

writ *v pa 3 sg* wrote 197/19; **writt** *pp* 216/28

writing tables *n phr pl* writing-tablets 363/39

writt of suppena *n phr* writ issued by a court
of justice commanding the presence of a
witness under a penalty for failure 197/33;
writtes of subpena *pl* 188/37

wyf, wyff, wyffe *see* **wif**

wynding *vb n* hoisting, lifting 341/6; **wyniige**
(*error for* 'wyninge') 341/4

yat *relative pron* that 90/28, 117/20, 119/13,
etc; **yt** 146/8; **yat** what, that which 117/19;
yat *conj* that 219/25, 219/30, 219/35

yate *n* gate 294/22, 295/28

yem *pron* them 76/4

yeoman *n* commoner or countryman of
respectable standing, especially one who
cultivates his own land 286/17, 286/40,
287/28; **yoman** 314/19; **yeomene of the
bottelles** *n phr pl* minor officials of the
royal household 303/21

yeve *n* eve 301/30(2), 336/34

yfayth *interj literally,* in faith! 381/26

yoman *see* **yeoman**

yis *pron* this 172/8, 174/19

yrdes *n pl* yards 214/5

yt *see* **yat**

Index

The index combines subject headings with places and names for ease of reference. Where the same word occurs in more than one category, the order of headings is people, places, subjects, and book or play titles (eg, Berkeley, Thomas precedes Berkeley, Glouc).

Place names, titles, and given names appear in their modern form where this is ascertainable; surnames are normally cited in the most common form used in the text and are capitalized (I, J, U, and V therefore appear in accordance with modern usage). Both places and surnames are followed by their variant spellings in parentheses. Names of saints are indexed under St; their identification and precise dates of feast days conform to David Hugh Farmer, *The Oxford Dictionary of Saints* (Oxford, 1979). The major sources used for identification of civil and ecclesiastical officials are *The Dictionary of National Biography* and F. Maurice Powicke and E.B. Fryde (eds), *The Handbook of British Chronology*. Sources for identification of patrons, monarchs, and other peers are specified in the headnote to Patrons and Travelling Companies, to which the index refers throughout.

The format for names and titles has been largely taken from R.F. Hunnisett, *Indexing for Editors* (Leicester, 1972). Thus family relationships, where known, have been used rather than succession numbers to distinguish members of noble families. Occupations known and considered relevant are supplied (eg, Bodell, Will, fiddler). Mayors are identified as such and their dates of office supplied in parentheses from the year of election or appointment where known.

Modern subject headings are provided with some complex groupings, such as costumes (individual) and musical instruments (kinds of), to aid research.

RECORDS OF EARLY ENGLISH DRAMA

York edited by Alexandra F. Johnston and Margaret Rogerson. 2 volumes. 1979.

Chester edited by Lawrence M. Clopper. 1979.

Coventry edited by R.W. Ingram. 1981.

Newcastle upon Tyne edited by J.J. Anderson. 1982.

Norwich 1540-1642 edited by David Galloway. 1984.

Cumberland/Westmorland/Gloucestershire
   edited by Audrey Douglas and Peter Greenfield. 1986.